Time and Logic

Originally published in 1995 *Time and Logic* examines understanding and application of temporal logic, presented in computational terms. The emphasis in the book is on presenting a broad range of approaches to computational applications. The techniques used will also be applicable in many cases to formalisms beyond temporal logic alone, and it is hoped that adaptation to many different logics of program will be facilitated. Throughout, the authors have kept implementation-orientated solutions in mind. The book begins with an introduction to the basic ideas of temporal logic. Successive chapters examine particular aspects of the temporal theoretical computing domain, relating their applications to familiar areas of research, such as stochastic process theory, automata theory, established proof systems, model checking, relational logic and classical predicate logic. This is an essential addition to the library of all theoretical computer scientists. It is an authoritative work which will meet the needs both of those familiar with the field and newcomers to it.

Time and Logic

A Computational Approach

Edited by Leonard Bolc and Andrzej Szałas

Routledge
Taylor & Francis Group

First published in 1995
by UCL Press Limited

This edition first published in 2019 by Routledge
2 Park Square, Milton Park, Abingdon, Oxon, OX14 4RN
and by Routledge
711 Third Avenue, New York, NY 10017

Routledge is an imprint of the Taylor & Francis Group, an informa business

Publisher's Note

The publisher has gone to great lengths to ensure the quality of this reprint but points out that some imperfections in the original copies may be apparent.

Disclaimer

The publisher has made every effort to trace copyright holders and welcomes correspondence from those they have been unable to contact.

A Library of Congress record exists under LCCN: 94020061

ISBN 13: 978-0-367-33653-0 (hbk)
ISBN 13: 978-0-429-32104-7 (ebk)
ISBN 13: 978-0-367-33657-8 (pbk)

Time and logic

Time and logic
a computational approach

Edited by

Leonard Bolc

Polish Academy of Sciences

&

Andrzej Szałas

University of Warsaw

UCL
PRESS

First published in 1995 by UCL Press

UCL Press Limited
University College London
Gower Street
London WC1E 6BT

The name of University College London (UCL) is a registered trade mark used by UCL Press with the consent of the owner.

ISBN: 1-85728-233-7 HB

British Library Cataloguing in Publication Data.
A catalogue record for this book is available from the British Library.

Library of Congress Cataloging-in-Publication Data

Time and logic: a computational approach / edited by Leonard Bolc & Andrzej Szalas.
p. cm.
Includes bibliographical references and index.
ISBN 1-85728-233-7
1. Logic programming. 2. Time. I. Bolc. Leonard, 1934–
II. Szalas, Andrzej, 1956–
QA76.63.T58 1994
005.1'01'5113—dc20 94-20061
CIP

Printed and bound by
Page Bros (Norwich) Ltd., England.

Contents

Preface

During the past decade a great deal of attention has been devoted to formalisms dealing with various concepts of time. One of the most important motivations, besides those of a linguistic and philosophical nature, arises from the needs of applications of those formalisms in computer science. The main goal of this book is then to introduce the reader to concepts of time as they are understood and applied in the theory of programming.

This book reviews various approaches and evaluates their advantages. The overall strategy is quite simple. We try to investigate the concept of time from a variety of contexts and viewpoints that you can easily recognize and adapt to your own needs. Moreover, the presented techniques are often very general and applicable not only to temporal phenomena, but also to other formalisms. For instance, many theorems on temporal logics can easily be adapted to various modal logics, in particular to most logics of programs. Particular attention is devoted to effective, implementation-oriented solutions. On the other hand, the book is not intended to present *all* contexts where time is essential. This area is developing much too rapidly to allow anyone to achieve such an ambitious goal. We nevertheless expect that the formalisms and methods we present will occupy a central position within that developing theory.

The chapters we present are the following:

- Chapter 1, by A. Szałas, presents the basic ideas of logics, in particular, temporal logics. Temporal logic is considered via a standard notion of time. The chapter surveys fundamental aspects of propositional and predicate temporal logic and discusses methodological properties of several proof systems for proving time-dependent properties. Formal specification of algorithms and data structures by means of temporal logic are also discussed.
- Chapter 2, by H. Andréka, V. Goranko, S. Mikulás, I. Németi and I. Sain, gives a comprehensive study of effective proof theory for temporal logics

of programs. Making the considered temporal logic effective may be a little surprising, as standard semantics makes the logic totally undecidable. However, the approach presented in this chapter considers time via non-standard model theory. The framework obtained allows the authors to present many different proof systems and to compare their power.

- Chapter 3, by P. Wolper, applies automata theoretic techniques to formal verification of temporal properties of programs. The author is more concerned about satisfiability and model checking than about proving tautologies. He presents and classifies various temporal program verification methods. Both deterministic and nondeterministic programs are studied, and linear, branching time and partially ordered time structures are considered.
- Chapter 4, by W. Penczek, surveys temporal logics with branching and partially ordered time. Those logics are mainly motivated by semantical considerations of concurrency that go beyond interleaving models. The chapter presents various proof systems and provides discussion of model checking issues
- Chapter 5, by B. Strulo, D. Gabbay and P. G. Harrison, describes a very new approach to modelling a temporal logic system in a random environment. The underlying model is based on stochastic process theory. The authors argue that the natural model of a temporal logic system in a stochastic environment is a finite state Markov chain. Once one accepts such a conclusion, further analysis becomes possible, based on a rich apparatus of stochastic analysis.
- Chapter 6, by E. Orlowska, provides so-called relational proof systems for applied temporal logics. More precisely, temporal logics are interpreted within a relational logic, based on relation algebras. This formalization places various notions of time within a new, very interesting context.
- Chapter 7, by E. Hajnicz, analyzes various time structures applied in computer science. Both point and interval structures are characterized and compared within the framework of classical predicate logic.

The surveys contained in this book are largely self-contained. They present well established and known results together with the most recent achievements. We thus hope that they can serve well both for newcomers to the area and for those who are well acquainted with the subject. Our work on the book was partially supported by the KBN grant 307069101, and by the Institute of Informatics of Warsaw University.

L. Bolc & A. Szałas

Chapter 1

Temporal logic of programs: a standard approach

*A. Szalas**

Institute of Informatics
University of Warsaw
ul. Banacha 2, 02-097 Warsaw, Poland
e-mail: szalas@mimuw.edu.pl

Abstract

This chapter discusses propositional and first-order temporal logic of programs with time corresponding to integers. The logic contains past and future temporal operators. We concentrate mainly on the formal verification of temporal properties. A variety of proof systems is presented in both Hilbert and Gentzen styles. Various notions of soundness and completeness are investigated. We also discuss applications of the logic in the formal specification and verification of properties of algorithms and data structures.

1.1 Introduction

This chapter concerns a standard approach to the temporal logic of programs. We thus first of all feel obliged to explain what we mean by both *temporal logic of programs* and *standard approach*. In general, temporal logics are those nonclassical (multi-modal, to be more precise) logics that allow us to formulate and verify sentences about situations dynamically changing in time. One can, for instance, formulate and verify such opinions as *Bob likes Susan since he met her*, *John drinks tea every day at five* or, getting even closer to computer science, *if initial state of a program is safe (whatever* safety *means here) then every state reached by the program in future is safe.* Despite the fact that

*This work was partly supported by the KBN grant 3 P406 019 06.

time is involved in every aspect of human activity, and is thus more or less explicitly inherited by systems of artificial intelligence, various notions of time naturally appear when one wishes to specify and verify properties of programs and their computations. In other words, programs, when run on computers, do cause time-dependent phenomena. Any execution of a program constitutes a sequence of situations, or states, determined by the program's statements. Thus any natural notion of time, adequate for program specification and verification, has to reflect the nature of execution sequences of programs. Although the choice of time structure is not quite obvious, as we shall see in Chapter 4, for the purpose of this chapter we shall assume that time exactly corresponds to execution sequences of programs. As those sequences are determined step by step by program instructions, time is assumed to be discrete, with points corresponding to natural numbers. This simple and most apparent notion of time has appeared powerful enough to be widely accepted as a basis for the temporal logic which has successfully been applied in the specification and verification of program properties. Thus, when using the term *temporal logic of programs*, we shall always mean the temporal logic in which points of time are labelled by natural numbers.

In fact two slightly different versions of temporal logic of programs have been investigated in the literature. They accept the same notion of time, but differ, in the definition of truth. The first of them is the logic with so called *initial semantics*. Informally speaking, a formula is valid in some interpretation if the first state of interpretation (perhaps together with its suffix) satisfies the formula. This version was investigated by the Manna and Pnueli school of temporal logic (cf. e.g. [29,30,31]). The second version of temporal logic admits so called *normal semantics*, where a formula is valid under some interpretation whenever all suffixes of the temporal sequence satisfy the formula (cf. e.g. [24]). Both versions have the same set of tautologies. They differ, however, when one considers properties of temporal theories. We shall consider a more enriched version of temporal logic. First, we shall add modalities that allow us to formulate sentences about the past. For the sake of simplicity we shall consider time as points which correspond to integers. Both of the previously mentioned versions of temporal logic of programs are, however, covered by our approach; namely, all properties expressible and provable by means of those logics still remain expressible and provable.

As usual, after establishing the semantic properties of considered logic and finding the logic worthy of interest because of its expressive power, elegance, applicability, or yet other benefits it offers, one of our main goals is to search for proof systems for reasoning about properties expressible by means of the logic. One can imagine many different proof systems for a given logic. However, it is quite clear that not all proof systems are equally convenient and powerful. Some of them are even unacceptable. First of all, it may appear that using some particular proof system, one can prove validity of invalid formulas. In such a case we say that proof system is not *sound*. Soundness is then the first and most important criterion for estimating proof systems. On the other hand, one can propose a proof system in which nothing can be proved. Such a proof system is of course sound, but again totally unacceptable. Thus one is obliged to search for such sound proof systems that allow us to prove the validity of as many valid formulas as possible. A proof system that allows us to prove the validity of all valid formulas is called *complete*. When defining proof systems for logics, we are therefore obliged to struggle for their completeness. The most convenient proof systems for both humans and computers are those with computable proofs, i.e. those that allow us to check automatically whether any proof rule leading to the desired conclusion is applied correctly. Unfortunately, even when dealing with logics of programs in which one can express at least the most basic properties of programs, e.g. the halting property, one cannot obtain complete proof systems with computable proofs. Regrettable enough, temporal logic is, in this sense, a typical logic of programs. One can thus either reject the demand for computability of temporal proofs or weaken the notion of completeness. One of the most fruitful approaches that weakens the notion of completeness is known as the *nonstandard approach*, where the notion of time is not precisely fixed, but rather given by a set of postulates. This approach has been proposed and investigated in the case of logics of programs, among others, by a group of Hungarian researchers (cf. e.g. [3,4,5,38,39]). As Chapter 2 gives a detailed introduction to this approach, we shall not discuss it in detail here. We mention it just to explain the term *standard approach*, as opposed to the nonstandard one. That is, to say, the standard approach is always understood via standard semantics which assumes that time corresponds exactly to natural numbers. Thus, when dealing with completeness issues, we shall be forced to admit proof systems that allow proofs whose correctness cannot be checked automatically. We shall, however, pay much attention to defining proof systems that allow us to carry out proofs with computable parts as large as possible.

As we mentioned earlier, the temporal logic of programs belongs to the much larger family of logics of programs developed to serve as a basic tool in defining semantics of programs and proving them correct. Logics of programs play a similar rôle in computer science to that of the classical logic in "pure" mathematics. Classical formulas, however, mirror the static nature of mathematical notions. On the other hand, the dynamic behaviour of programs requires another approach. Currently, in general, researchers agree that the dynamic character of phenomena appearing in most areas of computer science has its counterpart in modal logics of programs. Temporal logic of programs falls into this class of logics. In fact, it is a multi-modal logic with a time-dependent interpretation of modalities.

As there is a great variety of modal logics of programs, let us now put the case for temporal logic. First of all, time is present more or less explicitly in all aspects of computations. The specification and verification of time dependent properties of computations is thus one of the most important tools for design and implementation of software systems. Secondly, temporal logic goes beyond the traditional approach which considers the relational model of programs, i.e. a model which characterizes the behaviour of processes by relations between data and results. It allows us to deal with the model of reactive systems which takes into consideration the whole history of computations. Such a model is necessary when one deals with systems that are not supposed to terminate, and thus cannot be properly described in a relational model. Operating systems, airline reservation systems and industrial process control systems are typical examples of such reactive systems. Thirdly, most logics of programs are associated with specific programming tools, and moreover, usually the most basic ones. Specification of software modules by means of such logics is then strongly dependent on those tools. Temporal logic itself assumes nothing about the specific syntax and semantics of programs. Specification is then truly independent of the programming language to be used for implementation purposes. It just says, in a clear and elegant way, what should be achieved by a module and how it should interact with its environment. Fourthly, temporal logic has many successful applications in the management of databases, knowledge representation, natural language processing, specification and verification of concurrent programs and communication protocols, to mention a few. And last, but not least, understanding temporal logic has become, in many areas of software engineering, as useful and profitable as understanding the algorithms themselves.

One of the main aims of this chapter is to introduce the reader to the temporal logic of programs. We shall show techniques of both specification and verification of time dependent properties of programs and data types, trying to make our presentation as informal and intuitively convincing as possible. As formal verification of program properties must always be accompanied by specific proof systems, we shall present some of them, concentrating on the underlying proof techniques as well as on their most important methodological properties. Let us emphasize here that we shall discuss only those methodological aspects concerning proof theory that are common to most logics of programs and are thus particularly worthy of presentation. Many interesting aspects of temporal logics with only indirect relevance to this chapter will also be omitted. The reader interested in temporal logics themselves is referred to monographs [12,16,36,37,51]. An approach to program verification based on satisfiability and model checking is presented in Chapter 3. Thus we shall not discuss this matter here.

This chapter is organized as follows. First, in section 1.2, we give a general introduction to logics. In particular we discuss and define such notions as logic, semantic consequence, theory and proof systems. The next section contains an introduction to temporal logics. In section 1.4, we define and investigate propositional temporal logic. Among others, we discuss the expressiveness of the logic, present Gentzen and Hilbert-like proof systems and indicate most important properties of those systems and the logic itself. The last section presents first-order temporal logic together with several proof systems and a guide to proving properties of programs and data structures. The presentation of proof systems is accompanied by examples of their application. We have tried to make this introductory chapter as easy to read as possible. One can then read and understand most of the text without any particular knowledge of logic, except perhaps a few very basic notions of classical predicate (first-oder) logic that can be found in any manual on foundations of mathematics. Understanding of all proofs, however, requires some deeper knowledge of logical techniques. We usually give guides to such proofs, without the technicalities that can be found in the literature.

1.2 General logical framework

In this section we establish a general logical framework. We define notions of logic, theory, semantic consequence and proof systems. Let us then start with the very basic notion of logic. Recall first the rôle of logic in the clarification of human reasoning. In order to make the reasoning fruitful, first of all we have to decide what is the subject of reasoning or, in other words, what are we going to talk about and what language are we going to use. The next step is to associate a precise meaning to basic notions of the language, just to avoid ambiguities and misunderstandings. Finally we have to state clearly what kind of opinions (sentences) can be formulated in the language we deal with and, moreover, which of those opinions are true (valid), and which are false (invalid). Now we can investigate the subject of reasoning via the validity of expressed opinions. Such an abstraction just defines a specific logic.

Example Let us illustrate the very general discussion above with an example of well known classical propositional logic. The logic is used to investigate properties of complex sentences built from elementary sentences by using propositional connectives like negation, conjunction, disjunction, implication, etc. Whether complex sentences are true or not, depends solely on logical values of elementary sentences involved in them. For example, elementary sentence p implies elementary sentence q if and when p is false or q is true. Thus in classical propositional logic we need a language containing a set of propositional variables that serve to represent elementary sentences, and the set of propositional connectives used to build complex sentences. The sentences (or formulas) of the logic are formed from elementary sentences by applying propositional connectives. The meaning associated with complex sentences is given by valuations of elementary sentences together with a method of calculating values of complex sentences from their components. □

The above discussion leads to the following definition.

Definition 1.1 By a *logic* we mean triple $L = \langle F, Mod, \models \rangle$, where

- F is a set called the *set of well formed formulas*,

- Mod is a class, called the ***class of admissible interpretations***,
- $\models \subseteq Mod \times F$ is a binary relation, called the ***validity relation***; for $\mathcal{M} \in Mod$ and $p \in F$, $\mathcal{M} \models p$ intuitively means that formula p is true in interpretation $\mathcal{M}$.

For set of formulas $A \subseteq F$ and class of interpretations $B \subseteq Mod$, by $B \models A$ we mean that for any formula $p \in A$ and interpretation $\mathcal{M} \in B$, $\mathcal{M} \models p$. If $\mathcal{M} \models p$ or $\mathcal{M} \models A$ then we say that $\mathcal{M}$ is a *model* of formula p, or set of formulas A, respectively. □

Note that some authors use the term *model* somewhat ambiguously, to mean both an interpretation and a model. This convention is also used in some other chapters in this book. This, however, should not lead to misunderstandings.

Example Returning to our example of classical propositional logic, we note that the set of well formed formulas is just the set of sentences. More precisely, every propositional variable is a formula and $\neg p$ (not p), $p \wedge q$ (p and q) are formulas if p and q are (for simplicity we consider two propositional connectives only, the rest, such as $\vee, \leftarrow, \leftrightarrow$ are definable from these in the usual way). The class (set, in this case) of admissible interpretations consists of valuations of elementary sentences. Those valuations assign logical values T or F to propositional variables representing elementary sentences. Given valuation v of propositional variables, one can define the semantic consequence relation inductively:

- for propositional variable p, $v \models p$ iff $v(p) = \mathsf{T}$,
- if p is a formula then $v \models (\neg p)$ iff not $v \models p$,
- if p and q are formulas, then $v \models (p \wedge q)$ iff $v \models p$ and $v \models q$. □

One of the most important notions concerning semantics of logics is that of semantic consequence relation. Namely, the most fundamental application of logics depends on specifying and proving properties of classes of interpretations. For instance, one may be interested in the classical first-order theory of rings, groups, real numbers, natural numbers, stacks, queues, trees or arrays, to mention only a few typical examples. Thus, having chosen a logic, one usually selects the data and operations one is interested in and then specifies their properties by means of formulas of the logic. In other words, one builds a theory of operations and data. When choosing specified properties, a compromise must be found between the completeness of a specification and its simplicity and applicability. *Completeness* means here that the specification should contain answers to all possible questions one can ask about operations and data. *Simplicity and applicability* means, among others, that the specification should be effective, i.e. accompanied by a method of checking automatically whether a given formula belongs to the specification or not. As completeness and effectiveness do sometimes exclude each other, one has to decide which one is more important. In general, effectiveness has priority over completeness. Thus specification is found to be "nice" whenever it is effective and is as close to completeness as possible. The chosen set of basic properties of the specification should then be as small as possible, with a rich set of consequences. As a given specification can often have different models, one can talk only about consequences as facts which are valid in all models of the specification. The semantic consequence of a set of formulas is then defined as set of such consequences. Its rôle in logics and theories is then the basic one. As we shall show later, the rôle of theories in the temporal logic of programs is fundamental, for the semantics of algorithms and data structures in this logic are, one way or another, given by temporal theories. Let us conclude this discussion with the following definitions.

Definition 1.2 Let $L = \langle F, Mod, \models \rangle$ be a logic and let $A \subseteq F$ be a set of formulas. The set of ***semantic consequences*** of A, denoted by $Cn_L(A)$, is defined as the set of those formulas of F which are true in every model of A, i.e. $Cn_L(A) = \{p \in F \mid \text{for all } \mathcal{M} \in Mod, \mathcal{M} \models A \text{ implies } \mathcal{M} \models p\}$; $p \in Cn_L(A)$ is often denoted as $A \models p$ (somewhat ambiguously). □

Definition 1.3 Let $L = \langle F, Mod, \models \rangle$ be a logic. Then by ***theory based on*** L we mean a pair $T = \langle F_T, A_T \rangle$ where

- $F_T \subseteq F$ is a set of formulas, called a ***language*** of T,
- $A_T \subseteq F_T$ is a set of formulas expressed in the language of T, called a set of ***specific axioms*** of T.

By a set of formulas ***valid*** in theory T we mean $Cn_L(A_T) \cap F_T$. □

Usually, F_T in the above definition is not an arbitrary subset of F. Namely, the definition of L usually also contains a distinguished $Lang \subseteq 2^F$ and then $F_T \in Lang$ is required. Whenever F is defined by fixing a set of logical connectives (such as $\wedge, \neg, \Box$, in case of modal logic), then $Lang = \{F_T \mid F_T \subseteq F \text{ and } F_T \text{ is closed under all the logical connectives of } L\}$. For simplicity, we will ignore this here, but see e.g. [19].

Note that the definition of truth itself almost never gives explicit answers on the validity of opinions, since it depends on classes of interpretations. In particular, semantic proofs based on the above definitions cannot be automated. On the other hand, some methods of proving theorems are necessary to make the reasoning formal and verifiable. There are two goals one can achieve by formal reasoning. The first one is to establish those properties that are valid in all interpretations (so-called *tautologies*). The second is to establish properties valid in some interesting classes of interpretations, described by means of theories. Gentzen-like proof systems are found suitable for proving tautologies.

They can be implemented directly, or at least can suggest such an implementation. (For a more comprehensive study of implementing proof systems see e.g. [11,17].)

Although very important, tautologies can only support reasoning about validities. On the other hand, when analyzing properties of programs, one always deals with some specific theories describing certain interpretations, such as natural numbers, stacks, trees or lists. Hilbert-like axiomatic methods based on proof systems are accepted as a basis for formal and verifiable reasoning about both tautologies and properties of interpretations. They are more intuitive and easier to understand. However, there are currently much more open questions concerning the implementation of Hilbert-like proof systems than there are suitable solutions. The reasoning with Hilbert-like proof systems depends on accepting a set of basic axioms (i.e. "obvious" formulas admitted without proof), together with derivation rules, and then on deriving conclusions directly from axioms and/or theorems proved previously. Derivation rules are usually formulated according to the following scheme (we shall return to Gentzen style later):

> if all formulas from a set of formulas (so-called *premises*) A are proved then formula p (so-called *conclusion*) is proved, too.

Such a rule is denoted by $A \vdash p$. The set of *provable formulas* is defined inductively as the least set of formulas satisfying the following conditions:

- Every axiom is provable (note that some of the axioms may be so-called nonlogical axioms coming from the specific theory we are working in).
- If the premises of a rule are provable then its conclusion is provable, too.

One can then think of proof systems as nondeterministic procedures, for the process of proving theorems can be formulated as follows, where formula p is the one to be proved valid:

> if p is an axiom, or is already proved, then the proof is finished, otherwise select (nondeterministically) a set of axioms or previously proved theorems and then apply a nondeterministically chosen applicable derivation rule. Accept the thus obtained conclusion as the new theorem and repeat the described procedure.

As axioms are special kinds of derivation rules (namely those with the empty set of premises), nondeterminism can appear only when there are several derivation rules that can be applied during the proof. Note, however, that the procedure just described is not always computable. Uncomputability, for example, appears when one accepts infinitary derivation rules, i.e. those with infinitely many premises. Both nondeterminism and uncomputability make the search for proofs difficult or even impossible to mechanize.

Gentzen-like proof systems, also called ***sequent calculus***, offer a more general form of derivation rules. The key rôle is played here by the notion of sequents taking the form $A \Rightarrow B$, where both A and B are finite sets of formulas. Intuitively, sequent $A \Rightarrow B$ means the following:

> conjunction of formulas of set A implies disjunction of formulas of B, where, by convention, conjunction of the empty set of formulas is T, while its disjunction is F.

There is, however, an essential difference between the Hilbert and Gentzen methods of proofs. Namely, as Hilbert-like calculus is used to derive single formulas from sets of formulas, so sequent calculus allows us to derive sequents from other sequents. Moreover, Gentzen- and Hilbert-like proofs go in opposite directions. That is to say, in Hilbert-like systems the formula to be proved is obtained in the final stage of the proof, while in a Gentzen-like proof it is a starting point of the proof. The Gentzen-like (naive) proof procedure can then be formulated as follows, where formula p is to be proved valid.

> Start the whole proof from sequent $\emptyset \Rightarrow \{p\}$. If the sequent (or all other sequents obtained during derivation, if any) is (are) indecomposable (i.e. rules are no longer applicable) then check whether all of the final sequents are axioms. If the answer is yes, then p is proved valid, otherwise it is invalid. If some sequent is decomposable then first decompose it and then repeat the described procedure.

Axioms in Gentzen-like proof systems are usually very simple. For instance, any sequent $A \Rightarrow B$ such that $A \cap B \neq \emptyset$ is an axiom in many proof systems for tautologies. Derivation rules, however, take the more complicated form $S \vdash B$, where S is a set of sequents and B is a sequent.

Note that Hilbert-like proof systems are easy to use while reasoning about theories. One has only to add specific axioms of a theory to axioms of logic and then to apply derivation rules. Many theories do have nice Gentzen-like axiomatizations. However, obtaining them is often not a trivial task. Moreover, implementation of Gentzen-like axiomatizations of theories raises new problems and considerably complicates the process of finding proofs.

Let us summarize the above discussion with the following definitions.

Definition 1.4 Let $L = \langle F, Mod, \models \rangle$ be a logic.

- By a ***sequent*** of logic L we mean any expression of the form $A \Rightarrow B$, where A and B are finite sets of formulas of L.
- By a ***Gentzen-like proof system*** for logic L we mean any pair $\langle GAx, G\rangle$ such that
  - GAx, called a set of ***axioms***, is any set of sequents of L,

- G is any set of derivation rules of the form $S \vdash s$, where S is a set of sequents of L, and s is a sequent of L.

- We say that sequent s is ***indecomposable*** in a given Gentzen-like proof system iff s is an axiom or no rule of the system is applicable to s. A sequent is called ***decomposable*** iff it is not indecomposable.

- By a ***Hilbert-like proof system*** for logic L we mean any pair $\langle HAx, H\rangle$ such that
  - HAx, called a set of ***axioms***, is any set of formulas of L,
  - H is any set of derivation rules of the form $A \vdash p$, where A is a set of formulas of L, and p is a formula of L. □

Note that separating axioms from rules in the case of Hilbert-like proof systems is not necessary. Such a separation, however, allows us to treat both Gentzen- and Hilbert-like proof systems uniformly. Note also that axioms and derivation rules are usually given by schemes rather than by specific sequents, formulas or sets. For instance, writing $p, p \rightarrow q \vdash q$ we always think of p and q as variables ranging over set of formulas. Thus the above scheme of rules defines (usually infinitely) many rules that can be obtained by substituting p and q with specific formulas.

Definition 1.5 Let $P = \langle Ax, C\rangle$ be a Gentzen (Hilbert)-like proof system for logic $L = \langle F, Mod, \models\rangle$. By a *proof* in P we mean a rooted tree labelled by sequents (formulas) such that

- the height of the tree is finite,
- all leaves are labelled by elements of Ax (sequents or formulas, respectively),
- any node n in the tree is labelled either by an element of Ax, or by sequent (formula) s for which there is a derivation rule $D \vdash s$ in C with $D = \{t | t \text{ is a label of a son of } n \text{ in the tree}\}$.

We say that the sequent (formula) s is provable in P iff there is a proof in P with a root labelled by s. □

Since we are not going to discuss here applications of Gentzen-style proofs of theories, the next definition concerns Hilbert-like proof systems only. The reader interested in a more comprehensive presentation of Gentzen-like systems is referred to [50].

Definition 1.6 Let $P = \langle HAx, H\rangle$ be a Hilbert-like proof system for logic $L = \langle F, Mod, \models\rangle$. By a ***syntactic consequence*** (w.r.t. P) of a set of formulas A we mean any formula provable in the proof system $\langle HAx \cup A, H\rangle$. The set of syntactic consequences (w.r.t. P) of set A is denoted by $C_P(A)$. □

We conclude this section with an informal discussion of soundness and completeness. As mentioned in the introduction, soundness is always the most fundamental property of any reasonable proof system. Soundness means that all proved conclusions are semantically true. In terms of procedures, one can define soundness as correctness of the procedure implementing the proof system. All the results of the procedure must then be correct. Completeness, however, means that all semantically true conclusions can be obtained as results of the procedure. In other words, soundness means that all answers given by a proof system are correct, while completeness means that all correct answers can be obtained using the proof system. As soundness is then always required, completeness serves as a measure of the quality of proof systems. Since we shall deal with several notions of soundness and completeness, precise definitions of those notions will be given later, when necessary.

1.3 Introduction to temporal logics

As temporal logics serve as a tool for expressing and verifying properties dynamically changing in time, one first of all has to decide what is the structure of time, and what are time-dependent properties. Both time structure and time-dependent properties are strongly dependent on the specific application. As we are now mainly interested in the temporal logics of programs, we shall not attempt to give any general definition of temporal logics. Instead, we shall present a definition that follows intuitions related to programs and their computations. Consider then typical programs. Usual programs are algorithms that compute over fixed, time-independent data structures. Program variables are thus those symbols that change while passing from one program state to another. For our purposes it is then sufficient to admit that the only time-dependent symbols are program variables, and that all other symbols are independent of the flow of time. Time-dependent symbols are usually called *flexible* or *local*, while time-independent ones are *rigid* or *global*. The situation with the notion of time is not that simple, for temporal logics of programs are mainly applied to specification and verification of concurrent computations. Thus there can be as many reasonable structures of time as there are possible models of computations. Accepting the so-called interleaving model, where actions of processes are shuffled, one deals with a linear time. For semantics based on partial orders, partially ordered time is the most natural and apparent. It is not difficult to give examples of applications where multilinear time suits best. Even when one deals with linear time, there is a wide choice. The following are typical examples:

- time is reals, ordered by the usual relation $\leq$, i.e. the corresponding time structure is $\langle R, \leq \rangle$,

- time is integers ordered by the usual relation $\leq$, i.e. the time structure is $\langle Z, \leq \rangle$,
- time is natural numbers with a successor function (corresponding to next-time modality) ordered by the relation $\leq$, i.e. the time structure is $\langle N, succ, \leq \rangle$,
- time is natural numbers with distinguished constants 0, 1, addition, multiplication and ordered by the relation $\leq$, i.e. the time structure is $\langle N, 0, 1, +, *, \leq \rangle$.

In the general definition of the temporal logic of programs we have to accept all possible notions of time. We shall assume that time is given by means of classical first-order interpretation. Since data structures are usually defined by first-order interpretations, too, we have the following definition.

Definition 1.7 By *temporal logic* we mean any logic $TL = \langle F, Mod, \models \rangle$ such that

- F contains a distinguished set of constants C (elements of C are called *flexible constants*); no symbols except those of C can have a time-dependent meaning,
- Mod is a class of classical two-sorted interpretations of the form $\langle T, D, (f_c)_{c \in C} \rangle$, where
  - T is a *time structure*,
  - D is a *data structure* that gives meaning to function and relation symbols (as in classical first-order logic),
  - for any $c \in C$, $f_c : T \longrightarrow D$ is a function from T to D which serves to interpret constant c (the value of c at time t is $f_c(t)$). □

Note that in the case of propositional versions of temporal logics, data structure D of the above definition consists of two-element boolean algebra (with universe $\{\mathsf{T}, \mathsf{F}\}$).

Observe also that flexible constants are usually called *variables* in the literature as they correspond to program variables. In what follows we shall often use similar terminology.

1.4 Propositional temporal logic of programs

1.4.1 Introduction

Let us now define the propositional version of temporal logic of integer time (PTL). First of all, recall that *propositionality* means that we accept the two-element boolean algebra as the underlying data structure. Such a choice of data structure has many important consequences. From our point of view the most important of them is that the set of tautologies is decidable. As we shall show later, any infinite data structure, together with first-order quantifiers, makes the set of tautologies undecidable. Propositional temporal logic, then, plays a vital rôle in automated temporal theorem proving. In particular, temporal properties of programs that do not compute over infinite domains (many communication protocols among them) can be verified automatically.

In the following definition we shall introduce only two temporal operators, A and $\overline{A}$. These operators are similar. Their main difference is that A concerns the future, while $\overline{A}$ deals with the past. Intuitively, pAq means that p will be satisfied at the nearest of the future time points with q satisfied and $p\overline{A}q$ means that p has been satisfied at the nearest of the past time points with q satisfied. Note that we deal with the strong versions of the temporal operators, in that we require that pAq implies satisfiability of q at some future time point and $p\overline{A}q$ implies its satisfiability somewhere in the past.

Definition 1.8 By propositional temporal logic of programs we mean triple

$$PTL = \langle F_0, Mod_0, \models_0 \rangle,$$

where

- F_0 is the set of propositional temporal formulas containing a distinguished set P of flexible ***propositional variables*** and closed under the following formation rules
  1. if $p, q \in F_0$ then also $\neg p$, $p \wedge q \in F_0$ (other usual propositional connectives are regarded as abbreviations),
  2. if $p, q \in F_0$ then also pAq, $p\overline{A}q \in F_0$;
- Mod is the class of two-sorted first-order interpretations $\langle \mathbf{Z}, D, (f_p)_{p\in P} \rangle$, where
  1. $\mathbf{Z}$ is the structure of integers ordered by the usual relation $\leq$, i.e. $\mathbf{Z} = \langle Z, \leq \rangle$,
  2. D is the two-element boolean algebra with universe $\{\mathsf{T}, \mathsf{F}\}$,
  3. for any $p \in P$, $f_p : Z \longrightarrow \{\mathsf{T}, \mathsf{F}\}$ is a function assigning boolean values to propositional variables (intuitively $f_p(t)$ is the value of p at time point t)
- for $\mathcal{M} \in Mod_0$, and $p \in F_0$, $\mathcal{M} \models_0 p$ iff for all $t \in Z$, $\mathcal{M}, t \Vdash p$, where
  1. $\mathcal{M}, t \Vdash p$, for $p \in P$, iff $f_p(t) = \mathsf{T}$
  2. $\mathcal{M}, t \Vdash \neg p$, for $p \in F_0$, iff not $\mathcal{M}, t \Vdash p$
  3. $\mathcal{M}, t \Vdash p \wedge q$, for $p, q \in F_0$, iff $\mathcal{M}, t \Vdash p$ and $\mathcal{M}, t \Vdash q$

4. $\mathcal{M}, t \Vdash pAq$, for $p, q \in F_0$, iff there is $t_1 \in Z$ such that $t_1 > t$, $\mathcal{M}, t_1 \Vdash p \wedge q$ and for all $t < t_2 < t_1$, $\mathcal{M}, t_2 \Vdash \neg q$
5. $\mathcal{M}, t \Vdash p\overline{A}q$, for $p, q \in F_0$, iff there is $t_1 \in Z$ such that $t_1 < t$, $\mathcal{M}, t_1 \Vdash p \wedge q$ and for all $t_1 < t_2 < t$, $\mathcal{M}, t_2 \Vdash \neg q$. □

Note that all propositional variables are flexible. Observe also that the only temporal operators introduced in the above definitions are A and $\overline{A}$. One can, however, prove that for integer time ($\langle Z, \leq \rangle$) those operators are *fully expressive*. Let us explain this more precisely. First note that usual definitions of temporal operators take the following form

- $\overline{\Diamond} q$ is true at time point t iff there is time point $t' < t$ such that q is true at t',
- $\Box q$ is true at time point t iff for all time points $t' > t$, q is true at t',

and so on. When defining operators formally, we deal with *monadic* first-order theory of the flow of time. This means that we allow, besides $\leq$, unary predicates over time and quantifiers over time points. For instance, defining the above operators in the formal language, we have the following definitions, where Q is a predicate corresponding to q

- $\overline{\Diamond}$ is defined by formula $\exists t' < t[Q(t')]$ (the formula $\exists t' < t[Q(t')]$ is the so-called *truth table* for operator $\overline{\Diamond}$),
- the truth table of operator $\Box$ is the formula $\forall t' > t[Q(t')]$.

Full expressiveness of A and $\overline{A}$ means then, that for any monadic first-order formula p of the flow of time there is a formula q of PTL with p as its truth table, i.e.

q is true at time point t iff $p(t)$ holds.

Informally, any temporal operator over integer time definable by means of the usual definitions is also definable in the temporal logic we deal with. The sketch of proof of this fact is to be found in [13]. In fact, the proof concerns operators $\overline{U}$ and U. As those are expressible by means of A and $\overline{A}$, the theorem still remains valid for our version of propositional temporal logic.

Let us define the other usual temporal operators. In what follows, $s = t$ and $s < t$ are abbreviations for $(s \leq t \wedge t \leq s)$ and $(s \leq t \wedge s \neq t)$, respectively.

- the operator $\overline{U}$ with truth table $\exists t' < t[P(t') \wedge \forall s(t' < s < t \rightarrow Q(s))]$ is defined by
$$(q\overline{U}p) \leftrightarrow [p\overline{A}(q \rightarrow p)]$$
- the operator U with truth table $\exists t' > t[P(t') \wedge \forall s(t < s < t' \rightarrow Q(s))]$ is defined by
$$(qUp) \leftrightarrow [pA(q \rightarrow p)]$$

- the operator $\overline{\bigcirc}$ with truth table $\exists t' < t\ [\forall t'' < t(t'' \leq t') \wedge Q(t')]$ (i.e. Q is true at the immediate predecessor of t) is defined by

$$(\overline{\bigcirc} q) \leftrightarrow q\overline{A}\mathsf{T}$$

- the operator $\bigcirc$ with truth table $\exists t' > t\ [\forall t'' > t(t'' \geq t') \wedge Q(t')]$ (i.e. Q is true at the immediate successor of t) is defined by

$$(\bigcirc q) \leftrightarrow qA\mathsf{T}$$

- the operator $\overline{\Diamond}$ with truth table $\exists t' < t[Q(t')]$ is defined by

$$(\overline{\Diamond} q) \leftrightarrow \mathsf{T}\overline{A}q$$

- the operator $\Diamond$ with truth table $\exists t' > t[Q(t')]$ is defined by

$$\Diamond q \leftrightarrow \mathsf{T}Aq$$

- the operator $\overline{\Box}$ with truth table $\forall t' < t[Q(t')]$ is defined by

$$\overline{\Box} q \leftrightarrow (\neg\overline{\Diamond}(\neg q))$$

- the operator $\Box$ with truth table $\forall t' > t[Q(t')]$ is defined by

$$\Box q \leftrightarrow (\neg\Diamond(\neg q))$$

- the operator $\boxdot$ with truth table $\forall t[Q(t)]$ is defined by

$$\boxdot\, q \leftrightarrow (\overline{\Box} q \wedge q \wedge \Box q)$$

- the operator $\diamonddot$ with truth table $\exists t[Q(t)]$ is defined by

$$\diamonddot\, q \leftrightarrow (\neg\boxdot\neg q).$$

It is worth emphasizing here that our definitions of temporal operators concern *strict* past and future (without *now*). Another, equally expressive, possibility is to consider past and future that include *now* (see Chapter 2).

Observe that both initial and normal semantics for the temporal logic of programs (cf. [29,30,31] and [24], respectively) can be expressed by means of *PTL*. Since both semantics concern time with a structure of nonnegative integers ($\langle Z_+, \leq\rangle$), we first of all have to define the first time point, corresponding to 0. Such a definition can take, for instance, the following form, where $\circledast$ is a propositional variable

$$\diamonddot(\circledast) \wedge (\circledast \rightarrow (\overline{\Box}(\neg\circledast) \wedge \Box(\neg\circledast)))$$

i.e. $\circledast$ is true exactly at one time point. Now we can treat the time point in which $\circledast$ is true as the starting point of the temporal sequence. As operator *A* is expressively complete for time $\langle Z_+, \leq \rangle$ we can consider formulas of temporal logics of programs with operator A only and translate any formula p into

$$p\overline{A}\circledast$$

in the case of initial semantics, and into

$$(\overline{\Diamond}\circledast) \wedge p$$

in the case of normal semantics.

Let us now consider a few examples of properties of programs expressible by means of temporal logics of programs (thus by PTL, too). Some other examples can be found in [24,29,30,31]. In the following examples we assume that formulas p and q do not contain past time operators. Another classification of program properties, including the past, is given in [28] and [31].

- **Invariance (safety) properties**
  - $p \rightarrow \Box q$ (all states reached by a program after the state satisfying p will satisfy q)
  - $(\circledast \rightarrow p) \rightarrow \Box(AtEnd \rightarrow q)$ (partial correctness w.r.t conditions p and q, where propositional variable $\circledast$ is true only at the beginning of the specified program, while $AtEnd$ is true only when the program reaches its terminal state)
  - $\Box((\neg q) \vee (\neg p))$ (the program cannot enter critical regions p and q simultaneously (mutual exclusion)).
- **Eventuality properties**
  - $p \rightarrow \Diamond q$ (there is a program state satisfying q reached by a program after the state satisfying p)
  - $(\circledast \rightarrow p) \rightarrow qA\, AtEnd$ (total correctness w.r.t. conditions p and q)
  - $\Box\Diamond p \rightarrow \Diamond q$ (repeating a request p will force a response q)
  - $\Box p \rightarrow \Diamond q$ (permanent holding a request p will force a response q).

Note that precedence properties are easier and more natural to express by past time operators than by future time ones. For instance, a typical precedence property stating that any occurrence of a program state (event) satisfying p (if any) must be preceded by a state (event) satisfying q, can be formulated by past time operator $\overline{\Diamond}$ as follows

$$p \rightarrow \overline{\Diamond} q$$

while a suitable formula involving future time operators only would have to look like

$$\Diamond p \rightarrow (\neg p U q).$$

The propositional temporal logic we deal with, *PTL*, is decidable. This means that there is an algorithm to decide whether a given formula is satisfiable. More precisely, given a formula p of *PTL*, we can automatically check whether there is an interpretation $\mathcal{M} = \langle \mathbf{Z}, D, (f_p)_{p \in P} \rangle \in Mod_0$ satisfying p (i.e. such that $\mathcal{M} \models p$). Such an algorithm can, for instance, use the following important theorem.

Theorem 1.1 If a formula of *PTL* is satisfiable then it is satisfiable by a finitely representable interpretation. Moreover, the size of the interpretation can be calculated from size of the formula. □

A (naive) procedure of checking satisfiability could then be the following:

> given a formula p, calculate the size k of the interpretation and generate all possible interpretations of size k, testing whether they do satisfy p (as interpretations are finitely representable, such tests can easily be programmed).

The proof of Theorem 1.1 can be carried out using a standard technique of filtration (cf. Chapter 2 & [16]). The technique, in the case of temporal logics, has been applied in [6,13,24,28]. Chapter 2 and the last of the quoted works are of particular interest for us, as they concern temporal logic with (bounded) past, and give a detailed procedure of checking satisfiability. The procedure of Lichtenstein et al. ([28]) can easily be modified to cover the case of an unbounded past (i.e. that of *PTL*). As a full presentation of the procedure would have to be a bit too technical here, the interested reader is referred to the quoted paper. Let us only mention that given a formula p, time complexity of the procedure is $O(length.of.p * 2^{4*length.of.p})$. An automata theoretic technique of obtaining satisfiability procedures for temporal logics is also presented in this book, in Chapter 3 (also [40]).

As p is a tautology iff $\neg p$ is not satisfiable, the procedure of checking satisfiability can also be used to check whether a given formula p is a tautology.

1.4.2 Hilbert-like proof system for *PTL*

Let us now define the Hilbert-like proof system for the propositional temporal logic *PTL*.

Definition 1.9 By the Hilbert-like proof system *HP* for logic *PTL* we mean the system $\langle HAx, H \rangle$, where

- set *HAx* consists of the following (schemes of) axioms
    1. $\vdash \neg \bigcirc p \leftrightarrow \bigcirc(\neg p)$
    2. $\vdash (\bigcirc p \wedge \bigcirc q) \rightarrow \bigcirc(p \wedge q)$

3. $\vdash pAq \leftrightarrow \bigcirc((p \wedge q) \vee (\neg q \wedge pAq))$
4. $\vdash \neg\overline{\bigcirc}p \leftrightarrow \overline{\bigcirc}(\neg p)$
5. $\vdash (\overline{\bigcirc}p \wedge \overline{\bigcirc}q) \rightarrow \overline{\bigcirc}(p \wedge q)$
6. $\vdash p\overline{A}q \leftrightarrow \overline{\bigcirc}((p \wedge q) \vee (\neg q \wedge p\overline{A}q))$
7. $\vdash p \leftrightarrow \bigcirc(\overline{\bigcirc}p)$
8. $\vdash p \leftrightarrow \overline{\bigcirc}(\bigcirc p)$
9. $\vdash \Box(p \rightarrow \bigcirc p) \rightarrow (\bigcirc p \rightarrow \Box p)$
10. $\vdash \overline{\Box}(p \rightarrow \overline{\bigcirc}p) \rightarrow (\overline{\bigcirc}p \rightarrow \overline{\Box}p)$

- set H consists of the following (schemes of) derivation rules

  1. for each substitution instance of a classical propositional tautology $p, \vdash p$
  2. $p,\ p \rightarrow q\ \vdash\ q$
  3. $p \rightarrow q\ \vdash\ pAr \rightarrow qAr$
  4. $\bigcirc(p \wedge q) \rightarrow r,\ \bigcirc(\neg q \wedge r) \rightarrow r,\ r \rightarrow s\ \vdash\ pAq \rightarrow s$
  5. $p \rightarrow q \vdash\ p\overline{A}r \rightarrow q\overline{A}r$
  6. $\overline{\bigcirc}(p \wedge q) \rightarrow r,\ \overline{\bigcirc}(\neg q \wedge r) \rightarrow r,\ r \rightarrow s\ \vdash\ p\overline{A}q \rightarrow s$ □

Although the above proof system is influenced by those in the literature (cf. [24, 28,31]), it differs essentially from them. The main difference is that the proof system defined above offers proof rules which make the search for proofs easier. In particular, no other propositional proof system we know gives proof rules that explicitly characterize the most important temporal operators, such as $\overline{A}, A$ The only characterization of those operators is usually given by recursive axioms (like axioms 3 and 6 of HP). The presence of proof rules dealing directly with A and $\overline{A}$ (rules 3, 5 and particularly useful 4 and 6) makes the process of proving propositional temporal tautologies more goal-oriented. Similar rules were for the first time proposed in [45] in case of first-order temporal logic of programs (cf. also section 1.5.4).

A few examples of applications of HP now follow.

Example First we shall show (trivial) formal proofs that the following usual axioms of many propositional temporal proof systems

$$pAr \rightarrow \Diamond r, \tag{1.1}$$

$$\bigcirc(p \wedge q) \rightarrow (\bigcirc p \wedge \bigcirc q), \tag{1.2}$$

$$\overline{\bigcirc}(p \wedge q) \rightarrow (\overline{\bigcirc}p \wedge \overline{\bigcirc}q) \tag{1.3}$$

are derivable in system HP.

First note that $\Diamond r$ is, by definition, equivalent to $\mathbf{T}Ar$. Formula $p \rightarrow \mathbf{T}$ is derivable in system HP by application of rule 1, as it is simply a classical propositional tautology. Thus, applying rule 3 with q substituted by $\mathbf{T}$ we obtain $pAr \rightarrow \mathbf{T}Ar$, i.e., by definition, $pAr \rightarrow \Diamond r$. This proves (1.1).

As proofs of (1.2) and (1.3) are similar, we shall present the second of them. According to the definition, $\overline{\bigcirc}p \leftrightarrow p\overline{A}\mathbf{T}$, thus, by rule 1, it suffices to prove that

$$(p \wedge q)\overline{A}\mathbf{T} \rightarrow p\overline{A}\mathbf{T} \tag{1.4}$$

and

$$(p \wedge q)\overline{A}\mathbf{T} \rightarrow q\overline{A}\mathbf{T}. \tag{1.5}$$

Since formulas $(p \wedge q) \rightarrow p$ and $(p \wedge q) \rightarrow q$ are classical propositional tautologies, we prove (1.4) and (1.5) by application of rule 1 and then 5 with r substituted by $\mathbf{T}$.

Note that the following tautologies can be proved applying axioms 1, 4, tautologies (1.2), (1.3) and rule 1

$$\vdash \bigcirc(p \rightarrow q) \leftrightarrow (\bigcirc p \rightarrow \bigcirc q), \tag{1.6}$$

$$\vdash \overline{\bigcirc}(p \rightarrow q) \leftrightarrow (\overline{\bigcirc}p \rightarrow \overline{\bigcirc}q). \tag{1.7}$$

□

The following example shows a formal proof of a temporal property that combines past and future. It also displays the usefulness of proof rule 4.

Example Let us present a formal proof of the following temporal tautology

$$p \rightarrow \Box(\overline{\Diamond}p).$$

Reformulating using suitable definitions of operators $\Box$ and $\overline{\Diamond}$ we obtain the following equivalent formula

$$p \rightarrow \neg(\mathbf{T}A(\neg(\mathbf{T}\overline{A}p))),$$

i.e., by classical propositional reasoning, we have to prove the formula

$$\mathbf{T}A(\neg(\mathbf{T}\overline{A}p)) \rightarrow \neg p.$$

Its form suggests the use of rule 4 of proof system HP. It is then sufficient to find an invariant r such that premises of the rule can be proved valid. After applying suitable substitutions, those premises take the following form

$$\bigcirc(\mathbf{T} \wedge (\neg(\mathbf{T}\overline{A}p))) \rightarrow r, \tag{1.8}$$

$$\bigcirc(\mathbf{T}\overline{A}p \wedge r) \rightarrow r, \tag{1.9}$$

$$r \rightarrow (\neg p). \tag{1.10}$$

At first glance it seems that substituting r by $\neg p$ should work. Unfortunately, it is not the case. It is, however, quite a usual situation in the logics of programs (e.g. in that of Hoare for partial correctness of **while**-programs) that the invariant has to be stronger than the desired conclusion suggests. No wonder then, that a similar phenomenon is inherited by the temporal logic of programs. In our proof we shall accept formula $\bigcirc(\overline{\Box}(\neg p))$ as a suitable invariant. By the definition of $\overline{\Box}$, the invariant takes the form $\bigcirc(\neg(\mathbf{T}\overline{A}p))$.

The premise (1.8) reduces now to $\bigcirc(\neg(\mathbf{T}\overline{A}p)) \rightarrow \bigcirc(\neg(\mathbf{T}\overline{A}p))$, which as an obvious classical propositional tautology is provable (by rule (1) of HP).

After replacing r by our invariant and applying classical propositional reasoning, the second premise (1.9) takes the form

$$\bigcirc(\mathbf{T}\overline{A}p \wedge \bigcirc(\neg(\mathbf{T}\overline{A}p))) \rightarrow \bigcirc(\neg(\mathbf{T}\overline{A}p)).$$

Note that provability of formula $\bigcirc\bigcirc(\neg(\mathbf{T}\overline{A}p)) \rightarrow \bigcirc(\neg(\mathbf{T}\overline{A}p))$ implies, by axiom 1, tautology (1.6) of the previous example and rule (1) of HP, provability of the premise (1.9). By tautology (1.6) it suffices to show provability of the formula $\bigcirc(\neg(\mathbf{T}\overline{A}p)) \rightarrow (\neg(\mathbf{T}\overline{A}p))$, i.e. by axiom 1 and rule 1, provability of formula

$$\mathbf{T}\overline{A}p \rightarrow \bigcirc(\mathbf{T}\overline{A}p). \tag{1.11}$$

Consider the right-hand side of the implication (1.11). After application of axiom 6 we can rewrite it as $\bigcirc(\overline{\bigcirc}(\mathbf{T} \wedge p) \vee \overline{\bigcirc}(\neg p \wedge \mathbf{T}\overline{A}p))$. By applying axioms 1, 7 and tautology (1.6), we obtain the formula $p \vee (\neg p \wedge \mathbf{T}\overline{A}p)$, i.e. by rule 1, formula $(p \vee \mathbf{T}\overline{A}p)$, which, again by rule 1, is implied by the left-hand side of implication (1.11).

The premise (1.8), $r \rightarrow (\neg p)$, takes the form $\bigcirc(\neg(\mathbf{T}\overline{A}p)) \rightarrow (\neg p)$. To prove this formula it suffices to apply axiom 1 together with rule 1 in order to obtain the formula $p \rightarrow \bigcirc(\mathbf{T}\overline{A}p)$. This formula can be proved by applying axiom 6 and then 7 together with axiom 1, tautology (1.6) and rule 1.
To complete the proof it now suffices to apply rule 4 of HP. □

As it follows from the completeness theorem (see Theorem 1.3), HP offers a sufficient set of axioms and proof rules. This means that no new axiom or proof rule could possibly strengthen HP to prove more propositional temporal tautologies. On the other hand, so-called ***derived proof rules*** are very useful in practical applications. The following example shows a derivation of such a rule.

Example Let us now show that the usual rule

$$p \vdash \overline{\Box}p$$

is derivable in HP. Formulating the rule in terms of $\overline{A}$, we have to prove the derivability of rule $p \vdash \neg(\mathbf{T}\overline{A}(\neg p))$, i.e. by rule 1, $p \vdash (\mathbf{T}\overline{A}(\neg p)) \rightarrow \mathbf{F}$. The conclusion suggests using rule 6. The invariant has now to be equivalent to F, i.e. we have to prove the following premises

$$\overline{\bigcirc}(\mathsf{T} \wedge \neg p) \rightarrow \mathsf{F}, \tag{1.12}$$

$$\overline{\bigcirc}((\neg\neg p) \wedge \mathsf{F}) \rightarrow \mathsf{F}, \tag{1.13}$$

$$\mathsf{F} \rightarrow \mathsf{F}. \tag{1.14}$$

By the premise of the rule to be derived together with rule 1, we have that formula $(\neg p) \rightarrow \mathsf{F}$ is a tautology. Thus, by applying tautology (1.7), we have provability of $\overline{\bigcirc}(\neg p) \rightarrow \overline{\bigcirc}\mathsf{F}$. Since, by definition of F, $\overline{\bigcirc}(\mathsf{F}) \leftrightarrow \overline{\bigcirc}(q \wedge \neg q)$, by combining axioms 4 and 5 together with the definition of F, we have $\overline{\bigcirc}(q \wedge \neg q) \leftrightarrow (\overline{\bigcirc}q \wedge \overline{\bigcirc}\neg q) \leftrightarrow (\overline{\bigcirc}p \wedge \neg\overline{\bigcirc}p) \leftrightarrow \mathsf{F}$ i.e. $\overline{\bigcirc}(\neg p) \rightarrow \mathsf{F}$.

The provability of premises (1.13) and (1.14) is obvious. We are then allowed to apply rule 6 in order to obtain the desired conclusion. □

Observe that the rule *modus ponens* (rule 2 of *HP*) has not been applied in the above example. However, *modus ponens* is very useful in formal justification of derived proof rules. The technique of such a justification is based on the following simple observation:

> if implication $p \rightarrow q$ is a tautology then proof rule $p \vdash q$ is correct (sound), for the second premise of *modus ponens*, as tautology, needs no additional proof.

The following example illustrates the technique.

Example Note that formula $(\bigcirc p \wedge \bigcirc q) \rightarrow \bigcirc(p \wedge q)$ is an axiom in system *HP*. Thus, applying the rule *modus ponens* we derive a new proof rule $\bigcirc p \wedge \bigcirc q \vdash \bigcirc(p \wedge q)$. □

Let us now discuss soundness and completeness of *HP*. As the satisfiability (validity) problem for *PTL* is decidable, we were able to present an "ideal" proof system, i.e. one that was both sound and complete in classical sense. Recall then the classical notions of soundness and completeness.

Definition 1.10 We shall say that proof system *PS* for logic *PTL* is ***sound*** iff any formula provable in *PS* is a tautology of *PTL*. If any tautology of *PTL* is provable in *PS* then we say that *PS* is ***complete***. □

One can easily show that all axioms are true in all admissible interpretations of *PTL*. Moreover, if the premises of proof rules of *HP* are true in all admissible interpretations, then the respective conclusions are true as well. Thus we have the following theorem.

Theorem 1.2 Proof system *HP* for propositional temporal logic *PTL* is sound. □

The following theorem can be proved using standard techniques (essentially the same as in the case of proving decidability of the satisfiability problem; cf. Chapter 2, [16,24,28]).

Theorem 1.3 Proof system HP for propositional temporal logic PTL is complete. □

Combining theorems 1.2 and 1.3 we obtain the following important characterization of proof system HP:

> the set of formulas provable in HP is equal to the set of all tautologies of PTL.

1.4.3 Gentzen-like proof system for PTL

Let us now present a Gentzen-like proof system for PTL. According to the notational conventions used in the literature we denote finite sets of formulas by Δ, Γ, Π and Σ. Similarly, by Δ, p, Γ we mean set $\Delta \cup \{p\} \cup \Gamma$. Thus a colon corresponds to the set-theoretical union. A semicolon will be used to separate different sequents.

Definition 1.11 By Gentzen-like proof system GP for logic PTL we mean system $\langle GAx, G\rangle$ such that

- GAx consists of a single (scheme of) axioms of the form

  1. $\vdash\ \Gamma \Rightarrow \Delta$ when $\Gamma \cap \Delta \neq \emptyset$

- G is the set containing the following (schemes of) derivation rules

  1. $\Gamma \Rightarrow \Delta\ \vdash\ \Pi, \Gamma \Rightarrow \Delta, \Sigma$
  2. $p, \Gamma \Rightarrow \Delta\ \vdash\ \Gamma \Rightarrow \Delta, \neg p$
     $\Gamma \Rightarrow \Delta, p\ \vdash\ \neg p, \Gamma \Rightarrow \Delta$
  3. $p, q, \Gamma \Rightarrow \Delta\ \vdash\ p \wedge q, \Gamma \Rightarrow \Delta$
     $\Gamma \Rightarrow \Delta, p;\ \Gamma \Rightarrow \Delta, q\ \vdash\ \Gamma \Rightarrow \Delta, p \wedge q$
  4. $\Gamma \Rightarrow \Delta, p;\ p, \Pi \Rightarrow \Sigma\ \vdash\ \Pi, \Gamma \Rightarrow \Delta, \Sigma$
  5. $\neg \bigcirc p, \Gamma \Rightarrow \Delta\ \vdash\ \bigcirc(\neg p), \Gamma \Rightarrow \Delta$
     $\Gamma \Rightarrow \Delta, \neg \bigcirc p\ \vdash\ \Gamma \Rightarrow \Delta, \bigcirc(\neg p)$
  6. $\neg \overline{\bigcirc} p, \Gamma \Rightarrow \Delta\ \vdash\ \overline{\bigcirc}(\neg p), \Gamma \Rightarrow \Delta$
     $\Gamma \Rightarrow \Delta, \neg \overline{\bigcirc} p\ \vdash\ \Gamma \Rightarrow \Delta, \overline{\bigcirc}(\neg p)$
  7. $\Gamma \Rightarrow \Delta\ \vdash\ \Gamma Ap \Rightarrow \Delta Ap$, where ΣAr denotes set $\{qAr \mid q \in \Sigma\}$
  8. $\Gamma \Rightarrow \Delta\ \vdash\ \Gamma \overline{A} p \Rightarrow \Delta \overline{A} p$, where $\Sigma \overline{A} r$ denotes set $\{q\overline{A}r \mid q \in \Sigma\}$
  9. $p, \Gamma \Rightarrow \Delta\ \vdash\ \overline{\bigcirc}(\bigcirc p), \Gamma \Rightarrow \Delta$
     $\Gamma \Rightarrow \Delta, p\ \vdash\ \Gamma \Rightarrow \Delta, \overline{\bigcirc}(\bigcirc p)$

10. $p, \Gamma \Rightarrow \Delta \vdash \bigcirc(\overline{\bigcirc}p), \Gamma \Rightarrow \Delta$
$\Gamma \Rightarrow \Delta, p \vdash \Gamma \Rightarrow \Delta, \bigcirc(\overline{\bigcirc}p)$
11. $\Gamma, \bigcirc((p \wedge q) \vee (\neg q \wedge pAq)) \Rightarrow \Delta \vdash \Gamma, pAq \Rightarrow \Delta$
$\Gamma \Rightarrow \Delta, \bigcirc((p \wedge q) \vee (\neg q \wedge pAq)) \vdash \Gamma \Rightarrow pAq, \Delta$
12. $\bigcirc(p \wedge q) \Rightarrow r;\ \bigcirc(\neg q \wedge r) \Rightarrow r;\ \Gamma, r \Rightarrow \Delta \vdash pAq, \Gamma \Rightarrow \Delta$
13. $\Gamma, \overline{\bigcirc}((p \wedge q) \vee (\neg q \wedge p\overline{A}q)) \Rightarrow \Delta \vdash \Gamma, p\overline{A}q \Rightarrow \Delta$
$\Gamma \Rightarrow \Delta, \overline{\bigcirc}((p \wedge q) \vee (\neg q \wedge p\overline{A}q)) \vdash \Gamma \Rightarrow pAq, \Delta$
14. $\overline{\bigcirc}(p \wedge q) \Rightarrow r;\ \overline{\bigcirc}(\neg q \wedge r) \Rightarrow r;\ \Gamma, r \Rightarrow \Delta \vdash p\overline{A}q, \Gamma \Rightarrow \Delta$
15. $\Gamma \Rightarrow \Delta, \Box(p \rightarrow \bigcirc p) \vdash \Gamma \Rightarrow \Delta, \bigcirc p \rightarrow \Box p$
16. $\Gamma \Rightarrow \Delta, \overline{\Box}(p \rightarrow \overline{\bigcirc}p) \vdash \Gamma \Rightarrow \Delta, \overline{\bigcirc}p \rightarrow \overline{\Box}p$ □

The proof system *GP* is a new one. One can, however, observe its similarities to that given in [34] for temporal logic of future time. Note also that the axioms and proof rules presented in the above definition reflect the axioms and proof rules of the Hilbert-like proof system *HP* given in Definition 1.9.
The following table shows the respective correspondences:

Hilbert-like proof system *HP*	Gentzen-like proof system *GP*
axiom 1	rule 5
axiom 2	rule 7 (with $\Gamma = \{q, r\}, \Delta = \{q \wedge r\}$ and $p = \mathbf{T}$)
axiom 3	rule 11
axiom 4	rule 6
axiom 5	rule 8 (with $\Gamma = \{q, r\}, \Delta = \{q \wedge r\}$ and $p = \mathbf{T}$)
axiom 6	rule 13
axiom 7	rule 10
axiom 8	rule 9
axiom 9	rule 15
axiom 10	rule 16
rule 1	axiom 1, rules 1, 2, 3
rule 2	rule 4 (with $\Gamma, \Delta, \Pi = \emptyset, \Sigma = \{r\}$)
rule 3	rule 7
rule 4	rule 12
rule 5	rule 8
rule 6	rule 14

Observe that implementation of the above proof system is not straightforward. When implementing the system one meets two serious problems. The first follows from the presence of the so-called ***cut rule*** (rule 4 of *GP*). Application of other rules is directed by the syntax of sequents. The cut rule makes the search for a proof much more difficult, as direction by syntax is no longer possible. However, a careful analysis of the proof system, similar to that presented in [34], shows that the cut rule can be eliminated from the proof system without losing its power. We introduced the rule only to show an intuitive argument for completeness of the above proof system. Namely, as all Hilbert-like rules have their counterparts in GP, Hilbert-like proofs can be repeated using Gentzen-like formalism. Completeness of HP implies then the completeness of GP.

The second difficulty in implementing GP follows from the presence of rules (rules 12 and 14 of GP), where invariants are to be found in order to make those rules applicable. The search for invariants can be very expensive. Difficulties with searching for invariant are illustrated in the second example given in section 1.4.2. Some heuristics should then be worked out in order to make implementations of GP useful.

Let us now present a few examples of formal Gentzen-like proofs. In the following examples, by

$$\frac{S_1}{S_2}(number)$$

we denote the application of a rule (axiom) of GP enumerated by ***number***, with S_1 (S_2) as premises (conclusion) of the applied rule. Proofs should then be read top down, althought constructed bottom up.

Example Let us first show that the following rules can be derived in GP:

$$\Gamma \Rightarrow \bigcirc p, \Delta;\ \Gamma \Rightarrow \bigcirc q, \Delta \ \vdash\ \Gamma \Rightarrow \Delta, \bigcirc(p \wedge q) \tag{1.15}$$

$$\Gamma, \bigcirc p, \bigcirc q \Rightarrow \Delta \ \vdash\ \Gamma, \bigcirc(p \wedge q) \Rightarrow \Delta. \tag{1.16}$$

Derivation of (1.15) is the following:

$$\dfrac{\dfrac{\Gamma \Rightarrow \bigcirc p, \Delta; \quad \Gamma \Rightarrow \bigcirc q, \Delta}{\Gamma \Rightarrow \bigcirc p \wedge \bigcirc q, \Delta}(3) \qquad \dfrac{\dfrac{\dfrac{p, q \Rightarrow p; \quad p, q \Rightarrow q}{p, q \Rightarrow p \wedge q}(3)}{\bigcirc p, \bigcirc q \Rightarrow \bigcirc(p \wedge q)}(7)}{\bigcirc p \wedge \bigcirc q \Rightarrow \bigcirc(p \wedge q)}(3)}{\Gamma \Rightarrow \Delta, \bigcirc(p \wedge q)}(4)$$

The right-hand branch of this derivation reduces to axioms. Observe then that the conclusion of the derivation depends only on premises $\Gamma \Rightarrow \bigcirc p, \Delta$; $\Gamma \Rightarrow \bigcirc q, \Delta$. This justifies rule (1.15).

The derivation of rule (1.16) can look as follows:

$$\dfrac{\dfrac{\dfrac{\bigcirc p, \bigcirc q, \Gamma \Rightarrow \Delta}{(\bigcirc p \wedge \bigcirc q), \Gamma \Rightarrow \Delta}(3)}{\Gamma \Rightarrow \Delta, \neg(\bigcirc p \wedge \bigcirc q)}(2) \qquad \dfrac{\dfrac{\dfrac{\dfrac{\dfrac{p, q \Rightarrow p}{p \wedge q \Rightarrow p}(3)}{\bigcirc(p \wedge q) \Rightarrow \bigcirc p}(7) \quad \dfrac{\dfrac{p, q \Rightarrow q}{p \wedge q \Rightarrow q}(3)}{\bigcirc(p \wedge q) \Rightarrow \bigcirc q}(7)}{\bigcirc(p \wedge q) \Rightarrow \bigcirc p \wedge \bigcirc q}(3)}{\neg(\bigcirc p \wedge \bigcirc q), \bigcirc(p \wedge q) \Rightarrow}(2)}{\Gamma, \bigcirc(p \wedge q) \Rightarrow \Delta}(4)$$

As before, in order to complete the justification of rule (1.16) it now suffices to forget those branches of the proof that reduce to axioms.

Observe that we used the cut rule (rule 4) while justifying both rules (1.15) and (1.16). Note that the cut rule corresponds to rule *modus ponens* of system HP. No wonder then that the technique we applied here is essentially the same as the technique of applying *modus ponens* of HP (see the last example of Section 1.4.2.). □

Example Let us now show examples of two simple proofs of temporal tautologies $\neg\bigcirc\mathsf{F}$ and $pAq \rightarrow \Diamond q$.
The proof of the first tautology can be the following:

$$\dfrac{\dfrac{\dfrac{\dfrac{\dfrac{\bigcirc p \Rightarrow \bigcirc p}{\bigcirc p, \neg\bigcirc p \Rightarrow}(2)}{\bigcirc p, \bigcirc(\neg p) \Rightarrow}(5)}{\bigcirc(p \wedge \neg p) \Rightarrow}(\mathit{rule}\ 1.16)}{\Rightarrow \neg\bigcirc(p \wedge \neg p)}(2)}{\Rightarrow \neg\bigcirc\mathsf{F}}(\mathit{definition})$$

Note that the second tautology has already been proved in section 1.4.2. Observe, however, how the former proof can be automated in Gentzen-like formalism.

$$\dfrac{\dfrac{\dfrac{\dfrac{\dfrac{\dfrac{\dfrac{\dfrac{p, p \Rightarrow p}{p, p, \neg p \Rightarrow}(2)}{p, p \wedge \neg p \Rightarrow}(3)}{p \Rightarrow \neg(p \wedge \neg p)}(2)}{p \Rightarrow \mathsf{T}}(\mathit{definition})}{pAq \Rightarrow \mathsf{T}Aq}(7)}{\Rightarrow \neg(pAq) \vee \mathsf{T}Aq}(2)}{\Rightarrow pAq \rightarrow \mathsf{T}Aq}(\mathit{definition})}{\Rightarrow pAq \rightarrow \Diamond q}(\mathit{definition})$$

□

Recall that sequent $\Gamma \Rightarrow \Delta$ is interpreted as

$$\bigwedge_{p\in\Gamma} p \rightarrow \bigvee_{p\in\Delta} p.$$

Thus definitions of soundness and completeness given in section 1.4.2. can easily be reformulated to cover Gentzen-like formalism.

Definition 1.12

- We say that Gentzen-like proof system PS for logic PTL is *sound* iff for any sequent $\Gamma \Rightarrow \Delta$ provable in PS, $\models_0 \bigwedge_{p\in\Gamma} p \rightarrow \bigvee_{p\in\Delta} p$.

- If any sequent $\Gamma \Rightarrow \Delta$ such that $\models_0 \bigwedge_{p \in \Gamma} p \rightarrow \bigvee_{p \in \Delta} p$ is provable in PS then we say that PS is *complete*. □

One can easily show that the axiom of GP, interpreted as above, is true in all admissible interpretations of PTL. Moreover, if the premises of proof rules of GP are true in all admissible interpretations, then the respective conclusions are true as well. Thus we have the Theorem 1.4.

Theorem 1.4 Proof system GP for propositional temporal logic PTL is sound. □

As pointed out above, any sequent can be interpreted as a single formula. Moreover, as shown in the table given just after Definition 1.11, any derivation rule of HP has its counterpart in GP. Thus the following theorem can be proved as a corollary of Theorem 1.3 by showing equivalence between HP and GP.

Theorem 1.5 Proof system GP for propositional temporal logic PTL is complete. □

Note also that the above theorem can be proved directly, by applying standard techniques ([33,34]). The second of these papers shows that the above theorems remain true also for GP without the cut rule (rule 4).

Combining Theorems 1.4 and 1.5 one obtains the following important characterization of proof system GP, similar to that of HP:

> the set of sequents provable in GP is equal to the set of all sequents $\Gamma \Rightarrow \Delta$ for which $\models_0 \bigwedge_{p \in \Gamma} p \rightarrow \bigvee_{p \in \Delta} p$. In particular, the set of all formulas p for which sequent $\Rightarrow p$ is provable in GP is equal to the set of all tautologies of logic PTL.

1.5 First-order temporal logic of programs

1.5.1 Introduction

Up to now we have been considering propositional temporal logic PTL. We have shown that PTL is interesting as a formal tool for the specification of properties of programs. Moreover, PTL has a nice finitary axiomatization, which makes it even more interesting from a practical point of view. This section is devoted to first-order temporal logic. This means that, besides all features of PTL, we allow arbitrary data structures and quantifiers over individuals. First-order temporal logic allows us then to get closer to the practice of programming. Namely, it allows us to formulate and verify temporal properties of "real" programs that compute over "real" data types like natural numbers, arrays, stacks, queues, trees, etc. In what follows we shall define first-order temporal logic and show some of its most important methodological properties, with standard incompleteness among them. Then we shall present a few proof systems for the logic and give an overview of specification and verification techniques related to those temporal properties of programs that do require first-order notions.

According to Definition 1.7, the only flexible symbols we allow are propositional and individual variables. As most properties of data types are time-independent, it is also convenient to have, besides flexible individual variables, rigid individual ones, too. Flexible variables are sometimes called flexible constants (see [1,5]). Moreover, as in classical first-order logic, we need (rigid) symbols denoting functions (***function symbols***) and (rigid) symbols denoting relations (***relation symbols***). Given sets VF_I, VR_I of flexible and rigid individual variables, and *Func* of function symbols, the set of temporal terms is defined as follows.

Definition 1.13 By the set *Terms* of temporal terms, we mean the least set containing VF_I and VR_I, closed under the following formation rule

- if $t_1, t_2, ..., t_k \in Terms$ and $f \in Func$ is a k-argument function symbol, then also
$$f(t_1, t_2, ..., t_k) \in Terms.$$

Terms without flexible variables are called ***classical terms.*** □

Note that the above definition differs from the classical one since we accept flexible variables as terms, too. That makes terms time dependent. The value of a term is then defined as follows.

Definition 1.14 Let $J = \langle T, D, (f_c)_{c \in C}\rangle$ be a two-sorted interpretation with T as time structure and D as data structure (cf. Definition 1.7), and let $v : VR_I \longrightarrow D$ be a valuation of rigid individual variables. Value of term *trm* in interpretation $\mathcal{M}$ under valuation v at time $t \in T$, $trm^{\mathcal{M}}(v,t)$ is defined inductively as follows

- if $trm \in VR_I$ then $trm^{\mathcal{M}}(v,t) = v(trm)$, i.e. the value of a rigid variable is given by valuation v
- if $trm \in VF_I$ then $trm^{\mathcal{M}}(v,t) = f_{trm}(t)$, i.e. the value of a flexible variable is given by the respective function of interpretation $\mathcal{M}$
- if $trm = f(t_1, t_2, ..., t_k)$ then $trm^{\mathcal{M}}(v,t) = f^{\mathcal{M}}(t_1{}^{\mathcal{M}}(v,t), t_2{}^{\mathcal{M}}(v,t), ...,$ $t_k\mathcal{M}(v,t))$ where $f^{\mathcal{M}}$ means a function of interpretation J corresponding to function symbol f. □

As propositional and flexible individual variables have a very similar meaning, in what follows we do not distinguish between them. Such a convention will simplify our notation without introducing ambiguities and misunderstandings. One only has to remember that data type D of interpretation is (at least) two-sorted, with two-element boolean algebra as one of the sorts. Accordingly, respective functions giving meaning to propositional variables range over the boolean algebra. As the set of flexible variables contains from now on both individual and propositional variables, we shall denote it by VF rather than by VF_I.

In the following definition of first-order temporal logic we assume that the set of basic symbols of the logic consists of sets *Pred* of relation symbols, *Func* of function symbol and VF, VR_I of flexible and rigid variables, respectively.

Definition 1.15 By first-order temporal logic of programs we mean triple

$$FTL = \langle F_1, Mod_1, \models_1 \rangle,$$

where

- F is the set of first-order temporal formulas containing all propositional variables of set VF of flexible variables (in another terminology, flexible constants) and closed under the following formation rules
  1. if $p, q \in F$ then also $\neg p$, $p \wedge q \in F$ (other usual propositional connectives, as before, are regarded as abbreviations)
  2. if $p \in Pred$ is a k-argument relation symbol and $t_1, ..., t_k \in Terms$ then $p(t_1, ..., t_k) \in F$
  3. if $p, q \in F$ then also pAq, $p\overline{A}q \in F$
  4. if $x \in VR_I$ and $q \in F$ then $\forall x(q) \in F$ (existential quantifier is introduced by usual definition, $\exists x(q) \leftrightarrow \neg\forall x(\neg q)$)
- Mod_1 is the class of two-sorted first-order interpretations $\langle \mathbf{Z}, D, (f_z)_{z \in VF} \rangle$, where
  1. $\mathbf{Z}$ is the structure of integers ordered by the usual relation $\leq$, i.e. $\mathbf{Z} = \langle Z, \leq \rangle$,
  2. D is a many-sorted data structure, containing, among others, the two-element boolean algebra,
  3. for any $z \in VF$, $f_z : T \longrightarrow D$ is a function assigning values to flexible variables (intuitively $f_z(t)$ is the value of z at time point t)
- for $\mathcal{M} \in Mod_1$, and $p \in F_1$, $\mathcal{M} \models_1 p$ iff for all $i \in Z$ and all valuations v of rigid variables, $\mathcal{M}, v, i \Vdash p$, where
  1. $\mathcal{M}, v, i \Vdash p$, for propositional variable $p \in VF$, iff $f_p(i) = \mathbf{T}$,

2. $\mathcal{M}, v, i \Vdash p(t_1, t_2, ..., t_k)$, for k-argument relation symbol $p \in Pred$ and temporal terms $t_1, ..., t_k$, iff

$$(t_1{}^{\mathcal{M}}(v,i), t_2{}^{\mathcal{M}}(v,i), ..., t_k{}^{\mathcal{M}}(v,i)) \in p^{\mathcal{M}},$$

where $p^{\mathcal{M}}$ is the relation of D corresponding to relation symbol p

3. definitions for $\neg p$, $p \wedge q$, pAq, $p\overline{A}q$ remain unchanged (cf. Definition 1.8 of PTL)

4. $\mathcal{M}, v, i \Vdash \forall x(q(x))$ iff $\mathcal{M}, v', i \Vdash q(x)$ for any valuation v' which differs from v at most in the value of variable x. □

Let us now concentrate on axiomatizability of FTL. We shall show that the logic is *incomplete*. This means that there is no finitistic proof system which is sound and complete for the logic or, equivalently, that the set of tautologies of the logic is not partially decidable (i.e. not recursively enumerable). Let us adapt here a proof from [48]. Some other proofs that can also be adapted here, and even strengthen the result, can be found in [3,1,41] (see also *Temporal specification of data types*, Section 1.5.6).

The argument we are going to present depends on showing that finite sets can be characterized by a formula of the logic FTL. Then we shall apply Trakhtenbrot's theorem to show the result. Let us then recall the theorem (the proof can be found, for example, in [10]):

> the set of classical first-order formulas valid in all finite interpretations is not partially decidable.

Having a temporal formula, say Fin, characterizing finite sets, one can apply Trakhtenbrot's theorem in order to show that the set $FIN = \{p \mid p \text{ is a classical first-order formula and } \models Fin \rightarrow p\}$, i.e. the set of formulas valid in all finite interpretations, is not partially decidable. Were the logic complete, one would have a partial procedure for deciding whether $p \in FIN$, and thus the set would be partially decidable. The formula Fin we are looking for can be defined as follows, where $=$ stands for equality, and z is a flexible individual variable:

$$\exists x[z = x \ \wedge \forall y(z \neq x \, U z = y)].$$

The formula characterizes finite sets, as at any time point, if flexible variable z equals some element e of the domain then it eventually has again to be equal to e, but in the meantime, at successive time points, has to be equal to all other elements of the domain. As distances between time points are finite, the domain of data structure must be finite as well.

We thus have the following important theorem.

Theorem 1.6 First-order temporal logic is incomplete for standard semantics. □

Observe that the above theorem remains valid also for first-order temporal logics of programs that accept natural numbers as a time structure. As incompleteness means that there is no finitistic sound and complete proof system for the logic, in the following sections we shall present infinitary sound and complete proof systems and relatively complete ones.

The Trakhtenbrot's theorem we applied above requires some function and relation symbols in the signature of the data structure. However, even if the set of all tautologies of a logic is not partially decidable, a set of tautologies over some fixed signature may be partially decidable. In the case of FTL, if the signature contains the equality symbol $=$ then for no extension of the signature the set of tautologies over this signature is partially decidable. The proof of this fact depends on reducing the complement of the halting property for Turing machines to the validity problem of first-order temporal tautologies (with $=$). Namely, it appears that for any Turing machine one can effectively construct a formula that encodes the computation of the machine. As the complement of the halting property can be expressed by a temporal formula such as $AtBegin \rightarrow \Box(\neg AtEnd)$ (cf. Section 1.4.1), and the complement of the halting problem is not partially decidable, we obtain the desired result. For a precise proof see [48]. Some hints can also be found in Section 1.5.6, ***Indirect approach***). See also [3].

1.5.2 A complete Hilbert-like proof system for FTL

The process of program verification requires a full formalization which manifests in the completeness of proof systems. We thus give in this section a complete (in the classical sense) proof system for FTL. As the logic is incomplete, the proof system we present is an infinitary one. It can be applied both in metamathematical investigations on FTL and in proving the correctness of programs directly (see [42]). Moreover, it can be used in formal justification of any proof rule that is useful in proving temporal properties of programs. The form of infinitary proof rules suggests a method of implementation of the proof system by approximating those rules by meta-induction on their premises. The status of infinitary proof rules is also discussed in [15,32].

The infinitary proof system for first-order temporal logic defined below is a new one. It is strongly influenced by the infinitary proof system of [42]. Other, essentially weaker, infinitary proof systems for different versions of first-order temporal logics can be found in [22,23].

In what follows, by $q(x \leftarrow t)$ we denote the formula obtained from q by replacing x by t, renaming the variables of t which appear in q in the scope of a quantifier.

Definition 1.16 By Hilbert-like proof system HF for logic FTL we mean system $\langle HAx, H\rangle$, where

- set HAx consists of the following (schemes of) axioms

1. $\forall x[q(x)] \rightarrow q(x \leftarrow t)$, where $t \in Terms$ is a temporal term such that substitution $x \leftarrow t$ does not create any new occurrences of flexible terms in the scope of temporal operators in q
2. $\forall x(\bigcirc p(x)) \rightarrow \bigcirc(\forall x(p(x)))$
3. $\forall x(\overline{\bigcirc} p(x)) \rightarrow \overline{\bigcirc}(\forall x(p(x)))$

- set H consists of the following (schemes of) derivation rules

1. for each substitution instance of a propositional temporal tautology $p, \vdash p$
2. rules 2, 3 and 5 of proof system HP (cf. Definition 1.9)
3. $p \rightarrow q \vdash p \rightarrow \forall x[q(x)]$, where x does not appear in p
4. $\{[\bigwedge_{0<j<i} \bigcirc^j(\neg q) \wedge \bigcirc^i(p \wedge q)] \rightarrow r\}_{i \in N-\{0\}} \vdash pAq \rightarrow r,$
   where N denotes the set of natural numbers, and $\bigcirc^k$ means $\bigcirc\bigcirc...\bigcirc$ repeated k times
5. $\{[\bigwedge_{0<j<i} \overline{\bigcirc}^j(\neg q) \wedge \overline{\bigcirc}^i(p \wedge q)] \rightarrow r\}_{i \in N-\{0\}} \vdash p\overline{A}q \rightarrow r,$
   where $\overline{\bigcirc}^k$ means $\overline{\bigcirc}\,\overline{\bigcirc}...\overline{\bigcirc}$ repeated k times. □

Note that rule 1 of the above proof system can equivalently be replaced by axioms of the Hilbert-like proof system HP for PTL, defined in Definition 1.9.

Let us now look at a few examples of applications of HF.

Example Observe that axiom 2 of proof system HF is a variant of the Barcan axiom for modality $\bigcirc$. Let us show that its inverse, $\bigcirc(\forall x(p(x))) \rightarrow \forall x(\bigcirc p(x))$, holds in FTL as well. In fact we shall show a stronger version of the above tautology, namely

$$\forall x(p(x))Aq \rightarrow \forall x(p(x)Aq),$$

where x is not free in q. (The version for $\bigcirc$ can be obtained from the above by substituting q by $\mathbf{T}$.)

Let us show that $(\forall x(p(x)))Aq \rightarrow p(x)Aq$ (once we have proved this formula, we can simply apply rule 3 of HF to obtain the desired conclusion). By axiom 1 of HF we have that $\forall x(p(x)) \rightarrow p(x)$. Thus, in order to complete the proof it suffices to apply rule 2 of HF (more precisely, rule 3 of HP). □

In the following example we show an application of the infinitary proof rule 4.

Example Let us show that the following rule of HP is derivable in HF:

$$\bigcirc(p \wedge q) \rightarrow r,\ \bigcirc(\neg q \wedge r) \rightarrow r,\ r \rightarrow s \vdash pAq \rightarrow s. \tag{1.17}$$

We shall use rule 4 in order to show the derivability of rule

$$\bigcirc(p \wedge q) \rightarrow r,\ \bigcirc(\neg q \wedge r) \rightarrow r, \vdash pAq \rightarrow r. \tag{1.18}$$

Once rule (1.18) is derived, rule (1.17) can easily be derived by classical propositional reasoning.

Since the conclusion of rule (1.18) takes the form $pAq \to r$, we have to show that the following set of premises

$$\{[\bigwedge_{0<j<i} \bigcirc^j(\neg q) \wedge \bigcirc^i(p \wedge q)] \to r\}_{i \in N - \{0\}}$$

of rule 4 can be derived from premises of rule (1.18). We proceed by induction on i. We first have to show that

$$\bigcirc^1(p \wedge q) \to r.$$

That is, however, just the first of premises of rule (1.18). We denote by P_i the formula

$$\bigwedge_{0<j<i} \bigcirc^j(\neg q) \wedge \bigcirc^i(p \wedge q).$$

We now have to prove that for all $i > 1$, if $P_i \to r$ is derivable, then $P_{i+1} \to r$ is derivable as well. Observe that, by rule 1 of HF,

$$P_{i+1} \leftrightarrow \bigcirc(\neg q \wedge P_i).$$

By inductive assumption we have that $P_i \to r$. Thus P_{i+1} implies $\bigcirc(\neg q \wedge r)$. By the second premise of rule (1.18) we then have $P_{i+1} \to r$, which is just the required conclusion. □

Let us now discuss the most important methodological properties of the proof system HF. Careful analysis (similar to that given in [42]) shows that HF is both sound and complete for standard semantics. Notions of soundness and completeness are again classical here, but are even stronger than for the proof system HP for propositional temporal logic. Namely, by strengthening the following definitions and theorems, we can consider theories, too.

Definition 1.17 We say that proof system PS for logic FTL is ***sound*** iff for any set of formulas A, the set of syntactic consequences of A, $C_{PS}(A)$, is contained in the set of semantic consequences of A (in the sense of logic FTL). If the set of syntactic consequences of A contains the set of semantic consequences of A then we say that PS is ***complete***. □

One can easily show that all axioms are true in all admissible interpretations of FTL. Moreover, if the premises of proof rules of HF are true in all admissible interpretations, then the respective conclusions are true as well. Thus we have the following theorem.

Theorem 1.7 Proof system HF for first-order temporal logic FTL is sound. □

The following theorem can be proved by using the technique of ultrafilters (cf. [42], note also that the theorem follows directly from more general theorem given in [46]).

Theorem 1.8 Proof system HF for first-order temporal logic FTL is complete. □

Combining Theorems 1.7 and 1.8 one obtains the following important characterization of proof system HF:

> the set of syntactic consequences $C_{HF}(A)$ of any set of formulas A is equal to the set of all semantic consequences of A (in the sense of logic FTL).

There is yet another important property of HF, which follows easily from the completeness theorem. Namely, in order to facilitate reasoning about temporal theories, one often uses some variant of the so-called ***deduction theorem***. The deduction theorem for proof system HF can be formulated as follows.

Theorem 1.9 Let A be a set of temporal formulas, let p, q be formulas and let $\mathbf{x}$ be the vector of all rigid variables that are free in p. Then

$$A \cup \{p\} \vdash q \text{ implies } A \vdash Cl(p) \rightarrow q,$$

where $\vdash$ is the syntactic consequence relation of HF, and $Cl(p)$ denotes the formula $\boxdot(\forall \mathbf{x}(p))$. □

1.5.3 A complete Gentzen-like proof system for FTL

Let us now present a Gentzen-like proof system for FTL. By Δ and Γ we denote finite sets of formulas. Recall that Δ, p, Γ denotes set $\Delta \cup \{p\} \cup \Gamma$. Note that the proof system defined below is a new one. The only complete Gentzen-like proof system for first-order temporal logic (with time corresponding to natural numbers) we know is that of Kawai ([21]). As the temporal logic considered in the quoted paper has $\bigcirc$, $\Diamond$, and $\Box$ as the only temporal operators, the proof system given below concerns an essentially stronger version of first-order temporal logic.

Definition 1.18 By the Gentzen-like proof system GF for logic FTL we mean system $\langle GAx, G\rangle$ such that

- GAx consists of a single (scheme of) axioms of the form

  1. $\vdash \Gamma \Rightarrow \Delta$ when $\Gamma \cap \Delta \neq \emptyset$

- G is the set containing the following (schemes of) derivation rules

  1. rules 1-11, 13 of proof system GP (cf. Definition 1.11)

2. $\Gamma, p(x \leftarrow t) \Rightarrow \Delta \ \vdash \ \Gamma, \forall x(p(x)) \Rightarrow \Delta$
   $\Gamma \Rightarrow \Delta, p(x) \ \vdash \ \Gamma \Rightarrow \Delta, \forall x(p(x))$,
   where $t \in Terms$ is a temporal term such that substitution $x \leftarrow t$ does not create any new occurrences of flexible terms in the scope of temporal operators in p and, in the case of the second rule, variable x does not appear in Γ and Δ

3. $\Gamma, \bigcirc(\forall x(p(x))) \Rightarrow \Delta \ \vdash \ \Gamma, \forall x(\bigcirc p(x)) \Rightarrow \Delta$

4. $\Gamma, \overline{\bigcirc}(\forall x(p(x))) \Rightarrow \Delta \ \vdash \ \Gamma, \forall x(\overline{\bigcirc} p(x)) \Rightarrow \Delta$

5. $\{\Gamma, [\bigwedge_{0<j<i} \bigcirc^j(\neg q) \wedge \bigcirc^i(p \wedge q)] \Rightarrow \Delta\}_{i \in N-\{0\}} \ \vdash \ \Gamma, pAq \Rightarrow \Delta$,
   where N denotes the set of natural numbers

6. $\{\Gamma, [\bigwedge_{0<j<i} \overline{\bigcirc}^j(\neg q) \wedge \overline{\bigcirc}^i(p \wedge q)] \Rightarrow \Delta\}_{i \in N-\{0\}} \ \vdash \ \Gamma, p\overline{A}q \Rightarrow \Delta$ □

Note that the axioms and proof rules presented in the above definition reflect the axioms and proof rules of the Hilbert-like proof system HF given in Definition 1.16. The following table shows the respective correspondences:

Hilbert-like proof system HF	Gentzen-like proof system GF
axiom 1	rule 2 (with $\Gamma = \emptyset$ and $\Delta = \{p(x \leftarrow t)\}$
axiom 2	rule 3 (with $\Gamma = \emptyset$ and $\Delta = \{\bigcirc(\forall x(p(x)))\}$
axiom 3	rule 4 (with $\Gamma = \emptyset$ and $\Delta = \{\overline{\bigcirc}(\forall x(p(x)))\}$
rule 1, rule 2	axiom 1, rule 1
rule 3	rule 2
rule 4	rule 5
rule 5	rule 6

Observe that the following rules for the existential quantifier are easily derivable:

$$\Gamma, p(y) \Rightarrow \Delta \ \vdash \ \Gamma, \exists x[p(x)] \Rightarrow \Delta, \tag{1.19}$$

$$\Gamma \Rightarrow \Delta, p(t) \ \vdash \ \Gamma \Rightarrow \Delta, \exists x[p(x)], \tag{1.20}$$

where t is a classical term and y does not appear in Γ and Δ.

Let us now look at an example of a formal derivation of a Gentzen-like proof rule.

Example In order to illustrate the use of infinitary rule 6 of GF we shall show that the following rule

$$p \wedge q \Rightarrow \vdash \ p\overline{A}q \Rightarrow$$

is derivable in GF.

Observe that the following derivation

$$\cfrac{\cfrac{\cfrac{\{\overrightarrow{\bigcirc}^{i}(p \wedge q) \Rightarrow\}_{i \in N-\{0\}}}{\{\bigwedge_{0<j<i} \overrightarrow{\bigcirc}^{j}(\neg q), \overrightarrow{\bigcirc}^{i}(p \wedge q) \Rightarrow\}_{i \in N-\{0\}}}(1)}{\{\bigwedge_{0<j<i} \overrightarrow{\bigcirc}^{j}(\neg q) \wedge \overrightarrow{\bigcirc}^{i}(p \wedge q) \Rightarrow\}_{i \in N-\{0\}}}(1)}{p \overline{\mathcal{A}} q \Rightarrow}(6)$$

reduces our derivation to showing provability of all sequents $\overrightarrow{\bigcirc}^{i}(p \wedge q) \Rightarrow$, with $i \in N - \{0\}$ from sequent $p \wedge q \Rightarrow$. We proceed by induction on i. First note that the following simple derivation shows the case of $i = 1$:

$$\cfrac{p \wedge q \Rightarrow}{\overrightarrow{\bigcirc}^{1}(p \wedge q) \Rightarrow}(1)$$

Now we have to show the induction step. Assume that $\overrightarrow{\bigcirc}^{i}(p \wedge q) \Rightarrow$ is derivable. Owing to the following derivation

$$\cfrac{\overrightarrow{\bigcirc}^{i}(p \wedge q) \Rightarrow}{\overrightarrow{\bigcirc}^{i+1}(p \wedge q) \Rightarrow}(1)$$

we can show that provability of $\overrightarrow{\bigcirc}^{i}(p \wedge q) \Rightarrow$ implies provability of $\overrightarrow{\bigcirc}^{i+1}(p \wedge q) \Rightarrow$. This proves the result. □

Since for Gentzen-like proof systems we are mainly interested in proving tautologies, the definitions of soundness and completeness given in Section 1.4.3 can easily be adapted to fit well here.

Definition 1.19

- We say that Gentzen-like proof system PS for logic FTL is *sound* iff for any sequent $\Gamma \Rightarrow \Delta$ provable in PS, $\models_1 \bigwedge_{p \in \Gamma} p \rightarrow \bigvee_{p \in \Delta} p$.
- If any sequent $\Gamma \Rightarrow \Delta$ such that $\models_1 \bigwedge_{p \in \Gamma} p \rightarrow \bigvee_{p \in \Delta} p$ is provable in PS then we say that PS is *complete*. □

As in the case of GP for propositional temporal logic, one can easily show that any axiom of GF is true in all admissible interpretations of FTL. Moreover, if premises of proof rules of GF are true in all admissible interpretations, then the respective conclusions are true as well. Thus we have the following theorem.

Theorem 1.10 Proof system GF for first-order temporal logic FTL is sound. □

As we pointed out before (Sections 1.2 and 1.4.3), any sequent can be interpreted as a single formula. Moreover, as shown in the table following

Definition 1.18, any axiom and derivation rule of HF has its counterpart in GF. Thus the following theorem can be proved as a corollary of Theorem 1.8 by showing equivalence between HF and GF. Another proof can be carried out by a simple application of a general theorem given in [47].

Theorem 1.11 Proof system GF for first-order temporal logic FTL is complete. □

Note also that Theorem 1.11 can be proved directly, by applying standard techniques (cf. [32]). One can also show that the above theorems remain true also for GF without the cut rule.

Combining Theorems 1.10 and 1.11 we obtain the following important characterization of GF, similar to that of GP,

> the set of sequents provable in GF is equal to the set of all sequents $\Gamma \Rightarrow \Delta$ for which $\models_1 \bigwedge_{p\in\Gamma} p \rightarrow \bigvee_{p\in\Delta} p$. In particular, the set of all formulas p for which sequent $\Rightarrow p$ is provable in GF is equal to the set of all tautologies of logic FTL.

1.5.4 Hilbert-like relatively complete proof system for FTL

In the previous section we investigated complete, in the classical sense, but infinitary proof systems. However, there are a number of responses to the incompleteness of first-order temporal logic of programs, trying to weaken the classical notion of completeness and staying within a finitary framework. Investigations of the logics of programs have led to various nonclassical notions of completeness. The most interesting of those notions are ***relative completeness*** and that offered by the nonstandard school of computer science. As the comprehensive study of the latter is presented in Chapter 2, let us now concentrate on the former. Relative completeness, introduced in [9] in the context of Hoare logic for partial correctness of **while**-programs, has been widely accepted in the world of computer science.

Cook, in his paper, separated the reasoning about programs and reasoning about underlying data structures. He insisted that one should reduce the reasoning about programs to reasoning about classical first-order properties of data structures. There are, however, data structures for which such a reduction is, in general, impossible. Relative completeness concerns then a restricted class of admissible interpretations, namely those where the reduction is guaranteed. The related notion of soundness has also to be modified, for it has to concern the restricted class of interpretations only. Let us now recall the general definition of relative soundness and completeness.

Definition 1.20 Let $L = \langle F, Mod, \models\rangle$ be a logic and PS be a Hilbert-like proof system for L. We shall say that PS is ***sound (complete) for L relative to class*** $\wp \subset Mod$ provided that for any interpretation $I \in \wp$ and formula $p \in F$,

$$Th_I \vdash p \text{ implies (is implied by) } I \models p,$$

where Th_I denotes the set of classical first-order formulas true in interpretation I. □

Cook considered a class of *expressive* interpretations. Further investigations have shown that expressive interpretations are either *finite* or *arithmetical*, i.e. those with finite domain or those that contain a standard model of natural numbers and satisfy some minor condition.

Later it turned out that one is restricted to arithmetical interpretations when considering logics of programs more expressive than that of Hoare. Arithmetical completeness, reflecting this restriction, has been derived from relative completeness in [18], in the context of dynamic logic. Harel gave finitary proof rules for first-order dynamic logic that allow us to eliminate programs from formulas of the logic. There is, of course, a price to be paid, namely the set of axioms forms a totally undecidable set. On the other hand, those axioms as classical first-order properties of data structures are supposed to be known by a programmer who should never write programs based on unknown properties of data. We shall return to arithmetical completeness for first-order temporal logic later. Now let us define a new proof system for FTL. Note that the proof system defined below differs from that of [45] only in the presence of past time temporal operators.

Definition 1.21 By the Hilbert-like proof system HR for logic FTL we mean system $\langle HAx, H\rangle$, where

- set HAx consists of the following (schemes of) axioms
  1. axioms 2 and 3 of proof system HF (cf. Definition 1.16)
- set H consists of the following (schemes of) derivation rules
  1. for each substitution instance of a temporal propositional tautology $p, \vdash p$
  2. $s \to \exists n(r(n)),\ r(n \leftarrow n{+}1) \to (\bigcirc(p \wedge q) \vee \bigcirc(\neg q \wedge r(n))),\ \neg r(n \leftarrow 0) \vdash s \to pAq$,
     where n appears neither in p nor in q
  3. $s \to \exists n(r(n)),\ r(n \leftarrow n{+}1) \to (\overline{\bigcirc}(p \wedge q) \vee \overline{\bigcirc}(\neg q \wedge r(n))),\ \neg r(n \leftarrow 0) \vdash s \to p\overline{A}q$,
     where n appears neither in p nor in q
  4. rules 2-6 of proof system HP (cf. Definition 1.9). □

Note that rule 1 of the above proof system can be replaced by all the axioms of HP for propositional temporal logic.

Now, instead of presenting a particular example, we shall briefly discuss a general method of proving temporal formulas with HR. In order to prove that a formula, say p, is valid, one can apply the following procedure:

> find the innermost occurrence of a temporal operator (A or $\overline{A}$). If no such operators appear then the reasoning is finished, for it is now reduced to reasoning about the classical first-order theory of a data structure. Otherwise prove the equivalence of the temporal formula to a classical first-order formula, say q, using proof rules 2 or 3 for implication $\rightarrow$ and rule 4 (more precisely rules 4 or 6 of HP) for implication $\leftarrow$. Substitute the innermost temporal formula by q (rules (3) and (5) of HP are, among others, applied here) and repeat the procedure.

Note that the existence of formulas r and s required in the premises of rules 2 and 3 of HR and 4 and 6 of HP is guaranteed since the class of admissible interpretations is now restricted to contain strictly arithmetical interpretations only (cf. [45]). Consider first the case of rules 2 and 3 of HR. The formula $r(n)$ that satisfies premises of those rules can be defined inductively as follows:

$$r(0) \leftrightarrow \mathsf{F}$$
$$r(n+1) \leftrightarrow (\bigcirc(p \wedge q) \vee \bigcirc(\neg q \wedge r(n)))$$

where $\bigcirc$ is either $\circ$, in the case of rule 2, or $\overline{\circ}$, in the case of rule 3. Note that formula s, which occurs in the premises of those rules, can now take the form $\exists n(r(n))$. Similarly, formulas r and s from premises of rules 4 and 6 of HP can be substituted by $\exists n(r(n))$.

The only problem to be solved is that we must now eliminate the inductive definition of formula $r(n)$ and find a formula that explicitly defines $r(n)$. There is, however, a theorem of recursion theory (cf. Theorem 3.5 in [20], p. 92) that guarantees that such an elimination is possible (cf. also [45]).

Let us now discuss informally the notion of arithmetical completeness for FTL, since it requires some modifications because of the unusual approach to proving the properties of programs offered by temporal logic. In dynamic logic programs are involved in formulas. In temporal logic the situation is different (see Section 1.5.6). One has then to fix the whole interpretation rather than its data structure only (a different approach is presented in [43], where functions interpreting flexible constants are not fixed). The presence of a time structure within interpretations of FTL raises some new methodological problems, as we would like to avoid explicit references to time points within temporal formulas (cf. [1]). One possible solution, given in [45], is to allow data structures that can be embedded into time structure. The class of admissible interpretations thus obtained contains *strictly arithmetical* interpretations. The obtained class is a proper subclass of the class of arithmetical interpretations. The class is, however, still interesting as strictly arithmetical interpretations, with natural numbers, stacks, arrays, queues, trees, lists, etc., among them, reject only those arithmetical interpretations that are of no practical interest because of their uncomputability. The following definition summarizes the above discussion.

Definition 1.22 Let $FTL = \langle F_1, Mod_1, \models_1 \rangle$ be the first-order temporal logic (cf. Definition 1.15).

- Interpretation $I \in Mod_1$ is *strictly arithmetical* provided that:
  - data structure of I contains sort N of natural numbers together with constants 0 and 1, functions $+$ and $*$ and relation $\leq$ (interpreted as usual)
  - for each sort s of data structure of I there is an effective binary relation e_s *encoding elements of sort* e, i.e. such that for each x of sort s there is exactly one $i \in N$ with $e_s(x, i)$ true in I.
- We say that proof system PS is *strictly arithmetically sound (complete)* iff PS is sound (complete) for FTL relative to the class of strictly arithmetical interpretations. □

The following theorem can be proved by simple application of the general theorems given in [45].

Theorem 1.12 Proof system HR for logic FTL is both strictly arithmetically sound and complete. □

Thus we have the following important characterization of proof system HR:

> if interpretation I is strictly arithmetical, then the set of (first-order temporal) formulas provable in HR from set Th_I of specific axioms, $C_{HR}(Th_I)$ is equal to the set of formulas valid in interpretation I.

1.5.5 A Gentzen-like relatively complete proof system for *FTL*

Let us complete our presentation of proof systems for FTL with a strictly arithmetically sound and complete Gentzen-like proof system GR. Although influenced by proof system HR, system GR is a new one.

Definition 1.23 By Gentzen-like proof system GR for logic FTL we mean system $\langle GAx, G \rangle$, where

- set GAx consists of the following (scheme of) axioms

  1. $\Gamma \Rightarrow \Delta$ when $\Gamma \cap \Delta \neq \emptyset$

- set G consists of the following (schemes of) derivation rules
  1. rules 1-14 of proof system GP (cf. Definition 1.11)
  2. rules 2-4 of proof system GF (cf. Definition 1.18)
  3. $r(n \leftarrow n+1), \Gamma \Rightarrow \bigcirc(p \wedge q) \vee \bigcirc(\neg q \wedge r(n)), \Delta;\ r(n \leftarrow 0) \Rightarrow ; \Gamma \Rightarrow \exists n(r(n)), \Delta \ \vdash\ \Gamma \Rightarrow pAq, \Delta,$
     where n appears neither in p nor in q
  4. $r(n \leftarrow n+1), \Gamma \Rightarrow \overline{\bigcirc}(p \wedge q) \vee \overline{\bigcirc}(\neg q \wedge r(n)), \Delta;\ r(n \leftarrow 0) \Rightarrow ; \Gamma \Rightarrow \exists n(r(n)), \Delta \ \vdash\ \Gamma \Rightarrow p\overline{A}q, \Delta,$
     where n appears neither in p nor in q □

Note that the axioms and proof rules presented in the above definition reflect the axioms and proof rules of the Hilbert-like proof system HR given in Definition 1.21. The following table shows the respective correspondences:

Hilbert-like proof system HR	Gentzen-like proof system GR
axiom 1	rule 2
rule 1	axiom 1, rule 1
rule 2	rule 3
rule 3	rule 4
rule 4	rule 1

Observe that the general method of finding formula $r(n)$ (cf. rules 3 and 4), discussed in Section 1.5.4, applies to proof system GR as well.

Since any sequent is equivalent to a single formula, the definitions of relative soundness and completeness given in Section 1.5.4 can easily be adapted to fit well here.

Definition 1.24 Let $L = \langle F, Mod, \models \rangle$ be a logic and PS be a Gentzen-like proof system for L. We shall say that PS is *sound (complete) for L relative to class $\wp \subset Mod$* provided that for any interpretation $I \in \wp$ and sequent $\Gamma \Rightarrow \Delta$ of L,

$$\vdash_{Th_I} s \text{ implies (is implied by) } I \models \bigwedge_{p \in \Gamma} p \rightarrow \bigvee_{p \in \Delta} p,$$

where $\vdash_{Th_I}$ denotes the syntactic consequence relation of proof system PS augmented with the following set of axioms:

$$\{\Rightarrow p \mid p \in Th_I\}.$$

□

As shown by the table following Definition 1.23, any axiom and derivation rule of HR has its counterpart in proof system GR. Thus the following theorem can be proved as a corollary of Theorem 1.12 by showing equivalence between HR and GR. Another proof can be carried out by the simple application of a general theorem given in [47].

Theorem 1.13 Proof system GR for first-order temporal logic FTL is both sound and complete for FTL relative to the class of strictly arithmetical interpretations. □

The above theorem gives the following important characterization of proof system GR, similar to that of GP and GF,

> if interpretation I is strictly arithmetical, then the set of sequents provable in GR augmented with set $\{\Rightarrow p \mid p \in Th_I\}$ of axioms is equal to the set of all sequents $\Gamma \Rightarrow \Delta$ for which $I \models_1 \bigwedge_{p\in\Gamma} p \rightarrow \bigvee_{p\in\Delta} p$.
>
> In particular, the set of all formulas p for which sequent $\Rightarrow p$ is provable in GR is equal to the set of all formulas valid in interpretation I.

1.5.6 On proving temporal properties of programs

Introduction

Programs do not appear in temporal formulas explicitly. This makes the logic independent of any particular programming language and thus comfortable for specification purposes. On the other hand, when it comes to formal verification of temporal properties of programs, one first of all has to fill the gap between temporal logic and the programming language used. There are (at least) two approaches to solving the problem. The first, which we call *direct approach* depends on supplying the user of a programming language with proof rules that allow the temporal properties of programs to be proved. Such proof rules usually define methods of proving properties related to the specific programming tools of the language. The second, *indirect*, approach depends on defining first the temporal semantics of programs axiomatically, via temporal theories. The temporal properties of programs are then simply semantic consequences of the respective temporal theories. This means that in the direct approach one proves properties of programs by applying proof rules directly, while indirectness of the second approach follows from the intermediate step of defining temporal theory related to a given program and then deriving the properties of the program.

The direct approach is usually more comfortable, but less general, than the indirect one. This follows from the fact that specific temporal properties usually each require a separate rule. One can, for instance, prove that a program satisfies formula pAq, but can have difficulty proving its more complicated properties such as, say, $pAq \vee \overline{\Diamond}(r \wedge q \wedge \neg p)$. In the indirect approach, after building the temporal theory of a program, one simply uses one of the existing proof systems for FTL (note that the direct approach also has to be supported by proof systems for "pure" temporal logic). There is yet another advantage of the indirect approach. Namely, it allows us to specify, analyze and verify algorithms and data structures uniformly, as temporal theories (see later).

As we shall present only a guide to both approaches, the reader interested in the underlying techniques is referred to [7,8,28,24,31] for the direct approach and to [5,24,39,49] for the indirect approach. In fact, the quoted works of Kröger, Andréka, Németi, Sain present combinations of both approaches. The matter is also discussed in Chapter 3.

Direct approach

As we noticed earlier, the direct approach depends on supplying programmers with proof rules for proving interesting classes of properties of programs (cf. [7, 8,28,31]). The simplest and oldest example for the direct approach is the Floyd-Hoare method of proving the partial correctness of **while**-programs. Safety (invariance) properties, with partial correctness among them, are recognized the most fundamental ones (cf. [26]). Proof rules dealing with safety properties usually match the following pattern:

$$\Pi \triangleright p \hookrightarrow p \ \vdash \ \Pi \triangleright p \rightarrow \Box\, p,$$

where:

- Π is a program
- $\Pi \triangleright q$ means that all computations of program Π satisfy temporal formula q
- $p \hookrightarrow q$ means that for every computation c of Π and every time point t, satisfiability of formula p at time t implies satisfiability of formula q at time $t+1$ (intuitively, formula $p \hookrightarrow q$ means "Π leads from p to q").

Another fundamental class of program properties consists of eventuality properties (see Section 1.4.1). The general pattern of proof rules for those properties is the following (cf. [28]):

$$\Pi \triangleright p \hookrightarrow (p \vee q),\ \mathit{Eventually}\ \Pi \triangleright p \hookrightarrow q \ \vdash \ \Pi \triangleright p \rightarrow \Diamond q,$$

where

- the "*Eventually* $\Pi \triangleright p \hookrightarrow q$" usually corresponds to some fairness requirement that guarantees an eventual execution of a step that leads from p to q.

Observe that a kind of principle of well founded orderings or induction (computational or structural) is almost always reflected by a proof rule of direct proof systems (cf. [24,38,39]).

As direct approach proof systems are strongly influenced by the specific goals they are supposed to achieve, we are not able to give a comprehensive survey of those proof systems here. The reader interested in details is referred to the quoted papers. It is however worth emphasizing here that, besides soundness and completeness, ***compositionality*** is one of the most important criteria of estimating the quality of proof systems for temporal properties of concurrent programs. Namely, while proving properties of a program, one would like to be able to divide the program into smaller subprograms (according to some syntax rules), prove properties of subprograms and then compose the proved properties in order to derive the desired property of the whole program. As programs do not appear in "pure" temporal formulas, the compositionality issue appears only when one attempts to prove properties of programs written in specific programming languages (cf. [7,8,28]).

Indirect approach

The approach we are going to present in this section is indirect in that no direct proof rules for temporal properties of programs are given. Before reasoning about programs, one has first to define (axiomatically) the temporal semantics of the programming language being used. Then, using the semantics of a given program, one can derive its properties.

Let us describe the method more precisely. We first have to concentrate on the formalization of defining the temporal semantics of programming languages. The formalization we are going to present is mainly based on a papers by Szałas & Petermann [49]. As this paper formalizes the semantics of a programming language of distributed processes with asynchronous communication, the semantics of which is rather complicated, the paper introduces the logic of multi-linear time. However, the techniques applied in the paper can easily be adapted to other programming languages, remaining within the framework of temporal logic we deal with. Let PL be a programming language. The basic idea of the indirect approach is to define an effective method (algorithm) which, for every program Π of PL, constructs temporal theory T_Π such that

- any model of theory T_Π corresponds to a computation of program Π
- any computation of program Π defines a model of theory T_Π.

The temporal semantics of program Π is then characterized via class of models of theory T_Π. Such a method ensures *completeness* of reduction of the formal verification of program properties to reasoning in "pure" temporal logic, for we have the following obvious observation

> temporal formula q is true in all computations of program Π iff $T_\Pi \models q$.

For illustration of the method, consider the following examples.

Example Let us sketch the definition of the temporal semantics of **while**-programs. In order to express the properties of the computations of a program, we need some flexible propositional variables representing *control* of the program (see also [24,29]). We shall denote those variables by $at[K]$, where K is a program. The intuitive meaning of variable atK is *program K is ready to execute*. The temporal semantics of **while**-programs is given by the following (schemes of) axioms:

1. $at[\Lambda; K] \to \bigcirc(atK)$, where Λ denotes the empty statement
2. $at[z := t; K] \to (t = x \to \bigcirc(z = x \wedge at[K]))$, where x is a rigid variable and z is a flexible variable
3. $at[\textbf{if } p \textbf{ then } K \textbf{ else } M \textbf{ fi}; L] \to [(p \to \bigcirc(at[K; L])) \wedge (\neg p \to \bigcirc(at[M; L]))]$
4. $at[\textbf{while } p \textbf{ do } K \textbf{ od}; L] \to [(p \to \bigcirc(at[K; \textbf{while } p \textbf{ do } K \textbf{ od}; L])) \wedge (\neg p \to \bigcirc(at[L]))]$.

In order to obtain complete theories of programs, we have to add some other axioms stating that exactly one variable $at[K]$ is true at a given time point, and that substitution is the only statement that can change the values of program variables. We have also to express that initially the whole program is ready to execute (e.g. by formula $\circledast \to at[\Pi]$, where $\circledast$ is a flexible propositional variable, defined in Section 1.4.1). One can show that theories thus obtained are complete for the standard semantics of **while**-programs. Recall that in the standard semantics computations are defined as (possibly infinite) sequences of states representing valuations of program variables. Program variables change their values as a result of execution of assignment statements. Values of control variables (of the form $at[K]$) change according to changes of program control.

Consider, for example, a program

$$\Pi = [\textbf{while } z \neq y \textbf{ do } z := z + 1 \textbf{ od}].$$

Theory T_Π contains the the following axioms

1. $at[z := z + 1; \Pi] \to (z + 1 = x \to \bigcirc(z = x \wedge at[\Pi]))$
2. $at[\Pi] \to [(z \neq y \to \bigcirc at[z := z + 1; \Pi]) \wedge (\neg z \neq y \to \bigcirc(at\Lambda))]$
3. additional axioms (as mentioned above).

Now, in order to prove that all computations of program Π satisfy a temporal formula, say p, one has to prove that p is a semantic consequence of the above set of axioms, i.e. 1, 2, 3 $\models p$. Moreover, completeness of theory T_Π ensures that every property of program Π valid for the standard semantics of **while**-programs is a semantic consequence of the set of axioms of T_Π. □

The following example presents a definition of the temporal semantics of a simple programming language with concurrency.

Example Let us consider programs of the form $K_1||K_2||...||K_n$, where K_1, $K_2, ..., K_n$ are **while**-programs. We accept *interleaving* of actions as the underlying semantics. This means that from the many statements that are ready to execute exactly one is chosen to go on (cf. also [24,29]). We shall thus introduce two kinds of flexible propositional variables corresponding to the control of programs, $at[K]$ and $in[K]$. The meaning of variables of the form $at[K]$ is the same as in the previous example, i.e. $at[K]$ means that statement K is ready to execute. Variable $in[K]$ is true at a given time point when statement K is currently being executed. Temporal specification of our language is given by the following set of (schemes of) axioms

1. $at[\Lambda; K] \rightarrow (\bigcirc at[K])A(in[\Lambda; K])$
2. $at[z := t; K] \rightarrow (t = x \rightarrow (\bigcirc(z = x \wedge at[K]))A(in[z := t; K]))$
3. $at[\textbf{if } p \textbf{ then } K \textbf{ else } M \textbf{ fi}; L] \rightarrow$
   $((p \rightarrow \bigcirc(at[K; L])A(in[\textbf{if } p \textbf{ then } K \textbf{ else } M \textbf{ fi}; L])) \wedge$
   $(\neg p \rightarrow \bigcirc(at[M; L])A(in[\textbf{if } p \textbf{ then } K \textbf{ else } M \textbf{ fi}; L])))$
4. $at[\textbf{while } p \textbf{ do } K \textbf{ od}; L] \rightarrow$
   $((p \rightarrow \bigcirc(at[K; \textbf{while } p \textbf{ do } K \textbf{ od}; L]))A(in[\textbf{while } p \textbf{ do } K \textbf{ od}; L])) \wedge$
   $(\neg p \rightarrow \bigcirc(at[L]))A(in[\textbf{while } p \textbf{ do } K \textbf{ od}; L]).$

As before, in order to obtain complete theories of programs, one has to add some other axioms stating that exactly one variable $in[K]$ is true at a given time point, and that substitution is the only statement that can change the values of program variables. We have also to express that initially the whole program is ready to execute. □

Temporal specification of data types

Formal specification and analysis of abstract data types occupies an important place in current research on the description of semantics of programming languages and on the process of program design and verification. The previous section showed how to specify temporal semantics of programs. This section is devoted to the specification of data structures by means of temporal formulas.

Temporal specification of abstract data types was initiated by Lamport [27]. Later the problem was considered in a paper by Kröger [25]. A different approach, which better suits our presentation, has been proposed in a paper by Szałas [44]. The approach we shall discuss is free of many of the limitations common to all methods that consider data structures via formalized theories of classical first-order logic. In particular, any formalized theory of classical first-order logic has nonstandard, unexpected models (cf. the Upward Skolem, Löwenheim and Tarski Theorem). This is no longer valid in the case of logic FTL. Similarly, Gödel's results on the incompleteness of first-order arithmetics cannot be transferred to FTL. Moreover, contrary to classical first-order logic, such important properties of data like ***every natural number (stack, queue, tree etc.) is finite***, are expressible within the logic we deal with. An example of a property not expressible in classical first-order logic but expressible in *FTL* has already been considered in Section 1.5.1, where finite sets were characterized by a formula of *FTL*.

The method of data structure specification we discuss here follows a widely accepted axiomatic style. The basic notion in the method is that of semantic consequence (cf. also discussion in Section 1.2). Let us sketch the method by considering the following example (the reader interested in a more comprehensive description, accompanied by more examples is referred to Szałas [44]).

Example Let us specify natural numbers by means of first-order temporal logic. First, assume that the operations we are interested in are constant 0, functions *succ* (successor), + (addition), $*$ (multiplication) and the equality relation =. We shall accept well known Peano axioms as a part of our specification. However, as mentioned before, our specification can be essentially strengthened, namely, by labelling consecutive states of temporal sequence by natural numbers and expressing that every natural number is a label of a state, we exclude nonstandard elements of the domain and thus obtain a "perfect" specification, all models of which are identical (up to isomorphism). Thus the specification we shall present has no unexpected, or even counterintuitive implementations (models). The specification of natural numbers can then be the following, where x, y are rigid variables and z is a flexible variable of sort N.

- **sort** N
- **operations**
  - $0 : \longrightarrow N$
  - $succ : N \longrightarrow N$
  - $+, * : N \times N \longrightarrow N$
  - $=: N \times N \longrightarrow \{\mathsf{T}, \mathsf{F}\}$
- **axioms**
  1. $0 \neq succ(x)$
  2. $succ(x) = succ(y) \rightarrow x = y$
  3. $x + 0 = x \wedge x * 0 = 0$
  4. $x + succ(y) = succ(x + y) \wedge x * succ(y) = x * y + x$
  5. $\overline{\Diamond}(z = 0) \vee z = 0 \vee \Diamond(z = 0)$
  6. $(\overline{\Diamond}(z = 0) \wedge z = x) \rightarrow \bigcirc(z = succ(x))$
  7. $\forall x[z = 0 \rightarrow (x = 0 \vee \Diamond(z = x))]$

Note that axioms 1-4 are Peano axioms, axioms 5 and 6 define labelling of states and the last axiom says that every element of the domain has to be a label of a state.

One can prove that the above specification is *first-order complete*, i.e. all classical first-order formulas true in the standard model of natural numbers are semantic consequences of the above specification. As the set of classical first-order formulas true in the standard model of natural numbers is totally undecidable (not arithmetical in sense of Kleene and Mostowski hierarchy), we can conclude that the set of tautologies of FTL is totally undecidable as well. □

Acknowledgment

I would like to thank I. Németi and I. Sain for careful reading of the manuscript and contributing helpful comments and suggestions.

References

[1] Abadi, M. 1988. *The power of temporal proofs.* Report 30, Systems Research Center, Palo Alto, California.

[2] Abadi, M. & Z. Manna 1986. A timely resolution. In *Proceedings of the 1st Annual Symposium on Logics in Computer Science*, 176–89, IEEE.

[3] Andréka, H., I. Németi, I. Sain 1979. Completeness problems in verification of programs and program schemes. *Lecture Notes in Computer Sceince* **74**, 208–218.

[4] Andréka, H., I. Németi & I. Sain 1982. A complete logic for reasoning about programs via nonstandard model theory (parts I and II), *Theoretical Computer Science*, **17**(2), 193–212 and **17**(3) 213–16.

[5] Andréka, H., I. Németi & I. Sain 1991. On the strength of temporal proofs. *Theoretical Computer Science* **80**, 125–51.

[6] Andréka, H. et. al. 1994. Chapter 2 of this volume.

[7] Barringer, H., R. Kuiper & A. Pnueli 1984. Now you may compose temporal logic specifications. In *Proceedings of 16th Annual ACM Symposium on Theory of Computing*, 51–63.

[8] Barringer, H., R. Kuiper & A. Pnueli 1985. A compositional temporal approach to a CSP-like language. In *Proceedings of the IFIP Working Conference on Formal Models in Programming*, E. J. Neuhold & G. Chroust (eds), 207–28. Amsterdam: North Holland.

[9] Cook, S. A. 1978. Soundness and completeness of axiom system for program verification. *SIAM Journal of Computing* **7**(1), 70–90.

[10] Ebbinghaus, H. D., J. Flum & W. Thomas 1984. *Mathematical logic*. Berlin: Springer.

[11] Fitting, M. 1990. *First-order logic and automated theorem proving*. Berlin: Springer.

[12] Gabbay, D. M. 1976. *Investigations in modal and tense logics with applications to problems in philosophy and linguistics*. Dordrecht: D. Reidel.

[13] Gabbay, D. M., I. Hodkinson & M. Reynolds 1994. *Temporal logic. Mathematical foundations and computational aspects*. Oxford: Oxford University Press.

[14] Gabbay, D. M., et al. 1980. On the temporal analysis of fairness. In *Proceedings 7th Annual Symposium on the Principles of Programming Languages*, 163–73.

[15] Goldblatt, R. 1982. Axiomatizing the logic of computer programming. *Lecture Notes in Computer Science* **130**.

[16] Goldblatt, R. 1987. *Logics of time and computation*. Stanford Center for the Study of Language and Information.

[17] Gordon, M. J., A. J. Milner & C. P Wadsworth 1979. Edinburgh LCF. *Lecture Notes in Computer Science* **130**.

[18] Harel, D. 1978. First-order dynamic logic. *Lecture Notes in Computer Science* **68**.

[19] Henkin, L., J. D. Monk & A. Tarski 1985. *Cylindric algebras*, Part II. Amsterdam: North Holland.

[20] Hinman, P. G. 1978. *Recursion-theoretic hierarchies*. Berlin: Springer.

[21] Kawai, H. 1987. Sequential calculus for a first order infinitary temporal logic. *Zeitschrift für Mathematische Logic und Grundlagen der Mathematik* **33**, 423–32.

[22] Kawai, H. 1988. Completeness theorems for temporal logics T_Ω and $\Box T_\Omega$. *Zeitschrift für Mathematische Logic und Grundlagen der Mathematik* **34**, 393–8.

[23] Kröger, F. 1978. A uniform logical basis for the description, specification and verification of programs. In *Proceedings of the IFIP Working Conference on Formal Description of Programming Concepts*, E. J. Neuhold (ed), 441–60. Amsterdam: North Holland.

[24] Kröger, F. 1987. *Temporal logic of programs.* Berlin: Springer.

[25] Kröger, F. 1987b. Abstract modules: combining algebraic and temporal logic specification means, *TSI* **6**, 559–73.

[26] Lamport, L. 1980. The 'Hoare logic' for concurrent programs. *Acta Informatica* **14**, 21–37.

[27] Lamport, L. 1983. Specifying concurrent program modules. *ACM Transactions on Programming Languages and Systems* **5**, 190–222.

[28] Lichtenstein, O., A. Pnueli & L. Zuck 1985. The glory of the past. *Lecture Notes in Computer Science* **193**, 196–218.

[29] Manna, Z. & A. Pnueli 1981a. Verification of concurrent programs: the temporal framework. In *The correctness problem in computer science*, R. S. Boyer & R. S. Moore (eds), 215–73. New York: Academic Press.

[30] Manna, Z. & A. Pnueli 1981b. Verification of concurrent programs: temporal proof principles. *Lecture Notes in Computer Science* **131**, 200–252.

[31] Manna, Z. & A. Pnueli 1988. The anchored version of the temporal framework. *Lecture Notes in Computer Science* **354**, 201–84.

[32] Mirkowska, G. & A. Salwicki 1987. *Algorithmic logic.* Dordrecht: D. Reidel & Warsaw: Polish Scientific Publishers.

[33] Nishimura, H. 1979. Sequential method in propositional dynamic logic. *Acta Informatica* **12**, 377–400.

[34] Paech, B. 1988. *Gentzen-systems for propositional temporal logics*, Report 88/01, Ludwig Maximilians Universität, Munich.

[35] Penczek, W. 1994. Chapter of 4 this volume.

[36] Prior, A. 1967. *Past, present and future.* Oxford: Oxford University Press.

[37] Rescher, N. & A. Urquhart 1971. *Temporal logic.* Berlin: Springer.

[38] Sain, I. 1987. Total correctness in nonstandard logics of programs. *Theoretical Computer Science* **50**, 285–321.

[39] Sain, I. 1988. Comparing and characterizing the power of established program verification method. In *Proceedings of the Conference on Many Sorted Logic and its Applications*, J. Tucker & K. Meinke (eds), 215–314. Chichester: John Wiley.

[40] Sistla, A. P., Y. Vardi & P. Wolper 1987. The complementation problem for Büchi automata with applications to temporal logics. *Theoretical Computer Science* **49**, 217–37.

[41] Szałas, A. 1986. Concerning the semantic consequence relation in first-order temporal logic. *Theoretical Computer Science* **47**, 329–34.

[42] Szałas, A. 1987. A complete axiomatic characterization of first-frder temporal logic of linear time. *Theoretical Computer Science* **54**, 199–214.

[43] Szałas A. 1987/88. Arithmetical axiomatization of first-order temporal logic. *Information Processing Letters* **26**, 111–16.

[44] Szałas, A. 1988. Towards the temporal approach to abstract data types. *Fundamenta Informaticae* **11**, 49–64.

[45] Szałas, A. 1991. On strictly arithmetical completeness in logics of programs. *Theoretical Computer Science* **79**, 341–55.

[46] Szałas, A. 1992. Axiomatizing fixpoint logics, *Information Processing Letters* **41**, 175–80.

[47] Szałas, A. 1992. *On natural deduction in fixpoint logics*, Report MPI-I-92-203, Max-Planck-Institut für Informatik, Saarbrücken.

[48] Szałas, A. & L. Holenderski 1988. Incompleteness of first-order temporal logic with until, *Theoretical Computer Science* **57**, 317–25.

[49] Szałas, A. & U. Petermann 1989. On Temporal Logic for distributed systems and its application to processes communicating by interrupts, *Fundamenta Informaticae* **12**, 191–204.

[50] Takeuti, G. 1975. *Proof theory*, Amsterdam: North-Holland.

[51] VanBenthem, J. 1983. *The Logic of time. A model theoretic investigation into varieties of temporal ontology and temporal discourse.* Dordrecht: Reidel.

[52] Wolper, P. 1994. Chapter 3 of this volume.

Chapter 2

Effective temporal logics of programs

H. Andréka, V. Goranko†, S. Mikulás*, I. Németi* and I. Sain**

***Mathematical Institute**
Hungarian Academy of Sciences
Budapest, Pf. 127, H-1364, Hungary

†***Department of Mathematics, UniQwa***
Private Bag X13, Phuthaditjhaba 9866, South Africa

Abstract

In this chapter we investigate effective proof systems for temporal logics both propositional and first-order. The issue of effective proof systems for propositional temporal logic is much easier than for the first-order one. Partly because of this and partly because of applications we dwell on the first-order case much longer than on the propositional case. We prove soundness and completeness theorems for various effective proof systems and compare the program verifying - power of those systems.

2.1 Introduction

In this chapter we investigate effective inference systems (i.e. proof systems or calculi) $\vdash$ for temporal logics both propositional (PTL) and first-order (FTL). The issue of effective inference systems for PTL is much easier than for FTL. Partly because of this, and partly because of motivation coming from applications, we will dwell on the FTL case much longer than on the PTL case. (However, the PTL case will be thoroughly presented too.)

An inference system $\vdash$ for a logic $\mathcal{L}$ is *effective* if the set of $\vdash$-proofs is a Turing enumerable (or equivalently, recursively enumerable) set of finite sequences of strings. This restriction is motivated by the applications, but independently

*The research of has been supported by Hungarian NSF grant no. 1810.

†The work was partly supported by research grant GUN 2019536 of the Foundation for Research Development of South Africa

of that, Church [26] writes that any logic should have an effective inference system, and if $\vdash$ of $\mathcal{L}$ does not satisfy this criterion then it is not really a logic (i.e. not an inference system for a logic). Church writes this on the basis of purely logical considerations. According to this opinion, the study of inference systems $\vdash^{\infty}$, not satisfying this effectiveness criterion, when being pursued in mathematical logic, is a field of ***pure*** mathematics motivated by ideas coming from logic but not necessarily applicable to logic. All the same, these investigations can be very interesting and valuable. (This opinion seems to be implicitly present throughout the fundamental work the Handbook of philosophical logic [36]). Independently of this opinion, we focus our attention on effective logics in this chapter, because effectiveness is needed for applicability. This is true not only for machine implementations (even interactive ones), but also for applications in the human sphere, i.e. specification, documentation, or proving some properties (such as safety or fairness) of programs, systems, networks, etc., by hand. For more on general motivation and introductory material we refer the reader to Chapter 1. While this chapter is consistent with Chapter 1, it can also be read independently, since it is self-contained.

2.2 On temporal logic in general

2.2.1 Preliminaries

Throughout this chapter we use the general logical framework introduced in Section 1.2. According to that, by a *logic* we understand a triple

$$\mathcal{L} = \langle \mathsf{F}_{\mathcal{L}}, \mathsf{Mod}_{\mathcal{L}}, \models_{\mathcal{L}} \rangle$$

where

- $\mathsf{F}_{\mathcal{L}}$ is a set or sometimes a class (called the set of *formulas* of $\mathcal{L}$),
- $\mathsf{Mod}_{\mathcal{L}}$ is a class (called the class of ***models*** of $\mathcal{L}$), and
- $\models_{\mathcal{L}} \subseteq \mathsf{Mod}_{\mathcal{L}} \times \mathsf{F}_{\mathcal{L}}$, i.e. $\models_{\mathcal{L}}$ is a binary relation between models and formulas (called the ***validity relation of*** $\mathcal{L}$).

(cf. Definition 1.1. We note that more elaborate approaches to the abstract study of logics and related concepts can be found e.g. in [14], [17], [77].)

We will often omit the subscripts $\mathcal{L}$ from $\mathsf{F}_{\mathcal{L}}$, $\mathsf{Mod}_{\mathcal{L}}$, and $\models_{\mathcal{L}}$ for brevity.

The intuitive meaning (and reading) of "$\langle \mathcal{M}, \varphi \rangle \in \models$" is that "the formula φ is valid in the model $\mathcal{M}$" or "$\mathcal{M}$ is a model of φ". As it is customary in the literature of logic (and is done in Chapter 1 too), we adopt the "infix notation" $\mathcal{M} \models \varphi$ for $\langle \mathcal{M}, \varphi \rangle \in \models$.

Convention

For an arbitrary binary relation R, $\langle x, y\rangle \in R$ and xRy both abbreviate the claim that x and y are in relation R. $x\not R y$ means that x and y are not in relation R, that is $\langle x, y\rangle \notin R$. In particular $\mathcal{M} \not\models \varphi$ means that the formula φ is not valid in the model $\mathcal{M}$. □

As generally done in the literature of logic (and also in Chapter 1), the symbol $\models$, besides denoting the validity relation, will also be used, ambiguously, for denoting other relations too, all of which, however, are derived from or closely related to this validity relation. Context will help to overcome this ambiguity. Our first examples for using $\models$ for denoting relations other than validity are the following.

Notation

Let $\mathcal{L} = \langle \mathsf{F}, \mathsf{Mod}, \models\rangle$ be a logic, let $\Sigma, \Gamma \subseteq \mathsf{F}$ be two arbitrary sets of formulas, let $\mathsf{K} \subseteq \mathsf{Mod}$ be an arbitrary class of models. Then

(a) $\mathsf{K} \models \Sigma$ is defined to hold iff $\mathsf{K} \times \Sigma \subseteq \models$ that is iff $(\forall \mathcal{M} \in \mathsf{K})(\forall \varphi \in \Sigma)\mathcal{M} \models \varphi$.

We write $\mathcal{M} \models \Sigma$ instead of $\{\mathcal{M}\} \models \Sigma$ for brevity. Similarly, $\mathsf{K} \models \varphi$ abbreviates $\mathsf{K} \models \{\varphi\}$ for any $\varphi \in \mathsf{F}$. (Thus $\mathcal{M} \models \varphi$ as a special case of the present new notation gives back the original meaning, i.e. validity, of the symbol $\models$.)

We read $\mathsf{K} \models \Sigma$ as "Σ *is valid in* K"; $\mathcal{M} \models \Sigma$ as "Σ *is valid in* $\mathcal{M}$" or "$\mathcal{M}$ *is a model of* Σ".

We abbreviate $\mathsf{Mod} \models \varphi$ as $\models_{\mathcal{L}} \varphi$ or, ambiguously, as $\models \varphi$. If $\models \varphi$ then φ is called a *valid* formula of $\mathcal{L}$.

(b) $\Gamma \models \Sigma$ is defined to hold iff $(\forall \mathcal{M} \in \mathsf{Mod})(\mathcal{M} \models \Gamma \Longrightarrow \mathcal{M} \models \Sigma)$.

Similarly to the conventions in (a), we write $\Gamma \models \varphi$ and $\varphi \models \Sigma$ to abbreviate $\Gamma \models \{\varphi\}$ and $\{\varphi\} \models \Sigma$ respectively.

We read $\Gamma \models \Sigma$ as "Σ *is a semantical consequence of* Γ". Recall from Definition 1.2 that $Cn_{\mathcal{L}}(\Gamma)$ denotes the set of all semantical consequences of Γ in the logic $\mathcal{L}$, that is $Cn_{\mathcal{L}}(\Gamma) = \{\varphi \in \mathsf{F} : \Gamma \models \varphi\}$. □

In Section 1.2, the concept of an ***inference system*** for an arbitrary logic $\mathcal{L}$ is discussed. As explained in Chapter 1, the purpose of an inference system for a logic $\mathcal{L}$, roughly speaking, is to provide a formal, "mechanizable" tool for finding semantical consequences of sets of formulas, or for finding valid formulas of $\mathcal{L}$. An arbitrary inference system IS determines a so-called ***syntactical consequence*** or ***derivability*** or ***provability*** relation $\vdash_{IS} \subseteq \mathcal{P}(\mathsf{F}) \times \mathsf{F}$, where, for an arbitrary set A, $\mathcal{P}(A)$ denotes the ***powerset*** of A (that is $\mathcal{P}(A) \stackrel{def}{=} \{B :$

$B \subseteq A\}$). Therefore, in cases when it causes no confusion, we call $\vdash_{IS}$ itself the inference system (instead of IS).

Definition 2.1 Let $\mathcal{L} = \langle \mathsf{F}, \mathsf{Mod}, \models \rangle$ be a logic, and $\vdash \subseteq \mathcal{P}(\mathsf{F}) \times \mathsf{F}$ an inference system for $\mathcal{L}$.

(a) $\vdash$ is called ***sound*** for $\mathcal{L}$ if for any $\Sigma \subseteq \mathsf{F}$ and $\varphi \in \mathsf{F}$ we have

$$(\Sigma \vdash \varphi \text{ implies } \Sigma \models \varphi) \tag{2.1}$$

Weakly sound means postulating (2.1) only for the $\Sigma = \emptyset$ case, that is ($\vdash \varphi$ implies $\models \varphi$).

(b) $\vdash$ is called (weakly) ***complete*** for $\mathcal{L}$ if for any $\varphi \in \mathsf{F}$ we have

($\models \varphi$ implies $\vdash \varphi$). $\vdash$ is said to be ***strongly complete*** for $\mathcal{L}$ if for any $\Sigma \subseteq \mathsf{F}$ and $\varphi \in \mathsf{F}$ we have

$$(\Sigma \models \varphi \text{ implies } \Sigma \vdash \varphi) \tag{2.2}$$

□

Instead of saying that $\vdash$ is sound (complete) for $\mathcal{L}$, we will sometimes say that $\vdash$ is sound (complete) for Mod (when the rest of $\mathcal{L}$ can be unambiguously recovered from knowing that $\mathsf{Mod}_{\mathcal{L}} = \mathsf{Mod}$).

We will make sure that all our inference systems are sound. Weak soundness is too restrictive for our purposes, but see, e.g. Abadi [2] for such systems.

Chapter 1 distinguishes two kinds of inference systems: Gentzen-type and Hilbert-type. Recall from Section 1.2 that a ***derivation rule*** or ***rule of inference*** of a Hilbert-type inference system for a logic $\mathcal{L}$ is a pair $\langle \Sigma, \varphi \rangle$, where Σ is a set of formula schemata (called the set of ***premises***), and φ is a formula schema (called the ***conclusion*** of the rule). One of the characteristic features of this chapter is that here Σ is ***always finite***. When writing down such a rule $\langle \Sigma, \varphi \rangle$, we will always use one of the traditional forms: $\frac{\Sigma}{\varphi}$ or $\Sigma \vdash \varphi$, instead of $\langle \Sigma, \varphi \rangle$; moreover, if $\Sigma = \{\psi_1, \ldots \psi_k\}$, then we often write $\frac{\psi_1, \ldots, \psi_k}{\varphi}$ and $\psi_1, \ldots, \psi_k \vdash \varphi$ instead of $\frac{\Sigma}{\varphi}$ and $\Sigma \vdash \varphi$ respectively. One of the best known examples for such a rule is $\frac{\psi, \psi \to \varphi}{\varphi}$ or $\psi, \psi \to \varphi \vdash \varphi$, using the other notation (***modus ponens***). If $\Sigma = \emptyset$, then the rule is called an ***axiom schema***.

Definition 2.2 Let $\vdash$ be a Hilbert-type inference system for a logic $\mathcal{L} = \langle \mathsf{F} \ldots \rangle$.

(a) By a $\vdash$-***proof*** for $\mathcal{L}$ we understand a finite sequence $\langle \varphi_0, \ldots, \varphi_n \rangle$ of formulas from F such that for every $i \leq n$ there exists a $\Sigma \subseteq \{\varphi_j : j < i\}$ such that $\Sigma \vdash \varphi_i$ is an instance of some derivation rule of $\vdash$.

(b) The inference system $\vdash$ is called ***effective*** if the set of $\vdash$-proofs is decidable.

(c) Let $\Gamma \subseteq \mathsf{F}$ and $\varphi \in \mathsf{F}$ be arbitrary. Then $\Gamma \vdash \varphi$ means that there exists a finite sequence $\langle \varphi_0, \ldots, \varphi_n \rangle$ of formulas from F such that for every $i \leq n$ there exists $\Sigma \subseteq \{\varphi_j : j < i\} \cup \Gamma$ such that $\Sigma \vdash \varphi_i$ is an instance of some derivation rule of $\vdash$ or $\varphi_i \in \Gamma$. If $\Gamma \vdash \varphi$ then we say that φ is *provable* or *derivable* from Γ. □

The main aim of the approaches surveyed herein is investigating effective inference systems (and their semantical aspects too).

Notation

Throughout this chapter, we use the following notation:

ω is the *set of all natural numbers*.

$\mathsf{N} = \langle \omega, 0, succ, \leq \rangle$ is the *standard model of successor arithmetic with ordering* (i.e. 0 is the usual zero, *succ* is the usual successor function, and $\leq$ is the usual ordering relation on ω).

If f is a function (i.e. a class of ordered pairs such that $\{\langle x, y\rangle, \langle x, z\rangle\} \subseteq f$ implies $y = z$) then

- $\mathsf{Dom}(f) \stackrel{def}{=} \{a : \langle a, b\rangle \in f\}$ (*domain* of f), and
- $\mathsf{Rng}(f) \stackrel{def}{=} \{b : \langle a, b\rangle \in f\}$ (*range* of f).

${}^{A}B$, for two arbitrary sets A and B, denotes the set of all functions with domain A and range contained in B, i.e. ${}^{A}B = \{f : \text{we have } f : A \longrightarrow B\}$. □

Remark

The reason why (following the standard notation in set theory) we write ${}^{A}B$ instead of B^A is that the latter is ambiguous for the following reasons. Recall that $0 = \emptyset$ and $1 = \{0\}$. Now, ${}^{1}1 = {}^{\{0\}}\{0\} = \{\langle 0, 0\rangle\} \neq \{0\} = 1 = 1^1$. Therefore for certain sets A and B we have $A^B \neq$ "set of all functions mapping A into B". Cf. [46] for more explanation. □

2.2.2 Propositional temporal logics and their completeness theorems

First we define the basic (most general) propositional temporal logic PT we will use throughout this chapter. Let us keep in mind that a temporal logic, technically, is nothing but a special multi-modal logic. We will make extensive use this fact in Section 2.2.4. Our propositional temporal logic PT is a special instance of that given in Definition 1.8. The time frame of PT is the standard model $\mathsf{N} = \langle \omega, 0, succ, \leq \rangle$ of successor arithmetic with ordering. We use three basic modalities, all of them unary. They are called *next-time*, *always-in-the-future*, and *always-in-the-past*, and are denoted by $\bigcirc$, $\Box$, and $\overline{\Box}$ respectively.

Sometimes we want to talk about all these special modalities (and perhaps some more special ones as well) at the same time. Through this paper, we use the symbols $\widehat{\Box}$ and $\widehat{\Diamond}$ for metavariables ranging over modalities. Recall from the literature of modal logic (see [20], [24],[42],[47], [94],[95]) that the *dual* $\widehat{\Diamond}$ of a unary modality $\widehat{\Box}$ is defined as follows:

$$\widehat{\Diamond}\varphi = \neg\widehat{\Box}\neg\varphi \text{ for every formula } \varphi.$$

The duals of $\Box$ and $\overline{\Box}$ are denoted by $\Diamond$ and $\overline{\Diamond}$ respectively, and are called ***sometime-in-the-future*** and ***sometime-in-the-past***. ($\bigcirc$ is self-dual, i.e. $\neg\bigcirc\neg = \bigcirc$).

Definition 2.3 The propositional temporal logic $\mathsf{PT} = \langle \mathsf{F}^0, \mathsf{Mod}^0, \models \rangle$ is defined as follows.

Let P be an arbitrary but fixed set (called the set of ***propositional variables***). The set F^0 of formulas of PT is defined to be the smallest set satisfying the following (recursive) condition:

$$P \cup \{(\neg\varphi), (\varphi \wedge \psi), \bigcirc\varphi, \Box\varphi, \overline{\Box}\varphi : \varphi, \psi \in \mathsf{F}^0\} \subseteq \mathsf{F}^0.$$

Cf. Definition 1.8.

The class Mod^0 is defined to be the class of all (propositional) Kripke models for F^0 with time frame N, that is

- $\mathcal{M} \in \mathsf{Mod}^0$ iff $\mathcal{M} = \langle \mathsf{N}, V \rangle$

where $\mathsf{N} = \langle \omega, 0, succ, \leq \rangle$, and V is a valuation of the propositional variables, that is $V : P \longrightarrow \mathcal{P}(\omega)$. Since the time frame of every model $\mathcal{M} \in \mathsf{Mod}^0$ is the standard model N, we will sometimes refer to these Kripke models as ***standard-time models*** or ***standard models***.

The validity relation $\models \subseteq \mathsf{Mod}^0 \times \mathsf{F}^0$ is defined as follows. First we will define the forcing (or "local truth") relation $\Vdash \subseteq \mathsf{Mod}^0 \times \omega \times \mathsf{F}^0$. We abbreviate $\langle \mathcal{M}, t, \varphi \rangle \in \Vdash$ by $\mathcal{M}, t \Vdash \varphi$, and read it as "$\varphi$ is true in the model $\mathcal{M}$ at time point t". The recursive definition of $\Vdash$ is given by items (1-6) below.

Let $\mathcal{M} = \langle \mathsf{N}, V \rangle \in \mathsf{Mod}^0$, $t \in \omega$, and $\varphi, \psi \in \mathsf{F}^0$ be arbitrary. Then

1.	If $\varphi \in P$ then $\mathcal{M}, t \Vdash \varphi$	iff	$t \in V(\varphi)$.
2.	$\mathcal{M}, t \Vdash (\neg\varphi)$	iff	$\mathcal{M}, t \nVdash \varphi$.
3.	$\mathcal{M}, t \Vdash (\varphi \wedge \psi)$	iff	$(\mathcal{M}, t \Vdash \varphi$ and $\mathcal{M}, t \Vdash \psi)$.
4.	$\mathcal{M}, t \Vdash \bigcirc\varphi$	iff	$\mathcal{M}, succ(t) \Vdash \varphi$.
5.	$\mathcal{M}, t \Vdash \Box\varphi$	iff	$\mathcal{M}, u \Vdash \varphi$ for every $u \geq t$.
6.	$\mathcal{M}, t \Vdash \overline{\Box}\varphi$	iff	$\mathcal{M}, u \Vdash \varphi$ for every $u \leq t$.

Now, for every $\mathcal{M} \in \mathsf{Mod}^0$ and $\varphi \in \mathsf{F}^0$, $\mathcal{M} \models \varphi$ iff $\mathcal{M}, t \Vdash \varphi$ for every $t \in \omega$. □

Besides $\bigcirc$, $\Box$, and $\overline{\Box}$, we will use the following two derived modalities (i.e. definable ones in F^0) as well:

$\odot\varphi \stackrel{def}{=} \overline{\Diamond}\,\overline{\Box}\varphi$ called "*first* φ(self – dual), and (2.3)

$\boxdot\varphi \stackrel{def}{=} \varphi \wedge \Box\varphi \wedge \overline{\Box}\varphi$ called "*always* φ". ($\boxdot$ is an S5 modality). (2.4)

The dual $\diamondsuit$ of $\boxdot$ is called "*sometime*".

Notice that, for every $\mathcal{M} \in \mathsf{Mod}^0$, $t \in \omega$, and $\varphi \in \mathsf{F}^0$, we have

- $\mathcal{M} \models \odot\varphi$ iff $\mathcal{M}, t \Vdash \odot\varphi$ iff $\mathcal{M}, 0 \Vdash \varphi$ and (2.5)
- $\mathcal{M} \models \boxdot\varphi$ iff $\mathcal{M}, t \Vdash \boxdot\varphi$ iff $\mathcal{M}, u \Vdash \varphi$ for every $u \in \omega$. (2.6)

Remark

Modalities $\widehat{\Box}_1$ and $\widehat{\Box}_2$ with accessibility relations R and R^{-1} respectively are called ***conjugate modalities***, cf. Jónsson & Tarski [50], [51]. Notice that our $\Box$ and $\overline{\Box}$ are conjugate modalities. The presence of conjugate modalities in temporal logics is most typical. The first abstract (syntactic) characterization of such pairs of modalities was given in [50] and [51] (in algebraic form). (The syntactic form used in [50] is slightly different from the one, $K_t(\widehat{\Box}_1, \widehat{\Box}_2)$, we will adopt from the literature below). Kripke models for propositional (multi-) modal logics were first defined in [50] and [51], too. These papers use the expression "atom structures" for Kripke models. $\Box$

Remark

We could have based our temporal logic on the irreflexive ordering "$<$" as opposed to the reflexive one $\leq$ as the accessibility relation interpreting $\Box$. Both versions are present in the literature, e.g. Goldblatt [42]. In our case, the choice is not too important, since in all the fragments we will investigate the modality $\bigcirc$ interpreted by *succ* is available, and by using *succ*, $<$ and $\leq$ are interdefinable. More concretely, let $\Box_<$ be interpreted by $<$. Then $\Box_< \varphi \leftrightarrow \bigcirc\Box\varphi$, and in the other direction $\Box\varphi \leftrightarrow (\varphi \vee \Box_< \varphi)$. $\Box$

Besides investigating PT, we will investigate some of its fragments, too. By a *fragment* of PT we mean a propositional multi-modal logic, the modalities of which are some (not necessarily all) of the modalities $\bigcirc$, $\Box$, $\overline{\Box}$, $\odot$, $\boxdot$. The class of models is fixed to be Mod^0 (the class of standard models) for all fragments of PT (and the semantics of our modalities is also fixed by Definition 2.3 and items (2.5), (2.6)). For example, a fragment of PT is the propositional multi-modal logic with modalities $\odot$ and $\bigcirc$ only. In this fragment, naturally, $\odot$ is a basic modality and not a derived one, since we do not have $\overline{\Box}$ (the meaning of $\odot$ is defined then by (2.5). When in a fragment of PT we have a certain modality, say $\overline{\Box}$, then we have its dual, $\overline{\Diamond}$, as well (since every fragment is closed under negation, by definition).

Fragments of PT will be important for us, e.g. in Section 2.3, where we will prove that certain distinguished logics of programs are equivalent with certain fragments of (first-order) temporal logic[1]. For example, we will see that Floyd-Hoare logic is equivalent to the $\{\odot, \bigcirc\}$ fragment of (first-order) temporal logic, and that the Intermittent assertions method is equivalent to the $\{\odot, \bigcirc, \boxdot\}$ fragment of temporal logic. See Theorems 2.45 and 2.46 in Section 2.4.

Notation

Throughout this chapter, a fragment of PT will be denoted as PT_X where the subscript X of PT indicates the modalities of the fragment PT_X. More specifically, X will always be a list of some elements of the five-element set $\{\bigcirc, \odot, F, P, S\}$, where F, P and S refer to $\Diamond$, (future), $\overline{\Diamond}$ (past), and $\diamondsuit$ (sometime) respectively. Thus, for example, $\mathsf{PT}_{\bigcirc F}$ stands for the fragment of PT having $\Diamond$ and $\bigcirc$ only. Further, $\mathsf{PT}_{F\bigcirc} = \mathsf{PT}_{\bigcirc F}$, and $\mathsf{PT} = \mathsf{PT}_{\bigcirc\odot FPS}$. $\square$

Next we will define and investigate ***Hilbert-type inference systems*** for several fragments PT_X of PT. We will denote the inference system for PT_X by $\vdash^0_X$. All the inference systems $\vdash^0_X$ given below are sound, and we will prove their ***completeness***. In this section completeness is understood in its weaker sense (see Definition 2.1(a)), that is $\vdash^0_X$ is said to be complete for PT_X iff ($\models \varphi$ implies $\vdash^0_X \varphi$) for every formula φ of PT_X. In contrast with the present propositional section, the issue of ***strong*** completeness will be thoroughly investigated in the first-order sections. We note that neither PT nor its fragments has strongly complete and sound inference systems (e.g. none of these logics is compact[2]).

We say that a logic $\mathcal{L}$ has the ***finite model property*** if we may restrict it to its finite models without changing the set of valid formulas, in other words, if every satisfiable formula is also satisfiable in some finite model. $\mathcal{L}$ is called ***decidable*** if the set of all valid formulas of $\mathcal{L}$ is decidable. In items I-IX below, we state and prove that the inference system $\vdash_X$ for PT_X given in the item is complete, and that PT_X is decidable.

In the rest of this section, for didactical reasons we will introduce and study more inference systems than are needed in the rest of the chapter. What we will really use are the ones in items III-V and VIII. We note that the basic techniques used here and most of the results (especially those for the fragments PT_F, $\mathsf{PT}_{\bigcirc F}$, PT_{FP}) are known, and some of them can be found, for example, in Segerberg [95], Goldblatt [42]. In the proofs we will assume that the reader is familiar with such basic constructions as the generated submodel, p-morphism, maximal consistent set and the canonical model. These concepts can easily be

[1]By first-order temporal logic we mean the first-order version of PT.

[2]A logic $\mathcal{L} = \langle, F, \ldots, \models\rangle$ is called *compact* iff for every $\Sigma \subseteq F$ and $\varphi \in F$, if $\Sigma \models \varphi$ then there is a finite subset $\Sigma_0 \subseteq \Sigma$ such that $\Sigma_0 \models \varphi$. It is easy to see that every logic having a strongly complete and sound inference system is compact.

found in the first chapter of the following classical sources: Segerberg [95], Hughes & Cresswell [47], Goldblatt [42], van Benthem [20] and Burgess [24]. Nevertheless, we will briefly recall some of the basic definitions and properties inside the proofs, in order to make this chapter self-contained.

I. (*F and P*)

We start with the classical mono-modal logic PT_F (known in the literature of modal logic as S4.3 Dum). The proof of the completeness for PT_F includes most of the basic techniques and is built into the completeness proof for every extended logic. That is why this proof will be given in detail, although it is essentially a combination of the proofs in Goldblatt [42] and Segerberg [94].

Here is the inference system $\vdash^0_F$:

- Axiom schemata:

1.	(BOOL)	all boolean tautologies
2.	(K(□))	$\Box(\varphi \rightarrow \psi) \rightarrow (\Box\varphi \rightarrow \Box\psi)$
3.	(ref)	$\Box\varphi \rightarrow \varphi$
4.	(tran)	$\Box\varphi \rightarrow \Box\Box\varphi$
5.	(wcon)	$\Box(\Box\varphi \rightarrow \psi) \vee \Box(\Box\psi \rightarrow \varphi)$
6.	(Dum)	$\Box(\Box(\varphi \rightarrow \Box\varphi) \rightarrow \varphi) \rightarrow (\Diamond\Box\,\varphi \rightarrow \Box\varphi)$.

- Rules of inference:

1. (MP) $\frac{\varphi,\varphi\rightarrow\psi}{\psi}$,
2. ($\mathrm{NEC}_\Box$) $\frac{\varphi}{\Box\varphi}$.

We note that wcon abbreviates *weak connectedness*, explained in the proof of Theorem 2.1. The same axiom 5 can also be interpreted as expressing that the pre-ordering of the time frame is linear (5 has this effect only under assuming the other axioms).

Remark

$\mathsf{K}(\widehat{\Box})$ refers to the fact that this axiom (together with 1 and the two rules) ensures that Kripke models provide an adequate semantics for $\widehat{\Box}$ as was proved by Jónsson and Tarski in 1948 (cf. [50], [51], [46] §2.7) by using boolean algebras with operators (BAO's). (Here $\widehat{\Box}$ stands for an arbitrary unary modality.) In particular, 1, 2, MP and $\mathrm{NEC}_{\widehat{\Box}}$ yield $\vdash \widehat{\Diamond}(\varphi \vee \psi) \leftrightarrow (\widehat{\Box}\varphi \vee \widehat{\Box}\psi)$ and $\widehat{\Box}\mathsf{T}$. The generalized Kripke models (rediscovered by Lemmon) needed for the weaker modal logic without $\widehat{\Box}\mathsf{T}$ (and hence without the rule $\mathrm{NEC}_{\widehat{\Box}}$) were also discovered and provided with the corresponding completeness proof in Jónsson & Tarski [50], [51]. We will not need these so-called non-normal modal logics. (But it will be useful to know what part of the Jónsson & Tarski completeness technique using BAOs is needed for which kind of Kripke models.) □

Theorem 2.1 The inference system $\vdash_F^0$ is complete and sound for PT_F, further PT_F has the finite model property, and PT_F is decidable.

Proof: Let φ be a PT_F-consistent formula, i.e. $\not\vdash_F^0 \neg\varphi$, and let w be a maximal PT_F-consistent set of formulas, containing φ (see [47] for the construction of such a set). Take the submodel $\mathcal{M}_w = \langle W_w, R, V\rangle$ of the canonical model of $\mathsf{PT}_F\,\Box$ - generated by w, that is W_w consists of all maximal PT_F - consistent sets accessible by R-paths from w, where the binary relation R is canonically defined: xRy iff $\Box x \subseteq y$ where $\Box x = \{\theta : \Box\theta \in x\}$, and V is the restriction of the canonical valuation over W_w: for every propositional variable p, $V(p) = \{x \in W_w : p \in x\}$.

From the classical literature of modal logics (see the previous references), we recall the most important property of a canonical model (and of all of its generated submodels), the truth lemma:

Truth Lemma:

> For every maximal consistent set x and every formula θ, $x \Vdash \theta$ iff $\theta \in x$. In particular, $\mathcal{M}_w, w \Vdash \varphi$.

What can we say about $\mathcal{M}_w$? It is well known that the schemata ref, tran, and wcon ensure reflexivity, transitivity, and weak connectedness:

$$\forall y, z(\exists x(xRy \wedge xRz) \rightarrow (yRz \vee zRy))$$

respectively for every frame validating them. All of them are canonical, i.e. they are valid in every canonical frame. Therefore R is reflexive, transitive and connected, since $\mathcal{M}_w$ has a root. The last schema (Dum) is more complicated: it is valid in those frames which enjoy the following second-order condition: for every x, y, if xRy, then no infinite R-path $x = x_0Rx_1 \ldots Rx_n \ldots$ exists such that $x_i \neq x_{i+1}$ and $\neg yRx_i$ for all x_i. Clearly, $\langle \omega, \leq\rangle$ validates all the schemata of PT_F, and hence PT_F is sound.

It is not difficult to see that $\mathcal{M}_w$ is not a standard model, so we need additional constructions to satisfy φ in such a model. One of the most frequently used techniques for this purpose is *filtration*.

Digression: filtration
For completeness, we give here the definition of this construction. Let $\mathcal{M} = \langle W, R, V\rangle$ be a model, and Γ be a set of formulas closed under subformulas. I.e. $\theta \in \Gamma \Rightarrow sf(\theta) \subseteq \Gamma$, where $sf(\theta)$ is the set of all subformulas of θ. For every $x \in W$ we define

$$\Gamma_x \stackrel{def}{=} \{\theta \in \Gamma : \mathcal{M}, x \Vdash \theta\}.$$

Thus we obtain an equivalence relation on W : $x \equiv_\Gamma y$ iff $\Gamma_x = \Gamma_y$. We put $|x| = \{y \in W : x \equiv_\Gamma y\}$ and $W_\Gamma = \{|x| : x \in W\}$. Note that if Γ is finite and has n elements then W_Γ has at most 2^n elements. Now we construct a model $\mathcal{M}_\Gamma = \langle W_\Gamma, R_\Gamma, V_\Gamma \rangle$ as follows: $V_\Gamma(p) = \{|x| : x \in V(p)\}$ for every variable $p \in \Gamma$, and arbitrary for the others. Finally, R_Γ must obey two conditions:

1. $xRy \Rightarrow |x|R_\Gamma|y|$;
2. $|x|R_\Gamma|y| \Rightarrow$ for every $\Box\theta \in \Gamma$, if $\mathcal{M}, x \Vdash \Box\theta$ then $\mathcal{M}, y \Vdash \theta$.

Every relation R_Γ obeying these condition is called a Γ-filtration of R, and the corresponding model $\mathcal{M}_\Gamma$, a Γ-filtration of $\mathcal{M}$. The main property of the filtration is given by the filtration lemma:

Filtration Lemma:

> For every $\theta \in \Gamma$ and $x \in W$, $\mathcal{M}, x \Vdash \theta$ iff $\mathcal{M}_\Gamma, |x| \Vdash \theta$. Especially, when filtrating the canonical model: $|x| \Vdash \theta$ iff $\theta \in x$ for every $\theta \in \Gamma$.

Another important fact is that every model $\mathcal{M}_\Gamma$ obtained by filtration is distinguishable, i.e. for every $s \in W_\Gamma$ there exists a formula χ_s characteristic for s, i.e. for every $t \in W_\Gamma$, $t \Vdash \chi_s$ iff $t = s$. Indeed, one can take

$$\chi_s = \bigwedge\{\theta : \theta \in \Gamma \text{ and } \mathcal{M}_\Gamma, s \Vdash \theta\} \wedge \bigwedge\{\neg\theta : \theta \in \Gamma \text{ and } \mathcal{M}_\Gamma, s \nVdash \theta\}$$

Moreover, $\mathcal{M}, x \Vdash \chi_s$ iff $\mathcal{M}_\Gamma, |x| \Vdash \chi_s$ iff $|x| = s$. In the same way, we can distinguish every finite subset Y in W_Γ by the disjunction χ_Y of the characteristic formulas of its elements. At that $\mathcal{M}, x \Vdash \chi_Y$ iff $\mathcal{M}_\Gamma, |x| \Vdash \chi_Y$ iff $|x| \in Y$.

At least two filtrations always exist:

> the *minimal* filtration defined by $|x|R_\Gamma|y|$ iff $x'Ry'$ for some $x' \in |x|$ and $y' \in |y|$, and
>
> the *maximal* filtration defined by condition (2) above, with $\Rightarrow$ replaced by $\Leftrightarrow$.

We have to mention another possible filtration, the *transitive* one: $|x|R_\Gamma|y|$ iff for every $\Box\theta \in \Gamma$, if $\mathcal{M}, x \Vdash \Box\theta$ then $\mathcal{M}, y \Vdash \Box\theta \wedge \theta$. It plays an important rôle in our proof, since when R is transitive, then R_Γ thus defined is indeed a filtration; moreover, R_Γ is transitive, too. □

Now, let us come back to the proof. Let $\Gamma = sf(\varphi)$, and take the transitive Γ-filtration $\mathcal{M}_\Gamma = \langle W_\Gamma, R_\Gamma, V_\Gamma \rangle$ of $\mathcal{M}$. Note that R_Γ is reflexive, transitive and connected (if $\neg|x|R_\Gamma|y|$ then $\neg xRy$ hence yRx, so $|y|R_\Gamma|x|$). Therefore, the relation $\underline{R}_\Gamma$ defined by $|x|\underline{R}_\Gamma|y|$ iff ($|x|R_\Gamma|y|$ and $|y|R_\Gamma|x|$) is an equivalence relation in W_Γ, and divides W_Γ into a finite number of finite R_Γ-*clusters* in which R_Γ is universal. A cluster is *proper* if it has more than one element. We will investigate the R_Γ-clusters more closely.

Definition 2.4 Let ξ be an R_Γ-cluster. We say that $s \in \xi$ is a *final element* in ξ if there exists $x \in s$, call it an *end of* s, such that for every $y \in W_\Gamma$, if $|y| \in \xi$ and xRy then $|y| = s$. □

Dummet lemma: Every proper non-last R_Γ-cluster has a final element.
Proof of Dummet lemma: We will introduce a new relation R^f in W_Γ: for $s, t \in W_\Gamma$, $sR^f t$ iff $(\forall x \in s)(\exists y \in t)xRy$. It is easy to check that R^f is also reflexive, transitive and connected, moreover, $R^f \subseteq R_\Gamma$. Defining the corresponding R^f-generated equivalence relation $\underline{R^f}$, we obtain a finite chain of finite R^f-clusters such that every R^f-cluster is included in some R_Γ-cluster, i.e. every R_Γ-cluster consists of a finite chain of R^f-clusters.

Now we will show the following equivalence: the existence of a final element in an R_Γ-cluster ξ means that the last R^f-cluster in ξ is a singleton and consists of this final element.

Indeed, if a final element $|f|$ with an end f exists in ξ, then it is in the last R^f-cluster in ξ which must be a singleton, because of the following. Suppose $|f|R^f t$ for some $t \in \xi$. Then for some $y \in t$, fRy, hence $t = |y| = |f|$.

Vice versa, if the last R^f-cluster in ξ is a singleton $\{s\}$, then s is a final element in ξ, because of the following. Let t belong to the last but one R^f-cluster of ξ (it exists since ξ is proper). Then $\neg sR^f t$, hence for some $f \in s$, $\neg fRy$ for every $y \in t$. Then f is an end of s: first, yRf for every $y \in t$ because of connectedness of R; now if fRx and $|x| \in \xi$ then $|x| = s$, otherwise $|x|R^f t$, hence xRy for some $y \in t$, and then fRy, which is a contradiction.

Now we are ready to prove the Dummet lemma. Let ξ be a proper non-last R_Γ-cluster. Suppose there are two elements s and t in the last R-cluster of ξ. Let χ_s be the characteristic formula of s. Take an element u from the R_Γ-cluster immediately following ξ. Then $\neg uR_\Gamma s$, hence for some $\Box\theta \in \Gamma$, $u \Vdash \Box\theta$, and $s \not\Vdash \Box\theta$. Then $t \not\Vdash \Box\theta$ as well, since otherwise $t \Vdash \Box\Box\theta$, and $tR_\Gamma s$ implies $s \Vdash \Box\theta$. Denote $\alpha = \chi_s \vee \Box\theta$. Then the following hold:

1. for every $x \in s$, $x \Vdash \alpha$;
2. for every $x \in t$, $x \not\Vdash \alpha$, and hence $x \not\Vdash \Box\alpha$;
3. for every $|x|$ in an R_Γ-cluster following ξ, $x \Vdash \alpha$ (because $uR_\Gamma|x|$);
4. for every $x \in t$, $x \Vdash \Diamond\Box\alpha$ (since $sR^f u \Rightarrow tR^f u$).

But then for any set $x \in t$, $x \not\Vdash \Diamond\Box\alpha \rightarrow \Box\alpha$, hence by (Dum), $x \Vdash \Diamond(\Box(\alpha \rightarrow \Box\alpha) \wedge \neg\alpha)$, i.e. for some y such that xRy, $y \Vdash \Box(\alpha \rightarrow \Box\alpha)$ and $y \Vdash \neg\alpha$. Then $|y|$ must belong to ξ, and hence $|y|R_\Gamma s$. Then $s \Vdash \alpha \rightarrow \Box\alpha$, so $s \Vdash \Box\alpha$, but then $t \Vdash \alpha$, which is a contradiction. Dummet lemma is proved. □

Using the Dummet lemma, we are able to unwind all but the last R_Γ-clusters into finite chains of elements, preserving the truth lemma. For every proper non-last R_Γ-cluster ξ with a final element f_ξ we take an arbitrary linear ordering $\leq_\xi$ of the elements of ξ with a greatest element f_ξ. Thus we obtain a finite "balloon" $\mathcal{M}'_\Gamma = \langle W_\Gamma, \leq, V_\Gamma \rangle$, where $s \leq t$ iff either the R_Γ-cluster of s precedes that of t, or both s and t belong to the last cluster, or both s and t belong to a non-last cluster ξ and $s \leq_\xi t$. Three observations on $\mathcal{M}'_\Gamma$ complete the proof:

1. **Truth lemma**: For every $s \in W_\Gamma$ and $\theta \in \Gamma$, $\mathcal{M}_R, s \Vdash \theta$ iff $\mathcal{M}'_\Gamma, s \Vdash \theta$.

   The proof is by induction on θ, and the crucial step is for $\theta = \Box\psi$ (provided the assertion holds for ψ). Since $\leq$ is included on R_Γ, if $\mathcal{M}_\Gamma, s \Vdash \Box\psi$, then $\mathcal{M}'_\Gamma, s \Vdash \Box\psi$. Let now $\mathcal{M}_\Gamma, s \nVdash \Box\psi$. If s belongs to the last R_Γ-cluster or to a singleton cluster, then $\leq$-successors and R_Γ-successors of s coincide, and trivially $\mathcal{M}'_\Gamma, s \nVdash \Box\psi$. Assume that s belongs to a non-last proper R_Γ-cluster ξ with a final element $|f|$ with an end f. Then $\mathcal{M}_\Gamma, |f| \nVdash \Box\psi$, since otherwise $\mathcal{M}_\Gamma, |f| \Vdash \Box\Box\psi$ and hence $\mathcal{M}_\Gamma, s \Vdash \Box\psi$. So by filtration lemma, $\Box\psi \notin f$, hence $\psi \notin x$ for some x such that fRx. Then either $|x| = |f|$ or $|x|$ belongs to a cluster following ξ. In both cases $s \leq |x|$, and $\mathcal{M}_\Gamma, |x| \nVdash \psi$, hence $\mathcal{M}'_\Gamma, |x| \nVdash \psi$, so $\mathcal{M}'_\Gamma, s \nVdash \Box\psi$. Thus, in particular, $\mathcal{M}'_\Gamma, |w| \Vdash \varphi$.

2. $\mathcal{M}'_\Gamma$ is a model for PT_F, since the underlying frame validates the axiom schemata. So, every PT_F-consistent formula is satisfied in a finite PT_F-model, i.e. PT_F has the finite model property and, being finitely axiomatized, is decidable.

3. Finally, to show completeness, it is sufficient to observe that $\mathcal{M}'_\Gamma$ is a p-morphic image of a standard PT_F-model. Indeed, let the last R_Γ-cluster in $\mathcal{M}_\Gamma$ be $\eta = \{s_0, \ldots, s_{k-1}\}$, and let the elements of W_Γ not in η and ordered by $\leq$ be $t_0, \ldots, t_m$. Then the mapping $\pi : \omega \longrightarrow W_\Gamma$ defined by

   $$\pi(n) = \begin{cases} t_n, & \text{if } n \leq m \\ s_\ell, & \text{where } \ell \text{ is the remainder of } n \text{ modulo } k\text{, otherwise} \end{cases}$$

   is a p-morphism from $\langle \omega, \leq \rangle$ onto $\langle W_\Gamma, \leq \rangle$, which means:

   - for every $i, j \in \omega$, $i \leq j \Rightarrow \pi(i) \leq \pi(j)$,
   - for every $i \in \omega$, $s \in W_\Gamma$, $\pi(i) \leq s \Rightarrow s = \pi(j)$ for some j, such that $i \leq j$.

   Then the model $\langle \omega, \leq, V \rangle$, where $V(p) = \pi^{-1}(V_\Gamma(p))$ verifies φ at any $n \in \pi^{-1}(|w|)$ due to Segerberg's well-known theorem (see [95] or [47]). We completed the proof of Theorem 2.4. □

Let us notice without proof that the logic PT_P can be axiomatized as PT_F with $\Box$ replaced by $\overline{\Box}$, and the Dummet schema (Dum) replaced by the stronger Grzegorczyc schema (cf. [94]):

$$(Grz_{\overline{\Box}}) \quad \overline{\Box}(\overline{\Box}(\varphi \to \overline{\Box}\varphi) \to \varphi) \to \varphi.$$

II. ($\bigcirc F$)

Now we enrich PT_F with the modality $\bigcirc$ (next-time), and thus obtain the logic $\mathsf{PT}_{\bigcirc F}$. It is axiomatized as follows (cf. Goldblatt [42]):

- Axiom schemata:

1. (BOOL)
2. (K ($\Box$))
3. (K ($\bigcirc$)) $\quad \bigcirc(\varphi \to \psi) \to (\bigcirc\varphi \to \bigcirc\psi)$
4. ($fun_{\bigcirc}$) $\quad \bigcirc\neg\varphi \leftrightarrow \neg\bigcirc\varphi$
5. (mix) $\quad \Box\varphi \to (\varphi \wedge \bigcirc\Box\varphi)$
6. ($ind_{\Box}$) $\quad \Box(\varphi \to \bigcirc\varphi) \to (\varphi \to \Box\varphi)$.

- Rules of inference:

1. (MP), ($\mathrm{NEC}_{\Box}$) and
2. ($\mathrm{NEC}_{\bigcirc}$) $\frac{\varphi}{\bigcirc\varphi}$.

It turns out that all dropped schemata of $\vdash^0_F$: ref, tran, wcon, and Dum are provable in $\mathsf{PT}_{\bigcirc F}$ (see [42]) so $\mathsf{PT}_{\bigcirc F}$ is indeed an extension of PT_F.

Theorem 2.2 $\vdash^0_{\bigcirc F}$ is complete and sound for $\mathsf{PT}_{\bigcirc F}$, and $\mathsf{PT}_{\bigcirc F}$ is decidable.

Sketch of the proof: We follow the schema of the proof of Theorem 2.1 with some necessary changes:

1. We start again with an arbitrary $\mathsf{PT}_{\bigcirc F}$-consistent formula φ, some maximal $\mathsf{PT}_{\bigcirc F}$-consistent set w containing φ, and the submodel $\mathcal{M}_w = \langle W_w, succ, R, V\rangle$ of the canonical $\mathsf{PT}_{\bigcirc F}$-model, $\Box$-generated by w, where $succ$ has the canonical definition: $(x \; succ \; y)$ iff $succ(x) \stackrel{def}{=} \{\theta : \bigcirc\theta \in x\} \subseteq y$. It is easy to see that $succ$ is a function and is included in R (use the derivable schema $\Diamond\bigcirc\varphi \to \Diamond\varphi$).

2. We take the minimal Γ-filtration $succ_\Gamma$ of $succ$, where

   $\Gamma = sf(\varphi) \cup \{\bigcirc\Box\theta : \Box\theta \in sf(\varphi)\}$.

   The following lemma gives us an appropriate Γ-filtration of R.

Ancestral lemma ([42]): If $succ_\Gamma$ is a Γ-filtration of $succ$, then its reflexive and transitive closure $succ^*_\Gamma$ is a Γ-filtration of R.

Proof of ancestral lemma: We have to check conditions (1) and (2) of filtration.

1. Let xRy. In order to show $|x| succ^*_\Gamma |y|$, we consider the set $S_x = \{s \in W_\Gamma : |x| succ^*_\Gamma\}$.
   Let χ be the characteristic formula of S_x, i.e. for every $u \in W_w$, $\chi \in u$ iff $|u| \in S_x$. We will show that $\Box(\chi \to \bigcirc\chi) \in x$. Indeed, let xRu and $\chi \in u$. Then $|u| \in S_x$, hence $|x| succ^*_\Gamma |u|$, i.e. $|x| succ^n_\Gamma |u|$ for some $n \geq 0$. Now, $(u \ succ \ z)$ implies $|u| succ_\Gamma |z|$, hence $|x| succ^{n+1}_\Gamma |z|$, so $|z| \in S_x$, whence $\chi \in z$. Now by (ind$_\Box$), $\chi \to \Box\chi \in x$, and $\chi \in x$, since $|x| \in S_x$, hence $\Box\chi \in x \Rightarrow \chi \in y$, so $y \in S_x$.

2. We will show that for every $n \geq 0$, $|x| succ^n_\Gamma |y|$ implies $\Box\theta \in y$ for every $\Box\theta \in x \cap \Gamma$. Induction by n: the case $n = 0$ is trivial; assume the statement holds for some n, and that $|x| succ^{n+1}_\Gamma |y|$. Then for some z, we have $|x| succ^n_\Gamma |z| succ_\Gamma |y|$. Let $\Box\theta \in x \cap \Gamma$. Then $\Box\theta \in z$, hence $\bigcirc\Box\theta \in z$ by (mix), and $\bigcirc\Box\theta \in \Gamma$ as well. But then $|z| \Vdash \bigcirc\Box\theta$, hence $|y| \Vdash \Box\theta$, so $\Box\theta \in y$.

Now, if $|x| succ^*_\Gamma |y|$, then for some $n \geq 0$, $|x| succ^n_\Gamma |y|$, whence if $\Box\theta \in x \cap \Gamma$, then $\Box\theta \in y$, so $\theta \in y$. Ancestral lemma is proved. □

Thus we have a Γ-filtration $R_\Gamma = succ^*_\Gamma$ of R, which is reflexive, transitive, connected, and fitting to the Γ-filtration of *succ*.

3. As in Theorem 2.1, we prove the Dummet lemma for R_Γ. However, when unwinding the R_Γ-clusters, we have to take care about $succ_\Gamma$. The problem is that it is not necessarily a function. But the following observation will help us:

   For every $x \in W_w$ and $\bigcirc\theta \in x \cap \Gamma$, $\exists y(|x| succ_\Gamma |y|$ and $\theta \in y)$ iff $\forall y(|x| succ_\Gamma |y| \to \theta \in y)$. To see this, let $|x| succ_\Gamma |y|$ for some y (such a y exists, so the "if direction" is trivial). Then $(x' \ succ_\Gamma \ y')$ for some $x' \in |x|$, $y' \in |y|$. Suppose $\theta \notin y$. Then $\theta \notin y' \Rightarrow \neg\theta \in y' \Rightarrow \bigcirc\neg\theta \in x' \Rightarrow \neg\bigcirc\theta \in x'$ by (fun$_\bigcirc$) $\Rightarrow \bigcirc\theta \notin x' \Rightarrow \bigcirc\theta \notin x$, which is a contradiction.

   This observation shows that in order to ensure the truth lemma, every element of W_Γ needs only one $succ_\Gamma$-successor, and any of them works. Thus we are ready to unwind.

   Take a non-last, proper R_Γ-cluster ξ, and order its elements $s_1, \ldots, s_k$, putting the final element at the end. For every $i = 1, \ldots, k-1$ there exists a $succ_\Gamma$-path $s_i \, succ_\Gamma s^1_i \, succ_\Gamma \ldots s^m_i \, succ_\Gamma s_{i+1}$ (the elements may appear in these paths in many copies). Filling in the sequence $s_1, \ldots, s_k$ into these paths, we obtain a finite $succ_\Gamma$-sequence containing all elements of ξ. We do the same with all proper R_Γ-clusters, and in the last one also connect, by a $succ_\Gamma$-path, the end with the beginning, and thus obtain a $succ_\Gamma$-cycle there. The result is a finite balloon $\mathcal{M}' = \langle W', S, S^*, V' \rangle$, where S is the successor relation in this balloon, S^* is the reflexive and transitive closure of S, and $V'(p)$ consists of all copies of elements from

$V_\Gamma(p)$. Note that the underlying frame of $\mathcal{M}'$ validates all schemata of $\mathsf{PT}_{\bigcirc F}$, and hence $\mathcal{M}'$ is a $\mathsf{PT}_{\bigcirc F}$-model. As in Theorem 2.1, we prove the following:

Truth lemma: For every $\theta \in \Gamma$ and $s \in W_\Gamma$, $\mathcal{M}_\Gamma, s \Vdash \theta$ iff $\mathcal{M}', s' \Vdash \theta$ for any copy s' of s. Thus we obtain a finite $\mathsf{PT}_{\bigcirc F}$-model satisfying φ, which proves the finite model property, and hence the decidability of $\mathsf{PT}_{\bigcirc F}$.

4. Finally we cut the S-cycle in $\mathcal{M}'$ at any point, and repeat it finitely many times, thus obtaining a standard $\mathsf{PT}_{\bigcirc F}$-model, mapped by a p-morphism (in the language of $\mathsf{PT}_{\bigcirc F}$) onto $\mathcal{M}'$. This last model satisfies φ, which gives completeness of $\mathsf{PT}_{\bigcirc F}$. With this, the proof of Theorem 2.2 is completed. □

III. $(\odot \bigcirc F)$

The next enrichment of the logic is adding the modality $\odot$ (first) referring to the first moment of the time - the zero. Here is the inference system $\vdash^0_{\odot\bigcirc F}$:

- Axiom schemata: those of $\vdash^0_{\bigcirc F}$ augmented with

7. (K($\odot$)) $\odot(\varphi \to \psi) \to (\odot\varphi \to \odot\psi)$
8. (fun$_\odot$) $\odot\neg\varphi \leftrightarrow \neg\odot\varphi$
9. (first) $\varphi \to \odot\Diamond\varphi$
10. (const) $\odot\varphi \to \Box\odot\varphi$.

- Rules of inference:

1. (MP), (NEC$_\Box$) (NEC$_\bigcirc$) and
2. (NEC$_\odot$) $\frac{\varphi}{\odot\varphi}$.

Let us notice that the induction principle $(\odot\varphi \wedge \Box(\varphi \to \bigcirc\varphi)) \to \varphi$ is derivable by $\vdash^0_{\odot\bigcirc F}$, as well as the schemata $\odot\Box\varphi \to \varphi$ and $\Diamond\odot\varphi \to \odot\varphi$, which will be used below.

Theorem 2.3 $\vdash^0_{\odot\bigcirc F}$ is complete and sound for $\mathsf{PT}_{\odot\bigcirc F}$, and $\mathsf{PT}_{\odot\bigcirc F}$ is decidable.

Sketch of the proof:

1. Let w be a maximal $\mathsf{PT}_{\odot\bigcirc F}$-consistent set containing a fixed $\mathsf{PT}_{\odot\bigcirc F}$-consistent formula φ. Denote $z \stackrel{def}{=} \odot w = \{\theta : \odot\theta \in w\}$. The schema (fun$_\odot$) ensures that z is a maximal $\mathsf{PT}_{\odot\bigcirc F}$-consistent set. Now we take the submodel $\mathcal{M}_z = \langle W_z, fst, succ, R, V\rangle$ of the canonical $\mathsf{PT}_{\bigcirc F}$-model $\Box$-generated by z, where fst, $succ$, and R are canonically defined according to the modalities $\odot$, $\bigcirc$, and $\Box$. Then the following hold:

- $w \in W_z$, since if $\theta \in \Box z$ then $\Box\theta \in z \Rightarrow \odot\Box\theta \in w \Rightarrow \theta \in w$; hence $\Box z \subseteq w$.
  - For every $x \in W_z$, $\odot x = \odot w = z$. Indeed, R is connected as we have already noticed, so either $\Box x \subseteq w$ or $\Box w \subseteq x$. Both cases are analogous, so we may assume $\Box x \subseteq w$. Then, if $\theta \in \odot x$ then $\odot\theta \in x \Rightarrow \Box\odot\theta \in x \Rightarrow \odot\theta \in w \Rightarrow \theta \in \odot w$. Thus $\odot x \subseteq \odot w$, hence $\odot x = \odot w$, because $\odot x$ is a maximal set.

2. From now on we proceed as in the proof of Theorem 2.2. We have to notice only that, after a Γ-filtration, $|z|$ will belong to the first R_Γ-cluster, and we can unwind this cluster starting from $|z|$, and thus ensuring $|z|$ is the zero of the obtained baloon. This will verify the inductive step for $\odot\theta$ in the truth lemma. $\Box$

IV. $(\odot\bigcirc)$

Now we will consider the fragment $\mathsf{PT}_{\odot\bigcirc} = \mathsf{PT}_0$ of $\mathsf{PT}_{\odot\bigcirc F}$, namely the logic with modalities $\odot$ and $\bigcirc$ only. This fragment will play a central rôle in the computer science applications.

- Axiom schemata:

1. (BOOL)
2. (K ($\odot$))
3. (K ($\bigcirc$))
4. (fun$_\odot$) $\quad \odot\neg\varphi \leftrightarrow \neg\odot\varphi$
5. (fun$_\bigcirc$)
6. (con$'_\odot$) $\quad \odot\varphi \leftrightarrow \odot\odot\varphi$
7. (con$''_\odot$) $\quad \odot\varphi \leftrightarrow \bigcirc\odot\varphi$.

- Rules of inference:

1. (MP), (NEC$_\odot$), (NEC$_\bigcirc$), and
2. (induction rule) $\frac{\{\odot\varphi,\ \varphi\rightarrow\bigcirc\varphi\}}{\varphi}$.

Theorem 2.4 $\vdash^0_{\odot\bigcirc}$ is complete and sound for $\mathsf{PT}_{\odot\bigcirc}$, and $\mathsf{PT}_{\odot\bigcirc}$ is decidable.

Sketch of the proof: Let w be a maximal PT_0-consistent set containing a PT_0-consistent formula φ. We take, as before, $z \stackrel{def}{=} \odot w = \{\theta : \odot\theta \in w\}$. z is a maximal PT_0-consistent set. Now we take the canonical submodel $\mathcal{M}_0 = \langle W_0, fst, succ, V_0\rangle$ $\bigcirc$-generated from $\{z, w\}$. Note that every element $x \in W_0$ is either of the form $succ^n z$ or of $succ^n w$ for some $n \in \omega$. In both cases $\odot x = z$, because of the following. Suppose $x = succ^n w$. We prove $\odot x = z$. Let $\psi \in \odot x$ be arbitrary. Then $\odot\psi \in x$ implies $\bigcirc^n \odot \psi \in w$, hence $\odot\psi \in w$, whence $\psi \in z$

(by con$''_{\odot}$ + Nec$_{\bigcirc}$($\vdash \bigcirc^{n-1}(\odot\varphi \leftrightarrow \bigcirc\odot\varphi)) + K(\vdash \bigcirc^{n-1}\odot\varphi \leftrightarrow \bigcirc^n\odot\varphi)$). Let $\psi \in z$. Then $\odot\psi \in w$ implies $\bigcirc^n \odot \psi \in w$, hence $\bigcirc\psi \in x$, whence $\psi \in \bigcirc x$ (by nec+K+con$''_{\bigcirc}$). If $x = succ^n w$ and $\odot\psi \in x$, then $\bigcirc^n \odot \psi \in w$ and $\vdash^0_{\odot\bigcirc} \bigcirc^n \odot \psi \leftrightarrow \odot\psi$ by (con$''_{\odot}$), hence $\odot\psi \in w$, i.e. $\psi \in z$, so $\odot x \subseteq z$, whence $\odot x = z$. If $x = succ^n z$ and $\odot\varphi \in x$, then $\bigcirc^n \odot \varphi \in z$, hence $\odot\varphi \in z$. Therefore $\odot\odot\varphi \in w$, so $\odot\varphi \in w$ by (con$'_{\odot}$), i.e. $\varphi \in z$, and again $\odot x \subseteq z$.

Thus we obtain a non-standard model (because it might be the case that w is not $succ^n z$ for any $n \in \omega$) of PT$_0$, which satisfies φ at w.

Now we shall show that φ is satisfied in a standard model. Let $d(\varphi)$ denote the ***modal depth*** of φ defined as follows. $d(p) \stackrel{def}{=} 0$; $d(\neg\alpha) \stackrel{def}{=} d(\alpha)$; $d(\alpha \wedge \beta) \stackrel{def}{=} max(d(\alpha), d(\beta))$; $d(\bigcirc\alpha) \stackrel{def}{=} d(\odot\alpha) \stackrel{def}{=} d(\alpha) + 1$. Suppose $d(\varphi) = n$. Consider a valuation V in $\langle \omega, 0, succ\rangle$ defined as follows.

$$V(p) \stackrel{def}{=} \{m : succ^m z \in V_0(p),\ 0 \le m \le n\} \cup \{m : succ^{m-(n+1)} w \in V_0(p),\ n < m\}.$$

Thus we obtain a standard model $\mathcal{M} = \langle \omega, 0, succ, V\rangle$. We shall prove that for every formula ψ such that $d(\psi) = k \le n$,

$$\mathcal{M}, m \Vdash \psi \text{ iff } \mathcal{M}_0, succ^m z \Vdash \psi \text{ for } 0 \le m \le n-k, \text{ and}$$
$$\mathcal{M}, m \Vdash \psi \text{ iff } \mathcal{M}_0, succ^{m-(n+1)} w \Vdash \psi \text{ for } n < m. \tag{2.7}$$

We use induction on $d(\psi)$.

(a) If $d(\psi) = 0$ then (2.7) follows from the definition of V.

(b) Assume that, for every θ with $d(\theta) < k$, (2.7) holds, and that $d(\psi) = k$.

Clearly, it is enough to prove (2.7) for the cases $\psi = \odot\theta$ and $\psi = \bigcirc\theta$.

When $\psi = \odot\theta$, then $\mathcal{M}, m \Vdash \psi$ iff $\mathcal{M}, 0 \Vdash \theta$ iff $\mathcal{M}_0, z \Vdash \theta$ by the induction hypothesis, which holds iff $\mathcal{M}_0, x \Vdash \psi$ for any $x \in W_0$.

Let $\psi = \bigcirc\theta$. If $0 \le m \le n-k$, then $\mathcal{M}, m \Vdash \psi$ iff $\mathcal{M}, m+1 \Vdash \theta$ iff $\mathcal{M}_0, succ^{m+1} z \Vdash \theta$ (by the induction hypothesis, since $d(\theta) = k-1$ and $m+1 \le n-(k-1)$) iff $\mathcal{M}_0, succ^m z \Vdash \psi$. The case $n < m$ is even easier.

The induction is completed. In particular, $\mathcal{M}, n+1 \Vdash \varphi$. Completeness is proved. Decidability follows from the decidability of the next system PT$_{\odot\bigcirc S}$, which is a conservative extension of PT$_0$. □

It might be of interest to note that the induction rule of $\vdash^0_{\odot\bigcirc}$ was not used in the proof of the ("weak") completeness Theorem 2.4 of $\vdash^0_{\odot\bigcirc}$ (above). The reason why we do not omit this rule from $\vdash^0_{\odot\bigcirc}$ despite its irrelevance for Theorem 2.4 is the following. As mentioned before, since propositional temporal logics (PT$_i$s) are not compact, we restrict our attention to weak completeness investigations, i.e. to theorems of the form

$$\Gamma \models \varphi \text{ iff } \Gamma \vdash \varphi \tag{2.8}$$

but restricted to the case when $\Gamma = \emptyset$. (Cf. Definition 2.1a & b.) Strong completeness would mean (2.8) for arbitrary Γ and φ. We know that strong completeness fails by failure of compactness. However, there is an intermediate property called "medium completeness". Medium completeness means (2.8) restricted to *finite* Γs. It is at this point where we need the induction rule. Namely, there are formulas γ, φ of $PT_{\odot\bigcirc}$ such that $\gamma \models \varphi$ in the sense of Definitions 2.1 and 2.3 (i.e. in every Kripke model $\mathcal{M}$ with $\mathcal{M} \models \gamma$ we have $\mathcal{M} \models \varphi$), but $\gamma \not\vdash \varphi$ if $\vdash$ is obtained from $\vdash^0_{\odot\bigcirc}$ by deleting the induction rule. That is, though we do not need the induction rule for deriving validities like $\models \varphi$, we do need it when deriving one nonlogical theorem from another. That is, this rule is needed when we use $\vdash^0_{\odot\bigcirc}$ as a binary (syntactical consequence) relation instead of only as a unary theoremhood relation. This usage of $\vdash^0_{\odot\bigcirc}$ will be crucial to its first - order temporal logic application, and even more to its computer science applications.

Open problem

Is $\vdash^0_{\odot\bigcirc}$ medium complete for $PT_{\odot\bigcirc}$? (If not, can it be extended to a nice medium complete system?) □

The reason why in the literature (and hence here too) medium completeness is somewhat neglected in comparison with weak and strong completeness is the following. If a logic $\mathcal{L} = \langle F_{\mathcal{L}}, M_{\mathcal{L}}, \models_{\mathcal{L}}\rangle$ has certain basic properties, then medium completeness coincides with weak completeness. These properties are the following:

(a) availability of "$\wedge$", and

(b) the weak deduction property (cf. [14] and the works of W. J. Blok and D. Pigozzi quoted therein).

Property (b) means the existence of a derived binary logical connective Δ, in $\mathcal{L}$, such that $\varphi \models_{\mathcal{L}} \psi$ iff $\models \mathcal{L}\Delta(\varphi, \psi)$ for all $\varphi, \psi \in F_{\mathcal{L}}$. All our PT_is have (a), and every PT_i in which $\Box$ is expressible, has (b) too ($\Delta(\varphi, \psi)$ being $\Box(\varphi \rightarrow \psi)$). However, PT_0 does not have (b).

V. $(\odot \bigcirc S)$

Now let us enrich PT_0 with $\boxdot$ (Always) and thus obtain the system $PT_{\odot\bigcirc S}$.

- Axiom schemata: those of $\vdash^0_{\odot\bigcirc}$ $\{\text{con}'_{\odot}, \text{con}''_{\odot}\}$ augmented with

6.	$(S5(\boxdot))$	which is $(\Diamond\varphi \rightarrow \boxdot\Diamond\varphi) + (\text{rel}_{\boxdot}) + K(\boxdot)$
7.	(incl)	$\boxdot\varphi \rightarrow \odot\varphi \wedge \bigcirc\varphi$
8.	$(\text{con}_{\odot})$	$\odot\varphi \rightarrow \boxdot \odot \varphi$
9.	$(\text{ind}_{\boxdot})$	$\odot\varphi \wedge \boxdot(\varphi \rightarrow \bigcirc\varphi) \rightarrow \varphi$.

- Rules of inference:

  1. (MP), (NEC$_\boxdot$).

Theorem 2.5 $\vdash^0_{\odot\bigcirc s}$ is complete and sound for $\mathsf{PT}_{\odot\bigcirc s}$, and $\mathsf{PT}_{\odot\bigcirc s}$ is decidable.

Sketch of the proof:

1. Given a $\mathsf{PT}_{\odot\bigcirc s}$-consistent formula φ, we start with a maximal $\mathsf{PT}_{\odot\bigcirc s}$-consistent set w containing φ and z as defined in item IV. z is a maximal $\mathsf{PT}_{\odot\bigcirc s}$-consistent set. Now take the canonical submodel $\mathcal{M}_z = \langle W_z, fst, succ, U, V\rangle$ $\boxdot$-generated by z. Note that U is the universal relation on W_z. Let fst_Γ and $succ_\Gamma$ be the minimal Γ-filtrations of fst and $succ$, where $\Gamma = sf(\varphi)$. Then

   (a) For every $|x|, |y| \in W_\Gamma$, $|x| fst_\Gamma |y|$ iff $|y| = |z|$.

   (b) Ancestral lemma: For every $|x| \in W_\Gamma$, $|z| succ^*_\Gamma |y|$, because of the following. Let $X \stackrel{def}{=} \{|y| \in W_\Gamma : |z| succ^*_\Gamma |y|\}$ and let χ be the characteristic formula of X. Then:

   (i) $\odot\chi \in x$ since $|z| \in X$;

   (ii) $\boxdot(\chi \to \bigcirc\chi) \in x$, which is verified by the following.
   Assume $\diamonddot(\chi \wedge \bigcirc\neg\chi) \in x$. Now $\diamonddot(\chi \wedge \bigcirc\neg\chi) \in x \Rightarrow \chi \to \bigcirc\chi \in u$ for some $u \in W_\Gamma \Rightarrow |u| \in X$ and for some v, $u\, succ\, v$ and $v \notin X$, which is impossible.
   Thus, in particular, $|z| succ^*_\Gamma |w|$.

2. Now we unwind as in Theorem 2.2, and prove the truth lemma. □

□From now on we investigate temporal systems involving both $\Box$ and $\overline{\Box}$.

VI. (*FP*)

We start with the classical temporal logic PT_{FP}. We will use $\boxdot$ as well, as a derived modality ($\boxdot\varphi \stackrel{def}{=} \varphi \wedge \Box\varphi \wedge \overline{\Box}\varphi$).

- Axiom schemata: those of PT_F augmented with

  7. (K ($\overline{\Box}$)) $\overline{\Box}(\varphi \to \psi) \to (\overline{\Box}\varphi \to \overline{\Box}\psi)$
  8. (K$_t$($\Box, \overline{\Box}$)) $\varphi \to \Box\overline{\Diamond}\varphi \wedge \overline{\Box}\Diamond\varphi$
  9. (con) $\boxdot\varphi \to \Box\overline{\Box}\varphi \wedge \overline{\Box}\Box\varphi$
  10. (Grz$_{\overline{\Box}}$) $\overline{\Box}(\overline{\Box}(\varphi \to \overline{\Box}\varphi) \to \varphi) \to \varphi$.

- Rules of inference:

  1. (MP), (NEC$_\Box$).

Remark

Schema $K_t(\widehat{\Box}_1, \widehat{\Box}_2)$ expresses that modalities $\widehat{\Box}_1$ and $\widehat{\Box}_2$ are conjugates of each other in the Jónsson & Tarski sense, who proved in 1948 that this is sufficient and necessary for completeness for frames in which $\widehat{\Box}_1$ is interpreted by the inverse of the accessibility relation of $\widehat{\Box}_2$, cf. [50], [51]. The abbreviation K_t refers to temporal Kripke frames.

Some theorems of PT_{FP}:

(a) The schema con is stronger than wcon, and so the latter can be dropped here.

(b) $\vdash_{FP} (\mathrm{ref}_{\overline{\Box}}) \wedge (\mathrm{tran}_{\overline{\Box}}) \wedge (\mathrm{Dum}_{\overline{\Box}}) \wedge (\overline{\Box}(\overline{\Box}(\varphi \to \overline{\Box}\varphi) \to \varphi) \to \overline{\Box}\varphi)$. These are easy exercises, left to the reader.

(c) $\vdash_{FP} (\mathrm{MC}_{\overline{\Box}})$, where

$(\mathrm{MC}_{\overline{\Box}}): \quad \overline{\Box}\overline{\Diamond}\varphi \to \overline{\Diamond}\overline{\Box}\varphi$

Here is a short inference in PT_{FP}: $\overline{\Box}\overline{\Diamond}\varphi \wedge \overline{\Box}\overline{\Diamond}\neg\varphi \vdash_{FP}$ $\overline{\Box}\overline{\Diamond}\varphi \wedge \overline{\Box}\overline{\Box}\overline{\Diamond}\neg\varphi \vdash_{FP} \overline{\Box}(\overline{\Diamond}\varphi \wedge \overline{\Box}\overline{\Diamond}\neg\varphi) \vdash_{FP} \overline{\Box}\overline{\Diamond}(\varphi \wedge \overline{\Diamond}\neg\varphi) \vdash_{FP}$ $\overline{\Box}(\neg\varphi \to \overline{\Diamond}(\varphi \wedge \overline{\Diamond}\neg\varphi)) \vdash_{FP} \overline{\Box}(\overline{\Box}(\varphi \to \overline{\Box}\varphi) \to \varphi) \vdash_{FP} \overline{\Box}\varphi$, and also $\overline{\Box}\overline{\Diamond}\varphi \wedge \overline{\Box}\overline{\Diamond}\neg\varphi \vdash_{FP} \overline{\Diamond}\neg\varphi$ hence $\overline{\Box}\overline{\Diamond}\varphi \wedge \overline{\Box}\overline{\Diamond}\neg\varphi \vdash_{FP} \mathsf{F}$.

Theorem 2.6 $\vdash^0_{FP}$ is complete and sound for PT_{FP}, and PT_{FP} is decidable.

Sketch of the proof: As a basis, we take the proof of Theorem 2.1, but we make changes and additional steps:

1. We start with a PT_{FP}-consistent formula $\varphi \in w$, and denote $z \stackrel{def}{=} \{\theta : \overline{\Diamond}\overline{\Box}\theta \in w\}$. z is a maximal PT_{FP}-consistent set, since $\vdash_{FP} \overline{\Diamond}\overline{\Box}\alpha \wedge \overline{\Diamond}\overline{\Box}\beta \to \overline{\Diamond}\overline{\Box}(\alpha \wedge \beta)$ and $\vdash_{FP} \overline{\Diamond}\overline{\Box}\alpha \vee \overline{\Diamond}\overline{\Box}\neg\alpha$.
   Now we take the submodel $\mathcal{M}_z = \langle W_z, U, R, V\rangle$ of the canonical PT_{FP}-model $\boxdot$-generated by w, where xUy iff $\boxdot x \subseteq y$. It is an easy exercise to show that $\boxdot$ is an S5 modality, whence U is an equivalence relation containing R. Moreover, U is the universal relation on W_z. So $W_z = \langle x : \boxdot z \subseteq x\rangle$. As usual, R is reflexive, transitive and connected. Also observe the following facts:

   (a) $w \in W_z$ since zRw, i.e. $w \subseteq \Diamond z$, because if $\alpha \in w$ then $\overline{\Diamond}\alpha \in W \Rightarrow \overline{\Diamond}\overline{\Box}\Diamond\alpha \in w \Rightarrow \Diamond\alpha \in z$.

   (b) For every $x \in W_z$, $\{\theta : \overline{\Diamond}\overline{\Box}\theta \in x\} = z$, because of the following. Suppose xRw. Then $x \subseteq \overline{\Diamond}w$, so if $\overline{\Diamond}\overline{\Box}\theta \in x$ then $\overline{\Diamond}\overline{\Diamond}\overline{\Box}\theta \in w$, hence $\overline{\Diamond}\overline{\Box}\theta \in \omega$. Thus $\{\theta : \overline{\Diamond}\overline{\Box}\theta \in x\} \subseteq z$. But these are maximal sets, so they coincide.

(c) For every $x \in W_z$, zRx.
Suppose xRz, i.e. $x \subseteq \overline{\Diamond} z$ and $\theta \in z$. Then $\overline{\Diamond\Box}\theta x \Rightarrow \overline{\Diamond\Box}\theta \in x \Rightarrow \alpha \in \overline{\Diamond} x$. Thus $z \subseteq \overline{\Diamond} x$, so zRx.

2. Let us remember that in a temporal language with modalities $\Box$ and $\overline{\Box}$, condition (2) on a Γ-filtration is replaced by

   (a) $|x|R_\Gamma|y| \Rightarrow$
   for every $\Box\theta \in \Gamma$, if $\mathcal{M}, x \Vdash \Box\theta$ then $\mathcal{M}, y \Vdash \theta$; and
   for every $\overline{\Box}\theta \in \Gamma$, if $\mathcal{M}, y \Vdash \overline{\Box}\theta$ then $\mathcal{M}, x \Vdash \theta$.

   An appropriate filtration preserving transitivity is the *Priorian* one:

   (b) $|x|R_\Gamma|y|$ iff
   for every $\Box\theta \in \Gamma$, if $\mathcal{M}, x \Vdash \Box\theta$ then $\mathcal{M}, y \Vdash \Box\theta \wedge \theta$, and
   for every $\overline{\Box}\theta \in \Gamma$, if $\mathcal{M}, y \Vdash \overline{\Box}\theta$ then $\mathcal{M}, x \Vdash \overline{\Box}\theta \wedge \theta$.

   We will use this filtration over the set $\Gamma = sf(\varphi)$.

3. Now we define a notion dual to that of a final element of a Γ-cluster: an element s of the R_Γ-cluster ξ is called an *initial element* in ξ, if there exists $x \in s$, call it the *beginning of* s, such that for every $y \in W_\Gamma$, if $|y| \in \xi$ and yRx then $|y| = s$.

   If we consider the relation R^p dual to R^f, defined by sR^pt iff $(\varphi\forall y \in t)(\exists x \in s)xRy$, then the following dual correspondence holds: an R_Γ-cluster ξ has an initial element iff the first R^p-cluster in R_Γ is a singleton.

   Now, since we have both $\mathrm{Dum}_\Box$ and $\mathrm{Dum}_{\overline{\Box}}$ derivable in PT_{FP}, we can prove a double Dummet lemma: every proper non-last R_Γ-cluster has a final element, and every proper non-first R_Γ-cluster has an initial element. The proof consists of two parts completely analogous to those in Theorem 2.1, with one additional argument only. Namely, the Priorian filtration requires consideration of two cases when $\neg uR_\Gamma s$ (in the proof on a final element):

   (a) For some $\Box\theta \in \Gamma$, $u \Vdash \Box\theta$ and $s \nVdash \Box\theta$. Then, as before, take $\alpha = \chi_s \vee \Box\theta$.

   (b) For some $\overline{\Box}\theta \in \Gamma$, $s \Vdash \overline{\Box}\theta$ and $u \nVdash \overline{\Box}\theta$. In this case, take $\alpha = \chi_s \vee \neg\overline{\Box}\theta$.

   Both cases can be dealt with analogously. Considerations symmetric with those in the proof on an initial element can be made.

   In addition to the above, we will prove that, because of $\mathrm{MC}_{\overline{\Box}}$, the first R_Γ-cluster ξ_0 has an initial element too. Actually, we will prove that $|z|$ is this initial element, as follows. Assume that s belongs to the first

R^p-cluster of ξ_0. Then $sR^p|z|$, hence xRz for some $x \in s$. Note that for every α, if $\overline{\Diamond}\,\overline{\Box}\alpha \in x$ then $\overline{\Box}\alpha \in y$ for some y such that yRx. But zRy, so xRy, hence $\alpha \in x$. Vice versa, if $\alpha \in x$ then $\overline{\Diamond}\,\overline{\Box}\alpha \in x$ since otherwise $\overline{\Diamond}\,\overline{\Box}\neg\alpha \in x$ by $MC_{\overline{\Box}}$, and $\neg\alpha \in x$. Now, if $\theta \in \Gamma \cap x$ then $\overline{\Diamond}\,\overline{\Box}\theta \in x$, hence $\theta \in z$, and if $\theta \in \Gamma \cap z$ then $\overline{\Diamond}\,\overline{\Box}\theta \in x$, hence $\theta \in x$. Therefore $x \cap \Gamma = z \cap \Gamma$, hence $s = |z|$. So, $|z|$ is the first initial element in W_Γ, and will be the zero in the final model.

4. Finally, we unwind, as usual, all R_Γ-clusters except the last one, starting from the initial element and finishing with the final one. The last R_Γ-cluster is unwound, starting from its initial element. The truth lemma is proved as in Theorem 2.1.

VII. ($\bigcirc FP$)

Now we consider the system $\vdash^0_{\bigcirc FP}$: we add to the schemata and rules of $\vdash^0_{\bigcirc FP}$ those of $\vdash^0_{\bigcirc F}$ as well as the additional

($\bigcirc\overline{\Box}$) $\quad \overline{\Box}\varphi \wedge \bigcirc\varphi \rightarrow \bigcirc\overline{\Box}\varphi.$

Theorem 2.7 $\vdash^0_{\bigcirc FP}$ is complete and sound for $\mathsf{PT}_{\bigcirc FP}$, and $\mathsf{PT}_{\bigcirc FP}$ is decidable.

Sketch of the proof: This proof combines those of Theorem 2.2 and Theorem 2.6.

1. Let φ be $\mathsf{PT}_{\bigcirc FP}$-consistent, w be a maximal $\mathsf{PT}_{\bigcirc FP}$-consistent set containing φ, and $z = \{\theta : \overline{\Diamond}\,\overline{\Box}\theta \in w\}$. Take, as in Theorem 2.6, the canonical submodel $\mathcal{M}_z = \langle W_z, succ, U, R, V\rangle$ $\boxdot$-generated by z. We have to show that W_z is closed under $succ$. Proving that the schema $\bigcirc\overline{\Box} \rightarrow \overline{\Box}\bigcirc\varphi$ is derivable in $\mathsf{PT}_{\bigcirc FP}$ is left to the reader as an exercise. Now, if zRx and $x\ succ\ y$ then zRy, so $y \in W_z$ by virtue of the derivable schema $\Diamond\bigcirc\varphi \rightarrow \Diamond\varphi$. We will show that if xRz and $x\ succ\ y$ then either $z\ succ\ y$ or yRz, hence, in both cases, $y \in W_z$.

   Suppose $\bigcirc z \notin y$ and $\overline{\Box} z \notin y$. Then for some α, $\bigcirc\alpha \in z$ and $\neg\alpha \in y$ and for some β, $\overline{\Box}\beta \in z$ and $\neg\beta \in y$. Denote $\gamma = \alpha \vee \beta$. Then $\bigcirc\gamma \wedge \overline{\Box}\gamma \in z$ and $\neg\gamma \in y$. Therefore, by ($\bigcirc\overline{\Box}$), $\bigcirc\overline{\Box}\gamma \in z$, hence $\overline{\Box}\bigcirc\gamma \in z \Rightarrow \bigcirc\gamma \in x \Rightarrow \gamma \in y$ — a contradiction.

2. We make a minimal Γ-filtration of $succ$ as in Theorem 2.2, where

$$\Gamma = sf(\varphi) \cup \{\bigcirc\Box\theta : \Box\theta \in sf(\varphi)\} \cup \{\bigcirc\overline{\Box}\theta : \overline{\Box}\theta \in sf(\varphi)\}.$$

   We have to prove a lemma analogous to the ancestral lemma: if $succ_\Gamma$ is a Γ-filtration of $succ$, then $succ^*_\Gamma$ is such a Γ-filtration of R, which is appropriate for $\Box$ and $\overline{\Box}$. The additional step in the proof is the following. For every $n \geq 0$, $|x|succ^n_\Gamma|y|$ implies $\overline{\Box}\theta \in x$ for every $\overline{\Box}\theta \in y \cap \Gamma$. It is done by induction on n. The inductive step is ensured by the derivable schema $\bigcirc\overline{\Box}\theta \rightarrow \overline{\Box}\theta$, as follows. Assume that the assertion holds for some n, and assume $|x|succ^{n+1}_\Gamma|y|$ and $\overline{\Box}\theta \in y \cap \Gamma$. Then $|x|succ^n_\Gamma|u|succ_\Gamma|y|$. By the filtration lemma, $\mathcal{M}_\Gamma, |x| \Vdash \overline{\Box}\theta \Rightarrow \mathcal{M}_\Gamma, |u| \Vdash \bigcirc\overline{\Box}\theta$ and $\bigcirc\overline{\Box}\theta \in \Gamma \Rightarrow \bigcirc\overline{\Box}\theta \in u \Rightarrow \overline{\Box}\theta \in u \Rightarrow \overline{\Box}\theta \in x$. The ancestral lemma is proved.

3. Now we take $succ^*_\Gamma$ as a Γ-filtration of R, and the proof proceeds as in Theorems 2.2 and 2.6. □

VIII. ($\odot\bigcirc$ *FPS*)

We arrived at the full logic $\mathsf{PT} = \mathsf{PT}_{\odot\bigcirc FPS}$.

- Axiom schemata: those of $\mathsf{PT}_{\bigcirc FP}$ augmented with

  $(\odot\overline{\Box})$ $\quad \odot\varphi \leftrightarrow \overline{\Diamond}\,\overline{\Box}\,\varphi$

- Rules of inference:

  (MP), ($\mathrm{NEC}_{\boxdot}$), ($\mathrm{NEC}_{\bigcirc}$), ($\mathrm{NEC}_{\odot}$).

Theorem 2.8 $\vdash^0_{PT}$ is complete and sound for PT, and PT is decidable.

Sketch of the proof: The only step we have to add to the proof of Theorem 2.7 is that, by virtue of $(\odot\overline{\Box})$, $\{\theta : \overline{\Diamond}\,\overline{\Box}\theta \in w\} = \{\theta : \odot\theta \in w\} = \odot w$, so $|\odot w|$ is the zero of the final model, hence it is a model for PT. □

IX.

Finally, a modification of PT: instead of the constant modality $\odot$ referring to the zero, one can introduce a *modal constant* $\circledast$, presenting the zero itself. Note that Szalas [97] uses this modality. Having $\boxdot$ and $\circledast$, the modality $\odot$ is derivable: $\odot\theta = \diamonddot(\circledast \wedge \theta)$. With $\boxdot$ we can axiomatize $\circledast$ as follows:

($\circledast$1) $\quad \diamonddot\circledast$

($\circledast$2) $\quad \diamonddot(\circledast \wedge \varphi) \rightarrow \boxdot(\circledast \rightarrow \varphi)$

Adding $\bigcirc$, two more schemata appear:

($\bigcirc\circledast$) $\quad \bigcirc\neg\circledast$

($\mathrm{ind}_{\circledast}$) $\quad \diamonddot(\circledast \wedge \varphi) \wedge \boxdot(\varphi \rightarrow \bigcirc\varphi) \rightarrow \varphi$

$\Box$ adds the schema:

($\Box\circledast$) $\quad \varphi \rightarrow \boxdot(\circledast \rightarrow \Diamond\varphi)$

And $\overline{\Box}$ replaces ($\circledast$1) by $\overline{\Diamond}\circledast$.

The proofs of completeness and decidability are left to the reader.

Next we turn to first-order temporal logic. For more on propositional temporal logic (in particular, for completeness investigations via automata theory) refer to Chapter 3.

2.2.3 First-order temporal logics

In this section we investigate the first-order versions of some of the propositional temporal logics introduced in Section 2.2.2; that is, first-order temporal logics, the modalities of which are some of $\bigcirc$, $\Box$, $\overline{\Box}$, $\odot$, $\boxdot$.

First we give the definition of our first-order temporal logics. A general notion of a temporal logic is given in Definition 1.7. All our temporal logics can easily be seen to be special cases of that notion.

Let a first-order *similarity type* (i.e. signature or vocabulary) d be given. (Then, by definition, d consists of a set of *predicate symbols*, a set of *function symbols*, and a function assigning a natural number to every predicate and function symbol, thus specifying the *rank* of the symbol. Function symbols of rank 0 are called *constant symbols*.) All the symbols from d are considered to be *rigid* in our temporal logics, that is, their meanings do not change in time (cf. Section 1.3 and 1.5.1 and [36]). Similarly, the individual variables x_i $(i \in \omega)$ are rigid. A symbol is called *flexible* as opposed to rigid if its meaning is allowed to change over time. To d and $\{x_i : i \in \omega\}$, we add an infinity $C = \{c_i : i \in \omega\}$ of flexible constant symbols. That is, the meaning of c_i is allowed to change over time. (The word "constant" is slightly misleading here, since these symbols (c_i s) may have different meanings in different time instances or possible worlds $t \in T$, see Gabbay [34], p. 92_4.) Now, the formulas of the first-order temporal logic, F^1_d, of similarity type d are built up the usual way, using the propositional logical connectives $\neg, \wedge$, quantifiers $\exists x_i$ $(i \in \omega)$, and modalities $\bigcirc$, $\Box$, $\overline{\Box}$ ($\odot$ and $\boxdot$ are defined from the rest as in Section 2.2.2, items (2.3), (2.4)). In more detail:

Definition 2.5 Let d, C, $\{x_i : i \in \omega\}$ be as above. (Of course, all these sets are assumed to be disjoint etc.) Then the (recursive) definition of the set F^1_d of all *first-order temporal formulas of similarity type* d is the following:

(a) First, the set of all terms for F^1_d is defined to be the smallest set Trm_d such that

  (i) $(\{x_i : i \in \omega\} \cup C) \subseteq \mathsf{Trm}_d$, and

  (ii) for every function symbol f from d with rank k and for any $\tau_1, \ldots, \tau_k \in \mathsf{Trm}_d$ $f(\tau_1, \ldots, \tau_k) \in \mathsf{Trm}_d$.

(b) Now F^1_d is defined to be the smallest set satisfying the following closure conditions:

(i) For every predicate symbol Γ with rank k and any $\tau_1, \ldots, \tau_k \in \mathsf{Trm}_d$, $\{\tau_1 = \tau_2, r(\tau_1, \ldots, \tau_k)\} \subseteq \mathsf{F}^1_d$.

(ii) F^1_d is closed under all the logical connectives, that is, for every $\varphi, \psi \in \mathsf{F}^1_d$, $i \in \omega$, and $\widehat{\Box} \in \{\bigcirc, \Box, \overline{\Box}\}$, $\{(\neg\varphi), (\varphi \wedge \psi), \exists x_i\varphi, \widehat{\Box}\varphi\} \subseteq \mathsf{F}^1_d$. □

Remark

Most of the results of this chapter remain true even if we allow flexible predicate and function symbols as well as flexible constant symbols; and when this is not the case, then it is straightforward to reformulate the result when we allow any kind of symbols to be flexible. We have chosen to restrict ourselves to flexible constants only in order to keep this chapter short and easier to read. □

For semantic purposes, we use the usual first-order Kripke models (cf. [36]), that is, classical two-sorted structures $\mathcal{M} = \langle \mathbf{T}, \mathbf{D}, f_0, \ldots, f_i, \ldots \rangle_{i \in \omega}$, where $\mathbf{D}$ is a classical first-order model of similarity type d, $\mathbf{T} = \langle T, 0, succ, \leq \rangle$ is a structure similar to (of the same similarity type as) the standard model $\mathsf{N} = \langle \omega, 0, succ, \leq \rangle$ of successor arithmetic with ordering, and for $i \in \omega$, $f_i : T \longrightarrow D$ is a function from T into D, serving to interpret the flexible constants c_i. $\mathbf{T}$ is called the *time frame* of $\mathcal{M}$, and, except for its similarity type, is arbitrary (ambiguously, *succ* denotes both the arbitrary unary function of a time frame $\mathbf{T}$ and the standard successor function "$n + 1$" on ω; we will use the same ambiguity in the cases of 0 and $\leq$). For simplicity, we often write c_i for f_i. Mod_d denotes the class of all Kripke models $\mathcal{M}$ of the above kind. We will often write Mod instead of Mod_d for brevity.

To associate meanings to F^1_d-formulas in models from Mod, we could follow the style of Definitions 2.3 and 1.15. This would be the most traditional way for defining the meanings of the F^1_d-formulas. Instead, in this section we follow the standard procedure of *correspondence theory* ([36], §II.4.2.5 pp. 214—217), defining the validity of F^1_d-formulas in Kripke models via a translation function $tr : \mathsf{F}^1_d \longrightarrow \mathsf{Fmcl}(\mathsf{Mod})$ mapping the set F^1_d of temporal formulas into the *classical two-sorted first-order language* $\mathsf{Fmcl}(\mathsf{Mod})$ of Kripke models; then validity of $tr(\varphi)$ in $\mathcal{M}$ defines the validity of φ in $\mathcal{M}$, for every $\varphi \in \mathsf{F}^1_d$ and $\mathcal{M} \in \mathsf{Mod}$. In $\mathsf{Fmcl}(\mathsf{Mod})$, the c_is are unary function symbols with arguments of sort T (*time*) and value of sort D (*data*); x_i ($i \in \omega$) are the variables of sort D, and t_i ($i \in \omega$) are the variables of sort T. The interpretation of c_j in a model $\mathcal{M} = \langle \mathbf{T}, \mathbf{D}, f_0, \ldots, f_i, \ldots \rangle_{i \in \omega}$ is defined to be f_j, for every $j \in \omega$. We may assume that all occurrences of the flexible constants c_i are of the form $c_i = x_j$ in the F^1_d-formulas (every formula is easily seen to be equivalent to one of this form as it is well known, see e.g. [18]). It is enough to give the definition of tr for the modalities $\bigcirc, \Box, \overline{\Box}$ only, since $\odot, \boxdot$ are definable from them.

Definition 2.6 Let d be an arbitrary similarity type. First we define a function

$$tr^* : \mathsf{F}^1_d \times \{t_i : i \in \omega\} \longrightarrow \mathsf{Fmcl(Mod)}.$$

Intuitively, $tr^*(\varphi, t_i)$ means that φ is true at time t_i. For every $t \in \{t_i : i \in \omega\}$, $i, j \in \omega$, and $\varphi, \psi \in \mathsf{F}^1_d$, we choose $t_k \neq t$, and

- $tr^*(c_i = x_j, t) \stackrel{def}{=} (c_i(t) = x_j)$,
- $tr^*(\psi, t) \stackrel{def}{=} \psi$ whenever ψ is atomic and rigid (i.e. contains none of the c_is),
- tr^* preserves classical connectives and quantifiers (i.e. $tr^*(\varphi \wedge \psi, t) \stackrel{def}{=} tr^*(\varphi, t) \wedge tr^*(\psi, t)$, $tr^*(\neg\varphi, t) \stackrel{def}{=} \neg tr^*(\varphi, t)$, $tr^*(\exists x_i \varphi, t) \stackrel{def}{=} \exists x_i\, tr^*(\varphi, t)$), and
- $tr^*(\bigcirc\varphi, t) \stackrel{def}{=} \exists t_k (t_k = succ(t) \wedge tr^*(\varphi, t_k))$,
- $tr^*(\Box\varphi, t) \stackrel{def}{=} (\forall t_k \geq t) tr^*(\varphi, t_k)$,
- $tr^*(\overline{\Box}\varphi, t) \stackrel{def}{=} (\forall t_k \leq t) tr^*(\varphi, t_k)$.

This completes the definition (by recursion) of tr^*.
We let, for every $\varphi \in \mathsf{F}^1_d$; $tr(\varphi) \stackrel{def}{=} tr^*(\varphi, t_0)$; further, for every $\mathcal{M} \in \mathsf{Mod}_d$,

$$\mathcal{M} \models_d \varphi \text{ iff (by definition) } \mathcal{M} \models tr(\varphi). \qquad \square$$

Note that the choice of t_0 in the definition of tr is rather ad-hoc; we could have chosen any element of $\{t_i : i \in \omega\}$, e.g. $tr(\varphi)$ could be $tr^*(\varphi, t_{17})$ instead of $tr^*(\varphi, t_0)$. We just have to fix one of the t_is to obtain to a precise definition for tr.

Now, given an arbitrary similarity type d, the ***first-order temporal language of similarity type d*** is defined to be the following triple:

$$\mathsf{FT}_d = \langle \mathsf{F}^1_d, \mathsf{Mod}_d, \models_d \rangle$$

where F^1_d was defined in Definition 2.5, Mod_d in the following, and $\models_d$ in Definition 2.6. For brevity, we will often omit the subscript d from F^1_d, Mod_d, and $\models_d$.

Without restricting generality, we may assume that the class of all similarity types is "not controversial", that is, whenever f is a function symbol in a similarity type with rank k then it cannot occur as a function symbol of rank different from k or as a relation symbol, in any similarity type. The same restriction is applied to relation symbols too. This has the consequence that to any d_1 and d_2 there is a d such that $\mathsf{F}^1_{d_1} \cup \mathsf{F}^1_{d_2} \subseteq \mathsf{F}^1_d$. (This can actually be done, for example, by defining symbols such that every symbol contains some code carrying the information whether it is a function or relation symbol, further what its rank is.) Let SymType denote the class of all similarity types, i.e.

$$\mathsf{SymType} \stackrel{def}{=} \{d : d \text{ is a similarity type}\}.$$

Now first-order temporal logic is defined to be

$$\mathsf{FT} = \langle \mathsf{F}^1, \mathsf{Mod}, \models \rangle,$$

where

- $\mathsf{F}^1 \stackrel{def}{=} \bigcup\{\mathsf{F}^1_d : d \in \mathsf{SymType}\}$,
- $\mathsf{Mod} \stackrel{def}{=} \bigcup\{\mathsf{Mod}_d : d \in \mathsf{SymType}\}$, and
- $\models \stackrel{def}{=} \bigcup\{\models_d : d \in \mathsf{SymType}\}$. Notice that this means that for arbitrary $\mathcal{M} \in \mathsf{Mod}$ and $\varphi \in \mathsf{F}^1$, if $\mathcal{M} \models \varphi$ then there is a d such that $\mathcal{M} \in \mathsf{Mod}_d$, $\varphi \in \mathsf{F}^1_d$, and $\mathcal{M} \models_d \varphi$.

Next, similarly to Section 2.2.2, we will define fragments of FT, and a fragment will be determined, again, by the modalities allowed in the fragment. By a fragment of FT we understand a first-order multi-modal logic, the modalities of which are some of $\bigcirc$, $\square$, $\overline{\square}$, $\odot$, $\boxdot$. The class of models is fixed to be **Mod**. The semantics of a fragment is given by tr as defined in Definition 2.6, *unless* $\odot$ or $\boxdot$ is not definable in the fragment. For such cases, we introduce

(*a*) $tr^*(\odot\varphi, t) \stackrel{def}{=} \exists t_1\,(t_1 = 0 \land tr^*(\varphi, t_1))$, and

(*b*) $tr^*(\boxdot\varphi, t) \stackrel{def}{=} \forall t_1\, tr^*(\varphi, t_1)$,

filling the gaps. (a) and (b) will be justified in later sections where we will see that in the classes of models we seriously consider, $tr^*(\odot\varphi, t)$, according to (a) will be equivalent to its old definition when we have $\overline{\square}$, and similarly for $tr^*(\boxdot\varphi, t)$. (We note that the more elegant equivalent form $tr^*(\boxdot\varphi, t) = \forall t\, tr^*(\varphi, t)$ of (b) has been replaced with the present one, because some of our undergraduate students found the latter easier to read: the same applies to (a). In parallel to the notation given in Section 2.2.2, we introduce the following notation.

Notation

Throughout this chapter, a fragment of FT will be denoted as FT_X where X is a list of some elements of $\{\bigcirc, \odot, F, P, \mathsf{S}\}$.

$\mathsf{F}^1_{X,d}$ denotes the set of formulas (of similarity type d) of the logic FT_X.

In later sections, the following four fragments of FT will turn out to be important for us: $\mathsf{FT}_{\odot\bigcirc}$, $\mathsf{FT}_{\odot\bigcirc S}$, $\mathsf{FT}_{\odot\bigcirc SF}$, and $\mathsf{FT}_{\odot\bigcirc SFP} = \mathsf{FT}$. Since we will use these fragments very frequently, we give them shorter names too, as follows:

$\mathsf{FT}_0 \stackrel{def}{=} \mathsf{FT}_{\odot\bigcirc}$, $\mathsf{FT}_1 \stackrel{def}{=} \mathsf{FT}_{\odot\bigcirc S}$, $\mathsf{FT}_2 \stackrel{def}{=} \mathsf{FT}_{\odot\bigcirc SF}$, $\mathsf{FT}_3 \stackrel{def}{=} \mathsf{FT}_{\odot\bigcirc SFP} = \mathsf{FT}$.

Example Here are some simple examples for first-order temporal formulas:

(a) $\varphi_1 \stackrel{def}{=} \odot \Box \exists x_0 (x_0 = c_1 \wedge \bigcirc x_0 \neq c_1) \in \mathsf{F}^1$.

φ_1 expresses, intuitively, that c_1 always changes.

(b) Let $\bar{x} = \langle x_1, ..., x_k \rangle$ and $\bar{c} = \langle c_1, ..., c_k \rangle$. $\exists \bar{x}$ abbreviates $\exists x_1 \exists x_2 ... \exists x_k$ and $\bar{x} = \bar{c}$ abbreviates $x_1 = c_1 \wedge x_2 = c_2 \wedge ... \wedge x_k = c_k$. Assume that a certain similarity type d contains a $2k$-ary relation symbol R. We abbreviate the formula $R(x_1, ..., x_k, c_1, ..., c_k)$ by its "infix" version $\bar{x} R \bar{c}$. Now we let

$$Exe \stackrel{def}{=} \Box \exists \bar{x} (\bar{x} = \bar{c} \wedge \bigcirc \bar{x} R \bar{c}).$$

Clearly $Exe \in \mathsf{F}^1_d$. Let us imagine that $x_1, \ldots, x_k$ are the variables used in a program p, and that $c_1, \ldots, c_k$ are the *locations* or *registers* where the (changing) values of $x_1, \ldots, x_k$ are, respectively, stored. Assume that the relation R is interpreted as the state-transition relation defined by the program p (*not* the input - output relation, but instead the "next-state" relation). Then the intuitive meaning of Exe is that $\bar{c}$ is an *execution sequence* of p.

(c) Here we use the notation introduced in (b). We let

$$Fair \stackrel{def}{=} (Exe \rightarrow \Box \varphi \forall \bar{x} (\bar{c} R \bar{x} \rightarrow \Diamond \bar{c} = \bar{x})).$$

Using the intuition sketched in (b), *Fair* expresses that the execution $\bar{c}$ of p is *fair*.

(d) Let $\bar{x}$ and $\bar{c}$ be as in (b); further let $\bar{y} = \langle x_{k+1}, \ldots, x_{2k} \rangle$. We let

$$Det(\bar{c}) \stackrel{def}{=} \Box \exists \bar{x} \exists \bar{y} (\bar{x} = \bar{c} \wedge \bigcirc \bar{y} = \bar{c} \wedge \Box (\bar{x} = \bar{c} \rightarrow \bigcirc \bar{y} = \bar{c})).$$

If we imagine that $\bar{c}$ carries all the information of a possible state of a "world" (e.g. $\bar{c}$ represents a process running in a certain data domain), then the intuitive meaning of *Det* is that "the world is deterministic". For more about this formula (and the next one $Cl(c)$) see the beginning of Section 2.2.5.

(e) Let c be an arbitrary flexible constant, and x an arbitrary individual variable. We say that c is a *clock* if

$$Cl(c) \stackrel{def}{=} \Box \exists x (x = c \wedge \bigcirc \Box x \neq c)$$

holds. This definition of a clock originates from Abadi [2]. □

Convention

Throughout this paper, d denotes an arbitrary but fixed similarity type unless we state explicitly otherwise. □

Next we define the first-order version of the forcing relation $\Vdash$ introduced in Definition 2.3.

Intuitively, what we want to define now is the meaning of the claim that a first-order temporal formula φ is satisfied at a certain time instance t in a Kripke model $\mathcal{M}$. We want to define this through satisfiability of Fmcl(Mod) -formulas, which are, by definition, classical two-sorted first-order formulas. Because of possible free occurrences of the variables in such formulas, we must consider the possible *valuations* of the variables. A valuation is a pair $\langle v, w\rangle$ where $v : \{x_i : i \in \omega\} \longrightarrow D$ and $w : \{t_i : i \in \omega\} \longrightarrow T$. For an arbitrary $\psi \in$ Fmcl(Mod) and $\mathcal{M} = \langle \mathbf{T}, \mathbf{D}, f_i\rangle_{i\in\omega} \in$ Mod, the standard notation for the fact that ψ is satisfied in $\mathcal{M}$ at a valuation $\langle v, w\rangle$ is $\mathcal{M} \models \psi[v, w]$. For example,

$$\mathcal{M} \models x_0 = c_2(t_1)[v, w] \text{ iff } v(x_0) = f_2(w(t_1)).$$

Let $\mathcal{M}$ and v be as above, further let $s \in T$. Let $\varphi \in \mathsf{F}^1_d$, and $w : \{t_i : i \in \omega\} \longrightarrow T$ be such a valuation of the time variables that $w(t_0) = s$. Now we define

$$\mathcal{M}, s \Vdash \varphi[v] \text{ iff } \mathcal{M} \models tr^*(\varphi, t_0)[v, w].$$

(Note that this definition is correct, because, by definition, $tr^*(\varphi, t_0)$ may contain at most one free variable of sort time, which is t_0.) We read $\mathcal{M}, s \Vdash \varphi[v]$ as *"φ is satisfied in $\mathcal{M}$ at time s by the valuation of the variables v"*. We say that "*φ is satisfied in $\mathcal{M}$ at time s*", in symbols $\mathcal{M}, s \Vdash \varphi$, iff $\mathcal{M}, s \Vdash \varphi[v]$ for every valuation v.

For any $\varphi \in \mathsf{F}^1_d$, φ is called a *rigid formula* if it contains no flexible constants. Otherwise we call φ a *flexible formula*.

$\mathcal{M} \in$ Mod is called a *standard-time model* if its time frame $\mathbf{T}$ is the standard model $\mathbf{N} = \langle \omega, 0, succ, \leq\rangle$.

Next we will look at Hilbert-type inference systems for first-order temporal logics FT_X with $X \subseteq \{\bigcirc, \Box, \overline{\Box}, \odot, \boxdot\}$. A Hilbert-type inference system for FT is the following.

- **A1 propositional axioms:** Here we take the collection (union) of all the propositional axioms that occurred in Section 2.2.2.

1.	(BOOL)	all boolean tautologies
2.	$(\mathrm{K}(\widehat{\Box}))$	$\widehat{\Box}(\varphi \to \psi) \to (\widehat{\Box}\varphi \to \widehat{\Box}\psi)$ where $\widehat{\Box} \in \{\bigcirc, \Box, \overline{\Box}, \odot, \boxdot\}$
3.	$(\mathrm{fun}_{\widehat{\Box}})$	$\widehat{\Box}\neg\varphi \leftrightarrow \neg\widehat{\Box}\varphi$ where $\widehat{\Box} \in \{\odot, \bigcirc\}$
4.	(mix)	$\boxdot\varphi \to (\varphi \wedge \bigcirc\boxdot\varphi)$
5.	$(\mathrm{ind}_{\Box})$	$\Box(\varphi \to \bigcirc\varphi) \to (\varphi \to \Box\varphi)$
6.	(first)	$\varphi \to \odot\Diamond\varphi$
7.	(const)	$\odot\varphi \to \Box\odot\varphi$
8.	$(\mathrm{Grz}_{\overline{\Box}})$	$\overline{\Box}(\overline{\Box}(\varphi \to \overline{\Box}\varphi) \to \varphi) \to \varphi$

9. $(\bigcirc\overline{\Box})$ $\overline{\Box}\varphi \wedge \bigcirc\varphi \rightarrow \bigcirc\overline{\Box}\varphi$
10. $(\mathrm{K}_t(\Box,\overline{\Box}))$ $\varphi \rightarrow \Box\overline{\Diamond}\varphi \wedge \overline{\Box}\Diamond\varphi$
11. (con) $\boxdot\varphi \rightarrow \Box\overline{\Box}\varphi \wedge \overline{\Box}\Box\varphi$
12. (ref) $\Box\varphi \rightarrow \varphi$
13. (tran) $\Box\varphi \rightarrow \Box\Box\varphi$
14. (linearity) $\Box(\Box\varphi \rightarrow \psi) \vee \Box(\Box\psi \rightarrow \varphi)$
15. (Dum) $\Box(\Box(\varphi \rightarrow \Box\varphi) \rightarrow \varphi) \rightarrow (\Diamond\Box\varphi \rightarrow \Box\varphi)$
16. $(\mathrm{con}'_{\odot})$ $\odot\varphi \leftrightarrow \odot\odot\varphi$
17. $(\mathrm{con}''_{\odot})$ $\odot\varphi \leftrightarrow \bigcirc\odot\varphi$
18. (incl) $\boxdot\varphi \rightarrow \odot\varphi \wedge \bigcirc\varphi$
19. $(\mathrm{con}_{\odot})$ $\odot\varphi \rightarrow \boxdot\odot\varphi$
20. $(S5(\boxdot))$

- **A2 first-order** (i.e. quantifier) **axioms:**

1. $\varphi \leftrightarrow \widehat{\Box}\varphi$ for every $\widehat{\Box} \in \{\bigcirc, \Box, \overline{\Box}, \odot, \boxdot\}$ if φ is rigid
2. $\forall x\widehat{\Box}\varphi \leftrightarrow \widehat{\Box}\varphi\forall x\varphi$ for every $\widehat{\Box} \in \{\bigcirc, \Box, \overline{\Box}, \odot, \boxdot\}$
3. $\varphi \rightarrow \forall x\varphi$ if x is not a free variable of φ
4. All the usual equality axioms of first-order logic
5. $(\exists x\neg\varphi \leftrightarrow \neg\varphi\forall x\varphi)$
6. $\forall x\varphi \rightarrow \varphi(x/\tau)$ for any term τ such that the substitution $x \mapsto \tau$ does not create new bound occurrences of variables or new occurrences of flexible symbols in the scope of modalities in φ.

- Rules:

(R1) $\frac{\varphi, \varphi \rightarrow \psi}{\psi}$ (modus ponens)
(R2) $\frac{\varphi}{\widehat{\Box}\varphi}$ ($\widehat{\Box}$-generalization) for every
$\widehat{\Box} \in (\{\bigcirc, \Box, \overline{\Box}, \odot, \boxdot\} \cup \{\forall x_i : i \in \omega\})$
(R3) $\frac{\odot\varphi, \varphi \rightarrow \bigcirc\varphi}{\varphi}$ (induction).

Proposition 2.1 For any propositional temporal formula schema ψ (from PT) valid in the standard-time models $\langle\, \omega \ldots \rangle$, all FT-instances of ψ are provable from A1, A2 and R1—R3.

Proof: First we check that all the axioms of $\vdash^0_{PT}$ are provable from A1 to R3 as follows. (The rules of $\vdash^0_{PT}$ are explicitly stated in R1 and R2, so we need not think about them.) The only axiom of $\vdash^0_{PT}$ missing from A1 is $(\odot\,\Box)$. This $(\odot\,\Box)$ can be derived from A1 and R1—R3 using the methods of Section 2.2.2. The reader unable to derive $(\odot\,\Box)$ is invited to add this schema as an extra axiom to A1; we omitted $(\odot\,\Box)$ for purely aesthetic reasons; we will never use the fact that it is not listed in A1. Now, Theorem 2.8 completes the proof of

Proposition 2.1. (We proved a little bit more, namely we do not need A2 in deriving propositional validities.) □

We denote the inference system A1—R3 given above, for the logic FT, by $\vdash_{FT}$. For a fragment FT_X of FT, $\vdash_X$ denotes that inference system which we obtain from $\vdash_{FT}$ by omitting those axiom schemata and derivation rules from the above in which such modalities occur which do not occur in X. For the distinguished fragments FT_i ($i \leq 3$) of FT (see the notation given earlier), we will use the notation $\vdash_i$ ($i \leq 3$) as well. Thus, for example, $\vdash_{\odot\bigcirc} = \vdash_0$ and $\vdash_{FT} = \vdash_{\odot\bigcirc SFP} = \vdash_3$.

Corollary 2.1 For $i \leq 3$, $\vdash_i$ is propositionally complete for the class of standard models of FT_i, that is:

> for every propositional formula schema ψ (from PT) using the modalities of FT_i which is valid in the standard models $\langle\omega,\ldots\rangle$, all FT-instances of ψ are provable by $\vdash_i$.

Proof: For $i = 3$ this is the same as Proposition 2.1. For $i = 0$, Corollary 2.1 follows from Theorem 2.4; for $i = 1$, from Theorem 2.5; for $i = 2$, from Theorem 2.3. □

Remark

The statement of Corollary 2.1 does not hold for every $\vdash_X$ and FT_X in place of $\vdash_i$ and FT_i ($i \leq 3$). However, it remains true for those $\vdash_X$ and FT_X for which we have corresponding theorems in Section 2.2.2. *We note that if* $(\odot\overline{\Box})$ *is included as an axiom into A1, then the conclusion of Corollary 2.1 becomes true for practically all fragments studied in Section 2.2.2.* □

On the first-order level, the situation is different, e.g. the following was proved by Sain around 1980, see e.g. Németi [65], [6], [84], [91].

Theorem 2.9 None of the extensions $\vdash_0 \mapsto \vdash_S \mapsto \vdash_{SF} \mapsto \vdash_{FP}$ is conservative, i.e. there are formulas $\varphi_0, \varphi_1, \varphi_2$ in the fragment of $\vdash_0$ such that $\not\vdash_0 \varphi_0$ but $\vdash_S \varphi_0$, $\not\vdash_S \varphi_1$ but $\vdash_{SF} \varphi_1$ etc.

On the proof: The last ($\vdash_{SF} \mapsto \vdash_{SFP}$) part follows from our Theorem 2.19, as well as Theorem 2.22 or 2.23. The proofs of the remaining two statements can be found in [92]. □

Proposition 2.2 Recall that d denotes an arbitrary but fixed similarity type. Let $\varphi \in F^1_d$ be arbitrary. Then

(a) $\mathsf{Mod}_d \models \varphi$ implies $\vdash_{FT}\varphi$ (completeness). Moreover,

(b) for every $\Gamma \subseteq F^1_d$, $\Gamma \models \varphi$ implies $\Gamma\vdash_{FT}\varphi$ (strong completeness).

Proof: This theorem is part of Theorem 2.10 (sandwich completeness theorem) formulated later in this section. □

In connection with Proposition 2.2(b), we would like to call the reader's attention to the fact that from now on we will heavily use systems like $\vdash_{FT}$ for inferences $\Gamma \vdash_{FT} \varphi$, where the elements of Γ are arbitrary formulas (and not logical validities). This is in contrast with the usage in Section 2.2.2, where the emphasis was on deriving validities only, i.e. on derivations $\emptyset \vdash_{FT} \varphi$ only. The definition of $\Gamma \vdash_{FT} \varphi$, where the elements of Γ need not be logical theorems, is given in Definition 2.2(c).

Notation: Let $\mathsf{K} \subseteq \mathsf{Mod}_d$. Then $\models^K$ denotes the semantic consequence relation induced by the logic $\langle \mathsf{F}^1_d, \mathsf{K}, \models_d \rangle$ in the sense of the notation given in Section 2.1.1. That is, for any $\Sigma \subseteq \mathsf{F}^1_d$ and $\varphi \in \mathsf{F}^1_d$, we let $\Sigma \models^K \varphi$ denote that $(\{\mathcal{M} \in \mathsf{K} : \mathcal{M} \models_d \Sigma\}) \models_d \varphi$. □

In the remark preceding Def. 2.6 we introduced the notation $\mathsf{Fmcl}(\mathsf{Mod})$ for denoting the set of all classical two-sorted first-order formulas, the class of models of which is that of Kripke models Mod. Thus the classical logic we consider is $\mathsf{Fmcl}(\mathsf{Mod}), \mathsf{Mod}, \models^{cl})$. Here $\models^{cl}$ denotes the classical validity relation of first-order logic. Often we omit the superscript *cl* for brevity (as we already did in Definition 2.6). We call the sort of the time frames *time*, and the other sort *data* (the intuition behind the latter name comes from the computer science applications discussed in later sections). In $\mathsf{Fmcl}(\mathsf{Mod})$, we use the set $\{t_i : i \in \omega\}$ for variables of sort *time*, and $\{x_i : i \in \omega\}$ for variables of sort *data*.

In Definition 2.7 we will define a class $\mathsf{K}^{Ind+Tord} \subset \mathsf{Mod}$ of Kripke models via axioms formulated in the language $\mathsf{Fmcl}(\mathsf{Mod})$. This class was first introduced in [10], [11], [13], [65], [6], and investigated in various other papers, e.g. in [44], [1], [3], [2], [93], [16], [92], [40], [67], [68], [70], [85].

A soundness and completeness theorem w.r.t. a distinguished subset F^{1pca} of F^1 was proved in [83], [84], [92], [85]. (For every block diagram or regular program p, every partial correctness assertion about p is expressed by some $\varphi \in \mathsf{F}^{1pca}$.) The theorem concerning F^{1pca} states that for every $\varphi \in \mathsf{F}^{1pca}$ and for every $\Gamma \subseteq \mathsf{F}^1$,

$$\Gamma \models^{K^{Ind+Tord}} \varphi \quad \text{iff} \quad \Gamma \vdash_{FT} \varphi. \tag{2.9}$$

In this section we state completeness and soundness theorems similar to (2.9), but we will consider only such subsets of F^1 which form the set of all formulas of one of the fragments FT_i ($i \leq 3$).

Notation: Let $\mathsf{K} \subseteq \mathsf{Mod}$ (be arbitrary).

(a) *Thcl*(K) denotes the set of all classical first-order formulas valid in K, that is:

$$Thcl(\mathsf{K}) \stackrel{def}{=} \{\varphi \in \mathsf{Fmcl}(\mathsf{Mod}) : \mathsf{K} \models^{cl} \varphi\}.$$

$Tht(\mathsf{K})$ denotes the set of all first-order temporal formulas valid in K (in the sense of temporal logic, defined in our Definition 2.6), that is:

$Tht(\mathsf{K}) \stackrel{def}{=} \{\varphi \in \mathsf{F}^1_d : \mathsf{K} \models_d \varphi\}$.

(b) Let $\Sigma \subseteq \mathsf{Fmcl(Mod)}$ and $\Gamma \subseteq \mathsf{F}^1_d$. Then $Mdcl(\Sigma)$ denotes the class of all Kripke models in which Σ is valid in the classical sense, and $Mdt(\Gamma)$ denotes the class of all Kripke-models in which Γ is valid in the sense of temporal logic. That is:

$$Mdcl(\Sigma) \stackrel{def}{=} \{\mathcal{M} \in \mathsf{Mod} : \mathcal{M} \models^{cl} \Sigma\} \text{ and}$$

$$Mdt(\Gamma) \stackrel{def}{=} \{\mathcal{M} \in \mathsf{Mod} : \mathcal{M} \models_d \Gamma\}$$

(c) Whenever it will be necessary or desirable, we will indicate the similarity type of the logic in subscripts, like $Thcl_d$, Tht_d, $Mdcl_d$, Mdt_d. □

For the definition of $\mathsf{K}^{Ind+Tord}$, first we need to define two sets, Ind and $Tord$ of formulas, formulated in the language $\mathsf{Fmcl(Mod)}$ (in fact, $Tord$ is formulated in the sublanguage of $\mathsf{Fmcl(Mod)}$ consisting of formulas purely of sort *time*, i.e. using the function and predicate symbols 0, $succ$, $\leq$ and variables from $\{t_i : i \in \omega\}$ only.) Ind is an ***induction principle***, while $Tord$ expresses that the time frame is linearly ordered ("*Tord*" abbreviates "Time is linearly ordered".)

Definition 2.7

(a) For every $\varphi \in \mathsf{Fmcl(Mod)}$ and $t \in \{t_i : i \in \omega\}$ we let $ind(\varphi, t)$ be the formula

$$(\varphi(0) \wedge \forall t(\varphi \rightarrow \varphi[t/succ(t)])) \rightarrow \forall t\varphi,$$

where $\varphi(0)$ and $\varphi[t/succ(t)]$ denote the formulas obtained from φ by substituting respectively 0 and $succ(t)$ for every free occurrence of t in φ. We define

$$Ind \stackrel{def}{=} \{ind(\varphi, t) : \varphi \in \mathsf{Fmcl(Mod)} \text{ and } t \in \{t_i : i \in \omega\}\}.$$

(b) We let $Tord$ be the full first-order theory of (all first-order formulas valid in) the standard model $\mathsf{N} = \langle \omega, 0, succ, \leq \rangle$ using the set $\{t_i : i \in \omega\}$ of variables.

(c) Now $\mathsf{K}^{Ind+Tord}$ is defined to be the set of all Kripke models in which $Ind \cup Tord$ is valid in the classical sense, that is

$$\mathsf{K}^{Ind+Tord} \stackrel{def}{=} Mdcl(Ind \cup Tord).$$ □

For brevity, we shall often write $ind(\varphi)$ instead of $ind(\varphi, t)$. We call $ind(\varphi)$ the ***full induction*** axiom for the formula $\varphi(\in \mathsf{Fmcl(Mod)})$ (along the time frame). Accordingly, Ind is called the set of all full induction formulas, or the ***principle of full induction on time***.

Notice that a full induction formula $ind(\varphi,t)$ may contain free variables of both sorts *time* and *data* of the Kripke models $\mathcal{M}$. (Except for t, every free variable occurring in φ remains free in $ind(\varphi,t)$.) The free variables of $ind(\varphi,t)$ are called the ***parameters*** of $ind(\varphi,t)$.

Tord can be given by a finite set of axioms, such as:

$$
\begin{array}{lll}
\Sigma \stackrel{def}{=} \{ & t_0 \leq t_1 \leq t_2 \rightarrow t_0 \leq t_2 & \text{(transitivity of } \leq), \\
& 0 \leq t_0 & \text{(0 is the smallest element)}, \\
& t_0 \leq t_1 \leq t_0 \rightarrow t_0 = t_1, & \\
& t_0 \leq t_1 \vee t_1 \leq t_0 & \text{(linearity and reflexivity of } \leq), \\
& t_0 < succ(t_0) & (succ \text{ is strictly increasing}), \\
& t_0 < t_1 \rightarrow succ(t_0) \leq t_1, & \\
& t_0 = 0 \leftrightarrow \varphi\forall t_1(t_0 \neq succ(t_1)) & \text{(0 has no predecessor)} \},
\end{array}
$$

where $\tau < \sigma$ abbreviates $\sigma \neq \tau \leq \sigma$, for any terms τ and σ.

Using the notation introduced in Definition 2.1(a), $Tord = Cn(\Sigma) = (Thcl(Mdcl(\Sigma)))$, see e.g. Chang Keisler [28], Exam. 3.4.4, p. 159 for a proof. Therefore we shall often identify $Tord$ with Σ.

Notation

For two sets Γ_1 and Γ_2 of formulas, instead of $\Gamma_1 \cup \Gamma_2$, we will often write $\Gamma_1 + \Gamma_2$ (according to wide spread custom in the literature of logic). Thus, for example, $Ind + Tord = Ind \cup Cn(\Sigma)$. □

Theorem 2.10 (sandwich completeness theorem)

(a) $\vdash_{FT}$ is strongly complete for Mod, and sound (in the stronger sense) for $\mathsf{K}^{Ind+Tord}$. That is, for every similarity type d, for every $\Gamma \subseteq \mathsf{F}^1_d$ and for every $\varphi \in \mathsf{F}^1_d$,

$\Gamma \models_d \varphi$ implies $\Gamma \vdash_{FT} \varphi$ implies $\Gamma \models^{K^{Ind+Tord}} \varphi$.

(b) $\{\varphi \in \mathsf{F}^1_d : \mathsf{Mod} \models_d \varphi\} \subset \{\varphi \in \mathsf{F}^1_d : \vdash_{FT} \varphi\} \subset \{\varphi \in \mathsf{F}^1_d : \models^{K^{Ind+Tord}} \varphi\}$.

Proof: (b) is an immediate consequence of (a).

The proof of the ***soundness part*** of (a) goes as follows: let $\Gamma \subseteq \mathsf{F}^1$, $\varphi \in \mathsf{F}^1$, and assume $\Gamma \vdash_{FT} \varphi$. We need to prove $\Gamma \models^{K^{Ind+Tord}} \varphi$. For proving this, it is enough to prove that in every Kripke-model $\mathcal{M} \in \mathsf{K}^{Ind+Tord}$, all the axiom schemata A1, A2 of $\vdash_{FT}$ are valid in $\mathcal{M}$, and all the rules R1—R3 are sound in $\mathcal{M}$. The former is easy to check and is left to the reader. The latter is easy too, but we check below the soundness of R3 (induction rule).

Let us assume that $\mathcal{M} \models \odot\varphi$ and $\mathcal{M} \models \varphi \rightarrow \bigcirc\varphi$. We need to prove $\mathcal{M} \models \varphi$. By our assumptions, $\mathcal{M} \models^{cl} tr(\varphi)[t_0/0]$ and $\mathcal{M} \models^{cl} \forall t(tr(\varphi) \rightarrow$

$tr(\varphi)[t_0/succ(t_0)]$). Therefore, by $\mathcal{M} \models^{cl} Ind$, we have $\mathcal{M} \models^{cl} tr(\varphi)$. Therefore $\mathcal{M} \models_d \varphi$. □

We will prove the *completeness part* of this theorem in Section 2.2.4. For the purposes of this chapter, Theorem 2.10 is enough. However, next we formulate another completeness theorem, one of a more traditional form. We will prove that it follows from Theorem 2.10.

We let K^{FT} be the following class of Kripke models:

$$\mathsf{K}^{FT} \stackrel{def}{=} Mdt(\{\varphi \in \mathsf{F}^1_d : \vdash_{FT} \varphi\}).$$

Theorem 2.11 $\vdash_{FT}$ is strongly complete and sound for K^{FT}, that is, for every

$$\Gamma \subseteq \mathsf{F}^1 \text{ and } \varphi \in \mathsf{F}^1, \Gamma \models^{\mathsf{K}^{FT}} \varphi \text{ iff } \Gamma \vdash_{FT} \varphi$$

Proof: Theorem 2.11 follows from Theorem 2.10 above and Proposition 2.3 below. □

Remark

Using van Benthem's correspondence theory (see [19]), another version of Theorem 2.11 could be given such that, instead of using the set $\{\varphi \in \mathsf{F}^1_d : \vdash_{FT} \varphi\}$ of temporal formulas and the operator Mdt in defining K^{FT}, one would use a subset of Fmcl(Mod) and the operator $Mdcl$; thus selecting K^{FT} from Mod similarly to the way we selected $\mathsf{K}^{Ind+Tord}$. We leave such a reformulation to the (interested) reader. □

Next we formulate the generalization of Theorem 2.10 to the inference systems $\vdash_i$ of the distinguished fragments FT_i ($i \leq 3$) of FT. Let the set of all formulas of FT_i be denoted by $\mathsf{F}^{1i}(= \mathsf{F}^{1i}_d)$.

Theorem 2.12 Let $i \leq 3$.

(a) $\vdash_i$ is strongly complete for Mod, and sound for $\mathsf{K}^{Ind+Tord}$. That is, for every $\Gamma \subseteq \mathsf{F}^{1i}$ and $\varphi \in \mathsf{F}^{1i}$,

$$\Gamma \models \varphi \text{ implies } \Gamma \vdash_i \varphi \text{ implies } \Gamma \models^{\mathsf{K}^{Ind+Tord}} \varphi.$$

(b) $\{\varphi \in \mathsf{F}^{1i} : \mathsf{Mod} \models_d \varphi\} \subset \{\varphi \in \mathsf{F}^{1i} : \vdash_i \varphi\} \subset \{\varphi \in \mathsf{F}^{1i} : \models^{\mathsf{K}^{Ind+Tord}} \varphi\}$.

Proof: The soundness part of (a) follows from that of Theorem 2.10. The completeness part of (a) will be proven in Section 2.2.5. (b) is a straightforward consequence of (a). □

The formulation of an analogous generalization of Theorem 2.11 is left to the reader.

Proposition 2.3 Theorem 2.10 implies Theorem 2.11. That is, Theorem 2.11 can be proved from assuming that Theorem 2.10 is true.

Proof:

Claim (1): Assume that

$$\vdash_{FT} \text{ is strongly complete (but not necessarily sound) for Mod} \tag{2.10}$$

Then $\vdash_{FT}$ is strongly complete for K^{FT}, that is, for all $\Gamma \subseteq F^1$ and $\varphi \in F^1$,

$$\Gamma \models^{K^{FT}} \models \varphi \text{ implies } \Gamma \vdash_{FT} \varphi \qquad \square$$

Proof: Assume (2.10), and let Γ, φ be as above. Let $\Theta \stackrel{def}{=} \{\varphi \in F^1 : \vdash_{FT} \varphi\}$. (Then $K^{FT} = Mdt(\Theta)$). Assume $\Gamma \models^{K^{FT}} \varphi$. Then $(\Gamma \cup \Theta) \models \varphi$ by the definition of K^{FT}. By Corollary 2.1, this implies $(\Gamma \cup \Theta) \vdash_{FT} \varphi$. But since "$\vdash_{FT}\Theta$" holds by definition, $(\Gamma \cup \Theta) \vdash_{FT} \varphi$ implies $\Gamma \vdash_{FT} \varphi$.

Claim (2): $\vdash_{FT}$ is sound for K^{FT}, that is, for all $\Gamma \subseteq F^1$ and $\varphi \in F^1$,

$$(\Gamma \vdash_{FT} \varphi \text{ implies } \Gamma \models^{K^{FT}} \varphi) \tag{2.11}$$

Proof: Obviously $\vdash_{FT}\varphi$ implies $\models^{K^{FT}} \varphi$. Thus weak soundness holds.

Let $\Gamma \subseteq F^1$, $\varphi \in F^1$, and assume $\Gamma \vdash_{FT} \varphi$. We want to prove $\Gamma \models^{K^{FT}} \varphi$. By $\Gamma \vdash_{FT} \varphi$, there is a finitely long derivation $\langle \psi_1, \ldots, \psi_k \rangle$ such that $\psi_k = \varphi$. We will proceed by induction on the length of this derivation.

If $k = 1$ then ψ_1, that is, φ is either an axiom of $\vdash_{FT}$ or an element of Γ. Therefore $\Gamma \models^{K^{FT}} \varphi$.

Let $n \leq k$, and assume that $\Gamma \models^{K^{FT}} \{\psi_1, \ldots, \psi_n\}$. We want to prove $\Gamma \models^{K^{FT}} \psi_{n+1}$.

By the definition of a derivation, $\{\psi_1, \ldots, \psi_n\} \vdash_{FT} \psi_{n+1}$ in one step. By (2.11), here a problem can occur only when applying *inference rules* of $\vdash_{FT}$ to $\{\psi_1, \ldots, \psi_n\}$. So assume that ψ_{n+1} was obtained by applying one of the rules (R1—R3) to $\{\psi_1, \ldots, \psi_n\}$, and the rule yielded ψ_{n+1} *in one single step* from $\{\psi_1, \ldots, \psi_n\}$. Now checking our three rules one by one, we have to make sure that $\{\psi_1, \ldots, \psi_n\} \models^{K^{FT}} \psi_{n+1}$. This is left to the reader (we did a similar checking of rule 3 in the proof of the soundness part of Theorem 2.10). Thus $\Gamma \models^{K^{FT}} \psi_{n+1}$.

Then, by induction on the length of the derivation $\Gamma \vdash_{FT} \varphi$, we are done. We have proved Claim (2). $\square$

Claims (1) and (2) together prove Proposition 2.3.

By proving the (completeness parts of the) sandwich completeness theorems (2.10 and 2.12), all the proofs in this section will be completed. In these proofs we will use the basic completeness theorem of ***first-order multi-modal logics***, since temporal logics are special multi-modal logics. This basic completeness theorem is formulated and proved in the following Section 2.2.4.

Remark

The basic completeness theorem for ***propositional*** multi-modal logics was proved first by Jónsson and Tarski in 1948 (see [50], [51]). They called it the ***representation theorem*** of boolean algebras with operators, by atom structures. An atom structure is nothing but the Kripke frame (called a time frame in temporal logic) of a Kripke model, while a boolean algebra with operators corresponds to the set of all formulas of a multi-modal logic (the extra-boolean operators are the modalities). Thus a main tool for investigating completeness problems for multi-modal logics (on the propositional level) became and is still the theory of boolean algebras with operators. For basic literature on this subject, besides [50] and [51], see also [49] and [46].

In Section 2.2.4 we prove the first-order version of the basic completeness theorem for multi-modal logics. □

2.2.4 First-order multi-modal logics: basic completeness investigations

Let I be a set and $X = \{\Box_i : i \in I\}$ be a new set of symbols (modalities). Let d be a similarity type as in Definition 2.5. Then the set $\mathsf{F}^1_{I,d}$ of first-order multi-modal formulas with modalities from X is defined to be $\mathsf{F}^1_{X,d}$ as the latter was defined in the notation of Section 2.2.3. That is, all symbols of d are rigid, and there is a set $C = \{c_i : i \in \omega\}$ of *flexible* constant symbols in $\mathsf{F}^1_{X,d}$. $\mathsf{Mod}_{I,d}$ is as was defined in the remark following Definition 2.5 with the exception that if $\mathcal{M} \in \mathsf{Mod}_{I,d}$ then $\mathcal{M} = \langle \mathbf{T}, \mathbf{D}, f_i \rangle_{i\in\omega}$ with $\mathbf{T} = \langle T, R_i \rangle_{i\in I}$, $R_i \subseteq T \times T$. That is, the difference is that now we do not assume anything about the accessibility relations R_i interpreting $\Box_i$. First-order multi-modal logic is defined to be

$$\mathsf{FMM}_{I,d} = \langle \mathsf{F}^1_{I,d}, \mathsf{Mod}_{I,d}, \models_{I,d} \rangle,$$

where $\models_{I,d}$ is defined following Definition 2.6 with the obvious generalizations. As usual, $\Diamond_i \varphi$ denotes $\neg \Box_i \neg\varphi$.

Definition 2.8 The inference system $\vdash_{mm}$ is defined by 1—11 below. Let us recall from the beginning of Section 2.2.3 that we call a term or a formula ***rigid*** if it does not contain any c_is.

1. all classical propositional tautologies
2. $\Box_i(\varphi \to \psi) \to (\Box_i \varphi \to \Box_i \psi)$ for all $i \in I$
3. $\varphi \leftrightarrow \Box_i \varphi$ for all $i \in I$, provided φ is rigid
4. $\forall x \Box_i \varphi \leftrightarrow \Box_i \forall x\varphi$ for all $i \in I$
5. $\varphi \to \forall x\varphi$ if x is not free in φ
6. all the usual equality axioms of classical first-order logic
7. $\exists x\neg\varphi \leftrightarrow \neg\forall x\varphi$

8. $\forall x\varphi \to \varphi(x/\tau)$ for any term τ such that the substitution $x \mapsto \tau$ does not create new bound occurrences of variables or new occurrences of flexible symbols in the scope of the modalities in φ
9. $\{\varphi, \varphi \to \psi\} \vdash_{mm} \psi$
10. $\varphi \vdash_{mm} \Box_i \varphi$ for all $i \in I$
11. $\varphi \vdash_{mm} \forall x\varphi$. □

Theorem 2.13 $\vdash_{mm}$ **is strongly complete and sound for** $\mathsf{FMM}_{I,d}$ **(for any choice of** I **and** d**), i.e.**

$$\Gamma \models_{I,d} \varphi \text{ iff } \Gamma \vdash_{mm} \varphi \quad \text{for any } \Gamma \cup \{\varphi\} \subseteq \mathsf{F}^1_{I,d}.$$

Proof: For soundness one has to check that all substitution instances (by concrete formulas) of 1—8 are valid and 9—11 preserve validity.

For completeness we consider the following calculus $\vdash^*_{mm}$, and prove its completeness, which clearly implies the completeness of $\vdash_{mm}$. By $\vdash^*_{mm}$ we mean the inference system whose axioms are the substitution instances of 1—8, and if φ is an axiom, then so are $\forall x\varphi$ and $\Box_i \varphi$ for all $i \in I$. The only rule of inference is 9. Proving completeness of $\vdash^*_{mm}$ we follow Strategy 1 in [38], 273—6. Given a consistent set of formulas Σ, we extend it to Δ, an omega complete (for every rigid term τ, $\varphi(\tau) \in \Delta \Rightarrow \forall x\varphi(x) \in \Delta$) and maximal consistent (Δ is consistent and if $\varphi \notin \Delta$, then $\Delta \cup \{\varphi\}$ is inconsistent) set. Such a Δ is *saturated*. We will construct a Kripke model satisfying Δ. First we need the following

Lemma 2.1 If w is an omega complete set of formulas, then so is $w \cup \Phi$, provided Φ is a finite set of formulas.

Proof: Let us assume that $w \cup \Phi \vdash^*_{mm} \varphi(\tau)$ for all rigid terms τ. By the deduction theorem for $\vdash^*_{mm}$ (which is easy to prove by induction), we get $w \vdash^*_{mm} \wedge\Phi \to \varphi(\tau)$, where $\wedge\Phi$ is the conjunction of the members of Φ. Since w is omega complete, it follows that $w \vdash^*_{mm} \forall x(\wedge\Phi \to \varphi(x))$. Without loss of generality we can assume that x is foreign to Φ, so $w \vdash^*_{mm} \wedge\Phi \to \forall x\varphi(x)$, and then $w \cup \Phi \vdash^*_{mm} \forall x\varphi(x)$. □

Lemma 2.2 Any consistent omega complete set w can be extended to a saturated set written in the same language.

Proof: Enumerate the set of all formulas $\{\varphi_i : i \in \omega\}$, and let $M_0 = w$. Suppose that M_i is constructed, $M_i \cup \{\varphi_i\}$ is consistent, and φ_i is $\exists x\varphi(x)$. By Lemma 2.1, M_i is omega complete, so $M_i \cup \varphi(\tau)$ is consistent for some rigid term τ. Since $\varphi(\tau)$ entails $\exists x\varphi(x)$, $M_{i+1} = M_i \cup \{\varphi(\tau), \exists x\varphi(x)\}$ is consistent. It is easy to see that $\bigcup_{i\in\omega} M_i$ is the desired saturated extension of w. □

Lemma 2.3 If w is a saturated set which contains $\neg \Box_i \psi$, then $w^* = \{\varphi : \Box_i \varphi \in w\} \cup \{\neg\psi\}$ is consistent and omega complete.

Proof: w^* is consistent, for if it were not, then there would be a deduction of ψ from it, which would yield a deduction of $\Box_i \psi$ from w, just putting $\Box_i$ in front of each element of the deduction. By Lemma 2.1, w^* is omega complete if $\{\varphi : \Box_i \varphi \in w\}$ is, so assume $\{\varphi : \Box_i \varphi \in w\} \vdash^*_{mm} \theta(\tau)$ for every rigid term τ. By the above argument, $w \vdash^*_{mm} \Box_i \theta(\tau)$ for rigid τs, and by the omega completeness of w, it follows that $w \vdash^*_{mm} \forall x \Box_i \theta(x)$. By the Barcan formula 4 (Definition 2.8), $w \vdash^*_{mm} \Box_i \varphi \forall x \theta(x)$. Since w is maximal $\Box_i \varphi \forall x \theta(x) \in w$, and so $\forall x \theta(x) \in \{\varphi : \Box_i \varphi \in w\}$, i.e. $\{\varphi : \Box_i \varphi \in w\} \vdash^*_{mm} \forall x \theta(x)$. □

Lemma 2.4 If w is saturated and $\neg \Box_i \psi \in w$, then $w^* = \{\varphi : \Box_i \varphi \in w\} \cup \{\neg\psi\}$ can be extended to a saturated set written in the same language.

Proof: (By Lemmas 2.2 and 2.3). □

Given a consistent set Σ, we extend it to an omega complete set Σ' by the well known method of Henkin, adding new rigid constants to the language of Σ. Then by Lemma 2.2 we can consider the saturated extension Δ of Σ'. Note that, by the maximality of Δ, for each flexible constant c_i there is a rigid constant τ such that $\tau = c_i \in \Delta$. Now we construct a model $\mathcal{M}$ as follows.

Let $\Delta_0 \stackrel{def}{=} \{\varphi : \varphi \in \Delta$ and φ is a rigid atomic formula$\}$, and let T be the set of those saturated extensions of Δ_0 in the language of Δ which contain each rigid atomic formula φ iff $\varphi \in \Delta_0$. Note that T is not empty, since $\Delta \in T$. For all $i \in I$, let

$$w_1 R_i w_2 \quad \text{iff} \quad w_1, w_2 \in T \quad \text{and} \quad w_2 \supseteq \{\varphi : \Box_i \varphi \in w_1\}.$$

Next we define the semantic value of a term τ at time w:

(a) if τ is a constant, then $a(\tau)(w) \stackrel{def}{=} \{\tau' : \tau = \tau' \in w$ and τ' is rigid$\}$,

(b) if $\tau = F_n(\tau_1 \ldots \tau_n)$, then $a(\tau)(w) \stackrel{def}{=} a(\tau')(\Delta)$, where τ' is a rigid term such that $\Delta \ni \tau = \tau'$.

Of course, we let $f_i(c_i)(w) = a(c_i)(w)$ for all $i \in \omega$ and $w \in T$. Let

$$D \stackrel{def}{=} \{a(\tau)(\Delta) : \tau \text{ is a term}\}.$$

We continue the definition of the assignment function a:

$$a(P_n)(w) \stackrel{def}{=} \{\langle d_1 \ldots d_n\rangle \in {}^nD : \text{there are rigid } \tau_1 \ldots \tau_n \text{ such that for all } i \leq n,\ a(\tau_i)(w) = d_i \text{ and } P_n(\tau_1 \ldots \tau_n) \in w\}$$

$$\begin{aligned}
a(P_n(\tau_1 \dots \tau_n))(w) = 1 &\text{ iff } \langle a(\tau_1)(w) \dots a(\tau_n)(w) \rangle \in a(P_n)(w) \\
a(\neg\varphi)(w) = 1 &\text{ iff } a(\varphi)(w) = 0 \\
a(\varphi \to \psi)(w) = 1 &\text{ iff } a(\varphi)(w) = 0 \text{ or } a(\psi)(w) = 1 \\
a(\Box_i \varphi)(w) = 1 &\text{ iff } \text{for all } w' \in T, \text{if } wR_iw' \text{ then } a(\varphi)(w') = 1 \\
a(\forall x \varphi)(w) = 1 &\text{ iff } \text{for all } u \in D,\ a[x:u](\varphi)(w) = 1,
\end{aligned}$$

where $a[x:u]$ is the same as a except that the value of $a[x:u]$ at x is u, i.e. $a[x:u](x)(w) = u$ for all $w \in T$.

Clearly, $\mathcal{M} = \langle \mathbf{T}, \mathbf{D}, f_i \rangle_{i \in \omega}$, where $\mathbf{D} = \langle D, a \rangle$, is a Kripke model.

Truth lemma For all $w \in T$

$$\varphi \in w \text{ iff } a(\varphi)(w) = 1.$$

Proof: By induction on the complexity of formulas.

(a) φ has the form $P_n(\tau_1 \dots \tau_n)$. If $P_n(\tau_1 \dots \tau_n) \in w$, then there are rigid terms $\sigma_1 \dots \sigma_n$ such that $\sigma_i = \tau_i \in \omega$, and so $a(\tau_i)(w) = a(\sigma_i)(w)$ for all $i \leq n$. So

$$\begin{aligned}
P_n(\tau_1 \dots \tau_n) \in w &\text{ iff } P_n(\sigma_1 \dots \sigma_n) \in w \\
&\text{ iff } \langle a(\tau_1)(w) \dots a(\tau_n)(w) \rangle \in a(P_n)(w) \\
&\text{ iff } a(P_n(\tau_1 \dots \tau_n))(w) = 1.
\end{aligned}$$

(b) φ is $\neg\psi$ or $\psi \to \theta$.
Straightforward.

(c) φ is $\forall x \psi$.

$$\begin{aligned}
a(\forall x \psi)(w) = 1 &\text{ iff } \text{for all } u \in D,\ a[x:u](\psi)(w) = 1 \\
&\text{ iff } \text{for all rigid terms } \tau,\ a[a(\tau)(w):x](\psi)(w) = 1 \\
&\text{ iff } \text{for all rigid terms } \tau,\ a(\psi(x/\tau))(w) = 1 \\
&\text{ iff } \text{for all rigid terms } \tau,\ \psi(x/\tau) \in w \\
&\text{ iff } \forall x \psi \in w.
\end{aligned}$$

(d) φ is $\Box_i \psi$.

$$\begin{aligned}
a(\Box_i \psi)(w) = 1 &\text{ iff } \text{for all } w', wR_iw' \to a(\psi)(w') = 1 \\
&\text{ iff } \text{for all } w', wR_iw' \to \psi \in w' \\
&\text{ iff } \Box_i \psi \in w.
\end{aligned}$$

For the last equivalence we use $\neg \Box_i \psi \in w$ which implies there is a $w' \in T$ such that wR_iw' and $\neg\psi \in w$, which is true because by Lemma 2.4, there is a $w' \supset \{\varphi : \Box_i \varphi \in w\} \cup \{\neg\psi\}$ which is saturated. By the definition of R_i, wR_iw' holds if $w' \in T$. To show that $w' \in T$ let us assume that $\theta \in \Delta_0$. Then $\theta \in w$ and by 3 (Definition 2.8) $\Box_i \theta \in w$, so $\theta \in w'$. If $\theta \notin \Delta_0$, then $\theta \notin w$, so $\neg\theta \in w$. By 3 (Definition 2.8) again $\Box_i \neg\theta \in w$, so $\neg\theta \in w'$, i.e. $\theta \notin w'$. □

By the truth lemma it follows that all members of Δ and of Σ are true at Δ on the model $\mathcal{M}$, which finishes our proof of Theorem 2.13. □

Let $\mathsf{FMM}^+_{I,d}$ be obtained from $\mathsf{FMM}_{I,d}$ by adding a new modality $\boxdot$ which is interpreted by the accessibility relation $T \times T$ in every model $\mathcal{M}$.

Let $\vdash^+_{mm}$ obtained from $\vdash_{mm}$ by

(a) extending all axioms and rules from $\Box_i$ also to $\boxdot$,

(b) adding the axioms $\boxdot\varphi \to \varphi$ and $\Diamond\boxdot\varphi \to \boxdot\varphi$, and

(c) adding $\boxdot\varphi \to \Box_i \varphi$ for all $i \in I$.

Theorem 2.14 $\vdash^+_{mm}$ is strongly complete and sound for the first-order multi-modal logic $\mathsf{FMM}^+_{I,d}$.

Proof: The proof is nearly the same as that of Theorem 2.13, we just have to construct T more carefully. First note that when we extend a consistent set to a saturated one, say Δ, then we have to add all logical axioms to the set, including those formulas which are given by substituting new constants (that we need in the omega complete extension) in the axioms. So each saturated set contains all logical axioms, and thus all those formulas of the extended language, which are deducible (from the empty set).

Let T' be the time structure constructed in the proof of Theorem 2.13. Let us define R (the relation interpreting $\boxdot$) as follows:

$$w_1 R w_2 \;\text{ iff }\; w_1, w_2 \in T' \;\text{ and }\; w_2 \supseteq \{\varphi : \boxdot\varphi \in w_1\}\,.$$

Since $\boxdot\varphi \to \varphi$, wRw for all $w \in T'$. If $w_1Rw_2Rw_3$, then if $\boxdot\varphi \in w_1$, then by $\boxdot\boxdot\varphi \leftrightarrow \boxdot\varphi$ (which is an easy consequence of $\boxdot\varphi \to \varphi$ and $\Diamond\boxdot\varphi \to \boxdot\varphi$), $\boxdot\boxdot\varphi \in w_1$, so $\boxdot\varphi \in w_2$, and thus $\varphi \in w_3$, i.e. w_1Rw_3. If w_1Rw_2, then if $\boxdot\varphi \in w_2$, then $\neg\boxdot\varphi \notin w_2$, so $\boxdot\neg\boxdot\varphi \notin w_1$. By $\Diamond\boxdot\varphi \to \boxdot\varphi$ and $\boxdot\varphi \to \varphi$ we get $\varphi \in w_1$, so w_2Rw_1. Thus R is an equivalence relation. Moreover, $R_i \subseteq R$ for all $i \in I$, because $\boxdot\varphi \to \Box_i \varphi$. We can consider the equivalence class T which contains the saturated set Δ. Then $\mathcal{M} = \langle\langle T, R, R_i\rangle_{i\in I}, \mathbf{D}, f_j\rangle_{j\in\omega}$ turns out to be the suitable model, because Δ is satisfiable in $\mathcal{M}$ (at time Δ). □

Let us recall that the sandwich completeness theorem for FT was formulated in Section 2.3.3 as Theorem 2.10, and claimed that $\vdash_{FT}$ was strongly complete and sound for the class $\mathsf{K}^{Ind+Tord}$ of Kripke models. We proved the soundness of $\vdash_{FT}$ right after the formulation of the theorem, but we did not prove its completeness. We are going to fill this gap now, using Theorems 2.13 and 2.14.

Proof: (of completeness part of the sandwich completeness theorem for FT) Assume that $\Sigma \subseteq \mathsf{F}^1_d$ is an $\vdash_{FT}$-consistent set of formulas. It is enough to show that Σ is satisfiable in a model $\mathcal{M} \in \mathsf{Mod}_d$. We will check that the model constructed for Σ in the proof of Theorem 2.14 is already in Mod_d (after the obvious, purely formal changes).

The proof is analogous with that of Theorem 2.14. We repeat the construction in the proof of Theorem 2.13, but now in the framework of the inference system $\vdash_{FT}$ instead of the weaker one $\vdash^+_{mm}$. As a result, we obtain a model $\mathcal{M} = \langle\langle T, \ldots\rangle$ such that the elements of T are maximal consistent sets of formulas in a fixed language $\mathsf{F}m_{d+}$ extending the original F^1_d. Since we use $\vdash_{FT}$ this time, for each $w \in T$, w contains all $\mathsf{F}m_{d+}$-instances of all logical axioms of $\vdash_{FT}$. Since w is maximal consistent,

$$w \supseteq \{\varphi \in \mathsf{F}^1_{d+} : \vdash_{FT} \varphi\}$$

Otherwise $\mathcal{M}$ is exactly as at the end of the proof of Theorem 2.14. Let this $\mathcal{M}$ be fixed.

Now, we will use techniques known from the proof of Stalqvist's theorem (see [99], van Benthem's paper in [19] and Venema [102]) for showing $\mathcal{M} \in \mathsf{Mod}_d$. Following the terminology of Goldblatt [41], let $\mathbf{T} = \langle T, R_i\rangle_{i\in I}$ be a frame with T consisting of certain maximal consistent subsets of F^1_{d+}. $\mathbf{T}$ is *refined* iff

$$(\forall w_1, w_2 \in T)(\forall i \in I)(w_i \not R_i w_2 \text{ iff } (\exists \psi \in w_2) \Diamond_i \psi \notin w_1).$$

By the definition of R_i in the proof of Theorem 2.6 we know that the frame of our $\mathcal{M}$ is refined. We will use this property for checking $\mathcal{M} \in \mathsf{Mod}_d$. Let R_F and R_P be the accessibility relations interpreting $\Box$ and $\overline{\Box}$ in $\mathcal{M}$. The hardest task (in showing $\mathcal{M} \in \mathsf{Mod}_d$) is to show that $R_F = (R_P)^{-1}$.

Claim (3): If $\mathcal{M}$ is refined then in $\mathcal{M}$ we have

$$\Diamond\overline{\Box}\varphi \to \varphi \text{ implies } R_F = (R_P)^{-1}.$$

Proof: Assume $\mathcal{M} \models \Diamond\overline{\Box}\varphi \to \varphi$ and that $\mathcal{M}$ is refined.

Assume that $R_F \neq (R_P)^{-1}$. Then there are Γ, Δ in T with

$$\Gamma \underset{R_P}{\overset{R_F}{\underset{\not\leftarrow}{\rightarrow}}} \Delta.$$

Using the facts that $\mathcal{M}$ is refined and that $\Delta \underset{R_P}{\not\leftarrow} \Sigma$, there is a ψ with $\underline{\psi \in \Gamma}$ and $\overline{\Diamond}\psi \notin \Delta$. By Δs being maximal consistent, $\overline{\Diamond}\psi \notin \Delta$ implies $\neg\overline{\Diamond}\psi \in \Delta$, the latter being equivalent to $\overline{\Box}\neg\psi \in \Delta$. So we have

$$\psi \in \Gamma \underset{R_P}{\overset{R_F}{\underset{\not\leftarrow}{\rightarrow}}} \Delta \in \overline{\Diamond}\neg\psi.$$

From this, using the definition of R_F and that $\Gamma \xrightarrow{R_F} \Delta$, we obtain $\Diamond\overline{\Box}\neg\psi$. This, using our hypothesis $\Diamond\overline{\Box}\varphi \rightarrow \varphi$, yields $\underline{\neg\psi \in \Gamma}$. But this is a contradiction (as we have $\psi \in \Gamma$, see above, and Γ is maximal consistent), therefore our hypothesis $R_F \neq (R_P)^{-1}$ is false. $\square$

By Claim (3) we proved $R_F = (R_P)^{-1}$ in $\mathcal{M}$. Proving that $R_{\bigcirc}$ is a function $\bigcirc : T \longrightarrow T$ and that $R_{\odot} = T \times \{w\}$ for some w go by the same method, but are easier, and are left to the reader.

We have seen $\mathcal{M} \in \mathsf{Mod}_d$. Since our original Σ is satisfiable in $\mathcal{M}$, this proves that $\vdash_{FT}$ is strongly complete w.r.t. Mod_d. By this, the sandwich completeness theorem is proved. $\square$

We can improve our sandwich completeness theorem to obtain the following proposition.

Proposition 2.4 For every $\varphi \in \mathsf{F}^1_d$,

$$Mdcl(Tord) \models \varphi \text{ implies } \vdash_{FT}\varphi \text{ implies } Mdcl(Ind + Tord) \models \varphi. \square$$

The proof goes by pushing the techniques we used in proving the sandwich completeness theorem above, i.e. inspecting the "canonical" model $\mathcal{M}$ constructed in the proof of Theorem 2.13, and noticing that it is refined in Goldblatt's sense etc. We will not need this proposition, so we do not go into the details of the proof.

This proposition seems to be closer to a nicer completeness theorem (than the sandwich one), because *Mdcl(Tord)* is closer to *Mdcl(Ind + Tord)* than Mod_d was. So why can we not apply the same technique to push the completeness part even closer and to obtain a completeness result for (*Ind + Tord*) instead of *Tord*? For some reason, this method (of inspecting the canonical $\mathcal{M}$ and perhaps restricting ourselves to a part of its frame as we did in the proof of Theorem 2.14) does not seem to work. One reason might be that *Ind* cannot be translated to modal formulas to which [46], 2.1.16 (p. 440) could be applied (positive multi-modal formulas being preserved under taking canonical frames), or to which the improved version of this result (of boolean algebras with operators) known as Stalqvist's theorem (cf. Venema [102], Stalqvist [99]) could be applied. It is not clear that this is the reason, but we certainly used techniques from the proof of Stalqvist's theorem in our above proof of the sandwich completeness theorem. Anyway, we will see below that handling (*Ind+Tord*) in completeness issues is much harder than the tasks encountered so far.

2.2.5 A closer look at the completeness problem of first-order temporal logic

In this section we turn to the problem of finding completeness theorems for first order temporal logic as nice the ones were in Section 2.2.2 proved for propositional temporal logics. There we defined our class Mod^0 of Kripke models by postulating that $\mathcal{M} = \langle \mathbf{T} \ldots \rangle \in \mathsf{Mod}^0$ iff $\mathbf{T} = \langle \omega, 0, succ, \leq \rangle$ is the standard model of successor arithmetic. Now, we would like to find a class $\mathsf{K}_1 \subseteq \mathsf{Mod}_d$ of *first order* Kripke models characterized in a similarly explicit and mathematically transparent manner and then prove that for every $\varphi \in \mathsf{F}^1_d$, $\mathsf{K}_1 \models \varphi$ iff $\vdash_1 \varphi$ for some inference system $\vdash_1$.

As we indicated in Section 2.2.3, a natural choice for K_1 is $\mathsf{K}^{Ind+Tord} = Mdcl(Ind + Tord)$ first suggested for this purpose in [10], Andréka [6], Németi [65], [13], and related works. We will study this one as well as a few other natural choices.

As pointed out in [36], obtaining satisfactory completeness theorems for first order multi modal systems like FT is much harder (and is much less developed) than the same for propositional temporal logics.

Open problem

(a) Is the inference system $\vdash_{FT}$ complete for the logic

$\mathsf{FT}^{Ind+Tord} \stackrel{def}{=} \langle \mathsf{F}^1_d, \mathsf{K}^{Ind+Tord}, \models_d \rangle$?

More concisely, is $\vdash_{FT}$ complete for $\mathsf{K}^{Ind+Tord}$?

(b) If not, then can we strengthen $\vdash_{FT}$ (without radically changing its style) such that it would become complete for $\mathsf{FT}^{Ind+Tord}$?

It would be very nice to know the answer. A positive answer for either (a) or (b) would yield a satisfactory completeness theorem for FT. This problem was investigated (with several partial results) in e.g. Abadi [2], [1], [3], Sain [93], Andréka et al. [16], Pasztor & Sain [70].

Since we do not know the answer, we will introduce slight restrictions under which completeness is available. One is the so-called *deterministic world hypothesis* (DWH), another one is *existence of clocks*. It is important to point out that DWH does *not* imply that the *part* of the world which we are investigating would be deterministic. DWH means only that knowing the state of the *whole* world at a time instance t determines the state at $succ(t)$. However, knowing the state of our computer only at time t might have no predicting power for its state at $succ(t)$[3]. Therefore this assumption does not prevent us from reasoning about nondeterminism, concurrency, etc. It was proved in the full version of Sain [84], [85] that DWH renders $\vdash_{FT}$ complete for $\mathsf{K}^{Ind+Tord}$, that is for $\mathsf{FT}^{Ind+Tord}$.

[3] Assuming DWH does not amount to more than what was generally assumed in the philosophy of science beginning with Laplace. This assumption was seriously questioned only by the Copenhagen interpretation of quantum mechanics. Of course, it would be nice to have a completeness theorem for *FT* which is applicable also to the Copenhagen interpretation, but as Abadi's works argue, we hope that such subtleties will not hamper applicability of *FT* in the near future.

Below we will recall the assumption $C(\gamma)$ of the existence of clocks. Since $C(\gamma) \Longrightarrow$ DWH, the results below stating that $C(\gamma)$ renders $\vdash_{FT}(=\vdash_{SFP})$ and $\vdash_{SF}$ complete for $\mathsf{K}^{Ind+Tord}$ are slightly weaker than the original results concerning DWH. In other words, the completeness results under assuming clocks are immediate consequences of completeness under assuming DWH because of the following. Assume $C(\gamma)$. Then by $C(\gamma) \Longrightarrow$ DWH, we have DWH. But DWH does imply completeness. Hence $C(\gamma)$ implies completeness.

For certain reasons we will concentrate on $C(\gamma)$ and its weaker version below. A corollary of the above mentioned completeness theorem using DWH can easily be formulated by using the formula $Det(\bar{c})$ given in Example (d) in Section 2.2.3. Recall that $\bar{c}$ is a sequence of flexible constants, and the definition of $Det(\bar{c})$ was

$$\Box\exists\bar{x}\exists\bar{y}(\bar{x} = \bar{c} \wedge \bigcirc\bar{y} = \bar{c} \wedge \Box(\bar{x} = \bar{c} \rightarrow \bigcirc\bar{y} = \bar{c}))$$

Theorem 2.15 (Sain 1984) Assume that all the flexible constants occurring in $\varphi \in \mathsf{F}^1_d$ also occur in the sequence $\bar{c}$. Then

$$(Ind + Tord + Det(\bar{c}) \models_d \varphi) \text{ iff } (Det(\bar{c}) \vdash_{FT} \varphi).$$

Proof: The proof of this theorem is immediate from Theorem 2.16. $\Box$

For $n \in \omega$, let $Det_n \stackrel{def}{=} Det(\langle c_0, \ldots, c_n\rangle)$. Let $Det_n^+ \stackrel{def}{=} \{Det_k : n \leq k \in \omega\}$.

Theorem 2.16 (Sain 1984) Let $n \in \omega$ be arbitrary. Then

(a) $(Ind + Tord + Det_n^+ \models \varphi)$ iff $(Det_n^+ \vdash_{FT} \varphi)$ for any $\varphi \in \mathsf{F}^1_d$. Moreover,

(b) For any $\Gamma \cup \{\varphi\} \subseteq \mathsf{F}^1_d$, we have
$(\Gamma + Ind + Tord + Det_n^+ \models \varphi)$ iff $(\Gamma + Det_n^+ \vdash_{FT} \varphi)$

Proof: For a proof (in slightly different form) see Sain [85], [92]. $\Box$

In the fragment without $\overline{\Box}$ it is harder to obtain a completeness theorem, therefore we need some more definition. (Theorem 2.16 does not generalize to the fragment $\mathsf{FT}_{\odot\bigcirc SF}$ without $\overline{\Box}$.)

Let $\overline{c_n} = \langle c_0, \ldots, c_n\rangle$ and $\overline{x_n} = \langle x_0, \ldots, x_n\rangle$. Let $Det_n^\infty \stackrel{def}{=} Det_n \wedge \Diamond\exists\overline{x_n}(\overline{x_n} = \overline{c_n} \wedge \bigcirc\overline{x_n} = \overline{c_n})$. Let $Det_n^{+\infty} \stackrel{def}{=} \{Det_k^\infty : n \leq k \in \omega\}$.

Theorem 2.17 (Sain 1983) Let $n \in \omega$ be fixed. Then

(a) For any $\Gamma \cup \{\varphi\} \subseteq \mathsf{F}_{\odot\bigcirc SF}$, we have
$(\Gamma + Ind + Tord + Det_n^{+\infty} \models \varphi)$ iff $(\Gamma + Det_n^{+\infty} \vdash_{SF} \varphi)$. Further

(b) $(\Gamma + Ind + Det_n^{+\infty} \models \varphi)$ iff $(\Gamma + Det_n^{+\infty} \vdash_S \varphi)$,
if φ is a formula of $\mathsf{FT}_{\odot\bigcirc S}$.

Proof: For a proof (in slightly different form) see Sain [85], [92]. □

We note that Theorem 2.17 becomes false if we replace $Det_n^{+\infty}$ with Det_n^+.

Recall from Abadi [1], [2], [3] that a *clock* is a temporal formula $\gamma(\bar{x})$ satisfying

$$C(\gamma) \stackrel{def}{=} \Box(\exists\bar{x}\gamma(\bar{x}) \wedge (\gamma(\bar{x}) \rightarrow \bigcirc\Box\neg\gamma(\bar{x})).$$

More precisely, $C(\gamma)$ is a formula "saying" that the formula γ is a clock. So a clock γ never "shows the same time" in two different time instances t and t_1.

Theorem 2.18 (Pasztor & Sain) Even if we permit flexible predicate and function symbols, the temporal logics $\vdash_{SF}$ and $\vdash_{SFP}(=\vdash_{FT})$ are complete for the semantics $\mathsf{K}^{Ind+Tord}$, if we assume the existence of a clock. That is, for any temporal formulas φ and γ, (a) implies (b) below.

(a) $Ind + Tord + C(\gamma) \models \varphi$

(b) $C(\gamma) \vdash_{SFP} \varphi$.

The same holds with everything restricted to the language of $\vdash_{SF}$.

The proof is based on the ideas in the proof given in Sain [85], [92] for Theorem 2.16, but some more work is needed. A detailed proof is available from Sain. For a different proof (using a result of Abadi) see that in Pasztor & Sain [70]. □

Theorem 2.18 generalizes the completeness result for "T_1" in Abadi [1], [2], [3] to Hilbert-style proof systems. In particular, for the formula φ constructed in §§3–4 therein to show incompleteness for $(Ind + Tord)$ of the Hilbert-style T_0, we have $\vdash_{SF}\varphi$ (while $\nvdash_{T_0} \varphi$). Theorem 2.16 improves the $\vdash_{SFP}$-case of the above result by weakening the clock assumption.

The following theorem says that Theorem 2.16 fails for $\vdash_{SF}$ in place of $\vdash_{SFP}$, i.e. $\vdash_{SF}$ is incomplete for $(Ind + Tord)$ under Det_n^+ (but not under $C(\gamma)$ by Theorem 2.18).

Theorem 2.19 There is a similarity type d, a formula $\varphi \in \mathsf{F}^1_{\odot\bigcirc SF,d}$ (i.e. $\varphi \in \mathsf{F}^1_d$ but $\overline{\Box}$ does not occur in φ) such that

$$\mathsf{K}^{Ind+Tord} \models \varphi \qquad \text{but, for all } n \in \omega, \quad Det_n^+ \nvdash_{SF} \varphi.$$

Proof: We will prove a slightly stronger statement, that φ can be chosen to be a commonly investigated property called the *safety property* or *invariance property* of a simple program p described below. That is, we will define the program p, postulate a temporal formula $Ax(p)$ expressing that the flexible constants $\bar{c}$ constitute an execution sequence of p. Then we will show that a simple temporal statement about $\bar{c}$ (i.e. about the execution of p) has the above desired property, i.e. it is true in $\mathsf{K}^{Ind+Tord}$, but it is not provable by $\vdash_{SF}$. (Of course, it is provable by $\vdash_{SFP}$, because of Theorem 2.18).

Consider the data domain $\mathbf{D} = \langle \mathbf{Z}, 0, succ, R\rangle$ where $\langle \mathbf{Z}, 0, succ\rangle$ is the standard structure of the integers, and $R = \{\langle z, -z\rangle : z \in \mathbf{Z}\}$.

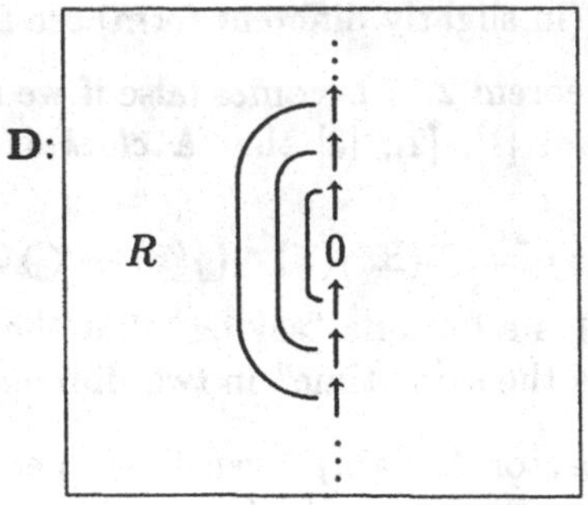

Let the program p start with $c := 0$ and then increase the value of c by 1 in each step. (So, in particular, p never terminates.)

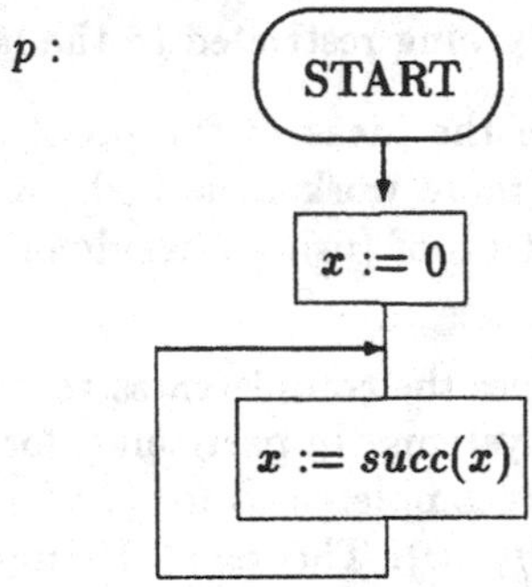

For this choice of p, $Ax(p)$ is the following temporal formula: $\exists x(x = c \wedge \bigcirc c = succ(x)) \wedge \odot c = 0$. The invariance property ψ of p states that during any execution of p, c (i.e. the program register x) will never have the value -1. This is expressible e.g. by the temporal formula $\boxdot Ax(p) \rightarrow \boxdot(succ(c) \neq 0)$. Let $Th \stackrel{def}{=} Th(\mathbf{D})$ be the full first-order (nontemporal!) theory of $\mathbf{D}$. It is enough to show that

(a) $Th \vdash_{SFP} \psi$, and
(b) $Det_1^+ + Th \nvdash_{SF} \psi$.

Remark

(a) and (b) yield more than claimed in the theorem, because of the following. By (a) and compactness, there is a sentence $\gamma \in Th$ such that $\gamma \vdash_{SFP} \psi$. Since γ is a rigid sentence, $\vdash_{SFP}(\gamma \rightarrow \psi)$. Let φ be $(\gamma \rightarrow \psi)$. Then φ is an invariance property, since $\gamma \rightarrow (\boxdot Ax(p) \rightarrow \boxdot(succ(c) \neq 0))$ is equivalent to $\gamma \wedge \boxdot Ax(p) \rightarrow \boxdot(succ(c) \neq 0)$ i.e. $\boxdot Ax(p) \rightarrow (\gamma \rightarrow \boxdot(succ(c) \neq 0))$ which is equivalent to $\boxdot Ax(p) \rightarrow \boxdot(\gamma \rightarrow succ(c) \neq 0)$ since γ is rigid. Now we have

$\vdash_{SFP}\varphi$ and $\not\vdash_{SF}\varphi$, proving the stronger, invariance property version of the theorem, even for deterministic programs.

To prove (ii), consider the Kripke model $\mathcal{M} = \langle\langle \mathbf{Z}, 0, succ, \mathbf{Z}\times\mathbf{Z}\rangle, \mathbf{D}, \mathsf{Id}\rangle$ where Id is the identity function. The point here is that the relation $\leq^{\mathcal{M}}$ interpreting $\Box$ in $\mathcal{M}$ is the "nihilistic" relation $\mathbf{Z}\times\mathbf{Z}$. Clearly

(c) $\quad \mathcal{M}\models Th\cup\{\neg\psi\}\cup Det_1^+$.

It is not hard to check that all the axioms (and rules) of $\vdash_{SF}$ are true in $\mathcal{M}$ except for induction (which appears both in A1 and in R3).

In the language of $\vdash_{SF}$, R3 is equivalent to the induction formula

$$(\mathrm{ind}_{\Box,\odot}) \qquad \odot\varphi\wedge\Box(\varphi\rightarrow\bigcirc\varphi)\rightarrow\Box\varphi.$$

This was proved e.g. in [91], Lemma 2.4 (i), p. 85.

To prove $\mathcal{M}\models(\mathrm{ind}_{\Box,\odot})$, it is enough to prove that $\mathbf{D}\models$ *Indcl* where *Indcl* is classical first-order induction

$$Indcl = \{\varphi(0)\wedge\forall x(\varphi(x)\rightarrow\varphi(succ(x)))\rightarrow\forall x\varphi(x):$$
$$\varphi(x)\text{ is an arbitrary first-order formula in the language of }\mathbf{D}\}.$$

This can be proved by the usual ultraproduct constructions in e.g. [13], [65], [85], [92]. We omit the details of the latter. So we have $\mathcal{M}\models(\mathrm{ind}_{\Box,\odot})$. This in turn implies that *all* axioms and rules of $\vdash_{SF}$ are true in $\mathcal{M}$. So by induction on the length of proofs, for any formula ρ we have $\vdash_{SF}\rho\Rightarrow\mathcal{M}\models\rho$. Therefore, by (c), we have $\mathcal{M}\not\models\varphi$ hence $Det_1^+\not\vdash_{SF}\varphi$ proving (b).

To prove (i), one proves by temporal induction

(d) $\quad \exists x\,(c = x\wedge\overline{\Box}c\neq succ(x)\rightarrow\overline{\Box}\neg(cRx))$.

Now we assume $\neg\psi$, that is $\Diamond c = -1$. Then $\Diamond(c = -1\wedge\Diamond c = 1)$ which implies $\Diamond(c = 1\wedge\overline{\Diamond}c = -1)$ which, by $-1R1$, contradicts (d). It is very easy to formalize this informal argument in $\vdash_{SFP}$. This proves (a). We have proved (some more than) Theorem 2.19. $\Box$

Let us turn to the fragments $\vdash_{SF}, \vdash_S, \vdash_0$ of $\vdash_{SFP} = \vdash_{FT}$.

The natural semantics for $\vdash_{SF}$ seems to be $\mathsf{K}^{Ind+Tord} = Mdcl(Ind+Tord)$. However, $\mathsf{K}^{Ind+Tord}$ is *not* a natural semantics for $\vdash_S$, since the relation $\leq$ on T described by *Tord* is not represented by any modality in $\vdash_S$, i.e. $\mathsf{FT}_{\odot\bigcirc S}$. Therefore, the natural semantics for $\vdash_S$ is $\mathsf{K}^{Ind}\overset{def}{=}Mdcl(Ind)$. It does not matter that the relation symbol $\leq$ is still around in K^{Ind}, the important thing is that there are no axioms postulated for it. That is, if $\mathbf{T} = \langle T, 0, succ, \leq\rangle$ is a (time) frame in K^{Ind} then if we change $\leq$ completely arbitrarily, i.e. we choose $\leq^+ = \emptyset$, then still $\mathbf{T} = \langle T, 0, succ, \leq^+\rangle$ will remain a frame in K^{Ind}. This makes K^{Ind} equivalent with its reduct where $\leq$ is deleted from the time frames. This is true because the elements of Mod are models of classical first-order (two-sorted) logic, and this logic has basic properties like Beth's definability property and Craig's interpolation property. Having found that of $\vdash_S$, we ask what the natural semantics for $\vdash_0$ should be. This is harder to answer, because the accessibility relation of $\diamondsuit$ (i.e. of "sometime") is $T \times T$, therefore we cannot delete it as easily as we deleted $\leq$ interpreting $\diamondsuit$. However, there is a natural answer: $\diamondsuit$ is interpreted by quantification over T (i.e. $t \vdash \diamondsuit\varphi$ iff $(\exists t_1 \in T)t_1 \vdash \varphi$). (So, what we want to remove this time is quantification over T.) Let Ind^{qf} be obtained from Ind by restricting induction to those formulas $\varphi \in$ Fmcl(Mod) which contain no quantifiers over the domain T. Here the superscript qf intends to refer to quantifier free w.r.t. the time domain T. It is important to emphasize that quantifiers over D are allowed (in arbitrary complexity) in Ind^{qf}. Therefore Ind^{qfT} would have been a more natural notation, but the literature on this semantics for computer science logics goes back to Andréka & Németi [8], [13], so we decided to be consistent at least with part of this literature.

Definition 2.9

$$Ind^{qf} \stackrel{def}{=} \{(\varphi(0) \wedge \forall t(\varphi(t) \rightarrow \varphi(succ(t))) \rightarrow \forall t\varphi(t)) :$$
$\varphi(t) \in$ Fmcl(Mod) contains no quantifiers ranging over the domain T, i.e. no quantifiers of form $\exists t_i$ with $i \in \omega$ }.

□

$Mdcl(Ind^{qf})$ will be regarded as the natural semantics for $\vdash_0$.

The uses of the semantics K^{Ind} and $Mdcl(Ind^{qf})$ for, more or less, the present purposes go back to [10], [6], [13], [65]. They were obtained in the quoted works from their earlier version in Andréka & Németi [8], by using the insights coming from Csirmaz's early results on the problems left open in [8]. In particular, Csirmaz's result clarified the difference between K^{Ind} and $Mdcl(Ind^{qf})$ from the point of view of computer science applications. This way Csirmaz answered a question going back to Andréka et al. [7] which, independently of Burstall [25], suggested using a version of $\vdash_S$ for program verification and asked how its proof theoretic power relates to that of the Floyd–Hoare method. Csirmaz's results were published in [30], [31], [33]. (Some of the proofs in [30] and [31] were simplified later by Sain in [82], [88].)

For simplicity, from now on, when $\varphi \in F^1_d$ (i.e. φ is temporal), we will sometimes write $Ind^{qf} \models \varphi$ as shorthand for $Mdcl(Ind^{qf}) \models_d \varphi$. We will sometimes do the same for other $\Gamma \subseteq$ Fmcl(Mod) in place of Ind^{qf}. (The sloppiness here is that Γ comes from the nontemporal language Fmcl(Mod), while φ comes from the temporal one, F^1_d. The connection between the two languages is that $Mdcl(\Gamma)$ is also a class of temporal Kripke models. To make it explicit that we are using this connection, we should write $Mdcl(\Gamma) \models_d \varphi$ instead of $\Gamma \models \varphi$. From now on, however, we will be less careful about this notational principle.)

Theorem 2.20 $\vdash_S$ is not complete even for the semantics K^{Ind} (here everything is restricted to the $\vdash_S$ - fragment, of course). Moreover, there is a formula φ in the $\vdash_S$ - fragment $FT_{\odot\bigcirc S}$ such that $K^{Ind} \models \varphi$ but $Det^+_1 \not\vdash_S \varphi$.

The proof is immediate from that of Theorem 2.19 above. □

Neither Det_n^+ nor $C(\gamma)$ helps. In case of the latter the reason is that $C(\gamma)$ is not expressible in the language of $\vdash_S$. According to Theorem 2.17 (b), $Det_n^{+\infty}$ helps.

We conjecture that for any temporal formula φ in the $\vdash_S$ - fragment, $\vdash_S \varphi$ iff $Ind_1 \models \varphi$. Here the set $Ind_1 \subset Ind$ is induction over those formulas which contain only one variable of sort **T**.

Theorem 2.21 $\vdash_0$ is complete for the semantics Ind^{qf}, i.e. for any temporal formula φ in the language of $\vdash_0$,

$$\vdash_0 \varphi \quad \text{iff} \quad Ind^{qf} \models \varphi$$

The proof is based on Theorem 2.4 and is available from the authors. □

In connection with the problems raised at the end of the important works of Abadi [1], [2], [3], among others, we obtain the following: Abadi [2], [3] proved that the inference systems in Manna & Pnueli [61] become incomplete for the semantics ($Ind+Tord$) if we add flexible predicate (or function) symbols. ([61] does not allow these.) In Theorem 2.22 we state that this incompleteness remains true even without allowing (or adding) flexible predicates (or functions).

Theorem 2.22 The inference system introduced in Manna & Pnueli [61] for temporal logic with $\bigcirc$ and $\Box$ is incomplete for the semantics $\mathsf{K}^{Ind+Tord}$. Moreover, it remains incomplete after adding all propositionally valid formulas (cf. A1 herein) and any finite number of new axioms (valid in $\mathsf{K}^{Ind+Tord}$).

The proof is a refinement of that of Theorem 2.19, and is available from the authors. □

The next result seems to answer Abadi's open question (2) in [2], §9, p. 72.

Theorem 2.23 The inference system T_1 introduced in Abadi's papers [1], [2], [3] is incomplete for $\mathsf{K}^{Ind+Tord}$ if used without "until". This is so even if we assume DWH, and despite T_1's being reinforced with a rule permitting the use of auxiliary definitions in proofs. From the remark at the end of §7 of [2] discussing "T_1 without until", we conclude that clocks do increase the power of this system.

For a proof see that of Theorem 2.19 (Further explanation is available from the authors.) □

We did not check whether the counterexample in the proof of Theorem 2.19 proves perhaps that T_1 together with "until" is still incomplete for $\mathsf{K}^{Ind+Tord}$. Either way, it would be nice to check this.

Open problem

Is Theorem 2.15 true without any extra assumptions like existence of clocks or any kind of DWH? □

Recent attempts and ideas for solving the completeness problem for FT

Next we turn to solving some open problems raised in recent publications of the computer science temporal logic school represented by Manna & Pnueli [61], [62], Abadi & Manna [5], Abadi [1], [2], [3]. These problems concern the proof theoretic powers of the inference systems: T_0, introduced by Manna & Pnueli [61], [62], and reformulated by Abadi [1], [2], [3]; the resolution system **R** of Abadi & Manna [5] with its final form in [3], [2]; and T_1, T_2 of Abadi [1], [2], [3]. It was proved in Pasztor & Sain [70] taken together with Abadi [3] that (for our present purposes at least) $\vdash_{SFP}$, T_1, and **R** are equivalent. So the reader unfamiliar with the Abadi & Manna works cited here should substitute $\vdash_{SFP}$ for T_1 or **R**. On the other hand, T_2 will be defined (recalled) soon. The last sentence in the "Open problems" sections of Abadi [1], [2], [3] (§9 in [1], §9 in [2], §5.9 in [3]) asks if a clock adds power to T_1 or **R**. (The question is understood modulo infinite data domains, of course.) We will answer this problem affirmatively. To recall the second problem we are going to solve, we need the following definition.

Definition 2.10 Consider the following "Gabbay-type rule" or so-called *consistency rule* (CR):

If

$$\vdash (\exists\overline{x}(\odot\overline{c} = \overline{x} \wedge \varphi(\overline{x})) \wedge \Box\exists\overline{x}\overline{x'}(\overline{x} = \overline{c} \wedge \bigcirc\overline{x'} = \overline{c} \wedge \psi(\overline{x},\overline{x'}))) \rightarrow \gamma \qquad (2.12)$$

then also $\vdash \gamma$

whenever no member of $\overline{c}$ occurs in φ, ψ, or γ.

Let $\vdash_{SFP}{}^{+}$ be the inference system $\vdash_{SFP}$ augmented with the new rule (2.12). That is, whenever $\vdash_{SFP}{}^{+} [(\ldots) \rightarrow \gamma]$ then we also have $\vdash_{SFP}{}^{+}\gamma$. Otherwise we are allowed to use $\vdash_{SFP}$ in $\vdash_{SFP}{}^{+}$ - derivations. Then $\vdash_{T_2}$ (or simply T_2) is defined to be $\vdash_{SFP}{}^{+}$.

It is important to note that now we are allowed to use $\vdash_{T_2}$ for $\vdash_{T_2} \varphi$, but *never* to use it in the context $\Gamma \vdash_{T_2} \varphi$ (with Γ a set of arbitrary formulas, i.e. nonlogical axioms). Namely, a well known property of the consistency rules, a special case of which is (2.12), is that they are usually far from being sound in the latter context. That is, usually $(\Gamma \vdash_{T_2}) \not\Rightarrow (\Gamma \models^{K})$ for any reasonable choice of **K**. In other words, these consistency rules were designed for use only in the $\vdash_{T_2}$ (or more dramatically $(\emptyset \vdash_{T_2})$) context and *not* in the $(\Gamma \vdash_{T_2})$ context. □

The formulation of $\vdash_{T_2}$ in Abadi [2] is slightly different from the above one, but for the purpose of this chapter we may consider the above formulation equivalent to Abadi's original one.

Consistency rules like CR have been used successfully for obtaining complete inference systems for logics which had been proved to have *no* complete Hilbert-style inference systems, see Venema [101], Def.3.2, [102], Simon [98]. As far as we know, the rule goes back to Gabbay [35], but see [102] for historical background of this rule.

It is interesting to note that certain aspects of this rule turn out to be useful in connection with the ⟨Some – other – times⟩ modality, i.e. the irreflexive version of $\Diamond$, which, to our knowledge, was first discovered and proved useful by G.H. von Wright, see Segerberg [96]; its usefulness in computer science was first pointed out in Sain [79], [87], see also Pasztor [69]. This ⟨Some – other – times⟩ modality is denoted by D for "difference", in Venema [102] and van Benthem [22].

Because of this record of success of the consistency rules (the price we have to pay for completeness is that we are restricted to proving validities like $\emptyset \vdash \varphi$), there seems to be hope that adding CR to $\vdash_{SFP}$ and obtaining $\vdash_{T_2}$ this way, one might be able to obtain a nice completeness theorem for FT. (Perhaps one will have to fine-tune the system, modifying T_2 slightly etc., but the approach seems to be promising.) Below we will see how far this approach has been able to go till now.

The inference system $\vdash_{T_2}$ is ***not sound*** for $\mathsf{K}^{Ind+Tord}$. This, however, is not a weakness but rather a virtue. Namely, T_2 was designed for a smaller class $\mathsf{K}^{Ind+Tpa} \neq\subset \mathsf{K}^{Ind+Tord}$ of Kripke models by Abadi, because he wanted a stronger inference system. The semantics $\mathsf{K}^{Ind+Tpa}$ goes back to Andréka & Németi [8], and was suggested for computer science logics of programs and actions, e.g. in Andréka et al. [13], Németi [65], Sain [76]. Later, Abadi [2], [3] presented convincing arguments that this is a rather suitable (or reasonably adequate) semantics from the point of view of computer science applications.

Let us turn to recalling $\mathsf{K}^{Ind+Tpa}$ from these works.

Definition 2.11

(a) We begin by *expanding* our time frames

$\mathbf{T} = \langle T, 0, succ, \leq \rangle$ with two new binary operations $+$ and $\times$, obtaining $\mathbf{T}^+ = \langle T, 0, succ, \leq, +, \times \rangle$. Then we require the usual set *PA* of Peano's axioms for arithmetic to be valid in our expanded frames $\mathbf{T}^+$.

Now we have two-sorted models $\mathcal{M}^+ = \langle\langle \mathbf{T}, \ldots, \times\rangle, \mathbf{D}, f_0, f_1, \ldots\rangle$, which are expansions of our old models in **Mod**. Let us denote the class of these new models $\mathcal{M}^+$ by $\mathbf{Mod}^+$. Then $\mathsf{Fmcl}(\mathbf{Mod}^+)$ contains more formulas than $\mathsf{Fmcl}(\mathbf{Mod})$, because now we have the new symbols $+$ and $\times$ acting on the time sort T.

Let *Ind* be the same as before, but now *Ind* postulates induction over all formulas of $\mathsf{Fmcl}(\mathbf{Mod}^+)$, including the ones containing $+$ and $\times$ for sort T. We define

$$\mathsf{K}^{Ind+Tpa} \stackrel{def}{=} \{\mathcal{M}^+ = \langle \mathbf{T}^+, \mathbf{D}, f_i \rangle_{i\in\omega} : \mathbf{T}^+ \models PA \text{ and } \mathcal{M}^+ \models Ind\}.$$

Equivalently, let $Tpa \subseteq \mathsf{Fmcl}(\mathsf{Mod}^+)$ be a copy of PA postulated for the time sort T of our models $\mathcal{M}^+$. Then

$$\mathsf{K}^{Ind+Tpa} = Mdcl(Ind + Tpa).$$

(b) Let $\varphi \in \mathsf{F}^1_d$ and let $\mathcal{M}^+ = \langle\langle T, 0, succ, \leq, +, \times\rangle, \mathbf{D}, f_i\rangle_{i\in\omega}$. Then $\mathcal{M}^+ \models_d \varphi$ is defined to hold iff $\langle\langle T, 0, succ, \leq\rangle, \mathbf{D}, f_i\rangle_{i\in\omega} \models \varphi$. □

We use the expanded models $\mathcal{M}^+ \in \mathsf{K}^{Ind+Tpa}$ for interpreting the same old temporal modalities $\odot$, $\bigcirc$, $\Box$, $\overline{\Box}$. That is, we use only the old part "0, *succ*, $\leq$" of our new models $\mathcal{M}^+$ when interpreting temporal formulas. One could ask then: "What is the use of the new operations $+$ and $\times$ on T?" The answer is that their use is *indirect*. They enable us to postulate the stronger axioms $Ind + Tpa$ which in turn force 0, *succ*, $\leq$ to be more similar to the standard time frame $\langle \omega, 0, succ, \leq\rangle$ of PT. Let

$$\mathsf{Rd}(\mathsf{K}^{Ind+Tpa}) \stackrel{def}{=} \mathsf{RdK}^{Ind+Tpa} \stackrel{def}{=} \{\mathcal{M} \in \mathsf{Mod} : \mathcal{M} \text{ it can be expanded with } + \text{ and } \times \text{ to an } \mathcal{M}^+ \in \mathsf{K}^{Ind+Tpa}\}.$$

Rd stands for "*reduct*", i.e. for forgetting $+$ and $\times$. Now,

$$\mathsf{RdK}^{Ind+Tpa} \neq\subset \mathsf{K}^{Ind+Tord}.$$

When there is no danger of confusion, we will omit the "forgetful" operator Rd. That is, we will write $\mathsf{K}^{Ind+Tpa} \models \varphi$ instead of $\mathsf{RdK}^{Ind+Tpa} \models \varphi$ or $\mathsf{K}^{Ind+Tpa} \subset \mathsf{K}^{Ind+Tord}$.

Proposition 2.5

(a) All standard models are in $\mathsf{K}^{Ind+Tpa}$, i.e.
$\langle\langle \omega, 0, succ, \leq\rangle, \mathbf{D}, f_i\rangle_{i\in\omega} \in \mathsf{RdK}^{Ind+Tpa}$ for all choices of $\mathbf{D}$ and f_i.

(b) There are temporal formulas φ already in $\mathsf{FT}_{\odot\bigcirc}$ such that

$$\mathsf{K}^{Ind+Tpa} \models \varphi \quad \text{but} \quad \mathsf{K}^{Ind+Tord} \not\models \varphi.$$

Proof: Relatively easy, see Sain [76], Andréka et al. [10], [13]. □

Proposition 2.5 says that $\mathsf{K}^{Ind+Tpa}$ is a much stronger semantics for all fragments of our temporal logic than $\mathsf{K}^{Ind+Tord}$.

Of course, it is a challenge to devise a nice, complete inference system for

$$\mathsf{FT}^{Ind+Tpa} = \langle \mathsf{F}^1_d, \mathsf{K}^{Ind+Tpa}, \models_d\rangle.$$

This problem has been implicitly raised already in Németi [65], and also in other early publications of the so called nonstandard logics of programs (NLP) school. The requirement that the inference system be nice is essential since ugly complete inference systems have already been published in Andréka et al. [13], Sain [80] (for a slightly different syntax whose translation to the present syntax is a routine exercise). Abadi [2], [3] designed the inference system $\vdash_{T_2}$ (sometimes denoted as T_2) to meet this challenge.

As we will see, under assuming the existence of clocks, he was successful. That is, under assuming clocks (as we did in Theorem 2.18), T_2 is complete for $\mathsf{FT}^{Ind+Tpa}$. But it was proved in Sain [93] (see also Andréka et al. [16]) that T_2 is *not* complete for $\mathsf{FT}^{Ind+Tpa}$ in general.

Theorem 2.24 (Abadi [2]) Under assuming the existence of clocks ($C(\gamma)$), T_2 is complete for $\mathsf{FT}^{Ind+Tpa}$. That is, for any $\varphi, \gamma \in \mathsf{F}^1_d$, we have

$$(\mathsf{K}^{Ind+Tpa} \models C(\gamma) \to \varphi) \text{ implies } \vdash_{T_2} C(\gamma) \to \varphi$$

The proof is in [2]. □

Unfortunately the soundness direction "⇐" for the above theorem fails.

Theorem 2.25 (Sain [92]) Even under assuming clocks, T_2 remains unsound for $\mathsf{FT}^{Ind+Tpa}$. That is, there is $\varphi \in \mathsf{F}^1_d$ such that

(a) $\mathsf{K}^{Ind+Tpa} \not\models \varphi$, but

(b) $\vdash_{T_2} C(c = x) \to \varphi$.

Proof: [92]. □

~~The defect shown by Theorem 2.40 *can* be mended though.~~ Namely, the semantics $\mathsf{K}^{Ind+Tpa} = Mdcl(Ind + Tpa)$ was strengthened in [13], p. 264, [78], [86], [65] etc. to one denoted by $Mdcl(Ind{+}Tpa{+}Ex^b)$. Here Ex^b is a restricted version of the *comprehension axiom* Ex. Since the standard terminology in logic is "comprehension", some of the quoted works (e.g.[86]) denote these two sets of axioms as Cm^b and Cm respectively. (The abbreviation Ex refers to "existence axiom".) Here we do not recall Ex^b (which, however, is a standard tool of nonstandard second-order logic, see e.g. Makowsky & Sain [59]), but we will recall Ex at the end of this chapter. It was proved by Sain around 1982–3 that Ex adds to the program verifying powers of these logics[4].

Theorem 2.26 (Sain) Under assuming clocks, T_2 is sound and complete for the semantics $Mdcl(Ind + Tpa + Ex^b)$, i.e.

$$(Mdcl(Ind + Tpa + Ex^b) \models C(\gamma) \to \varphi) \text{ iff } \vdash_{T_2} C(\gamma) \to \varphi,$$

[4]Using different terminology, this means that quantifying over flexible variables increases the program-verifying power of temporal logics.

for any $\gamma, \varphi \in \mathsf{F}^1_d$.
The proof is based partly on Abadi's methods [2] and partly on the methods concerning Ex, Ex^b and Peano's arithmetic [85], [93]. It is available from Sain. □

Let us look at the problem whether assuming clocks can be eliminated, or at least weakened.

Theorem 2.27 (Sain 1988) T_2 is not complete for $\mathsf{K}^{Ind+Tpa}$. Moreover, T_2 remains incomplete under the deterministic world hypothesis Det_n^+, and even under the stronger $Det_n^{+\infty}$.

Proof: Sain [93]; the details left unchecked are fully supplied in Csirmaz [32]. (See also Andréka et al. [16].) □

The above outlined limitative results on T_2, e.g. Theorem 2.27, were recalled from (an early version of) [16], and their consequences were discussed in Abadi [4]. The ideas presented are similar to these above, where we argue that DWH will not limit applicability too much.

Open problem

Find a nice, Hilbert-style inference system $\vdash$ for first-order temporal logic which is sound and complete for $(Ind + Tpa \models)$, i.e. for the semantics Abadi denotes as $\vdash_P$. □

2.3 Expressing and proving properties of programs in temporal logics: fairness and concurrency

Let p be an arbitrary program (cf. Definition 2.12 below). For proving statements about p, the various ***program verification methods*** (see e.g. Pnueli [71], p.56, Burstall [25] and Németi [65]) develop a theory $Ax(p)$ "around" this program p, and prove the statement in question inside of this particular theory $Ax(p)$. Burstall's and Pnueli's program verification methods (to be recalled in Section 2.4) are concrete examples for this. Instead of "program verification method", we will simply write "method" for brevity. Probably the first descriptions of Burstall's method are in [25] and independently in [7]. Pnueli and others extended Burstall's method from the basically modal framework $\vdash_{\odot\bigcirc S}$ to more truly temporal ones like $\vdash_{FT}$, e.g. in Pnueli [71], [72], Gabbay et al. [37], Manna & Pnueli [61], [62], [63]. Both of these methods are suitable for proving both partial and total correctness of programs. In this chapter we concentrate only on partial correctness assertions (pcas from now on). This is our reason for defining here provability of pcas only, by temporal logic methods. Intuitively, a pca $[p]\psi$ states that every possible output of program p will satisfy formula ψ. (Note that it does not claim that there will be such an output, that is, a pca says nothing about termination.)

An *intuitive summary* of item (2.13) is given in the following 30 or so lines.

If p is a program then $Ax(p)$ is the temporal logic formula expressing that c is an execution sequence of p (i.e. c is a time sequence of values of the data variable or "register" of the program p; if p contains more data variables then the formula becomes more complicated in the obvious way). For example if $\ell_1 \xrightarrow{x:=x+2} \ell_2$ is an edge (or command) of p then $Ax(p)$ contains the subformula

$$(\text{“at } \ell_1\text{”}) \rightarrow \exists x(x = c \wedge \bigcirc(c = x + 2 \wedge \text{“at } \ell_2\text{”})).$$

Now,

> a *temporal proof* of a partial correctness assertion $\varphi \rightarrow [p]\psi$ (more classically expressed as $\{\varphi\}p\{\psi\}$) is a proof of the temporal formula γ expressing
> ("c is at the halt label of p" $\rightarrow \psi(c)$),
> from $Ax(p)$ and $\odot\varphi(c)$, using one of the inference systems $\vdash_0 = \vdash_{\odot\bigcirc}$, $\vdash_{\odot\bigcirc S}$, $\vdash_{\odot\bigcirc SF}$, or $\vdash_{\odot\bigcirc SFP} = \vdash_{FT}$. The formulas γ, $Ax(p)$, and $\odot\varphi(c)$ belong to the fragment $\vdash_0$, cf. e.g. Pnueli [73]).
> We write $\vdash_{\odot\bigcirc S} (\varphi \rightarrow [p]\psi)$ for $\{Ax(p), \odot\varphi(c)\} \vdash_{\odot\bigcirc S} \gamma$ and similarly for the other inference systems $\vdash_{\odot\bigcirc SF}$, $\vdash_0$, etc. (2.13)

We note that this definition of $\vdash_{\odot\bigcirc S} \varphi \rightarrow [p]\psi$ is equivalent to

$$\vdash_{\odot\bigcirc S} \Box Ax(p) \wedge \odot\varphi(c) \rightarrow \Box\gamma .$$

The advantage of our original definition is that it is applicable to the fragment $\mathsf{F}^1_{\odot\bigcirc}$ where $\Box$ is not available.

Let Form_d denote the set of all (ordinary classical) first-order formulas of similarity type d. Very often, by a pca we understand a formula of the form $[p]\psi$ which in the classical Hoare notation would read as $\{\mathsf{TRUE}\}p\{\psi\}$. Traditionally, a pca is a formula of the form $\varphi \rightarrow [p]\psi$ with $\varphi, \psi \in \mathsf{Form}_d$. So our pcas seem to be special cases only of traditional pcas. However, this restriction does not restrict generality of the investigation. Namely, every traditional pca $\varphi \rightarrow [p]\psi$ is equivalent to a "restricted" one $[p']\psi'$ because of the following. Let $\bar{x}$ contain all the data variables in φ, p and ψ. Let $\bar{x}'$ be a disjoint copy of $\bar{x}$. Let p' be the program obtained from p which first copies $\bar{x}$ into $\bar{x}'$ and then executes p (on $\bar{x}$ as before). Then $[p'](\varphi(\bar{x}') \rightarrow \psi(\bar{x}))$ is equivalent to $\varphi(\bar{x}) \rightarrow [p]\psi(\bar{x})$.

In Definition 2.12 below we give a set $Ax(p) \subseteq \mathsf{F}^1_{\odot\bigcirc}$ of axioms for an arbitrary program p. Intuitively, $Ax(p)$ expresses that the flexible constant symbols $c_0, \ldots, c_k$ (the denotation of which may change in time!) form an *execution sequence* or *trace* of the program p, where k is the number of variables occurring in p. In this part of the chapter by a *program* we always mean a deterministic block-diagram program. For fixing our notation, in Definition 2.12 we recall the definition of a program, too. Of course, this does *not* apply to the places where we discuss fairness, concurrency, etc.

Definition 2.12

(a) *Lab* denotes the set of all (rigid) constant terms of similarity type d (i.e. *Lab* is the set of those terms which do not contain variables). The elements of *Lab* are called *labels*. (*Lab* is chosen this way for simplicity only. This is an ad-hoc choice designed only to avoid irrelevant distractions. There are many other possible ways for handling labels, see the remark below.)

The set U_d of *commands* of type d is defined by

$$U_d \stackrel{def}{=} \{(i : x_j \leftarrow \tau), (i : IF \chi GOTO\, v), (i : HALT) : \\ i, v \in Lab,\ j \in \omega, \tau \text{ is a rigid term of type } d, \chi \in \mathsf{Form}_d \\ \text{is a quantifier-free formula, and } i \neq v\}.$$

A constant term i in a command standing on the left-hand side of ":" is called the *label of the command*. By a (deterministic) *program (of type d)* we understand a finite sequence $p \in (U_d)^*$ of commands in which no two members have the same label and there is exactly one halt command: the last command of p. Further, if $(i : IF\chi GOTO\, v)$ occurs in p then there is a command in p the label of which is v. If the restriction that a label can occur at most in one command is lifted then we obtain *nondeterministic* programs.

The set of all deterministic programs of type d is denoted by P_d.

(b) Let $p \in P_d$. We define functions $n(p)$, $k(p)$, $i_m(p)$, $u_m(p)$ of p. When using these functions, we almost always omit the arguments "(p)" and simply write n, k, $i_m u_m$ instead of $n(p)$ etc. We do this already in their definitions: $n(p) = n$, i_m, and u_m, for $m \leq n$, are defined by the equation $p = \langle (i_0 : u_0), \ldots, (i_n : u_n) \rangle$ (thus u_n is $HALT$).

$$k \stackrel{def}{=} min\{w \in \omega : (\forall v \geq w)(x_v \text{ does not occur in } p)\}.$$

The variable x_k (which does not occur in p) is called the *control variable* of p.

(c) Let $p = \langle (i_0 : u_0), \ldots, (i_n : u_n) \rangle \in P_d$. Let $\bar{x} = \langle x_0, \ldots, x_k \rangle$ and $\bar{c} = \langle c_0, \ldots, c_k \rangle$. $\bar{x} = \bar{c}$ abbreviates $\bigwedge \{x_i = c_i : i \leq k\}$.

We define a set $Ax(p) \subseteq \mathsf{F}^1_{\odot\bigcirc}$ of axioms as follows:

$$Ax(p) \stackrel{def}{=} \{(c_k = i_m \rightarrow \kappa(i_m, u_m, \bar{x}, \bar{c})) : m < n\} \cup \{\odot(c_k = i_0)\}$$

where: if $u_m =$ "$x_w \leftarrow \tau$" then

$$\kappa(i_m, u_m, \bar{x}, \bar{c}) \stackrel{def}{=} ((\bar{c} = \bar{x}) \rightarrow \bigcirc(c_k = i_{m+1} \wedge c_w = \tau(\bar{x}) \wedge \bigwedge\{c_j = x_j : j < k \text{ and } j \neq w\})),$$

if $u_m =$ "*IF*χ*GOTO* v" then

$$\kappa(i_m, u_m, \bar{x}, \bar{c}) \stackrel{def}{=} ((\bar{c} = \bar{x} \wedge \chi) \rightarrow \bigcirc(c_k = v \wedge \bigwedge\{c_j = x_j : j < k\})) \wedge ((\bar{c} = \bar{x} \wedge \neg\chi) \rightarrow \bigcirc(c_k = i_{m+1} \wedge \bigwedge\{c_j = x_j : j < k\})),$$

and if $u_m =$ "*HALT*" then

$$\kappa(i_m, u_m, \bar{x}, \bar{c}) \stackrel{def}{=} (\bar{c} = \bar{x} \rightarrow \bigcirc(\bar{c} = \bar{x})).$$

□

Remark

Throughout, we use the convention that whenever we discuss the provability of some property of a program p from a data theory Th, we always assume that Th postulates that all the terms occurring as labels in p are different. So, for example, let p be $\langle(0 : x \leftarrow 3), (1 : x \leftarrow x + 1), (2 : HALT)\rangle$. Then $\vdash [p]x = 4$ or equivalently $\emptyset \vdash [p]x = 4$ means $\{0 \neq 1 \neq 2 \neq 0\} \vdash [p]x = 4$. Similarly for $\models$ in place of $\vdash$. The only reason for this fairly ad hoc convention is to simplify our framework. Namely, the values of the control variable have to be labels, but for simplicity we use these labels as possible values of the functions we call *intensions*. For those readers who dislike the above ad hoc solution of the "labels as data" problem, we outline here our original formalism.

In the original version of NLP including its temporal logic (and intensional logic) versions, the classical logic counterparts (in the correspondence theoretic sense) denoted by $\langle \mathsf{F}^1 cl(\mathsf{Mod}), \mathsf{Mod}, \models^{cl}\rangle$ herein, were a five-sorted logic with models like $\mathcal{M} = \langle \mathbf{T}, \mathbf{D}, \mathbf{L}, I_D, I_L\rangle$, where $\mathbf{L} = \langle L, 0^L, s^L, \leq^L\rangle$ satisfies the usual *finite* axiomatization of $\langle, \omega, 0, succ, \leq \rangle$, cf. Andréka et.al [10]. Further, $D \cap L = \emptyset$, $I_D \subseteq {}^T D$, and $I_L \subseteq {}^T L$. Then the labels in a program were required to be elements of $Lab = \{0^L, s^L 0^L, s^L \ldots s^L 0^L, \ldots\} =$ variable-free terms of the language of $\mathbf{L}$. A trace of a program p was defined to be a pair $\langle a, b\rangle$ with $b \in I_L$, and $a \in {}^k(I_D)$ with k the number of variables occurring in p.

This approach completely eliminates the "labels as data" problem. The price we had to pay was that we had to drag along two extra sorts throughout our investigations. The ad hoc solution for the "labels as data" problem described above (and used throughout this chapter) was designed to create a situation where we have the same results as in the five-sorted (more systematic) formalism, but the whole machinery is considerably simpler. All our definitions, proofs, and results can easily be translated from the three-sorted formalism to the five-sorted one so that the ad hoc elements of our dealing with the "labels as data" problem disappears completely. □

Having introduced the set P_d of programs, let us turn to statements (e.g. pcas) about programs and their temporal provability.

By a pca of similarity type d we understand a new kind of formula $[p]\psi$, where $p \in P_d$ and $\psi \in \mathsf{Form}_d$. The more general-looking $\varphi \to [p]\psi$ where $\varphi, \psi \in \mathsf{Form}_d$ is also called a pca (we already explained why this is always reducible to a pca of the simpler $[p]\psi$ form). As was already mentioned, the Hoare-style notation for a pca $\varphi \to [p]\psi$ reads as $\{\varphi\}\ p\ \{\psi\}$. Occasionally we will use this notation too.

Definition 2.13

(a) Recall from items (in Section 2.2.3) that $\{\vdash_0, \vdash_1, \vdash_2, \vdash_3\} = \{\vdash_0, \vdash_{\odot\bigcirc S}, \vdash_{\odot\bigcirc SF}, \vdash_{\odot\bigcirc SFP}\}$ are the inference systems for the temporal logics extending the fragment $\mathsf{FT}_0 = \mathsf{FT}_{\odot\bigcirc}$ of FT.

For each temporal inference system $\vdash_i$ ($i \leq 3$), we will define the $\vdash_i$-definability of pcas. That is, for each $Th \subseteq \mathsf{Form}_d$ and pca $[p]\psi$, we will define what $Th \vdash_i [p]\psi$ means, for $i \leq 3$.

(b) Let $Th \cup (\varphi, \psi) \subseteq \mathsf{Form}_d$ and $p \in P_d$, and $i \leq 3$. Then

$$Th \vdash_i (\varphi \to [p]\psi) \text{ is defined to hold iff}$$
$$Th \cup Ax(p) \vdash_i (\exists \bar{x}(\varphi \wedge \odot\bar{c} = \bar{x} \wedge c_k = i_{HALT}) \to \exists \bar{x}(\bar{x} = \bar{c} \wedge \psi))$$

where $\bar{c} = \langle c_0 \ldots c_k \rangle$ with $k = k(p)$ exactly as in Definition 2.12(b) above.

(c) The same (as in (b)) applies for any other temporal inference system $\vdash$ (in place of $\vdash_i$) extending $\vdash_0$. (We need the condition that $\vdash$ extends $\vdash_0$ because the formulas $Ax(p)$ etc. involved in (b) are formulated in the language $\mathsf{F}^1_{\odot\bigcirc}$ of $\vdash_0$.) So we need this part, for (b) to make sense.

(d) We write $\vdash_i [p]\psi$ to denote $\emptyset \vdash_i \mathsf{TRUE} \to [p]\psi$. We might occasionally use the notation $\vdash_i \{\varphi\}\ p\ \{\psi\}$ for the same thing. Here $\vdash_i$ is a temporal inference system of course. □

An *invariance property* of a program $p \in P_d$ is a statement of the kind

$$\boxdot Ax(p) \to \boxdot(\text{“}at(\ell_i)\text{''} \to \psi(c))$$

for some arbitrary but fixed classical first order formula $\psi(x)$ and arbitrary but fixed label ℓ_i. It is an obvious generalization of the concept of a pca discussed above. Its temporal provability is defined completely analogously.

Recall that $Ax(p)$ was our set of temporal axioms expressing that the vector $\bar{c}$ of flexible constants $c_0, c_1, \ldots$ constitutes an execution sequence of our program p. $Ax(p)$ was expressed according to the following ideas.

Let p be a program with $\bar{x} = \langle x_0, \ldots, x_k \rangle$ its data variables (or its registers) and control variable. That is, a state of p in a data domain $\mathbf{D} = \langle D, \ldots \rangle$ is an evaluation $f : \{x_0, \ldots, x_k\} \longrightarrow D$ of $\bar{x}$ into $\mathbf{D}$. Then there is a classical first order formula $\pi(\bar{x}, \bar{x}')$ describing the state transition relation of p (π contains no modalities and no flexible symbols). Intuitively, $\pi(\bar{x}, \bar{x}')$ means that $\bar{x}$ is a possible state of p, and $\bar{x}'$ is a ***possible successor*** state of $\bar{x}$ in some execution of p. Further, $\pi(\bar{x}, \bar{x})$ means that $\bar{x}$ is a halting state of p. Now, $Ax(p)$ was defined to be $\forall \bar{x}(\pi(\bar{c}, \bar{x}) \to \bigcirc(\bar{c} = \bar{x}))$.

Clearly $Ax(p)$ is a temporal formula, and for any Kripke model $\mathcal{M}$, if $\mathcal{M} \models Ax(p)$ then $\mathcal{M} \models \boxdot Ax(p)$. Actually the intended meaning of $Ax(p)$ is $\boxdot Ax(p)$. The only reason for dropping $\boxdot$ was that this way we were expressing the same thing by using fewer modalities, permitting greater flexibility in applications.

Let $\vdash^*$ be a temporal logic (e.g. $\vdash^*$ can be $\vdash_{\odot\bigcirc S}$, $\vdash_{\odot\bigcirc SF}$ etc. introduced at the beginning of this chapter). Let $\varphi \to [p]\psi$ be a pca where $\pi(\bar{x}, \bar{x}')$ defines the state transition relation of p (as above). (Here φ and ψ are $\varphi(\bar{x})$ and $\psi(\bar{x})$, and they contain no modalities or flexible symbols.)

We say that $\varphi \to [p]\psi$ is $\vdash^*$-provable, in symbols $\vdash^* \varphi \to [p]\psi$, iff

$$\{Ax(p), \odot\varphi(\bar{c})\} \vdash^* \pi(\bar{c}, \bar{c}) \to \psi(\bar{c}). \tag{2.14}$$

In (2.14), $\varphi(\bar{c})$, $\psi(\bar{c})$, and $\pi(\bar{c}, \bar{c})$ can be formalized more carefully as $\exists x(\bar{x} = \bar{c} \wedge \varphi(\bar{x}))$ and the same for ψ or π.

Temporal provability of other program properties (e.g. invariance properties, termination, etc.) are defined analogously to (2.13)[5]. In passing we note the following. An important feature of (2.14) is that it uses no modality other than $\bigcirc$ and $\odot$. Therefore $\vdash^*$-provability of pcas makes sense in any fragment $\vdash^*$ of temporal logic containing $\bigcirc$ and $\odot$, even in $\vdash_0$ not containing any other modality (not even "plain sometime" $\diamondsuit$). This fragment $\vdash_0$ is interesting because it is equivalent to Floyd-Hoare logic w.r.t. provability of pcas (see Theorem 2.28). Availability of (2.14) in all fragments makes it possible to compare the pca-proving powers of these fragments.

Let us turn to concurrency. In this subsection we will concentrate on some basic concerns about the question; what kind of temporal logics are most suitable for representing and proving properties of concurrent processes? We will not go into the details of what kinds of concurrency we are dealing with, because this is not needed for addressing the general question about choosing an adequate temporal logic. The basic problem is that in reasoning about programs, the next-time modality $\bigcirc$ has proved to be immensely useful (as the references of this chapter illustrate). At ane point, there was an impression that concurrency could be better handled in temporal logic without $\bigcirc$. If this impression had proven to be right, then we would have faced a lot of new work for finding new completeness techniques of temporal logic without $\bigcirc$. (For

[5] In particular, for invariance properties the definition given in (2.14) becomes $\{Ax(p), \odot\varphi(\bar{c})\} \vdash^* \psi(\bar{c})$ (with exactly the same restrictions on φ, ψ as above, i.e. as in the pca case).

example, how would we prove all those things we used to prove by induction?) Fortunately, this is not the case, as will be outlined below.

For certain reasonings about concurrent situations, $\Box Ax(p)$ is too strong a description. If we are executing several processes $p_1, \ldots, p_\ell$ in a concurrent fashion which are *not* synchronized then the use of $\bigcirc$ in $\Box Ax(p_1)$ introduces an artificial synchronization. For this and related reasons we have to revise $Ax(p)$ and replace it with more subtle formalizations (of basically the same idea). Let p and π be as above. Then $Axinv(p)$ is the formula

$$(\forall \bar{x}, \bar{x}')(\bar{c} = \bar{x} \wedge \pi(\bar{x}, \bar{x}') \to \bigcirc(\bar{c} = \bar{x}' \vee \bar{c} = \bar{x})).$$

Now, $Axinv(p)$ differs from $Ax(p)$ in that it expresses that we do not know how long it takes to execute a transition step $\pi(\bar{x}, \bar{x}')$ of the program p, but as long as the step is not finished, we remain in the old state $\bar{x}$, and when it is finished we get into the new state $\bar{x}'$. The only thing that can go wrong with this formula is that it does not express that executing a step takes only a finite amount of time. (Actually if the process p has to wait for something then this finiteness condition may not even be true, but let us come back to this later.) Already, $Axinv(p)$ is strong enough to prove all invariance properties (in FT) that were provable from $Ax(p)$. That is, let $\vdash$ be a temporal logic containing at least $\odot$ and $\bigcirc$ and the induction rule (R3 in Section 2.2.3). (Actually we assume that $\vdash$ contains $\vdash_0$.) Let φ be an invariance property of p. Then

$$Ax(p) \vdash \varphi \qquad \text{iff} \qquad Axinv(p) \vdash \varphi.$$

This is what the "inv" part refers to in the abbreviation $Axinv$. In particular, we can prove the same pcas from $Axinv(p)$ as from $Ax(p)$. But we cannot prove eventualities like total correctness, termination, fairness etc. from $Axinv(p)$. To this end let $Axfair(p)$ be the formula

$$\forall \bar{x}(\pi(\bar{c}, \bar{x}) \to \Diamond \bar{c} = \bar{x}).$$

Now, from $Axinv(p) \wedge Axfair(p)$, the same program properties (invariance, eventualities, etc.) can be proved in FT as from $Ax(p)$. The advantage is that the new axioms do not imply any undesired synchronization and hence can be applied to concurrent situations more realistically. At the same time we can use the same axiomatizations of FT as before (see the beginning of this chapter and/or Abadi [2], Abadi & Manna [5]) and they will have basically the same proof theoretic powers for deriving the same program properties as they had with $Ax(p)$.

For some concurrent situations $Axfair(p)$ might be too strong. (For example, because it might be $Axfair(p)$ itself what we want to prove from some more basic assumptions. Or we might want to prove deadlock freedom (and then assuming $Axfair$ to start with is not quite fair).) We might have a temporal formula $Enabled(p_i)$ associated with each program p_i which expresses that the execution of p_i can proceed whenever $Enabled(p_i)$ is true. Then $Axfair^+(p)$ is the formula

$$\forall\bar{x}((\pi(\bar{c},\bar{x}) \wedge \Box\Diamond Enabled(p)) \rightarrow \Diamond\bar{c} = \bar{x})$$

Using the new $Axinv(p) \wedge Axfair^+(p)$, we can reason about concurrent situations quite realistically, without having to change our basic temporal logic $\vdash_{\odot\bigcirc SF}$ (or $\vdash_{\odot\bigcirc SFP}$).

Remark

If we do not need $Axfair^+$ but only $Axfair$ then the necessity of using all modalities of $\vdash_{\odot\bigcirc SF}$ to express $Axinv(p) \wedge Axfair(p)$ might seem a high price. Do we really need $\Diamond$ here? Let $Axfair^0$ be $\varphi\forall\bar{x}(\pi(\bar{c},\bar{x}) \rightarrow \Diamond\bar{c} = \bar{x})$. If $Ax^0(p)$ is $Axinv(p) \wedge Axfair^0(p)$, then we can write up $Ax^0(p)$ in $\vdash_{\odot\bigcirc S}$ already. For many purposes $Ax^0(p)$ might be just as good as $Ax(p)$ or $Axinv + Axfair$. Clearly the same invariance properties can be proved from $Ax^0(p)$ as from the rest (as was observed earlier), and it seems likely that this extends to total correctness and termination properties (we did not check this, though). We do not know how suitable $Ax^0(p)$ is (in comparison with $Ax(p)$ and $Axinv + Axfair$) for proving temporal properties of programs in general.

2.4 On special properties of programs

2.4.1 Comparing and characterizing program-verifying powers of temporal logics

For an arbitrary similarity type d, let PCA_d denote the set of all pcas of similarity type d, i.e.

$$\mathsf{PCA}_d \stackrel{def}{=} \{[p]\psi : p \in P_d \text{ and } \psi \in \mathsf{Form}_d\}.$$

Let $\vdash_i$ and $\vdash_j$ $(i,j \leq 3)$ be two inference systems for the temporal logics extending the fragment $\mathsf{FT}_0 = \mathsf{F}_{\odot\bigcirc}$ of FT. Recall from Definition 2.13 the concept of $\vdash_i$–provability $(i < 3)$ of pcas from data theories $Th \subseteq \mathsf{Form}_d$.

We say that $\vdash_i$ *has greater (or equal) program verifying power than* $\vdash_j$ (w.r.t. pcas), in symbols $\vdash_i \geq_\Box \vdash_j$ or $\vdash_j \leq_\Box \vdash_i$, if for every similarity type d, for every $Th \subseteq \mathsf{Form}_d$ and $\rho \in \mathsf{PCA}_d$, the following holds:

$$(Th \vdash_j \rho) \text{ implies } (Th \vdash_i \rho).$$

We say that $\vdash_i$ and $\vdash_j$ *have the same* (or *equal*) *program verifying power* (w.r.t. pcas), in symbols $\vdash_i \equiv_\Box \vdash_j$, if

$$\vdash_i \leq_\Box \vdash_j \leq_\Box \vdash_i .$$

We say that $\vdash_i$ ***has strictly greater program verifying power than*** $\vdash_j$, in symbols $\vdash_i >_\Box \vdash_j$ or $\vdash_j <_\Box \vdash_i$, if

$$(\vdash_i \geq_\Box \vdash_j \qquad \text{and} \qquad \vdash_i \not\equiv_\Box \vdash_j).$$

Distinguished program verification methods

Let $[p]\psi$ be a pca. Then,

- $[p]\psi$ is provable by ***Burstall's method*** (which is the same as the ***intermittent assertions method***), iff $\vdash_{\odot\bigcirc S} [p]\psi$.
- $[p]\psi$ is provable by ***Pnueli's method***, iff $\vdash_{\odot\bigcirc SF} [p]\psi$.
- $\vdash^{\mathbf{FH}} [p]\psi$ denotes the claim that the pca $[p]\psi$ is provable by the well known classical ***Floyd–Hoare method***. The Floyd–Hoare method $\vdash^{\mathbf{FH}}$ is an inference system designed for proving pcas, i.e. statements of the form $\varphi \to [p]\psi$. $\vdash^{\mathbf{FH}}$ is of a style different from Burstall's or Pnueli's methods (which will be briefly referred to as $\vdash_{\odot\bigcirc S} [p]\psi$ and $\vdash_{\odot\bigcirc SF} [p]\psi$) in the following sense. $\vdash^{\mathbf{FH}}$ is based solely on classical one-sorted first- order logic. That is, $\vdash^{\mathbf{FH}}$ makes no use of modal logic or nonclassical logic of any kind. $\vdash^{\mathbf{FH}}$ works inside the classical one–sorted logic $\langle \mathsf{Form}_d, \{\mathbf{D} : \mathbf{D}$ is a "data domain" of type $d\}, \models\rangle$. The definition of $\vdash^{\mathbf{FH}}$ goes back to Naur, moreover, Alan Turing himself used it. $\vdash^{\mathbf{FH}}$ is the same as what is sometimes called ***invariant assertions method*** and sometimes ***Hoare logic***. We do not recall $\vdash^{\mathbf{FH}}$ here because it is well covered in the literature, see, e.g. Manna [60], Gergely & Szőts [39], González & Artalejo [43], [13], Csirmaz [30], [88], Makowsky & Sain [59].

The above definitions of Burstall's, Pnueli's and Floyd–Hoare methods are naturally extended to the derivability of a pca from a data theory (or, equivalently, a data type specification) Th. For example,

$$Th \vdash^{\mathbf{FH}} (\varphi \to [p]\psi) \text{ or equivalently } Th \vdash^{\mathbf{FH}} \{\varphi\}p\{\psi\}$$

is defined the natural way (see the above references for details, which are pretty obvious though).

In accordance with what we said earlier, the relations $\equiv_\Box$, $\leq_\Box$, $<_\Box$ are applicable to the formal system (or program verification method) $\vdash^{\mathbf{FH}}$ too, E.g. $\vdash^{\mathbf{FH}} \equiv_\Box \vdash_i$ means that for any pca $[p]\psi$ we have

$$\vdash^{\mathbf{FH}} [p]\psi \qquad \text{iff} \qquad \vdash_i [p]\psi.$$

It is important to note that this is equivalent to saying that for any d, any $Th \cup \{\psi\} \subseteq \mathsf{Form}_d$, any $p \in P_d$ we have $\vdash^{\mathbf{FH}} [p]\psi$ iff $\vdash_i [p]\psi$.

Although $\vdash^{\mathbf{FH}}$ has nothing in common with nonclassical (e.g. modal) logics, Burstall [25] has already raised the problem of matching $\vdash^{\mathbf{FH}}$ up with modal and temporal logics of programs. As far as we know, Theorem 2.28 is the first definitive answer in this direction (though informal conjectures such as $\vdash^{FH}$ is equivalent to "*always*" logic but not with "*sometime*" logic, have appeared already in Manna & Waldinger [64]).

Theorem 2.28 (Sain) $\vdash^{FH} \equiv_{\Box} \vdash_0$.

That is, exactly those pcas are provable by the Floyd-Hoare method which are provable by the weak temporal logic $\vdash_0$. This result extends to non-deterministic programs, too.
For a proof see [16], p. 129. □

One of the uses of the relation (between proof systems) $\equiv_{\Box}$ defined above is in formulating ***characterization theorems*** for distinguished, well known program verification methods. The purpose of such a theorem is to characterize the proof theoretic power of the method in question in terms of clear, well understood mathematical concepts. For more intuitive motivation see e.g. [92], [16], [84].

Recall the definitions of *Ind* and *Tord* from Definition 2.7, Section 2.2.3. Our first group of characterizations of program-verifying powers first, the Csirmaz (1981) (vastly improving on a result of Andréka & Németi (1977), the second two from Sain (1981–82)) is as follows.

Theorem 2.29

$$\vdash^{FH} \quad \equiv_{\Box} \quad Ind^{qf}$$
$$\vdash_{\odot\bigcirc S} \quad \equiv_{\Box} \quad Ind$$
$$\vdash_{\odot\bigcirc SF} \quad \equiv_{\Box} \quad (Ind + Tord) \equiv_{\Box} \vdash_{\odot\bigcirc SFP} = \vdash_{FT}.$$

The proofs of these statements can be found in [92]. Concerning the proof and history of the first statement, see also Andréka et al. [16], p. 127. □

Corollary 2.2

$\vdash_{\odot\bigcirc SF} \equiv_{\Box} (\vdash_{\odot\bigcirc SFP}$ *expanded with "until"* and "*since*". □

Corollary 2.2 can be even further generalized to obtain $\vdash_{\odot\bigcirc SF} \equiv_{\Box}$ ANY, where ANY is temporal logic with modalities based on discrete linear ordering on time and containing $\vdash_{\odot\bigcirc SF}$. This follows from the fact that by having the *Tord* axiom in Theorem 2.29, one can describe all possible temporal modalities based on discrete linear ordering of time. As was mentioned earlier, from the point of view of proving invariance properties of programs, $\vdash_{\odot\bigcirc S}$ and $\vdash_{\odot\bigcirc SF}$ are the same as the established program verification methods known as intermittent assertions method (IAM) (or sometime method or Burstall's method) and Pnueli's temporal method respectively. (Recall that pcas are special invariance properties.) However, if we want to extend this remark (defining IAM as $\vdash_{\odot\bigcirc S}$ etc.) to provability of *total correctness, termination* or ***eventualities*** in general, then something has to be added. Namely, IAM and Pnueli's method for eventualities (hence for termination too) are "$Dia_g \vdash_{\odot\bigcirc S}$" and "$Dia_g \vdash_{\odot\bigcirc SF}$" respectively, where Dia_g is an induction principle on data (as opposed to time), explained more carefully in Section 2.4.2.

Already, from the point of view of proving ***deterministic pcas*** only, Floyd–Hoare method is strictly weaker than $\vdash_{\odot\bigcirc S}$ which is strictly weaker than $\vdash_{\odot\bigcirc SF} \equiv_{\Box} \vdash_{\odot\bigcirc SFP}$ which in turn is strictly weaker than some new methods to be introduced and discussed later. In symbols, we have the following theorem.

Theorem 2.30 $\vdash^{\mathrm{FH}}, <_{\Box}\vdash_{\odot\bigcirc S}, <_{\Box}\vdash_{\odot\bigcirc SF} \equiv_{\Box}\vdash_{FT} <_{\Box}$ (*certain new methods*) where, e.g., $\vdash^{\mathrm{FH}} <_{\Box}\vdash_{\odot\bigcirc S}$ means that strictly more deterministic pcas are provable by $\vdash_{\odot\bigcirc S}$ than by $\vdash^{\mathrm{FH}}$.
For the proof and more careful formulation of the third inequality the reader is referred to Theorem 2.34. The remaining (first two) inequalities follow from theorems in [92] or [85]. The $\Box$ part was stated in Theorem 2.29. $\Box$

As we have already seen that the symbols $\equiv_{\Box}$, $\leq_{\Box}$, and $<_{\Box}$ are naturally applicable between $\vdash^{\mathrm{FH}}$ and the $\vdash_i$s, let us now notice that they are applicable between ***any*** formalisms $\vdash_u$ and $\vdash_w$ which are suitable for proving pcas. So Harel's axiomatization of dynamic logic [45] or any other logic of programs can take the place of $\vdash_i$ in $\vdash_u \equiv_{\Box} \vdash_w$ or $\vdash_u <_{\Box} \vdash_w$. (We note that, unless otherwise specified, $\Box$ and $<_{\Box}$ are defined with our attention restricted to deterministic programs.) We note that such comparisons of proof theoretic powers of different kinds of formalisms from the point of view of provability of special kinds of formulas (in our present case these constitute PCA_d but later we will look at the same with, for example, total correctness assertions in place of PCA_d) are well known in logic. Examples are the equiconsistency investigations in set theory or many of the investigations in Tarski & Givant [100].

In connection with the differences in proof theoretic (or program verifying) power discussed so far, the following question of practical relevance arises:

What happens if the data domain **D** is rich enough to encode finite sequences with single elements? More precisely, what we assume is that the data theory (or specification) forces the data domain to be such. Examples for such "rich" data theories are Peano's arithmetic, the specification of LISP and finite (or arbitrary) set theory with or without urelements. The answer to this question is that if the data theory ensures codability of finite sequences then Floyd–Hoare method $\vdash^{\mathrm{FH}}$ becomes as strong as Pnueli's $\vdash_{\odot\bigcirc SFP}$ which in turn remains still strictly weaker than the new methods mentioned above.

Theorem 2.31

$$\left(\vdash^{\mathrm{FH}} \Box \vdash_{\odot\bigcirc S} \Box \vdash_{\odot\bigcirc SFP} <_{\Box} (\textit{certain new methods})\right) \Big/ \begin{array}{c}\textit{modulo Peano's}\\ \textit{arithmetic}\\ \textit{for data}\end{array}$$

This theorem is proved in detail in Sain [85], but the equivalences follow from Andréka & Németi [8], [9] or [16], while the inequality follows from Theorem 2.34. □

Theorem 5.1 (iv) of Sain [86], p. 312 contains more information on the "$<_{\Box}$ (*certain new methods*)" part above, and Theorem 5.1 (vi) in the same paper is the *total correctness* version of the above theorem.

At this point a further characterization result can be presented. Namely let $\vdash^{\text{HAREL}}$ be the inference system of (standard) dynamic logic as presented in Harel [45] and also in Def. 10 on p. 493 of Sain [80].

Theorem 2.32

$$\left(\vdash^{\text{HAREL}} \equiv_{\Box} \textit{(Ind+Peano's arithmetic for time)}\right) \Big/ \begin{array}{c}\textit{modulo Peano's}\\ \textit{arithmetic}\\ \textit{for data}\end{array}$$

This follows from two theorems of Harel and Sain, see [45], Thm. 5, p. 496 and [86], Thm. 5.1(v), p. 312. Actually Thm.5 of [86] gives a more general characterization of $\vdash^{\text{HAREL}}$ too, namely w.r.t. all statements of programs expressible in standard dynamic logic. Instead of recalling that characterization in full detail, we mention that it uses, besides $(Ind + Tord)$, a restricted form of Ex defined in Section 2.4.2 below, together with three-sorted induction on data Dia_g (i.e. the same as Ind but for $\mathbf{D}$ instead of $\mathbf{T}$) which is sometimes called "structural induction". We note that full Ex would be too strong. □

Motivated by the above results, Gergely and Úry raised the question ([40]) whether $(\vdash^{\text{FH}} \equiv_{\Box} \vdash_{FT})/(\ldots)$ remains true if Peano's arithmetic on data is replaced with some weaker data theory. In particular, they suggested linear ordering of data (and for the case when this would not be sufficient they suggested adding Dia_g (see Section 2.4.2) too, in order to be able to recover the fullest possible power of the so called method of well founded relation). The answer is Theorem 2.33.

Theorem 2.33 (Andréka [6])

$$\left(\vdash^{\text{FH}} <_{\Box} \vdash_{\odot\bigcirc S}\right) \Big/ \textit{(modulo linear ordering on data} + Dia_g\textit{)}.$$

The proof is that of the main result of [6]. □

We conjecture that the methods in Sain [92] can be refined to generalize Theorem 2.33 to

$$\left(\vdash_{\odot\bigcirc S} <_{\Box} \vdash_{\odot\bigcirc SF}\right) \Big/ \textit{(modulo linear ordering on data)}.$$

2.4.2 Quantifying over flexible variables

In temporal logic it is not absurd to introduce new variables y_i $(i \in \omega)$ ranging over the domain $I \subseteq {}^T D$ of individuals changing in time. Consider for example the sentence "There is a quantity y_0 which changes whenever the temperature does but this y_0 is always greater than 100." This translates to a formula of the form $\exists y_0 \varphi$. We have to distinguish the new flexible variables y_i $(i \in \omega)$ from our rigid variables x_i $(i \in \omega)$. We obtain an extended language F^2_d where $\mathsf{F}^1_d \subseteq \mathsf{F}^2_d$, and the y_is may occur in F^2_d exactly as the c_is may in F^1_d. Actually, F^2_d is obtained from F^1_d by replacing C with $C \cup \{y_i : i \in \omega\}$, and then adding $\varphi \in \mathsf{F}^2_d \Longrightarrow \exists y_i \varphi \in \mathsf{F}^2_d$ if $i \in \omega$. F^2_d is the smallest set with this property. The Kripke models of F^2_d are classical three-sorted structures $\mathcal{M} = \langle \mathbf{T}, \mathbf{D}, I, f_i \rangle_{i \in \omega}$, where $\langle \mathbf{T}, \mathbf{D}, f_i \rangle_{i \in \omega} \in \mathsf{Mod}_d$, and I is a set of functions mapping T into D, i.e. $I \subseteq {}^T D$. Usually $\{f_i : i \in \omega\} \subseteq I$ is assumed. So the flexible constants c_i denote elements of the universe I. Let us denote this extended temporal logic permitting quantification over flexible variables y_i with

$$\mathsf{FT}^2 = \langle \mathsf{F}^2_d, \{\langle \mathbf{T}, \mathbf{D}, I, f_i \rangle_{i \in \omega} : \ldots\}, \models \rangle .$$

In the early papers by Sain [76], [77] and Andréka et al. this generalized temporal logic was called "intensional logic", the reason for which is indicated in Janssen [48].

In the framework of this extended temporal logic more programs can be proved correct than in the ones without flexible quantification. If we apply correspondence theory to this extended temporal logic FT^2, we obtain a classical three-sorted logic suitable for reasoning about programs (among other dynamical phenomena) called nonstandard logics of programs (NLP) in the literature, cf. Andréka et al. and Sain [13], [15], [16], [84], [86], [87] etc.

Using NLP, i.e. the extended temporal logic FT^2, it is easy to construct program verification methods strictly stronger than Pnueli's temporal logics of programs. Some of these strong methods have been defined in terms of temporal logics like FT^2 (see Andréka et al. [15], [16]). An example for a program, the partial correctness of which is provable by such a strong method but ***not provable by Pnueli's method***, is: a program verifier for LISP programs. A more mundane example is a proof checker for theorems about LISP or about Peano's arithmetic. Some of these new methods remain strictly stronger than Pnueli's one ***even if the data theory ensures codability of finite sequences*** (e.g. if it contains Peano's arithmetic).

In more detail, $(Ind + Tpa + Ex)$ is a set of axioms in the three-sorted classical first-order language of NLP (i.e. of $\langle \mathbf{T}, \mathbf{D}, I, f_i \rangle_{i \in \omega}$ discussed above). Ex, "existence axioms", postulates the existence of those elements of I which are definable by first-order three-sorted formulas. In traditional logic Ex is usually called a ***comprehension schema***, see [18], §D.4.5 (p. 937). More concretely, if $\mathcal{M} = \langle \mathbf{T}, \mathbf{D}, I, f_i \rangle_{i \in \omega}$ with $I \subseteq {}^T D$ being a third sort of $\mathcal{M}$, and $\varphi(z, x)$ is a formula (in the first-order language of $\mathcal{M}$) with $\mathcal{M} \models (\varphi \forall t \in T)(\exists x \in D)\varphi(t, x)$

then Ex postulates the existence of a $y \in I$ with $\mathcal{M} \models (\varphi \forall t \in T)\varphi(t, y(t))$. Further, let us recall from Definition 2.11 that Tpa abbreviates "Peano's axioms for the time scale $\mathbf{T}$ expanded with $+$ and $\times$". (Note that "Peano's axioms for the data domain $\mathbf{D}$", in short "Peano's arithmetic for data", is disjoint from Tpa since it speaks about a different sort of $\mathcal{M}$.)

Theorem 2.34 (Sain 1983a)

(a) $\vdash_{\odot\bigcirc SFP} <_{\square} (Ind + Tpa) <_{\square} (Ind + Tpa + Ex)$, and

(b) $((Ind + Tpa) <_{\square} (Ind + Tpa + Ex)) \Big/$ *modulo Peano's arithmetic for data* □

One concludes that $(Ind{+}Tpa{+}Ex)$ is strictly stronger than the strongest proof system T_2 studied in Abadi [1], [2], [3], Abadi & Manna [5], Manna & Pnueli [62] etc. because theorems therein state that $\vdash_{T_2} \leq_{\square} (Ind + Tpa)$. (This fact, however, entails *no* kind of value judgement one way or other.)

Actually we have a strictly increasing infinite hierarchy of methods between $\vdash_{\odot\bigcirc SFP}$ and $(Ind + Ex)$ (even *modulo Peano's arithmetic for data!*).

Theorem 2.35 (Sain 1983)

$$\vdash_{\odot\bigcirc SFP} <_{\square} (Ind + \Sigma_1 Ex) <_{\square} \ldots <_{\square} (Ind + \Sigma_n Ex) <_{\square} \ldots <_{\square} (Ind + Ex)$$

where $\Sigma_n Ex$ postulates Ex only for those formulas $\varphi(t, x)$ in which the prenex complexity of quantifiers over sort I is at most Σ_n. This statement holds "modulo Peano's arithmetic for data" too. Further, it remains valid if we add Tpa to every axiom system in it (besides *Peano's arithmetic for data*). □

A proof is given in Sain [85], but for completeness we note that the proof of Theorem 2.34 can be refined (using ideas in Remark 8.7 of [16]) to prove this theorem; further, another outline of the proof is available in Hájek [44].

Remark

The literature often considers I as a second-order sort, and then $\Sigma_n Ex$ is called Σ_1^n-comprehension, see [18], p. 937.

Theorems 2.34 and 2.35 above can be used to conclude that:

> Adding flexible variables (y_i, $i \in \omega$, see in Section 2.2.3) to temporal logic ($\vdash_{\odot\bigcirc SF}$ or $\vdash_{\odot\bigcirc SFP}$) increases its proof theoretic power profoundly (if the axioms Ex are postulated for these new variables).

More material on the subject of this section is found in Biró & Sain [23], [86], §5, [85], Hájek [44] and Gergely & Úry [40].

Until now we have characterized and compared formal systems w.r.t. pcas. One can treat provability of eventualities (like total correctness assertions) in NLP, as well as other kinds of statements about programs, see e.g. Sain [86], [80], [91]. The following result is an illustration for this.

First we note that, when used for proving eventualities, the intermittent assertions method as well as Pnueli's method are understood to be extended with a ***structural induction*** principle Dia_g acting on the ***data*** domain. The following theorem is formulated with this implicit understanding. This will be discussed in more detail later in this section.

Theorem 2.36 (Sain 1983a, 1987) From the point of view of *total correctness* assertions, intermittent assertions method is strictly weaker than Pnueli's method. But the difference between the powers of these two methods disappears if we assume that the data theory ensures codability of finite sequences (e.g. if it contains Peano's arithmetic).

The equivalence part of this theorem is proved in Sain [86]. The inequivalence part follows from the Sain's proof of Thm. 2.3. To see this, one can check that provability from the stronger system considered in that theorem there implies provability by Pnueli's method in that special concrete case which was used there for establishing inequivalence. □

A characterization of the IAM from the point of view of total correctness assertions (tcas) is given in Theorems 2.7 and 4.2.4 of Sain [86] under the assumption that the data theory (or equivalently specification) contains Peano's axioms (postulated for the data sort, of course). See also p. 286, lines 16–17 of [86]. It seems likely that the condition that the data theory has to contain Peano's arithmetic can be eliminated from Sain's characterization if we change the frame of characterization slightly. Namely, the assertion "the program p terminates" was represented (in the formalism of NLP) by Sain by saying that "p has an execution sequence which terminates". If instead, we use the statement saying "every execution sequence of p terminates", we get a slightly different representation of tcas. We conjecture that under this new representation the characterizations in Sain can be improved.

In Sain, the key device for handling total correctness and termination is the three-sorted *structural* induction Dia_g formulated in the language of NLP as well as in first-order temporal logic with flexible variables. Here, *Dia* abbreviates Data induction axioms, while g is that part of d which plays the rôle of $\{0, succ\}$ in number theoretic induction. (This axiom scheme also appears in Manna & Pnueli [61].) The school represented by Abadi & Manna [5] and Abadi [1], [2], [3] studies the same subject we do in Section 2.4, namely (comparison and characterization of) the proof theoretic powers of various temporal logics. However, exactly as we did in Section 2.2, they concentrate on provability of arbitrary temporal formulas as opposed to that of special kinds of program properties such as pcas, tcas, etc. One might think that this general kind of investigation renders studies of provabilities of special program properties such as the subject of this section superfluous, since tcas are special temporal formulas. Actually, this view seems to be implied in [2], §8, see also [1], pp. 123, 129. However, putting the results in [1], [2], [3] together with those in Sain [86], apparently disproves this view the following way. By [1], [2], [3], all the temporal inference systems in [1], [2], [3], [5] are sound for the semantics "$(Ind{+}Tpa) \models$". However, by Sain, no inference system sound for $(Ind{+}Tpa)$ can prove nontrivial tcas (more concretely, $(Ind{+}Tpa)$ in itself does not imply any nontrivial tca). The reasons for this are basically the same as the ones explained in the celebrated historical Kfoury & Park paper [53]. The modification in Sain of the earlier argument is the following: Kfoury and Park conclude that termination is an essentially higher-order property. [86] shows that this higher-orderness can be eliminated by using the nonstandard second-order sort I thus making a higher-order property first-order (but many-sorted) (The idea of course comes from Henkin's historical nonstandard higher-order logic.) A key step is that we have to postulate structural induction Dia_g for all sorts (especially for the nonstandard second-order one I). These considerations (together with the further subtleties discovered in Sain [86]) based on the classical Kfoury & Park ideas point in the direction that the investigations in [1], [2], [3], [5] cannot replace (or generalize) the ones initiated and pursued in [86], [78], Luezas et al. 1985, [80]. The above observations do *not* diminish the importance of the research direction advocated in the quoted works of Abadi and Manna, namely the direction reported and pursued in Section 2.2.

Many works in computer science logics, when dealing with proving eventualities, emphasize the ***principle of well founded orderings***, see e.g. §III.10 of Kröger [55] or the total correctness section of Gergely & Úry [40]. Well founded relations are only one of the many equivalent tools for providing induction, as it is well known, cf. e.g. Cohn [29]. The point here, as well as in the quoted literature, is that we use ***induction on data*** (structural induction) as opposed to ***induction on time*** (computational induction). (The former is important for proving eventualities, the latter for invariance properties.) Therefore this principle of well founded relations (on data!) is the same as Dia_g discussed above, introduced in the 1979 version of Andréka et al. [13] for computer science first-order temporal logic to treat eventualities. (Therein the notation DIA was used for Dia_g.) Therefore Theorem 2.36 as well as the other results in Sain [78], [86] apply to the well founded framework in Kröger [55] and to any other form of induction on the data domain. See also Theorem 2.33 and the remarks preceding it, in this connection.

Theorem 2.37 $\vdash_{\odot\bigcirc SFP}$ is complete and sound for $Mdcl(Ind + Tord)$ from the point of view of provability of all properties of deterministic programs.

This is not true for $\vdash_{\odot\bigcirc SF}$ in place of $\vdash_{\odot\bigcirc SFP}$.

Proof: Available from the authors, but see also Sain [92]. □

Certain important aspects of temporal logic were onitted from this chapter (for lack of space) for these see e.g. van Benthem [22] and Venema [102]. Also, while Theo Janssen's work on model theoretic semantics of natural languages was mentioned, the important convergence phenomenon between dynamic logic (e.g. as conceived in Sain [80] and Pratt [74]) coming from computer science and its applications in semantics and natural languages, see e.g. van Benthem [21] was left out almost completely.

Acknowledgement

We are indebted to Andrzej Szalas for asking us to write this chapter, and for his insisting that we really complete it.

Thanks are due to Yde Venema for his helpful suggestions concerning mathematical techniques in temporal logics.

References

[1] Abadi, M. 1987. The power of temporal proofs. *Proceedings of the Second Annual IEEE Symposium on Logic in Computer Science*, 123–30.

[2] Abadi, M. 1989. The power of temporal proofs. *Theoretical Computer Science* **64**, 35–84.

[3] Abadi, M. 1987. *Temporal-logic theorem proving*. Dissertation, Department of Computer Science, Stanford University.

[4] Abadi, M. 1990. Errata for "The power of temporal proofs" *Theoretical Computer Science* **70**, 275.

[5] Abadi, M. & Z. Manna 1986. A timely resolution. In *First Annual Symposium on Logic in Computer Science*, 176–89.

[6] Andréka, H. 1980. Sharpening the characterization of the power of Floyd's method. *Lecture Notes in Computer Science* **148**, 1–26.

[7] Andréka, H., K. Balogh, K. Lábadi, I. Németi & P. Tóth 1974. Plans to improve our program verifier program (in Hungarian). Working paper, NIM IGÚSZI, Department of Software Techniques.

[8] Andréka, H. & I. Németi 1977. *Completeness of Floyd method w.r.t. nonstandard time models*. Seminar Notes, Mathematical Institute of the Hungarian Academy of Sciences, Budapest. Abstracted in [9].

[9] Andréka, H. & I. Németi 1978. Completeness of Floyd logic. *Bulletin of Section of Logic (Wrocław)* **7**(3), 115–21.

[10] Andréka, H., I. Németi & I. Sain 1978. *On the completeness of Floyd-Hoare logic* Preprint, Mathematical Institute of the Hungarian Academy of Sciences, Budapest.

[11] Andréka, H., I. Németi & I. Sain 1979. Completeness problems in verification of programs and program schemes. *Lecture Notes in Computer Science* **74**, 208–18.

[12] Andréka, H., I. Németi & I. Sain 1979. Henkin-type semantics for program schemes to turn negative results to positive. In *Fundamentals of Computation Theory'79*, L. Budach (ed), 18-24. Berlin: Akademie Verlag.

[13] Andréka, H., I. Németi & I. Sain 1982. A complete logic for reasoning about programs via nonstandard model theory, Parts I-II. *Theoretical Computer Science* **17**(2), 193–212 and **17**(3), 259–278.

[14] Andréka, H., I. Németi & I. Sain 1984. *Abstract model theoretic approach to algebraic logic*. Manuscript.

[15] Andréka, H., I. Németi & I. Sain 1989. On the strength of temporal proofs (extended abstract). *Lecture Notes in Computer Science* **379**, 135–44. Full paper appeared as [16].

[16] Andréka, H., I. Németi & I. Sain 1980. On the strength of temporal proofs. *Theoretical Computer Science* **80**, 125–51.

[17] Andréka, H. & I. Sain 1981. Connections between algebraic logic and initial algebra semantics of CF languages. In *Mathematical Logic in Computer Science* **26**, 25-83. Amsterdam: North-Holland.

[18] Barwise, J. 1977. *Handbook of mathematical logic*. Amsterdam: North Holland.

[19] Van Benthem, J. F. 1984. Correspondence theory. In *Handbook of philosophical logic*, D. Gabbay & F. Guenthner (eds), 167–247. Dordrecht: Reidel.

[20] Van Benthem, J. F. 1986. *Modal logics and classical logic*. Napoli: Bibliopolis.

[21] Van Benthem, J. F. 1990. *General dynamics.* ITLI report no. LP–90–11.

[22] Van Benthem, J. F. 1991. Temporal logic. In *Handbook of logic in artificial intelligence and logic programming* **3**, D. Gabbay, Cht. Hogger, J. Robinson (eds). Oxford: Oxford University Press.

[23] Biró, B. & I. Sain 1984. Peano arithmetic for the time scale of non-standard models for logics of programs. *Annals of pure and applied logic* (forthcoming), Mathematical Institute of the Hungarian Academy of Science, Budapest.

[24] Burgess, J. 1984. Basic tense logic. In *Handbook of philosophical logic*, D. Gabbay & F. Guenthner (eds), 89–133. Dordrecht: Reidel.

[25] Burstall, R. M. 1974. Program proving as hand simulation with a little induction. IFIP Congress, Stockholm.

[26] Church, A. 1956. *Introduction to mathematical logic.* Princeton, New Jersey: Princeton University Press.

[27] Cartwright, R. & J. McCarthy 1979. First order programming logic. In *Proceedings of the 6th Annual ACM Symposium on Principles of Programming Languages*, 68–80.

[28] Chang, C. C. & H. J. Keisler 1973. *Model theory.* Amsterdam: North-Holland.

[29] Cohn, P. M. 1965. *Universal algebra.* New York: Harper & Row.

[30] Csirmaz, L. 1981. Programs and program verification in a general setting. *Theoretical Computer Science* **16**, 199–210.

[31] Csirmaz, L. 1985. A completeness theorem for dynamic logic. *Notre Dame Journal of Formal Logic* **26**(1), 51–60.

[32] Csirmaz, L. 1990. *Induction and Peano models.* DIMACS Technical Report 90–28. Department of Computer Science, Rutgers University.

[33] Csirmaz, L. & J. Paris 1984. A property of 2-sorted Peano models and program verification. *Zeitschrift für Mathematik Logic und Grundlagen der Mathematik* **30**, 324–34.

[34] Gabbay, D. M. 1976. *Investigations in modal and tense logics.* Dordrecht: Reidel.

[35] Gabbay, D. M. 1981. An irreflexivity lemma with applications to axiomatisations of conditions in linear frames. In *Aspects of philosophical logic*, U. Mönnich (ed), 67–89. Dordrecht: Reidel.

[36] Gabbay, D. & F. Guenthner 1984. ***Handbook of philosophical logic***, vol. II. Dordrecht: Reidel.

[37] Gabbay, D. et al. 1980. On the temporal analysis of fairness. In ***Proceedings of the 7th Annual ACM Symposium on Principles of Programming Languages.***

[38] Garson, J. W. 1984. Quantification in modal logic. In ***Handbook of philosophical logic***, D. Gabbay & F. Guenthner (eds), 249–307. Dordrecht: Reidel.

[39] Gergely, T. & M. Szőts 1979. Model theoretic investigations in programming theory. *Acta Cybernetica* **4**, 45–57.

[40] Gergely, T. & L. Úry 1991. ***First-order programming theories.*** SZÁMALK Technical Report, Budapest.

[41] Goldblatt, R. 1991. Metamathematics of modal logic. ***Reports on Mathematical Logic*** **6**, 4–77; 21–52.

[42] Goldblatt, R. 1987. ***Logics of time and computation.*** Center for the Study of Language and Information.

[43] González, T. H. & M. R. Artalejo 1989. A nonstandard completeness theorem. ***Theoretical Computer Science*** **68**, 277–302.

[44] Hájek, P. 1986. Some conservativeness results for nonstandard dynamic logic. In ***Algebra, combinatorics, and logic in computer science, Colloq. Math. Soc. J. Bolyai*** **42**, 443–9. Amsterdam: North Holland.

[45] Harel, D. 1979. First-order dynamic logic. ***Lecture Notes in Computer Science*** **68**.

[46] Henkin, L., J. D. Monk & A. Tarski 1985. ***Cylindric algebras***, part II. Amsterdam: North-Holland.

[47] Hughes, G. E. & M. J. Cresswell 1984. ***A companion to modal logic.*** London: Methuen.

[48] Janssen, T. M. V. 1983. ***Foundations and applications of Montague grammar.*** Dissertation, Mathematisch Centrum, Amsterdam.

[49] Jónsson, B. 1991. The theory of binary relations. ***Algebraic logic, Colloq. Math. Soc. J. Bolyai*** **56**, 245–92. Amsterdam: North Holland.

[50] Jónsson, B. & A. Tarski 1948. ***Boolean algebras with operators.*** American Mathematical Society Bulletin 54, 79–80.

[51] Jónsson B. & Tarski, A. 1952. ***Boolean Algebras with Operators Parts I and II*** (Full version of [50]) American Journal of Mathematis **73** 1951, 891–939; **74** 1952, 127–162.

[52] Kamp, J.A.W. 1971. Formal properties of "now". *Theoria* **37**, 227–73.

[53] Kfoury, D.J. & D.M.R. Park 1975. On the termination of program schemes. *Information and Control* **29**, 243–51.

[54] Krajíček, J. 1989. Personal communication.

[55] Kröger, F. 1988. *Temporal logic of programs* Berlin: Springer.

[56] Leivant, D. 1985. Logical and mathematical reasoning about imperative programs. In *Proceedings of the 12th Annual ACM Symposium on Principles of Programming Languages*, 132–40. New Orleans.

[57] Lichtenstein, O., A. Pnueli & L. Zuck 1985. The glory of the past. *Lecture Notes in Computer Science* **193**, 196–218.

[58] Luezas, A.G., T.H. Gonzalez, M.R. Artalejo 1989. *Standard versus nonstandard semantics in logics for functional programs.* Preprint, Dept. Informatica y Automatica, University Complutense, Madrid.

[59] Makowsky, J. A. & I. Sain 1989. Weak second order characterizations of various program verification systems. *Theoretical Computer Science* **66**, 299–321.

[60] Manna, Z. 1974. *Mathematical theory of computation*, New York: McGraw Hill.

[61] Z. Manna, Z. & A. Pnueli 1979. The modal logic of programs. *Lecture Notes in Computer Science* **71**, 385–409.

[62] Manna, Z. & A. Pnueli 1983. *Verification of concurrent programs: a temporal proof system.* Report No. STAN-CS-83–967, Department of Computer Science, Stanford University.

[63] Manna, Z. & A. Pnueli 1987. *A hierarchy of temporal properties.* Technical Report STAN-CS-87–1186, Department of Computer Science, Stanford University.

[64] Manna, Z. & R. Waldinger 1978. Is "sometime" sometimes better than "always"? *Communications of the ACM*, **21**, 159–72.

[65] Németi, I. 1982. Nonstandard dynamic logic. *Lecture Notes in Computer Science* **131**, 311–48.

[66] Parikh, R. 1978. A decidability result for second order process logic. In *IEEE Symposium on Foundation of Computer Science*, 177–83.

[67] Pasztor, A. 1986. Non-standard algorithmic and dynamic logic. *Journal of Symbolic Computation* **2**, 59–81.

[68] Pasztor, A. 1991. Recursive programs and denotational semantics in absolute logics of programs. *Theoretical Computer Science* **70**, 127-50.

[69] Pasztor, A. 1991. An infinite hierarchy of program verification methods. In *Many sorted logic and its applications*, J.Tucker & K.Meinke (eds), 315-42. New York: John Wiley.

[70] Pasztor, A. & I. Sain 1990. A streamlined temporal completeness theorem. *Lecture Notes in Computer Science* **440**.

[71] Pnueli, A. 1981. The temporal semantics of concurrent programs. *Theoretical Computer Science* **13**, 45–60.

[72] Pnueli, A. 1981. *The temporal logic of programs* Preprint. Weizman Institute of Science. Department of Applied Mathematics.

[73] Pnueli, A. 1986. Specification and development of reactive systems. In *Information Processing (IFIP'86)*, H.-J. Kugler (ed), 845-58. Amsterdam: North-Holland.

[74] Pratt, W. 1988. Dynamic algebras as a well-behaved fragment of relation algebras. *Lecture Notes in Computer Science* **425**, 77–110.

[75] Richter, M. M. & M. E. Szabo 1986. Nonstandard computation theory. In *Algebra, combinatorics, and logic in computer science, Colloq. Math. Soc. J. Bolyai)*, 667–93. Amsterdam: North-Holland.

[76] Sain, I. 1978. *Abstract model theory and completeness of languages.* Preprint, SZKI, Budapest. Part of this appeared as [77].

[77] Sain, I. 1979. There are general rules for specifying semantics: observations on abstract model theory. *Computational Linguistics and Computer Languages* **XIII**, 195–250.

[78] Sain, I. 1983a. Total correctness in nonstandard dynamic logic. *Bulletin of Section of Logic (Wrocław-Łódź)* **12**(2), 64–70.

[79] Sain, I. 1983b. *Successor axioms for time increase the program verifying power of full computational induction.* Preprint no. 23/1983. Mathematical Institute of the Hungarian Academy of Sciences, Budapest.

[80] Sain, I. 1984a. Structured nonstandard dynamic logic. *Zeitschrift für Math. Logic u. Grundlagen der Math.* **30**(3), 481–97.

[81] Sain, I. 1984b. *On Burstall' method, Parts I and II.* Preprint no. 57/1984. Mathematical Institute of the Hungarian Academy of Sciences. Budapest.

[82] Sain, I. 1985a. A simple proof for completeness of Floyd method. *Theoretical Computer Science*, **35**, 345–48.

[83] I.Sain 1985b. *Relative program verifying powers of the various temporal logics.* Preprint no. 40/1985. Mathematical Institute of the Hungarian Academy of Sciences. Budapest. An extended abstract of this is [84]

[84] Sain, I. 1985c. The reasoning powers of Burstall's modal logic and Pnueli's temporal logic program verification methods. *Lecture Notes in Computer Science* **193**, 302–319.

[85] Sain, I. 1986. *Nonstandard logics of programs.* Dissertation, Hungarian Academy of Sciences, (in Hungarian).

[86] Sain, I. 1987. Total correctness in nonstandard logics of programs. *Theoretical Computer Science* **50**, 285–321.

[87] Sain, I. 1988. Is "Some-other-time" sometimes better than "sometime" in proving partial correctness of programs? *Studia Logica* **XLVII**(3), 279–301.

[88] Sain, I. 1989a. An elementary proof for some semantic characterizations of nondeterministic Floyd-Hoare logic. *Notre Dame Journal of Formal Logic* **30**(4), 563–73.

[89] Sain, I. 1989b. *Computer science temporal logics need clocks.* Abstracts of the AMS.

[90] Sain, I. 1989c. Computer science temporal logics need their clocks. *Bulletin of the Section of Logic (Wrocław-Łódź)* **18**(4), 153–60.

[91] Sain, I. 1990. Past proves more invariance properties but not pca's. *Lecture Notes in Computer Science* **464**, 80–92.

[92] Sain, I. 1991. Comparing and characterizing the power of established program verification methods. In: *Many sorted logic and its applications*, J. Tucker & K. Meinke (eds), 215–314. New York: John Wiley.

[93] Sain, I. 1992. Temporal logics need their clocks. *Theoretical Computer Science* **95**, 75-95.

[94] Segerberg, K. 1970. Modal logics with linear alternative relations. *Theoria* **36**, 301–22.

[95] Segerberg, K. 1971. An essay in classical modal logic. *Filosofiska Studier* **13**, 301–22.

[96] Segerberg, K. 1976. "Somewhere else" and "Some other time". In ***Wright and wrong – mini essays in honor of Georg Henrik von Wright.*** Stiftersens wid Abo Akademi Forskiningsinstitut, 61–64.

[97] Szalas, A. 1994. Chapter 1 of this volume.

[98] Simon, A. 1991. Finite schema completenes for typeless logic and representable cylindric algebras. In *Algebraic Logic, Colloq. Math. Soc. J. Bolyai*, 665-70. Amsterdam: North-Holland.

[99] Salqvist, H. 1975. Completeness and correspondence in the first- and second-order semantics for modal logic. In *Proceedings of the 3rd Skandinavian Logic Symposium*. Amsterdam: North-Holland.

[100] Tarski, A. & S. Givant 1987. A formalization of set theory without variables. *AMS Colloquium publications* **41**.

[101] Venema, Y. 1991. *Cylindric Modal Logic*, ITLI – prepublication series, ML-91-01, University of Amsterdam, also to appear in *Journal of Symbolic Logic*.

[102] Venema, Y. 1992. *Many - dimensional modal logic*, PhD dissertation, University of Amsterdam.

Chapter 3

On the relation of programs and computations to models of temporal logic

P. Wolper

Institut Montéfiore, B28
Université de Liège
4000 Liège Sart-Tilman, Belgium
e-mail: pw@montefiore.ulg.ac.be

Abstract

In recent years there has been a proliferation of program verification methods that use temporal logic. These methods differ by the version of temporal logic they are based upon and by the way they use this logic. In this chapter we attempt to give a simple, unified and coherent view of the field. For this, we first characterize the models and model generators of different versions of temporal logic using automata theory. From this characterization, we build a classification of verification and synthesis methods that use temporal logic.

3.1 Introduction

Among the nonclassical logics used in computer science, temporal logic has probably been the most successful. Since it was first suggested by Pnueli [40] as a tool for the verification of concurrent programs, a large body of work on its theory and applications has developed. Not only has the original use advocated by Pnueli been studied further, but other variants of temporal logic and other ways of using it have also been investigated.

The variant of temporal logic initially presented by Pnueli is the linear version [40,41,31,34,59]. In this version, time is viewed as linear, which means that each time instant has a unique successor. In other words, the structures over which linear time temporal logic is interpreted are linear sequences. A second common version of temporal logic is branching time temporal logic [4,15]. In this version, each time instant may have several immediate successors which correspond to different futures, for instance those resulting from nondeterminism in a program. The structures over which branching time temporal logic is interpreted can be viewed as infinite trees. Still further versions of temporal logic have been developed to deal with structures that are partial orders [43,25]. The motivation there is to reason about computations that are usefully viewed as partial orders, for instance those of distributed systems.

Interestingly, the two main versions of temporal logic (linear time and branching time) have been used in a variety of ways. The oldest method uses either branching or linear time temporal logic for program verification as follows: the program is described by a set of temporal formulas; the desired property of the program is stated in temporal logic; and an axiomatic system is used to prove that the program formulas imply the desired property [41,22,26,39,31,34]. In most cases, this method is built around a first-order version of temporal logic.

The other uses of temporal logic are based on propositional temporal logic. The first of these is synthesis. There, one starts with a formula describing the desired behaviour of the program and one synthesizes a program by building a structure that satisfies the formula. This structure, which is a set of states and an accessibility relation[1] can then be interpreted as a program. This can be done either with linear time [58,37] or with branching time temporal logic [14]. Moreover, the method for building the structure is completely algorithmic and is based on the decision procedure for the propositional temporal logic being considered.

A second use of propositional temporal logic is model checking. Here, instead of building a program from a formula, one checks that a given finite-state program, viewed as a structure over which the formula is interpreted, actually satisfies it. This gives a fully algorithmic verification procedure for finite-state programs. It was first proposed in [9] and further developed in [11], [18] and [27]. It has also been extended to the verification of probabilistic finite-state programs in [52,44,56].

The number of variants of temporal logic and the number of ways of using these variants can make the field seem rather confusing to the uninitiated or even to the well read nonexpert. A thorough understanding of all the issues involved and of the applicability of the various methods and variants of the logic can be difficult to grasp.

In this chapter, our (ambitious?) goal is to give a simple, unified and coherent view of the field. Our approach is twofold. First, we study the models and model generators for each variant of temporal logic. The models are the structures satisfying the formulas of the logic. For instance, they are linear sequences for linear time temporal logic and trees for branching time temporal logic. Model generators are mathematical structures that represent the set of models of a given formula of the logic. For linear time they are

[1] a relation which for each state gives the next states

automata on infinite words [8] and for branching time they are automata on infinite trees [45].

Once we have this characterization of the logics, we consider several possible views of programs and their computations. For instance, a finite-state program can be viewed as a nondeterministic automaton and its computations as linear sequences. Another possibility is to view the computations of a distributed system as partially ordered sets of states.

Our description of the applications of temporal logic to program verification is based on the fact that to verify a program one needs two things: a description of the program and a description of the property to be verified. Depending on the type of program considered (e.g. deterministic or nondeterministic), the program and its computations can be different types of structures (e.g. branching or linear). Once this is fixed, we can choose to describe the program either by a formula, a model or a model generator of the adequate logic. A similar choice is made for the property. It is these choices of description formalisms that determine the verification method. For instance, model checking with linear time temporal logic is obtained by describing the program as a model generator of that logic and the desired property of its computations by a formula of the logic. In the branching time approach to model checking, the program is considered as a model of the logic and the properties of the set of computations of the program are described by a formula of the logic.

With this view of things, each application of temporal logic to verification can be analyzed by answering a few questions: what is a program? what is a computation? how is the program described? how is the desired property described? Once this is known, it is very easy to understand the method at hand. Another advantage is that most algorithms used in this area can be derived from the correspondence between the various types of descriptions of structures: formulas, models and model generators. This approach also extends to synthesis. Of course, in this application, one needs only a description of the desired program in a form that is not directly executable: a formula. The synthesis algorithm then transforms this description in one that is executable: a model or a model generator. Finally, let us note that our approach extends to recent verification work where the properties to be verified are described by an automaton [2,3,36].

Even though our coverage of temporal logic and its applications is quite extensive, it is not comprehensive. For instance, we do not deal with interval temporal logic [30,23,50], continuous time temporal logic and compositional approaches to temporal verification [5,6,7,38]. Nevertheless, our systematic way of looking at applications of temporal logic could also be useful in these areas.

3.2 Temporal logic

In this section, we will describe three versions of temporal logic: linear time temporal logic, branching time temporal logic and the partial order temporal logic of [43]. For each of these logics, we will give syntax and semantics and discuss their models and model generators. We limit ourselves to the propositional versions of the logic. For completeness and to show the techniques used to establish them, we give proofs for the results stated in this section. However, in a first reading of this chapter these proofs can be skipped.

3.2.1 Linear time

We have chosen one of the most common versions of propositional temporal logic appearing in the computer science literature. We will refer to it as *linear temporal logic* (LTL).

Syntax

LTL formulas are built from

- a set P of atomic propositions: $p_1, p_2, p_3, \ldots$,
- boolean connectives: $\wedge$, $\neg$,
- temporal operators: $\bigcirc$ ("next"), U ("until").

The formation rules are:

- An atomic proposition $p \in P$ is a formula.
- If f_1 and f_2 are formulas, so are $f_1 \wedge f_2$, $\neg f_1$, $\bigcirc f_1$, $f_1 \, U f_2$.

We use $\Diamond f$ ("eventually") as an abbreviation for $(\mathrm{T} \, U f)$ and $\Box f$ ("always") as an abbreviation for $\neg \Diamond \neg f$. We also use $\vee$ and $\supset$ as the usual abbreviations, and parentheses to resolve ambiguities.

Semantics

A *structure* for an LTL formula (with set P of atomic propositions) is a triple $M = (W, R, \pi)$ where

- W is a finite or enumerable set of states (also called worlds).
- R: $W \to W$ is a total successor function that for each state gives a unique next state.
- π: $W \to 2^P$ assigns truth values to the atomic propositions of the language in each state.

For a structure M and a state $w \in W$ we have

- $\langle M, w\rangle \models p$ iff $p \in \pi(w)$, for $p \in P$
- $\langle M, w\rangle \models f_1 \wedge f_2$ iff $\langle M, w\rangle \models f_1$ and $\langle M, w\rangle \models f_2$
- $\langle M, w\rangle \models \neg f$ iff not $\langle M, w\rangle \models f$
- $\langle M, w\rangle \models \bigcirc f$ iff $\langle M, R(w)\rangle \models f$

In the following definitions, we denote by $R^i(w)$ the ith successor of w, that is the ith element in the sequence
$w,\ R(w),\ R(R(w)),\ R(R(R(w))),\ \ldots$

- $\langle M, w\rangle \models f_1 U f_2$ iff for some $i \geq 0$,
  $\langle M, R^i(w)\rangle \models f_2$ and for all $0 \leq j < i$, $\langle M, R^j(w)\rangle \models f_1$

Models and model generators

A structure $M = (W, R, \pi)$ together with a state $w \in W$ constitutes an *interpretation* for LTL formulas. If this interpretation satisfies a formula f ($\langle M, w\rangle \models f$), it is said to be a *model* of f. We want to give a characterization of the models of LTL formulas. To do this, we first need to define a notion of a *canonical* model. Indeed, we want to identify models that are not different in any essential way (for instance isomorphic models) and represent them in a standard form. For this, we define a notion of equivalence of interpretations (and hence models) based on bisimulation [29].

Definition 3.1 Two interpretations $\langle M_1, w_{01}\rangle$ and $\langle M_2, w_{02}\rangle$ where $M_1 = (W_1, R_1, \pi_1)$ and $M_2 = (W_2, R_2, \pi_2)$ are equivalent iff there exists a relation $\phi \subseteq W_1 \times W_2$ such that:

- $(w_{01}, w_{02}) \in \phi$;
- if $(w_1, w_2) \in \phi$, then $\pi_1(w_1) = \pi_2(w_2)$;
- if $(w_1, w_2) \in \phi$, then $(R(w_1), R(w_2)) \in \phi$. □

Intuitively, Definition 3.1 states that two interpretations are equivalent if one can find a relation between their states such that the initial states are in correspondence, the labels of related states are identical and the relation is preserved by the transitions. The following lemma shows the rather obvious fact that equivalent interpretations satisfy the same LTL formulas.

Lemma 3.1 If two interpretations $\langle M_1, w_{01}\rangle$ and $\langle M_2, w_{02}\rangle$ are equivalent, then for any LTL formula f, $\langle M_1, w_{01}\rangle \models f$ iff $\langle M_2, w_{02}\rangle \models f$.

Proof: Assume that $M_1 = (W_1, R_1, \pi_1)$ and $M_2 = (W_2, R_2, \pi_2)$. If $\langle M_1, w_{01}\rangle$ and $\langle M_2, w_{02}\rangle$ are equivalent, there is a relation $\phi \subseteq W_1 \times W_2$ satisfying the conditions of Definition 3.1. We show that for any LTL formula f and for every pair of states $(w_1, w_2) \in \phi$, $\langle M_1, w_1\rangle \models f$ iff $\langle M_2, w_2\rangle \models f$. The proof is by induction on the structure of f. The case where f is an atomic proposition follows directly from the fact that $\pi_1(w_1) = \pi_2(w_2)$. The inductive cases are also straightforward. In the case of the operator U, notice that if $(w_1, w_2) \in \phi$, then for all i, $(R_1^i(w_1), R_2^i(w_2)) \in \phi$. □

We can now establish the existence of canonical interpretations for LTL formulas. Canonical interpretations for LTL formulas are of the form $\langle M, 0\rangle$, where $M = (N, succ, \pi)$, N being the set of natural numbers and $succ$ the successor function on the natural numbers (i.e., $succ(i) = i+1$ for all $i \in N$). Since in a canonical interpretation, the set of states, the successor function and the initial state are all fixed, such a model is characterized by a function $\pi : N \rightarrow 2^P$. We now establish that every interpretation for an LTL formula is equivalent to a canonical interpretation.

Lemma 3.2 Every interpretation $\langle M, w_0\rangle$ where $M = (W, R, \pi)$ is equivalent to a canonical interpretation $\pi' : N \rightarrow 2^P$.

Proof: The canonical interpretation π' is defined by $\pi'(i) = \pi(R^i(w_0))$, for all $i \geq 0$. To check that the canonical interpretation π' is equivalent to $\langle M, w_0\rangle$, consider the relation ϕ defined by $\phi = \{(i, R^i(w_0)) \mid i \geq 0\}$. □

Basically, to obtain a canonical interpretation from an arbitrary interpretation, one simply *unwinds* the interpretation into an infinite sequence. Now that we have established the existence of canonical interpretations which are mappings from the natural numbers to the set 2^P, we will consider only these. Doing this is not restrictive, as every other interpretation is equivalent in the strong sense of Definition 3.1 to a canonical interpretation.

Our goal is to give a description of the set of canonical models of an LTL formula. It is this description that we will call the *model generator* for an LTL formula. The model generators for LTL formulas are automata on infinite words. Before defining these automata, let us note that a canonical interpretation π can be viewed as an infinite word $w = a_1a_2a_3\ldots$ over the alphabet 2^P, where $a_i = \pi(i-1)$, $i \geq 1$

The type of finite automata on infinite words we consider is the one defined by Büchi [8]. A *Büchi sequential automaton* is a tuple $A = (\Sigma, S, \rho, S_0, F)$, where

- Σ is an alphabet,
- S is a set of states,
- $\rho : S \times \Sigma \rightarrow 2^S$ is a nondeterministic transition function,
- $S_0 \subseteq S$ is a set of starting states, and
- $F \subseteq S$ is a set of designated states.

A *run* of A over an infinite word $w = a_1a_2\ldots$ is an infinite sequence $s_0, s_1, \ldots$, where $s_0 \in S_0$ and $s_i \in \rho(s_{i-1}, a_i)$, for all $i \geq 1$. A run $s_0, s_1, \ldots$

is *accepting* if there is some designated state that repeats infinitely often, i.e., for some $s \in F$ there are infinitely many is such that $s_i = s$. The infinite word w is *accepted* by A if there is an accepting run of A over w. The set of denumerable words accepted by A is denoted $L(A)$.

Example Consider the automaton of Fig. 3.1 where $F = \{s_1\}$ and $S_0 = \{s_0\}$.

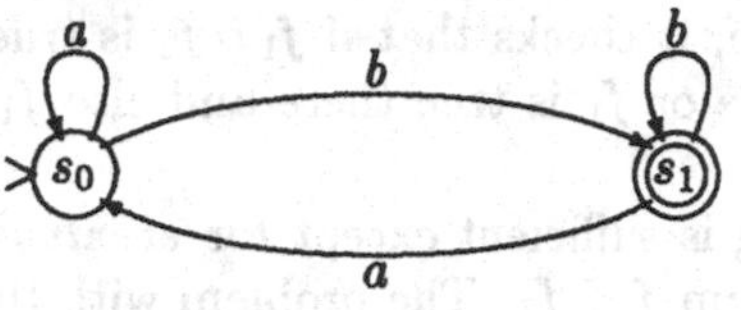

Figure 3.1: A Büchi sequential automaton

The language it accepts consists of all words of the form $(a^*bb^*)^\omega$, where $*$ denotes finite repetition and ω denotes infinite repetition. Note that the words of the form $(a^*bb^*)^*a^\omega$ are not accepted by this automaton. Intuitively, a word is accepted if it contains b infinitely often. □

We can now give the result relating LTL and Büchi automata. We show that given an LTL formula, we can build a Büchi sequential automaton that accepts exactly the canonical models of that formula. In the statement of the following theorem, we use $|f|$ to denote the length of a formula f, i.e., the number of symbols (propositions or connectives) it contains.

Theorem 3.1 [60] Given an LTL formula f, one can build a Büchi sequential automaton $A_f = (\Sigma, S, \rho, S_0, F)$, where $\Sigma = 2^P$ and $|S| \leq 2^{O(|f|)}$, such that $L(A_f)$ is exactly the set of sequences satisfying the formula f.

Proof: The construction uses the notion of the *closure* of an LTL formula f, denoted $cl(f)$. For a formula f, $cl(f)$ consists of all the subformulas of f and their negation, where we identify $\neg\neg f_1$ with f_1. Precisely, $cl(f)$ is defined as follows:

- $f \in cl(f)$
- if $f_1 \wedge f_2 \in cl(f)$ then $f_1, f_2 \in cl(f)$
- if $\neg f_2 \in cl(f)$ then $f_2 \in cl(f)$
- if $f_2 \in cl(f)$ then $\neg f_2 \in cl(f)$
- if $\bigcirc f_2 \in cl(f)$ then $f_2 \in cl(f)$
- if $f_1 U f_2 \in cl(f)$ then $f_1, f_2 \in cl(f)$.

Note that we have $|cl(f)| \leq 2|f|$. To build a Büchi automaton accepting the models of a formula f, we first build an automaton over the alphabet $2^{cl(f)}$.

This automaton will recognize the set of words that are obtained from models of f by extending the label of each state with the elements of $cl(f)$ true in that state.

The Büchi automaton we build is the combination of two automata: the *local automaton* and the *eventuality automaton*. The local automaton checks for "local inconsistencies" in the model. More precisely, it checks that there are no propositional inconsistencies and that the temporal operators are locally satisfied. For instance, it checks that if $f_1 \, U f_2$ is true in a state, then either f_2 is true in that state or f_1 is true there and also $f_1 \, U f_2$ is true in the next state.

The local checking is sufficient except for *eventuality formulas*. These are the formulas of the form $f_1 \, U f_2$. The problem with these formulas is that the local conditions imposed do not guarantee that a point where f_2 is true is indeed eventually reached. Checking this will be the role of the eventuality automaton.

Constructing the local automaton

The local automaton is $L = (2^{cl(f)}, N_L, \rho_L, N_f, N_L)$. The state set N_L is the set of all sets $\mathbf{s}$ of formulas in $cl(f)$ that do not have any propositional inconsistency. Namely they must satisfy the following conditions:

(i) For all $f_1 \in cl(f)$, we have that $f_1 \in \mathbf{s}$ iff $\neg f_1 \notin \mathbf{s}$.

(ii) For all $f_1 \wedge f_2 \in cl(f)$, we have that $f_1 \wedge f_2 \in \mathbf{s}$ iff $f_1 \in \mathbf{s}$ and $f_2 \in \mathbf{s}$.

For the transition relation ρ_L, we have that $\mathbf{t} \in \rho_L(\mathbf{s}, a)$ iff $a = \mathbf{s}$ (i.e., all transitions leaving a state have the same label as that state) and:

(i) For all $\bigcirc f_1 \in cl(f)$, we have that $\bigcirc f_1 \in \mathbf{s}$ iff $f_1 \in \mathbf{t}$, and

(ii) For all $f_1 \, U f_2 \in cl(f)$, we have that $f_1 \, U f_2 \in \mathbf{s}$ iff either $f_2 \in \mathbf{s}$ or both $f_1 \in \mathbf{s}$ and $f_1 \, U f_2 \in \mathbf{t}$.

Finally, the set of starting states N_f consists of all sets $\mathbf{s}$ such that $f \in \mathbf{s}$. The local automaton does not impose any acceptance conditions and so its set of designated states is the whole set of states.

The eventuality automaton

Given an LTL formula f, we define the set $e(f)$ of its eventualities as the subset of $cl(f)$ that contains all formulas of the form $f_1 \, U f_2$. The eventuality automaton is $E = (2^{cl(f)}, 2^{e(f)}, \rho_E, \{\emptyset\}, \{\emptyset\})$, where for the transition relation ρ_E, we have that $\mathbf{t} \in \rho_E(\mathbf{s}, a)$ iff:

(i) $\mathbf{s} = \emptyset$ and for all $f_1 \, U f_2 \in a$, we have that $f_1 \, U f_2 \in \mathbf{t}$ iff $f_2 \notin a$.

(ii) $\mathbf{s} \neq \emptyset$ and for all $f_1 \, U f_2 \in \mathbf{s}$, we have that $f_1 \, U f_2 \in \mathbf{t}$ iff $f_2 \notin a$.

Intuitively, the eventuality automaton tries to satisfy the eventualities in the model. When the current state is $\emptyset$, it looks at the model to see which eventualities have to be satisfied. Thereafter, the current state says which eventualities have yet to be satisfied. Note that it is sufficient to check only periodically what eventualities have to be satisfied in the model. Indeed, eventualities that are not satisfied in a given state of the model also appear in the next state because of the conditions imposed by the local automaton. We often describe this by saying that eventualities are *propagated.*

Combining the automata

We now combine the local and eventuality automata to get the *model automaton.* The model automaton $M = (2^{cl(f)}, N_M, \rho_M, N_{M0}, F_M)$ is obtained by taking the cross product of L and E. Its sets of states is $N_M = N_L \times 2^{e(f)}$. The transition relation ρ_M is defined as follows: $(\mathbf{p}, \mathbf{q}) \in \rho_M((\mathbf{s}, \mathbf{t}), a)$ iff $\mathbf{p} \in \rho_L(\mathbf{s}, a)$ and $\mathbf{q} \in \rho_E(\mathbf{t}, a)$. The set of starting states is $N_{M0} = N_f \times \{\emptyset\}$, and the set of designated states is $F_M = N_L \times \{\emptyset\}$. Note that $|N_M| \leq 2^{|cl(f)|} \times 2^{|e(f)|} \leq 2^{3|f|}$.

The automaton we have constructed, accepts words over $2^{cl(f)}$. However, the models of f are defined by words over 2^P. So, the last step of our construction is to take the projection of our automaton on 2^P. This is done by mapping each element $b \in 2^{cl(f)}$ into $b \cap P$. □

The construction we have given for the model generator of LTL formulas is one of the simplest to describe. However, it leads to an automaton that can contain numerous unnecessary states. It is possible to make the construction less wasteful essentially by constructing only the states that are reachable from the initial state. Note however that this does not influence the worst case complexity of the algorithm.

Example The Büchi automaton of Fig. 3.1 is a model generator for the formula $\Box\Diamond p$ when a is taken to be $\emptyset$ and b to be $\{p\}$. Note that the automaton obtained from the construction given in the proof of Theorem 3.1 is somewhat more complicated, though it is equivalent to (generates the same infinite words as) the automaton we have described. □

The construction we have given can be extended to most versions of linear time propositional temporal logic, such as the extended temporal logic defined in [59,60,57] and the temporal logic with past operators of [28]. The inverse construction (building a temporal formula from a Büchi automaton) is possible if one uses extended temporal logic [59,60,57].

Theorem 3.1 makes the theory of Büchi automata very relevant to temporal logic. The following theorem states important results on the *nonemptiness problem* for Büchi sequential automata, i.e. the problem of determining for a given Büchi sequential automaton A whether $L(A)$ is nonempty.

Theorem 3.2

(a) The nonemptiness problem for Büchi sequential automata is solvable in nondeterministic logspace [51].
(b) The nonemptiness problem for Büchi sequential automata is solvable in linear time [17,18]. □

One can easily obtain a decision procedure for LTL by combining Theorems 3.1 and 3.2a. Given a formula f, one builds the automaton accepting the models of this formula (using Theorem 3.1) and then checks whether this automaton is nonempty (using Theorem 3.2a). By combining the construction of the automaton with the algorithm checking for nonemptiness, it is possible to obtain a PSPACE upper bound for the decidability of LTL (see [51,57]). The PSPACE upper bound for LTL was originally proven in [48] and [49] where a matching lower bound was also established.

3.2.2 Branching time

What distinguishes ***branching temporal logic*** (BTL) from LTL is its ability to specify whether a property is true of some computations or of all computations in a set. Syntactically, it is essentially LTL with two ***path quantifiers*** ($\forall$ and $\exists$) that indicate to which computations (paths) the LTL formulas apply. Semantically, these paths will be extracted from a branching structure, i.e. a set of states and an accessibility relation such that each state may have several successors. There are several variants of branching temporal logic. The main distinction between these is the type of LTL formula that can appear in the scope of a path quantifier. We will consider two versions of branching temporal logic: the logics CTL and CTL* defined in [15,16]. In CTL (***computation tree logic***), the formulas appearing in the scope of path quantifiers are restricted to be a single temporal operator. In CTL*, they can be arbitrary LTL formulas. When we do not need to distinguish between versions of branching time temporal logic, we will use the acronym BTL.

Syntax

In defining the syntax of CTL and CTL*, we distinguish between state and path formulas. Path formulas will be interpreted over linear sequences of states extracted from the branching structure. In contrast, state formulas will be interpreted in a state of the branching structure. They will be either formulas that can be interpreted by considering just one state (e.g., a boolean combination of atomic propositions) or built from path formulas to which a path quantifier ($\forall$ or $\exists$) is applied. Intuitively a state formula $\forall g$, where g is a path formula, is true in a state if g is true on all paths leaving that state. The CTL and CTL* formulas built from a set of atomic propositions P are defined as follows:

- **State formulas**
  (i) An atomic proposition $p \in P$ is a state formula.
  (ii) If f_1 and f_2 are state formulas, so are $f_1 \wedge f_2$ and $\neg f_1$.
  (iii) If g is a path formula, then $\exists g$ and $\forall g$ are state formulas.

- **Path formulas** (CTL)
  (i) If g_1 and g_2 are state formulas, then $\bigcirc g_1$, and $g_1 U g_2$ are path formulas.

- **Path formulas** (CTL*)
  (i) A state formula is a path formula.
  (ii) If g_1 and g_2 are path formulas, so are $g_1 \wedge g_2$ and $\neg g_1$.
  (iii) If g_1 and g_2 are path formulas, then $\bigcirc g_1$ and $g_1 U g_2$ are path formulas.

Finally, the formulas of CTL and CTL* are their respective state formulas. Intuitively, the difference between the two logics is that in CTL*, a path formula can be any boolean combination or nesting of temporal operators applied to state formulas. By contrast, in CTL, path formulas are a single temporal operator applied to a state formula. In CTL*, we will use $\Box$ and $\Diamond$ as the abbreviations defined in LTL. In CTL, we will use $\exists \Diamond f$ and $\forall \Diamond f$ to abbreviate $\exists(\mathbf{T}\, U f)$ and $\forall(\mathbf{T}\, U f)$ respectively. Also, $\exists \Box f$ will be an abbreviation for $\neg\forall\Diamond\neg f$ and $\forall\Box f$ for $\neg\exists\Diamond\neg f$.

Example $\forall\Box\Diamond p$ and $\exists(\Box\Diamond p \supset \Box\Diamond q)$ are CTL* formulas, but not CTL formulas. Indeed, the path formula in $\forall\Box\Diamond p$ is $\Box\Diamond p$ and thus contains nested temporal operators. On the other hand, $\forall\Box\forall\Diamond p$ is a CTL formula. In this case, we have a single temporal operator ($\Box$) applied to a state formula ($\forall\Diamond p$). □

Semantics

A ***structure*** for a BTL (CTL or CTL*) formula (with set P of atomic propositions) is a triple $M = (W, Q, \pi)$ where

- W is a finite or enumerable set of states (also called worlds).
- $Q \subset W \times W$ is a total accessibility relation that for each state gives a nonempty set of successors.
- π: $W \rightarrow 2^P$ assigns truth values to the atomic propositions in each state.

Note that the only difference between a structure for LTL and a structure for BTL is that we have an accessibility relation Q rather than a successor function R. This means that each state can have several immediate successors rather than a unique one.

To give the semantics of a BTL formula for an interpretation $\langle M, w\rangle$, we need to define the notion of a path (or linear interpretation) extracted from a branching interpretation. Intuitively, one extracts a linear interpretation from a branching one by choosing one specific successor for each state. Formally, we have the following definition.

Definition 3.2 A linear interpretation extracted from a branching interpretation $\langle M_B, w_0\rangle$ where $M_B = (W_B, Q_B, \pi_B)$ is a pair $\langle M_L, w_0\rangle$ where $M_L = (W_L, R_L, \pi_L)$ with $w_0 \in W_L \subseteq W_B$, $\pi_L(w) = \pi_B(w)$ and $(w, R_L(w)) \in Q_B$ for all $w \in W_L$. □

We can now give the semantics of BTL. For path formulas, the semantics are identical to those of LTL except that we interpret path formulas that are also state formulas according to the semantics of state formulas.

For state formulas, we define the truth of a formula g in an interpretation $\langle M_B, w_0\rangle$ by the following clauses:

- $\langle M_B, w_0\rangle \models p$ iff $p \in \pi(w)$, for $p \in P$
- $\langle M_B, w_0\rangle \models g_1 \wedge g_2$ iff $\langle M_B, w_0\rangle \models g_1$ and $\langle M_B, w_0\rangle \models g_2$
- $\langle M_B, w_0\rangle \models \neg g$ iff not $\langle M_B, w_0\rangle \models g$
- $\langle M_B, w_0\rangle \models \forall g$ iff for all linear structures $\langle M_L, w_0\rangle$ extracted from $\langle M_B, w_0\rangle$, $\langle M_L, w_0\rangle \models g$
- $\langle M_B, w_0\rangle \models \exists g$ iff for some linear structure $\langle M_L, w_0\rangle$ extracted from $\langle M_B, w_0\rangle$, $\langle M_L, w_0\rangle \models g$

Example The state w_0 of the interpretation described in Fig. 3.2 satisfies the CTL formula $\exists \Box \exists \Diamond p$, but does not satisfy the CTL* formula $\exists \Box \Diamond p$. Indeed, from that state there is no single path on which p is **T** infinitely often. On the other hand, there exists a path (the one going infinitely through w_0) from all points of which there is a path containing a state where p is **T**. In the interpretation of Fig. 3.3, the state w_0 satisfies both the CTL formula $\forall \Box \forall \Diamond p$ and the CTL* formula $\forall \Box \Diamond p$.

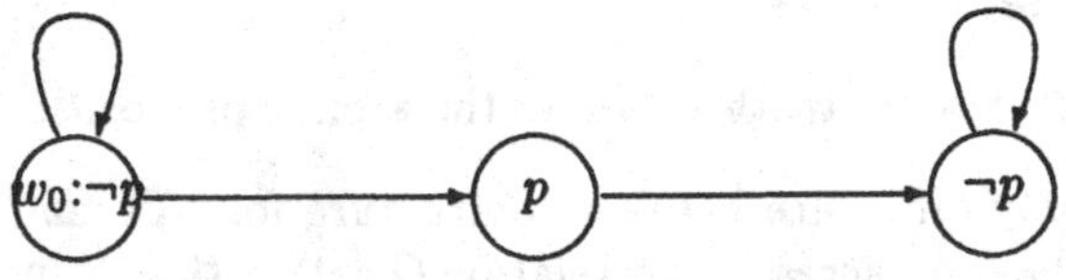

Figure 3.2: A model of $\exists \Box \exists \Diamond p$

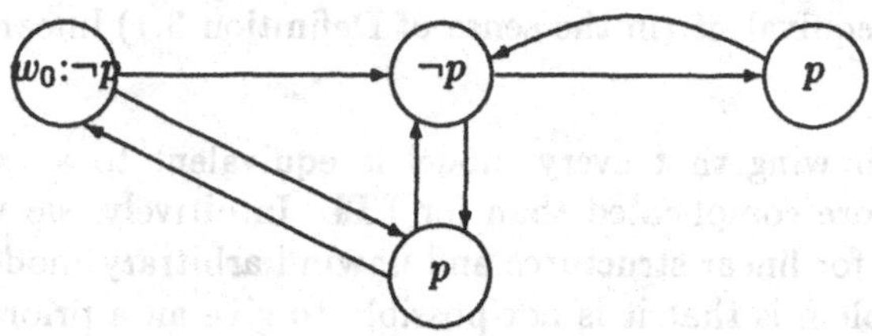

Figure 3.3: A model of $\forall\Box\Diamond p$

Models and model generators

As we did in the linear time case, we now consider the problem of constructing model generators for BTL. Again, the model generators will deal only with canonical models which are here infinite trees. To justify our notion of canonical model, we use a notion of equivalence of interpretations similar to the one we used for linear interpretations.

Definition 3.3 Two branching interpretations $\langle M_1, w_{01}\rangle$ and $\langle M_2, w_{02}\rangle$ where $M_1 = (W_1, Q_1, \pi_1)$ and $M_2 = (W_2, Q_2, \pi_2)$ are equivalent iff there is relation $\phi \subseteq W_1 \times W_2$ such that:

- $(w_{01}, w_{02}) \in \phi$;
- if $(w_1, w_2) \in \phi$, then $\pi_1(w_1) = \pi_2(w_2)$;
- if $(w_1, w_2) \in \phi$, and there is a $w_1' \in W_1$ such that $(w_1, w_1') \in Q_1$ then there is a $w_2' \in W_2$ such that $(w_2, w_2') \in Q_2$ and $(w_1', w_2') \in \phi$;
- if $(w_1, w_2) \in \phi$, and there is a $w_2' \in W_2$ such that $(w_2, w_2') \in Q_2$ then there is a $w_1' \in W_1$ such that $(w_1, w_1') \in Q_1$ and $(w_1', w_2') \in \phi$. □

The notion of equivalence given by Definition 3.3 is essentially Milner's bisimulation [29]. It is also related to the definition given for different purposes in [12]. As in the linear case, we can easily establish that equivalent branching structures satisfy the same BTL formulas.

Lemma 3.3 If two branching interpretations $\langle M_1, w_{01}\rangle$ and $\langle M_2, w_{02}\rangle$ are equivalent, then for any BTL formula f, $\langle M_1, w_{01}\rangle \models f$ iff $\langle M_2, w_{02}\rangle \models f$.

Proof: Assume that $M_1 = (W_1, Q_1, \pi_1)$ and $M_2 = (W_2, Q_2, \pi_2)$. If $\langle M_1, w_{01}\rangle$ and $\langle M_2, w_{02}\rangle$ are equivalent, there is a relation $\phi \subseteq W_1 \times W_2$ satisfying the conditions of Definition 3.3. We show for any BTL state formula f and for every pair of states $(w_1, w_2) \in \phi$, $\langle M_1, w_1\rangle \models f$ iff $\langle M_2, w_2\rangle \models f$. The proof is by induction on the structure of f. The interesting case is when f is of the form $\forall g$ or $\exists g$. For this it is sufficient to observe that if one can extract a linear interpretation from one of two equivalent branching interpretations, then one can extract an equivalent (in the sense of Definition 3.1) linear interpretation from the other. □

For BTL, showing that every model is equivalent to a canonical model is somewhat more complicated than for LTL. Intuitively, we want to do the same as we did for linear structures and unwind arbitrary models into infinite trees. The problem is that it is not possible to give an a priori bound on the branching factor (the maximum number of immediate successors of each node) of the tree. Indeed, in a branching structure a node can have an arbitrary number of successors and it is not always possible to find an equivalent model where the branching factor is smaller. The best we can do if we choose k-ary infinite trees as canonical models is to show that there is a k-ary tree canonical model equivalent to any model whose branching factor is at most k. As we will see below, this is indeed possible. First, we need to give some definitions concerning k-ary trees.

To define k-ary trees, we use $[k]$ to denote the set $\{1, \ldots, k\}$. The set $[k]^\star$ then denotes the set of nodes of the tree, the root being the empty string λ. The successors of a node x are thus the nodes xi, $i \in [k]$. A node x is said to be of depth i if the length of x is equal to i. A k-ary infinite tree T labelled by the elements of an alphabet Σ is then a function $T : [k]^\star \rightarrow \Sigma$. A k-ary tree canonical interpretation for BTL is of the form $\langle M, \lambda \rangle$, where $M = ([k]^\star, succ, \pi)$, the relation $succ$ being defined by $succ = \{(x, xi) | x \in [k]^\star, i \in [k]\}$. Since in these interpretations, the set of states, the initial state and the successor relation are all fixed, they reduce to a function $\pi : [k]^\star \rightarrow 2^P$, that is, to a labelled tree over the alphabet 2^P. We now show how to construct k-ary canonical models from models whose branching factor is $\leq k$ (by definition, the branching factor of a structure (W, Q, π) is the largest ℓ such that for some $w \in W$, we have $\ell = |\{w' | (w, w') \in Q\}|$).

Lemma 3.4 Every branching interpretation $\langle M, w_0 \rangle$ where $M = (W, Q, \pi)$ and whose branching factor is $\leq k$ is equivalent to a k-ary tree canonical interpretation $\pi' : [k]^\star \rightarrow 2^P$.

Proof: To define the canonical interpretation π', we first define the relation ϕ that will enable us to establish that π' is equivalent to $\langle M, w_0 \rangle$. The relation ϕ is actually a function in $[k]^\star \rightarrow W$. We define it in stages. At stage i, ϕ_i will be defined on all nodes of the tree of depth $\leq i$. We start with $\phi_0(\lambda) = w_0$. We obtain ϕ_{i+1} from ϕ_i by extending its definition to all nodes of the tree of depth $i + 1$ as follows. For each node $x \in [k]^\star$ of depth i, let $\{w_1, \ldots, w_\ell\}$, $\ell \leq k$, be the successors of $\phi_i(x)$. We define $\phi_{i+1}(xj) = w_j$ for $1 \leq j \leq \ell$ and $\phi_{i+1}(xj) = w_\ell$ for $\ell < j \leq k$. In other words the first ℓ successors of x simulate the ℓ successors of $\phi_i(x)$, and if $\ell < k$ we simply replicate the last successor. Finally, the relation ϕ is the limit ϕ_ω of the relations ϕ_i, and $\pi'(x) = \pi(\phi(x))$

for all $x \in [k]^*$. With this definition of π', it is quite straightforward to show that ϕ satisfies all the conditions of Definition 3.3. □

Lemma 3.4 tells us that if a formula has models of branching factor at most k then these models are equivalent to k-ary canonical models. The next natural step would thus be to describe a model generator for the k-ary canonical models of BTL formulas. However, for the model generator to be interesting, we need to choose k large enough for the set of k-ary canonical models to be nonempty if the formula is satisfiable. Fortunately, this is always possible. The next lemma shows that any satisfiable BTL formula that contains n path quantifiers has at least one $(n+1)$-ary canonical model. The idea of the proof of that lemma is that one needs only sufficient paths from each state of a model to satisfy all the existential path formulas that have to be **T** in that state (those of the form $\exists g$ or $\neg\forall g$). Moreover, the number of existential state formulas that can appear in a formula is bounded by the number of path quantifiers in that formula. This then makes it possible to show that a satisfiable formula with n path quantifiers always has an $(n+1)$-tree model. Indeed, having $n+1$ branches out of each node of the tree makes it possible to embed in the tree the n paths that are necessary from each node, without these interfering with one another. This is done by embedding the jth path out of a node x into the path $x(j+1)1^*$ of the tree. That path is the one that goes to the $(j+1)$th successor of the node in the tree and then always takes the leftmost branch of the tree.

Lemma 3.5 If a BTL formula f containing n path quantifiers has a model, then it has an $(n+1)$-ary canonical model.

Proof: Before giving the proof, we define the state closure of a CTL or CTL* formula f ($scl(f)$) as the set of state subformulas of f and their negation, where we identify $\neg\neg f_1$ with f_1. We also define existential state formulas as those of the form $\exists g$ or $\neg\forall g$ where g is a path formula.

Now, suppose f is satisfied by a branching interpretation $\langle M, w_0\rangle$ where $M = (W, Q, \pi)$. We construct an $(n+1)$-ary canonical model $\pi' : [n+1]^* \to 2^P$ satisfying f by inductively constructing a mapping $\psi : [n+1]^* \to W$ and taking $\pi'(x) = \pi(\psi(x))$. We start with a mapping ψ_0 defined on the set $X_0 = 1^*$ (i.e., the leftmost path starting at λ). To define ψ_0, we choose some linear interpretation $\langle M_L, w_0\rangle$ extracted from $\langle M, w_0\rangle$ where $M_L = (W_L, R_L, \pi_L)$ and define $\psi_0(1^k) = R_L^k(w_0)$, $k \geq 0$. Note that each node $x \in X_0$ has exactly one successor in X_0 which is its leftmost successor $x1$.

Now, given the mapping ψ_i defined on a set of nodes X_i, we show how to define ψ_{i+1} and the set X_{i+1}. Our construction ensures that all nodes in X_i either have $n+1$ successors within X_i or have only their leftmost successor in X_i. Consider the nodes in X_i that have only a leftmost successor in X_i. For each such node x, we extend ψ_i as follows. Consider the existential state formulas $E \in scl(f)$ such that $\langle M, \psi(x)\rangle \models E$. There are at most n such formulas, say $E_1, \ldots, E_n$, where n is the number of path quantifiers in f and where E_j is either $\exists g_j$ or $\neg\forall g_j$. For each formula E_j, we choose a linear interpretation $\langle M_{Lj}, \psi_i(x)\rangle$ extracted from $\langle M, \psi_i(x)\rangle$ such that $\langle M_{Lj}, \psi_i(x)\rangle \models g_j$ if E_j is $\exists g_j$ and $\langle M_{Lj}, \psi_i(x)\rangle \models \neg g_j$ if E_j is $\neg\forall g_j$. We then define $\psi_{i+1}(x(j+1)) = R_{L_j}(\psi_i(x))$ and $\psi_{i+1}(x(j+1)1^k) = R^k_{L_j}(\psi_i(x))$ for $k \geq 1$. If there are only $0 \leq \ell < n$ formulas E_j, for $j = \ell + 1, \ldots, n$, we choose $\langle M_{Lj}, \psi_i(x)\rangle$ to be an arbitrary linear interpretation extracted from $\langle M, \psi_i(x)\rangle$.

Finally, take ψ to be ψ_ω. The last step is to show that for all $f_s \in scl(f)$ and all nodes in $x \in [n+1]^*$ we have $\langle \pi', x\rangle \models f_s$ iff $\langle M, \psi(x)\rangle \models g$ and hence in particular, $\langle \pi', \lambda\rangle \models f$ iff $\langle M, w_0\rangle \models f$. This is done by induction on the structure of state formulas. The case of atomic propositions and boolean combinations is immediate and the construction ensures that if a state formula of the form $\exists g$ is satisfied in a state w of M, it will be satisfied in any state $x \in [n+1]^*$ such that $\psi(x) = w$. Also, as all paths in π' are paths in M, the same is true for formulas of the form $\forall g$. □

Note that the canonical model π' constructed in the proof of Lemma 3.5 is not equivalent to the initial model M. Indeed it might contain only a limited part of the states and paths of M. However, it contains sufficient states and paths to satisfy f if M satisfies f.

We are now ready to study the model generators for BTL formulas. We will establish the results only for CTL. Similar results can be obtained for CTL*, though the complexity bounds are quite different [20,54]. The model generators for the k-ary tree canonical models of CTL will be Büchi tree automata. Büchi tree automata are similar to Büchi sequential automata, except that they operate on trees rather than sequences. They are identical to the *special automata* of [46].

A k-ary *Büchi tree automaton* is a tuple $A = (\Sigma, S, \rho, S_0, F)$, where

- Σ is an alphabet,
- S is a set of states,
- $\rho : S \times \Sigma \rightarrow 2^{S^k}$ is a nondeterministic transition function (for each state and letter it gives the possible tuples of k successors)
- $S_0 \subseteq S$ is a set of starting states, and
- $F \subseteq S$ is a set of designated states.

The only difference between a Büchi sequential automaton and a Büchi tree automaton is that in the latter, the transition function maps states and letters to sets of k-tuples of states rather than to sets of states.

A run of an automaton A over a tree $T : [k]^* \rightarrow \Sigma$ is an n-ary tree $\phi : [k]^* \rightarrow S$ where $\phi(\lambda) \in S_0$ and for every $x \in [k]^*$, we have $(\phi(x1), \ldots, \phi(xn)) \in \rho(\phi(x), T(x))$. In intuitive terms, one can think of a run of a Büchi tree automaton A on a tree T as a labelling of T with states of A that is compatible with the transition relation of A. To define accepting runs, we consider paths in the run ϕ. A path from a node x in an infinite tree is an infinite sequence $p = x_0, x_1, x_2, \ldots, x_i, \ldots$ of nodes of the tree such that $x_0 = x$ and for all $i \geq 0$, x_{i+1} is an immediate successor of x_i (i.e., $x_{i+1} = x_i j$ for some $1 \leq j \leq k$). A run ϕ of A over T is *accepting* iff, on all infinite paths p starting at λ, some state in F appears infinitely often. The automaton A accepts T if it has an accepting run on T. We denote by $T(A)$ the set of trees accepted by A.

Example The Büchi tree automaton of Fig. 3.4 where $F = \{s_1\}$ and $S = \{s_0\}$ accepts all binary trees in which all paths contain b infinitely often. □

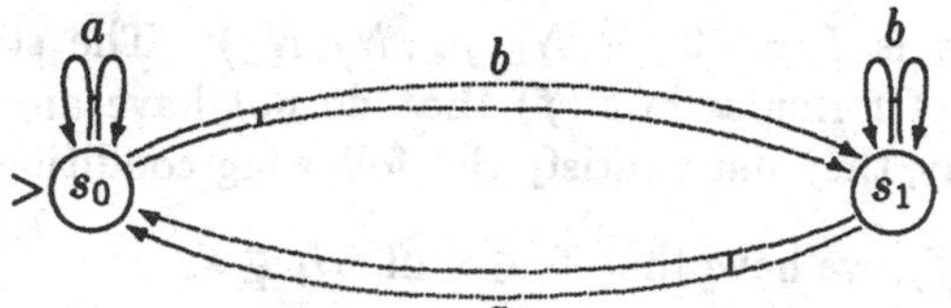

Figure 3.4: A Büchi tree automaton

Theorem 3.3 Given a CTL formula f and a constant k, one can construct a k-ary Büchi tree automaton $A = (\Sigma, S, \rho, S_0, F)$, where $\Sigma = 2^P$, and $|S| \leq 2^{O(|f|)}$, such that A accepts exactly all the k-ary tree models of f. □

Proof: A proof of this theorem can be obtained by the techniques described in [55]. Here, we will describe a different construction that we have made as simple as possible and that is quite similar to the proof we have given for Theorem 3.1.

The construction uses the notion of the closure of a formula f, denoted $cl(f)$. In the case of CTL, the notions of closure and *state closure* coincide. This is not the case for CTL*. For a CTL formula f, $cl(f)$ consists of all the subformulas of f and their negation, where we identify $\neg\neg f_1$ with f_1. Precisely, $cl(f)$ is defined as follows:

- $f \in cl(f)$
- if $f_1 \wedge f_2 \in cl(f)$ then $f_1, f_2 \in cl(f)$
- if $\neg f_2 \in cl(f)$ then $f_2 \in cl(f)$
- if $f_2 \in cl(f)$ then $\neg f_2 \in cl(f)$
- if $\exists\bigcirc f_2 \in cl(f)$ then $f_2 \in cl(f)$
- if $\forall\bigcirc f_2 \in cl(f)$ then $f_2 \in cl(f)$

- if $\exists f_1 U f_2 \in cl(f)$ then $f_1, f_2 \in cl(f)$
- if $\forall f_1 U f_2 \in cl(f)$ then $f_1, f_2 \in cl(f)$

Note that we have $|cl(f)| \leq 2|f|$. The Büchi tree automaton we build for a formula f is taken as the combination of three automata: the *local automaton*, the *existential eventuality automaton* and the *universal eventuality automaton*. As in the proof of Theorem 3.1, the local automaton checks that the tree satisfies local consistency conditions. On the other hand, the eventuality automaton has to be split into two parts: one that checks eventualities that have to be satisfied on some path (existential eventualities) and eventualities that have to be satisfied on all paths (universal eventualities).

Constructing the local automaton

The local automaton is $L = (2^{cl(f)}, N_L, \rho_L, N_f, N_L)$. The state set N_L is the set of all sets $\mathbf{s}$ of formulas in $cl(f)$ that do not have any propositional inconsistency. Namely, they must satisfy the following conditions:

(i) For all $f_1 \in cl(f)$, we have that $f_1 \in \mathbf{s}$ iff $\neg f_1 \notin \mathbf{s}$.

(ii) For all $f_1 \wedge f_2 \in cl(f)$, we have that $f_1 \wedge f_2 \in \mathbf{s}$ iff $f_1 \in \mathbf{s}$ and $f_2 \in \mathbf{s}$.

For the transition relation $\rho_L : N_L \times 2^{cl(f)} \rightarrow 2^{N_L^k}$, we have that $(\mathbf{t}_1, \ldots, \mathbf{t}_k) \in \rho_L(\mathbf{s}, a)$ iff $a = \mathbf{s}$ and:

(i) For all $\exists \bigcirc f_1 \in cl(f)$, we have that $\exists \bigcirc f_1 \in \mathbf{s}$ iff $f_1 \in \mathbf{t}_j$, for some $1 \leq j \leq k$

(ii) For all $\forall \bigcirc f_1 \in cl(f)$, we have that $\forall \bigcirc f_1 \in \mathbf{s}$ iff $f_1 \in \mathbf{t}_j$, for all $1 \leq j \leq k$

(iii) For all $\exists f_1 U f_2 \in cl(f)$, we have that $\exists f_1 U f_2 \in \mathbf{s}$ iff either $f_2 \in \mathbf{s}$ or $f_1 \in \mathbf{s}$ and $f_1 U f_2 \in \mathbf{t}_j$ for some $1 \leq j \leq k$.

(iv) For all $\forall f_1 U f_2 \in cl(f)$, we have that $\forall f_1 U f_2 \in \mathbf{s}$ iff either $f_2 \in \mathbf{s}$ or $f_1 \in \mathbf{s}$ and $f_1 U f_2 \in \mathbf{t}_j$ for all $1 \leq j \leq k$.

Finally, the set of starting states N_f consists of all sets $\mathbf{s}$ such that $f \in \mathbf{s}$. The local automaton does not impose any acceptance conditions and so its set of accepting states is the whole set of states.

The universal eventuality automaton

Given a CTL formula f, we define the set $ue(f)$ of its universal eventualities as the subset of $cl(f)$ that contains all formulas of the form $\forall f_1 U f_2$. The eventuality automaton is $UE = (2^{cl(f)}, 2^{ue(f)}, \rho_{UE}, \{\emptyset\}, \{\emptyset\})$, where for the transition relation ρ_{UE}, we have that $(\mathbf{t}_1, \ldots, \mathbf{t}_k) \in \rho_{UE}(\mathbf{s}, a)$ iff:

(i) $\mathbf{s} = \emptyset$ and for all $\forall f_1 U f_2 \in a$, we have that $\forall f_1 U f_2 \in \mathbf{t}_j$ for all $1 \leq j \leq k$ iff $f_2 \notin a$.

(ii) $\mathbf{s} \neq \emptyset$ and for all $\forall f_1 U f_2 \in \mathbf{s}$, we have that $\forall f_1 U f_2 \in \mathbf{t}_j$ for all $1 \leq j \leq k$ iff $f_2 \notin a$.

Intuitively, the universal eventuality automaton defined here is the same as the eventuality automaton used in the proof of Theorem 3.1 except that it runs down all the branches of the tree. Note that this can be done quite easily as the eventuality automaton is deterministic.

The existential eventuality automaton

Given a CTL formula f, we define the set $ee(f)$ of its existential eventualities as the subset of $cl(f)$ that contains all formulas of the form $\exists f_1 U f_2$. The existential eventuality automaton is similar to the universal eventuality automaton. Indeed, it has to allow for different existential eventualities being satisfied on different paths while ensuring that all of them are satisfied on some path. $EE = (2^{cl(f)}, 2^{ee(f)}, \rho_{EE}, \{\emptyset\}, \{\emptyset\})$, where for the transition relation ρ_{EE}, we have that $(\mathbf{t}_1, \ldots, \mathbf{t}_k) \in \rho_{EE}(\mathbf{s}, a)$ iff:

(i) $\mathbf{s} = \emptyset$ and for all $\exists f_1 U f_2 \in a$, we have that $\exists f_1 U f_2 \in \mathbf{t}_j$ for some $1 \leq j \leq k$ iff $f_2 \notin a$.

(ii) $\mathbf{s} \neq \emptyset$ and for all $\exists f_1 U f_2 \in \mathbf{s}$, we have that $\exists f_1 U f_2 \in \mathbf{t}_j$ for some $1 \leq j \leq k$ iff $f_2 \notin a$.

It is slightly more difficult to understand why the existential eventuality automaton indeed checks that all existential eventualities are satisfied. Let us sketch a proof of the fact that a tree is accepted by the existential eventuality automaton iff all the existential eventualities labelling its nodes are satisfied. First, let us assume that the tree T is accepted. Consider an existential eventuality ee labelling a node x of the tree T. We consider two possible cases. In the first case, in the accepting run of EE over T, EE is in state $\emptyset$ at node x. It is clear that the eventuality ee will be satisfied. In the second case, at node x, EE is not in the state $\emptyset$. As the run is accepting it will reach the state $\emptyset$ on every path from x. Now, because of the conditions imposed by the local automaton, ee will appear in one of these nodes unless it has been satisfied previously. The second case thus reduces to the first case.

Proving that a tree on which the existential eventualities are satisfied is accepted is easier. One can generate an accepting computation of EE by choosing transitions of EE in such a way that the computation corresponding to each eventuality follows a path on which that eventuality is satisfied. The fact that all eventualities are satisfied ensures that such a computation exists.

Combining the automata

To obtain the automaton accepting the k-ary canonical models of the formula f, we take the intersection of the three automata we have just described. This can be done by the construction given in [55]. The number of states of the resulting automaton will be twice the number of states in the product of the component automata and will thus be bounded by $2^{O(|f|)}$.

This automaton accepts words over $2^{cl(f)}$ so we still have to take its projection on the set 2^P which is done exactly as in the proof of Theorem 3.1. □

Example The Büchi tree automaton of Fig. 3.4 is a model generator for the formula $\forall\Box\forall\Diamond p$ when a is taken to be $\emptyset$ and b to be $\{p\}$. Note that the automaton obtained from the construction given in the proof of Theorem 3.3 is somewhat more complicated, though it is equivalent to (generates the same infinite trees) the automaton we have described. □

We can now give the analogue of Theorem 3.2 concerning the *emptiness problem* for Büchi tree automata, i.e. the problem of determining, for a given Büchi tree automaton A, whether $T(A)$ is empty.

Theorem 3.4

(a) The emptiness problem for Büchi tree automata is solvable in quadratic time [46].

(b) The emptiness problem for Büchi tree automata is logspace complete for PTIME [55]. □

It is straightforward to obtain a decision procedure for CTL by combining Theorems 3.3, 3.4a and Lemma 3.5. Given a formula f, one builds (using Theorem 3.3) the tree automaton accepting the k-ary tree models of this formula for a k greater than the number of path quantifiers in the formula. By Lemma 3.5 it is then sufficient to check using Theorem 3.4a that this automaton is nonempty. This yields the exponential time upper bound for the satisfiability problem of CTL (originally proven in [15]). A matching lower bound is also proven in [15]. Note that for the logic CTL*, the best known decision procedure (also obtained by automata theoretic techniques) is of nondeterministic double exponential time complexity [19,54]. For that logic, the best known lower bound is double exponential time [54].

3.2.3 Partial order temporal logic

In [43] a new version of temporal logic was introduced to reason about partially ordered computations. However, from a purely logical point of view, this logic is a version of branching time temporal logic that includes past operators. Its connection to partial orders is not intrinsic, but is due to the way in which it is used. We will study this issue in detail in a later section. Here, we will define POLT (partial order temporal logic) and study its inherent properties such as its models and model generators.

Syntax

We will consider only one version of POTL, namely the one corresponding to CTL. This version is a slight generalization of the logic defined in [43] where the operator U was not considered. The syntax of POTL is identical to that of CTL except that we also allow two ***backwards path operators***: $\overline{\bigcirc}$ (previous) and $\overline{U}$ (since). As in CTL, path formulas (either backwards or forwards) can contain only a single temporal operator. Besides the abbreviations used in CTL, we use $\exists\overline{\Diamond} f$ and $\forall\overline{\Diamond} f$ to abbreviate $\exists(\mathbf{T}\overline{U}f)$ and $\forall(\mathbf{T}\overline{U}f)$ respectively. Also, $\exists\overline{\Box} f$ will be an abbreviation for $\neg\forall\overline{\Diamond}\neg f$ and $\forall\overline{\Box} f$ for $\neg\exists\overline{\Diamond}\neg f$.

In POTL, we will need to distinguish between forwards and backwards path formulas (i.e. path formulas where the temporal operator is $\overline{\bigcirc}$ or $\overline{U}$). Note that in POTL path formulas contain only one operator and hence do not mix forwards and backwards operators. For ease of exposition, we define the *reverse* $\overline{g}$ of a path formula g as g where $\bigcirc$ is replaced by $\overline{\bigcirc}$ and U by $\overline{U}$ if g is a forwards path formula, and as g where $\overline{\bigcirc}$ and $\overline{U}$ are respectively replaced by $\bigcirc$ and U if g is a backwards formula.

Example $\forall\overline{\Box}\exists\bigcirc\forall p\overline{U}q$ is a POTL formula. □

Semantics

The logic POTL is interpreted over exactly the same type of structure as BTL. The only additional requirement is that the accessibility relation should be total in both directions. In other words, each state should have at least one successor and at least one predecessor. To define the semantics of POTL, we need to talk about backwards paths extracted from structures. This leads us to a definition symmetric to Definition 3.2.

Definition 3.4 A backwards linear interpretation extracted from a branching interpretation $\langle M_B, w_0\rangle$ where $M_B = (W_B, Q_B, \pi_B)$ is a pair $\langle M_L, w_0\rangle$ where $M_L = (W_L, R_L, \pi_L)$ with $w_0 \in W_L \subseteq W_B$, $\pi_L(w) = \pi_B(w)$ and $(R_L(w), w) \in Q_B$ for all $w \in W_L$. □

The only difference between Definitions 3.2 and 3.4 is that in Definition 3.4, we have extracted the linear interpretation in the direction opposite to the one defined by the relation Q_B. In other words, moving forwards in the backwards linear interpretation corresponds to moving backwards in the branching model.

The semantics of POTL are identical to those of CTL except where backwards path formulas appear. For these, we have the following two clauses:

- $\langle M_B, w_0\rangle \models \forall g$ where g is a backwards path formula iff for all backwards linear structures $\langle M_L, w_0\rangle$ extracted from $\langle M_B, w_0\rangle$, $\langle M_L, w_0\rangle \models \overline{g}$
- $\langle M_B, w_0\rangle \models \exists g$ where g is a backwards path formula iff for some backwards linear structures $\langle M_L, w_0\rangle$ extracted from $\langle M_B, w_0\rangle$, $\langle M_L, w_0\rangle \models \overline{g}$

Models and model generators

Partial order temporal logic does not have trees as canonical models. Indeed, a formula like $\exists\overline{\bigcirc}p \wedge \exists\overline{\bigcirc}\neg p$ is only true in a node that has at least two predecessors. This is clearly not possible in a tree where each node has only one successor. In [43] a class of models called *backwards-forwards trees* is considered. An easy way to understand backwards-forwards trees is to think of trees where the edges leaving each node point either forwards or backwards (see Fig. 3.5).

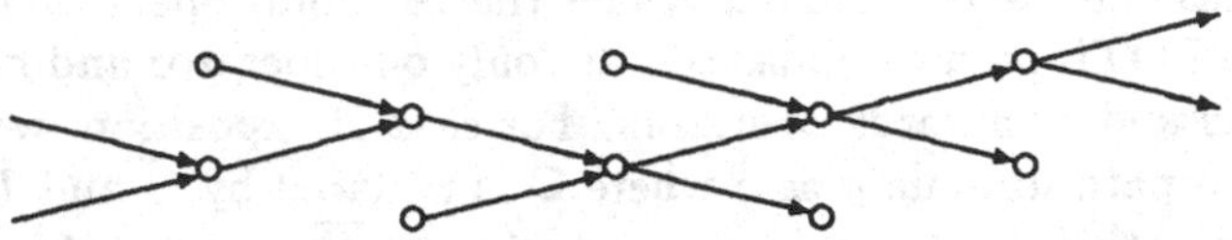

Figure 3.5: A backwards-forwards tree

An equivalent representation is to have all the edges of the tree in the same direction, but to label them with either + or − depending on their direction (see Figure 3.6).

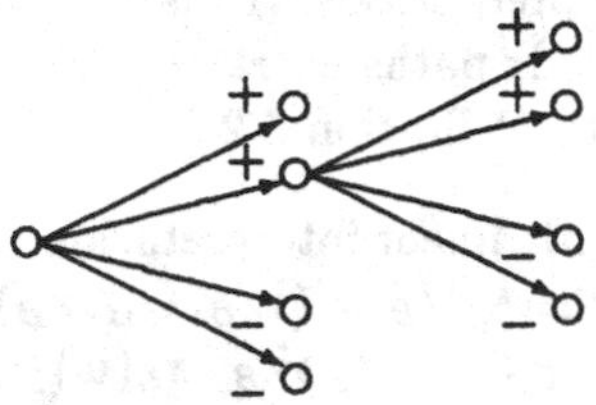

Figure 3.6: A backwards-forwards labelled tree

As in a tree each node has only one edge leading to it, the + and − labels can be placed on the nodes rather than on the edges. We will call such a tree with nodes labelled + or − a $\pm$ tree. If besides the $\pm$ labels, the tree also has labels from an alphabet Σ, we will call it a labelled $\pm$ tree. Formally, a k-ary labelled $\pm$ tree T is a function $T : [k]^\star \rightarrow \Sigma \times [\pm]$, where $[\pm]$ denotes the set $\{+, -\}$. For POTL, our canonical models will be k-ary $\pm$ trees labelled over the alphabet 2^P, i.e. interpretations $\langle M, \lambda \rangle$ where $M = ([k]^\star, succ, \tau)$, τ being a function from $[k]^\star$ to $2^P \times [\pm]$. Note that a $\pm$ tree is simply a representation of a special type of branching structure. The branching structure corresponding to a ± tree can be obtained by simply inverting all the edges leading to nodes labelled −. As a matter of terminology, we will use the words "son" and "father" when referring to the respective position of nodes in a ± tree. We will use the words "successor" and "predecessor" to talk about the respective position of such nodes when taking into account the polarity (± label) of the nodes. For instance, the − son of a node is its predecessor, whereas the father of a − node is its successor.

Now we turn to our notion of the equivalence of interpretations. It needs to be adapted as equivalent interpretations should have the same transitions *in both directions.* We will call the notion of equivalence we use on interpretations for POTL formulas *two-way equivalence.*

Definition 3.5 Two branching interpretations $\langle M_1, w_{01}\rangle$ and $\langle M_2, w_{02}\rangle$ where $M_1 = (W_1, Q_1, \pi_1)$ and $M_2 = (W_2, Q_2, \pi_2)$ are two-way equivalent iff there is relation $\phi \subseteq W_1 \times W_2$ such that:

- $(w_{01}, w_{02}) \in \phi$;
- if $(w_1, w_2) \in \phi$, then $\pi_1(w_1) = \pi_2(w_2)$;
- if $(w_1, w_2) \in \phi$, and there is a $w'_1 \in W_1$ such that $(w_1, w'_1) \in Q_1$ then there is a $w'_2 \in W_2$ such that $(w_2, w'_2) \in Q_2$ and $(w'_1, w'_2) \in \phi$;
- if $(w_1, w_2) \in \phi$, and there is a $w'_2 \in W_2$ such that $(w_2, w'_2) \in Q_2$ then there is a $w'_1 \in W_1$ such that $(w_1, w'_1) \in Q_1$ and $(w'_1, w'_2) \in \phi$;
- if $(w_1, w_2) \in \phi$, and there is a $w'_1 \in W_1$ such that $(w'_1, w_1) \in Q_1$ then there is a $w'_2 \in W_2$ such that $(w'_2, w_2) \in Q_2$ and $(w'_1, w'_2) \in \phi$;
- if $(w_1, w_2) \in \phi$, and there is a $w'_2 \in W_2$ such that $(w'_2, w_2) \in Q_2$ then there is a $w'_1 \in W_1$ such that $(w'_1, w_1) \in Q_1$ and $(w'_1, w'_2) \in \phi$. □

The difference between two-way equivalence and the equivalence notion of Definition 3.3 is that two-way equivalence considers both the edges leaving and the edges leading to a node. Note that in the restricted case of ± trees, an equivalent way to state Definition 3.5 is to use Definition 3.3 and require that if $(w_1, w_2) \in \phi$, then w_1 and w_2 also agree on their ± label. We now establish the analogue of Lemma 3.3.

Lemma 3.6 If two branching interpretations $\langle M_1, w_{01}\rangle$ and $\langle M_2, w_{02}\rangle$ are two-way equivalent, then for any POTL formula f, $\langle M_1, w_{01}\rangle \models f$ iff $\langle M_2, w_{02}\rangle \models f$.

Proof: The proof is identical to the proof of Lemma 3.3, except that here, we have to notice that if $\langle M_1, w_{01}\rangle$ and $\langle M_2, w_{02}\rangle$ are two-way equivalent branching structures, then, from these interpretations, one can extract equivalent forwards *and backwards* linear interpretations. □

To establish the existence of canonical models for POTL, we establish the analogue of Lemma 3.4. For this, we need to take into account both incoming and outgoing edges in the definition of the branching factor of a structure. To distinguish this branching factor from the one used in Lemma 3.4, we will call it the *two-way branching factor*. By definition, the two-way branching factor of a structure (W, Q, π) is the largest ℓ such that for some $w \in W$, we have $\ell = |\{w'|(w, w') \in Q \vee (w', w) \in Q\}|)$.

Lemma 3.7 Every branching interpretation $\langle M, w_0\rangle$ where $M = (W, Q, \pi)$ and whose two-way branching factor is $\leq k$ is equivalent to a k-ary $\pm$ tree canonical interpretation $\tau : [k]^* \rightarrow 2^P \times [\pm]$.

Proof: We define the canonical interpretation τ simultaneously with the relation ϕ that will enable us to establish that it is equivalent to $\langle M, w_0\rangle$. The relation ϕ is actually a function in $[k]^* \rightarrow W$. We define τ and ϕ in stages. At stage i, ϕ_i will be defined on all nodes of the $\pm$ tree of depth $\leq i$. We start with $\phi_0(\lambda) = w_0$ and $\tau_0(\lambda) = (\pi(\phi_0(\lambda), +)$. Note that for $\tau_0(\lambda)$, the choice of the label $+$ is arbitrary. We obtain ϕ_{i+1} from ϕ_i by defining it on all nodes of depth $i+1$ as follows. For each node $x \in [k]^*$ of depth i, let $\{w_{s_1}, \ldots, w_{s_\ell}\}$, be the successors of $\phi_i(x)$ (i.e. nodes w_j such that $(\phi(x), w_j) \in Q$) and let $\{w_{p_1}, \ldots, w_{p_\ell}\}$ be the predecessors of $\phi_i(x)$ (i.e. nodes w_j such that $(w_j, \phi(x)) \in Q$). By hypothesis, we have that $s_\ell + p_\ell \leq k$. We define $\phi_{i+1}(xj) = w_j$ for $s_1 \leq j \leq s_\ell$ or $p_1 \leq j \leq p_\ell$ and for all other $1 \leq j \leq k$, we take $\phi_{i+1}(xj) = w_{s_\ell}$. In other words, the first s_ℓ sons of x simulate the s_ℓ successors of $\phi_i(x)$, the next p_ℓ sons of x simulate the p_ℓ predecessors of x and if $s_\ell + p_\ell < k$, we simply replicate the last successor. We define τ_{i+1} on the nodes xj of depth $i+1$ by $\tau_{i+1}(xj) = (\pi(\phi_{i+1}(xj)), +)$ for $s_1 \leq j \leq s_\ell$ and $s_\ell + p_\ell < j \leq k$ and by $\tau_{i+1}(xj) = (\pi(\phi_{i+1}(xj)), -)$ for $p_1 \leq j \leq p_\ell$. The relation ϕ and the function τ are taken to be ϕ_ω and τ_ω. □

Our next step is to show that $\pm$-tree models with limited arity are an interesting class of models for POTL formulas. For this, we prove that if a POTL formula containing n path quantifiers has a model, then it has an $(n+1)$-ary $\pm$ canonical tree model. The proof is basically identical to the proof of Lemma 3.5 except that $\pm$ labels have to be introduced appropriately and we have to ensure that each node has at least one successor and one predecessor.

Lemma 3.8 If a POTL formula f containing n path quantifiers has a model, then it has an $(n+1)$-ary $\pm$ tree model.

Proof: Suppose f is satisfied by an interpretation $\langle M, w_0\rangle$ where $M = (W, Q, \pi)$. We construct a $(n+1)$-ary $\pm$ tree model τ satisfying f by inductively constructing a mapping $\psi : [n+1]^* \rightarrow W$ and defining τ in terms of ψ. We start with a mapping ψ_0 and a labelling τ_0 defined on the set $X_0 = 1^*$

(i.e. the leftmost path starting at λ). To define ψ_0 and τ_0, we choose either a forwards or a backwards linear interpretation $\langle M_L, w_0\rangle$ extracted from $\langle M, w_0\rangle$ where $M_L = (W_L, R_L, \pi_L)$. If all the eventualities that are satisfied in w_0 are forwards, we choose a backwards path. If they are all backwards, we choose a forwards path. If some are forwards and some are backwards, the choice does not matter. The reason for this particular choice is to ensure that the root of the tree has both at least one + son and one − son. If the chosen path is forwards, we define $\psi_0(1^k) = R_L^k(w_0)$ and $\tau_0(1^k) = (\pi(\psi_0(1^k)), +)$; if it is backwards, τ_0 is defined by $\tau_0(1^k) = (\pi(\psi_0(1^k)), -)$. Note that each node $x \in X_0$ has exactly one son in X_0 which is its leftmost son $x1$.

Now, given the mapping ψ_i defined on the set of nodes X_i, we show how to define ψ_{i+1} and the set X_{i+1}. Our construction ensures that all nodes in X_i either have $n+1$ sons within X_i or have only their leftmost son in X_i. Consider the nodes in X_i that have only a leftmost successor in X_i. For each such node x, we extend ψ_i as follows. Consider all existential state formulas $E \in scl(f)$ such that $\langle M, \psi_i(x)\rangle \models E$. There are at most n such formulas, say $E_1, \ldots, E_n$, where n is the number of path quantifiers in f and where E_j is either $\exists g_j$ or $\neg\forall g_j$. For each formula E_j, we choose a linear interpretation $\langle M_{Lj}, \psi_i(x)\rangle$ extracted from $\langle M, \psi_i(x)\rangle$ (forwards or backwards depending on whether g_j is a forwards or backwards formula). This linear interpretation must be such that $\langle M_{Lj}, \psi_i(x)\rangle \models g_j$ if E_j is $\exists g_j$ and g_j is a forwards formula, and such that $\langle M_{Lj}, \psi_i(x)\rangle \models \overline{g_j}$ if g_j is a backwards formula. If E_j is $\neg\forall g_j$, then the linear interpretation must satisfy either $\neg g_j$ or $\overline{\neg g_j}$ depending on whether g_j is forwards or backwards. We then define $\psi_{i+1}(x(j+1)) = R_{L_j}(\psi_i(x))$ and $\psi_{i+1}(x(j+1)1^k) = R_{L_j}^k(\psi_i(x))$ for $k \geq 1$. The mapping τ_{i+1} is then defined on these points by $\tau_{i+1}(x(j+1)^k) = (\pi(\psi_i(x(j+1)^k)), +)$ if the eventuality E_j is forwards. If it is backwards, the + in the definition of τ_{i+1} is replaced by −. If there are only $0 \leq \ell < n$ formulas E_j, for $j = \ell+1, \ldots, n$, we choose $\langle M_{Lj}, \psi_i(x)\rangle$ to be an arbitrary linear interpretation extracted from $\langle M, \psi_i(x)\rangle$. Note that this construction ensures that each node of the $\pm$ tree model has a successor and a predecessor. Indeed, a node and its leftmost son always have the same $\pm$ label. Hence if the son of that node is a successor, its father is a predecessor and vice versa. The relation ϕ and the function τ are taken to be ϕ_ω and τ_ω. □

Our last step is to show how to build a Büchi tree automaton that accepts all the k-ary $\pm$ tree models of a POTL formula f. The apparent difficulty in this construction is that we might have to go up and down the tree to take into account the fact that we are dealing with forwards and backwards formulas. Fortunately, it is possible to avoid checking conditions going up the tree by constructing an automaton that operates on trees labelled with elements of an extension of the closure of the formula f. This technique was introduced in [55] and further developed in [53].

Theorem 3.5 Given a POTL formula f and a constant k, one can construct a k-ary Büchi tree automaton $A = (\Sigma, S, \rho, S_0, F)$, where $\Sigma = 2^P \times [\pm]$, and $|S| \leq 2^{O(|f|)}$, such that A accepts exactly all the k-ary $\pm$ tree models of f. $\Box$

Proof: To build the automaton, we use an extension of the closure of the formula f. The extended closure of f ($ecl(f)$) is defined by the following rules:

- $f \in ecl(f)$
- if $f_1 \wedge f_2 \in ecl(f)$ then $f_1, f_2 \in ecl(f)$
- if $\neg f_2 \in ecl(f)$ then $f_2 \in ecl(f)$
- if $f_2 \in ecl(f)$ then $\neg f_2 \in ecl(f)$
- if $\exists \bigcirc f_2 \in ecl(f)$ then $f_2, \exists_d \bigcirc f_2, \exists_u \bigcirc f_2 \in ecl(f)$
- if $\forall \bigcirc f_2 \in ecl(f)$ then $f_2, \forall_d \bigcirc f_2, \forall_u \bigcirc f_2 \in ecl(f)$
- if $\exists f_1 U f_2 \in ecl(f)$ then $f_1, f_2, \exists_d f_1 U f_2, \exists_u f_1 U f_2 \in ecl(f)$
- if $\forall f_1 U f_2 \in ecl(f)$ then $f_1, f_2, \forall_d f_1 U f_2, \forall_u f_1 U f_2 \in ecl(f)$
- if $\exists \overline{\bigcirc} f_2 \in ecl(f)$ then $f_2, \exists_d \overline{\bigcirc} f_2, \exists_u \overline{\bigcirc} f_2 \in ecl(f)$
- if $\forall \overline{\bigcirc} f_2 \in ecl(f)$ then $f_2, \forall_d \overline{\bigcirc} f_2, \forall_u \overline{\bigcirc} f_2 \in ecl(f)$
- if $\exists f_1 \overline{U} f_2 \in ecl(f)$ then $f_1, f_2, \exists_d f_1 \overline{U} f_2, \exists_u f_1 \overline{U} f_2 \in ecl(f)$
- if $\forall f_1 \overline{U} f_2 \in ecl(f)$ then $f_1, f_2, \forall_d f_1 \overline{U} f_2, \forall_u f_1 \overline{U} f_2 \in ecl(f)$

Besides the addition of clauses for the past temporal operators, the difference between the $cl(f)$ defined in the proof of Theorem 3.3 and the $ecl(f)$ we have here is that for formulas of the form $\exists g$ and $\forall g$, we add the formulas $\exists_d g$, $\exists_u g$ and $\forall_u g$, $\forall_d g$ respectively. The intended use of these formulas is that $\exists_d g$ will be true in a node of a tree iff the path formula g is satisfied on a path going strictly down the tree whereas $\exists_u g$ will be true on a path initially going up the tree. This distinction will, for instance, make it possible to decide whether, to check a formula $\exists \bigcirc p$ is satisfied in a node of the tree, we have to look at the father or at the sons of this node. Note that if the node is labelled $-$, the father as well as all the sons of the node labelled $+$ are successors of the node. Similarly, $\forall_d g$ will be true in a node if g is true in all paths from that node going strictly downwards in the tree and $\forall_u g$ will be true if g is true on all paths initially going through the father of the node. Note that we take for the meaning of $\forall_d g$ that g is true on all paths that are strictly downwards. This makes things a little simpler and it is sufficient as it is easy to show that for the path formulas of POTL, a formula is satisfied on all paths iff it is satisfied on all upwards and strictly downwards paths. Indeed, once a forwards path starts going down the tree, it cannot go back up (the $\pm$ label would be wrong) and similarly for a backwards path.

As in the proof of Theorem 3.3, the automaton we are constructing is defined as the combination of three parts: the local automaton, the existential eventuality automaton and the universal eventuality automaton. We start with the local automaton.

Constructing the local automaton

The local automaton is $L = (2^{ecl(f)} \times [\pm], N_L, \rho_L, N_f, N_L)$. The state set N_L is the subset of elements (s, ℓ) of $2^{ecl(f)} \times [\pm]$ that satisfy the following conditions:

(a) For all $f_1 \in ecl(f)$, we have that $f_1 \in s$ iff $\neg f_1 \notin s$.

(b) For all $f_1 \wedge f_2 \in ecl(f)$, we have that $f_1 \wedge f_2 \in s$ iff $f_1 \in s$ and $f_2 \in s$.

In the case where $\ell = +$, we also require:

- For all $\exists \bigcirc f_1 \in ecl(f)$ we have that $\exists \bigcirc f_1 \in s$ iff $\exists_d \bigcirc f_1 \in s$.
- For all $\exists f_1 U f_2 \in ecl(f)$ we have that $\exists f_1 U f_2 \in s$ iff $\exists_d f_1 U f_2 \in s$.
- For all $\forall \bigcirc f_1 \in ecl(f)$ we have that $\forall \bigcirc f_1 \in s$ iff $\forall_d \bigcirc f_1 \in s$.
- For all $\forall f_1 U f_2 \in ecl(f)$ we have that $\forall f_1 U f_2 \in s$ iff $\forall_d f_1 U f_2 \in s$.
- For all $\exists \overline{\bigcirc} f_1 \in ecl(f)$ we have that $\exists \overline{\bigcirc} f_1 \in s$ iff $\exists_d \overline{\bigcirc} f_1 \in s$ or $\exists_u \overline{\bigcirc} f_1 \in s$.
- For all $\exists f_1 \overline{U} f_2 \in ecl(f)$ we have that $\exists f_1 \overline{U} f_2 \in s$ iff $\exists_d f_1 \overline{U} f_2 \in s$ or $\exists_u f_1 \overline{U} f_2 \in s$.
- For all $\forall \overline{\bigcirc} f_1 \in ecl(f)$ we have that $\forall \overline{\bigcirc} f_1 \in s$ iff $\forall_d \overline{\bigcirc} f_1 \in s$ and $\forall_u \overline{\bigcirc} f_1 \in s$.
- For all $\forall f_1 \overline{U} f_2 \in ecl(f)$ we have that $\forall f_1 \overline{U} f_2 \in s$ iff $\forall_d f_1 \overline{U} f_2 \in s$ and $\forall_u f_1 \overline{U} f_2 \in s$.

On the other hand, if $\ell = -$, we require:

- For all $\exists \bigcirc f_1 \in ecl(f)$ we have that $\exists \bigcirc f_1 \in s$ iff $\exists_d \bigcirc f_1 \in s$ or $\exists_u \bigcirc f_1 \in s$.
- For all $\exists f_1 U f_2 \in ecl(f)$ we have that $\exists f_1 U f_2 \in s$ iff $\exists_d f_1 U f_2 \in s$ or $\exists_u f_1 U f_2 \in s$.
- For all $\forall \bigcirc f_1 \in ecl(f)$ we have that $\forall \bigcirc f_1 \in s$ iff $\forall_d \bigcirc f_1 \in s$ and $\forall_u \bigcirc f_1 \in s$.
- For all $\forall f_1 U f_2 \in ecl(f)$ we have that $\forall f_1 U f_2 \in s$ iff $\forall_d f_1 U f_2 \in s$ and $\forall_u f_1 U f_2 \in s$.

- For all $\exists\overline{\bigcirc} f_1 \in ecl(f)$ we have that $\exists\overline{\bigcirc} f_1 \in \mathbf{s}$ iff $\exists_d\overline{\bigcirc} f_1 \in \mathbf{s}$.
- For all $\exists f_1 \overline{U} f_2 \in ecl(f)$ we have that $\exists f_1 \overline{U} f_2 \in \mathbf{s}$ iff $\exists_d f_1 \overline{U} f_2 \in \mathbf{s}$.
- For all $\forall\overline{\bigcirc} f_1 \in ecl(f)$ we have that $\forall\overline{\bigcirc} f_1 \in \mathbf{s}$ iff $\forall_d\overline{\bigcirc} f_1 \in \mathbf{s}$.
- For all $\forall f_1 \overline{U} f_2 \in ecl(f)$ we have that $\forall f_1 \overline{U} f_2 \in \mathbf{s}$ iff $\forall_d f_1 \overline{U} f_2 \in \mathbf{s}$.

For the transition relation $\rho_L : N_L \times (2^{ecl(f)} \times [\pm]) \rightarrow 2^{N_L^k}$, we have that $((\mathbf{t}_1, \ell_1), \ldots, (\mathbf{t}_k, \ell_k)) \in \rho_L((\mathbf{s}, \ell), (a, \ell'))$ iff $(a, \ell') = (\mathbf{s}, \ell)$ and the conditions we are going to describe hold. We separate them in two groups: those dealing with downwards path formulas and those dealing with upwards path formulas. First, we deal with downwards formulas:

- For all $\exists_d \bigcirc f_1 \in ecl(f)$ we have that $\exists_d \bigcirc f_1 \in \mathbf{s}$ iff for some $1 \leq j \leq k$, $f_1 \in \mathbf{t}_j$ and $\ell_j = +$.
- For all $\forall_d \bigcirc f_1 \in ecl(f)$ we have that $\forall_d \bigcirc f_1 \in \mathbf{s}$ iff for all $1 \leq j \leq k$ such that $\ell_j = +$, we have $f_1 \in \mathbf{t}_j$.
- For all $\exists_d f_1 U f_2 \in ecl(f)$ we have that $\exists_d f_1 U f_2 \in \mathbf{s}$ iff either $f_2 \in \mathbf{s}$ or $f_1 \in \mathbf{s}$ and for some $1 \leq j \leq k$, $\exists_d f_1 U f_2 \in \mathbf{t}_j$ and $\ell_j = +$.
- For all $\forall_d f_1 U f_2 \in ecl(f)$ we have that $\forall_d f_1 U f_2 \in \mathbf{s}$ iff either $f_2 \in \mathbf{s}$ or $f_1 \in \mathbf{s}$ and for all $1 \leq j \leq k$ for which $\ell_j = + \; \forall_d f_1 U f_2 \in \mathbf{t}_j$.
- For all $\exists_d \overline{\bigcirc} f_1 \in ecl(f)$ we have that $\exists_d \overline{\bigcirc} f_1 \in \mathbf{s}$ iff for some $1 \leq j \leq k$, $f_1 \in \mathbf{t}_j$ and $\ell_j = -$.
- For all $\forall_d \overline{\bigcirc} f_1 \in ecl(f)$ we have that $\forall_d \overline{\bigcirc} f_1 \in \mathbf{s}$ iff for all $1 \leq j \leq k$ such that $\ell_j = -$, we have $f_1 \in \mathbf{t}_j$.
- For all $\exists_d f_1 \overline{U} f_2 \in ecl(f)$ we have that $\exists_d f_1 \overline{U} f_2 \in \mathbf{s}$ iff either $f_2 \in \mathbf{s}$ or $f_1 \in \mathbf{s}$ and for some $1 \leq j \leq k$, $\exists_d f_1 \overline{U} f_2 \in \mathbf{t}_j$ and $\ell_j = -$.
- For all $\forall_d f_1 \overline{U} f_2 \in ecl(f)$ we have that $\forall_d f_1 \overline{U} f_2 \in \mathbf{s}$ iff either $f_2 \in \mathbf{s}$ or $f_1 \in \mathbf{s}$ and for all $1 \leq j \leq k$ for which $\ell_j = -$, $\forall_d f_1 \overline{U} f_2 \in \mathbf{t}_j$.

We now give the conditions for upwards formulas. As each node in a tree has only one father, these conditions are identical for formulas of the form $\exists_u g$ and of the form $\forall_u g$. We thus give them only for existential formulas, but they do apply to both existential and universal upwards formulas.

- For all $\exists_u \bigcirc f_1 \in ecl(f)$ we have that $\exists_u \bigcirc f_1 \in \mathbf{t}_j$ for some $1 \leq j \leq k$ iff $\ell_j = -$ and $f_1 \in \mathbf{s}$.
- For all $\exists_u f_1 U f_2 \in ecl(f)$ we have that $\exists_u f_1 U f_2 \in \mathbf{t}_j$ for some $1 \leq j \leq k$, iff either $f_2 \in \mathbf{t}_j$ or $f_1 \in \mathbf{t}_j$, $\exists f_1 U f_2 \in \mathbf{s}$ and $\ell_j = -$.

- For all $\exists_u \overline{O} f_1 \in ecl(f)$ we have that $\exists_u \overline{O} f_1 \in \mathbf{t}_j$ for some $1 \leq j \leq k$ iff $\ell_j = +$ and $f_1 \in \mathbf{s}$.
- For all $\exists_u f_1 \overline{U} f_2 \in ecl(f)$ we have that $\exists_u f_1 \overline{U} f_2 \in \mathbf{t}_j$ for some $1 \leq j \leq k$, iff either $f_2 \in \mathbf{t}_j$ or $f_1 \in \mathbf{t}_j$, $\exists f_1 \overline{U} f_2 \in \mathbf{s}$ and $\ell_j = +$.

Finally, the set of starting states N_f consists of all pairs $(\mathbf{s}, \ell)$ such that $\mathbf{s}$ does not contain any $\exists_u$ or $\forall_u$ formulas and such that $f \in \mathbf{s}$. The local automaton does not impose any acceptance conditions and thus its set of accepting states is the whole set of states.

The universal eventuality automaton

The eventuality automata (universal and existential) have to check that in all nodes of the tree, all eventualities are satisfied. The important observation here is that it is sufficient to do this for downwards eventualities. Indeed, if an eventuality is satisfied on an upwards path, either it will be satisfied while the path is moving up the tree and no further checking is necessary or it will eventually propagate into a downwards eventuality. This is the case as the local automaton forces unsatisfied eventualities to propagate and, when moving up the tree, one eventually reaches the root which is not allowed to contain upwards formulas.

These observations make the universal and existential eventuality automata very similar to the ones we used for CTL. Given a POTL formula f, we define the set $due(f)$ of its downwards universal eventualities as the subset of $ecl(f)$ that contains all formulas of the form $\forall_d f_1 U f_2$ and $\forall_d f_1 \overline{U} f_2$. The eventuality automaton is $UE = (2^{ecl(f)} \times [\pm], 2^{due(f)}, \rho_{UE}, \{\emptyset\}, \{\emptyset\})$, where for the transition relation ρ_{UE} we have that $((\mathbf{t}_1, \ell_1), \ldots, (\mathbf{t}_k, \ell_k)) \in \rho_{UE}((\mathbf{s}, \ell), (a, \ell'))$ iff:

(a) $\mathbf{s} = \emptyset$ and

  (i) for all $\forall_d f_1 U f_2 \in a$, we have that $f_2 \notin a$ iff $\forall_d f_1 U f_2 \in \mathbf{t}_j$ for all $1 \leq j \leq k$ such that $\ell_j = +$,

  (ii) for all $\forall_d f_1 \overline{U} f_2 \in a$, we have that $f_2 \notin a$ iff $\forall_d f_1 U f_2 \in \mathbf{t}_j$ for all $1 \leq j \leq k$ such that $\ell_j = -$.

(b) $\mathbf{s} \neq \emptyset$ and

  (i) for all $\forall_d f_1 U f_2 \in \mathbf{s}$, $f_2 \notin a$ iff we have that $\forall_d f_1 U f_2 \in \mathbf{t}_j$ for all $1 \leq j \leq k$ such that $\ell_j = +$,

  (ii) for all $\forall_d f_1 \overline{U} f_2 \in \mathbf{s}$, $f_2 \notin a$ iff we have that $\forall_d f_1 \overline{U} f_2 \in \mathbf{t}_j$ for all $1 \leq j \leq k$ such that $\ell_j = -$.

This automaton is essentially identical to the one defined in the proof of Theorem 3.3 except that it checks forwards eventualities on + nodes and backwards eventualities on − nodes.

The existential eventuality automaton

Given an POTL formula f, we define the set $dee(f)$ of its downwards existential eventualities as the subset of $ecl(f)$ that contains all formulas of the form $\exists_d f_1 \, U f_2$ and $\exists_d f_1 \overline{U} f_2$. The existential eventuality automaton is also very similar to the one used in the proof of Theorem 3.3. It is the following: $EE = (2^{ecl(f)} \times [\pm], 2^{dee(f)}, \rho_{EE}, \{\emptyset\}, \{\emptyset\})$, where for the transition relation ρ_{EE} we have that $((\mathbf{t}_1, \ell_1), \ldots, (\mathbf{t}_k, \ell_k)) \in \rho_{EE}((\mathbf{s}, \ell), (a, \ell'))$ iff:

(a) $\mathbf{s} = \emptyset$ and

- (i) for all $\exists_d f_1 \, U f_2 \in a$ we have that $f_2 \notin a$ iff $\exists_d f_1 \, U f_2 \in \mathbf{t}_j$ for some $1 \leq j \leq k$ such that $\ell_j = +$,
- (ii) for all $\exists_d f_1 \overline{U} f_2 \in a$ we have that $f_2 \notin a$ iff $\exists_d f_1 \, U f_2 \in \mathbf{t}_j$ for some $1 \leq j \leq k$ such that $\ell_j = -$.

(b) $\mathbf{s} \neq \emptyset$ and

- (i) for all $\exists_d f_1 \, U f_2 \in \mathbf{s}$, $f_2 \notin a$ iff we have that $\exists_d f_1 \, U f_2 \in \mathbf{t}_j$ for some $1 \leq j \leq k$ such that $\ell_j = +$,
- (ii) for all $\exists_d f_1 \overline{U} f_2 \in \mathbf{s}$, $f_2 \notin a$ iff we have that $\exists_d f_1 \overline{U} f_2 \in \mathbf{t}_j$ for some $1 \leq j \leq k$ such that $\ell_j = -$.

Combining the automata

Combining the automata and projecting on the alphabet 2^P is done exactly as in the proof of Theorem 3.3. □

Combining Theorem 3.5 with Theorem 3.4 and Lemma 3.8, we obtain an exponential decision procedure for POTL. Clearly, the matching lower bound proven for CTL also applies.

3.2.4 Summary

We have described three versions of temporal logic: linear time, branching time and partial order. For each we have given syntax and semantics and shown how, given a formula, one can construct a model generator describing up to equivalence all the models of the formula that are in a given class. The results are summarized in Table 3.1.

3.3 Program verification

In this section, we review and classify the applications of temporal logic to program verification. Our classification is organized around the different views of programs and their computations. We will consider successively deterministic programs with linear executions, nondeterministic programs with linear

Table 3.1: *Summary of Temporal Logics.*

Logic	Models	Model generators	Class of models described
linear	sequences	Büchi sequential automata	all models
branching	trees	Büchi tree automata	k-ary models
partial order	$\pm$ trees	Büchi tree automata	k-ary models

executions and programs having partially ordered sets as executions. For each of these views, we show how verification methods can be obtained by relating the programs and computations to either models or model generators of the various temporal logics.

We will consider only finite-state programs. This has the advantage of simplifying the presentation and of relating nicely to the propositional temporal logics described in the previous section. However, our classification and a number of the results we state here are also applicable to infinite-state programs and first-order temporal logic.

3.3.1 First view: deterministic programs

Verifying deterministic programs is not the most usual application of temporal logic. However it is a simple case and serves as a good introduction to our methodology.

A deterministic program is a tuple (W, R, w_0, π) where

- W is a set of states,
- R is a total transition function,
- w_0 is a unique initial state,
- $\pi : W \to \Sigma$ is a labelling function.

One can think of the label of a state as describing the properties of that state and specifying the actions the program performs when entering that state. Notice that a deterministic program has a unique computation (or execution) which is the infinite sequence of states generated from the initial state: $w_0, R(w_0), R^2(w_0), \cdots$

Our approach is based on relating programs and their computations to either models or model generators for some version of temporal logic. In the case of deterministic programs this relation is straightforward. A deterministic program is exactly the same type of structure as a model for an LTL formula. The same is true of the computation of that program. Actually, the program and its computation are equivalent according to Definition 3.1, so we will not distinguish them in what follows.

As we explained in the introduction, to obtain a verification method, we need to choose some way of describing the program and some way of describing the desired properties of the program. Our choices are the following:

- *Program:* Can be described explicitly by its states and transitions or can be described by a formula. As we are considering deterministic programs, the formula should be such that it has only one model up to equivalence.

- *Property:* Even if the program is deterministic, the property need not be so, as it can be true of more than one program. The most natural way to describe the property is to use an LTL formula. Another possibility is to use a model generator (i.e. a Büchi sequential automaton) rather than an LTL formula.

Note that given Theorem 3.1 any property or program that can be described by an LTL formula can also be described by a Büchi automaton. However, strictly speaking, the converse is not true. To be able to give a formula corresponding to any automaton, one needs to extend LTL. One possibility is to use the extended temporal logic of [59,60,57]. Another possibility is to use additional propositions in the formula to encode the states of the automaton. The transitions of the automaton can then easily be described by LTL formulas. The problem with this approach is that the resulting formula conveys more information than is desired. Besides the description of the acceptable behaviors, it also includes the encoding of the states of the automaton. To hide this encoding, one can consider the propositions describing the states as existentially quantified. This takes us beyond LTL and towards ***quantified linear time propositional temporal logic***. Quantified temporal logic has been studied in [47,51]. It has been shown that it is possible to build Büchi automata from quantified temporal logic, but the complexity of the algorithm is much higher than for LTL (it is nonelementary). Fortunately, as the preceding discussion suggests, one level of existential quantification is sufficient for encoding automata and in this case Theorem 3.1 still applies. This type of encoding of the states by existentially quantified formulas is the method usually used when one wants to represent a program by a temporal formula.

The verification problem is, given a description of a program and a property, to determine if the program (or equivalently its computation) satisfies the property. Depending on how we choose to describe the program and the property, we get various methods as shown in Table 3.2.

We now give more details about the various methods.

Model checking

In this approach, the verification problem is to check that the program which is described explicitly satisfies (i.e. is a model of) the specification. This method was introduced in [9,10] for nondeterministic programs and BTL specifications,

Table 3.2: *Verification methods for deterministic programs.*

Program	Property	
	LTL formula	Büchi sequential automaton
States and transitions	Model checking	Automaton verification
LTL formula	Axiomatic verification	Reverse model checking

and was applied to nondeterministic programs and LTL specifications in [27] and [56] (see Section 3.3.2). It has not so far been advocated in the context of deterministic programs and LTL specifications, probably because in practice this is not an interesting case. Algorithmically, it is much simpler than the case of nondeterministic programs and LTL specifications. It can be solved with a simple polynomial time algorithm which is an adaptation of the algorithm used for doing model checking for nondeterministic programs and branching time logic (see [11,17,18]).

Automaton verification

This rather recent approach was introduced for nondeterministic programs in [2] and further developed in [3,36]. In the case we are considering now, the problem is to determine if the unique computation of a deterministic program is a word accepted by the automaton describing the desired property of the program. This can be done by viewing the program as a deterministic automaton, taking the product of this automaton with the automaton describing the property and checking that the result is nonempty.

Axiomatic verification

This is the earliest verification method based on temporal logic. It was introduced in [40] and [41] and was further developed in [31,39,32,33,34] and [35]. It is usually presented for nondeterministic or concurrent programs, but is applicable as is to deterministic programs. Here, one verifies the program by proving in a suitable axiomatic system that the formula describing the program implies the formula describing the property.

Reverse model checking

This verification method has never been studied. It uses the rather unnatural approach of specifying the program by a formula and the property to be verified by an automaton. Algorithms for this problem can be obtained by techniques similar to the ones used in model checking. Basically, one starts by building the Büchi automaton corresponding to the program formula. If the program is deterministic, this automaton should also be deterministic. It is then sufficient to check that the intersection of this automaton and the automaton specifying the desired property is nonempty. We do not advocate reverse model checking, but include it only for the sake of presenting a complete picture of possible verification methods.

3.3.2 Second view: nondeterministic programs

The most common use of temporal logic is for the verification of nondeterministic programs or of concurrent programs where the concurrency is modelled by nondeterminism.

A nondeterministic program is a tuple (W, Q, w_0, π) where

- W is a set of states,
- Q is a transition relation,
- w_0 is a unique initial state,
- $\pi : W \to \Sigma$ is a labelling function.

The computations of such programs are infinite sequences of states w_0, w_1, $\ldots w_i, \ldots$ such that w_0 is the initial state of the program, and for all $i \geq 0$, $(w_i, w_{i+1}) \in Q$. A program can have many computations.

The most straightforward way to relate nondeterministic programs to temporal logic is to view programs as interpretations for BTL formulas and computations as linear interpretations extracted from the branching interpretation. Given our definitions, this correspondence is immediate. Also, it is easy to see that if we consider the set of computations of a program and organize these into a tree, this tree will be equivalent to the program according to Definition 3.3. We will thus not distinguish between this tree and the program.

There is, however, a second way to relate nondeterministic programs to temporal logic. It consists of viewing the programs as model generators for LTL (i.e. as Büchi sequential automata) and the computations as models of LTL. This might require some clarification as the programs we have defined are different from Büchi automata in two respects: the labels are on states and not on edges and there is no set of accepting states. These differences are fortunately only superficial. Indeed, one can transform a nondeterministic program into a Büchi automaton by labelling all the edges leaving a state with the label of that state and by taking the set of accepting states to be the whole set of states. Notice that these conventions imply that the set of words accepted by the Büchi automaton associated with a program is exactly the set of computations of the program.

Given this correspondence between Büchi automata and programs, a question that occurs naturally is: why not allow a Büchi-style acceptance condition on the program? This is indeed possible and is considered to be a way of describing a *fairness* condition on the execution of the program [11,21,13,1]. The set of computations of the program is then restricted to those computations that satisfy the acceptance condition, i.e. that go infinitely often through one of the accepting states.

Pushing this line of thought one step further, one can think of interpreting BTL over structures that include a Büchi-style acceptance condition. This was done in [13]. There, one interprets a state formula $\exists g$ ($\forall g$) as meaning "g is true on some (all) paths satisfying the acceptance condition". Although the resulting logic is syntactically identical to BTL, it has different valid formulas and hence a different decision procedure than BTL interpreted over structures without an acceptance condition. We will not study this interpretation of branching time temporal logic further, but we will note that the results we give below for BTL interpreted over structures without an acceptance condition also apply to the case of branching time logic interpreted over structures with an acceptance condition. Interestingly, with this interpretation, the similarity between the model generators of LTL and the models of BTL is complete.

Our choices for verifying nondeterministic programs using temporal logic are summarized in Table 3.3.

Table 3.3: *Modelling nondeterministic programs.*

Computation	Program	
	LTL model generator	BTL model
LTL model	Linear approach	Mixed approach 1
BTL model (Computation tree)	Mixed Approach 2	Branching Approach

We will now examine in more details the linear and branching approaches to verifying nondeterministic programs. We will not consider further the mixed approaches. Indeed, they have not been used as such and there is little to learn from their study.

The linear approach for nondeterministic programs

Let us recall that in this context, a program is viewed as a model generator for LTL and computations as models of LTL. The possible verification methods are summarized in Table 3.4.

Table 3.4: *LTL-based verification for nondeterministic programs.*

Program	Property	
	LTL formula	Büchi sequential automaton
States, transitions and acceptance condition	Model checking	Automaton verification
LTL formula	Axiomatic verification	Reverse model checking

Our options are actually identical to the ones we had for verifying deterministic programs using LTL. The difference between the two cases is that finding algorithms for the various verification methods is more difficult for nondeterministic programs than for deterministic programs. Let us examine the known results.

Model checking

Here, one has to check that all the computations of the program satisfy a given LTL formula. This problem was considered in [27] and [56]. The result is that model checking can be done in time linear in the size of the program and exponential in the size of the formula. A very simple description of the algorithm can be given [56]. One takes the negation $\neg f$ of the formula f and builds the corresponding Büchi automaton $A_{\neg f}$. This automaton is at most exponential in the size of the formula. The next step is to combine $A_{\neg f}$ with the automaton A_P corresponding to the program and check that the resulting automaton is empty. This last step can be done in linear time. Note that we build the automaton for $\neg f$ and not for f. This is because it is much easier to check that the intersection of two Büchi automata is empty than to check that the language generated by one automaton is included in the language generated by the other (a PSPACE-complete problem).

Automaton verification

In this case, one has to check that all the computations of the program are accepted by the specification automaton. In other words, one has to verify that the language generated by the automaton corresponding to the program ($L(A_P)$) is a subset of the language accepted by the specification automaton ($L(A_{spec})$). Unfortunately, this is a PSPACE-complete problem. The usual algorithm to solve it is to build the complement $\overline{A}_{spec}$ of the automaton A_{spec} (this is the expensive part of the algorithm [51]) and check that $A_P \cap \overline{A}_{spec} = \phi$.

In the papers where this method is considered, the algorithm is simplified by imposing some restriction on the automaton A_{spec}. In [2] and [3], the automaton is a deterministic automaton or a combination of deterministic automata. In [36], “forall automata” are used for specification. These automata are the dual of nondeterministic automata in the sense that they accept a word iff *all* the computations of the automaton on that word are accepting. This makes these automata easy to complement into nondeterministic automata and hence they can easily be used for automaton verification. Their disadvantage is that they are a rather unnatural way of describing properties of programs. Finally, let us mention that in [2,3] as well as in [36], the method is applied to infinite-state programs and first-order specifications. In simple terms, the transitions of the automaton A_{spec} are labelled by first-order predicates on the states of the program and the verification is done by extracting *proof obligations* from the combination of the specification automaton and the program. These proof obligations are Hoare-like verification conditions on the transitions of the program that have to be satisfied for the program to meet its specification. However, the fundamental basis of the method is identical to that described in the finite-state case.

Axiomatic verification

This verification method is almost identical to the corresponding one for deterministic programs. The only difference is that the formula specifying the program can have several models, each of which corresponds to a computation of the program.

Reverse model checking

An algorithm for this verification method can be obtained by building the automaton corresponding to the formula describing the program. This reduces the problem to the automaton verification problem.

The branching approach for nondeterministic programs

We now consider the case of the program as well as its computation tree being viewed as models of BTL. The potential verification methods are described in Table 3.5.

Table 3.5: *BTL-based verification for nondeterministic programs.*

Program	Property	
	BTL formula	Büchi tree automaton
States and transitions	Model checking	Automaton verification
BTL formula	Axiomatic verification	Reverse model checking

Model checking

Model checking for BTL was introduced in [9] and [10]. The best algorithm for model checking for CTL is of linear complexity in both the size of the formula and the model. For CTL*, the complexity in the size of the formula is exponential while the complexity in the size of the model remains linear [18].

Automaton verification

In this case, the problem is to determine if the computation tree of the program is accepted by the Büchi tree automaton describing the desired property. This can be done by viewing the program as a trivial deterministic tree automaton (accepting only one tree), taking the product of this automaton with the automaton for the property and checking that the result is nonempty. This yields a quadratic time algorithm since the emptiness problem for Büchi tree automata is solvable in quadratic time (Theorem 3.4).

Axiomatic verification

Here, one uses an axiomatic system to prove that the formula specifying the program implies the specification formula. Note that as the computation tree of the program corresponds to a model of a BTL formula, the formula describing the program should have only one model up to equivalence.

Reverse model checking

We have to check that all the models of the formula describing the program are accepted by the automaton giving the specification. If, as should be the case, the program formula describes only one program, the corresponding tree automaton should accept only one tree and the problem can be reduced to the automaton verification problem we have just discussed.

3.3.3 Third view: partially ordered computations

We would like to attract the reader's attention to the fact that the branching approach for nondeterministic programs is analogous to the application of LTL to deterministic programs. In both cases, programs and their set of computations correspond to models of the logic: in one case they are models of LTL and in the other of BTL. In this section, we will consider a use of BTL that is the analogue of the use of LTL for nondeterministic programs.

A number of authors [43,42,25] have argued that, when considering distributed programs, it is necessary to view computations as partial orders of local states rather than as total orders of global states. Formally, one can say that a partially ordered computation is a tuple (W, Q, w_0, π) where

- W is a set of states,
- Q is a transition relation,
- w_0 is an initial state,
- $\pi : W \rightarrow \Sigma$ is a labelling function.

and where the transitive closure of the relation Q is irreflexive. This last condition is not very important given that we do not wish to distinguish between computations that are equivalent according to Definition 3.3 and hence we can always unwind one that is not a partial order into one that is. The important characteristic of partially ordered computations is that once they are unwound, some states might be incomparable by the transitive closure of the relation Q. This is never the case in the totally ordered computations we have considered so far. A special case of a partially ordered computation to which we will pay special attention is that of an infinite tree.

If a computation is a partial order, one might wonder what a program is. The natural answer is that it is a structure generating partial orders, a special case of which is a tree automaton generating infinite trees. It is, of course, possible to consider more general structures generating arbitrary partial orders and not just trees. However, we will limit ourselves to the case of tree automata for two reasons. The first is simplicity; the second is that, as we have shown, an arbitrary branching structure is always equivalent in the sense of Definition 3.5 to a labelled tree and such equivalent structures cannot be distinguished by formulas of the logics we are considering.

To make things more concrete, let us relate our abstract definition of partially ordered computations to distributed programs. One can consider a state of a computation having several successors as corresponding to a *fork* (i.e. a process splitting into several processes) and a state having several predecessors as corresponding to a *join* (i.e. several processes synchronizing and merging into a single process). Now a program will potentially generate several partial orders as it might include some nondeterminism beyond the fork and join operations.

There have been two attempts to use temporal logic for reasoning about partially ordered computations. The first deals directly with the partial orders [43], the second first converts them into a tree of global states [25].

Applying POTL to partially ordered computations

In [43], POTL is applied to partially ordered computations. The connection between the logic and the programs is established by identifying the models of POTL with partially ordered computations. Given our definition of partially ordered computations, this identification is immediate. It should be contrasted with the branching approach to verifying these programs (see Section 3.2.2) where a model of BTL corresponds to the *set* of computations (computation tree) of a program and not to a *single* computation as in this section. Once we have established that a computation is a model of POTL, a program is then a model generator for POTL which is an automaton on $\pm$ trees.

The possible verification methods are then those appearing in Table 3.6.

Table 3.6: *POTL-based verification.*

Program	Property	
	POTL formula	Büchi tree automaton
Tree automaton	Model checking	Automaton verification
POTL formula	Axiomatic verification	Reverse model checking

Model checking

To solve the model-checking problem for POTL and partially ordered computations, it is possible to use an automata-theoretic approach as in LTL-based model checking for nondeterministic programs. However, we will have to use tree automata rather than sequential automata, but the basic approach is the same. If the specification is f, we build the tree automaton for $\neg f$ and check that its intersection with the tree automaton describing the program is empty. There is however one difficulty, which is to make sure that the branching factors of the program and the automaton for the formula are identical. A description of a model-checking algorithm for POTL can be found in [24]

Automaton verification

Here, we have to check that all trees generated by the program automaton are accepted by the specification automaton. For this, one needs to complement the specification automaton and check that its intersection with the program automaton is empty. Unfortunately, Büchi tree automata are not closed under complementation. One thus needs a more general type of tree automata to solve this problem, for instance Rabin tree automata [45]. However, the complementation algorithm for Rabin tree automata is quite intricate and expensive.

Axiomatic verification

The axiomatic approach was the one advocated for verification in [43]. The program is described by a POTL statement and one then proves using an axiomatic system that this statement implies the specification.

Reverse model checking

This problem can be reduced to the automaton verification problem by building the tree automaton corresponding to the program formula.

Applying BTL to partially ordered computations

Katz & Peled [25] find a different way of using temporal logic to deal with partially ordered computations. That approach starts by mapping the partially ordered computation into a tree of global states. The goal is to make it possible to describe properties of the global state and those of the partially ordered computation. An important point to remember is that *one* tree of global states corresponds to *one* partially ordered computation whereas in the case of nondeterministic programs, *one* tree corresponds to *many* computations (the computation tree of the program).

To verify programs in this framework, it is thus natural to relate the models of BTL to computations and its model generators (automata on infinite trees) to programs, similarly to what we did in the case of POTL. The difference is in the way the trees representing the computations are interpreted. The applicable verification methods are thus the same as in the POTL case and we will not re-examine them. In [25], the axiomatic method is proposed for verification. Note that from a purely logical point of view, it is exactly BTL that is used. Indeed, the only difference between this and the use of BTL for nondeterministic programs is that in the latter a model of BTL is considered as a *single* computation rather than as a computation tree.

In [25], this method is pushed one step further. The idea is to develop a new logic that can talk simultaneously about several computations, each of which is an infinite tree. This logic is called QISTL (*quantified interleaving set temporal logic*) in [25] and can be thought of as a *branching branching temporal logic* (BBTL). It is to branching time logic what branching time logic is to linear time logic. To describe it schematically, one can say that it includes

- tree formulas interpreted over infinite trees, and
- state formulas that are either atomic propositions, tree quantifiers applied to tree formulas or boolean combinations of state formulas.

Its models are thus structures similar to tree automata or, equivalently, sets of trees. The model generators for this logic would have one more level of branching and have not yet been named.

To use BBTL for verification, one then takes a distributed program or its *set* of computations to be a model of BBTL. An interesting special case is when the only BBTL formula used are of the form $\forall_{tree} tf$ where tf is a BTL formula. In this case, a program (which is a set of trees) is verified if it satisfies the BBTL formula $\forall_{tree} tf$. Equivalently, all the trees (computations) of the program have to satisfy the BTL formula tf. This is exactly the verification that is done when applying BTL to partially ordered computations.

3.3.4 Summary

As a summary, we have collected in Table 3.7 the various connections established between models, model generators, programs and computations.

Table 3.7: *Summary of Verification Approaches.*

	View 1	View 2 (linear)	View 2 (branching)	View 3
Linear model	*Computation* Program	*Computation*		
Linear generator		*Computation* *Tree* Program		
Branching model			*Computation* *Tree* Program	*Computation*
Branching generator				Program

For each of the connections, we obtain verification methods by representing the program and the specification by either an automaton or a formula. Finally, let us note that the most common method of obtaining an algorithm for a verification method is to convert whatever is given as a formula into an automaton using the results of Section 3.2. One then "only" has to deal with an automata-theoretic problem.

3.4 Program synthesis

Here we examine the applications of temporal logic to program synthesis. In general, program synthesis is building an executable program from a non executable specification. In our case the nonexecutable specification will be a propositional temporal logic formula and the synthesis method will be based on the correspondence between formulas and their models or model generators. Clearly, only a limited class of programs can be specified in propositional temporal logic (in fact finite-state programs or a subset thereof depending on the version of propositional temporal logic that is used). However, it has been argued [58,14,37] that this type of synthesis is useful if the target is the synchronization part of a concurrent program. Indeed, synchronization code is usually finite state, but it is often complex and hard to write correctly.

We now review the various synthesis methods that have been proposed. Our classification of these methods follows the same lines as our classification of verification methods.

3.4.1 First view: deterministic programs

In Section 3.3.1, we noticed that a deterministic program is the same type of structure as a model of LTL. Thus, if one specifies a program by an LTL formula, a deterministic program whose only computation satisfies that formula can be constructed by building a model of the formula. Building a model is done by first building the model generator (Theorem 3.1) and then extracting a model from this model generator. This method was proposed in [58] and [37].

3.4.2 Second view: non-deterministic programs

Here we have the same choices as in Section 3.3.2. A nondeterministic program can be regarded either as a model of a BTL formula or as a model generator for an LTL formula. The first approach was taken in [14] and the second in [58,37].

To synthesize a program from a BTL specification, one thus constructs a model of this specification. This can be done by first building the tree automata that generates the models of the specification (Theorem 3.3), and then extracting a model from this automaton. In [14], the synthesis algorithm is described in terms of *semantic tableaux*. However, there is no essential difference between this algorithm and the one obtained by building the tree automaton for the formula and extracting a model from that automaton.

If one uses an LTL specification, the synthesis algorithm is then to build the sequential Büchi automaton that generates all the models of the specification. This can be done using Theorem 3.1. However, once this automaton is built, one problem remains to be solved: how does one implement the requirement that the only legal computations of the program are those that go infinitely often through some designated state of the Büchi automaton? In [58] and [37], this problem was solved by considering the acceptance condition of the Büchi automaton as a fairness condition [21]. The program was then split up into processes in such a way that it would satisfy this condition if the processes were executed under a reasonable fairness assumption. Finally, let us note that it is also possible to synthesize a program with a fairness condition from BTL if one uses the logic of [13].

Acknowledgement

I wish to thank M. Baudinet, P. Gribomont, V. Lovinfosse and M. Vardi for reading drafts of this paper and providing helpful comments.

References

[1] Aggarwal, S., C. Courcoubetis & P. Wolper 1990. Adding liveness properties to coupled finite- state machines. *ACM Transactions on Programming Languages and Systems* **12**, 303–39.

[2] Alpern, B. & F. Schneider 1985. *Verifying temporal properties without using temporal logic.* Technical Report TR 85-723. Department of Computer Science, Cornell University.

[3] Alpern, B. & F. Schneider 1987. Proving boolean combinations of deterministic properties. In *Proceedings of the IEEE Symposium on Logic in Computer Science* 131–7.

[4] Ben-Ari, M., Z. Manna & A. Pneuli 1984. The logic of nexttime. In *8th Annual ACM Symposium on Principles of Programming Languages*, 164–76.

[5] Barringer, H., R. Kuiper & A. Pneuli 1984. Now you may compose temporal logic specifications. In *Proceeding 16th Annual ACM Symposium on Theory of Computing*, 51–63.

[6] Barringer, H., R. Kuiper & A. Pneuli 1985. A compositional temporal approach to a CSP-like language. In *Proceedings of the IFIP Working*

Conference on the Role of Abstract Models in Information Processing, E. J. Neuhold & G. Chroust (eds), 207–27. Amsterdam: North Holland.

[7] Barringer, H., R. Kuiper & A. Pneuli 1986. A really abstract concurrent model and its temporal logic. In *Proceedings of the 13th Annual ACM Symposium on the Principles of Programming Languages*, 173–83.

[8] Büchi, J. R. 1962. On a decision method in restricted second order arithmetic. In *Proceedings of the Internationl Congress of Logic, Methodology and Philosophy of Science*, 1–12.

[9] Clarke, E. M. & E. A. Emerson 1982. Synthesis of synchronization skeletons from branching time temporal logic. *Lecture Notes in Computer Science* **131**, 52–71.

[10] Clarke, E. M., E. A. Emerson & A. P. Sistla 1984. Automatic verification of finite-state concurrent systems using temporal logic specifications: a practical approach. In *Proceedings of the 10th Annual ACM Symposium on Principles of Programming Languages*, 117–26.

[11] Clarke, E. M., E. A. Emerson & A. P. Sistla 1986. Automatic verification of finite-state concurrent systems using temporal logic specifications. *ACM Transactions on Programming Languages and Systems* **8**, 244–63.

[12] Clarke, E. M., O. Grumberg & M. C. Browne 1985. Reasoning about networks with many identical finite-state processes. In *Proceedings of the 5th Annual ACM Symposium on Principles of Distributed Computing*, 282–94 and *Proceedings of the 12th Annual ACM Symposium on Principles of Programming Languages*, 121–31.

[13] Courcoubetis, C., M. Y. Vardi & P. Wolper 1986. Reasoning about fair concurrent programs, In *Proceedings of the 18th Symposium on Theory of Computing*, 283–94.

[14] Emerson, E. A. & E. M. Clarke 1982. Using branching time logic to synthesize synchronization skeletons, *Science of Computer Programming* **2**, 241–66.

[15] Emerson, E. A. & J. Y. Halpern 1985. Decision procedures and expressiveness in the temporal logic of branching time, *Journal of Computer and System Sciences*, **30**, 1–24.

[16] Emerson, E. A. & J. H. Halpern 1986. “Sometimes” and “Not Never” revisited: on branching versus linear time temporal logic. *Journal of the ACM* **33**(1), 151–78.

[17] Emerson, E. A. & C-L. Lei 1985. Temporal model checking under generalized fairness constraints. In *Proceedings of the 8th Hawaii International Conference on System Sciences.*

[18] Emerson, E. A., C-L. Lei 1985. Modalities for model checking: branching time strikes back, In *Proceedings of the 12th Annual ACM Symp. on Principles of Programming Languages*, 84–96.

[19] Emerson, E. A. 1985. Automata, tableaux and temporal logics. *Lecture Notes in Computer Science* **193**, 79–88.

[20] Emerson, E. A., & A. P. Sistla 1984. Deciding branching time logic, *Information and Control* **61**, 175–201.

[21] Francez, N. 1986. *Fairness*, Berlin: Springer.

[22] Gabbay, D., A. Pnueli, S. Shelah & J. Stavi 1980. The temporal analysis of fairness. In *7th Annual ACM Symposium on Principles of Programming Languages*, 163–73.

[23] Halpern, J., Z. Manna & B. Moszkowski 1983. A hardware semantics based on temporal intervals. *Lecture Notes in Computer Science* **154**.

[24] Kornatsky, Y. & S. S. Pinter 1986. *A model checker for partial order temporal logic*, EE PUB no. 597, Department of Electrical Enginering, Technion-Israel Institute of Technology.

[25] Katz, S. & D. Peled 1987. Interleaving set temporal logic. In *Proceedings of the 6th Annual ACM Symposium on Principles of Distributed Computing*, 178–90.

[26] Lamport, L. 1980. Sometimes is sometimes not never, In *7th Annual ACM Symposium on Principles of Programming Languages*, 174–85.

[27] Lichtenstein, O. & A. Pnueli 1985. Checking that finite state concurrent programs satisfy their linear specifications. In *Proceedings of the 12th Annual ACM Symposium on Principles of Programming Languages*, 97–107.

[28] Lichtenstein, O., A. Pnueli & L. Zuck 1985. The glory of the past. *Lecture Notes in Computer Science* **193**, 196–218.

[29] Milner, R. 1980. A calculus of communicating systems, *Lecture Notes in Computer Science* **92**.

[30] Moszkowski, B. 1983. *Reasoning about digital circuits*, PhD thesis, Department of Computer Science, Stanford University.

[31] Manna, Z. & A. Pnueli 1981. Verification of concurrent programs: the temporal framework. In *The correctness problem in computer science*, R. S. Boyer & J. S. Moore (eds), 215–73. London: Academic Press.

[32] Manna, Z. & A. Pnueli 1984. How to cook a temporal proof system for your pet language. In *Proceedings of the 10th Annual ACM Symposium on Principles of Programming Languages*, 141–54.

[33] Manna, Z. & A. Pnueli 1983a. Proving properties: the temporal way. *Lecture Notes in Computer Science* **154**, 491–512.

[34] Manna, Z. & A. Pnueli 1983b. Verification of concurrent programs: a temporal proof system. *Mathematical Center Tracts* **159**, 163-225.

[35] Manna, Z. & A. Pnueli 1984. Adequate proof principles for invariance and liveness properties of concurrent programs. *Science of Computer Programming* **4**, 257–289.

[36] Manna, Z. & A. Pnueli 1987. Specification and verification of concurrent programs by ∀-automata. In *Proceedings of the 14th Annual ACM Symposium on Principles of Programming Languages*, 1–12.

[37] Manna, Z. & P. Wolper 1984. Synthesis of communicating processes from temporal logic specifications. *ACM Transactions on Programming Languages and Systems* **6**(1), 68–93.

[38] Nguyen, V., D. Gries & S. Owicki 1985. A model and temporal proof system for networks of processes. In *Proceedings of the 12th Annual ACM Symposium on Principles of Programming Languages*, 121–31.

[39] Owicki, S. & L. Lamport 1982. Proving liveness properties of concurrent programs. *ACM Transactions on Programming Languages and Systems* **4**, 455–96.

[40] Pnueli, A. 1977. The temporal logic of programs. In *Proceedings of the 18th IEEE Symposium on Foundations of Computer Science*, 46–57.

[41] Pnueli, A. 1981. The temporal logic of concurrent programs. *Theoretical Computer Science* **13**, 45–60.

[42] Pratt, V. R. 1982. On the composition of processes. In *Proceedings of the 9th ACM Symposium on Principles of Programming Languages*, 213–23.

[43] Pinter, S. S. & P. Wolper 1984. A temporal logic for reasoning about partially ordered computations. In *Proceedings of the 3rd ACM Symposium on Principles of Distributed Computing*, 28–37.

[44] Pnueli, A. & L. Zuck 1986. Probabilistic verification by tableaux. In *Proceedings of the IEEE Symposium on Logic in Computer Science*, 322–31.

[45] Rabin, M. O. 1969. Decidability of second order theories and automata on infinite trees. *Transactions of American Mathematical Society* **141**, 1–35.

[46] Rabin, M. O. 1970. Weakly definable relations and special automata. In *Proceedings of the Symposium on Mathematical Logic and Foundations of Set Theory*, Y. Bar-Hillel (ed), 1–23. Amsterdam: North Holland.

[47] Sistla, A. P. 1983. *Theoretical issues in the design and verification of distributed systems.* PhD thesis, Department of Computer Sciences, Harvard University.

[48] Sistla, A. P. & E. M. Clarke 1985. The complexity of propositional linear temporal logic. In *Proceedings of the 14th Annual ACM Symposium on Theory of Computing*, 159–68.

[49] Sistla, A. P. & E. M. Clarke 1985. The complexity of propositional linear temporal logics. *Journal of the ACM* **32**, 733–49.

[50] Schwartz, R. L., P. M. Melliar-Smith & F. H. Vogt 1983. An interval logic for higher-level temporal reasoning. In *Proceedings of the 2nd ACM Symposium on Principles of Distributed Computing*, 173–86.

[51] Sistla, A. P., M. Y. Vardi & P. Wolper 1987. The complementation problem for Büchi automata with applications to temporal logic. *Theoretical computer science* **49**, 217–37.

[52] Vardi, M. 1985a. Automatic verification of probabilistic concurrent finite-state programs. In *Proceedings of the 26th IEEE Symposium on Foundations of Computer Science*, 327–38.

[53] Vardi, M. Y. 1985b. The taming of converse: reasoning about two-way computations. *Lecture Notes in Computer Science* **193**, 413–24.

[54] Vardi, M. Y. & L. Stockmeyer 1985. Improved upper and lower bounds for modal logics of programs. In *Proceedings of the 17th Annual ACM Symposium on Theory of Computing* 240–51.

[55] Vardi, M. Y. & P. Wolper 1986a. Automata-theoretic techniques for modal logics of programs. *Journal of Computer and System Sciences* **32**, 183–321.

[56] Vardi, M. Y. & P. Wolper 1986b. An automata-theoretic approach ro automatic program verification. In *Proceedings of the ACM Symposium on Logic in Computer Science*, 322–31.

[57] Vardi, M. Y. & P. Wolper 1994. Reasoning about infinite computations. *Information and Computation* **110**(2), in press.

[58] Wolper, P. 1982. Synthesis of communicating processes from temporal logic specifications. PhD thesis, Computer Science Department, Stanford University.

[59] Wolper, P. 1983. Temporal logic can be more expressive. *Information and Control* **56**, 72–99.

[60] Wolper, P., M. Y. Vardi & A. P. Sistla 1983. Reasoning about infinite computation paths. In *Proceedings of the 24th IEEE Symposium on Foundations of Computer Science*, 185–94.

Chapter 4

Branching time and partial order in temporal logics

*W. Penczek**

Institute of Computer Science
Polish Academy of Sciences
Ordona 21, 01-237 Warsaw, Poland

Abstract

The aim of this chapter is to present existing propositional temporal logics with branching and partially ordered time. These logics are used for specifying and proving properties of programs and systems. The branching time approach is useful e.g. for nondeterministic programs and can be applied also for concurrent programs. The partial order approach is especially useful for concurrent programs and facilitates the study of more subtle properties than those based on branching time.

A survey of branching time logics, computation tree logics, partial order temporal logics and logics based on event structures is given. The following issues are also discussed: the completeness of proof systems, the finite model property, decidability, model checking and expressiveness of the logics.

4.1 Introduction

The aim of this chapter is to present the existing formal languages of propositional temporal logic with frames based on branching time structures or, more general, partial orders. Branching time and partial order logics differ not only in their underlying frames, but also in the way the logics are linked to the behaviour of concurrent systems. Therefore, the formal systems studied comprise both a syntax and a semantics of a logic; our motive for their study derives

***This work has been partly supported by a grant from The Wolfson Research Awards Scheme in The United Kingdom and by the Polish grant No. 2 2047 9203.**

from the way that the frames correspond to differing behavioural aspects of concurrent systems.

In a branching time approach, which adopts a tree-structured time, every time instant may have several immediate successors which correspond to different futures, for instance those resulting from nondeterminism from modelling concurrency by interleaving. In a partial order approach, where any partial order structure can be applied, the situation is similar, except that every time instant may also have several immediate predecessors corresponding to different pasts, resulting from interleaved or noninterleaved concurrency.

It has to be stressed that the difference in the approaches has very little to do with the philosophical question of the structure of physical time and the problems of determinancy versus free will. Instead, it is pragmatically based on the choice of the type of systems and on the choice of properties to be formalized and proved.

There are several reasons for developing logics based on branching time or partial order structures. The branching time approach considers, for a given program and a given input, an execution tree generated by the program. Over the execution tree, universal properties involving all computations (maximal sequences of states) can be studied, as well as existential properties referring to a specific computation. This approach is very useful for nondeterministic programs and can be also applied for concurrent programs. The partial order approach considers, for a given program and a given input, the set of trees or partial orders representing full runs. Over these structures, universal and existential properties of computations as well as properties involving runs can be studied. The use of the latter ability makes this approach especially useful for concurrent programs.

Partial order logics can be divided into two groups with respect to the structures serving as frames: configuration structures and event structures. Configurations represent states of an entire system, whereas events in event structure models represent local states of sequential agents. Moreover, another division can be made with respect to properties expressible about runs. Some logics, like ISTL [21] or ESL[δ], can express only universal properties about runs whereas others, e.g. QISTL [21], or Petri Net Logic [35], express also existential properties.

The first ideas about branching time logics appeared in the papers of Abrahamson [1], [2]. Later, Ben-Ari et al. defined the unified branching time system (UB) [3]. In the same year, Clarke & Emerson extended the expressiveness of UB by defining computation tree logic (CTL) [4], their results are fully described in [5]. In 1983, Emerson & Halpern gave the definition of CTL* [12]. The first logic based on partial orders (POTL) was defined by Pinter & Wolper in 1984 [34] and then extended by Kornatzky & Pinter in 1986 [18]. Three years after the first logic, Katz & Peled presented interleaving set temporal logic [21] based on configuration structures. The history of event structure logics is much shorter. The first logic dealing with n-sequential event structures was defined by Lodaya & Thiagarajan [25] in 1987. Then Penczek [29] presented a temporal logic based on unrestricted event structures. This logic has been extended and refined consequently in [30], [27], and [28].

In this chapter all the logics mentioned above are presented. The same pattern of presentation is followed for each logic. First, the syntax and the semantics of a logic are given. Then, it is shown how frames of the logic are linked with the behaviour of a concurrent system, if this is not obvious. Finally, expressiveness, a proof system and a characterization of the logic are presented and discussed. The following issues are involved: the completeness of proof systems, the finite model property, decidability and model checking. The first part of this chapter deals with the following branching time logics:

- UB-unified system of branching time,
- CTL-computation tree logic,
- CTL*-computation tree logic*.

The second part contains descriptions of the following partial order logics:

- POTL-partial order temporal logic,
- POTL[$U, \overline{U}$]-partial order temporal logic with until and since,
- ISTL-interleaving set temporal logic,

and temporal logics based on event structures:

- SESL-sequential agent event structure logic,
- ESL-event structure logic,
- ESL[δ]-event structure logic with a run proposition,
- DESL-discrete event structure logic,
- ESL[C]-event structure logic with a concurrency operator.

4.2 Branching time temporal logics

This section begins with a definition of a computation tree logic* (CTL*) formal language, restrictions of which will constitute the formal systems UB and CTL. CTL* is a very powerful temporal logic which can be used for specifying a variety of program properties due to its modal operators. These allow for quantifying over paths of CTL* models as well as over states of the paths. Trees are canonical models of CTL*. They can be easily defined as unwindings of standard Kripke models. The semantics of CTL* formulas is given now, but its characterization is postponed until UB and CTL have been defined.

4.2.1 Formal language of CTL*

The language of CTL* [12], [5] is composed of state and path formulas. As the names indicate, state formulas are interpreted over states and path formulas are interpreted over paths. In fact, path formulas contain all state formulas. There are two path quantifiers, $\exists$ and $\forall$, with the intuitive meanings: "there is a path" and "for all paths", respectively. Path modalities are: $\bigcirc$, at the next state; U, until; $\Diamond$, eventually; and $\Box$, always.

Syntax of CTL*

Let AP be a set of atomic propositions. Then, the set of state formulas and the set of path formulas is defined inductively. The set of state formulas is defined by:

- every member of AP is a state formula,
- if p and q are state formulas, then so are $\neg p$ and $p \wedge q$,
- if p is a path formula, then $\exists p$ is a state formula,

and the set of path formulas is:

- any state formula p is also a path formula,
- if p, q are path formulas, then so are $p \wedge q$ and $\neg p$,
- if p, q are path formulas, then so are $\bigcirc p$ and $(p U q)$.

The other connectives and modalities are used as abbreviations:

- $p \vee q \overset{def}{=} \neg(\neg p \wedge \neg q)$,
- $p \rightarrow q \overset{def}{=} \neg p \vee q$,
- $p \leftrightarrow q \overset{def}{=} (p \rightarrow q) \wedge (q \rightarrow p)$,
- $\mathbf{T} \overset{def}{=} p \vee \neg p$, for any p,
- $\forall p \overset{def}{=} \neg \exists \neg p$,
- $\Diamond p \overset{def}{=} (\mathbf{T} U p)$,
- $\Box p \overset{def}{=} \neg \Diamond \neg p$.

Semantics of CTL*

Let $\mathcal{M} = (W, R, V)$ be a model, where W is a nonempty set of states, $R \subseteq W \times W$ is a total binary (successor) relation on W (i.e. each state has at least one R-successor), and $V : W \longrightarrow 2^{AP}$ is a valuation function which assigns to each state a set of atomic propositions assumed to be true of this state. A *(forward) fullpath* starting at w_0 is an infinite sequence $x = (w_0, w_1, ...)$ of states such that $(w_i, w_{i+1}) \in R$ for each $i \geq 0$. x_i denotes the suffix $(w_i, w_{i+1}, \ldots)$ of x. $\mathcal{M}, w \Vdash p$ ($\mathcal{M}, x \Vdash p$) denotes that the state (path) formula p is true at the state w (in the fullpath x, resp.) in the model $\mathcal{M}$. $\mathcal{M}$ is omitted, if it is implicitly understood. $w \Vdash p$ ($x \Vdash p$) is defined inductively for an arbitrary state w (a fullpath $x = (w_0, w_1, ...)$, resp.) as follows:

- $w \Vdash p$ iff $p \in V(w)$ for any atomic proposition $p \in AP$,
- $w \Vdash p \wedge q$ iff $w \Vdash p$ and $w \Vdash q$,
  $w \Vdash \neg p$ iff not $w \Vdash p$,
- $w \Vdash \exists p$ iff $x \Vdash p$ for some forward fullpath x starting at w,
- $x \Vdash p$ iff $w_0 \Vdash p$ for any state formula p,
- $x \Vdash p \wedge q$ iff $x \Vdash p$ and $x \Vdash q$,
  $x \Vdash \neg p$ iff not $x \Vdash p$,
- $x \Vdash \bigcirc p$ iff $x_1 \Vdash p$,
  $x \Vdash (p\, U\, q)$ iff $(\exists i \geq 0)\ x_i \Vdash q$ and $(\forall j:\ 0 \leq j < i)\ x_j \Vdash p$.

A state formula p is *valid in the model* $\mathcal{M}$ (written $M \Vdash p$), if for every state w in $\mathcal{M}$, $\mathcal{M}, w \Vdash p$. A set of state formulas L is *valid in the model* $\mathcal{M}$ (written $M \Vdash L$), if for every formula $p \in L$, $M \Vdash p$. A state formula p is said to be *valid* (written $\Vdash p$), if for every model $\mathcal{M}$, $M \Vdash p$. A state formula p is *satisfiable*, if for some model $\mathcal{M}$ and some state w in $\mathcal{M}$, $\mathcal{M}, w \Vdash p$. In this case $\mathcal{M}$ is said to be a model of p. A state formula p is said to be a *semantical consequence* of a set of state formulas L (written $L \models p$), if $M \Vdash L$ implies $M \Vdash p$, for every model $\mathcal{M}$. The above notions are defined similarly for path formulas.

In what follows, for every logic UB, CTL and CTL*, a proof system, composed of axioms and inference rules, will be given. As usual $L \vdash p$ denotes that the formula p can be derived from the set of formulas L using axioms and inference rules. A proof system is said to be *sound and complete*, if $L \models p$ iff $L \vdash p$, for any finite set of formulas L and any formula p.

Before discussing the logical features of CTL*, its restrictions UB and CTL are considered.

4.2.2 Unified system of branching time (UB)

The first system discussed here, contained in CTL*, is the unified system of branching time (UB). UB was introduced by Ben-Ari et al. [3]. The UB basic modalities are $\exists\Diamond$, $\exists\bigcirc$ and $\exists\Box$ (and their duals $\forall\Box, \forall\bigcirc$, and $\forall\Diamond$). A formal syntax of a UB language is given here. As this language contains state formulas only, they will simply be called formulas.

Syntax of UB

The set of UB formulas is the maximal one generated by the rules:

- every member of AP is a formula,
- if p and q are formulas, then so are $\neg p$ and $p \wedge q$,
- if p is a formula, then so are $\exists \Box p$, $\exists \Diamond p$ and $\exists \bigcirc p$.

The derived basic modalities are:

- $\forall \Box p \stackrel{def}{=} \neg \exists \Diamond \neg p$,
- $\forall \Diamond p \stackrel{def}{=} \neg \exists \Box \neg p$,
- $\forall \bigcirc p \stackrel{def}{=} \neg \exists \bigcirc \neg p$.

Semantics of UB

The semantics of UB is the subset of the semantics of CTL* concerning UB formulas. It follows from the semantics of CTL* that UB formulas $\exists \Diamond p$ and $\exists \Box p$ have the following semantic meaning:

- $\mathcal{M}, w_0 \Vdash \exists \Diamond p$ iff there is a forward fullpath $x = (w_0, w_1, ..)$ such that for some $i \geq 0$, $\mathcal{M}, w_i \Vdash p$,
- $\mathcal{M}, w_0 \Vdash \exists \Box p$ iff there is a forward fullpath $x = (w_0, w_1, ..)$ such that for all $i \geq 0$, $\mathcal{M}, w_i \Vdash p$.

Expressiveness of UB

The system UB (as well as CTL and CTL*) is used to specify properties of concurrent (or nondeterministic) programs. A frame of the logic represents an execution tree generated by a program. Therefore, the class of possible models is restricted to the class of all execution trees of a given program. The properties which can be expressed about these execution trees are listed. A safety property is expressible as an invariance assertion of the form $\forall \Box p$, which expresses that p is true at all states of a computation tree. For example, mutual exclusion can be specified by the formula $\forall \Box(\neg(CS_1 \wedge CS_2))$, where CS_i is true at a state if the process i has entered a critical section. A liveness property is expressible as an inevitability assertion $\forall \Diamond p$, which says that p is true at some state of each path. For example, the absence of starvation can be expressed by the following formula $(TRY_i \rightarrow \forall \Diamond (CS_i))$, where TRY_i is true at a state, if the process i is ready to enter the critical section. A possibility property is expressed by a formula of form $\exists \Diamond p$. Fairness constraints are not expressible in UB.

A proof system for UB

The proof system for UB that can be extracted from the proof system for CTL is shown below. This proof system is equivalent to the original proof system for UB given in [3].

- Axioms:

  (A1) All substitution rules of propositional calculus
  (A2) $\exists\bigcirc(p \vee q) \leftrightarrow \exists\bigcirc p \vee \exists\bigcirc q$
  (A3) $\exists\Diamond p \leftrightarrow p \vee \exists\bigcirc\exists\Diamond p$
  (A4) $\exists\Box p \leftrightarrow p \wedge \exists\bigcirc\exists\Box p$
  (A5) $\exists\bigcirc\top$

- Inference rules:

  (R1) $p, p \rightarrow q \vdash q$
  (R2) $p \rightarrow q \vdash \exists\bigcirc p \rightarrow \exists\bigcirc q$
  (R3) $r \rightarrow (\neg q \wedge \exists\bigcirc r) \vdash r \rightarrow \exists\Box\neg q$
  (R4) $r \rightarrow (\neg q \wedge \forall\bigcirc(r \vee \neg\exists\Diamond q)) \vdash r \rightarrow \neg\exists\Diamond q$

Axioms A3 and A4 show that $\exists\Diamond p$ and $\exists\Box p$ can be defined by fixed point equalities. A5 says that each state does have a successor.

A characterization of UB

A logical characterization of UB is now presented. It contains results concerning the completeness of the given proof system, the finite model property and complexity of checking satisfiability. Firstly, it is stated formally that the proof system for UB are satisfactory.

Theorem 4.1 The proof system for UB is sound and complete. □

The finite model property is an important feature of a logic, enabling the application of standard constructions for checking satisfiability.

Theorem 4.2 UB has the finite model property. □

Below, it is shown that the satisfiability problem for UB is decidable and the complexity of the algorithm is given.

Theorem 4.3 There is a deterministic algorithm, for deciding whether a UB formula is satisfiable, of exponential complexity in the length of the tested formula. □

It turns out that there is no better algorithm for testing satisfiability since the complexity of the algorithm matches a lower bound for satisfiability.

Theorem 4.4 ([17], [11]) There is a deterministic exponential time lower bound for UB satisfiability. □

The proof sketches of the above theorems are given for CTL - an extension of UB.

4.2.3 Computation tree logic (CTL)

CTL was defined in [4], [5] and [1]. It extends UB by introducing the new path modality U. In the language of CTL, the single linear time operator ($\Diamond$, $\Box$, $\bigcirc$ or U) can follow the path quantifier ($\forall$ or $\exists$). Below, a formal syntax and semantics of CTL are given.

Syntax of CTL

The set of CTL formulas *FORM* is the maximal one generated by the rules:

- every member of AP is a formula,
- if p and q are formulas, then so are $\neg p$ and $p \wedge q$,
- if p, q are formulas, then so are $\forall(p\,U q)$, $\exists(p\,U q)$ and $\exists\bigcirc p$.

The derived basic modalities are:

- $\exists\Diamond p \stackrel{def}{=} \exists(\mathrm{T}\,U p)$,
- $\forall\Diamond p \stackrel{def}{=} \forall(\mathrm{T}\,U p)$.

Semantics of CTL

The semantics of CTL is the subset of the semantics of CTL* (defined in Section 4.2.1) concerning CTL formulas.

Expressiveness of CTL

All the properties expressible in UB are obviously expressible in CTL. Formulas expressing new properties contain the modality U. For example, the relative order of events can be specified, e.g. the fact that the process i must enter its trying region (TRY_i) before gaining access to its critical region (CS_i) along all computation paths, can be expressed as $\forall((\neg CS_i)\,U(TRY_i))$. As in UB, fairness constraints are not expressible in CTL.

A proof system for CTL

The proof system is given in terms of state formulas since CTL formulas are state formulas only.

- Axioms:

(A1) All substitution rules of propositional calculus
(A2) $\exists\bigcirc(p \vee q) \leftrightarrow \exists\bigcirc p \vee \exists\bigcirc q$
(A3) $\exists(p\,U q) \leftrightarrow q \vee (p \wedge \exists\bigcirc\exists(p\,U q))$
(A4) $\forall(p\,U q) \leftrightarrow q \vee (p \wedge \forall\bigcirc\forall(p\,U q))$

(A5) $\exists \bigcirc \top$

- Inference rules:

(R1) $p, p \rightarrow q \vdash q$
(R2) $p \rightarrow q \vdash \exists \bigcirc p \rightarrow \exists \bigcirc q$
(R3) $r \rightarrow (\neg q \wedge \exists \bigcirc r) \vdash r \rightarrow \neg\forall(p\, U\, q)$
(R4) $r \rightarrow (\neg q \wedge \forall \bigcirc (r \vee \neg\exists(p\, U\, q)) \vdash r \rightarrow \neg\exists(p\, U\, q)$

A characterization of CTL

CTL is shown to have the finite model property, to be decidable and to possess a complete proof system [11]. The first step consists in establishing that CTL has the finite model property, i.e., that if a formula p is satisfiable, then it is satisfiable in a finite model whose size is bounded by some function f of the length of the formula p. Having established this property a non-deterministic algorithm to determine the satisfiability of the formula p is given. This algorithm runs in time polynomial in the size of a model for p: it guesses a model of size no more than $f(length(p))$ and checks whether it is a model for p. However, it turns out that it is possible to find a faster algorithm testing CTL satisfiability. This is shown in Theorem 4.6.

Theorem 4.5 CTL has the finite model property.

Proof: There are two stages. Stage 1 defines the quotient structure of a Hintikka structure. In stage 2 the quotient structure is unwound in order to get a finite model.

Stage 1: The notion of a structure and a Hintikka structure has to be defined. A structure is a triple $\mathcal{M} = (W, R, L)$, where W is a nonempty set of states, $R \subseteq W \times W$ is a binary relation on W, and $L : W \longrightarrow 2^{FORM}$ is a function assigning to each state a set of formulas. Notice that a structure $\mathcal{M}$ is a model, if $(\forall w \in W)(\forall p \in L(w))$ $(\mathcal{M}, w \Vdash p$ iff $p \in L(w))$. Hintikka structures are dealt with. Roughly speaking, a Hintikka structure is a structure, where the formulas of $L(w)$ "true" at the state w satisfy certain consistency conditions which seem weaker than those required for L in the case of a model. However, it is shown that the notions of a model and of a Hintikka structure are in some sense equivalent.

Definition 4.1 A *Hintikka structure* (for p_0) is a structure $\mathcal{M} = (W, R, L)$, where R is a total relation (and $p_0 \in L(w)$ for some $w \in W$) and L satisfies the following conditions:

(H1) if $\neg p \in L(w)$ then $p \notin L(w)$,
(H2) if $\neg\neg p \in L(w)$ then $p \in L(w)$,
(H3) if $p \wedge q \in L(w)$ then $p,\ q \in L(w)$,
(H4) if $\neg(p \wedge q) \in L(w)$ then $\neg p \in L(w)$ or $\neg q \in L(w)$,
(H5) if $\exists(pUq) \in L(w)$ then $q \in L(w)$ or $p, \exists\bigcirc\exists(pUq) \in L(w)$,
(H6) if $\neg\exists(pUq) \in L(w)$ then $\neg q, \neg p \in L(w)$ or $\neg q, \neg\exists\bigcirc\exists(pUq) \in L(w)$,
(H7) if $\forall(pUq) \in L(w)$ then $q \in L(w)$ or $p, \neg\exists\bigcirc\neg\forall(pUq) \in L(w)$,
(H8) if $\neg\forall(pUq) \in L(w)$ then $\neg q, \neg p \in L(w)$ or $\neg q, \exists\bigcirc\neg\forall(pUq) \in L(w)$,
(H9) if $\exists\bigcirc p \in L(w)$ then $\exists v\ ((w, v) \in R$ and $p \in L(v))$,
(H10) if $\neg\exists\bigcirc p \in L(w)$ then $\forall v\ (((w, v) \in R)$ implies $\neg p \in L(v))$,
(H11) if $\exists(pUq) \in L(w)$ then there is a forward fullpath x starting at w and a state v on x such that for all v' before v on x, $q \in L(v)$ and $p \in L(v')$,
(H12) if $\forall(pUq) \in L(w)$ then for all forward fullpaths x starting at w there is a state v on x such that for all v' before v on x, $q \in L(v)$ and $p \in L(v')$. □

It can easily be proved that a CTL formula p is satisfiable iff there is a Hintikka structure for p. Now, looking for a finite model for a satisfiable formula p_0, the Fischer - Ladner closure (see [17]) of p_0 is defined. Let $C(p_0)$ be the least set of formulas containing p_0 and satisfying the following conditions:

(C1) if $\neg p \in C(p_0)$ then $p \in C(p_0)$,
(C2) if $p \wedge q \in C(p_0)$ then $p,\ q \in C(p_0)$,
(C3) if $\exists\bigcirc p \in C(p_0)$ then $p \in C(p_0)$,
(C4) if $\exists(pUq) \in C(p_0)$ then $q,\ p, \exists\bigcirc\exists(pUq) \in C(p_0)$,
(C5) if $\forall(pUq) \in C(p_0)$ then $q, p, \neg\exists\bigcirc\neg\forall(pUq) \in C(p_0)$.

Let $FL(p_0) = C(p_0) \cup \neg C(p_0)$, where $\neg C(p_0) = \{\neg p \mid p \in C(p_0)\}$. It can be shown by induction on the length of the formula that the cardinality of $FL(p_0)$, $card(FL(p_0)) \leq 2|p_0|$, where $card(S)$ denotes the number of the elements of a set S.

Let $\mathcal{M} = (W, R, V)$ be a model for p_0, and let $\leftrightarrow_{FL(p_0)}$ be an equivalence relation on W defined as follows: $w_1 \leftrightarrow_{FL(p_0)} w_2$ iff $(\forall q \in FL(p_0))$ $(w_1 \Vdash q$ iff $w_2 \Vdash q)$. $[w]$ denotes the set $\{v \in W \mid w \leftrightarrow_{FL(p_0)} v\}$. The quotient structure of $\mathcal{M}$ by $\leftrightarrow_{FL(p_0)}$ is the structure $\mathcal{M}' = (W', R', L')$, where $W' = \{[w] \mid w \in W\}$, $R' = \{([w], [v]) \in W' \times W' \mid \exists w' \in [w], \exists v' \in [v] :\ (w', v') \in R\}$, $L'([w]) = \{q \in FL(p_0) \mid w \Vdash q\}$. Unfortunately, $\mathcal{M}'$ does not need to be a Hintikka structure for p_0. The satisfiability of formulas of the form $\forall(pUq)$ may be unpreserved. However, the quotient structure $\mathcal{M}'$ provides some useful information. It is easy to check that $\mathcal{M}'$ satisfies all the conditions of the definition of a Hintikka structure except possibly H12. Instead, $\mathcal{M}'$ satisfies another important condition which makes it possible to prove $\mathcal{M}'$ to be modally equivalent to some Hintikka structure. The definition of modally equivalent structures is as follows. Two structures $\mathcal{M} = (W, R, L)$ and $\mathcal{M}' = (W', R', L')$ are said to be *modally equivalent*, if $(\forall p \in FORM)$ $((\exists w \in W)\ p \in L(w)$ iff $(\exists w' \in W')\ p \in L'(w'))$. The following definitions are used in the next part of the proof.

Definition 4.2 Given a structure $\mathcal{M} = (W, R, L)$, an *interior (frontier) node* of $\mathcal{M}$ is one having (not having, resp.) an R-successor. The *root* of $\mathcal{M}$ is the unique node (if it exists) from which all other nodes are accessible by the relation R. □

Directed acyclic graphs are known as *dags*.

Definition 4.3 A *fragment* $\mathcal{N} = (W, R, L)$ is a rooted structure for which all the interior nodes satisfy H1 – H10 and all the frontier nodes satisfy H1 – H8 and whose graph is a finite dag. Given $\mathcal{M}_1 = (W_1, R_1, L_1)$ and $\mathcal{M}_2 = (W_2, R_2, L_2)$, $\mathcal{M}_1$ is said to be contained in $\mathcal{M}_2$, written $\mathcal{M}_1 \subseteq \mathcal{M}_2$, iff $W_1 \subseteq W_2$, $R_1 \subseteq R_2$ and $L_1 = L_2/W_1$. □

Remember that $\mathcal{M} = (W, R, V)$ is a model for p_0 and $\mathcal{M}' = \mathcal{M}/\leftrightarrow_{FL(p_0)} = (W', R', L')$.

Lemma 4.1 Suppose $\forall(p\,U\,q) \in L'([w'])$. Then, there is a fragment $\mathcal{N}$ rooted at $[w']$ contained in $\mathcal{M}'$ such that for all the frontier nodes v of $\mathcal{N}$, $q \in L'(v)$ and for all the interior nodes u of $\mathcal{N}$, $p \in L'(u)$.

Now, a pseudo-Hintikka structure can be defined.

Definition 4.4 A *pseudo-Hintikka structure* (for p_0) is a structure $\mathcal{M} = (W, R, L)$ with R total (such that $p_0 \in L(w)$ for some $w \in W$, resp.) which satisfies H1 – H11 and such that for all $w \in W$ the following condition holds:

(H12′) $\forall(p\,U\,q) \in L(w)$ implies that there is a fragment $\mathcal{N}$ rooted at w, contained in $\mathcal{M}$ such that for all the frontier nodes v of $\mathcal{N}$, $q \in L(v)$, and for all the interior nodes u of $\mathcal{N}$, $p \in L(u)$. □

It can be proved that the quotient structure $\mathcal{M}'$ is a pseudo-Hintikka structure.

Stage 2: The only thing to show in the second stage of the proof is that the pseudo-Hintikka structure $\mathcal{M}'$ for p_0 is modally equivalent to some Hintikka structure for p_0. This is done by "unwinding" the pseudo-Hintikka structure in the way described fully in [11]. Here, the main steps of the proof are presented.

Formulas of the form $\exists\bigcirc p$, $\forall(p\,U\,q)$ and $\exists(p\,U\,q)$ are said to be *eventuality formulas*.

First, notice that for each w of W' and for each eventuality formula $p \in L'(w)$, there is a fragment, call it $DAG[w,p]$, contained in W' in which p is satisfied. This follows from the definition of a pseudo-Hintikka structure.

Secondly, it is shown how to use these $DAGs$ to construct for each node w of W' a fragment, call it $FRAG[w]$, such that every eventuality formula from $L'(w)$ is satisfied in $FRAG[w]$. It is noticed that if $p \in L'(w)$, then for every fragment containing w, either an appriopriate condition H holds for p in the fragment (e.g. H11 for $\exists(p_1\, U q)$, or H12 for $\forall(p_1\, U q)$) or the conditions required to fulfil it are propagated to the frontier nodes. For $\forall(p_1\, U q)$ this means that for every path in the fragment from w to a frontier node v, either $q \in L'(w')$ for some w' on the path and $p_1 \in w''$ for all w'' on the path before w and w', or $p_1, \forall(p_1\, U q) \in L(v')$ for every v' at the path. $FRAG[w]$ is constructed in an inductive way. Let $p_1, \ldots, p_n$ be a list of all eventuality formulas from $L'(w)$. $FRAG_0$ consists of w and enough successors to ensure H9. $FRAG_{j+1}$ is obtained from $FRAG_j$ by extending the frontier nodes as follows. If p_{j+1} is fulfiled for w in $FRAG_j$, then $FRAG_j = FRAG_{j+1}$. Otherwise, every or some (it depends on p_{j+1}) frontier node v is replaced by a copy of $DAG[v, p_{j+1}]$. Moreover, new frontier nodes that are copies of the same node are identified.

It is then shown how to get a Hintikka structure from $FRAGs$. The construction is performed inductively, in stages. Let $\mathcal{M}_1$ be $FRAG[w_0]$ with $w_0 \in W'$ and $p_0 \in w_0$. Now, for each frontier node w of $\mathcal{M}_i$, if there is an interior node w' of $\mathcal{M}_i$ such that $L'(w) = L'(w')$ and $FRAG[w']$ is contained in $\mathcal{M}_i$, and the only arcs from nodes of $FRAG[w']$ to nodes of $\mathcal{M}_i$ begin at frontier nodes of $FRAG[w']$, then w and w' are identified. Otherwise, w is replaced by a copy of $FRAG[w]$, constructed before. The construction terminates at the least m, when $\mathcal{M}_m$ has an empty set of frontier nodes; $\mathcal{M}_m$ is a Hintikka structure for p_0. It can be shown that if $|p_0| = n$, then the pseudo-Hintikka structure for p_0 is of size not larger than 2^n and the Hintikka structure for p_0 is of size not larger than $n8^n$. □

Next, it is shown that there is a better algorithm for testing the satisfiability of p_0 than that which would examine all the finite pseudo-Hintikka structures of size less than $2^{|p_0|}$ in order to find one for p_0.

Theorem 4.6 There is a deterministic algorithm for deciding whether a CTL formula is satisfiable, of exponential complexity in the length of the tested formula.

Proof: Let p_0 be a given formula which is to be tested for satisfiability. A pseudo-Hintikka structure for p_0 of size not larger than $2^{|p_0|}$ is constructed.

1. The first step starts with building a structure $\mathcal{M}_0 = (W_0, R_0, L_0)$, where $W_0 = \{w \mid w \subseteq FL(p_0)$, w is maximal and satisfies H1 – H8$\}$, (maximality means that for every $p \in FL(p_0)$ ($p \in w$ or $\neg p \in w$)), $L_0(w) = w$, $R_0 \subseteq W_0 \times W_0$ such that for every $w, v \in W_0$, $(w, v) \in R_0$ iff $\neg\exists \bigcirc p \in w$ implies $\neg p \in v$.

2. The next step consists in building a structure $\mathcal{M}_1$ obtained from $\mathcal{M}_0$ by repeatedly eliminating all nodes either for which the conditions H9 – H11 and H12′ are not satisfied or that do not have at least one successor. If the resulting structure is not empty and contains a state w_0 such that $p_0 \in w_0$, then it is a pseudo-Hintikka structure for p_0. Thus p_0 is satisfiable. The complexity of such an algorithm is $DTIME(2^{cn})$ for $c \geq 1$ and $|p_0| = n$.
Note that there is a deterministic exponential time lower bound for CTL satisfiability as UB is contained in CTL. □

Theorem 4.7 The proof system for CTL is sound and complete.

Proof: It has to be shown that any consistent formula p (i.e. $\not\vdash \neg p$) is satisfiable. So, p_0 is supposed to be a consistent CTL formula. A pseudo-Hintikka structure for p_0 is built as in the proof of the decidability theorem.

Let $w \in W_0$ and define the formula p_w as the conjunction of formulas in w, i.e. $p_w = \bigwedge_{q \in w} q$. By the maximality of w, it follows that if $q \in FL(p_0)$, then $q \in w$ iff $\vdash p_w \rightarrow q$. The proof consists in showing that if a state $w \in W_0$ is eliminated in the algorithm of the decidability theorem proof, then p_w is inconsistent. As this is shown, the continuation is as follows. It can be easily observed that:

$$\vdash p_0 \leftrightarrow \bigvee_{\{w \mid p_0 \in w,\ p_w \text{ is consistent}\}} p_w$$

Thus, if p_0 is consistent, some p_w is consistent as well. This w is not eliminated in the construction. A pseudo-Hintikka structure for p_0 is obtained. Therefore p_0 is satisfiable.

Next, it is proved by induction on when a state is eliminated, that if a state w is eliminated, then $\vdash \neg p_w$. It is easy to check that if w is eliminated at step 1, then p_w must be inconsistent. Then it is shown that if the formula p_w is consistent, w is not eliminated at step 2.

First observe that if $(w, v) \notin R_0$, then $p_w \wedge \exists \bigcirc p_v$ is inconsistent. By definition, $\neg\exists \bigcirc p \in w$ and $p \in v$ for some p. Now, $\vdash (p_w \wedge \exists \bigcirc p_v) \rightarrow (\neg\exists \bigcirc p \wedge \exists \bigcirc p)$. Thus, $p_w \wedge \exists \bigcirc p_v$ is inconsistent.

Secondly, it is shown that if a state w is eliminated at step 2, then $\vdash \neg p_w$. Only the case when H11 is not satisfied at w is considered here. The other cases have similar proofs. Therefore, suppose w is eliminated at step 2 on account H11 failing at w with respect to $\exists(p\,U q)$. The formula p_w is shown to be inconsistent. Let $V = \{v \mid \exists(pUq) \in v$ and v is eliminated at step 2 because H11 fails$\}$. Since H11 fails, $\vdash p_v \rightarrow \neg q$ for each $v \in V$. Let $r = \bigvee_{v \in V} p_v$. Of course, $\vdash r \rightarrow \neg q$. Suppose it can be shown that $\vdash r \rightarrow \forall\bigcirc(r \vee \neg\exists(p\,U q))$. Then by the inference rule (R4), $\vdash r \rightarrow \neg\exists(p\,U q)$. Since $w \in V$, $\vdash p_w \rightarrow \neg\exists(p\,U q)$. But, by assumption $\exists(p\,U q) \in w$, so p_w must be inconsistent.

In order to show that $\vdash r \rightarrow \forall\bigcirc(r \vee \neg\exists(p\,U q))$, it suffices to show that for each $v \in V$, $\vdash p_v \rightarrow \forall\bigcirc(r \vee \neg\exists(p\,U q))$. Suppose this is not true. Then for some $v \in V$, $p_v \wedge \exists\bigcirc(\neg r \wedge \exists(p\,U q))$ is consistent. As $(\neg r) \leftrightarrow \bigvee_{v' \notin V} p_{v'}$, so

$p_v \wedge \exists \bigcirc (p_{v'} \wedge \exists (p\, U q))$ is consistent for some $v' \notin V$. Therefore, both $p_v \wedge \exists \bigcirc p_{v'}$ and $p_{v'} \wedge \exists (p\, U q)$ are consistent. The former implies $(v, v') \in R_0$ and the latter implies $\exists (p\, U q) \in v'$ (by maximality). But if $\exists (p\, U q) \in v'$ and $v' \notin V$, then H11 must hold for v'. Since $(v, v') \in R_0$, $p \in v$ (as $\exists (p\, U q) \in v$), then H11 must also hold for v, contradicting the fact that $v \in V$.

In this way it has been shown that only states w with p_w inconsistent are eliminated. This ends the proof. □

Model checking for CTL

Model checking is a method of verifying algorithmically a formula against a model. Let us assume a finite model (representing behaviour of a concurrent system) $\mathcal{M}$ and a CTL formula p representing a property. In order to establish whether the concurrent system satisfies the property it is checked whether the formula p holds in the model $\mathcal{M}$. It turns out that the complexity of this problem is polynomial [5].

Theorem 4.8 There is a deterministic algorithm for determining whether a CTL formula p holds at the state w in the finite model $\mathcal{M} = (W, R, V)$, of complexity $O(|p| \times (card(W) + card(R)))$.

Proof: Let $\mathcal{M} = (W, R, V)$ be a finite model. It is checked whether $\mathcal{M}$ is a model for a formula p. The algorithm shown here is designed so that when it finishes, each state w of $\mathcal{M}$ is labelled with the subformulas of p which hold at w. The algorithm operates in stages. The ith stage handles all subformulas of p of length i for $i \leq |p|$. Thus, at the end of the last stage each state is labelled with all subformulas of p holding at it. It can be easily seen that the following equivalence holds:

$$\forall (p_1\, U p_2) \leftrightarrow \neg(\exists(\neg p_2\, U(\neg p_1 \wedge \neg p_2)) \vee \exists \Box (\neg p_2)).$$

Because of that, any of the following six cases may be considered, depending on whether p is atomic or has one of the following forms: $\neg p_1$, $p_1 \wedge p_2$, $\exists \bigcirc p_1$, $\exists (p_1\, U p_2)$, or $\exists \Box p_1$. The algorithm is discussed for the last two cases, as the others are straightforward. To handle a formula of the form $p = \exists (p_1\, U p_2)$, the algorithm first finds all states which are labelled with p_2 and labels them with p. Then, it goes backwards using the relation R^{-1} and finds all states that can be reached by a path in which each state is labelled with p_1. All such states are labelled with p. This step requires time $O(card(W) + card(R))$. Now, the case when $p = \exists \Box p_1$ is considered. First, a structure $\mathcal{M}' = (W', R', V')$ is constructed, where $W' = \{w \in W \mid \mathcal{M}, w \Vdash p_1\}$, $R' = R \cap (W' \times W')$ and $V' = V/W'$. Secondly, the graph (W', R') is partitioned into maximal strongly connected components, i.e., maximal subgraphs in which there is a path of arrows between each two nodes. Those states which either belong to components of size greater than one or have a self loop are selected. Consequently, the algorithm goes backwards using R^{-1} and finds all those states that can be reached by a path in which each state is labelled with p_1. This step also requires time $O(card(W) + card(R))$. In order to handle an arbitrary CTL formula p, the state-labelling algorithm is successively applied to the subformulas of p, starting with the shortest and most deeply nested one. Since each pass takes time $O(card(W) + card(R))$ and since p has at most $|p|$ different subformulas, the algorithm requires time $O(|p| \times (card(W) + card(R)))$. □

Next, the most powerful branching time logic CTL* is discussed. It subsumes UB as well as CTL.

4.2.4 Computation tree logic* (CTL*) again

UB and CTL cannot be used for specifying many important properties of concurrent programs since their languages are too weak. Therefore if one wants to specify more properties including e.g. fairness requirements, CTL* has to be applied.

Expressiveness of CTL*

All the properties expressible in CTL are obviously expressible in CTL*. The following combinations of linear time operators are useful for expressing fairness constraints in CTL*:

- $\Diamond \Box p$ (abbrev. $\Box^\infty p$), and
- $\Box \Diamond p$ (abbrev. $\Diamond^\infty p$).

Consider, for example, a simple computation fullpath, and let $enabled_i$ hold at all moments at the fullpath at which process i is ready for execution, and let $executed_i$ hold at each state at which it is actually scheduled for execution. Then, the fairness assumptions for a family of m processes are expressed by the following formulas:

- $\bigwedge_{i=1...m} \Diamond^\infty executed_i$ – impartiality,
- $\bigwedge_{i=1...m}(\Diamond^\infty enabled_i \rightarrow \Diamond^\infty executed_i)$ – fairness,
- $\bigwedge_{i=1...m}(\Box^\infty enabled_i \rightarrow \Diamond^\infty executed_i)$ – justice.

Some examples of CTL* formulas that are not CTL formulas are now given.

- $\exists((p U q) \vee \Box p)$, which expresses the weak until property along a path,
- $\exists \Box^\infty executed_i$, which describes an unfair computation path along which, after a certain point in time, only process i is scheduled for execution.

- Similarly, the condition that all execution sequences of a family of m processes are impartial, given by $\forall \bigwedge_{i=1..m} \Diamond^{\infty}$ *executed*$_i$, is not a CTL formula.

The question concerning axiomatizability of CTL* is still open.
Checking whether a CTL* formula is satisfiable is much more difficult than in the case of CTL. But this is still decidable.

Theorem 4.9 [13] There is an algorithm for deciding whether a CTL* formula is satisfiable, of deterministic double exponential complexity in the length of the formula. □

The proof of this theorem consists in showing that the satisfiability problem can be reduced to testing the nonemptiness of tree automata. A lower bound of deterministic double exponential time has also been established [42].

In [6], a deterministic double exponential algorithm for CTL* interpreted over fair structures has been defined.

Model checking for CTL*

Model checking problem for CTL is solvable in deterministic linear time. The situation is different for CTL*. Unfortunately, the method of assigning the subformulas of a tested formula to the states of the model cannot be applied. One has to use more powerful automata theoretic methods.

Theorem 4.10 [36] Model checking for CTL* is PSPACE-complete. □

The main reason that CTL* is not broadly applied is the high complexity of checking satisfiability and performing model checking. There are, however, many logics "between" CTL and CTL* (which are not mentioned here) like CTL$^+$ [11], ECTL and ECTL$^+$ [10], [7], and FCTL [14], which extend the expressiveness of CTL, but have still less complicated algorithms of testing satisfiablity and of model checking than CTL*.

It should also be mentioned that there are branching time logics with syntax like CTL or CTL*, the formulas of which are interpreted over fair structures [6], Abrahamson structures (suffix and fusion closed) [2] and probabilistic structures [24]. These logics have also been shown to be decidable and to have the finite model property.

4.3 Temporal logics on partial orders

The aim of this section is to present the existing formal languages of temporal logic which are used to specify the behaviours of concurrent systems represented by partial orders. These logics have either partial order frames (event structure logics and ISTL) or preorder frames (POTL, POTL[U, $\overline{U}$]) representing partially ordered computations.

First, the formal systems POTL, POTL[U, $\overline{U}$] and ISTL are discussed. Their frames can be linked with the behaviours of concurrent systems represented by general partial order structures. Then, the logics interpreted over event structures, SESL, ESL, ESL[δ], DESL and ESL[C] are presented.

There are two ways in which a frame can represent the behaviour of a concurrent system. The first possibility is as it is defined for branching time temporal logics, i.e. a frame represents an entire concurrent system (see SESL, ESL, DESL, ESL[C]). The second option is as it is defined for linear time temporal logics, i.e. a frame represents one run (full execution) of a concurrent system. In this case, a structure representing the full behaviour of a concurrent system is defined as a set of frames, one for each run (see POTL, POTL[U, $\overline{U}$], ISTL).

4.3.1 Partial order temporal logic (POTL)

First, the definitions of temporal logics for reasoning about partially ordered computations are given. These logics, called POTL and POTL[U, $\overline{U}$], were defined by Pinter & Wolper [34], and Kornatzky & Pinter [18]. POTL[U, $\overline{U}$] is the extension of POTL obtained by introducing *until* and *since*. POTL is intended to describe partially ordered computations directly. Thus, it is able to specify that states have several successors and several predecessors. A state with several successors can be viewed as corresponding to *fork* (creating new processes) and a state with several predecessors as representing *join* (merging processes). Hence POTL includes temporal operators to talk about several successors and several predecessors. POTL can be also viewed as a branching time temporal logic (UB) with "past" operators $\exists\overline{\bigcirc}$, $\exists\overline{\Diamond}$ and $\exists\overline{\Box}$. The language of POTL is an extension of the language of UB by allowing quantification over backward paths. Therefore, POTL also has basic modalities $\exists\overline{\bigcirc}$, $\exists\overline{\Diamond}$ and $\exists\overline{\Box}$ (and their duals $\forall\overline{\bigcirc}$, $\forall\overline{\Box}$ and $\forall\overline{\Diamond}$). A formal syntax of POTL formulas is now given.

Syntax of POTL

Let AP be a set of atomic propositions. The set of POTL formulas is defined inductively:

- every member of AP is a formula,
- if p, q are formulas, then so are $\neg p$ and $p \wedge q$,
- if p is a formula, then so are $\exists\bigcirc p$, $\exists\Diamond p\, \exists\Box p$,
- if p is a formula, then so are $\exists\overline{\bigcirc} p$, $\exists\overline{\Diamond} p$ and $\exists\overline{\Box} p$.

The other connectives $\vee$, $\rightarrow$ and $\leftrightarrow$ are defined in the standard way.

The derived basic forward paths modalities are as for UB. These dealing with backward paths are defined below:

- $\forall\overline{\Box}p \stackrel{def}{=} \neg\exists\overline{\Diamond}\neg p$,
- $\forall\overline{\Diamond}p \stackrel{def}{=} \neg\exists\overline{\Box}\neg p$,
- $\forall\overline{\bigcirc}p \stackrel{def}{=} \neg\exists\overline{\bigcirc}\neg p$.

Semantics of POTL

Let $\mathcal{M} = (W, R, V)$ be a model, where W is a nonempty set of states and $R \subseteq W \times W$ is a binary relation on W. R and R^{-1} are assumed to be total (i.e. each state has at least one R-successor and one R-predecessor) and $V : W \longrightarrow 2^{AP}$ is a valuation function which assigns to each state a set of atomic propositions. A *forward (backward) fullpath* is an infinite sequence $x = (w_0, w_1, ...)$ of states such that $(w_i, w_{i+1}) \in R$ ($\in R^{-1}$, resp.) for each $i \geq 0$. As before, x_i denotes the ith state of the fullpath x and $\mathcal{M}, w \Vdash p$ ($\mathcal{M}, x \Vdash p$) denotes that the state (path) formula p holds at the state w (in the fullpath x, resp.) in the model $\mathcal{M}$. $\mathcal{M}$ is omitted, if it is implicitly understood. Let $x = (w_0, w_1, ...)$ be a forward or backward fullpath, $w_0 \Vdash p$ is defined inductively for an arbitrary state w_0 as follows:

- $w_0 \Vdash p$ iff $p \in V(w_0)$ for any atomic proposition

  $p \in AP$,
- $w_0 \Vdash \neg p$ iff not $w_0 \Vdash p$,

  $w_0 \Vdash p \wedge q$ iff $w_0 \Vdash p$ and $w_0 \Vdash q$,
- $w_0 \Vdash \exists\bigcirc p$ iff for some forward fullpath x starting at w_0, $w_1 \Vdash p$,

  $w_0 \Vdash \exists\Diamond p$ iff for some forward fullpath x starting at w_0, $w_i \Vdash p$ for some $i \geq 0$,

  $w_0 \Vdash \exists\Box p$ iff for some forward fullpath x starting at w_0, $w_i \Vdash p$ for all $i \geq 0$,
- $w_0 \Vdash \exists\overline{\bigcirc} p$ iff for some backward fullpath x starting at w_0, $w_1 \Vdash p$,

  $w_0 \Vdash \exists\overline{\Diamond} p$ iff for some backward fullpath x starting at w_0, $w_i \Vdash p$ for some $i \geq 0$,

  $w_0 \Vdash \exists\overline{\Box} p$ iff for some backward fullpath x starting at w_0, $w_i \Vdash p$ for all $i \geq 0$.

It can be noticed that the semantics of POTL is identical to the semantics of UB except for the rules incorporating the new backward path modalities. The other notions like satisfiability, validity, and validity in the model are defined similarly to the case of UB.

Expressiveness of POTL

POTL can be used in the same framework as UB, where a structure represents an entire concurrent system. Then, it extends the expressiveness of UB by making it possible to refer to the past. For example, a formula $\exists\overline{\Diamond}p$ expresses that there is an earlier state at which p holds, a formula $\forall\overline{\Diamond}p$ says that at each backward fullpath there is a state at which p holds, whereas $\forall\overline{\Box}p$ specifies that p holds at all states in the past.

However, POTL was defined to be applied to a different framework, where a structure represents one possible run of a system composed of sequential processes. A run of such a system of processes can be viewed as a directed acyclic graph. Each node represents a process state, and an edge from a node w to a node w' represents that w' immediately follows w. In this framework, POTL is used to specify properties involving all runs. Therefore, a concurrent system P is represented by a POTL structure $\mathcal{A}_{\mathcal{P}} = \{\mathcal{M} \mid \mathcal{M}$ represents a run of the system $P\}$.

Let $\mathcal{A}$ be a POTL structure. $\mathcal{A}$ is said to validate a formula p (written $\mathcal{A} \Vdash p$) iff $\mathcal{M} \Vdash p$ for each model $\mathcal{M}$ in $\mathcal{A}$. The meaning of POTL formulas is as follows. $\mathcal{A} \Vdash p$ formulates that for every model of $\mathcal{A}$, for every state in it, p holds. For example, $\mathcal{A} \Vdash q \rightarrow \forall\overline{\Diamond}p$ expresses that for every run, for every backward fullpath ending at states where q holds, there is a state at which p holds.

A proof system for POTL

- Axioms:

(A1) All substitution rules of propositional calculus

(A2) $\exists\bigcirc(p \vee q) \leftrightarrow \exists\bigcirc p \vee \exists\bigcirc q$

(A3) $\exists\Diamond p \leftrightarrow p \vee \exists\bigcirc\exists\Diamond p$

(A4) $\exists\Box p \leftrightarrow p \wedge \exists\bigcirc\exists\Box p$

(A5) $\exists\bigcirc\mathbf{T}$

(A6) $\exists\overline{\bigcirc}(p \vee q) \leftrightarrow \exists\overline{\bigcirc}p \vee \exists\overline{\bigcirc}q$

(A7) $\exists\overline{\Diamond}p \leftrightarrow p \vee \exists\overline{\bigcirc}\exists\overline{\Diamond}p$

(A8) $\exists\overline{\Box}p \leftrightarrow p \wedge \exists\overline{\bigcirc}\exists\overline{\Box}p$

(A9) $\exists\overline{\bigcirc}\mathbf{T}$

(A10) $p \rightarrow \forall\bigcirc\exists\overline{\bigcirc}p$

(A11) $p \rightarrow \forall\overline{\bigcirc}\exists\bigcirc p$

- Inference rules:

(R1) $p, p \rightarrow q \vdash q$

(R2) $p \rightarrow q \vdash \exists\bigcirc p \rightarrow \exists\bigcirc q$

(R3) $r \rightarrow (\neg q \wedge \exists \bigcirc r) \vdash r \rightarrow \exists \Box \neg q$

(R4) $r \rightarrow (\neg q \wedge \forall \bigcirc (r \vee \neg \exists \Diamond q)) \vdash r \rightarrow \neg \exists \Diamond q$

(R5) $p \rightarrow q \vdash \exists \overline{\bigcirc} p \rightarrow \exists \overline{\bigcirc} q$

(R6) $r \rightarrow (\neg q \wedge \exists \overline{\bigcirc} r) \vdash r \rightarrow \exists \overline{\Box} \neg q$

(R7) $r \rightarrow (\neg q \wedge \forall \overline{\bigcirc} (r \vee \neg \exists \overline{\Diamond} q)) \vdash r \rightarrow \neg \exists \overline{\Diamond} q$

The above proof system can be viewed as of three parts: the first, part (A1 – A5, R1 – R4) contains the axioms and the inference rules for UB, the second, A6 – A9, R5 – R7) is its mirror image. The third part consists of the axioms A10 and A11 relating past and future.

A characterization of POTL

It turns out that adding backward operators to UB results in the lost of the finite model property [34].

Theorem 4.11 POTL does not have the finite model property.

Proof: The formula $q \stackrel{def}{=} p \wedge \forall \bigcirc \forall \Box \neg p \wedge \forall \Box \forall \overline{\Diamond} p$ is shown to be satisfiable in infinite models only. A model of the formula q contains a state w_0, where p holds and, for all states forward accessible from w_0, the formulas $\neg p$ and $\forall \overline{\Diamond} p$ hold. As R is a total relation, then either there are infinitely many states accessible from w_0 in a model or one state, say v, accessible from w_0 is also accessible from itself. The latter is, however, impossible because then it would be an infinite backward fullpath from v, at which p does not hold, contradicting $\forall \overline{\Diamond} p$ holding at v. □

The direct consequence of this theorem can be found in the proof of completeness, where the infinite model for a formula is built. Checking whether a formula is satisfiable requires an exponential time algorithm as in the case of CTL.

Theorem 4.12 There is a deterministic algorithm for deciding whether a POTL formula is satisfiable, of exponential complexity in the length of the tested formula. □

Theorem 4.13 The proof system for POTL is sound and complete. □

The proof sketches of the above theorems are given for POTL$[U, \overline{U}]$ – an extension of POTL.

4.3.2 Partial order temporal logic with until and since

POTL$[U, \overline{U}]$ is an extension of POTL as CTL is an extension of UB. However, in the case of POTL$[U, \overline{U}]$ a new path modality *since* is also introduced.

Syntax of POTL[$U, \overline{U}$]

The set of POTL[$U, \overline{U}$] formulas is the maximal set generated by the following rules:

- every member of AP is a formula,
- if p, q are formulas, then so are $\neg p$ and $p \wedge q$,
- if p, q are formulas, then so are $\exists \bigcirc p$, $\exists(p\,U q)$ and $\forall(p\,U q)$,
- if p, q are formulas, then so are $\exists \overline{\bigcirc} p$, $\exists(p\,\overline{U} q)$ and $\forall(p\,\overline{U} q)$.

The derived basic modalities are:

- $\exists \Diamond p \stackrel{def}{=} \exists(\mathbf{T}\,U p)$,
- $\forall \Diamond p \stackrel{def}{=} \forall(\mathbf{T}\,U p)$,
- $\exists \overline{\Diamond} p \stackrel{def}{=} \exists(\mathbf{T}\,\overline{U} p)$,
- $\forall \overline{\Diamond} p \stackrel{def}{=} \forall(\mathbf{T}\,\overline{U} p)$.

The other derived modalities are defined as for POTL.

The definition of a model for POTL[$U, \overline{U}$] is as for POTL, with the difference that the relations R and R^{-1} are not required to be total. This is motivated by the fact that the initial or the terminal state of some process may have no predecessors or successors, respectively. This kind of frame is required, for example, for reasoning about Petri nets [20].

The semantics of POTL[$U, \overline{U}$] formulas (except for the new ones) is like for POTL, involving the following new definition of a forward (backward) fullpath. A forward (backward) fullpath is a maximal sequence of states $x = (w_0, w_1, \ldots)$ such that $(w_i, w_{i+1}) \in R$ ($\in R^{-1}$, resp.) for each $i \geq 0$. Notice that a forward (backward) fullpath x is finite iff its last (first) state does not have any R-successor (R-predecessor, resp.). The semantics of formulas containing *until* and *since* is now given.

Let $\mathcal{M} = (W, R, V)$ be a model and $w_0 \in W$.

- $w_0 \Vdash \exists(p\,U q)$ iff for some forward fullpath x starting at w_0, $(\exists i \geq 0)\ w_i \Vdash q$ and $(\forall j :\ 0 \leq j < i)\ w_j \Vdash p$,

  $w_0 \Vdash \forall(p\,U q)$ iff for all forward fullpaths x starting at w_0, $(\exists i \geq 0)\ w_i \Vdash q$ and $(\forall j :\ 0 \leq j < i)\ w_j \Vdash p$,
- $w_0 \Vdash \exists(p\,\overline{U} q)$ iff for some backward fullpath x starting at w_0, $(\exists i \geq 0)\ w_i \Vdash q$ and $(\forall j :\ 0 \leq j < i)\ w_j \Vdash p$,

  $w_0 \Vdash \forall(p\,\overline{U} q)$ iff for all backward fullpaths x starting at w_0, $(\exists i \geq 0)\ w_i \Vdash q$ and $(\forall j : 0 \leq j < i)\ w_j \Vdash p$.

Expressiveness of POTL$[U, \overline{U}]$

POTL$[U, \overline{U}]$ extends the expressiveness of POTL similarly to the way in which CTL extends the expressiveness of UB. All properties expressible in POTL are expressible in POTL$[U, \overline{U}]$. Moreover, properties concerning the relative order of events in the future and in the past can be expressed using formulas of the form $\exists(pUq)$, $\forall(pUq)$, $\exists(p\overline{U}q)$ and $\forall(p\overline{U}q)$.

It has been shown in [18] that POTL$[U, \overline{U}]$ is a strict extension of POTL.

A proof system for POTL$[U, \overline{U}]$

- Axioms:

(A1) All substitution rules of propositional calculus

(A2) $\exists\bigcirc(p \vee q) \leftrightarrow \exists\bigcirc p \vee \exists\bigcirc q$

(A3) $\exists(pUq) \leftrightarrow q \vee (p \wedge \exists\bigcirc\exists(pUq))$

(A4) $\forall(pUq) \leftrightarrow q \vee (p \wedge \forall\bigcirc\forall(pUq) \wedge \exists\bigcirc \mathbf{T})$

(A5) $\exists\overline{\bigcirc}(p \vee q) \leftrightarrow \exists\overline{\bigcirc} p \vee \exists\overline{\bigcirc} q$

(A6) $\exists(p\overline{U}q) \leftrightarrow q \vee (p \wedge \exists\overline{\bigcirc}\exists(p\overline{U}q))$

(A7) $\forall(p\overline{U}q) \leftrightarrow q \vee (p \wedge \forall\overline{\bigcirc}\forall(p\overline{U}q) \wedge \exists\overline{\bigcirc}\mathbf{T})$

(A8) $p \rightarrow \forall\bigcirc\exists\overline{\bigcirc} p$

(A9) $p \rightarrow \forall\overline{\bigcirc}\exists\bigcirc p$

- Inference rules:

(R1) $p,\ p \rightarrow q \vdash q$

(R2) $p \rightarrow q \vdash \exists\bigcirc p \rightarrow \exists\bigcirc q$

(R3) $r \rightarrow (\neg q \wedge \exists\bigcirc r) \vdash r \rightarrow \neg\forall(pUq)$

(R4) $r \rightarrow (\neg q \wedge \forall\bigcirc(r \vee \neg\exists(pUq))) \vdash r \rightarrow \neg\exists(pUq)$

(R5) $p \rightarrow q \vdash \exists\overline{\bigcirc} p \rightarrow \exists\overline{\bigcirc} q$

(R6) $r \rightarrow (\neg q \wedge \exists\overline{\bigcirc} r) \vdash r \rightarrow \neg\forall(p\overline{U}q)$

(R7) $r \rightarrow (\neg q \wedge \forall\overline{\bigcirc}(r \vee \neg\exists(p\overline{U}q))) \vdash r \rightarrow \neg\exists(p\overline{U}q)$

The above proof system can be viewed as three parts: the first, A1–A4, R1 – R4 contains the axioms and the inference rules for CTL (except for $\forall\bigcirc\mathbf{T}$), the second, A5 – A7, R5 – R7 is its mirror image and the third contains axioms A8 and A9 relating past and future.

A characterization of POTL$[U, \overline{U}]$

Since POTL does not have the finite model property, as one might expect, POTL$[U, \overline{U}]$ does not have it either.

Theorem 4.14 POTL$[U, \overline{U}]$ does not have the finite model property. □

The proof is the same as for POTL using the formula $p \wedge \exists \bigcirc \mathbf{T} \wedge \forall \bigcirc \forall \Box(\neg p \wedge \exists \bigcirc \mathbf{T}) \wedge \forall \Box \forall \overline{\Diamond} p$, which differs from the formula q used in the proof for POTL in the subformulas $\exists \bigcirc \mathbf{T}$. These subformulas were added in order that the relation R is total.

It is now shown how to check whether a POTL$[U, \overline{U}]$ formula is satisfiable.

Theorem 4.15 There is a deterministic algorithm for deciding whether a POTL$[U, \overline{U}]$ formula is satisfiable, of exponential complexity in the length of the tested formula.

Proof: The proof of this theorem is similar to the proof for CTL. It consists in defining an algorithm which constructs a pseudo-Hintikka structure for a satisfiable POTL$[U, \overline{U}]$ formula. This construction is not repeated, but it is shown how to define a pseudo-Hintikka structure for a POTL$[U, \overline{U}]$ formula and how to "unwind" it into a Hintikka structure. As POTL$[U, \overline{U}]$ does not have the finite model property, a finite pseudo-Hintikka structure for a POTL$[U, \overline{U}]$ formula has to be unwound into an infinite Hintikka structure. This makes the construction slightly more complicated than it was in the case of CTL.

First, the definition of a Hintikka structure for a POTL$[U, \overline{U}]$ formula p_0 is given.

Definition 4.5 A Hintikka structure (for p_0) is a structure $\mathcal{M} = (W, R, L)$, where $R \subseteq W \times W$ is a relation (and $p_0 \in L(w)$ for some $w \in W$) and L satisfies the conditions H1-H12 in Definition 4.1 and the following conditions:

(H13) if $\exists(p\overline{U}q) \in L(w)$ then $q \in L(w)$ or $p, \exists\overline{\bigcirc}\exists(p\overline{U}q) \in L(w)$,

(H14) if $\neg\exists(p\overline{U}q) \in L(w)$ then $\neg q, \neg p \in L(w)$ or $\neg q, \neg\exists\overline{\bigcirc}\exists(p\overline{U}q) \in L(w)$,

(H15) if $\forall(p\overline{U}q) \in L(w)$ then $q \in L(w)$ or $p, \neg\exists\overline{\bigcirc}\neg\forall(p\overline{U}q) \in L(w)$,

(H16) if $\neg\forall(p\overline{U}q) \in L(w)$ then $\neg q, \neg p \in L(w)$ or $\neg q, \exists\overline{\bigcirc}\neg\forall(p\overline{U}q) \in L(w)$,

(H17) if $\exists\overline{\bigcirc}p \in L(w)$ then $\exists v\ ((w, v) \in R^{-1}$ and $p \in L(v))$,

(H18) if $\neg\exists\overline{\bigcirc}p \in L(w)$ then $\forall v\ (((w, v) \in R^{-1})$ implies $\neg p \in L(v))$,

(H19) if $\exists(p\overline{U}q) \in L(w)$ then there is a backward fullpath x starting at w and a state v on x such that for all v' before v on x, $q \in L(v)$ and $p \in L(v')$,

(H20) if $\forall(p\overline{U}q) \in L(w)$ then for all backward fullpaths starting at w there is a state v on x such that for all v' before v on x, $q \in L(v)$ and $p \in L(v')$. □

It can be easily proved that a POTL$[U, \overline{U}]$ formula p is satisfiable iff there is a Hintikka structure for p. Now, looking for a finite pseudo-Hintikka structure for the satisfiable formula p_0, the Fischer-Ladner closure (see [17]) of p_0 and then the quotient structure of a model is defined. Let $C(p_0)$ be the least set of formulas containing p_0 and satisfying the conditions C1-C5 as for CTL and moreover:

(C6) if $\exists\overline{\bigcirc} p \in C(p_0)$ then $p \in C(p_0)$,

(C7) if $\exists(p\overline{U}q) \in C(p_0)$ then $q,\ p, \exists\overline{\bigcirc}\exists(p\overline{U}q) \in C(p_0)$,

(C8) if $\forall(p\overline{U}q) \in C(p_0)$ then $q,\ p, \neg\exists\overline{\bigcirc}\neg\forall(p\overline{U}q) \in C(p_0)$.

Let $FL(p_0) = C(p_0) \cup \neg C(p_0)$, where $\neg C(p_0) = \{\neg p \mid p \in C(p_0)\}$. It can be shown by induction on the length of the formula that $card(FL(p_0)) \le 2|p_0|$. Let $\mathcal{M} = (W, R, V)$ be a model for p_0, and let $\leftrightarrow_{FL(p_0)}$ be an equivalence relation on W defined as follows: $w_1 \leftrightarrow_{FL(p_0)} w_2$ iff $(\forall q \in FL(p_0))$ $(w_1 \Vdash q$ iff $w_2 \Vdash q)$. The set $\{v \in W \mid w \leftrightarrow_{FL(p_0)} v\}$ is denoted by $[w]$. The quotient structure of $\mathcal{M}$ by $\leftrightarrow_{FL(p_0)}$ is the structure $\mathcal{M}' = (W', R', L')$, where $W' = \{[w] \mid w \in W\}$, $R' = \{([w],[v]) \in W' \times W' \mid \exists w' \in [w], \exists v' \in [v] : (w', v') \in R\}$, $L'([w]) = \{q \in FL(p_0) \mid w \Vdash q\}$. As in the case of CTL, $\mathcal{M}'$ does not need to be a Hintikka structure for p_0. The satisfiability for formulas of the form $\forall(pUq)$ and $\forall(p\overline{U}q)$ may not be preserved. However, analogously, the quotient structure $\mathcal{M}'$ provides useful information. It is easy to check that $\mathcal{M}'$ satisfies all the conditions of the definition of a Hintikka structure except possibly H12 and H20. Instead, $\mathcal{M}'$ satisfies another important condition which makes it possible to prove $\mathcal{M}'$ to be modally equivalent to some Hintikka structure. The following definitions are useful in the next part of the proof.

Definition 4.6 A *(backward) fragment* $\mathcal{N} = (W, R, L)$ is a (backward, resp.) rooted structure for which all the interior nodes satisfy H1 – H10, H13 – H16 and H18, (H1 – H8, H10 and H13 – H18, resp.) and all the frontier nodes satisfy H1 – H8, H13 – H16 and H18 (H1 – H8, H10 and H13 – H16, resp.) and whose graph is a finite dag. Given $\mathcal{M}_1 = (W_1, R_1, L_1)$ and $\mathcal{M}_2 = (W_2, R_2, L_2)$, $\mathcal{M}_1$ is said to be *contained* in $\mathcal{M}_2$, (written $\mathcal{M}_1 \subseteq \mathcal{M}_2$), iff $W_1 \subseteq W_2$, $R_1 \subseteq R_2$ and $L_1 = L_2/W_1$. □

Definition 4.7 A *pseudo-Hintikka structure* (for p_0) is a structure $\mathcal{M} = (W, R, L)$ (such that $p_0 \in L(w)$ for some $w \in W$, resp.), which satisfies H1 – H11, H13 – H19 and such that for all $w \in W$ the following conditions hold:

H12′ $\forall(pUq) \in L(w)$ implies that there is a fragment $\mathcal{N}$ rooted at w contained in $\mathcal{M}$ such that for all the frontier nodes v of $\mathcal{N}$, $q \in L(v)$, and for all the interior nodes u of $\mathcal{N}$, $p \in L(u)$.

H20′ $\forall(p\overline{U}q) \in L(w)$ implies that there is a backward fragment $\mathcal{N}$ rooted at w contained in $\mathcal{M}$ such that for all the frontier nodes v of $\mathcal{N}$, $q \in L(v)$, and for all the interior nodes u of $\mathcal{N}$, $p \in L(u)$. □

Now, it can be easily proved that $\mathcal{M}'$ is a pseudo-Hintikka structure.
It is shown in the second stage of the proof that the pseudo-Hintikka structure $\mathcal{M}'$ for p_0 is modally equivalent to some Hintikka structure for p_0. This is done by "unwinding" the pseudo-Hintikka structure in the way described fully in [34]. The method is based on the fact that for each state in a pseudo-Hintikka structure, a "forward tree" (ftree) and a "backward tree" (btree) can be built. These trees satisfy all formulas of the form $\forall(p\,U\,q)$ and $\exists(p\,U\,q)$, or $\forall(p\overline{U}q)$ and $\exists(p\overline{U}q)$. An ftree is simply a tree whereas a btree would be a tree if the directedness of edges were changed. The combination of an ftree and a btree is called fbtree. The construction proceeds by alternating and combining these forward and backward trees. The definition of a backward-forward unwinding BFU of the pseudo-Hintikka structure is given inductively on the i-step backward-forward unwinding BFU_i. The definition of BFU_i can be found in [34]. Then, BFU is defined as $\bigcup_{i=1}^{\infty} BFU_i$. □

There is a deterministic exponential time lower bound for POTL[$U, \overline{U}$] satisfiability since POTL[$U, \overline{U}$] includes UB, for which such a lower bound has been shown.

Theorem 4.16 The proof system for POTL[$U, \overline{U}$] is sound and complete. □

The proof is similar to that given for CTL using the new definition of a pseudo-Hintikka structure for a POTL[$U, \overline{U}$] formula. The main change is in adding symmetrical claims to handle the past components of POTL[$U, \overline{U}$] formulas and in not requiring R and R^{-1} to be total.

When the POTL[$U, \overline{U}$] models are required to have the relation R and R^{-1} total (as in the case of POTL), then the proof system has to be extended by formulas of the form $\exists \bigcirc \top$, $\exists \overline{\bigcirc} \top$, and all the results are still valid with small changes in the proofs.

Model checking for POTL[$U, \overline{U}$]

Model checking for POTL[$U, \overline{U}$] is more complicated than for CTL [19]. There are two reasons for this. First, formulas contain backward modalities. Secondly, formulas are interpreted over models corresponding to runs of concurrent systems.

Theorem 4.17 Model checking for POTL[$U, \overline{U}$] is exponential in the size of the model and doubly exponential in the length of the tested formula. □

The proof of the above theorem is very complicated. The interested reader is referred to [19].

POTL and POTL[$U, \overline{U}$] constitute a bridge between branching time and partial order logics. They can be viewed as extensions of branching time logics UB and CTL by past modalities. However, their semantic structures can be linked with partial orderings representing runs of concurrent systems.

4.3.3 Interleaving set temporal logic (ISTL)

So far, temporal logics have been interpreted over pre-order structures. Now, interleaving set temporal logic [21], [22], interpreted over partial order structures of global states, is introduced. The main aim in defining this logic was to express properties inherent in the partial order interpretations, more specifically, to distinguish concurrency from nondeterminism.

Syntax of ISTL

The formal language of ISTL is the same as that of CTL, i.e. it contains basic formulas of the form:

$$p \in AP,\ p \wedge q,\ \neg p,\ \forall(p\,U\,q),\ \exists(p\,U\,q),\ \text{and } \exists\bigcirc p.$$

The derived basic modalities are: $\forall\Diamond q$ abbreviating $\forall(\mathrm{T}\,U q)$, $\exists\Diamond q$ abbreviating $\exists(\mathrm{T}\,U q)$, $\forall\Box p$ abbreviating $\neg\exists\Diamond\neg q$, $\exists\Box q$ abbreviating $\neg\forall\Diamond\neg q$ and $\forall\bigcirc q$ abbreviating $\neg\exists\bigcirc\neg q$

To define the semantics for ISTL a lot of new notions have to be introduced, because frames of ISTL and CTL are connected with possible executions of distributed systems in different ways. In the case of CTL (as well as of UB and CTL*) an entire concurrent system is considered as defining one large partial order or branching structure. The branching modalities ($\exists(p\,U q)$ or $\exists\Diamond p$) can distinguish between different paths (interleaved runs). In the other view, which is given by ISTL, whenever there is an explicit nondeterministic choice in the code of a program, a single partial order includes only one specific choice made in that execution. Note that POTL and POTL$[U,\overline{U}]$ were connected with concurrent systems in the same way. Thus, a concurrent program is represented by a set of partial orders (or branching structures), each representing a run of a system.

A structure representing one possible run of a system is now defined. The approach of [21] is followed here; for the more general definition (concerning also nondiscrete and uncountable systems) the reader is referred to [26].

Definition 4.8 Let $(E,<)$ be an irreflexive *partial order* of events satisfying the following conditions:

- E is a countable set,
- $\{e' \in E \mid e' < e\}$ is finite, for each $e \in E$. □

The second condition says that the history of each event is finite.

The above partial order is used to represent a single execution of a system. Then, the notion of a global state can now be introduced.

Definition 4.9 A *global state* w is a subset of E satisfying the following condition:

$$(\forall e, e' \in E)\ [(e' < e \wedge e \in w) \rightarrow (e' \in w)] - \textit{backward} - \textit{closedness}. \quad \Box$$

A global state contains with each event all the events that happened in the past. Global states constitute states in frames. The set of all global states generated by $(E,<)$ is denoted by $W(E,<)$. If $(E,<)$ is understood, then W stands for $W(E,<)$.

A partial order of global states is now defined.

Definition 4.10 Let $R \subseteq W \times W$ be an irreflexive partial order of global states such that $w \, R \, w'$ iff $w \subset w'$. □

As R is a discrete partial order, the transition relation (next step relation) $\rightarrow$ on W can be defined as: $\rightarrow \, = \, R - R^2$. This means that $w \rightarrow w'$ iff $w \neq w'$ and there is an event $e \in E$ such that $w \cup \{e\} = w'$. As in case of branching time logics, maximal paths of global states are considered.

Definition 4.11 A forward fullpath $x = (w_0, w_1, \ldots)$ is a maximal sequence of global states such that $w_i \rightarrow w_{i+1}$ for each $i \geq 0$. □

Some forward fullpaths are of special interest.

Definition 4.12 A forward fullpath x is said to be an *observation* in W iff $(\forall w \in W)$ $(\exists w'$ on $x)$ $w \, R \, w'$. Let OBS denote the set of all observations in W. □

Observations are those special sequences of global states that represent the full executions of a system. It can be shown that OBS is not empty and, moreover, it is suffix and fusion closed.

Semantics of ISTL

A model is an ordered pair $\mathcal{M} = (F, V)$, where a frame $F = (W, R)$ is a partial order of global states and $V : W \longrightarrow 2^{AP}$ is a valuation fuction.

Let $x = (w_0, w_1, ...)$ be an observation in W. Now, the notion of a formula p holding at the state w_0 in a model $\mathcal{M}$, (written $\mathcal{M}, w_0 \Vdash p$ or simply $w_0 \Vdash p$) is defined inductively:

- $w_0 \Vdash p$ iff $p \in V(w_0)$, for $p \in AP$,
- $w_0 \Vdash p \wedge q$ iff $w_0 \Vdash p$ and $w_0 \Vdash q$,
  $w_0 \Vdash \neg p$ iff not $w_0 \Vdash p$,
- $w_0 \Vdash \exists (p \, U \, q)$ iff for some observation x in W starting at w_0, $(\exists i \geq 0)$ $w_i \Vdash q$ and $(\forall j : 0 \leq j < i)$ $w_j \Vdash p$,

  $w_0 \Vdash \forall (p \, U \, q)$ iff for each observation x in W starting at w_0, $(\exists i \geq 0)$ $w_i \Vdash q$ and $(\forall j : 0 \leq j < i)$ $w_j \Vdash p$,

  $w_0 \Vdash \exists \bigcirc p$ iff there is a state w_1 such that $w_0 \rightarrow w_1$ and $w_1 \Vdash p$.

A formula p is said to be valid in a model $\mathcal{M}$ (written $\mathcal{M} \Vdash p$) iff $w \Vdash p$ for each $w \in W$.

Expressiveness of ISTL

A concurrent system P is represented by an ISTL structure $\mathcal{A}_\mathcal{P} = \{\mathcal{M} \mid \mathcal{M}$ is the model representing a single execution of the system $P\}$. Let $\mathcal{A}$ be an ISTL structure. $\mathcal{A}$ is said to validate a formula p (written $\mathcal{A} \Vdash p$) iff $\mathcal{M} \Vdash p$ for each $\mathcal{M}$ in $\mathcal{A}$. The meaning of ISTL formulas is as follows. $\mathcal{A} \Vdash p$ expresses that for every model of $\mathcal{A}$, for every state in it, p holds.

All the properties expressible in CTL except for possibility ones are expressible in ISTL. Moreover, formulas are not quantified over all paths but over observations and all executions. Therefore, their semantics is related to all runs. For example, the following properties about $\mathcal{A}$ can be formulated. $\mathcal{A} \Vdash q \rightarrow \forall \Diamond p$ expresses that for all observations starting at states where q holds, there is a state at which p hols. $\mathcal{A} \Vdash \forall \Box p$ says that p is an invariant, and $\mathcal{A} \Vdash q \rightarrow \exists \Diamond p$ states that for each execution, for each state w where q holds, there is an observation starting at w containing a state at which p holds. This formula can be used to express the property of serializability of database transactions [33].

A characterization of ISTL

The price to be paid for extra expressiveness of ISTL is its undecidability. It was shown that if some more conditions are required about ISTL models, then ISTL is undecidable.

Theorem 4.18 [31] ISTL interpreted over full executions of trace systems is undecidable. □

The satisfiability problem for ISTL is reduced to the recurring tiling problem, which is known to be undecidable and Π_1^1-complete.

So far, no complete proof system for the whole language of ISTL has been defined. In [32], a complete infinitary axiomatization for ISTL without formulas of the form $\exists \Box p$ was presented.

There has also been defined the logic ISTL* [21], which uses the language of CTL* with the same models as ISTL, and the logic QISTL [21], which is a branching version of ISTL.

4.4 Logics on event structures

The behaviour of a concurrent system does not need to be represented by a structure of global states. It can also be described via events (occurrences of system actions). Then, two relations between events are needed: an earlier–later relation representing causality and a conflict relation reflecting choices made by the system.

This section contains definitions of formal systems based on event structures. The first such system was put forward by Lodaya & Thiagarajan [25]. Section 4.4.1 introduces event structures and related notions.

4.4.1 Event structures

The notion of an event structure was introduced by Winskel [37]. An event structure represents the behaviour of a distributed system by means of a set of event occurrences, a causality relation that partially orders the event occurrences and a conflict relation which reflects the choices available to the system.

Definition 4.13 An *event structure* is a triple $ES = (E, \leq, \sharp)$, where

- E is a nonempty set of *events*,
- $\leq \subseteq E \times E$ is a partial order, called the *causality relation*,
- $\sharp \subseteq E \times E$ is an irreflexive, symmetric relation, called the *conflict relation*,
- For any $e, e', e'' \in E$: $e \sharp e' \leq e''$ implies $e \sharp e''$ (the *conflict inheritance*).

□

The last clause in the definition captures the intuition that in the past of any event no two events can be in conflict. Notice that it follows from the definition that the relations $\leq$ and $\sharp$ are disjoint. Next, some notions related to event structures are defined. They are needed to understand how the behaviour of a system is described by an event structure.

Definition 4.14 Let $ES = (E, \leq, \sharp)$ be an event structure and $Rn \subseteq E$.

- Rn is conflict free iff $(Rn \times Rn) \cap \sharp = \emptyset$,
- Rn is backward closed iff $e' \leq e$ implies $e' \in Rn$, for each $e \in Rn$ and $e' \in E$,
- Rn is a run iff Rn is a maximal backward closed and conflict free subset of E,
- $Rn_{ES} = \{Rn \subseteq E \mid Rn \text{ is a run in } ES\}$ is a set of all runs in ES.

□

Runs represent possible full executions of event structures. They correspond to single executions, as defined for ISTL.

Definition 4.15 An event structure $ES = (E, \leq, \sharp)$ is said to be sequential iff for any two events $e_1, e_2 \in E$, $e_1 \; R \; e_2$, where $R \in \{\leq, \geq, \sharp\}$. □

Sequential event structures are used to represent sequential, but maybe non-deterministic, concurrent systems.

One of the important restrictions of event structures is the class n-agent event structures, defined below, representing concurrent systems consisting of n sequential components (agents). The individual agents become aware of the properties of other agents through explicit communication, modelled by the global partial ordering relation.

Definition 4.16 An *n-agent* event structure is the structure $ES = (E_1, \ldots, E_n, \leq, \sharp)$ with $n \in N$ satisfying the following conditions:

(a) $i \neq j$ implies $E_i \cap E_j = \emptyset$, for i, j: $1 \leq i, j \leq n$.

(b) $(E, \leq, \sharp)$ is an event structure, where $E = \bigcup_{i=1}^{n} E_i$.

(c) The agent $(E_i, \leq_i, \sharp_i)$ is a sequential event structure, where $\sharp_i = \sharp / E_i \times E_i$ and $\leq_i = \leq / E_i \times E_i$, for any i: $1 \leq i \leq n$.

(d) $\sharp = \{(e_1, e_2) \mid \exists (e_1', e_2') \in \sharp' : e_1' \leq e_1 \text{ and } e_2' \leq e_2\}$, where $\sharp' = \bigcup_{i=1}^{n} \sharp_i$. □

Part (d) of the definition captures the idea that choices are made "locally" by the individual sequential agents and that this information is propagated by the causality relation. Consequently, different agents can influence each other only through explicit communication, which is modelled by the "global" causality relation $\leq$.

4.4.2 Sequential agent event structure logic (SESL)

The temporal logic for a subclass of event structures, i.e. for n-agent event structures, is now presented. For example, the semantics of asynchronous co-municating sequential processes can be defined by n-agent event structures [38].

Syntax of SESL

Let AP be a countable set of atomic propositions. The set $T = \{t_1, ..., t_n\}$ consisting of n atomic type propositions is fixed. It is assumed that $AP \cap T = \emptyset$ and $\Phi = AP \cup T$. The type propositions are used to identify particuliar agents. Let i, j, k range over $\{1, \ldots, n\}$ for some fixed n. The logical connectives $\neg$ and $\wedge$, as well as n indexed forward modalities (one for each agent) $\Box_1, \Box_2, \ldots, \Box_n$ and n indexed backward modalities $\overline{\Box}_1, \overline{\Box}_2, \ldots, \overline{\Box}_n$ are used.

The set of formulas is now be built up inductively:

- every member of Φ is a formula,
- if p and q are formulas, then so are $\neg p$ and $p \wedge q$,
- if p is a formula, then so are $\Box_i p$ and $\overline{\Box}_i p$ for all $i \leq n$.

The derived logical connectives and modalities are:

- $\vee$, $\rightarrow$, $\leftrightarrow$ are defined in the standard way,
- $p \oplus q \stackrel{def}{=} (p \wedge \neg q) \vee (q \wedge \neg p)$,
- $\Diamond_i p \stackrel{def}{=} \neg \Box_i \neg p$, for all $i \leq n$ ($\Diamond_i$ - i-forward),
- $\overline{\Diamond}_i p \stackrel{def}{=} \neg \overline{\Box}_i \neg p$, for all $i \leq n$, ($\overline{\Diamond}_i$ - i-backward).

Semantics of SESL

A frame and a model for SESL are defined in the standard way with a restriction on a valuation function, which needs to assign type propositions to corresponding agents.

Definition 4.17 A frame is an n-agent event structure $ES = (E_1, E_2, \ldots, E_n, \leq, \sharp)$. □

It is convenient to specify an n-agent event structure as $ES = (E, \leq, \sharp)$ and assume implicitly a partitioning $E_1, \ldots, E_n$ of E.

Definition 4.18 A model is an ordered pair $\mathcal{M} = (ES, V)$, where

- $ES = (E, \leq, \sharp)$ is a frame,
- $V : E \longrightarrow 2^{\Phi}$ is a valuation function satisfying: $t_i \in V(e)$ iff $e \in E_i$, for any $e \in E$ and $t_i \in T$. □

$\mathcal{M}, e \Vdash p$ denotes that the formula p holds at the state e in the model $\mathcal{M}$. $\mathcal{M}$ is omitted, if it is implicitly understood. Then $e \Vdash p$ is defined inductively:

- $e \Vdash p$ iff $p \in V(e)$ for any atomic proposition $p \in \Phi$,
- $e \Vdash \neg p$ iff not $e \Vdash p$,

  $e \Vdash p \wedge q$ iff $e \Vdash p$ and $e \Vdash q$,
- $e \Vdash \Box_i p$ iff for some $e' \in E_i$, $e' \leq e$ and for all $e'' \in E_i$, $e' \leq e''$ implies $e'' \Vdash p$,

  $e \Vdash \overline{\Box}_i p$ iff for all $e' \in E_i$, $e' \leq e$ implies $e' \Vdash p$.

The notions of validity and satisfiability are defined in the standard way.

Expressiveness of SESL

The behaviour of a concurrent system is represented by a n-agent event structure. Safety and possibility properties concerning the whole system as well as separate agents can be expressed. For example, a formula $\Box_i\, p$ holds at a state e of the agent i, if p holds at e and for all later states of the agent i. This formula holds at a state e of the agent $j \neq i$, if there is an earlier state of the agent i, at which $\Box_i\, p$ holds (this means that the agent i communicated to the agent j the information $\Box_i\, p$). A formula $\overline{\Box}_i\, p$ holds at e if for all earlier states of the agent i the formula p has held. $\Diamond_i\, p$ holds at a state of the agent i, if p holds in some future state of the agent i. $\Diamond_i\, p$ holds at a state of the agent $j \neq i$, if at any earlier state of the agent i, the formula $\Diamond_i\, p$ held. $\overline{\Diamond}_i\, p$ says that there has been an earlier state of the agent i at which p held. Eventuality properties are not expressible. That type of properties is shown to be expressible in ESL[δ].

A proof system for SESL

The proof system for SESL is composed of 17 axioms and 3 inference rules reflecting properties of n-agent event structures.

- Axioms:

(A0)	(All the substitution rules of propositional calculus)	
(A1)	$\Box_i(p \rightarrow q) \rightarrow (\Box_i\, p \rightarrow \Box_i\, q)$	
(A2)	$\overline{\Box}_i(p \rightarrow q) \rightarrow (\overline{\Box}_i\, p \rightarrow \overline{\Box}_i\, q)$	(deductive closures)
(A3)	$t_i \rightarrow (\Box_i\, p \rightarrow p)$	(local reflexivity)
(A4)	$t_i \rightarrow (p \rightarrow \overline{\Diamond}_i\, p)$	
(A5)	$\Box_i\, p \rightarrow \Box_i \Box_i\, p$	(transitivity)
(A6)	$\overline{\Diamond}_i\, p \rightarrow \overline{\Diamond}_i \overline{\Diamond}_i\, p$	
(A7)	$\overline{\Diamond}_i\, p \wedge \overline{\Diamond}_i\, q \rightarrow \overline{\Diamond}_i(p \wedge \overline{\Diamond}_i\, q) \vee$ $\overline{\Diamond}_i(q \wedge \overline{\Diamond}_i\, p)$	(backward linearity of agents)
(A8)	$\overline{\Diamond}_i\, p \rightarrow \Box_i \overline{\Diamond}_i\, p$	(relating past and future)
(A9)	$\Diamond_i\, p \rightarrow \overline{\Box}_i \Diamond_i\, p$	
(A10)	$\Box_i\, p \rightarrow \overline{\Diamond}_i(t_i \wedge \Box_i\, p)$	
(A11)	$\overline{\Diamond}_i\, p \rightarrow \overline{\Diamond}_i(t_i \wedge \overline{\Diamond}_i\, p)$	(communication axioms)
(A12)	$\Diamond_i\, p \rightarrow \overline{\Box}_i(t_i \rightarrow \Diamond_i\, p)$	
(A13)	$\overline{\Box}_i\, p \rightarrow \overline{\Box}_i(t_i \rightarrow \overline{\Box}_i\, p)$	
(A14)	$t_1 \oplus \ldots \oplus t_n$	
(A15)	$t_i \rightarrow \Box_i\, t_i$	(type axioms)
(A16)	$t_i \rightarrow \overline{\Box}_i\, t_i$	

- Inference rules:

(R1)	$p,\ p \rightarrow q \vdash q$	(modus ponens)
(R2)	$p \rightarrow q \vdash \Box_i\, p \rightarrow \Box_i\, q$	(generalization rules)
(R3)	$p \vdash \overline{\Box}_i\, p$	

A characterization of SESL

The are two main results known about SESL. The first one is about completeness of the given proof system.

Theorem 4.19 The proof system for SESL is sound and complete. □

The proof is similar to the proof for ESL[C], a sketch of which is given later on.

The model built for a formula in the proof of the completeness theorem is infinite because the logic lacks the finite model property. The proof of this fact is similar to the corresponding proof for ESL, which will be given further.

Theorem 4.20 [23] SESL is decidable.

In fact in [23] the decidability of a slightly different logic is shown, but with a few changes, the same proof can be applied for SESL. There are no results about model checking for SESL.

Next, logics dealing with unrestricted event structures are presented. They have been introduced in [29], [30], and [27].

4.4.3 Syntax of logics on event structures

First, the definition of a very rich language of temporal logic is given. Its restrictions give rise to different formal systems discussed in this section. The language contains modalities corresponding to the relations of causality, conflict, backward and forward next step, and of concurrency. The meaning of the modalities is explained as soon as a system using these modalities is introduced.

Let $AP = \{p_1, p_2, \ldots\}$ be a countable set of atomic propositions. A distinguished symbol δ is fixed. It is assumed that $\delta \notin AP$ and $\Phi = AP \cup \{\delta\}$. The logical connectives $\neg$ and $\wedge$, as well as the modalities $\Box, \overline{\Box}, \otimes, \overline{\otimes}, \Box_{\|}$ and $\Box_c$ are used. The set *FORM* of formulas is built up inductively:

(E1) every member of *AP* is a formula,
(E1′) δ is a formula,
(E2) if p and q are formulas, then so are $\neg p$ and $p \wedge q$,
(E3) if p is a formula, then so are $\Box p$, $\overline{\Box} p$ and $\Box_{\|} p$,
(D4) if p is a formula, then so are $\otimes p$ and $\overline{\otimes} p$,
(C5) if p is a formula, then so is $\Box_c p$.

The following derived logical connectives and modalities are defined:

- $p \vee q \stackrel{def}{=} \neg(\neg p \wedge \neg q)$ (standard)
- $p \rightarrow q \stackrel{def}{=} \neg p \vee q$ (standard)
- $\Diamond p \stackrel{def}{=} \neg \Box \neg p$ ($\Diamond$ - forward)
- $\overline{\Diamond} p \stackrel{def}{=} \neg \overline{\Box} \neg p$ ($\overline{\Diamond}$ - backward)
- $\Diamond_{\sharp} p \stackrel{def}{=} \neg \Box_{\sharp} \neg p$ ($\Diamond_{\sharp}$ - dependent)
- $\bigcirc p \stackrel{def}{=} \neg \otimes \neg p$ ($\bigcirc$ - next forward)
- $\overline{\bigcirc} p \stackrel{def}{=} \neg \overline{\otimes} \neg p$ ($\overline{\bigcirc}$ - next backward)
- $\Diamond_I p \stackrel{def}{=} \delta \rightarrow \Diamond(p \wedge \delta)$ ($\Diamond_I$ - inevitable)
- $\bigcirc_I p \stackrel{def}{=} \delta \rightarrow \bigcirc(p \wedge \delta)$ ($\bigcirc_I$ - next inevitable)
- $\Diamond_c p \stackrel{def}{=} \neg \Box_c \neg p$ ($\Diamond_c$ - concurrent)

The meaning of $\Diamond_I$ and $\bigcirc_I$ will be explained in the section about ESL[δ]. Since event structure logics use slightly different frames, the semantics is defined separately for each logic considered.

4.4.4 Event structure logic (ESL)

Every logic discussed in this section is an extension of the formal system called event structure logic (ESL). Note that ESL itself is an extension of the well known axiomatic system S4. It contains a new modality $\Box_{\sharp}$ corresponding to the conflict relation. This operator is introduced in order to express important behavioural properties of event structures like conflict freeness and inevitability.

The syntax of ESL is now given.

Syntax of ESL

The set of ESL formulas is the maximal one generated by rules E1, E2, and E3 from the former page.

Semantics of ESL

The notion of a Kripke frame is extended by adding the second relation.

Definition 4.19 A frame $F = (E, \leq, \sharp)$ is an arbitrary event structure. □

A model is defined in the standard way.

Definition 4.20 A model is an ordered pair $\mathcal{M} = (F, V)$, where

- $F = (E, \leq, \sharp)$ is a frame,
- $V : E \longrightarrow 2^{AP}$ is a valuation function. □

Let $\mathcal{M} = (F, V)$ be a model, $e \in E$ be a state and p be a formula. $\mathcal{M}, e \Vdash p$ denotes that the formula p holds at the state e in the model $\mathcal{M}$ (as usual $\mathcal{M}$ is omitted, if it is implicitly understood). This notion is defined inductively as follows:

(E1) $e \Vdash p$ iff $p \in V(e)$, for $p \in AP$,
(E2) $e \Vdash \neg p$ iff not $e \Vdash p$,
$e \Vdash p \wedge q$ iff $e \Vdash p$ and $e \Vdash q$,
(E3) $e \Vdash \Box p$ iff $(\forall e' \in E)$ $(e \leq e'$ implies $e' \Vdash p)$,
$e \Vdash \overline{\Box} p$ iff $(\forall e' \in E)$ $(e' \leq e$ implies $e' \Vdash p)$,
$e \Vdash \Box_{\sharp} p$ iff $(\forall e' \in E)$ $(e \sharp e'$ implies $e' \Vdash p)$.

The following standard abbreviations are used:

- $\mathcal{M} \Vdash p$ iff $\mathcal{M}, e \Vdash p$ for each $e \in E$,
- $\mathcal{M} \Vdash L$ iff $\mathcal{M} \Vdash p$ for each $p \in L$,
- $\Vdash p$ iff $\mathcal{M} \Vdash p$ for each model $\mathcal{M}$,
- $L \models p$ iff $\mathcal{M} \Vdash L$ implies $\mathcal{M} \Vdash p$, for each model $\mathcal{M}$.

Expressiveness of ESL

Similarly to the case of SESL, the behaviour of a concurrent system is represented by an event structure. A safety property is expressible as an invariance formula of the form $\Box p$ which expresses that p holds at all states of an event structure. A possibility property is expressed by a formula of the form $\Diamond p$. The conflict-freeness property is expressible by a formula of the form $\Box_{\sharp} p$, which says that for all states in conflict, the formula p holds. In the other words, all states at which $\neg p$ holds are not in conflict. A formula $\overline{\Diamond} p$ says that p held in the past. Eventuality properties are not expressible in ESL. It is shown later than the operator $\Box_{\sharp}$ enables to axiomatize an extension of ESL, in which eventuality properties are expressible.

A proof system for ESL

The proof system for ESL is composed of twelve axioms and four inference rules reflecting the properties of causality and conflict relations.

- Axioms:

(A0)	All the substitution rules of the propositional calculus	
(A1)	$\Box(p \rightarrow q) \rightarrow (\Box p \rightarrow \Box q)$	
(A2)	$\overline{\Box}(p \rightarrow q) \rightarrow (\overline{\Box} p \rightarrow \overline{\Box} q)$	(deductive closures)
(A3)	$\Box_\sharp(p \rightarrow q) \rightarrow (\Box_\sharp p \rightarrow \Box_\sharp q)$	
(A4)	$\Box p \rightarrow p$	(reflexivity of $\leq$)
(A5)	$\overline{\Box} p \rightarrow p$	(reflexivity of $\leq^{-1}$)
(A6)	$\Box p \rightarrow \Box \Box p$	(transitivity of $\leq$)
(A7)	$\overline{\Box} p \rightarrow \overline{\Box}\,\overline{\Box} p$	(transitivity of $\leq^{-1}$)
(A8)	$p \rightarrow \Box \overline{\Diamond} p$	(relating past and future)
(A9)	$p \rightarrow \overline{\Box} \Diamond p$	(relating past and future)
(A10)	$p \rightarrow \Box_\sharp \Diamond_\sharp p$	(symmetry of $\sharp$)
(A11)	$\Box_\sharp p \rightarrow \Box_\sharp \Box p$	(conflict inheritance)

- Inference rules:

(R1)	$p,\ p \rightarrow q \vdash q$	(modus ponens)
(R2)	$p \vdash \Box p$	
(R3)	$p \vdash \overline{\Box} p$	(generalization rules)
(R4)	$p \vdash \Box_\sharp p$	

A characterization of ESL

It is shown now that the given proof system is sound and complete for ESL [29]. It is proved that ESL lacks the finite model property, but it is decidable.

Theorem 4.21 The proof system for ESL is sound and strongly complete, (i.e., $L \vdash p$ iff $L \models p$, for each set of formulas L and each formula p). $\Box$

Proof: Soundness of the proof system is easy to show, so the method of proving completeness is discussed here. Let L be a consistent set of formulas. It is assumed that $L \models p_0$ and supposed that $L \not\vdash p_0$. The aim is to construct a model satisfying $\neg p_0$ and validating L and to show in this way that the supposition was wrong. The set *MCSF* of maximal consistent sets of formulas containing L is defined in the standard way. Note that in the original paper [29] ultrafilters were used instead of *MCSF*, but this does not change the idea of the proof. Next, the canonical structure $\mathcal{M}_0 = ((E_0, \leq_0, \sharp_0), V_0)$ is defined as follows:

1. $E_0 = MCSF$,
2. $\leq_0 = \{(e, e') \in MCSF \times MCSF \mid \{p \mid \Box p \in e\} \subseteq e'\}$,
3. $\sharp_0 = \{(e, e') \in MCSF \times MCSF \mid \{p \mid \Box_\sharp p \in e\} \subseteq e'\}$,
4. $p \in V_0(e)$ iff $p \in e$, where $p \in AP$ and $e \in MCSF$.

For some $e^0 \in E_0$, $\neg p_0 \in e^0$.

The notion of a pseudo-model is now defined.

Definition 4.21 A structure $\mathcal{M} = ((E, \leq, \sharp), V)$ is a pseudo-model iff the following conditions are satisfied:

(a) E is a non-empty set,

(b) $\leq$ is reflexive and transitive,

(c) $\sharp$ is symmetric and for any $e, e', e'' \in E$: $e \sharp e' \leq e''$ implies $e \sharp e''$,

(d) $V : E \longrightarrow 2^{AP}$ is a valuation function. □

The notion of a formula p holding at a state e in the pseudo-model $\mathcal{M}$ (written $\mathcal{M}, e \Vdash p$) is defined as for models. It can be shown that $\mathcal{M}_0$ satisfies all the properties of pseudo-models. The next step in the proof consists in unwinding the canonical pseudo-model $\mathcal{M}_0$ into a modally equivalent model of ESL. The method, called "copying" (see [41]), is used.

The structure $\mathcal{M}_1 = ((E_1, \leq_1, \sharp_1), V_1)$ is defined as follows:

- $E_1 = E_0 \times I$, where I is a set of integers; e_j abbreviates (e, j) for $e \in E_0$ and $j \in I$.
- $\leq_1 = \{(e_i, e'_j) \mid (e = e' \text{ and } i = j) \text{ or } (e \leq_0 e', i < j \text{ and } j \equiv i (mod\ 2)\}$, where $j \equiv i(mod\ 2)$ iff $|j - i|$ is an even number.
- $\sharp_1 = \{(e_i, e'_j) \mid e \sharp_0 e' \text{ and } j \equiv i + 1 (mod\ 2)\}$,
- $V_1(e_i) = V_0(e)$, for all $i \in I$ and $e \in E_0$.

It can be shown that $\mathcal{M}_1$ satifies the following properties:

- $\leq_1$ is a partial order in E_1,
- $\sharp_1$ is irreflexive and symmetric,
- for any $e, e', e'' \in E_1$: $e \sharp_1 e' \leq_1 e''$ implies $e \sharp_1 e''$.

Therefore, $(E_1, \leq_1, \sharp_1)$ is an event structure. Then, the modal equivalence of $\mathcal{M}_0$ and $\mathcal{M}_1$ is proved. For any formula p and any state $e \in E_0$ the following equivalence holds: $(\forall i \in I)$ $(\mathcal{M}_1, e_i \Vdash p$ iff $\mathcal{M}_0, e \Vdash p)$. This implies that $\mathcal{M}_1 \Vdash L$ and that there is $e^0_j \in E_1$ for some $j \in I$ such that $\mathcal{M}_1, e^0_j \Vdash \neg p_0$. This completes the proof of completeness of ESL. □

Theorem 4.22 ESL does not have the finite model property.

Proof: It is shown that the formula $q \stackrel{def}{=} \Box(\Box(p \rightarrow \Box p) \rightarrow p) \rightarrow p$ $(p \in AP)$ is valid in each finite model and that q is not a theorem. Then, $\neg q$ is a formula satisfiable only in infinite models. Note that the formula q is equivalent to the formula $\Box(\Diamond(p \wedge \Diamond\neg p) \vee p) \rightarrow p$. Now, let $\mathcal{M} = (F, V)$ be a finite model with $F = (E, \leq, \sharp)$. Consider an arbitrary $e \in E$. Assume that $\mathcal{M}, e \Vdash \Box(\Diamond(p \wedge \Diamond\neg p) \vee p)$ and suppose that $\mathcal{M}, e \Vdash \neg p$. Then $\mathcal{M}, e \Vdash \Diamond(p \wedge \Diamond\neg p)$. Thus, there is $e_1 \in E$ such that $e < e_1$ and $\mathcal{M}, e_1 \Vdash \neg p \wedge \Box(\Diamond(p \wedge \Diamond\neg p) \vee p)$. In such a way, when an infinite sequence $e_1, e_2, \ldots$ of states of E is constructed such that $\forall i, j \in N$, $i \leq j$ implies $e_i < e_j$. This is a contradiction because E is finite. To show that q is not a theorem it is sufficient to construct a model in which $\neg q$ is satisfiable. Let $\mathcal{M} = (F, V)$ with $F = (I, \leq, \sharp)$, where I is a set of integers, $\leq$ is the standard less or equal relation in I, $\sharp = \emptyset$ and $p \in V(i)$ iff $|i|$ is odd. Then, $\mathcal{M}, 0 \Vdash \Box(\Diamond(p \wedge \Diamond\neg p) \vee p) \wedge \neg p$, i.e. $\mathcal{M}, 0 \Vdash \neg q$ and $\mathcal{M}$ is clearly an ESL model. □

Next, it is shown that ESL is decidable.

Theorem 4.23 ESL is decidable.

Proof: ESL is shown to have the finite model property with respect to the pseudo-models. This implies that ESL is decidable with respect to the pseudo-models. As any pseudo-model can be unwound into a modally equivalent model of ESL, decidability with respect to the pseudo-models is equivalent to decidability (with respect to the models) of ESL.

Let p_0 be a consistent formula. Thus, there is a canonical pseudo-model $\mathcal{M}_0$ for p_0. This pseudo-model is then filtrated to obtain a finite pseudo-model for p_0. The Fischer - Ladner closure $FL(p_0)$ of p_0 is defined. Let $FL(p_0)$ be the least set of formulas containing p_0 and satisfying the following conditions:

1. if $p \vee q \in FL(p_0)$ then $p, q \in FL(p_0)$,
2. if $\neg p \in FL(p_0)$ then $p \in FL(p_0)$,
3. if $\Box p$ or $\overline{\Box} p$ or $\Box_\sharp p \in FL(p_0)$ then $p \in FL(p_0)$,
4. if $\Box_\sharp p \in FL(p_0)$ then $\Box p \in FL(p_0)$.

It can be shown that $card(FL(p_0)) \leq 2|p_0|$. Let $\mathcal{M}_0 = ((E_0, \leq_0, \sharp_0), V_0)$ be a canonical pseudo-model for p_0, and $\equiv_{FL(p_0)}$ be an equivalence relation on E_0 defined as follows:

$$e_1 \equiv_{FL(p_0)} e_2 \text{ iff } e_1 \cap FL(p_0) = e_2 \cap FL(p_0).$$

Let $[e]$ denote the set $\{e' \in E_0 \mid e \equiv_{FL(p_0)} e'\}$. Then, the quotient structure of $\mathcal{M}_0$ by $\equiv_{FL(p_0)}$ is the structure $\mathcal{M}' = ((E', \leq', \sharp'), V')$, where:

- $E' = \{[e] \mid e \in E_0\}$,
- $\leq'$ is the transitive closure of $\leq_1 = \{([e], [f]) \in E' \times E' \mid \exists e' \in [e], \exists f' \in [f] : e' \leq_0 f'\}$,

- $\sharp' = (\leq')^{-1} \circ (\sharp_1) \circ (\leq')$, where $\sharp_1 = \{([e],[f]) \in E' \times E' \mid \exists e' \in [e], \exists f' \in [f] : e' \sharp_0 f'\}$,
- $V' : E' \longrightarrow 2^{AP}$ s.t. $p \in V'([e])$ iff $p \in e$, for $p \in AP \cap FL(p_0)$ and $e \in E_0$.

It can be shown that $\mathcal{M}'$ is a finite pseudo-model, moreover, that for each formula $p \in FL(p_0)$ and for each $e \in E_0 : \mathcal{M}', [e] \Vdash p$ iff $p \in e$. This completes the proof. □

As it was mentioned earlier, ESL formulas cannot express inevitability properties. Thus, the first extension to the formal system of ESL makes it possible to express these.

Next, the definition of inevitability properties for event structures is given.

Definition 4.22 Let $ES = (E, \leq, \sharp)$ be an event structure, $B, Q \subseteq E$ and $e \in E$.

- Q is said to be *inevitable* from e iff

  $(\forall Rn \in Rn_{ES})\,(e \in Rn \rightarrow \{e' \in E \mid e \leq e'\} \cap Rn \cap Q \neq \emptyset)$.

- Q is said to be inevitable from B iff Q is inevitable from each $e \in B$. □

Intuitively speaking, Q is inevitable from e if each run with e contains a state from Q in the future of e.

In order to express inevitability properties the notion of a run has to be incorporated into a frame. Then, the language is extended to make it possible to refer to runs.

4.4.5 ESL with run proposition (ESL[δ])

The idea is to extend ESL with a distinguished proposition, δ, marking a particular run of interest [29].

Syntax of ESL[δ]

The set of ESL[δ] formulas is the maximal one generated by the rules E1, E1′, E2, and E3.

Semantics of ESL[δ]

Definition 4.23 A frame is a quadruple $F = (E, Rn, \leq, \sharp)$, where $(E, \leq, \sharp) = ES$ is an event structure and Rn is a run in ES. A model is an ordered pair $\mathcal{M} = (F, V)$, where

- $F = (E, Rn, \leq, \sharp)$ is a frame,

- $V : E \longrightarrow 2^{\Phi}$ is a valuation function from the set E into the set of all subsets of Φ such that $\delta \in V(e)$ iff $e \in Rn$. □

The semantic rule E1′ for the run proposition δ is added to the semantic rules E1, E2, and E3 for the logical connectives and the ESL modalities:

(E1′) $e, M \Vdash \delta$ iff $\delta \in V(e)$ (i.e. iff $e \in Rn$).

Expressiveness of ESL[δ]

The behaviour of a concurrent system P is represented by a structure $\mathcal{A}_{\mathcal{P}}$ being the set of models $\mathcal{M} = ((E, Rn, \leq, \sharp), V)$ such that $(E, \leq, \sharp)$ represents the full behaviour of the system P, and Rn is a run.

Let $\mathcal{A}$ be an ESL[δ] structure. $\mathcal{A}$ is said to validate a formula p (written $\mathcal{A} \Vdash p$) iff $\mathcal{M} \Vdash p$ for each model $\mathcal{M}$ in $\mathcal{A}$. Now, the meaning of ESL[δ] formulas is as follows. $\mathcal{A} \Vdash p$ expresses that for every model of $\mathcal{A}$, for every state in it, p holds.

ESL[δ] extends the expressiveness of ESL by enabling us to express inevitability properties. Since the formula $\Diamond_I q$ was defined as $\delta \rightarrow \Diamond(q \wedge \delta)$, $\mathcal{A} \Vdash p \rightarrow \Diamond_I q$ says that q is inevitable from p in the structure $\mathcal{A}$.

A proof system for ESL[δ]

The proof system contains the proof system for ESL with two extra axioms reflecting the run properties:

(A12) $\delta \rightarrow \Box_{\sharp} \neg\delta$ (conflict-freeness of the run Rn)
(A13) $\Box_{\sharp} \neg\delta \rightarrow \delta$ (maximality of the run Rn)

A characterization of ESL[δ]

As in the case of ESL, it is shown that the proof system is sound and complete.

Theorem 4.24 The proof system for ESL[δ] is sound and complete.

Proof: Having the completeness theorem for ESL, it is sufficient to prove that for each model $\mathcal{M} = ((E, Rn, \leq, \sharp), V)$ the following condition holds:
$\mathcal{M} \Vdash \text{A12} \wedge \text{A13}$ iff Rn is a run in $(E, \leq, \sharp)$. □

Next, one can show that introducing δ does not change other properties of the logic. ESL[δ] does not have the finite model property, but it is decidable.
The next extension of Event Structure Logic (ESL) has been motivated by a great interest in specifying discrete systems.

4.4.6 Discrete event structure logic (DESL)

The class of frames is restricted to discrete event structures. A new modality reflecting a successor relation is introduced to the formal language of ESL [30].

Syntax of DESL

The set of DESL formulas is the maximal one generated by the rules E1, E2, E3, and D4.

Semantics of DESL

First, the notion of discrete event structure is introduced.

Definition 4.24 An event structure $ES = (E, \leq, \sharp)$ is *discrete* iff there exists an irreflexive, antisymmetric and intransitive relation $\rightarrow \subseteq E \times E$, called the *successor relation* such that $\leq = (\rightarrow)^*$. □

Definition 4.25 A frame is a structure $F = (E, \rightarrow, \leq, \sharp)$, where $(E, \leq, \sharp)$ is a discrete event structure with the successor relation $\rightarrow$. □

Definition 4.26 A model is an ordered pair $\mathcal{M} = (F, V)$, where F is a frame and $V : E \longrightarrow 2^{AP}$ is a valuation function. □

The semantic rules for DESL are composed of the rules E1, E2, and E3 of ESL and of new rules for the introduced modalities:

(D4) $\mathcal{M}, e \Vdash \otimes p$ iff $(\forall e' \in E)$ $(e \rightarrow e'$ implies $\mathcal{M}, e' \Vdash p)$,
$\mathcal{M}, e \Vdash \overline{\otimes} p$ iff $(\forall e' \in E)$ $(e' \rightarrow e$ implies $\mathcal{M}, e' \Vdash p)$.

Expressiveness of DESL

All the properties expressible in ESL are obviously expressible in DESL. Moreover, formulas $\otimes p$ and $\overline{\otimes} p$ enable us to speak about successors and predecessors. For example, $q \rightarrow \otimes p$ expresses that p holds at all successors of the states where q holds. $q \rightarrow \overline{\bigcirc} p$ guarantees that each state satisfying q has a predecessor at which p holds.

A proof system for DESL

The proof system for DESL contains the proof system for ESL with 8 new axioms:

(A12)	$\otimes(p \rightarrow q) \rightarrow (\otimes p \rightarrow \otimes q)$	
(A13)	$\overline{\otimes}(p \rightarrow q) \rightarrow (\overline{\otimes} p \rightarrow \overline{\otimes} q)$	(deductive closures)
(A14)	$\Box p \rightarrow \otimes \Box p$	$(\rightarrow^* \subseteq \leq)$
(A15)	$\overline{\Box} p \rightarrow \overline{\otimes}\, \overline{\Box} p$	$((\rightarrow^{-1})^* \subseteq \leq^{-1})$
(A16)	$\Box(p \rightarrow \otimes p) \rightarrow (p \rightarrow \Box p)$	$(\leq \subseteq \rightarrow^*)$
(A17)	$\overline{\Box}(p \rightarrow \overline{\otimes} p) \rightarrow (p \rightarrow \overline{\Box} p)$	$(\leq^{-1} \subseteq (\rightarrow^{-1})^*)$
(A18)	$p \rightarrow \otimes \overline{\bigcirc} p$	(relating next step past and future)
(A19)	$p \rightarrow \overline{\otimes} \bigcirc p$	(relating next step past and future)

A characterization of DESL

First, it is shown that the given proof system is complete and then the finite model property and decidability are discussed [30].

Theorem 4.25 The proof system for DESL is sound and complete.

Proof: Let p_0 be a consistent formula. First, a canonical structure $\mathcal{M}_0$ for p_0 is constructed in a similar way to that described for ESL. Then, as in the case of ESL, the quotient pseudo-model $\mathcal{M}'$ of $\mathcal{M}_0$ by the equivalence relation on E_0 induced by the Fischer - Ladner closure $FL(p_0)$ is defined. Elements of $E_0/\equiv_{FL(p_0)}$ are denoted by $[e]$. Now, $FL(p_0)$ is the least set of formulas containing p_0 and satisfying the following conditions:

1-4 as for ESL,

5. if $\otimes p$ or $\overline{\otimes} p \in FL(p_0)$ then $p_0 \in FL(p_0)$.

It can be shown that $\mathcal{M}' = ((E', \rightarrow', \leq', \sharp'), V')$ satisfies the following conditions:

- E' is not empty,
- $\leq'$ is reflexive and transitive,
- $\sharp'$ is symmetric,
- $\sharp' \circ \leq' \subseteq \sharp'$,
- $\rightarrow'^{*} = \leq'$.

Moreover, $(\forall e \in E_0)$ $(\forall p \in FL(p_0))$ $\mathcal{M}', [e] \Vdash p$ iff $p \in e$. Next, using the copying method, the pseudo-model is improved in order to obtain a model for p_0. A structure $\mathcal{M}_1 = ((E_1, \rightarrow_1, \leq_1, \sharp_1), V_1)$ is defined as follows:

- $E_1 = E' \times I$, where I is the set of integers,
- $\rightarrow_1 = \{(e_i, e'_j) \mid e \rightarrow' e' \text{ and } i + 2 = j\}$,
- $\leq_1 = \{(e_i, e'_j) \mid (e = e' \text{ and } i = j) \text{ or } (e \leq' e' \text{ and } i < j \text{ and } j \equiv i (mod\ 2)\}$, where $j \equiv i(mod\ 2)$ iff $|j - i|$ is an even number.
- $\sharp_1 = \{(e_i, e'_j) \mid e \sharp' e' \text{ and } j \equiv i + 1\ (mod\ 2)\}$,
- $V_1(e_i) = V'(e)$, for all $i \in I$ and $e \in E'$.

It can be shown that $\mathcal{M}_1$ is a model for p_0, modally equivalent with $\mathcal{M}'$. This completes the proof. □

Using the same argument as in the case of ESL, one can show that DESL does not have the finite model property.

Theorem 4.26 DESL is decidable. □

The proof follows from the finite pseudo-model property of DESL and the modal equivalence of the pseudo-models and the models.

As in the case of ESL, it is possible to extend the language by a run proposition, making it possible to refer to runs of an event structure. This would allow one to express that a formula p is inevitable in the next state of q: $q \rightarrow \bigcirc_I p$.

The next step towards extending ESL was made by Mukund & Thiagarajan [27]. They introduced the new modal operator $\Box_c$ corresponding to the concurrency relation.

4.4.7 ESL with a concurrency operator (ESL[C]) [27]

The definition of the concurrency relation in an event structure is first given.

Definition 4.27 Let $ES = (E, \leq, \sharp)$ be an event structure, then the *concurrency relation*, *co*, is defined as follows:

$$co = E \times E - (\leq \cup \leq^{-1} \cup \sharp).$$ □

Intuitively speaking, two events are in the concurrency relation, if they can occur concurrently.

Syntax of ESL[C]

The set of ESL[C] formulas is the maximal one generated by the rules E1, E2, E3, and C5.

Semantics of ESL[C]

The semantics is nearly the same as for ESL, with the exception that the causality relation in the event structure is assumed to be irreflexive. This extends expressiveness in case of the absence of the next step operators. There is also the new semantic rule for the modality $\Box_c$.

(C5) $e, M \Vdash \Box_c p$ iff $(\forall e' \in E)$ (e *co* e' implies $e', M \Vdash p$).

Expressiveness of ESL[C]

All the properties expressible in ESL are also expressible in ESL[C]. Moreover, properties incorporating the concurrency relation can be specified. For example, a formula $q \rightarrow \Box_c p$ expresses that for all states in the concurrency relation with a state satisfying q, the formula p holds. For example, this allows us to specify that each agent in an n-agent event structure is sequential: $t_i \rightarrow \Box_c \neg t_i$, for $1 \leq i \leq n$.

A proof system for ESL[C]

The proof system for ESL[C] contains the proof system for ESL without the reflexivity axioms A4 and A5, but with additional axioms for the operator $\Box_c$ and two new inference rules:

(A12)	$\Box_c(p \rightarrow q) \rightarrow (\Box_c p \rightarrow \Box_c q)$	(deductive closure)
(A13)	$p \rightarrow \Box_c \Diamond_c p$	(symmetry of *co*)
(A14)	$\Diamond_c p \rightarrow \overline{\Box}(\Diamond_c p \vee \Diamond p)$	(conflict-free past)
(A15)	(a) $\Diamond p \rightarrow \Box(p \vee \Diamond p \vee \overline{\Diamond} p \vee \Diamond_\sharp p \vee \Diamond_c p)$	(relating modalities)
	(b) $\Diamond_\sharp p \rightarrow \Box_\sharp(p \vee \Diamond p \vee \overline{\Diamond} p \vee \Diamond_\sharp p \vee \Diamond_c p)$	(relating modalities)
	(c) $\Diamond_c p \rightarrow \Box_c(p \vee \Diamond p \vee \overline{\Diamond} p \vee \Diamond_\sharp p \vee \Diamond_c p)$	(relating modalities)
	(d) $\overline{\Diamond} p \rightarrow \Box(p \vee \Diamond p \vee \overline{\Diamond} p \vee \Diamond_c p)$	(relating modalities)
(A16)	$\Diamond_\sharp p \rightarrow \Box_c(\Diamond p \vee \Diamond_\sharp p \vee \Diamond_c p)$	(relating $\Diamond_\sharp$ and $\Box_c$)
(A17)	$\Diamond_\sharp p \rightarrow \overline{\Box}(\Diamond p \vee \Diamond_\sharp p \vee \Diamond_c p)$	(relating $\Diamond_\sharp$ and $\overline{\Box}$)
(A18)	$\Diamond_c p \rightarrow \Box(\overline{\Diamond} p \vee \Diamond_\sharp p \vee \Diamond_c p)$	(relating $\Diamond_c$ and $\Box$)

Inference rules:

(R5)	$p \vdash \Box_c p$	(generalization rule)
(R6)	$\overline{p} \rightarrow q \vdash q$	(uniqueness rule)

$$\overline{p} \stackrel{def}{=} p \wedge \Box\neg p \wedge \overline{\Box}\neg p \wedge \Box_\sharp \neg p \wedge \Box_c \neg p,$$

where p is an atomic proposition not appearing in q. The formula $\overline{p}$ says that the proposition p holds in exactly one state. The uniqueness rule will be used to construct a model in which at each state e_i a different formula $\overline{p_i}$ holds.

A characterization of ESL[C]

Next it is shown that the given proof system is complete.

Theorem 4.27 [27] The proof system for ESL[C] is sound and complete.

Proof: Every consistent formula p_0 is shown to be satisfiable. In a standard way, maximal consistent sets of formulas (MCSF) and relations $\leq_0$, $\sharp_0$, and co_0 in MCSF are defined:

- $A \leq_0 B \stackrel{def}{=} \{p \mid \Box p \in A\} \subseteq B$,
- $A \sharp_0 B \stackrel{def}{=} \{p \mid \Box_\sharp p \in A\} \subseteq B$,
- $A\ co_0\ B \stackrel{def}{=} \{p \mid \Box_c p \in A\} \subseteq B$.

However, the method used before for proving completeness of ESL and DESL cannot be used. This follows from the fact that the modalities of ESL[C] correspond to relations which union is equal to the cartesian product of the states of a model. Therefore, it is not known how to "distribute" relations between copies of the states so that each two are in exactly one relation and all the conditions on relations are satisfied.

The new method relies on bulding a model in an iterative way, starting from a MCSF and adding more MCSF's if they are needed to make formulas in the existing MCSF's hold. Next, the notions of chronicle and chronicle structures are defined.

Definition 4.28 Let $ES = (E, \leq, \sharp)$ be a frame. Then the following notions are defined:

- A chronicle T on ES is a function $T : E \rightarrow MCSF$.
- A chronicle T is coherent iff it satisfies the following conditions:
    1. $\forall e, e' \in E: \ e \leq e'$ implies $T(e) \leq_0 T(e')$,
    2. $\forall e, e' \in E: \ e \sharp e'$ implies $T(e) \sharp_0 T(e')$,
    3. $\forall e, e' \in E: \ e \ co \ e'$ implies $T(e) \ co_0 \ T(e')$.

A chronicle structure is a pair (ES, T), where $ES = (E, \leq, \sharp)$ is a frame and T is a coherent chronicle. □

A requirement is a pair (e, Mp) (M stands for $\Diamond$, $\overline{\Diamond}$, $\Diamond_\sharp$ or $\Diamond_c$) such that $e \in E$, $Mp \in T(e)$ and there is no $e' \in E$ such that $e \ R \ e'$ (R stands for $\leq$, $\geq$, $\sharp$ or co, resp.) and $p \in T(e')$. In general, a coherent chronicle may contain some requirements and therefore does not define a model.

T is called r_0-*perfect* iff it is coherent and has no requirement (e, q) with $q \in FL(r_0)$, where $FL(r_0)$ contains all the subformulas of r_0 with their negations. A r_0-perfect chronicle can be viewed in some sense as a Hintikka structure for r_0. It can be easily shown that a r_0-perfect chronicle defines a model for the formula r_0. Therefore, the idea of proving completeness consists in constructing an r_0-perfect chronicle for the formula r_0 such that $r_0 \in T(e)$ for some $e \in E$.

To start with let $\{q_0, q_1, ..., q_n\}$ be the set of atomic propositions appearing in r_0. The enumeration of AP is fixed according to the position in the sequence $q_0, q_1, ..., q_n, p_0, p_1, ...$ Then, an injective function $f : E \times FL(r_0) \longrightarrow \mathcal{N}$ is defined. It gives a code number $f((e, q))$ to every pair (e, q) composed of the event e and the formula q. An infinite sequence of chronicle structures $CH_0, CH_1, ...$ is defined inductively. The chronicle structures have a r_0-perfect chronicle as the least upper bound.

CH_0 is defined as follows: $ES_0 = ((\{e_0\}, \emptyset, \emptyset), T_0)$, where $T_0(e_0) = A_0$. A_0 is an MCSF containing $\{\overline{p_0}\}$ and A', where A' is the set of formulas obtained by replacing each occurrence of an atomic proposition p_i by p_{i+1} (for all $i \geq 0$) in formulas of an MCSF A containing r_0.

It is assumed that each chronicle structure $CH_i = (ES_i, T_i)$, where $ES_i = (E_i, \leq_i, \sharp_i)$ is an event structure, $E_i = \{e_0, ..., e_i\}$, T_i is a coherent chronicle, and for $0 \leq j \leq i$, $\overline{p_j} \in T_i(e_j)$ (see (R6) for the definition of $\overline{p}$).

CH_{i+1} is obtained from CH_i in the following way. Let (e_j, Mp) be a requirement in CH_i that has the least code of all other requirements. If no such requirement exists, then $CH_{i+1} = CH_i$. Otherwise, CH_{i+1} is constructed such that the following conditions are satisfied: ES_{i+1} is an event struture, T_{i+1} is a coherent chronicle which does not have (e_j, Mp) as a requirement and every requirement (e_k, p') in CH_{i+1} for k: $1 \leq k \leq i$ was a requirement in CH_i.

This construction consists of the following steps:

1. Let A''_k be the set of formulas obtained by replacing all atomic propositions p_{l+1} by p_{l+2} (for all $l \geq i$) in $T_i(e_k)$ for all $e_k \in E_i$.

2. Construct an MCSF A'_{i+1} such that p and $\overline{p_{i+1}}$ belong to it. Extend A''_j to an MCSF A'_j such that $A'_j \; R \; A'_{i+1}$, where ($R = \leq$, $(\geq, \sharp, co)$ for $M = \Diamond$, $(\overline{\Diamond}$, $\Diamond_\sharp$, $\Diamond_c$, resp.)).

3. Extend all other A''_k (with $k \neq j$) to an MCSF's A'_k, preserving the semantic relationship existing between $T_i(e_k)$ and $T_i(e_j)$ and preserving all already fulfiled requirements.

4. $E_{i+1} = E_i \cup \{e_{i+1}\}$, $T_{i+1}(e_j) = A'_j$ for j: $1 \leq j \leq i+1$, and $e_k \; R \; e_l$ iff $A'_k \; R \; A'_l$, for $R \in \{\leq, \sharp, co\}$ and k, l: $1 \leq k, l \leq i+1$.

This sequence was defined so that ES_{i+1} is a proper extension of ES_i. Now the resulting event structure $ES = (E, \leq, \sharp)$ is defined, where $E = \bigcup_{i=1}^{\infty} E_i$, $\leq = \bigcup_{i=1}^{\infty} \leq_i$, $\sharp = \bigcup_{i=1}^{\infty} \sharp_i$, and a r_0-perfect chronicle is defined as follows. $T(e_i) = \bigcup_{j \geq i}(T_j(e_i) \cap L_j)$, where L_j the a set of formulas built over atomic propositions $\{q_0, q_1, ..., q_n, p_0, .., p_j\}$. The definition of T is correct since for all $k \geq j \geq i$: $T_k(e_i) \cap L_j = T_j(e_i) \cap L_j$. This allows to show that $T(e_i)$ is an MCSF indeed. □

Decidability of ESL[C] remains still an open problem.

In [28], the similar language with the modality corresponding to the minimal conflict relation has been introduced and axiomatized.

4.5 Conclusions

All the logics presented in this chapter can be used for specifying and proving properties of concurrent systems. Three kinds of logics have been introduced: those interpreted over branching time structures (UB, CTL, CTL*) over partial order structures (POTL, POTL[$U, \overline{U}$], ISTL); and over event structures (SESL, ESL, ESL[δ], DESL, ESL[C]). It was discussed how frames correspond to the behaviour of concurrent systems. The main emphasis was put on the logical characterization of the formal languages. Therefore, proof systems have been provided for axiomatizable logics, and the finite model property and decidability have been discussed. Moreover, the expressiveness of the logics interpreted over the same structures was compared and some attempt has been made to relate expressiveness of logics interpreted over different frames. It was shown that logics on partial orders can be more expressive than those on branching structures, but they may have more complicated algorithms for testing satisfiability and for model checking.

Acknowledgements:
The author wishes to thank Dr. Ruurd Kuiper and Dr. Brian Monahan for suggesting many valuable improvements.

References

[1] Abrahamson, K. 1979. Modal logics for concurrent programs. *Lecture Notes in Computer Science* **70**.

[2] Abrahamson, K. 1980. *Decidability and expressiveness of logics of processes*. PhD thesis, Department of Computer Science, University of Washington.

[3] Ben-Ari, M., Z. Manna & A. Pnueli 1981. The temporal logic of branching time. In *Proceedings of the 8th Annual ACM Symposium on Principles of Programming Languages*, 164–76.

[4] Clarke, E. M. & E. A. Emerson 1981. Design and synthesis of synchronization skeletons using branching time temporal logic. *Lecture Notes in Computer Science* **131**, 52–71.

[5] Clarke, E. M., E. A. Emerson & A. P. Sistla 1983. Automatic verification of finite state concurrent systems using temporal logic specifications: a practical approach. In *Proceedings of the 10th Annual ACM Symposium on Principles of Programming Languages*, 117–26.

[6] Courcoubetis, C., M. Y. Vardi & P. Wolper 1986. Reasoning about fair concurrent programs. In *Proceedings of the 18th Annual ACM Symposium on Theory on Computing*, 283–94.

[7] Emerson, E. A. 1981. *Branching time temporal logic and the design of correct concurrent programs*. PhD thesis, Harvard University.

[8] Emerson, E. A. 1983. Alternative semantics for temporal logics. *Theoretical Computer Science* **26**, 121–30.

[9] Emerson, E. A. 1985. Automata, tableaux, and temporal logics. *Lecture Notes in Computer Science* **193**, 79–88.

[10] Emerson, E. A. & E. M. Clarke 1982. Using branching time logic to synthesize synchronization skeletons. *Science of Computer Programming* **2**, 241–66.

[11] Emerson, E. A. & J. Y. Halpern 1982. Decision procedures and expressiveness in the temporal logic of branching time. In *Proceedings of the 14th Annual ACM Symposium on Theory of Computing*, 169–80; also in *Journal of Computer and System Sciences* **30**, 1, 1–24, 1985.

[12] Emerson, E. A. & J. Y. Halpern 1983. "Sometimes" and "Not Never" revisited. On branching versus linear time temporal logic. In *Proceedings of the 10th Annual Symposium on Principles of Programming Languages*, Austin, 127–40; also in *Journal of the ACM* **33**, 1, 151–78, 1986.

[13] Emerson, E. A. & C. S. Jutla 1988. The complexity of free automata and logics of programs. In *Proceedings of the 29th Annual IEEE-CS Symposium on Foundations of Computer Science*, 328–37.

[14] Emerson, E. A. & C-L. Lei 1985. Modalities for model checking: branching time strikes back. In *Proceedings of the 12th Annual ACM Symposium on Principles of Programming Languages*, 84–96; also in *Science of Computer Programming* **8**, 275–306, 1987.

[15] Emerson, E. A. & A. P. Sistla 1984. Deciding full branching time logic. *Information and Control* **61**(3), 175–201.

[16] Emerson, E. A. & J. Srinivasan 1988. Branching time temporal logic. *Lecture Notes in Computer Science* **354**.

[17] Fischer, M. J. & M. E. Ladner 1979. Propositional dynamic logic of regular programs. *Journal of Computer and Systems Science* **18**(2), 194–211.

[18] Kornatzky, Y. & S. S. Pinter 1986. *POTL*[U, $\overline{\text{U}}$] *an extension to partial order temporal logic (POTL)*. EE Publication no. 596, Department of Electrical Engineering, Technion-Israel Institute of Technology.

[19] Kornatzky, Y. & S. S. Pinter 1986. *A model checker for partial order temporal logic*. EE Publication no. 597, Department of Electrical Engineering, Technion-Israel Institute of Technology.

[20] Kornatzky, Y. & S. S. Pinter 1986. *Hyper finite state systems: a hypergraph model for distributed finite state systems*. EE Publication no. 598, Department of Electrical Engineering, Technion-Israel Institute of Technology.

[21] Katz, S. & D. Peled 1987. Interleaving set temporal logic. In *6th ACM Symposium on Principles of Distributed Computing*, 178–90.

[22] Katz, S. & D. Peled 1988. An efficient verification method for parallel and distributed programs. *Lecture Notes in Computer Science* **354**.

[23] Lodaya, K., R. Ramanujam & P. S. Thiagarajan 1993. Decidability of a partial order based temporal logic. *Lecture Notes in Computer Science* **700**, 582–92.

[24] Lehmann, S. & S. Shelah 1982. Reasoning with time and chance. *Information and Control* **53**(3), 165–98.

[25] Lodaya, K. & P. S. Thiagarajan 1987. A modal logic for a subclass of event structures. Lecture Notes in Computer Science **267**, 290–303.

[26] Mazurkiewicz, A., E. Ochmański & W. Penczek 1989. Concurrent systems and inevitability. *Theoretical Computer Science* **64**, 281–304.

[27] Mukund, M. & P. S. Thiagarajan 1989. An axiomatization of event structures, *Lecture Notes in Computer Science* **405**, 143–60.

[28] Mukund, M & Thiagarajan P. S. 1992. An axiomatization of well branching prime event structures, *Theoretical Computer Science* **96**(1), 35–72.

[29] Penczek, W. 1988. A temporal logic for event structures. *Fundamenta Informaticae* **11**(3), 297–326.

[30] Penczek, W. 1989. A temporal logic for the local specification of concurrent systems. In *Information Processing 89*, IFIP 1989, 857–62. Amsterdam: Elsevier.

[31] Penczek, W. 1992. On undecidability of propositional temporal logics on trace systems. *Information Processing Letters* **43**, 147–53.

[32] Penczek, W. 1993. Axiomatizations of temporal logics on trace systems. *Lecture Notes in Computer Science* **665**, 452–62.

[33] Peled, D. & A. Pnueli 1990. Proving partial order liveness properties. *Lecture Notes in Compter Science* **443**, 553–71.

[34] Pinter, S. S. & Wolper P. 1984. A temporal logic for reasoning about partially ordered computations. In *Proceedings of the 3rd Symposium on Principles of Distributed Computing*, 28–37.

[35] Reisig, W. 1988. Towards a temporal logic of causality and choice in distributed systems. *Lecture Notes in Computer Science* **354**, 606–27.

[36] Sistla, A. P. & M. N. Clarke 1982. The complexity of propositional temporal logic. ral logic. *ACM Symposium on Theory of Computing*.

[37] Winskel, G. 1980. Events in computation. PhD thesis, Department of Computer Science, University of Edinburgh.

[38] Winskel, G. 1982. Event structure semantics for CCS and realated languages. *Lecture Notes in Computer Science* **140**, 561–77.

[39] Winskel, G. 1986. Event structures. *Lecture Notes in Computer Science* **255**, 325–92.

[40] Winskel, G. 1989. An introduction to event structures. *Lecture Notes in Computer Science* **354**, 364–97.

[41] Vakarelow 1987. S4 + S5 together – S4+5. In em Proceedings of the 8th Conference of Logic, Methodology and Philosophy of Science **5**(3).

[42] Vardi, M. & L. Stockmeyer 1985. Improved upper and lower bounds for modal logics of programs. In *Proceedings of the 7th Annual Symposium on Theory of Computing*, 240–251.

Chapter 5

Temporal logic in a stochastic environment

B. Strulo, D. Gabbay and P. G. Harrison*

Department of Computing
Imperial College
180 Queens Gate, London SW7 2BZ
United Kingdom

Abstract

Temporal logic has proved to be a useful tool for the specification of computer systems interacting with their environment. Meanwhile, a common approach to the analysis of the performance of such systems has been based on stochastic process theory and, in particular, Markov chains. We describe an approach to modelling a temporal logic system in a random environment and how Markov chain techniques can be applied. We also survey some other approaches.

5.1 Introduction

Temporal logic has been used to good effect in specifying systems interacting with their environment [18,10,6,2]. These systems, often called reactive systems, are typically concurrent programs or real-time control systems whose job is to monitor and react to external events. Temporal logic is good at describing the structure in time required of the actions of the system. Standard methods of proof or synthesis then allow us to show that the system does have those properties. An example is an operating system where a resource is to be allocated to a requester. We might require that after any request the resource is eventually allocated. Temporal logic is a natural formalism for expressing this requirement and the hope is that appropriate proof techniques will allow a demonstration that a given operating system has the required property.

***Supported by a grant from the SERC.**

For information about the performance of a real-time system we may wish to describe the environment in a probabilistic manner. Numerical techniques are then available to predict the long-term behaviour of such a stochastic system. Thus suppose that, in our example, we know the probabilities for a transition from a state with no request to a state with one pending and vice versa. We may predict the probability of finding the system, in the long term, in either state.

Temporal logic has a large and interesting literature both as a topic in itself and in relation to computer science [20]. It emerged from study in philosophy and linguistics but its importance to computer science is now clear. A wide-ranging survey showing this movement and discussing the many different themes and perspectives on this central idea, but from a theoretical point of view, is provided by [21].

Much work relevant to computer science is on the use of temporal logic in specification, particularly for reactive systems of the type mentioned already. An introduction to this stream of work is [16] which uses a fairly standard linear temporal logic and clearly demonstrates its utility for proving important properties of concurrent programs. A complete example of a complex program and proof is in [10] which clearly and indisputably shows the importance of these ideas.

This chapter investigates the particular logic "until-since-fixed-point" (USF) and the temporal logic specification/programming style of [9]. This is the heart of a relatively new approach in which the specification is treated as a program and executed directly. The paper introduces the idea that the past component of a specification can be read as a querying of the past, while the future component is an imperative command that the future must meet.

Our use of stochastic process theory is limited to standard results taken from a well established literature. We have used in particular [15] and also [3]. We have used standard definitions of processes as random variables using conventional notions of probability and conditionals. We also use the usual ideas for classifying states by the accessibility relation and finally we use the steady-state theorem to find the steady-state solution.

In this chapter we first of all explain what we mean by a "temporal logic system". We then show that, for a wide class of such systems, there is a finite-state strategy that they may use to execute. Thus we show that we may regard that system as a finite-state automaton. We then show that such an automaton in an environment modelled by a finite-state Markov chain is itself such a Markov chain. Thus we show that the natural model of a temporal logic system in a stochastic environment is a finite-state Markov chain. Once we know the system is a finite-state Markov chain further analysis becomes possible. For example, we might be able to determine the probability that a specification will be satisfied in a given stochastic environment.

5.2 Fundamentals

What is a *temporal logic system*? Consider a system made up of an environment and what we will call a program (though it may in fact be some complex combination of programs and hardware). We model this system in a discrete time with a starting point. Thus without loss of generality we assume time to be the natural numbers.

To enable us to use a logical formalism we will describe the behaviour of the system in terms of the valuation of proposition letters. Thus we assume the environment and the program to have a finite number of controls each and to represent these controls by the state of some sets of proposition letters.

We will use a synchronous model. Thus we assume that the environment and the program take turns to assert their behaviour (by setting and resetting their proposition letters). Our temporal logic then comes in as some supplied specification of desired behaviour. The specification is a temporal formula in the proposition letters, and we say that a behaviour meets its specification if it is a model of the formula. A program meets the specification if all its possible behaviours do. We formalize this model below.

5.2.1 The model

We assume that our propositions are drawn from some set *Prop*. We will also assume this to be infinitely extensible so none of our constructions exhaust it. Given a set of propositions $P \subset Prop$ we say $h : P \to 2^{\mathbb{N}}$ is a P-structure, i.e. a function assigning a set of times at which it is true to each proposition. We write the set of P-structures as $S(P)$.

A propositional temporal logic L over such structures then assigns to a set of propositions a tuple $\langle L(P), \models \rangle$ where $L(P)$ is the set of well formed P-formulae and $\models$ a relation from $S(P) \times L(P)$ which, given $h \in S(P)$, gives the true formulae $A \in L(P)$ (we write $h \models A$ in that case).

Much work has gone into comparing the expressiveness of such propositional temporal logics. Typically, this has been concerned with the number of subsets of the natural numbers that may be "named" with formulae of the logic. This sort of definition distinguishes many different logics. In the context of specification we will use a different idea of expressiveness and show that this makes many propositional temporal logics equivalent.

How do we envisage formulae of our logic being used as specifications? We imagine our implementor being given a formula $A_1 \in L_1(P)$ for some logic $\langle L_1, \models_1 \rangle$. In this formula some of the propositions represent behaviours of the environment while others represent actions of the program. Our implementor is then obliged to build the program so that any of its behaviours, when considered as a P-structure h say, has the property $h \models_1 A_1$.

Given h_1, a P_1-structure, and h_2, a P_2-structure, and some $P \subset P_1 \cap P_2$

we say

$$h_1 =_P h_2 \quad \text{iff} \quad \forall p \in P \quad h_1(p) = h_2(p)$$

which is to say that they agree on the propositions in P. Note that the demand we have placed on our implementor is that the P-structures produced give appropriate interpretations to the propositions in P. Now let us say that our implementor produces a behaviour which assigns additional propositions (from P' say). These have no direct external interpretation and so we may make no restriction on the value of these propositions. Thus the demand on our implementor is that whatever behaviour is produced, say a $(P \cup P')$-structure h_2, for any P-structure h_1 with $h_1 =_P h_2$, then $h_1 \models_1 A_1$.

So now let us say that our implementor is given some alternative formula A_2 in a different logic $\langle L_2(P \cup P'), \models_2 \rangle$. This will be equally good as a specification if it requires the implementor to produce exactly the same behaviours. So we have

Definition 5.1 A *logic* L_2 is as *specificationally expressive* as a logic L_1

- iff $\forall P \subset Prop$, $\forall A_1 \in L_1(P)$, $\exists P' \subset Prop$ and $A_2 \in L_2(P \cup P')$ so that $\forall h \in S(P)$

$$h \models_1 A_1 \quad \text{iff} \quad \exists h' \in S(P \cup P') \quad h' \models_2 A_2 \quad \text{and} \quad h =_P h'$$

□

We will take a very simple future time logic, T, which has only a tomorrow and always operator and show that it is as specificationally expressive as a large and powerful logic — the USF of [9]. This is because by treating formulae as specifications we are giving our specifier additional power — essentially that of existentially quantifying over propositions.

5.2.2 The logic T

For a set of propositions P, the well formed formulae $L_2(P)$ are the least set including

$$p \quad \neg A \quad A \wedge B \quad \bigcirc A \quad \hat{\Box} A$$

where $p \in P$ and A, B are well formed formulae.

We define the semantics first by extending h to a valuation for all formulae. The valuation of a formula A in a P-structure, h, is A^h defined recursively by:

- if $A \in P$ then $A^h = h(A)$
- $(\neg A)^h = \mathbb{N} \setminus (A^h)$
- $(A \wedge B)^h = A^h \cap B^h$
- $(\bigcirc A)^h = \{n : n + 1 \in A^h\}$

- $(\widehat{\Box}A)^h = \{n : \forall m \geq n \; m \in p^h\}$

As usual we can define the additional logical connectives $\vee$, T, F, etc. in terms of $\neg$ and $\wedge$. We will also define the additional temporal connective $\widehat{\Diamond}A = \neg\widehat{\Box}\neg A$ meaning that A occurs at sometime in the future. Note that $\widehat{\Box}$ is "reflexive", i.e. it checks the present as well as the future.

To use these formulae as specifications we have a choice. If the specification is A, does this state that A is true at all times or at time 0? In other words, is the requirement on the model h that $A^h = \mathbb{N}$ or that $0 \in A^h$? The choice between these "floating" and "anchored" versions is discussed in [17]. For our simple logic we will choose the anchored version and say $h \models_2 A$ iff $0 \in A^h$.

5.2.3 The logic USF

For a set of propositions P, the well formed formulae $L_1(P)$ are the least set including

$$p \quad \neg A \quad A \wedge B \quad AUB \quad A\overline{U}B \quad \varphi pA$$

where $p \in P$ and A, B are well formed formulae. We define pure past formulae to be boolean combinations of formulae of the form $A\overline{U}B$ where A and B are formulae not including U. We then add a syntactic restriction that for a fixed point formula φpA to be well formed, A must be pure past.
As before, the semantics is defined recursively:

- if $A \in P$ then $A^h = h(A)$
- $(\neg A)^h = \mathbb{N} \setminus (A^h)$
- $(A \wedge B)^h = A^h \cap B^h$
- $(A\overline{U}B)^h = \{n : \exists m < n \; m \in B^h \wedge \forall l (m < l < n \rightarrow l \in A^h)\}$
- $(AUB)^h = \{n : \exists m > n \; m \in B^h \wedge \forall l (n < l < m \rightarrow l \in A^h)\}$
- $(\varphi pA)^h$ is the unique $T \subseteq \mathbb{N}$ such that $T = A^{h(p/T)}$

Here $h(p/T)$ is h with the original valuation of p replaced by T.

Thus the definition of $A\overline{U}B$ is the set of all times where B is true at some time in the past and A is true at all times (if any) strictly in between. Similarly the definition of AUB is all times where B is true in the future and A true at all times (if any) strictly in between.

The definition of φ, as usual for ***fixed point definitions***, requires justification. Rigorous proof is provided in [11] while an explanation is in [9]. To see intuitively why the fixed point φpA exists uniquely note that A is pure past (by the definition of well formedness). Given h we can consider A as an operator taking any valuation of p, say T, to $A^h(p/T)$. So to construct the fixed point start with p completely unknown. If we apply the A operator to such a valuation we do not know what we will get at *most* time points, but $A(p)$ *is* uniquely well defined at time 0 since A is pure past. If we now apply the A operator again and consider $A(A(r))$ the value at 0 will not change. The value at 1 will now also be uniquely well defined however. At each step of reapplying A the values defined so far cannot change but a new defined value is added. Thus the limit of this process (under the obvious metric) is the unique well defined fixed point we require.

As before we can define the additional logical connectives in terms of $\neg$ and $\wedge$. We can also define additional temporal connectives as follows:

Connective	Definition	Meaning
$\Diamond A$	$\mathsf{T}UA$	A at sometime in the future
$\overline{\Diamond} A$	$\mathsf{T}\overline{U}A$	A at sometime in the past
$\Box A$	$\neg\Diamond\neg A$	A always in the future
$\overline{\Box} A$	$\neg\overline{\Diamond}\neg A$	A always in the past
$\bigcirc A$	$\mathsf{F}UA$	A "tomorrow"(at the next time)
$\overline{\bigcirc} A$	$\mathsf{F}\overline{U}A$	A "yesterday" (at the previous time)
$\hat{\Box} A$	$\Box A \wedge A$	reflexive always
$\hat{\Diamond} A$	$\neg\hat{\Box}\neg A$	reflexive sometime

Note that we have defined not only the usual nonreflexive $\Box$ and $\Diamond$ from USF but also our reflexive operators from logic T. It should be plain that this valuation function is consistent with that defined for our logic T, in that it gives the same valuations to formulae that are syntactically in both languages.

Finally, we define our semantic relation, this time using the floating version i.e. $h \models_1 A$ iff $A^h = \mathsf{N}$. This choice is usual for USF and gives us the opportunity to compare the two.

5.3 Specificational equivalence

We will show that, as far as specifications go, it does not matter which logic we work in. First, note that USF is certainly as specificationally expressive as T. Assume we are given some formula A in T. Plainly A is a formula of USF, and given a P-structure h then A^h is the same in both logics. Now consider $\neg\overline{\bigcirc}\mathsf{T}$ in USF. This is true only at 0 and so $h \models_1 \neg\overline{\bigcirc}\mathsf{T} \rightarrow A$ iff $h \models_2 A$ as required.

Now we show the result in the other direction. We prove first that we can simulate the evaluation process of USF in our simple logic T.

Theorem 5.1 Given $A \in L_1(P)$, a formula in USF, a formula $A^*(q) \in L_2(P \cup P' \cup \{q\})$ where $q \notin P \cup P'$ can be constructed, with $\forall h' \in S(P \cup P' \cup \{q\})$

$$h' \models_2 A^*(q) \quad \text{implies} \quad (\forall h \in S(P) \quad h =_P h' \quad \text{implies} \quad h'(q) = A^h)$$

while

$$\forall h \in S(P) \quad \exists h' \in S(P \cup P' \cup \{q\}) \quad h' \models_2 A^*(q) \quad \text{and} \quad h =_P h'$$

□

Thus we construct a new formula $A^*(q)$ from T which includes the necessary specifications to make q the same value as A. Further, it will work whatever P-structure we give it.

Then consider A_2 defined by $A^*(q) \wedge \widehat{\Box} q$. Say $h' \models_2 A_2$. By requiring $A^*(q)$ we obtain $h'(q) = h(A)$ and by requiring $\widehat{\Box} q$ we obtain $h \models_1 A$. Conversely if $h \models_1 A$ then we know we can find $h' \models_2 A^*(q)$ with $h' =_P h$ and $h'(q) = A^h = \mathbb{N}$. Hence $h' \models_2 A_2$ as required and this A_2 is the formula we need to show T as specificationally expressive as USF.

The proof is constructive in that we show an algorithm to construct A^* inductively from A.

Proof: We proceed by induction over the structure of A.

1. A is $p \in P$

   (i) Define $A^*(q) = \widehat{\Box}(p \leftrightarrow q)$.

   (ii) First say $h' \models_2 A^*(q)$. Then $h'(q) = h'(p)$ and so $h' =_P h$ implies $h'(q) = A^h$ as required.

   (iii) Alternatively given h define $h'(q) = h(q)$ and $h' =_P h$. Then $h' \models_2 A^*(q)$ as required.

2. A is $\neg B$

   (i) Define $A^*(q) = B^*(\neg q)$.

   (ii) First say $h' \models_2 A^*(q)$. Thus $h' \models_2 B^*(\neg q)$ and so by induction $h' =_P h$ implies $h'(\neg q) = B^h$. Thus $h'(q) = A^h$ as required.

   (iii) Alternatively, given h we know inductively we can find h'' with $h'' =_P h$ and $h'' \models_2 B^*(q)$, so since $q \notin P$ we can define $h' = h''$ but with $h'(q) = \mathbb{N} \setminus h''(q)$ and we have $h' \models_2 A^*(q)$ as required.

3. A is $B \wedge C$

   (i) Define $A^*(q) = \widehat{\Box}(q \leftrightarrow r \wedge s) \wedge B^*(r) \wedge C^*(s)$ where r, s are new propositions from P'.

   (ii) Now if $h' \models_2 A^*(q)$ then $h' \models_2 B^*(r)$ and $h' \models_2 C^*(s)$ so by induction $h' =_P h$ implies $h'(r) = B^h$ and $h'(s) = C^h$. Thus $h'(q) = A^h$ as required.

(iii) Alternatively, given h we know inductively we can find h'_1 with $h'_1 =_P h$ and h'_2 with $h'_2 =_P h$ and $h'_1 \models_2 B^*(r)$ and $h'_2 \models_2 C^*(s)$. Thus by an appropriate choice of propositions from P' we can define h' but with $h'(q) = h'_1(r) \cap h'_2(s)$ and we have $h' \models_2 A^*(q)$ as required.

4. A is $C\overline{U}B$

(i) Define $A^*(q) = \neg q \wedge \hat{\Box}(\bigcirc q \leftrightarrow (r \vee (s \wedge q))) \wedge B^*(r) \wedge C^*(s)$.

(ii) Now if $h' \models_2 A^*(q)$ then $h' \models_2 B^*(r)$ and $h' \models_2 C^*(s)$ so by induction $h' =_P h$ implies $h'(r) = B^h$ and $h'(s) = C^h$. Now plainly at 0 we have $\neg q$ as required. Further assume by induction that at n, q correctly has the value of $C\overline{U}B$. Then q will be true at $n+1$ iff we have B at n or $C\overline{U}B$ at n and C at n giving $h'(q) = A^h$ as required.

(iii) Alternatively, given h we know inductively we can find h'_1 with $h'_1 =_P h$ and h'_2 with $h'_2 =_P h$ and $h'_1 \models_2 B^*(r)$ and $h'_2 \models_2 C^*(s)$. Thus by an appropriate choice of propositions from P' we can define h' but with $h'(q) = \{n : \exists m < n \; m \in h'_2(s) \wedge \forall l(m < l < n \rightarrow l \in h'_1(r))\}$. Then we plainly obtain $h' \models_2 A^*(q)$ as required.

5. A is CUB

(i) Define $A^*(q) = \hat{\Box}(q \leftrightarrow \bigcirc(r \vee (s \wedge q)) \wedge \hat{\Box}(q \leftarrow \Diamond r)) \wedge B^*(r) \wedge C^*(s)$.

(ii) Now if $h' \models_2 A^*(q)$ then $h' \models_2 B^*(r)$ and $h' \models_2 C^*(s)$ so by induction $h' =_P h$ implies $h'(r) = B^h$ and $h'(s) = C^h$. Now assume q has the correct value at time n. Then plainly it has the correct value at all times less than n (proof by induction on n). Now consider if r is true at n. Then plainly q is correct at $n-1$ and hence all $m < n$. Now either $h'(r)$ is infinite or finite. If it is the former then for all m there is such a larger n. Otherwise, at some point we have $\neg \Diamond r$ and hence $\neg q$ making q correct for all n as required.

(iii) Alternatively, given h we know inductively we can find h'_1 with $h'_1 =_P h$ and h'_2 with $h'_2 =_P h$ and $h'_1 \models_2 B^*(r)$ and $h'_2 \models_2 C^*(s)$. Thus by an appropriate choice of propositions from P' we can define h' but with $h'(q) = \{n : \exists m > n \; m \in h'_2(s) \wedge \forall l(n < l < m \rightarrow l \in h'_1(r))\}$. Then we plainly obtain $h' \models_2 A^*(q)$ as required.

6. A is $\varphi p B(p)$

(i) Note here that $B(p)$ has a free variable p which it retains after transformation. We will write $B^*(q; p)$ where the second variable is this p and then use $B^*(q; q)$ to indicate that we wish to transform B and then substitute q for the free p in B^*. We define $A^*(q) = B^*(q; q)$.

(ii) Now if $h' \models_2 A^*(q)$ then $h' \models_2 B^*(q;q)$ so by induction $h' =_P h$ implies $h'(q) = B^h$. But $B^h = B^{h'}$ and so by the fixed point semantics $h'(q) = A^h$.

(iii) Alternatively, given h we know inductively we can find h'' with $h'' =_P h$ and $h'' \models_2 B^*(q;q)$. If we define h' as h'' but with $h'(p) = h'(q)$ then plainly $h' \models_2 A^*(q)$ as required.

This completes the induction and gives the theorem. □

Thus we have shown that in the context of specification we might as well work in our simple T logic as with all the power of USF. The technique used to show this theorem is powerful. It shows that to obtain the required expressiveness as far as specifications are concerned, we need only three mechanisms:

- The ability to assign initial values to propositions. This is available in USF because of the yesterday operators which distinguish the initial time, while in T it is available because of the anchored interpretation of specification.
- The ability to constrain the valuation of formulae tomorrow by boolean operators given their value today. This single-step unfolding is essentially a (nondeterministic) finite-state automaton.
- The ability to impose some restriction on the eventual satisfaction of any commitments propagated in the above mechanism. We achieve this through the □ or $\hat{\Box}$ operators.

The relationship to automata (though excluding the past fragment) is discussed clearly in Chapter 3.

5.4 Showing the program to be finite state

5.4.1 Introduction

This study was motivated by considering the MetateM specification language described in [9]. However, we have shown that that logic and a wide variety of other propositional temporal logic specification languages are no more expressive as specifications than our simple logic T. We now wish to show that we can reasonably assume that our program has only a finite number of states.

5.4.2 Implementation of a specification

How does our implementor create the program to meet its specification? In general there may be many answers to this question. We will just show that if our specification is implementable then there is some implementation which is finite state and assume that the program we are dealing with is such an implementation.

We use directly the results from [19]. First, note that formulae of our logic T are path formulae in their logic. Their operators are reflexive but we have shown how to use reflexive operators only. Their logic is future only and they use the anchored interpretation exactly as in T. Thus it is straightforward to take our formula A_2 as their ϕ — the linear temporal logic formula to be satisfied. Then their Theorem 2 implies that, since we assume our specification implementable, there exists a "deterministic transducer" which, given the environment actions, gives the next program action. They show this transducer is finite state. Thus we have the result we require.

5.5 The main theorem

Having established a *Markov-like property* for the program and assuming it for the environment, we now show that the system as a whole is a Markov chain in some state space.

5.5.1 The model in Markov formalism

We describe the external state by a set of environment propositions whose values are encoded by a random variable value E_t, the value of the environment propositions at time t.

The actions of the MetateM interpreter are similarly encoded by A_t, the value of the actions at time t.

To model incomplete information we make the interpreter see not the external state but a visible representation of it encoded by V_t, the value of the visible environment at time t.

To model the uncertainty we make the visible environment dependent randomly on only the real environment at that time:

- **Assumption 1**

$$\begin{aligned}\Pr(V_t = i \mid E_t = j) = \Pr(V_t &= i \mid E_t = j, E_{t-1} = j_{t-1}, \ldots \\ &E_1 = j_1, A_t = k_t, \ldots, A_1 = k_1)\end{aligned}$$

This assumption is not restrictive since, on the one hand, the program has access to this visible environment at any point in the history. On the other, if we wish to have the visible environment dependent on more history, we can carry that dependence in the real environment (it is only the instantaneous uncertainty that the real environment cannot model).

As stated above we assume a *Markov type property* for the real environment:

- **Assumption 2**

$$\Pr(E_t = i \mid E_{t-1} = j, A_{t-1} = j') = \Pr(E_t = i \mid E_{t-1} = j, E_{t-2} = j_{t-2}, \ldots, E_1 = j_1, A_{t-1} = j', A_{t-2} = j'_{t-2}, \ldots, A_1 = j'_1)$$

As already remarked, although the environment need look only at its last state, in this discrete time framework we could transform any chain which required more information about its past into one which did not, by embedding the history into the state space. The only disadvantage here is that then the state space would be countably infinite.
As shown above we can encode all the information the program needs to make its decision into a finite-state space — the state space of the deterministic transducer along with the values of V_t and A_{t-1} (though note that the actions in A may need to be augmented by finitely many new ones).

We will assume that the encoding of A_t, E_t and V_t includes that information. Thus we may take it that the strategy gives A_t as a deterministic function of V_t and A_{t-1}. Thus:

- **Assumption 3**

$$\Pr(A_t = i' \mid V_t = v, A_{t-1} = j') = \Pr(A_t = i' \mid V_t = v, V_{t-1} = v_{t-1}, \ldots, V_1 = v_1, A_{t-1} = j', A_{t-2} = j'_{t-2}, \ldots A_1 = j'_1, E_t = i_t, \ldots, E_1 = i_1)$$

Thus the possible dependence is diagrammatically:

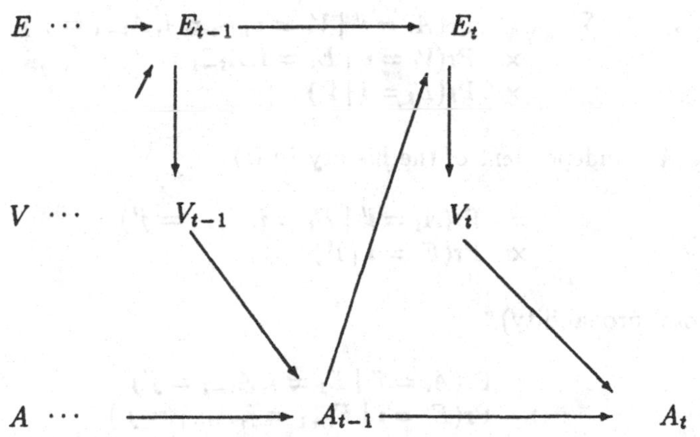

The proof of the Markov property for the complete process with state encoded by E_t and A_t proceeds by expanding over all possible visible environments to eliminate any dependency there. Then we can combine the properties for E and A to obtain the required overall property. Thus we have Theorem 5.2.

Theorem 5.2 The stochastic process $\{(E_t, A_t) \mid t \geq 0\}$ has the Markov property

$$\begin{aligned}\Pr(E_t = i, A_t = i' \mid (E_{t-1} = j, A_{t-1} = j', \ldots, A_1 = j_1')\\ = \Pr(E_t = i, A_t = i' \mid E_{t-1} = j, A_{t-1} = j')\end{aligned}$$

Proof: Let Π denote the history condition $E_{t-1} = j$, $A_{t-1} = j'$, $E_{t-1} = j_{t-1}$, ..., $A_1 = j'_1$. Writing VA for the set of visible actions:

$$\begin{aligned}&\Pr(E_t = i, A_t = i' \mid \Pi)\\ &= \Pr(A_t = i' \mid E_t = i, \Pi) \times \Pr(E_t = i \mid \Pi)\end{aligned}$$

(by expanding the conditional)

$$\begin{aligned}= \textstyle\sum_{v \in \mathrm{VA}} \quad & \Pr(A_t = i' \mid V_t = v, E_t = i, \Pi)\\ \times \quad & \Pr(V_t = v \mid E_t = i, \Pi)\\ \times \quad & \Pr(E_t = i \mid \Pi)\end{aligned}$$

(by total probability)

$$\begin{aligned}= \textstyle\sum_{v \in \mathrm{VA}} \quad & \Pr(A_t = i' \mid V_t = v, E_t = i, \Pi)\\ \times \quad & \Pr(V_t = v \mid E_t = i, A_{t-1} = j')\\ \times \quad & \Pr(E_t = i \mid \Pi)\end{aligned}$$

(since V is independent of the history in Π)

$$\begin{aligned}= \textstyle\sum_{v \in \mathrm{VA}} \quad & \Pr(A_t = i' \mid V_t = v, E_t = i, A_{t-1} = j')\\ \times \quad & \Pr(V_t = v \mid E_t = i, A_{t-1} = j')\\ \times \quad & \Pr(E_t = i \mid \Pi)\end{aligned}$$

(since A is independent of the history in Π)

$$\begin{aligned}= \quad & \Pr(A_t = i' \mid E_t = i, A_{t-1} = j')\\ \times \quad & \Pr(E_t = i \mid \Pi)\end{aligned}$$

(by total probability)

$$\begin{aligned}= \quad & \Pr(A_t = i' \mid E_t = i, A_{t-1} = j')\\ \times \quad & \Pr(E_t = i \mid E_{t-1} = j, A_{t-1} = j')\end{aligned}$$

(using the Markov property of E_t to remove the dependence on Π)

$$= \Pr(E_t = i, A_t = i' \mid E_{t-1} = j, A_{t-1} = j')$$

□

5.5.2 Discussion

We have shown that the system behaves as a Markov chain with a specific state space. This consists of the action propositions (possibly augmented by our transformation into T), the state space of the deterministic transducer, and whatever information is needed by the environment. Using [19] and assuming a finite-state space for the environment, we obtain a finite-state space overall.

5.5.3 An example

We use an example from [5]: the resource manager. We translate to the connectives used in this chapter as follows. The specification describes a process which manages a resource to be allocated to a maximum of one at any one time of two requesters.

The constraints are taken as:

- If the resource is requested by a process then it must eventually be allocated to that process.
- If the resource is not requested then it should not be allocated.
- At any time, the resource should be allocated to at most one process.

Restricting the example to just two processes, we use r_1 and r_2 to name the occurrence of requests from the two requesters. Then we use a_1 and a_2 to name the corresponding allocations. Note that the r_i are environment propositions (in E_t) while the a_i are actions in A_t. We will not use V_t in this example since we will assume the interpreter has complete information, i.e. that $V_t = A_t$.

Then the floating specification in USF is:

1. $\overline{\bigcirc} r_1 \rightarrow \Diamond a_1$
2. $\overline{\bigcirc} r_2 \rightarrow \Diamond a_2$
3. $(\neg r_1)\mathcal{Z}(a_1 \wedge \neg r_1) \rightarrow \neg a_1$
4. $(\neg r_2)\mathcal{Z}(a_2 \wedge \neg r_2) \rightarrow \neg a_2$
5. $\neg a_1 \vee \neg a_2$

We are using here the weak form of Since (Zince) which is true at time zero. Note that our yesterday operator is strong (unlike the treatment in Barringer), i.e. false at time zero.

We exhibit a transformation into logic T. This gives a new specification:

1. $\widehat{\Box}(r_1 \rightarrow \bigcirc \widehat{\Diamond} a_1)$
2. $\widehat{\Box}(r_1 \rightarrow \bigcirc \widehat{\Diamond} a_1)$
3. $\widehat{\Box}(p_1 \rightarrow \neg a_1)$
4. $\widehat{\Box}(p_2 \rightarrow \neg a_2)$

5. $\widehat{\Box}(\neg a_1 \vee \neg a_2)$

6. $p_1 \wedge \widehat{\Box}(\bigcirc p_1 \leftrightarrow (a_1 \wedge \neg r_1) \vee (\neg r_1 \wedge p_1))$

7. $p_2 \wedge \widehat{\Box}(\bigcirc p_2 \leftrightarrow (a_2 \wedge \neg r_2) \vee (\neg r_2 \wedge p_2))$

Here the p_i hold the current values of the relevant $\mathcal{Z}$. We are using a version of the transformation which translates the weak $\mathcal{Z}$ analogously to **S** (the proof is similar and straightforward). We have also eliminated unnecessary propositions.

Working from this specification in T to a deterministic transducer using the Pnueli & Rosner approach has a doubly exponential complexity and is far too long to do manually. Instead we will use a more straightforward approach modelled on the strategy adopted by the MetateM interpreter.

We use states that value these propositions and also our commitment to eventually allocate, i.e. $\Diamond a_i$. Thus there are 256 different states. Some of these are expressly forbidden by specifications 3, 4 and 5.

We use a notation in which we describe a state by the successive values (0 for false and 1 for true) of: $r_1\ r_2\ a_1\ a_2\ \Diamond a_1\ \Diamond a_2\ p_1\ p_2$.

Assuming the simplest strategy for the interpreter of always giving priority to the requester 1, the possible states and transitions are:

00 00 00 $p_1p_2 \rightarrow r_1r_2$ 00 00 p_1p_2	
00 01 01 $p_1 0 \rightarrow r_1r_2$ 00 00 $p_1 1$	
00 10 10 $0 p_2 \rightarrow r_1r_2$ 00 00 $1 p_2$	Here we have assumed the interpreter makes no allocation since there is no request.
00 10 11 00 $\rightarrow r_1r_2$ 01 01 10	Here the interpreter fulfils the outstanding allocation.
01 00 00 $p_1p_2 \rightarrow r_1r_2$ 01 01 $p_1 0$	
01 01 01 $p_1 0 \rightarrow r_1r_2$ 01 01 $p_1 0$	
01 10 10 $0 p_2 \rightarrow r_1r_2$ 01 01 10	
01 10 11 00 $\rightarrow r_1r_2$ 01 01 10	Here the interpreter makes an immediate allocation to 2 since 1 cannot be waiting (it has priority).

10 00 00 $p_1p_2 \rightarrow r_1r_2$ 10 10 $0p_2$	
10 01 01 $p_10 \rightarrow r_1r_2$ 10 10 01	
10 10 10 $0p_2 \rightarrow r_1r_2$ 10 10 $0p_2$	
10 10 11 00 $\rightarrow r_1r_2$ 10 11 00	Here the interpreter makes an immediate allocation to 1 since it has priority.
11 00 00 $p_1p_2 \rightarrow r_1r_2$ 10 11 00	
11 01 01 $p_10 \rightarrow r_1r_2$ 10 11 00	
11 10 10 $0p_2 \rightarrow r_1r_2$ 10 11 00	
11 10 11 00 $\rightarrow r_1r_2$ 10 11 00	If both are requesting then we allocate to 1 but ensure we propagate a commitment to allocate to 2.

Note that there are no states of the form xx 00 01 xx (outstanding request with no allocation) since any reasonable interpreter strategy would have satisfied them. Further, with this strategy no state of the form xx 01 11 xx (allocation to 2 with outstanding request from 1) is possible since the interpreter would have satisfied the first requester by preference.

Now we may perform analysis on this chain. There are 64 probabilities chosen by the environment for the new state of r_i given the previous r_i and a_i. We will assume them constant, so that this chain is time-homogeneous, and call them a_{ijklmn} where i, j, k, l are the previous values of the r_i and a_i and m, n are the new r_i values.

To start our analysis we will assume the a_{ijklmn} are all non-zero. Then we may analyze the states using the transition table above as follows. We need to find the irreducible part of the chain to find a steady-state solution.

Consider the sequence of states starting with the potential start state 00 00 00 11:

00 00 00 11	$\rightarrow$	01 00 00 11	$\rightarrow$	00 01 01 10	$\rightarrow$
10 00 00 11	$\rightarrow$	00 10 10 01	$\rightarrow$	11 00 00 11	$\rightarrow$
00 10 11 00	$\rightarrow$	01 01 01 10	$\rightarrow$	10 01 01 10	$\rightarrow$
01 10 10 01	$\rightarrow$	11 01 01 10	$\rightarrow$	01 10 11 00	$\rightarrow$
11 01 01 10	$\rightarrow$	10 10 11 00	$\rightarrow$	11 10 11 00	$\rightarrow$
00 10 11 00	$\rightarrow$	00 01 01 10	$\rightarrow$	00 00 00 11	

which takes us back to the first state. The existence of this cycle shows that no smaller set of states can be closed. To show the irreducibility of this set we look at the other states and see if they are accessible. If we find that they can be reached from a possible start state then they are accessible, otherwise they are inaccessible. We write "i" and "j" to indicate 0 or 1 and use "(loop)" to indicate a path which is not finding any more states and "(inac)" for states we have already shown to be inaccessible.

ij 00 00 00	$\leftarrow$	Can be reached only from 00 00 00 00 which is not a start state. Thus this state is inaccessible.

ij 00 00 01	←	00 00 00 01		(loop)		
	←	00 01 01 00	←	01 00 00 0j	←	00 00 00 00 (inac)
					←	00 00 00 01 (loop)
					←	00 01 01 00 (loop)
			←	01 01 01 00	←	01 00 00 0j (loop)
					←	01 0101 00 (loop)
ij 00 00 10	←	00 00 00 10		(loop)		
	←	00 10 10 00	←	10 00 00 00	←	00 00 00 00 (inac)
			←	10 10 10 00	←	10 00 00 00 (loop)
					←	10 00 00 10 ...
		continued	←	10 00 00 10	←	00 00 00 10 (loop)
					←	00 10 10 00 (loop)
ij 01 01 00		(inac)				
ij 10 10 10		(inac)				

None of these states are starting states and so none are accessible and part of the irreducible chain.

Thus the originally listed cycle is the irreducible set of states and because of the finite-state space it must be recurrent non-null.

We could now solve for steady-state probabilities using the steady-state theorem. Writing, for example $p_{00000011}$ for the probability of state 00000011 in the steady state (we use $p_{000000ij}$ to indicate summation over possible i,j values) we have balance equations such as:

$$p_{00000011} = a_{000000} \times p_{00000011} + a_{000100} \times p_{00010110} + a_{001000} \times p_{00101001}$$

$$p_{00010110} = a_{001000} \times p_{00101100} + a_{010000} \times p_{0100001i} + a_{010100} \times p_{01010110} + a_{011000} \times (p_{0110100i} + p_{01101100})$$

Solution of these equations would enable us to find the proportion of time spent in any one state or the mean time to move from one state to another or various other properties of the steady-state behaviour.

We may, however, make predictions about its behaviour even without solving these.

Note that the system will return infinitely often to 00 00 00 11. This shows that the system will meet its specifications since any commitment $\Diamond a_i$ will be eventually satisfied.

However, consider the system with different environmental transition probabilities so that $a_{ijkl0m} = 0$, in other words, the first requester never stops requesting. Then fewer transitions are possible so our cycle is no longer valid.

The maximal cycle is now

10 10 11 11 → 11 10 11 11 → 10 10 11 11

which takes us back to the first state. Thus this set of states is all part of the steady-state recurrent solution. As before, we can show that all other states are not part of the irreducible chain. Thus, with these environment transitions the system no longer successfully meets its commitments with this strategy.

5.6 Conclusion

We have considered a natural model to use in describing a system executing temporal logic specifications in an environment which is described randomly. We have shown that a USF specification need not use any past formulae (including fixed points) as long as it has some means of initializing its propositions at the time origin. We have seen that if the specification is implementable then it has a finite-state implementation.

This implies a Markov property for the actions of the program in a suitably but finitely augmented state space. We assumed such a Markov property for the environment and showed that, in conjunction with the property for the interpreter, this gives us the Markov property for the system with combined state-space.

Although this did allow us to obtain some results for a very simple example, it seems that the computation involved in any reasonable size problem is very large. Instead of providing this sort of numerical answer directly, we hope these ideas will provide a jumping off point for the examination of new interpreter execution strategies or for the analysis of probabilistic algorithms.

An important value to be found for our system is the probability of successfully satisfying a given specification for a given strategy in a given environment. Our approach, unfortunately, does not naturally lead to this sort of answer. If we consider a system in its steady state it will either be certain to satisfy its specification or certain not to. The interesting behaviour controlling satisfaction is intimately linked with the transient or initial behaviour of the chain before it reaches its steady state. Markov chain theory does not include easy solutions to this sort of behaviour, though some approximation techniques are available. The applicability of these is still to be investigated.

5.7 Alternative approaches

We have considered a program built without regard to probability. Our implementations have the property that they will succeed in meeting their specification for all possible behaviours of the environment. But in our example we have seen a simple program which is not an implementation in this sense. However, for most random environments (any with certain transitions non zero probability) our simple program succeeds in meeting its specification with probability 1.

There has been considerable work on this sort of verification, i.e. testing if a given program and system will meet a given specification with probability 1, e.g. [1], [12], [14], [13]. Essentially they work with logics which reason about probabilistic systems themselves. In [14] a logic containing a straightforward logic of linear time has a new modality added to it. This new modality is read "certainly" and indicates that its argument happens with probability 1. Three different axiomatizations are also provided, covering general, finite and bounded models. [13] gives logics (over branching models) to reason directly about what can or must happen in Markov systems. Thus with these logics we could take our system with known behaviour and then show it was certain to meet its specifications.

In [7] a different problem is attacked. It is assumed that some specification is given. The formalism used is ω-regular sets, but this is equivalent to Büchi automata and thus our temporal logic (see e.g. [22]). The problem tackled is to find an implementation (program) which maximizes the probability of meeting that specification. Courcoubetis & Yannakakis give an algorithm based on the Markov decision process theory to find such an implementation. Their implementation is finite state and, like the nonprobabilistic techniques, doubly-exponential in the size of specification.

References

[1] Alur R., C. Courcoubetis & D. Dill 1991. Model-checking for probabilistic real-time systems. *Lecture Notes in Computer Science* **510**, 115–26.

[2] Alur, R. & T. A. Henzinger 1991. Logics and models of real time: A survey. *Lecture Notes in Computer Science* **600**, 74–106.

[3] Bartlett, M. S. 1978. *An introduction to stochastic processes*, 3rd edn. Cambridge: Cambridge University Press.

[4] Banieqbal, B., H. Barringer & A. Pnueli (eds) 1987. *Lecture Notes in Computer Science* **398**.

[5] Barringer, H., M. Fisher, D. Gabbay, G. Gough & R. Owens 1989/90. MetateM: A framework for programming in temporal logic. *Lecture Notes in Computer Science* **430**.

[6] Chaochen, Z. 1987. Specifying communicating systems with temporal logic. In Banieqbal et al. [4].

[7] Courcobetis, C. & M. Yannakakis 1990. Markov decision processes and regular events. In *Proceedings of the 17th Colloquium on Automata Languages and Programming*, 336–49. Berlin: Springer.

[8] de Bakker, J. W., W.P. de Roever & G. Rozenberg (eds) 1989. Linear time, branching time and partial order in logics and models for concurrency. *Lecture Notes in Computer Science* **354**.

[9] Gabbay, D. 1987. Declarative past and imperative future: executable temporal logic for interactive systems. In Banieqbal et al. [4].

[10] Hailpern, B. T. 1982. Verifying concurrent processes using temporal logic. *Lecture Notes in Computer Science* **129**.

[11] Hodkinson, I. 1989. *Elimination of fixed point operators in the temporal logic yf.* Technical report, Imperial College.

[12] Hart, S. & M. Sharir 1983. Termination of probabilistic concurrent programs. *ACM Transactions on Programming Languages and Systems* **5**(3), 356–80.

[13] Hart, S. & M. Sharir 1984. Probabilistic temporal logics for finite and bounded models. In *Proceedings of the 16th ACM Symposium on the Theory of Computing*, 1–13.

[14] Lehmann, D. & S. Shelah 1983. Reasoning with time and chance. *Information and Control* **53**, 165–98.

[15] Mitrani, I. 1987. *Modelling of computer and communication systems.* Cambridge: Cambridge University Press.

[16] Manna, Z. & A. Pnueli 1981. Temporal verification of concurrent programs. In *The Correctness Problem in Computer Science*, R. S. Boyer & J. S. Moore (eds). London: Academic Press.

[17] Manna, Z. & A. Pnueli 1987. The anchored version of the temporal framework. In de Bakker et al. [8].

[18] Pnueli, A. 1986. Applications of temporal logic to the specification and verification of reactive systems: a survey of current trends. *Lecture Notes in Computer Science* **224**.

[19] Pnueli, A. & R. Rosner 1989. On the synthesis of a reactive module. *Conference Record of the 16th Annual ACM Symposium on Principles of Programming Languages.*

[20] Rescher, N. & A. Urquhart 1971. *Temporal Logic*, Berlin: Springer.

[21] Van Benthem, J. 1987. Time, logic and computation. In de Bakker et al. [8].

[22] Wolper, P. 1994. Chapter 3 of this volume.

Chapter 6

Temporal logics in a relational framework

E. Orłowska

Institute of Theoretical and Applied Computer Science
Polish Academy of Sciences

Abstract

The inspiration for relational formalization of logical systems comes from the need for the development of proof theory for information logics and from the successful relational modelling of programming constructs and phenomena. One of the main advantages of relational formalization is that the classical opposition between extensional and intensional or between compositional and noncompositional is eliminated. Similarly, the opposition between static and dynamic or between declarative and procedural is transformed into a coexistence in a uniform framework.

In this chapter we illustrate the methodology of relational formalization with examples taken from the areas of applied temporal logics, information logics and temporal information logics.

6.1 Introduction

Relational formalization **of nonclassical logics is realized on the following three methodological levels:**

- ***Semantics and model theory***
  With a logic $\mathcal{L}$ there is associated a class of relational models for $\mathcal{L}$.
- ***Proof theory***
  With logic $\mathcal{L}$ there is associated a relational logic for $\mathcal{L}$ such that its proof system provides a deduction method for $\mathcal{L}$.
- ***Algebraization***
  With a class of standard semantic structures for $\mathcal{L}$ there is associated a class of nonclassical algebras of relations that provide an algebraic semantics for $\mathcal{L}$.

The inspiration for relational formalization of logical systems came from the two sources: first, from the need for the development of proof theory for information logics that have been defined in connection with rough set-based knowledge representation (Pawlak [21], [23], Orlowska [14], [16], Vakarelov [32]); secondly, from the successful relational modelling of programming constructs and phenomena in the theory of programs (Hoare & Jifeng [5]). The standard methods of proof theory were found to be insufficient for providing deduction systems for information logics with the intended semantics, that is semantics determined by information systems.

Formalization of nonclassical logics within a suitably modified relational calculus has been proposed in Orlowska [15]. It has been shown that there is a very natural correspondence between formal systems of nonclassical logics and certain nonclassical relational calculi. Relational semantics, relational proof systems and nonclassical algebras of relations for various nonclassical logics have been proposed in Orlowska ([17], [18], [19]). The methodology suggested in these papers extends to information logics as well as to the other applied logics.

Relational formalization has several advantages. In most of the nonclassical logics their formulas, which are built with intensional propositional connectives, for example with modal or temporal operators, are not compositional. The meaning of a compound formula is not a function of meanings of its subformulas. In relational formalism all these formulas become compositional. The classical opposition between extensional and intensional or between compositional and noncompositional is eliminated when we pass to the relational counterpart of a given nonclassical logic. In several applications of nonclassical logics there is a need to distinguish between information about static facts and dynamic transitions in a domain which a given logic is intended to model. Relational representation of nonclassical formulas enables us to express an interaction between these two components of information in a single, uniform formalism. In relational logics an opposition between static and dynamic or between declarative and procedural is transformed into a coexistence and interaction of these two types of information in a uniform framework.

From the algebraic perspective, relational formalization of nonclassical logics leads to what might be called nonclassical algebras of relations. In these algebras "logical" relational operations are admitted which are relational counterparts of intensional propositional connectives. They are not always expressible in terms of the standard relational operations.

In this chapter we illustrate the methodology of relational formalization with examples taken from the area of temporal logics, in particular, temporal information logics. In Section 6.2 we develop relational semantics for standard temporal logics with modal operators of past and future, and for some of their extensions. In Section 6.3 we present a method of assigning a relational logic to a given nonclassical logic. In Section 6.4 relational proof system is recalled for classical relational logic. To define a deduction system for logics determined by classes of models satisfying some constraints, we have to expand this proof system by adjoining rules that reflect these constraints. In Section 6.5 definability of classes of constraints by means of relational rules is discussed. In Secs. 6.6–6.8 and relational formalization of some applied temporal logics is given and the respective nonclassical relational logics are introduced. Section 6.6 is devoted to logics with propositional constants. In information logics the constants represent objects in an information system, and in temporal logics they allow us an explicit reference to moments of time. In Section 6.7 a relational proof system is given for an event structure logic. In Section 6.8 a relational formalization of a temporal information logic is discussed.

We consider nonclassical logics whose relational counterpart is provided by algebras of binary relations, and therefore throughout this chapter by "relation" we always mean a binary relation. In Orlowska [18] a relational formalization of relevant logics is presented which requires algebras of ternary relations. We begin with basic definitions and facts about algebras of relations.

Let W be a nonempty set. The full algebra of binary relations over W is the algebra:

$$Re(W) = (Sb(W \times W), -, \cup, \cap, 1, 0, ;, ^{-1}, I)$$

where $(Sb(W \times W), -, \cup, \cap, 1, 0)$ is the boolean algebra of subsets of $W \times W$, $1 = W \times W$ is the universal relation, 0 is the empty relation, $I = \{(w, w) : w \in W\}$ is the identity in W, operations ; and $^{-1}$ are relational composition and conversion, respectively. Throughout this chapter the operations in $Re(W)$ are referred to as "standard relational operations". The class RRA of representable relation algebras consists of isomorphic copies of subalgebras and direct products of full algebras of relations. Every algebra from RRA is isomorphic to an algebra whose elements are binary relations, 1 is an equivalence relation, and I is an identity on the field of 1. If 1 has exactly one equivalence class, then such an algebra is simple. The class RRA is a variety (Tarski [30], [31]), but its equational theory is not finitely axiomatizable, and moreover, an infinite axiomatization of RRA requires infinitely many relation variables (Monk [10], [11]).

Proposition 6.1

For any relations P, Q in $Re(W)$ the following conditions are satisfied:

(a) $P \subseteq Q$ iff $-P \cup Q = 1$
(b) $P = Q$ iff $(-P \cup Q) \cap (-Q \cup P) = 1$
(c) $P \neq 1$ iff $1; (-P); 1 = 1$
(d) $P = 1$ and $Q = 1$ iff $P \cap Q = 1$
(e) $P = 1$ or $Q = 1$ iff $1; -(1; (-P); 1); 1 \cup Q = 1$
(f) $P = 1$ implies $Q = 1$ iff $1; (-P); 1 \cup Q = 1$

Conditions a-f show that any open formula of the equational theory of algebras of binary relations is expressible in the form of an equation.

In the relational representation of logical formulas the operations of right (/) and left (\) residuation play an important role:

$$R/P = \{(y,z) : (x,y) \in P \quad \text{implies} \quad (x,z) \in R \text{ for all } x\}$$
$$Q\backslash R = \{(x,y) : (y,z) \in Q \quad \text{implies} \quad (x,z) \in R \text{ for all } z\ \}.$$

Residuations are definable in terms of the standard relational operations:

$$R/P = -(P^{-1};-R) \quad Q\backslash R = -(-R;Q^{-1}).$$

A relation P is said to be a ***right ideal relation*** whenever $P;1 = P$.

Proposition 6.2

(a) If P, Q are ideal relations, then so are $-P$, $P \cup Q$, $P \cap Q$.

(b) If Q is an ideal relation, then for any P relations $P;Q$ and Q/P are ideal as well.

Ideal relations can be viewed as unary relations (or sets) which are "dummy embedded" into relations of a higher rank. It follows that class RRA is a generalized reduct of a class of subalgebras of algebras of relations of any rank higher than two. A comprehensive survey of the theory of algebras of relations can be found in Maddux [9].

6.2 Relational semantics for standard temporal logics

Semantic presentation of nonclassical logics with intensional operators is usually provided in terms of possible worlds semantics (Kripke [6], [7]). Under possible world interpretation, formulas are understood as subsets of a universe of possible worlds, and intensional propositional operations are defined in terms of an accessibility relation or a family of accessibility relations between possible worlds. Next, the inductively defined satisfiability of formulas at worlds provides truth conditions for the formulas. Let a frame $F = (W, R)$ be given such that W is a nonempty set of possible worlds and $R \subseteq W \times W$ is a binary accessibility relation in W. Frames generate semantical structures of logical systems. With each frame F we associate a family of models $M = (W, R, m)$, where m is a meaning function that assigns subsets of W to propositional variables. Let VARPROP be an infinite denumerable set of propositional variables. We consider nonclassical propositional languages whose formulas are generated from VARPROP by means of various propositional operations, including the classical operations and some intensional operations. Satisfiability of atomic formulas (propositional variables) and formulas built with the classical extensional operations of negation ($\neg$), disjunction ($\vee$), conjunction ($\wedge$), and implication ($\rightarrow$) is defined as follows:

- $M, w \Vdash p$ iff $w \in m(p)$ for any propositional variable p.
- $M, w \Vdash \neg A$ iff not $M, w \Vdash A$.
- $M, w \Vdash A \vee B$ iff $M, w \Vdash A$ or $M, w \Vdash B$.
- $M, w \Vdash A \wedge B$ iff $M, w \Vdash A$ and $M, w \Vdash B$.
- $M, w \Vdash A \rightarrow B$ iff not $M, w \Vdash A$ or $M, w \Vdash B$.

A formula A is true in M iff $M, w \Vdash A$ for all $w \in W$, A is true in frame $F = (W, R)$ iff it is true in every model $M = (W, R, m)$ based on this frame, and A is valid iff it is true in all frames.

In modal logics the operators $\Box_R$ and $\Diamond_R$ of necessity and possibility, respectively, determined by an accessibility relation R, are semantically defined as follows:

- $M, w \Vdash \Box_R A$ iff for all $u \in W$ if $(w, u) \in R$, then $M, u \Vdash A$.
- $M, w \Vdash \Diamond_R A$ iff there is an $u \in W$ such that $(w, u) \in R$ and $M, u \Vdash A$.

Various modal systems are obtained by imposing constraints on an accessibility relation R in the models. Let CT be a set of constraints, then $FRM(CT)$ is the class of frames (W, R) such that accessibility relation R satisfies all the constraints from CT. We do not specify here any particular formalism for representing these constraints. It may be a first-order or a second-order language, or a language of relational terms over a suitable algebra of relations. In particular, it can be a modal language. Any constraint C is a formula from the respective language of constraints in which a relational constant denoting an accessibility relation occurs. (If a constraint is given in the form of a modal formula, then the respective constant occurs within the modal operators.) A relation R satisfies a constraint C whenever the sentence obtained from C by interpreting the constant as R is true, according to the standard definition of truth in the given language of constraints.

Given a nonclassical propositional language, by logic $\mathcal{L}(CT)$ of the class $FRM(CT)$ of frames we mean the set of formulas from this language that are true in all frames from $FRM(CT)$:

$$\mathcal{L}(CT) = \{A : A \text{ is true in all frames from } FRM(CT)\}.$$

The well known modal logics are: K(all), T(reflexive), KB(symmetric), B(reflexive, symmetric), K4(transitive), KB4(symmetric, transitive), S4(reflexive, transitive), S5(reflexive, symmetric, transitive), S4.1(reflexive, transitive, atomic), KD(serial), KDB(symmetric, serial), KD4(transitive, serial), S4.3.1(reflexive, transitive, euclidean, discrete), G(transitive, well capped).

In the relational representation of formulas we are going to articulate explicitly information about both their syntactic structure and their semantic satisfiability condition. Generally speaking, formulas will be represented as terms over a class of algebras of relations, and the validity of a formula will be reflected by an equation over this class. Each of the propositional connectives will become a "logical" relational operation, and in this way an original syntactic form of formulas will be preserved. Semantic information about a formula which is included in a satisfiability condition consists of the two basic parts: first, we say which states satisfy the subformulas of the given formula; secondly, we say how those states are related to each other via the accessibility relation. Those two ingredients of semantic information are, of course, interrelated and inseparable. In the relational representation of formulas the terms representing accessibility relations are included explicitly in the respective relational terms corresponding to the formulas. They become the arguments of the relational operations in a term in the same way its other subterms are obtained from subformulas of the given formula. In this way semantic information is provided explicitly on the same level as syntactic information, and the traditional distinction between syntax and semantics disappears, in a sense. In the relational term corresponding to a formula, both syntactic and semantic information about the formula are integrated into a single information item.

Let VARREL be an infinite, denumerable set of relation variables, let $1, I$ be constants denoting the universal relation and the identity relation, respectively, and let R be a relational constant intended to represent an accessibility relation from models of a nonclassical logic. Let EXPREL be the smallest set of relational expressions (terms) such that VARREL $\subseteq$ EXPREL, $1, I, R \in$ EXPREL and for any two relational terms $P, Q \in$ EXPREL we have $-P, P \cup Q, P \cap Q, P;Q, P^{-1} \in$ EXPREL.

We define the translation function t from a set of modal propositional formulas into set EXPREL. Let t' : VARPROP $\rightarrow$ VARREL be a one-to-one mapping of propositional variables into relational variables. Next, we define function t as follows, where p is a propositional variable and A, B are formulas:

$$
\begin{aligned}
t(p) &= t'(p);1 \\
t(\neg A) &= -t(A), \\
t(A \vee B) &= t(A) \cup t(B), \\
t(A \wedge B) &= t(A) \cap t(B), \\
t(A \rightarrow B) &= -t(A) \cup t(B), \\
t(\Diamond_R A) &= R;t(A), \\
t(\Box_R A) &= -(R;-t(A)) = t(A)/R^{-1}
\end{aligned}
$$

Hence, when passing from logical formulas to relations we replace propositional operations by relational operations. The crucial point here is that the accessibility relation is "taken out" of the modal operator and the possibility operation is transformed into composition of the respective relations, and the necessity operation becomes right residuation. In this way, with any formula A of a modal logic there is associated a relational term $t(A)$. Given an algebra $Re(W)$ of binary relations, any homomorphism h from the algebra of relational terms into $Re(W)$ such that $h(R) = R$ provides meaning m_h of formulas in $Re(W)$, namely, $m_h(A) = h(t(A))$. In this way any system (W, m_h) is a relational model for a modal logic. From the perspective of relation algebras, the relationship between the possibility operation and relational composition is reflected more adequately by treating composition as a parametrized unary operation $;_R$:

$$\Diamond_R\, x = ;_R x = R \,;x$$

The class of algebras of relations that provides algebraization of standard modal logics consists of algebras determined by frames (W, R) that are standard semantic structures of the given logic. These algebras have the following form:

$$\{(U \times W : U \subseteq W\}, -, \cup, \cap, ;_R)$$

where $;_R x = R\,;\,x$.

Proposition 6.3

For any modal formula A its translation $t(A)$ represents an ideal relation.

Proof: For propositional variables this property is induced by making $t(p)$ invariant with respect to composition with the universal relation. Since boolean operators preserve the property of being ideal, the formulas built with the classical propositional operations become terms representing ideal relations. Since a result of composing any relation with an ideal relation is an ideal relation, the terms obtained from formulas built with modal operators represent ideal relations as well. □

Entailment can also be transformed into a relational term. We say that formulas $A_1, \ldots, A_n$ imply a formula B whenever for every model M of $\mathcal{L}$ if $A_1, \ldots, A_n$ are true in M, then B is true in M. The following relational term corresponds to this inference:

$$t(A_1, \ldots, A_n \text{ imply } B) = 1; -(t(A_1) \cap, \ldots, \cap t(A_n))\,; 1 \cup t(B).$$

To obtain relational formalization of any particular modal system of the form $\mathcal{L}(CT)$, we adjoin the system of equations $t(A) = 1$ obtained from formulas A of a logic $\mathcal{L}$, and the specific relational postulates which characterize accessibility relations from models of $\mathcal{L}$. For example, system KB is characterized by $R^{-1} \subseteq R$.

Given a modal logic $\mathcal{L}$, a class LRA of nonclassical algebras of relations can be assigned to $\mathcal{L}$ (Orlowska [17]) such that:

> formula A is valid iff $t(A) = 1$ holds in every algebra from LRA,
> inference $A_1, \ldots, A_n$ imply B is admissible iff $t(A_1, \ldots, A_n$ imply $B)=1$ holds in LRA.

In this chapter our main concern is providing representation of the above equations in the suitable logical framework and we will not consider here the underlying algebras. The language of relational terms is the first step towards development of a relational logic for any given nonclassical logic.

In frames for temporal logics, elements of set W are interpreted as moments of time and the accessibility relation reflects an earlier-later relationship. To get access to both past and future moments, in temporal frames we usually include an accessibility relation R and its converse R^{-1}. Modal operators determined by R refer to future states and those determined by its converse refer to past moments. It follows that $\Box_R$, $\Diamond_R$, $\Box_{R^{-1}}$, $\Diamond_{R^{-1}}$ are interpreted as "always in the future", "sometime in the future", "always in the past", "sometime in the past", respectively. Traditionally they are denoted by $\Box$, $\Diamond$, $\overline{\Box}$, $\overline{\Diamond}$, respectively. The logics with these operators as the only intensional operators are referred to as the ***standard temporal logics***. We obtain various classes of standard logics by assuming specific properties of the accessibility relation. Usually it is assumed that R is at least reflexive and transitive. However, since the timescale is not necessarily linearly ordered, we may imagine that at any given moment of time the future develops in different directions. Hence we can have linear or branching time temporal logics and, moreover, relation R might satisfy some additional conditions, for example seriality or weak density (Burgess [2]). The language of temporal logics with operators determined by a relation R and its converse is more expressive than the ordinary modal language with operators determined by R alone, for example continuity of a strict linear ordering is expressible only in the presence of both past and future operators.

In languages of temporal logics we often admit binary operators U and $\overline{U}$ with semantics:

- $M, w \Vdash A U B$ iff there is $t \in W$ such that $(w, t) \in R$ and $M, t \Vdash B$ and for all $u \in W$ if $(w, u) \in R$ and $(u, t) \in R$, then $M, u \Vdash A$.
- $M, w \Vdash A \overline{U} B$ iff there is $t \in W$ such that $(t, w) \in R$ and $M, t \Vdash B$ and for all $u \in W$ if $(t, u) \in R$ and $(u, w) \in R$, then $M, u \Vdash A$.

Hence AUB says that there is a future moment t at which B is satisfied and A is satisfied at all moments between now and t. Similarly, $A\overline{U}B$ means that there is a past moment t at which B is satisfied and at all moments between t and now A is satisfied. In the presence of U, the next-state operator $\bigcirc$ is definable in the modal language:

$M, w \Vdash \bigcirc A$ iff $M, w \Vdash (A \wedge \neg A) U A$.

To define relational representation of temporal formulas we extend the set EXPREL of relational expressions by admitting relational counterparts of logical operations U, $\overline{U}$, and $\bigcirc$ among the relational operations. For the sake of simplicity they are denoted in the same way as the respective propositional operators. Let A, B be binary relations and R be a constant relation corresponding to the accessibility relation, then we define:

- $AUB = \{(w,z)$: there is t such that $(w,t) \in R$ and $(t,z) \in B$ and for all u if $(w,u) \in R$ and $(u,t) \in R$, then $(u,z) \in A\}$,
- $A\overline{U}B = \{(w,z)$: there is t such that $(t,w) \in R$ and $(t,z) \in B$ and for all u if $(t,u) \in R$ and $(u,w) \in R$, then $(u,z) \in A\}$,
- $\bigcirc A = \{(w,z)$: there is t such that $(w,t) \in R$ and $(t,z) \in t(A)$ and there is no u such that $(w,u) \in R$ and $(u,t) \in R\}$.

These new relational operations are not definable by means of the standard relational operators. It is easy to see that if A and B are ideal relations, then so are AUB , $A\overline{U}B$ and $\bigcirc A$.

Set EXPREL_{TEMP} of relational expressions for temporal logics is obtained from $\mathsf{VARREL} \cup \{1, I, R\}$ by making its closure with respect to the standard relational operators and the operators defined above. Then the translation function t is extended to all the temporal formulas:

$$
\begin{aligned}
t(\Diamond A) &= t(\Diamond_R A) = R \,;\, t(A)\\
t(\Box A) &= t(\Box_R A) = t(A)/R^{-1}\\
t(\overline{\Diamond} A) &= t(\Diamond_{R^{-1}} A) = R^{-1} \,;\, t(A)\\
t(\overline{\Box} A) &= t(\Box_{R^{-1}} A) = t(A)/R\\
t(AUB) &= t(A)\,U t(B)\\
t(A\overline{U}B) &= t(A)\,\overline{U} t(B)\\
t(\bigcirc A) &= \bigcirc t(A)
\end{aligned}
$$

It is easy to check that the relational terms obtained from temporal formulas represent ideal relations. In logics of linear time we assume that R is weakly connected, which yields $-(R^{-1};(I \cup R \cup R^{-1})) = 1$. Seriality of the timescale corresponds to $R; 1 = 1$, weak density is reflected by $R \subseteq R; R$.

The class of algebras of relations for these temporal logics consists of the following algebras determined by temporal frames (W, R):

$$(\{U \times W : U \subseteq W\}, -, \cup, \cap, ;_R, U, \overline{U}, \bigcirc)$$

6.3 Relational logics

Given a nonclassical propositional logic $\mathcal{L}$, whose frames consist of a set W and an accessibility relation in this set (or a family of accessibility relations), we define a relational logic Rel$\mathcal{L}$ for $\mathcal{L}$. Let VAR be a set of individual variables and let $\mathsf{CON}_{\mathcal{L}}$ be a set of relational constants representing accessibility relations in models of $\mathcal{L}$. For example, if $\mathcal{L}$ is a modal or standard temporal logic, then $\mathsf{CON}_{\mathcal{L}} = \{R\}$ consists of a single constant. Set $\mathsf{EXPREL}_{\mathcal{L}}$ of relational expressions is generated from $\mathsf{VARREL} \cup \{1, I\} \cup \mathsf{CON}_{\mathcal{L}}$ with the standard relational operations and possibly with new relational operations which are not definable in terms of the standard ones, such as U and $\overline{U}$, that correspond to some of the intensional propositional operations of $\mathcal{L}$. Formulas of the relational logic are of the form xAy, where $x, y \in$ VAR and A is a relational expression from set EXPREL$_{\mathcal{L}}$. If in set W an algebraic structure is assumed, then we define a set TMS$_{\mathcal{L}}$ of terms generated by VAR with all these algebraic operations. For example, if in models of a temporal logic unary successor operation s is admitted in the set of moments of time, then the respective set TMS$_{\mathcal{L}}$ contains terms of the form $s(x)$. Next, formulas of the relational logic for $\mathcal{L}$ are defined as expressions of the form xAy, where $x, y \in$ TMS$_{\mathcal{L}}$ and $A \in$ EXPREL$_{\mathcal{L}}$. Semantic structures for relational logics are models of the form:

$$M = (W, m)$$

where W is a nonempty set and meaning function m : VARREL $\cup \{1, I\} \cup$ CON$_{\mathcal{L}} \rightarrow Sb(W \times W)$ assigns binary relations in W to relational variables and constants, in such a way that $1, I$ and constants from CON$_{\mathcal{L}}$ receive their intended interpretation as the universal relation, identity and accessibility relations from models of $\mathcal{L}$, respectively. Function m extends to all the relational expressions from EXPREL$_{\mathcal{L}}$ in a natural way:

- $m(R) \subseteq W \times W$ for every $R \in$ CON$_{\mathcal{L}}$, $m(1) = W \times W$, $m(I) = \{(w, w) : w \in W\}$,
- $m(-A) = -m(A)$, $m(A^{-1}) = m(A)^{-1}$,
- $m(A \cup B) = m(A) \cup m(B)$, $m(A \cap B) = m(A) \cap m(B)$, $m(A; B) = m(A); m(B)$,

and moreover, if a relation represented by $R \in$ CON$_{\mathcal{L}}$ satisfies some constraints in logic $\mathcal{L}$, then we assume that in models of the relational logic for $\mathcal{L}$ relation $m(R)$ satisfies the same constraints. For example, in temporal logic of linear time we assume that in every model relation $m(R)$ is weakly connected.

By a valuation in M we mean a function v : VAR $\rightarrow W$ assigning elements of W to individual variables. A relational formula xAy is satisfied by v in M whenever elements $v(x)$ and $v(y)$ stand in relation $m(A)$:

$$M, v \Vdash xAy \quad \text{iff} \quad (v(x), v(y)) \in m(A).$$

Formula xAy is true in M iff $M, v \Vdash xAy$ for all valuations v in M, and xAy is valid iff it is true in all models. In other words, formula xAy is true in a model M whenever $m(A) = m(1)$ holds. Relational logics defined according to the above scheme and such that set CON$_{\mathcal{L}}$ is nonempty, or the set of relational operations includes some nonstandard operations, are called ***nonclassical relational logics***. The classical relational logic is the logic with formulas xAy such that A is a term over the class of algebras $Re(W)$.

The semantic relationship between formulas of a nonclassical logic $\mathcal{L}$ and formulas of the relational logic for $\mathcal{L}$ is established in the lemmas of the following scheme.

Proposition 6.4

For every model of $\mathcal{L}$ of the form $M = (W$, family of relations, $m)$, there is a model $M' = (W, m')$ of the relational logic for $\mathcal{L}$ such that for any formula A of $\mathcal{L}$ and for any $w \in W$ we have:

$$M, w \Vdash A \text{ iff } (w, z) \in m'(t(A)) \text{ for all } z \in W \tag{6.1}$$

Proof: We define model M' as follows. Its universe coincides with the universe W of M. If $P \in \mathsf{VARREL}$ and $P = t'(p)$ for a propositional variable p, then we put $m'(P) = m(p) \times W$. If $R \in \mathsf{CON}_{\mathcal{L}}$, then we put $m'(R) = R$, that is the meaning of constant R in the relational model is the relation from model M denoted by that constant; as usual we use the same symbols for both of them. The proof of the required condition is by induction with respect to the complexity of F. We show the induction step for a modal logic $\mathcal{L}$ and a formula of the form $\Diamond_R A$. We have $M, w \Vdash \Diamond_R A$ iff there is $t \in W$ such that $(w, t) \in R$ and $M, t \Vdash A$. By the induction hypothesis there is t such that $(w, t) \in m'(R)$ and $(t, z) \in m'(t(A))$ for all $z \in W$ which yields $(w, z) \in m'(R); m'(t(A)) = m'(R; t(A)) = m'(t(\Diamond_R A))$. □

Proposition 6.5

For every model $M' = (W, m')$ of the relational logic for $\mathcal{L}$ there is a model M of $\mathcal{L}$ such that condition (6.1) is satisfied.

Proof: We define model M as follows. Its universe coincides with the universe W of M'. Accessibility relations in M are all the relations $m'(R)$ for $R \in \mathsf{CON}_{\mathcal{L}}$. For any propositional variable p we put $m(p)$ = domain of $m'(P)$ where $P = t'(p)$. By induction on the complexity of a formula A one can show that condition (6.1) is satisfied. □

Proposition 6.6

(a) A formula A of logic $\mathcal{L}$ is valid in $\mathcal{L}$ iff $xt(A)y$ is valid in $\mathsf{Rel}\mathcal{L}$

(b) Formulas $A_1, \ldots, A_n$ imply a formula B in $\mathcal{L}$ iff $x1; -(t(A_1) \cap \ldots \cap t(A_n)); 1 \cup t(B)y$ is valid in $\mathsf{Rel}\mathcal{L}$.

Proof: To prove (a) assume that a formula A is valid in logic $\mathcal{L}$. Suppose that there is a model $M' = (W', m')$ of the relational logic for $\mathcal{L}$ and there are $x, y \in W'$ such that $(x, y) \notin m'(t(A))$. By Proposition 6.5 there is a model M of $\mathcal{L}$ with the universe W' such that not $M, x \Vdash A$, which contradicts the assumption. Now assume that $xt(A)y$ is valid in the relational logic for $\mathcal{L}$ and suppose that A is not valid in L. Hence there is a model $M = (W$, family of accessibility relations, $m)$ of $\mathcal{L}$ and there is $w \in W$ such that not $M, w \Vdash A$. By Proposition 6.4 there is a model M' of the relational logic for $\mathcal{L}$ with the universe W, and there is $z \in W$ such that $(w, z) \notin m'(t(A))$, which contradicts the assumption.

We prove condition (b) for $n = 1$. Assume that for every model M of $\mathcal{L}$ if A is true in M, then B is true in M. Suppose that there is a model $M' = (W, m)$ of logic Rel$\mathcal{L}$ such that $m(1; -t(A); 1 \cup t(B)) \neq m(1)$. By Proposition 6.1(f) it yields $m(t(A)) = m(1)$ and $m(t(B)) \neq m(1)$. By Proposition 6.5 there is a model M of $\mathcal{L}$ having the same universe as M' such that A is true in M and B is not true in M, a contradiction. Now assume that $x1; -t(A); 1 \cup t(B)y$ is valid in Rel$\mathcal{L}$. Suppose that A does not imply B in $\mathcal{L}$, that is there is a model M of $\mathcal{L}$ such that A is true in M but B is not true in M. By Proposition 6.4 there is a model $M' = (W, m')$ of Rel$\mathcal{L}$ with the same universe as M such that $m'(t(A)) = m'(1)$ and $m'(t(B)) \neq m'(1)$. By Proposition 6.1(f) we obtain a contradiction which completes the proof. □

We conclude that, given a nonclassical logic $\mathcal{L}$, a deduction system of the relational logic for $\mathcal{L}$ can serve as a theorem prover for $\mathcal{L}$. In the following sections, relational proof systems will be outlined for some temporal logics.

6.4 Relational proof system for classical relational logic

Proof systems for relational logics are Rasiowa - Sikorski style systems (Rasiowa & Sikorski [27]). In this section we recall the deduction rules for the classical relational logic (Orlowska [15]), that is, the logic whose formulas xAy are built from terms A generated by VARREL $\cup \{1, I\}$ with the standard relational operations. The rules apply to finite sequences of relational formulas. There are two groups of rules: decomposition rules and specific rules. Decomposition rules allow us to decompose formulas in a sequence into some simpler formulas. Decomposition depends on relational operations occurring in a formula. As a result of decomposition, we usually obtain finitely many new sequences of formulas, and sometimes, as in the case of operation $- *$ in dynamic logic, infinitely many sequences. The specific rules allow us to modify a sequence to which they are applied; they have the status of structural rules. The role of axioms is played by what are called *fundamental sequences*. In what follows, K and H denote finite, possibly empty, sequences of formulas of a relational logic. A variable is said to be "restricted in a rule" whenever it does not appear in any formula of the upper sequence in this rule.

Decomposition rules for the standard relational operations:

$$(\cup)\ \frac{K, xA \cup By, H}{K, xAy, xBy, H} \qquad (-\cup)\ \frac{K, x-(A \cup B)y, H}{K, x-Ay, H \quad K, x-By, H}$$

$$(\cap)\ \frac{K, xA \cap By, H}{K, xAy, H \quad K, xBy, H} \qquad (-\cap)\ \frac{K, x-(A \cap B)y, H}{K, x-Ay, x-By, H}$$

$$(--)\ \frac{K, x - -Ay, H}{K, xAy, H}$$

$$(^{-1})\ \frac{K, xA^{-1}y, H}{K, yAx, H} \qquad (-^{-1})\ \frac{K, x - (A^{-1})y, H}{K, y - Ax, H}$$

$$(;)\ \frac{K, xA;By, H}{K, xAz, H, xA;By \quad K, zBy, H, xA;By} \quad z \text{ is a variable}$$

$$(-;)\ \frac{K, x - (A;B)y, H}{K, x - Az, z - By, H} \quad z \text{ is a restricted variable}$$

$$(\backslash)\ \frac{K, x - (A\backslash B)y, H}{K, yAz, H, x - (A\backslash B)y \quad K, x - Bz, H, x - (A\backslash B)y} \quad z \text{ is a variable}$$

$$(/)\ \frac{K, xA/By, H}{K, z - Bx, zAy, H} \quad z \text{ is a restricted variable}$$

$$(-/)\ \frac{K, x - (A/B)y, H}{K, zBx, H, x - (A/B)y \quad K, z - Ay, H, x - (A/B)y} \quad z \text{ is a variable}$$

Specific rules for identity relation:

$$(I\ 1)\ \frac{K, xAy, H}{K, xIz, xAy, H \quad K, zAy, xAy, H} \quad z \text{ is a variable}$$

$$(I\ 2)\ \frac{K, xAy, H}{K, xAz, xAy, H \quad K, zIy, xAy, H} \quad z \text{ is a variable}$$

$$(sym\ I)\ \frac{K, xIy, H}{K, yIx, H}$$

A sequence of formulas is said to be fundamental whenever it contains formulas of the following form:

(f1) $xAy, x - Ay$ **for any relational expression** A

(f2) $x1y$

(f3) xIx

A sequence K of relational formulas is valid iff for every model M of the relational logic and for every valuation v over M there is a formula in K which is satisfied by v in M. It follows that sequences of formulas are interpreted as disjunctions of their elements. A relational rule of the form $K/\{H_t : t \in T\}$ is admissible whenever sequence K is valid iff for all $t \in T$ sequence H_t is valid. It is easy to see that the fundamental sequences are valid and all the rules given above are admissible. Admissibility of the decomposition rules follows from definitions of the respective relational operations, and admissibility of specific rules follows from the properties of relational constants reflected by those rules. For example, rules I1 and I2 are admissible because we have $I; A = A = A; I$ for any relation A.

Relational proofs have the form of trees. Given a relational formula xAy, where A might be a compound relational expression, we successively apply decomposition or specific rules. In this way we form a tree whose nodes consist of finite sequences of relational formulas. We stop applying rules to formulas in a node after obtaining a fundamental sequence, or when none of the rules is applicable to the formulas in this node. A branch of a proof tree is said to be fundamental whenever it contains a node with a fundamental sequence of formulas. A tree is fundamental iff all of its branches are fundamental. The completeness theorem says that a relational formula F is valid iff there is a fundamental proof tree for F.

Example We can show that $-(A\backslash B) = (-B\backslash - A)\backslash - I$ in any $Re(W)$. In view of Proposition 6.1(b) it is sufficient to show that

$$((A\backslash B) \cup ((-B\backslash - A)\backslash - I)) \cap (-(A\backslash B) \cup -((-B\backslash - A)\backslash - I)) = 1$$
$$x((A\backslash B) \cup ((-B\backslash - A)\backslash - I)) \cap (-(A\backslash B) \cup -((-B\backslash - A)\backslash - I))y$$
$$(\cap)$$

$x(A\backslash B) \cup ((-B\backslash - A)\backslash - I)y$	$x - (A\backslash B) \cup -((-B\backslash - A)\backslash - I)y$
$(\cup)$	$(\cup)$
$xA\backslash By, x(-B\backslash - A)\backslash - Iy$	$x - (A\backslash B)y, F = x - ((-B\backslash - A)\backslash - I)y$
$(\backslash)$ twice	$(-\backslash)$ new variable:$= x$
new variables:$= z, t$	$x - (A\backslash B)y, y - B\backslash - Ax, F \quad ..., xIx, ...$
$y - Az, xBz, y - (-B\backslash - A)t, x - It$	$(\backslash)$ new variable:$= z$ \qquad\qquad fund.
$(-\backslash)$ new variable:$= z$	$x - (A\backslash B)y, xBz, y - Az$

$$
\begin{array}{ll}
y - Az, xBz & y - Az, xBz \\
t - Bz, x - It & yAz, x - It \\
\text{(I1) to } xBz & \text{fund.}
\end{array}
\qquad
\begin{array}{l}
(-\backslash) \text{ new variable:} = z \\
yAz, ... \qquad x - Bz, ... \\
\text{fund.} \qquad\ \text{fund.}
\end{array}
$$

new variable:$= t$

$$..., xIt, ... \quad ..., tBz, ...$$
$$\text{fund.} \qquad \text{fund.}$$

□

6.5 Relational proof systems for nonclassical relational logics

Relational proof systems are fully modular. Given a reduct of the relational language, we obtain a deduction system for it by restricting the set of rules and the set of fundamental sequences to those which refer to the respective operators and constants from this reduct. For example, in the relational logic corresponding to modal logic K we do not need constant I, and hence we do not need the rules and fundamental sequences referring to it. Similarly, given an extension of the basic relational language, to obtain a deduction system for the underlying logic we have to define decomposition rules for all the new operators and their complements and the specific rules reflecting the properties of the new constants.

Let CT be a set of constraints which a binary relation is supposed to satisfy. For a constraint $C \in CT$ and a relation R, we shall write $C(R)$ to denote a sentence obtained from formula C by interpreting the relational constant in C as R. Let $REL(CT)$ be the class of relations satisfying constraints from CT:

$$REL(CT) = \{R \in Re(W) : W \text{ is a set, and } C(R) \text{ is true for every } C * CT\}.$$

Let a nonclassical logic $\mathcal{L}(CT)$ be given such that in every frame $F = (W, R) \in FRM(CT)$ we have $R \in REL(CT)$. The formulas of relational logic Rel$\mathcal{L}(CT)$ for $\mathcal{L}(CT)$ are built from terms generated by VARREL $\cup \{1, I, R\}$ with the standard relational operations, and possibly with some nonclassical relational operations, like U and $\overline{U}$, defined in Section 6.2. We have to provide in the language of Rel$\mathcal{L}(CT)$ a relational counterpart of every propositional operation from the language of logic $\mathcal{L}(CT)$. Models of this relational language are systems $M = (W, m)$ such that meaning function m satisfies conditions given in Section 6.3, and moreover $m(R) \in$ Rel$\mathcal{L}(CT)$. The relational proof system for Rel$\mathcal{L}(CT)$ consists of the rules and fundamental sequences given in Section 6.4, decomposition rules for all the nonclassical relational operations admitted in the language of Rel$\mathcal{L}(CT)$, and specific rules for relation R, reflecting the fact that $R \in REL(CT)$. An example of decomposition rules for nonclassical relational operations is given below.

Decomposition rules for temporal operators U and $\overline{U}$:

$$(U) \quad \frac{K, xAUBy, H}{H1 \quad H2 \quad H3} \quad \text{where} \quad \begin{array}{l} H1 = K, xRt, H, xAUBy \\ H2 = K, tBy, H, xAUBy \\ H3 = K, x - Ru, u - Rt, \\ uAy, H, xAUBy \ t \text{ is a variable,} \\ u \text{ is a restricted variable} \end{array}$$

$(-U)$ $\dfrac{K, x-(AUB)y, H}{H1 \quad H2 \quad H3}$ where $H1 = K, x-Rt, t-By,$
$xRu, H, x-(AUB)y$
$H2 = K, x-Rt, t-By,$
$uRt, H, x-(AUB)y$
$H3 = K, x-Rt, t-By,$
$u-Ay, H, x-(AUB)y$
u is a variable,
t is a restricted variable

$(\overline{U})$ $\dfrac{K, xA\overline{U}By}{H1 \quad H2 \quad H3}$ where $H1 = K, tRx, H, xA\overline{U}By$
$H2 = K, tBy, H, xA\overline{U}By$
$H3 = K, t-Ru, u-Rx,$
$uAy, H, xA\overline{U}By$ t is a variable,
u is a restricted variable

$(-\overline{U})$ $\dfrac{K, x-(A\overline{U}B)y, H}{H1 \quad H2 \quad H3}$ where $H1 = K, t-Rx, t-By,$
$tRu, H, x-(A\overline{U}B)y$
$H2 = K, t-Rx, t-By,$
$uRx, H, x-(A\overline{U}B)y$
$H3 = K, t-Rx, t-By,$
$u-Ay, H, x-(A\overline{U}B)y$
u is a variable,
t is a restricted variable

Let $r(R)$ denote a relational rule of the form $K/\{H_t : t \in T\}$ in which the relational constant R occurs, and let $RL(R)$ be a set of these rules. They are called specific rules for R. In a similar way to that developed in Section 6.4 we define the admissibility of a rule in a nonclassical relational logic. Sequence K of relational formulas is valid in Rel$\mathcal{L}(CT)$ iff for every model M of Rel$\mathcal{L}(CT)$ and every valuation v in M there is a formula F in K such that $M, v \Vdash F$. We say that $r(R)$ is admissible in Rel$\mathcal{L}(CT)$ whenever sequence K is valid in Rel$\mathcal{L}(CT)$ iff for every $t \in T$ sequence H_t is valid in Rel$\mathcal{L}(CT)$. We say that a set $RL(R)$ of rules defines class $REL(CT)$ whenever $R \in REL(CT)$ iff every rule $r(R) \in RL(R)$ is admissible.

As usual, we use the same symbols for relations and the respective constants.

Proposition 6.7

If sets $RL_1(R)$, $RL_2(R)$ of specific rules for R define classes $REL(CT_1)$, $REL(CT_2)$ of relations, respectively, then class $REL(CT_1 \cup CT_2)$ is definable by $RL_1(R) \cup RL_2(R)$. □

In the following we give examples of classes of relations definable by means of rules. A relation R is euclidean if it satisfies:

$$\text{for all } x, y, z \quad \text{if} \quad (x, y) \in R \quad \text{and} \quad (x, z) \in R, \quad \text{then} (y, z) \in R.$$

The corresponding relational rule is:

$$(eucR) \quad \frac{K, xRy, H}{K, zRx, H, xRy \quad K, zRy, H, xRy} \quad z \text{ is a variable}$$

Proposition 6.8

Rule *eucR* defines *REL(euclidean)*.

Proof: Assume that rule *eucR* is admissible, and suppose that there are a, b, c such that $(a, b) \in R$, $(a, c) \in R$ and $(b, c) \notin R$. Consider an instance of rule (*eucR*) such that $K = z - Rx$, $z - Ry$ and H is empty. It follows that sequence $S = xRy$, $z - Rx$, $z - Ry$ is valid. However, a valuation v such that $v(x) = b$, $v(y) = c$, and $v(z) = a$ satisfies none of the formulas in S, a contradiction.

Now assume that $R \in REL(euclidean)$. If upper sequence $S = K$, xRy, H in rule *eucR* is valid, then so are the lower sequences $S1 = K$, zRx, H, xRy and $S2 = K$, zRy, H, xRy. Now assume that for every model M and every valuation v in M there are formulas $F1$ in $S1$ and $F2$ in $S2$ such that $M, v \Vdash F1$ and $M, v \Vdash F2$. If $F1 = zRx$ and $F2 = zRy$, then since R is euclidean, we have $M, v \Vdash xRy$. In all the remaining cases $F1$ or $F2$ occurs in S. We conclude that S is valid. □

Example We give a relational proof of formula $\Diamond A \rightarrow \Box \Diamond A$ which is valid in the class $FRM(euclidean)$ of frames with euclidean relations. To simplify notation we assume that $t(A) = A$.

$$x(-(R; A) \cup (R; A)/R^{-1})y$$
$$(\cup)$$
$$x - (R; A)y, x(R; A)/R^{-1}y$$
$$(-;) \text{ new variable:= } z$$
$$x - Rz, z - Ay, x(R; A)/R^{-1}y$$
$$(/) \text{ new variable:= } v \, (-^{-1})$$
$$x - Rz, z - Ay, x - Rv, vR; Ay$$
$$(;) \text{ new variable:= } z$$

$x - Rz, z - Ay, x - Rv, vRz, vR; Ay$ $zAy, \ldots$
(*eucR*) new variable:= x fund.
$xRv, \ldots$ $xRz, \ldots$
fund.   fund.

□

Applied nonclassical logics are usually multi-logics with several intensional propositional operations, and their models contain several accessibility relations. Moreover, very often these relations are not independent but are related to each other. The respective constraints, represented in the form of formulas of a suitable language of constraints, each of which contains finitely many relational constants denoting accessibility relations, are called ***multi-relational constraints***. If CT contains multi-relational constraints, then by $REL(CT)$ we mean a set of relations that satisfies the respective sentences obtained from formulas of CT by suitable interpretation of constants. Relational logics adequate to formalize nonclassical multi-logics have formulas that are built with terms generated from relation variables, constants $1, I$ and accessibility relation constants from a nonempty set $CON_{\mathcal{L}}$. In models of these relational logics the meaning function assigns relations satisfying all constraints from CT to constants from $CON_{\mathcal{L}}$. The corresponding relational proof systems contain specific rules $r(R_1, \ldots, R_n)$ that are proof theoretic counterparts of the admitted constraints. In a natural way we extend notion of definability by means of rules of this form to classes of relations satisfying multi-relational constraints.

Consider the following example. Let $CON_{\mathcal{L}} = \{P, Q, R\}$ and $CT = \{R \subseteq P \cap Q\}$. The following rule defines the respective set of relations:

$$\frac{K}{K, xRy \quad K, x - Py, x - Qy}$$

Rules of this form have been suggested by Dragalin [4]. They are called ***specialized cut rules***, and have the form of cut rule where the cut formula is restricted. In Section 6.7 several examples will be given of rules that provide definability of classes of relations in nonclassical relational logics.

6.6 Relational formalization of temporal logics with propositional constants

In Passy [24] an extension of modal languages was introduced and investigated, obtained by adjoining to a given modal language an infinite, denumerable set CONPROP of propositional constants interpreted as singleton sets. Given a model $M = (W, R, m)$, meaning function m assigns an element of W to every constant c:

$$m(c) \in W \quad \text{for} \quad c \in \text{CONPROP}$$

The constants as well as propositional variables become atomic formulas, and their satisfiability is defined as follows:

$$M, w \Vdash c \quad \text{iff} \quad m(c) = \{w\}$$

Dynamic logic with constants has been investigated in Passy & Tinchev [25], temporal logics with contants are considered in Blackburn [1]. Constants increase drastically the expressiveness of modal languages. The following examples give classes of relations which are definable in a modal language with a single accessibility relation, provided that the language contains the constants (Blackburn [1]).

Proposition 6.9

Relation $R \in REL(CT)$ iff formula A is true in every frame from $FRM(CT)$:

(a)	irreflexive	$c \rightarrow \neg \Diamond c$
(b)	antisymmetric	$c \rightarrow \Box(\overline{\Diamond} c \rightarrow c)$
(c)	directed	$\Diamond \overline{\Diamond} c$
(d)	connected	$\overline{\Diamond} c \vee c \vee \Diamond c$
(e)	discrete	$c \rightarrow (\Diamond(A \vee \neg A) \rightarrow \Diamond \overline{\Box}\overline{\Box} \neg c)$

These properties of temporal ordering are of great importance in temporal reasoning. The adequate modelling of timescale should guarantee that any moment does not precede itself. It seems that the most appropriate model for linear timescales is a strict total order which is irreflexive and connected. In several applications we need to distinguish between discrete and dense timescales, for example to model the execution of computer programs discrete time is appropriate.

To formalize logics with constants in a relational framework, we define binary relations whose domains are singleton sets. Let A be an ideal relation, that is, $A;1 = A$. The domain of A is a singleton set iff $A \neq \emptyset$ & $A; A^{-1} \subseteq I$. Ideal relations with this property are referred to as points (Schmidt & Stroehlein [28]).

Relational logics for modal logics with constants are obtained from the relational logics described in Section 6.3 by adjoining to the language of relational terms a denumerable set $CONP$ of point constants. The semantics of the extended relational language is provided by models $M = (W, m)$ such that $m(c)$ is a point in W for every $c \in CONP$. Let v be a valuation in M, then satisfiability of new relational formulas is defined as:

$$M, v \Vdash xcy \text{ iff } m(c) = \{v(x)\} \times W.$$

To the relational rules we add the following rules for constants:

$$\text{(c1)} \quad \frac{K, xIy, H}{K, xcz, H, xcy \quad K, ycz, H, xcy} \quad z \text{ is a variable}$$

$$\text{(c2)} \quad \frac{K, xcy, H}{K, xcz, H} \quad z \text{ is a variable}$$

$$\text{(c3)} \quad \frac{K}{K, x - cy} \quad x, y \text{ are restricted variables}$$

Proposition 6.10
Rules c1 - c3 are admissible iff in every model $M = (W, m)$ of a relational logic with constants $m(c)$ is a point.

Proof: Admissibility of c1 is equivalent to $m(c); m(c)^{-1} \subseteq m(I)$ for any meaning function m. Admissibility of c2 reflects the fact that $m(c)$ is an ideal relation; admissibility of c3 corresponds to $m(c) \neq \emptyset$. □

In the following we present relational rules which define the classes of relations listed in Proposition 6.9. In all these rules x, y are arbitrary variables.

$$(irrefR) \quad \frac{K}{K, xIy \quad K, xRy}$$

$$(antisymR) \quad \frac{K, xIy, H}{K, xRy, H, xIy \quad K, yRx, H, xIy}$$

$$(dirR) \quad \frac{K}{K, x-Rz, y-Rz} \quad z \text{ is a restricted variable}$$

$$(conR) \quad \frac{K}{K, x-Ry \quad K, y-Rx \quad K, x-Iy}$$

$$(disR) \quad \frac{K}{K, xRy \quad K, x-Iy, x-Ry, yR;Rx}$$

Example We give a relational proof of irreflexivity axiom from Proposition 6.9a. We assume that $t(c) = c$.

$$x - c \cup -(R;c)y$$
$$(\cup)$$
$$x - cy, x - (R;c)y$$
$$(-;) \text{ new variable:}= z$$
$$x - cy, x - Rz, z - cy$$
$$(irrefR)$$

$x - cy, z - cy, xIz$ $\qquad\qquad\qquad$ $\ldots, xRz, \ldots$
(c1) new variable:= y $\qquad\qquad\qquad$ fund.
$xcy, \ldots \quad zcy, \ldots$
fund. $\quad$ fund.

□

6.7 Relational formalization of event structure logic

The notion of event structure was introduced in Winskel [33] and investigated in Nielsen et al. [12], Winskel [34], Lodaya & Thiagarajan [8]. A logic *ESL* for event structures was introduced and investigated in Penczek [26]. An event structure is intended to model the behaviour of a distributed system in terms of a set of event occurrences, a causality relation, which is a partial order in a set of event occurrences, and a conflict relation, which determines forbidden successions of events. Two event occurrences which are neither comparable with respect to the causality relation nor in conflict, may occur concurrently. An event structure is a system $ES = (E, csl, cnf)$, where:

(e1) E is a nonempty set of events.

(e2) $csl \subseteq E \times E$ is a reflexive, antisymmetric and transitive relation in E, called the *causality relation*.

(e3) $cnf \subseteq E \times E$ is an irreflexive and symmetric relation in E, called the *conflict relation*.

(e4) For any $e, e1, e2 \in E$ if $(e, e1) \in cnf$ and $(e1, e2) \in csl$, then $(e, e2) \in cnf$.

Condition e4 is referred to as *conflict inheritance*. Conditions e3 and e4 imply that relations csl and cnf are disjoint. Let X be a subset of E. We say that:

(r1) X is conflict free iff for any $e, e' \in E$ if $e \in X$ and $(e, e') \in cnf$, then $e' \notin X$.

(r2) X is backward closed iff for any $e, e' \in E$ if $e \in X$ and $(e', e) \in csl$, then $e' \in X$.

(r3) X is a run in structure ES iff X is a maximal (with respect to inclusion) conflict free and backward closed subset of E.

The language of logic *ESL* is obtained from the language of temporal logic, described in Section 6.2, in the following way. Operations $\Diamond, \overline{\Diamond}, \Box, \overline{\Box}$ are interpreted as modalities determined by the causality relation. Moreover, we adjoin unary propositional operations $\Diamond_{\#}$ and $\Box_{\#}$ which are the modalities determined by the conflict relation, and a propositional constant "run". The semantics of the language is provided by frames of the form $M = (W, csl, cnf, RUN)$ such that (E, csl, cnf) is an event structure, and $RUN \subseteq E$ is a run in that structure. Satisfiability of formulas in models based on these frames is defined as follows:

- $M, w \Vdash \Diamond A$ iff there is $t \in W$ such that $(w, t) \in csl$ and $M, t \Vdash A$.
- $M, w \Vdash \overline{\Diamond} A$ iff there is $t \in W$ such that $(t, w) \in csl$ and $M, t \Vdash A$.

- $M, w \Vdash \Box A$ iff for all $t \in W$ if $(w,t) \in csl$, then $M, t \Vdash A$.
- $M, w \Vdash \overline{\Box} A$ iff for all $t \in W$ if $(t,w) \in csl$, then $M, t \Vdash A$.
- $M, w \Vdash \Diamond_{\#} A$ iff there is $t \in W$ such that $(w,t) \in cnf$ and $M, t \Vdash A$.
- $M, w \Vdash \Box_{\#} A$ iff for all $t \in W$ if $(w,t) \in cnf$, then $M, t \Vdash A$.
- $M, w \Vdash run$ iff $w \in RUN$.

Satisfiability of formulas built with classical propositional connectives is defined as in Section 6.2.

Relational logic corresponding to logic ESL is defined in a similar way to that developed in Section 6.3. Set $CON_{ESL} = \{csl, cnf, run\}$ and set $EXPREL_{ESL}$ of relational terms is generated by $VARREL \cup \{1, I, csl, cnf, run\}$. Translation of modal formulas into relational terms is as follows:

- $t(\Diamond A) = csl; t(A)$
- $t(\overline{\Diamond} A) = csl^{-1}; t(A)$
- $t(\Box A) = t(A)/csl^{-1}$
- $t(\overline{\Box} A) = t(A)/csl$
- $t(\Diamond_{\#} A) = cnf; t(A)$
- $t(\Box_{\#} A) = t(A)/cnf^{-1}$
- $t(run) = run$

The relational proof system for logic ESL consists of the rules given in Section 6.4, and the specific rules which reflect all the constraints imposed on the accessibility relations in models of ESL: reflexivity, antisymmetry and transitivity of the causality relation, irreflexivity and symmetry of the conflict relation, conflict inheritance, and the properties of run.

$$(ref\ scl) \quad \frac{K, xcsly, H}{K, xIy, xcsly, H}$$

$$(antisym\ csl) \quad \frac{K, xIy, H}{K, xcsly, xIy, H \quad K, ycslx, xIy, H}$$

$$(tran\ csl) \quad \frac{K, xcsly, H}{K, xcslz, H, xcsly \quad K, zcsly, H, xcsly} \quad z \text{ is a variable}$$

$$(irref\ cnf) \quad \frac{K}{K, xIy \quad K, xcnfy} \quad x, y \text{ are variables}$$

$$(sym\ cnf) \quad \frac{K, xcnfy, H}{K, ycnfx, H}$$

$$(inh)\quad \frac{K, xcnfy, H}{K, xcnfz, H, xcnfy \quad K, zcnfy, H, xcnfy}\ z \text{ is a variable}$$

$$(r1)\quad \frac{K, x*runy, H}{K, zruny, H, x-runy \quad K, zcnfx, H, x-runy}\ z \text{ is a variable}$$

$$(r2)\quad \frac{K, xruny, H}{K, zruny, H, xruny \quad K, xcslz, H, xruny}\ z \text{ is a variable}$$

$$(r3)\quad \frac{K}{K, x-runy \quad K, x-cnfz, z-runy}\ z \text{ is a restricted variable}$$

$$(r4)\quad \frac{K, xruny, H}{K, xrunz, H}\ z \text{ is a variable}$$

Fundamental sequences of the system are f1, f2, f3.

It is easy to see that the given specific rules define the class of relations satisfying conditions e1 - e4 and r1 - r3. Rule r1 reflects condition R1 of conflict freeness of a run. Rule r2 corresponds to condition R2 of backward closure of a run. Rules r1 and r3 guarantee that run is a maximal relation with those properties, that is, $cnf; run \cup run = 1$. Rule r4 reflects the property $run; 1 = run$, which is the characteristic feature of all the relational terms obtained from modal formulas by means of translation t.

Example We show that formula $A = run \rightarrow \overline{\Box} run$ is valid in ESL. We have $t(A) = -run \cup run/csl$.

$x(-run \cup run/csl)y$
(∪)
$x - runy, xrun/csly$
(/) new variable:= z
$x - runy, z - cslx, zruny$
(r1) new variable:= x

$xruny, \ldots$ — fund.

$xcnfx, x - runy, z - cslx, zruny$
(r2) new variable:=x

$xruny, \ldots$ — fund. $\qquad$ $zcslx, \ldots$ — fund.

□

Example We show that formula $A = \Box_{\#} \neg run \rightarrow run$ is valid in ESL. Its relational translation is $t(A) = -(-run/cnf^{-1}) \cup run$.

$$x(-(-run/cnf^{-1}) \cup run)y$$
$$(\cup)$$
$$x-(-run/cnf^{-1})y, xruny$$
$$(r3) \text{ new variable:} = u$$
$$x-(-run/cnf^{-1})y, x-cnfu, u-runy, xruny$$
$$(-/)(^{-1})(--) \text{ new variable:} = u$$
$$xcnfu, \ldots \quad uruny, \ldots$$
$$\text{fund.} \quad \text{fund.}$$

□

Example We show that if $cnf = \emptyset$, then $run = 1$. By Proposition 6.1(f) it is sufficient to show that $1; cnf; 1 \cup run = 1$.

$$x(1; cnf; 1 \cup run)y$$
$$(\cup)$$
$$x1; cnf; 1y, xruny$$
$$(\text{r3}) \text{ new variable:} = z$$
$$x1; cnf; 1y, x-cnfz, z-runy, xruny$$
$$(;) \text{ new variable:} = x$$
$$x1x, \ldots \quad xcnf; 1y, x-cnfz, z-runy, xruny$$
$$\text{fund.} \quad (;) \text{ new variable:} = z$$
$$xcnfz, \ldots \quad z1y, \ldots$$
$$\text{fund.} \quad \text{fund.}$$

□

6.8 Relational formalization of an information temporal logic

In this section we discuss the relational formalization of a temporal logic developed for representation of information in attribute-based information systems (Codd [3], Pawlak [21]). Information logics have emerged in connection with the following paradigm of knowledge representation (Orlowska and Pawlak [20]):

Representation = Semantics + Syntax + Deduction method.

Usually our primary concern about a given domain is semantic in character. Our views of the respective part of a real world are formed in abstraction from its language. Hence, the component "semantics" is to provide a conceptual model of the domain to be represented.

The component "syntax" provides a linguistic counterpart of the conceptual model adopted in the semantics. The point here is to define a formal language to be used in expressing information about those domains to which a given conceptual model pertains. There must be a strict correspondence between the model and the language connected with it. The primitive concepts included in the model should have their linguistic counterparts at the level of atomic formulas. Further, compound formulas should be constructed from atomic formulas using logical operations, selected according to the type of a domain.

The "deduction method" is to provide the method of handling information presented by means of the formal language introduced within the "syntax". The working out of such a deduction method should consist in formulating the logic to be used and the methods of inference that are admissible in that logic. Such logic should include classical propositional logic, but it turns out that classical logic alone does not suffice in many cases. For instance, consideration of the temporal dimension of information requires the use of a temporal logic.

Temporal information logic, TIL, considered in this section has been developed to provide a means of knowledge representation in domains that can be described by listing the following conceptual primitives: object, property of object. In attribute-based systems, properties are split into pairs of the form (attribute, value). For example, property "to be green" is articulated as (colour, green). To model real situations in which properties of objects change with time, we additionally include the parameter which represents the moment to which that information applies. We are interested in such attributes as height, temperature and blood pressure, usually at given moments of time. Further, their change in a given time interval may be of essential importance too. In TIL we intend to represent data that has the form of a description of time-varying properties of objects.

By ***dynamic information system*** (Orlowska [13]) we mean a system of the form:

$$S = (OB, T, ord, AT, \{VAL_a : a \in AT\}, f)$$

where OB is a nonempty set of objects, T is a nonempty set of moments of time, ord is an ordering on set T, AT is a nonempty set of attributes, VAL_a, for $a \in AT$, is a nonempty set of values of attribute a, f is a function $f : OB \times T \times AT \to VAL = \bigcup\{VAL_a : a \in AT\}$ such that for every $x \in OB$, $t \in T$, and $a \in AT$ we have $f(x,t,a) \in VAL_a$.

Example Consider a part of the table containing results of photoelectric observations of stars, presented in the *Astrophysical Journal*:

	JD	V	B-V
S CMi	1688.788	11.12	1.97
	1798.538	9.28	1.76
R Cnc	1719.750	3.38	1.47
	1800.558	9.51	2.02
R Leo	1688.821	6.27	1.62
	1833.481	9.91	2.87
T Cen	1687.826	6.05	1.44
	1717.816	6.12	1.73

The table can be treated as a dynamic information system such that: set OB of objects consists of the stars, $OB = \{S\ CanisMinoris, R\ Cancri, R\ Leonis,$

T Centauri}; set T of moments of time consists of non-negative real numbers representing Julian days given in the second column of the table; relation *ord* is the natural order in the set of real numbers restricted to set T; set AT of attributes consists of two wavelength regions of spectrum $AT = \{visual(V),$ $blue\text{-}visual\ (B-V)\}$; set VAL of values of attributes consists of the magnitudes of a star in the given wavelength regions. □

The language of TIL is a standard temporal language with specific atomic formulas. An atomic piece of information in an information system is a statement of the form: object x assumes value v of attribute a. Hence, instead of propositional variables, we admit structured atomic formulas built with syntactic components of three types. Let VAROB, VARAT and VARV be sets of object variables, attribute variables and attribute value variables, respectively. They are arbitrary, pairwise disjoint, denumerable sets. The atomic formulas of the language are of the form:

$$(o, a, v) \text{ for } o \in \mathsf{VAROB},\ a \in \mathsf{VARAT},\ v \in \mathsf{VARV}.$$

The need for explicit representation of a structure of constituents of propositions is often articulated in the modern semantic theories of natural language. It is becoming a common view that a logic of propositions adequate for modelling the cognitive abilities of a natural language should explicitly exhibit this structure together with truth conditions, and that atomic propositions should represent how the propositional constituents are related (Searle & Vanderveken [29]). Information logics developed for knowledge representation in attribute-based information systems, and in particular TIL, contribute to this trend. Atomic formulas have constituents that represent basic pieces of information about a domain that is modelled by means of an information system. Complex formulas are built in the usual way from the atomic ones with the classical propositional operations and temporal operations. Atomic formula (o, a, v) represents a statement that object x assumes value v of attribute a. However, in a dynamic information system, truth or falsity of such a statement depends on a moment of time. It follows that we should define intensional semantics for our language, namely, semantics which allows us to express the time dependence of statements. We define the semantics of TIL by the notion of a model determined by a dynamic information system.

By a "model" we mean any pair $M = (S, m)$, where $S = (OB, T, ord, AT,$ $\{VAL_a : a \in AT\}, f)$ is a dynamic information system, and m is a meaning function which assigns objects to object variables, attributes to attribute variables, and values of attributes to attribute value variables: $m(o) \in OB$, $m(a) \in AT$, $m(v) \in VAL$. In the usual way we define the satisfiability of formulas in a moment of time, and for atomic formulas we have:

$$M, t \Vdash (o, a, v) \text{ iff } f(m(o), t, m(a)) = m(v).$$

Axioms of logic TIL include the standard temporal axioms characterizing the admitted timescale, and the specific axiom:

$$(o,a,v) \wedge (o,a,v') \wedge (o',a',v) \rightarrow (o',a',v') \quad (6.2)$$

which says that every value of attribute for an object is determined uniquely. It is easy to see that, since that in every information system mapping f is a function, formula (6.2) is valid in TIL.

Relational logic corresponding to TIL is similar to the logics defined in Section 6.3. The minor difference is that instead of the relational variables we introduce in the language triples of the form (o,a,v). Models of the relational logic for TIL are determined by dynamic information systems in the same way as the respective models of TIL. Translation of formulas of TIL into relations is as follows:

- $t(\Box A) = t(A)/ord$
- $t(\overline{\Box} A) = t(A)/ord^{-1}$
- $t(\Diamond A) = ord; t(A)$
- $t(\overline{\Diamond} A) = ord^{-1}; t(A)$

The specific relational rules include the rules which reflect the constraints imposed on the admitted timescale, and the following rules for the atomic formulas:

$$(a1) \quad \frac{K, x(o,a,v)y, H}{K, x(o,a,v)z, H} \quad \text{for any variable } z$$

$$(a2) \quad \frac{K, x(o,a,v)y, H}{K, x(o',a',v')y, H \quad K, x(o',a',v)y, H \quad K, x(o,a,v')y, H}$$

Rule a1 guarantees that relations (o,a,v) are right ideal relations. Rule a2 replaces axiom (6.2); it defines a class of relations (o,a,v) such that in an underlying information system, mapping f (which assigns values of attributes to objects) is a function.

References

[1] Blackburn, P. 1990. ***Nominal tense logic and other sorted intensional frameworks.*** PhD dissertation, Department of Computer Science, University of Edinburgh.

[2] Burgess, J. P. 1979. Logic and time. ***Journal of Symbolic Logic*** **44**, 566–81.

[3] Codd, E. F. 1970. A relational model for large shared data banks. ***Communications of ACM*** **13**, 377–87.

[4] Dragalin, A. 1992. Personal communication.

[5] Hoare, C. A. R. & H. Jifeng 1986. The weakest prespecification. *Fundamenta Informaticae* **IX**, 51–84, 217–62.

[6] Kripke, S. 1963. Semantical analysis of modal logic. *Zeitschrift för Matheamtische Logik und Grundlagen der Mathematik* **9**, 67–96.

[7] Kripke, S. 1965. Semantical analysis of intuitionistic logic. In *Formal systems and recursive functions*, J. N. Crossley & M. A. Dummett (eds). Amsterdam: North-Holland.

[8] Lodaya, K. & P. S. Thiagarajan 1987. *A modal logic for a subclass of event structures*. Report 220, Computer Science Department, Aarhus University.

[9] Maddux, R. 1991. The origin of relation algebras in the development and axiomatization of the calculus of relations. *Studia Logica* **50**, 421–56.

[10] Monk, D. 1964. On representable relation algebras. *Michigan Mathematical Journal* **11**, 207–10.

[11] Monk, D. 1969. Nonfinitizability of classes of representable cylindric algebras. *Journal of Symbolic Logic* **34**, 331–43.

[12] Nielsen, M., G. Plotkin & G. Winskel 1981. Petri nets, event structures and domains, part I. *Theoretical Computer Science* **13**, 85–109.

[13] Orlowska, E. 1982. Dynamic information systems. *Fundamenta Informaticae* **V**, 101–18.

[14] Orlowska, E. 1985. Logic of nondeterministic information. *Studia Logica* **XLIV**, 93–102.

[15] Orlowska, E. 1988. Relational interpretation of modal logics. In *Algebraic logic*, H. Andréka, D. Monk, I. Németi (eds), 443–71. Amsterdam: North Holland.

[16] Orlowska, E. 1989. Logic for reasoning about knowledge. *Zeitschrift för Mathematische Logik und Grundlagen der Mathematik* **35**, 559–72.

[17] Orlowska, E. 1990. Algebraic aspects of the relational knowledge representation: modal relation algebras. *Lecture Notes in Artifical Intelligence* **619**, 1–22.

[18] Orlowska, E. 1992. Relational proof system for relevant logics. *Journal of Symbolic Logic* **57**, 1425–40.

[19] Orlowska, E. 1993. Relational semantics for nonclassical logics: formulas are relations. In *Philosophical logic in Poland*, J. Woleński (ed), 167–86. Dordrecht: Kluwer.

[20] Orlowska, E. & Z. Pawlak 1984. *Logical foundations of knowledge representation.* ICS PAS Report 537.

[21] Pawlak, Z. 1981. Information systems-theoretical foundations. *Information Systems* **6**, 205–18.

[22] Pawlak, Z. 1983 *Information systems. Theoretical foundations* (in Polish). Warsaw: WNT.

[23] Pawlak, Z. 1991. *Rough sets.* Dordrecht: Kluwer.

[24] Passy, S. 1984. *Combinatory dynamic logic.* PhD dissertation, University of Sofia.

[25] Passy, S. & T. Tinchev 1985. PDL with data constants. *Information Processing Letters* **20**, 35–41.

[26] Penczek, W. 1988. A temporal logic for event structures. *Fundamenta Informaticae* **XI**, 297–326.

[27] Rasiowa, H. & R. Sikorski 1963. *The mathematics of metamathematics.* Warsaw: Polish Scientific Publishers.

[28] Schmidt, G. & T. Stroehlein 1989. *Relationen und Graphen.* Berlin: Springer.

[29] Searle, J. R. & D. Vanderveken 1985. *Foundations of illocutionary logic.* Cambridge: Cambridge University Press.

[30] Tarski, A. 1941. On the calculus of relations. *Journal of Symbolic Logic* **6**, 73–89.

[31] Tarski, A. 1955. Contributions to the theory of models. *Indagationes Mathematicae* **17**, 56–64.

[32] Vakarelov, D. 1989. Modal logics for knowledge representation. *Lecture Notes in Computer Science* **363**, 257–77.

[33] Winskel, G. 1980. *Events in computation.* PhD dissertation, Department of Computer Science, University of Edinburgh.

[34] Winskel, G. 1986. Event structure semantics for *CCS* and related languages. *Lecture Notes in Computer Science* **224**, 510–584.

Chapter 7

An analysis of structure of time in the first order predicate calculus

E. Hajnicz

Institute of Computer Scence
Polish Academy of Sciences
Ordona 21, 01-237 Warsaw, Poland

Abstract

In this chapter we describe time structures in first-order predicate calculus. We assume that time is composed of points and intervals. We discuss and compare known solutions. As it turns out, a representation of time composed of points is easier than composed of intervals—there is a smaller set of basic relations linking objects. Because of that we pay more attention to interval structures. We mainly focus on three solutions: classical (following van Benthem), Allen & Hayes' and Tsang's.

7.1 Introduction

Time is an extremely important notion in many scientific domains. It also arouses great interest among researchers engaged in computer science and has broad applications in different branches of this scientific domain.

However, before an application of a notion is possible, we should think over its meaning and structure. Therefore, we should answer the basic question: what is the time composed of. (Philosophical considerations of whether time is a real being do not have too much significance for us.)

Since in the case of space it is thought that it appears only where matter occurs, and because these notions are inseparable, time (time passing as a matter of fact) must take place only where events occur. Because of that, many researchers ([5]; [11]; [6]) consider time to be composed of events and describe event structures. Nevertheless, in considerations space, scientists often treat matter as something that occurs in space (e.g. metric space). Analogously, in the case of time we can treat events as something occurring in time and consider time as a more basic notion. In this chapter we want to describe time in such an abstract manner. Then we can assume that time is composed of points or intervals.

In both cases we should meditate on how the considered objects form time. The obvious property of time that we all experience is its passing. McTaggart ([16]; [17]) formulates two opposite concepts of time, calling them "A-series" and "B-series". In his own words, dynamic A-series is "the series of positions which runs from the far past through the near past to the present, and then from the present through the near future to the far future". The static B-series is "the series of positions which runs from earlier to later". A-series can be treated as a representation of time experienced from the inside; in this way time is described by modal tense logics. On the other hand, B-series represent time viewed from the outside. Then objects forming time appear in a certain order. First-order predicate calculus is best suited for such a description of time. It is then necessary to think over this order, i.e. to consider and describe different temporal structures. The next question is whether objects form linear, left linear or partial order. Sometimes it is also important whether this order is dense or discrete, and whether structures are infinite or not.

As it turns out, a representation of time composed of points is easier to deal with than time composed of intervals—there is a smaller set of basic relations linking objects. Consequently, in this chapter we pay more attention to interval structures.

In the literature there are many descriptions of interval structures. Here we want to focus on three solutions: classical (following [5]), Allen & Hayes [2]; [3]; [4] and Tsang's [18]; [19]. All of them describe interval temporal structures in the first order predicate calculus. We will try to compare these solutions in order to indicate the differences between these approaches as well as their similarities.

Allen & Hayes [2] define their theory as a representation of Allen's [1] interval calculus. In [7]; [8] we present a formalization of the calculus based on the classical approach. Tsang [19] presents his theory as counterpart of Allen & Hayes' theory. Thus, the approaches presented here are not put together accidentally, but have been compared in different ways before. The formalization of Allen's interval calculus based on the relation algebras proposed in [14] is connected with the above theories. However, we will not consider it here because we focus on theories of first-order predicate calculus.

We assume that notions connected with first-order predicate calculus are familiar to the reader. In the considered theories, functional symbols do not appear, so we will use a restricted version of the calculus. Moreover, in considerations of temporal structures, i.e. "a totality of temporal individuals arranged in a temporal order" [5], these structures are often defined first, and only then is their logical description created. In this chapter we want to follow this order.

In Section 7.2 point structures and in Section 7.3 interval structures are described. Section 7.4 provides a comparison of different interval structures.

7.2 Point structures

Temporal structures for time composed of points are constructed by means of the *precedence relation* $<$. Therefore, a *point structure* $\mathfrak{T}$ is an ordered couple $\langle T, < \rangle$, where T is a nonempty set of time points and $<$ is a precedence relation over T. Such a temporal structure is naturally axiomatized by the following properties:

- transitivity $\forall x, y(x < y \wedge y < z \rightarrow x < z)$
- irreflexivity $\forall x \neg(x < x)$

In this way we obtain the basic theory $\mathcal{T}_P$ describing a class of structures with partial order. Furthermore, we can obtain the theory $\mathcal{T}_L$ describing linear structure by adding an axiom:

- linearity $\forall x, y(x < y \vee x = y \vee y < x)$

or theory $\mathcal{T}_B$ describing branching (left linear) structures by adding an axiom:

- left linearity $\forall x, y(x < z \wedge y < z \rightarrow x < y \vee x = y \vee y < x)$

Other important properties that can be satisfied in point structures are the following:

- density $\forall x, y(x < y \rightarrow \exists z(x < z \wedge z < y))$
- discreteness $\forall x, y(x < y \rightarrow \exists z(x < z \wedge \neg \exists u(x < u \wedge u < z)))$
  $\forall x, y(x < y \rightarrow \exists z(z < y \wedge \neg \exists u(z < u \wedge u < y)))$
- infinity $\forall x \exists y(y < x)$ $\quad \forall x \exists y(x < y)$
- finity $\exists x \forall y \neg(x < y)$ $\quad \exists x \forall y \neg(y < x)$

By selecting different sets of the above axioms we obtain different theories describing different classes of point structures. Evidently, there exist many other properties of point structures; in particular van Benthem [5] presents axiomatizations for the structures based on the set of moments isomorphic to **Z**, **Q** and **R**.

Another way of axiomatizing of point structures consists in replacement of the *strong precedence relation* $<$ by its weak counterpart $\leq$. It is connected with the replacement of the axiom of irreflexivity by the axiom of weak antisymmetry and with a small modification of other axioms. The differences between these two approaches are insignificant and we can hardly consider them as essentially different axiomatizations. As no other, really competitive descriptions of time structures exist, we have nothing to compare.

7.3 Interval structures

In contrast to points, interdependencies between intervals can be described in different ways—intervals can form different structures. In this section we present some well known axiomatizations of *interval structures* based on first-order predicate calculus.

7.3.1 The classical axiomatization

The most famous *interval structure*, presented for instance in [5] is $\Im = \langle I, <, \subseteq \rangle$, where I is a nonempty set of time intervals, $<$ is a *precedence relation* over I and $\subseteq$ is an *inclusion relation* over I. Since theories based on primitives $<$ and $\subseteq$ are the earliest and most widely discussed ones (not only in connection with AI) such theories are called *classical.*

Let a set of variables for classical theories be denoted as Z_C. Then we can define the set of well formed formulae $\mathcal{F}_C$ as the smallest set such that if $x, y \in Z_C$, then $x < y$, $x \subseteq y \in \mathcal{F}_C$ and for each $\alpha, \beta \in \mathcal{F}_C$ and $x \in Z_C$, $\neg\alpha \in \mathcal{F}_C, \alpha \rightarrow \beta \in \mathcal{F}_C$ and $\forall x\, \alpha(x) \in \mathcal{F}_C$ hold.

An axiomatization of such a structure is much more complicated than for point structures. The basic axiomatization of interval temporal structures, presented by van Benthem, is the following (abbreviations of names of properties are due to van Benthem):

- P_TRANS $\forall x, y, z(x < y \wedge y < z \rightarrow x < z)$
- P_IRREF $\forall x \neg(x < x)$
- I_TRANS $\forall x, y, z(x \subseteq y \wedge y \subseteq z \rightarrow x \subseteq z)$
- I_REF $\forall x(x \subseteq x)$
- I_ANTIS $\forall x, y(x \subseteq y \wedge y \subseteq x \rightarrow x = y)$
- MON $\forall x, y(x < y \rightarrow \forall z(z \subseteq x \rightarrow z < y))$
  $\forall x, y(x < y \rightarrow \forall z(z \subseteq y \rightarrow x < z))$
- CONJ $\forall x, y(\exists u(u \subseteq x \wedge u \subseteq y) \rightarrow \exists z(z \subseteq x \wedge (z \subseteq y \wedge \forall u(u \subseteq x \wedge u \subseteq y \rightarrow u \subseteq z)))$

The theory composed of these axioms will be called, as a basic one, $\mathcal{T}_{CB}$.

In [8], within the framework of presentation of formalization of Allen's interval calculus [1], interval structures have also to satisfy the following axioms (also presented by van Benthem):

- LIN $\forall x, y(x < y \vee \exists u(u \subseteq x \wedge u \subseteq y) \vee y < x)$
- FREE $\forall x, y(\forall z(z \subseteq x \rightarrow \exists u(u \subseteq z \wedge u \subseteq y)) \rightarrow x \subseteq y)$
- CONV $\forall x, y, z(x < y \wedge y < z \rightarrow \forall u(x \subseteq u \wedge z \subseteq u \rightarrow y \subseteq u))$

but they did not have to satisfy CONJ (conjunction). Certainly, LIN (linearity) had to be satisfied, as Allen's interval calculus concerns location of intervals on the time-axis; if we abandon it, we obtain a kind of a partial order. We can also consider a left linear order, replacing the axiom LIN by:

- L_LIN $\forall x, y, z(x < z \wedge y < z) \rightarrow (x < y \vee \exists u(u \subseteq x \wedge u \subseteq y) \vee y < x))$

Moreover, while analyzing different properties of interval structures, the following axioms can be formulated (also considered by van Benthem):

- NEIGH $\forall x, y(x < y \rightarrow \exists z(x < z \wedge \forall u \neg(x < u \wedge u < z)))$
  $\forall x, y(y < x \rightarrow \exists z(z < x \wedge \forall u \neg(z < u \wedge u < x)))$
- DISJ $\forall x, y(\exists u(x \subseteq u \wedge y \subseteq u) \rightarrow \exists z(x \subseteq z \wedge y \subseteq z \wedge \forall v(x \subseteq v \wedge y \subseteq v \rightarrow z \subseteq v)))$
- DIR $\forall x, y \exists z(x \subseteq z \wedge y \subseteq z)$
- SUCC $\forall x \exists y(x < y)$ $\forall x \exists y(y < x)$
- MOND $\forall x, y, z(x < z \wedge y < z \rightarrow \exists v(x \subseteq v \wedge y \subseteq v \wedge v < z \wedge \forall u(x \subseteq u \wedge y \subseteq u \rightarrow v \subseteq u)))$
  $\forall x, y, z(z < x \wedge z < y \rightarrow \exists v(x \subseteq v \wedge y \subseteq v \wedge z < v \wedge \forall u(x \subseteq u \wedge y \subseteq u \rightarrow v \subseteq u)))$
- DESC $\forall x \exists y(y \subseteq x \wedge y \neq x)$
- ATOM $\forall x \exists y(y \subseteq x \wedge \forall z(z \subseteq y \rightarrow z = y))$

DESC (endless descent) and ATOM (atomicity) are the counterparts of density and discreteness for intervals. These axioms have no counterparts in Allen & Hayes' and Tsang's theories and they will not be considered in the following discussion. MOND (duration monotonicity) makes sense only when DISJ (disjunction) and DIR (directedness) are satisfied and evidently implies them. On the other hand, when DIR and SUCC (succession, infinity) are satisfied, then CONJ and DISJ can be simplified, since their premises are always satisfied; so we can consider:

- CONJ* $\exists z(z \subseteq x \wedge z \subseteq y \wedge \forall u(u \subseteq x \wedge u \subseteq y \rightarrow u \subseteq z))$
- DISJ* $\exists z(x \subseteq z \wedge y \subseteq z \wedge \forall v(x \subseteq v \wedge y \subseteq v \rightarrow z \subseteq v))$

On the basis of these axioms many theories can be defined. For instance, van Benthem presents theories axiomatizing the interval temporal structures INT($\mathbf{Z}$) and INT($\mathbf{Q}$). In consideration of our need to compare with Allen & Hayes' and Tsang's theories, we distinguish a theory

$$\mathcal{T}_C = \{\text{P\_TRANS, P\_IRREF, I\_TRANS, I\_REF, I\_ANTIS, MON, CONJ, CONV, LIN, FREE, NEIGH, DISJ, DIR, SUCC, MOND}\}.$$

We will now consider the properties of these axioms and their interdependencies.

Lemma 7.1 The formula $x < y \rightarrow \neg(x \subseteq y) \wedge \neg(y \subseteq x)$ is a theorem of the classical theory $\mathcal{T}_C$.

Proof: Consider any structure $\Im = \langle I, <, \subseteq \rangle$ to be a model of the theory $\mathcal{T}_C$. Consider any $x, y \in I$ such that $x < y$. Suppose that $x \subseteq y$. By MON we have $x < x$, contrary to P_IRREF. Analogously $\neg(y \subseteq x)$ holds. □

Convexity, monotonicity and freedom are the properties of intervals and the relations ordering them that seems to be evident. Nevertheless, van Benthem included only monotonicity in the basic theory $\mathcal{T}_{CB}$. Also Ladkin [12] considers the notion of *unconvex intervals* (intervals "with holes"). However, *convexity* is such an evident, intuitive property of intervals that very often we assume it implicitly. For instance, van Benthem, even though he considers convexity explicitly, has not pointed out that **LIN**, **MON** and **FREE** imply **CONV**.

Lemma 7.2 The axioms **LIN**, **MON** and **FREE** imply the axiom **CONV**.

Proof: Consider any structure $\Im = \langle I, <, \subseteq \rangle$ which satisfies the axioms **LIN**, **MON** and **FREE**. Consider any $x, y, z \in I$ such that $x < y \land y < z$. Consider any $u \in I$ such that $x \subseteq u \land z \subseteq u$. Consider any $v \subseteq y$. Suppose that $u < v$. But $z \subseteq u$. So, by **MON**, $z < v$. As $y < z \land z < v$ by **P_TRANS** we have $y < v$. It contradicts the fact that $v \subseteq y$. Suppose that $v < u$. But $x \subseteq u$. So, by **MON**, $v < x$. Additionally $x < y$, so by **P_TRANS** $v < y$. It is contrary to the fact that $v \subseteq y$. Thus, by **LIN**, $\exists w(w \subseteq v \land w \subseteq u)$. Therefore $\forall v(v \subseteq y \rightarrow \exists w(w \subseteq v \land w \subseteq u))$. Eventually, by **FREE**, we have $y \subseteq u$. □

Therefore, we can use such a definition of linearity only for structures of convex intervals, though on the other hand unconvex intervals can form a kind of linear order, too (see Fig. 7.1.). Certainly it is more complicated than for convex intervals.

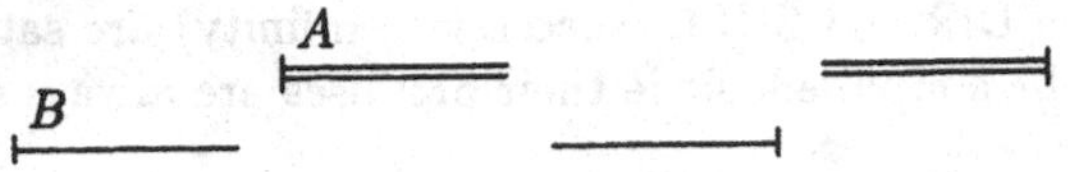

Figure 7.1. An example of the location of unconvex intervals on a linear time axis.

7.3.2 Allen and Hayes' axiomatization

Allen & Hayes [2], while encoding the interval calculus in first-order predicate calculus, define an interval temporal structure $\mathcal{J} = \langle J, \| \rangle$, where J is a nonempty set of temporal intervals and $\|$ is a binary relation of the meeting of intervals from J.

Let a set of variables for Allen & Hayes' theories be denoted as Z_A. Then we can define the set of well formed formulae $\mathcal{F}_A$ as the smallest set such that if $x, y \in Z_A$, then $x \| y \in \mathcal{F}_A$ hold and for each $\alpha, \beta \in \mathcal{F}_A$ and $x \in Z_A \neg\alpha \in \mathcal{F}_A, \alpha \rightarrow \beta \in \mathcal{F}_A$ and $\forall x\alpha(x) \in \mathcal{F}_A$ hold.

Allen & Hayes axiomatize the above structure as follows:

- M1 $\forall i, j(\exists k(i \| k \land j \| k) \rightarrow \forall l(i \| l \leftrightarrow j \| l))$
- M2 $\forall i, j(\exists k(k \| i \land k \| j) \rightarrow \forall l(l \| i \leftrightarrow l \| j))$
- M3 $\forall i, j, k, l((i \| j \land k \| l) \rightarrow i \| l$ **XOR** $\exists m(i \| m \land m \| l)$ **XOR** $\exists n(k \| n \land n \| j))$
- M4 $\forall i(\exists j, k(j \| i \land i \| k))$
- M5 $\forall i, j(i \| j \rightarrow \exists k, l, m((k \| i \land i \| j \land j \| l) \land (k \| m \land m \| l)))$

Axioms M1 and M2 determine the uniqueness of meeting places of intervals, axiom M3 determines a linear order of meeting places of intervals (see Fig. 7.2), axiom M4 determines infinity of time together with the assumption that no interval is infinite, and axiom M5 establishes the existence of a union of pairs of intervals (see Fig. 7.3).

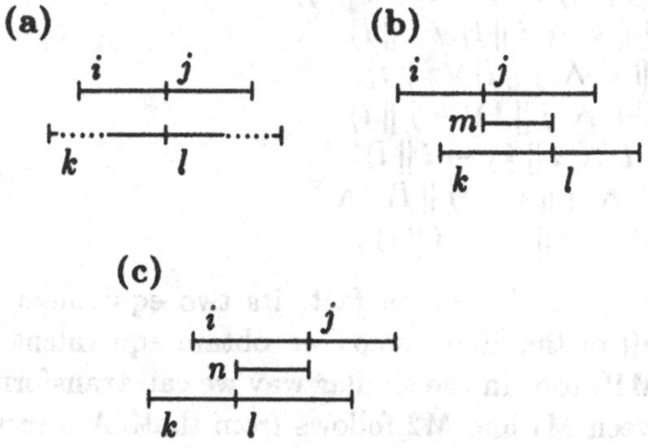

Figure 7.2 Three possible orders of pairs of meeting intervals

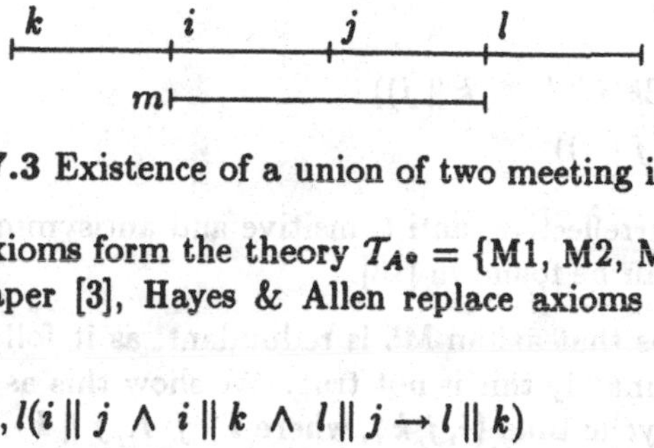

Figure 7.3 Existence of a union of two meeting intervals

The above axioms form the theory $T_{A^\bullet} = \{M1, M2, M3, M4, M5\}$.
In their next paper [3], Hayes & Allen replace axioms M1 and M2 by one axiom:

- M1′ $\forall i, j, k, l(i \parallel j \wedge i \parallel k \wedge l \parallel j \rightarrow l \parallel k)$

and they add a new axiom:

- M6 $\forall i, j, k, l(i \parallel k \wedge k \parallel j \wedge i \parallel l \wedge l \parallel j \rightarrow k = l)$

imposing the uniqueness of intervals with fixed "endings" (meeting places). So, we get the second theory $T_A = \{M1', M3, M4, M5, M6\}$. Because axioms M1 and M1′ are equivalent (see below), these theories differ only in the presence of axiom M6.
The above axiomatization ensures the validity of the basic properties of the relation of meeting of intervals.

Lemma 7.3 Axiom M1′ is equivalent to axioms M1 and M2. Moreover, axioms M1 and M2 are equivalent to each other.

Proof: Let us consider axiom M1.

$$\forall i,j(\exists k(i \parallel k \wedge j \parallel k) \rightarrow \forall l(i \parallel l \leftrightarrow j \parallel l)) \equiv$$
$$\forall i,j(\forall k(\neg(i \parallel k) \vee \neg(j \parallel k)) \vee \forall l((\neg(i \parallel l) \vee j \parallel l) \wedge (\neg(j \parallel l) \vee i \parallel l))) \equiv$$
$$\forall i,j,k,l(\neg(i \parallel k) \vee \neg(j \parallel k) \vee (\neg(i \parallel l) \vee j \parallel l) \wedge (\neg(j \parallel l) \vee i \parallel l)) \equiv$$
$$\forall i,j,k,l((\neg(i \parallel k) \vee \neg(j \parallel k) \vee \neg(i \parallel l) \vee j \parallel l) \wedge (\neg(i \parallel k) \vee \neg(j \parallel k) \vee \neg(j \parallel l) \vee i \parallel l)) \equiv$$
$$\forall i,j,k,l((\neg(i \parallel l \wedge j \parallel k \wedge i \parallel l) \vee j \parallel l) \wedge (\neg(i \parallel l \wedge j \parallel k \wedge j \parallel l) \vee i \parallel l)) \equiv$$
$$\forall i,j,k,l(((i \parallel k \wedge i \parallel l \wedge j \parallel k) \rightarrow j \parallel l) \wedge ((j \parallel k \wedge j \parallel l \wedge i \parallel k) \rightarrow i \parallel l)) \equiv$$
$$\forall i,j,k,l(i \parallel k \wedge i \parallel l \wedge j \parallel k \rightarrow j \parallel l) \wedge$$
$$\forall i,j,k,l(j \parallel k \wedge j \parallel l \wedge i \parallel k) \rightarrow i \parallel l)$$

We have obtained axiom M1′, and, in fact, its two equivalent instances together. Because in all of the above steps we obtain equivalent formulae, we can derive M1 from M1′, too. In the similar way we can transform M2 to M1′. The equivalence between M1 and M2 follows from that. A direct transformation between M1 and M2 is possible, too, but we do not present it here because it is rather complicated. □

Lemma 7.4 Axioms M1–M5 ensure that

(a) $\forall i \neg(i \parallel i)$

(b) $\forall i,j(i \parallel j \rightarrow \neg\exists k(i \parallel k \wedge k \parallel j))$

(c) $\forall i,j(i \parallel j \rightarrow \neg(j \parallel i))$

i.e. the relation $\parallel$ is irreflective, anti transitive and antisymmetric. The proof of these properties can be found in [18]. □

Ladkin [12] claims that axiom M5 is redundant, as it follows from axioms M3 and M4. Unfortunately this is not true. We show this as an example of a simple structure of cyclic time $\{i,j,k\}$, where $i \parallel j \wedge j \parallel k \wedge k \parallel i$.

Theorem 7.1 The above structure satisfies axioms M1–M4 and does not satisfy axiom M5.

Proof: We will check the satisfaction of the axioms only for the pair of meeting intervals i,j for the other pairs of intervals the reasoning is the same.

M1 There is no interval l such that $i \parallel l$ and $j \parallel l$.

M3 We have $i \parallel j$ and $j \parallel k$. Thus there exists $m = j$ such that $i \parallel m$ and $m \parallel k$. On the other hand, we have $i \parallel j$ and $k \parallel i$. Hence there exists $n = i$ such that $k \parallel n$ and $n \parallel j$.

M4 We have $k \parallel i \wedge i \parallel j$ and $i \parallel j \wedge j \parallel k$.

M5 We have $k \parallel i \wedge i \parallel j \wedge j \parallel k$, but there is no such interval m that $k \parallel m \wedge m \parallel k$.
If we added such an interval m, we would have $k \parallel i \wedge i \parallel j$ and $n = k$ such that $j \parallel n \wedge n \parallel i$ and $k \parallel m \wedge m \parallel k$, which would contradict M3.

□

The aim of Allen & Hayes was denotation of the intuitions possessed by people rather than the creation of the minimal theory. It is worth analyzing, however, whether all Allen & Hayes' axioms are "minimally" indispensable. Particular doubts are aroused by axiom M4. First, a set of intervals need not be infinite. Secondly, the exclusion of infinite intervals is not obvious; for instance McDermott [15] assumes the existence of the infinite fact *always*. A problem appears only for structures having a beginning or an ending it is possible that a union of an interval on the ending: of a structure with some other interval does not exist. However, if we replaced M4 by the weaker:

- M4′ $\forall i \exists j (i \parallel j) \vee \exists i \forall j (i \neq j \rightarrow j \parallel i \vee \exists k (j \parallel k \wedge k \parallel i)$
  $\forall i \exists j (j \parallel i) \vee \exists i \forall j (i \neq j \rightarrow i \parallel j \vee \exists k (i \parallel k \wedge k \parallel j)$

then as a result we would force each structure with one or two endings to have on each of its endings exactly one guard-interval preceding (succeeding) all other intervals, for which the required property of existence of a union would hold without any problem.

Certainly, it is not necessary for the union of any two meeting intervals to exist. Nevertheless, removing axiom M4 from the theory would admit degenerate structures, i.e. structures such that some (or even all) intervals in them could not meet any other interval. To avoid this we can introduce an even weaker variant of M4:

- M4″ $\forall i \exists j (i \parallel j \vee j \parallel i)$

It turns out that M4″ and M5 imply M4.

Lemma 7.5 Axioms M4 and M5 imply axiom M4. □

Proof: Let us consider any structure $\mathcal{J} = \langle J, \parallel \rangle$ such that axioms M4″ and M5 are satisfied in it, and any $i \in J$. Then, by M4, there exists $j \in J$ such that $i \parallel j \vee j \parallel i$. If $i \parallel j$, then, by M5, there exist $k, l \in J$ such that $k \parallel i \wedge i \parallel j \wedge j \parallel l$. Otherwise we have $j \parallel i$. Then, by M5, there exist $k', j' \in J$ such that $k' \parallel j \wedge j \parallel i \wedge i \parallel l'$. In both cases axiom M4 is satisfied. □

However, we can replace M5 by the weaker:

- M5″ $\forall i, j, k, l ((k \parallel i \wedge i \parallel j \wedge j \parallel l) \rightarrow \exists m (k \parallel m \wedge m \parallel l))$

Nevertheless, removing axiom M3 would undoubtly weaken the theory too much, since M3 not only concerns linearity, but also imposes some other important constraints on a structure (e.g. it is used in the proof of lemma 7.4). Because of that we can take $\mathcal{T}_{AB} = \{$ M1, M3, M4″$\}$ as a weakest basic theory of the axiomatization being considered (M4″ is included because a linearity condition together with the existence of isolated intervals looks strange).

In our discussion of classical theories we have paid much attention to the question of the convexity of intervals. Unfortunately, this property cannot be considered in any axiomatization based exclusively on the relation of meeting of intervals $\|$. This relation makes possible only the determination of a mutual location of endings of intervals, and does not refer to their "inside". Allen & Hayes assume implicitly that intervals are convex "in nature" (in other words their axiomatization concerns only the class of structures of convex intervals). It is evidenced by the way primitive relations of Allen's (1983) interval calculus (e.g. the *during* relation) are defined in Allen & Hayes' theory. Actually, it means treating intervals not as primitive notions, but (implicitly) as pairs of points being their beginnings and endings.

Therefore, if intervals were treated as really primitive notions, Allen & Hayes' axiomatization would not impose their convexity. We show this by an example of a particular structure of unconvex intervals:

$$\begin{aligned}\mathcal{J} = \quad & \{\langle m, n\rangle, \|: m, n \in Z, m < n,\\ & \langle m, n\rangle = \{x : m \leq x \leq m+1\} \cup \{x : n-1 \leq x \leq n\},\\ & \langle m_1, n_1\rangle \| \langle m_2, n_2\rangle \Rightarrow n_1 = m_2\}\end{aligned}$$

Such intervals are composed of one part if $n \leq m+2$, and they are composed of two parts otherwise. Thus it is a structure of unconvex intervals.

Theorem 7.2 The structure $\mathcal{J}$ defined above satisfies the axioms of Allen & Hayes' theory $\mathcal{T}_A$.

Proof: We show that $\mathcal{J}$ satisfies all Allen & Hayes' axioms.

M1 Consider any two intervals $i = \langle m_1, n_1\rangle, j = \langle m_2, n_2\rangle \in \mathcal{J}$. Consider any interval $k = \langle m_3, n_3\rangle \in \mathcal{J}$ such that $i \| k$ and $j \| k$. By the definition of $\|$ we have $n_1 = m_3$ and $n_2 = m_3$, so $n_1 = n_2$. Consider any interval $l = \langle m_4, n_4\rangle \in \mathcal{J}$. If $i \| l$, then $n_1 = m_4$, and then $n_2 = m_4$, hence $j \| l$. And if $j \| l$, then $n_2 = m_4$, and then $n_1 = m_4$, so $i \| l$.

M3 Consider any intervals $i, j, k, l \in \mathcal{J}$ such that $i \| j$ and $k \| l$. By the definition of $\mathcal{J}$ we can say that $i = \langle m_1, n_1\rangle, j = \langle n_1, k_1\rangle, k = \langle m_2, n_2\rangle$ and $l = \langle n_2, k_2\rangle$, and $m_1 < n_1 < k_1$ and $m_2 < n_2 < k_2$. As m_1, n_1, k_1, m_2, n_2, $k_2 \in Z$, there holds $n_1 = n_2$ or $n_1 < n_2$ or $n_1 > n_2$. If $n_1 = n_2$, then $\langle m_1, n_1\rangle = i \| l = \langle n_2, k_2\rangle$. If $n_1 < n_2$, then $m_1 < n_1 < n_2 < k_2$, so there exists an interval $m = \langle n_1, n_2\rangle$ and $\langle m_1, n_1\rangle = i \| m = \langle n_1, n_2\rangle = m \| l = \langle n_2, k_2\rangle$. If $n_1 > n_2$, then $m_2 < n_2 < n_1 < k_1$, so there exists an interval $n = \langle n_2, n_1\rangle$ and $\langle m_2, n_2\rangle = k \| n = \langle n_2, n_1\rangle = m \| j = \langle n_1, k_1\rangle$.

M4 Consider any interval $i = \langle m_1, n_1 \rangle \in \mathcal{J}$. Then there exist intervals $j = \langle k_1, m_1 \rangle$ and $k = \langle n_1, k_2 \rangle$ such that $j \parallel i$ and $i \parallel k$.

M5 Consider any intervals i, j, k, l such that $k \parallel i \wedge i \parallel j \wedge j \parallel l$. By the definition of $\mathcal{J}$ we can say that $k = \langle n_1, n_2 \rangle$, $i = \langle n_2, n_3 \rangle$, $j = \langle n_3, n_4 \rangle$ and $l = \langle n_4, n_5 \rangle$, where $n_1 < n_2 < n_3 < n_4 < n_5$. Then by the definition of $\mathcal{J}$ there exists $m = \langle n_2, n_4 \rangle$ and $k \parallel m \wedge m \parallel l$.

M6 Consider any $i, j, k, l \in \mathcal{J}$ such that $i \parallel k \wedge k \parallel j \wedge i \parallel l \wedge l \parallel j$. By the definition of $\mathcal{J}$ we can assume that $i = \langle k_1, m_1 \rangle, k = \langle m_1, n_1 \rangle, j = \langle n_1, l_1 \rangle$ and $l = \langle m_2, n_2 \rangle$. Since $i \parallel l$, by the definition of $\parallel$ we have $m_1 = m_2$. As also $l \parallel j$, by the definition of $\parallel$ we have $n_1 = n_2$. As there exists exactly one interval with certain interval endings in $\mathcal{J}$, there holds $k = l$. Thus the structure $\mathcal{J}$ satisfies all the axioms of the theory T_A. □

It is worth mentioning that for a similar structure of convex intervals:

$$\begin{aligned} \mathcal{J}' = \quad & \{\langle m, n \rangle, \parallel : m, n \in Z, \langle m, n \rangle = \{x : m \leq x \leq n\}, \\ & m < n, \langle m_1, n_1 \rangle \parallel \langle m_2, n_2 \rangle \iff n_1 = m_2\} \end{aligned}$$

(i.e. INT($\mathbf{Z}$)) the proof would be the same. It follows exactly from the fact that the relation of meeting of intervals gives us no chance to "look inside them". Moreover, in the class of structures with the relation of meeting of intervals $\parallel$ the structures $\mathcal{J}$ and $\mathcal{J}'$ are isomorphic!

On the other hand, the lack of a condition of convexity in Allen & Hayes' theory suggests that M3 is a linearity axiom also being satisfied in structures of unconvex intervals. However, more scrupulous examination of the axiom shows that it is true only when axiom M6 is satisfied. Otherwise we can imagine the next structure of (convex!) intervals with integer endings, but there exist two such intervals for every pair of points.

$$\begin{aligned} \mathcal{J}'' = \quad & \{\langle m, n \rangle^i, \parallel : m, n \in Z, m < n, i = 1 \vee i = 2, \\ & \langle m_1, n_1 \rangle^i \parallel \langle m_2, n_2 \rangle^j \iff n_1 = m_2\} \end{aligned}$$

Theorem 7.3 The structure $\mathcal{J}''$ defined above satisfies the axioms of Allen & Hayes' theory T_{A°.

The proof of this Theorem follows in the same way as the proof of Theorem 7.2. Certainly intervals considered in it should have upper indices, but they are not used in the proof, because the relation of meeting of intervals holds independently of values of these indices. □

Such a structure, composed of two axes often osculating with each other, can be recognized as degenerate it depends only on our "agreement" whether we treat these intervals as being located on different axes or as simultaneous ones. On the other hand, we have no kind of overlapping relation to determine whether they are simultaneous or not.

7.3.3 Tsang's axiomatization

The third, axiomatization of interval structures is that of Tsang [18]; [19]. It is worth mentioning here also because Tsang presents it as an alternative to Allen & Hayes' proposition, claiming that these approaches are equivalent.

Tsang uses an approach suggested by Kamp ([9]; [10]), based on a temporal structure $\mathcal{G} = \langle G, <, \mathcal{O} \rangle$, where G is a nonempty set of temporal intervals, $<$ is a precedence relation over G, and $\mathcal{O}$ is an overlapping relation over G. Hence, the Tsang axiomatization, like the classical one, is based on two relations, and $\mathcal{O}$, like $\subseteq$, is used to "look inside intervals". These two relations are similar to some extent, and because of that Tsang's approach seems to be closer to the classical one than to that of Allen & Hayes.

Let a set of variables for Tsang's theories be denoted by Z_T. Then we can define the set of well formed formulae $\mathcal{F}_T$ as the smallest set such that if $x, y \in Z_T$, then $x < y, x \mathcal{O} y \in \mathcal{F}_T$ and for each $\alpha, \beta \in \mathcal{F}_T$ and $x \in Z_T$, $\neg\alpha \in \mathcal{F}_T, \alpha \rightarrow \beta \in \mathcal{F}_T$ and $\forall x \alpha(x) \in \mathcal{F}_T$ hold.

For this structure Kamp suggests the following axiomatization:

- E1 $\forall x, y(x < y \rightarrow \neg(y < x))$ ANTISYM (<)
- E2 $\forall x, y, z(x < y \wedge y < z \rightarrow x < z)$ TRANS (<)
- E3 $\forall x, y(x \mathcal{O} y \rightarrow y \mathcal{O} x)$ SYM ($\mathcal{O}$)
- E4 $\forall x(x \mathcal{O} x)$ REF ($\mathcal{O}$)
- E5 $\forall x, y(x < y \rightarrow \neg(x \mathcal{O} y))$ SEP
- E6 $\forall x, y, z, u(x < y \wedge y \mathcal{O} z \wedge z < u \rightarrow x < u)$
- E7 $\forall x, y(x < y \vee x \mathcal{O} y \vee y < x)$ LIN

So we can speak about the original Kamp's theory $\mathcal{T}_{TB} = \{E1, E2, E3, E4, E5, E6, E7\}$. We will call it *basic* as it forms a basis for Tsang's considerations. In order to obtain equivalence of his description with Allen & Hayes' theory $\mathcal{T}_{A^\circ}$ Tsang defines the following additional axioms:

- E8 $\forall x \exists y(y < x \wedge \neg\exists u(y < u \wedge u < x))$
- E9 $\forall x \exists y(x < y \wedge \neg\exists u(x < u \wedge u < y))$
- E10 $\forall x, y(x \mathcal{O} y \rightarrow \exists z(z \text{ in } x \wedge z \text{ in } y \wedge \forall u(u \text{ in } x \wedge u \text{ in } y \rightarrow u \text{ in } z)))$ INTERSECTION
- E11 $\forall x, y \exists z(x \text{ in } z \wedge y \text{ in } z \wedge \forall u(u < x \wedge u < y \rightarrow u < z) \wedge \forall u(x < u \wedge y < u \rightarrow z < u))$ UNION

where $x \text{ in } y =_{def} \forall u(u \mathcal{O} x \rightarrow u \mathcal{O} y)$.

So, the basis of our further considerations concerning comparison of Tsang's concepts with other theories will be constituted by the theory $\mathcal{T}_T = \{E1, E2, E3, E4, E5, E6, E7, E8, E9, E10, E11\}$. Tsang also considers theories without the linearity axiom E7.

Unfortunately, the definition of the relation *in* given above is too weak to describe the real inclusion relation.

Example Imagine such a structure as presented in Fig. 7.4 (certainly the figure contains only a fragment of the structure). Relations $<$ and $\mathcal{O}$ are defined in it in a natural way. Then we have $x \mathcal{O} y \ \wedge \ x \mathcal{O} z \ \wedge \ y \mathcal{O} z$. The remaining intervals overlap either all of the intervals x, y, z or none of them. As a result we have x *in* y, x *in* z, y *in* x, y *in* z, z *in* x and z *in* y. Eventually, each of these intervals, according to axioms E10 and E11, can be a union as well as an intersection of any pair of these intervals. It is certainly contrary to intuition and follows either from the fact that this structure does not have a "real" intersection of intervals x and y, or from the fact that the relation *in*, defined in such a way, is not antisymmetric.

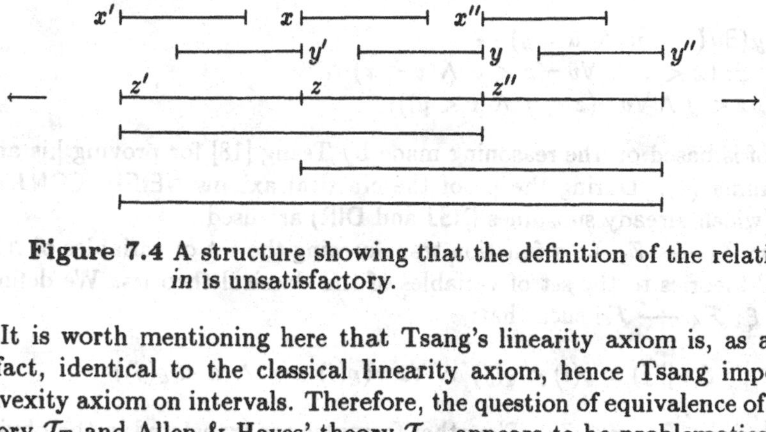

Figure 7.4 A structure showing that the definition of the relation *in* is unsatisfactory.

It is worth mentioning here that Tsang's linearity axiom is, as a matter of fact, identical to the classical linearity axiom, hence Tsang imposes the convexity axiom on intervals. Therefore, the question of equivalence of Tsang's theory $\mathcal{T}_T$ and Allen & Hayes' theory $\mathcal{T}_{A^\circ}$ appears to be problematical; it can be considered only in a class of structures of convex intervals.

7.4 Translations of axiomatizations of interval structures

As we have alternative presentations of interval temporal structures, a comparison of them appears to be necessary. Such a comparison for Allen & Hayes' theory, the classical one (the axiomatization presented by van Benthem for INT(Q)) and his own [14] was performed by Ladkin [13]. Namely, he enriched Allen & Hayes' theory $\mathcal{T}_A$ with the axiom imposing density of meeting places of intervals. The received theory constitutes an axiomatization of the interval structure INT(Q). Van Benthem proved it to be countably categorical; so all the three axiomatizations of this structure are logically equivalent.

In this chapter we want to perform such a comparison in a more straightforward way, by defining translations between the theories being considered and so examining interpretability of one of the theories in the other. First, we present a translation of Allen & Hayes' theory $\mathcal{T}_A$ into the classical theory $\mathcal{T}_C$.

7.4.1 A translation of Allen & Hayes' theory $\mathcal{T}_A$ into the classical theory $\mathcal{T}_C$

To be able to consider such a translation, we need a certain non trivial property of intervals, namely that either any two disjoint intervals meet each other, or there exists a third interval meeting both of them (see Fig. 7.5).

Figure 7.5 A problem of the meeting of intervals

Lemma 7.6 The classical theory $\mathcal{T}_C$ satisfies the following property:

$$\begin{aligned}&\forall x, y\, (\exists u\, (x < u \wedge u < y) \rightarrow \\ &\quad \exists z\, (x < z \wedge \forall v \neg (x < v \wedge v < z) \wedge \\ &\quad z < y \wedge \forall v \neg (z < v \wedge v < y)))\end{aligned}$$

The proof is based on the reasoning made by Tsang [18] for proving his analogous lemma (4). During the proof the classical axioms NEIGH, CONJ and MOND (which already subsumes DISJ and DIR) are used.

Let $\varrho\colon Z_A \longrightarrow Z_C$ be a function transforming the set of variables of Allen & Hayes' theories to the set of variables of the classical theories. We define a function $\xi\colon \mathcal{F}_A \longrightarrow \mathcal{F}_C$ such that:

$$\xi(i \parallel j) = \varrho(i) < \varrho(j) \wedge \forall x \neg (\varrho(i) < x \wedge x < \varrho(j))$$

Evidently $i, j \in Z_A$, $x \in Z_C$. The other formulae are translated in the obvious way. In what follows, we will not differentiate between the standard logical symbols in both theories since their meaning is the same and a context is always univocal.

Now we try to analyze translations of all the axioms of Allen & Hayes' theory.

Theorem 7.4 Translations of all the axioms of Allen & Hayes' theory $\mathcal{T}_A$ are satisfied in all models of the classical theory $\mathcal{T}_C$.

Proof: As all variables in axioms are bound, we omit the symbol ϱ in translations. Let $\Im = \langle I, <, \subseteq \rangle$ be a model of the theory $\mathcal{T}_C$.

$$\begin{aligned}\xi(\mathrm{M1}) = \quad &\forall i, j\, (\exists k\, (i < k \wedge \forall x \neg (i < x \wedge x < k) \wedge \\ &\qquad j < k \wedge \forall x \neg (j < x \wedge x < k)) \rightarrow \\ &\quad \forall l\, (i < l \wedge \forall x \neg (i < x \wedge x < l) \leftrightarrow \\ &\qquad j < l \wedge \forall x \neg (j < x \wedge x < l)))\end{aligned}$$

Consider any $i, j \in I$, and any $k \in I$ such that $i < k \wedge \forall x \neg (i < x \wedge x < k) \wedge j < k$ & $\forall x \neg (j < x \wedge x < k)$. Consider any l. Assume that $i < l \wedge \forall x \neg (i < x \wedge x < l)$. Suppose that $l < j$. Since $i < l$, so by P_TRANS

$i < j$. Then $i < j \land j < k$, which would mean that $\exists x\,(i < x \land x < k)$. This is a contradiction. Suppose that $\exists y\,(y \subseteq l \land y \subseteq j)$. There holds $y \subseteq l$ and $i < l$. So, by **MON**, we have $i < y$. At the same time $y \subseteq j$ and $j < k$. So, by **MON**, $y < k$. Thus $i < y$ and $y < k$, hence $\exists x\ (i < x \land x < k)$. This is a contradiction. Thus, by **LIN**, we have $j < l$. Suppose that $\exists x\,(j < x \land x < l)$. Since $x < l$, there must hold $\neg(i < x)$. Then suppose also that $x < i$. We then have $j < x \land x < i$. So, by **P_TRANS**, we have $j < i$. But at the same time $i < k$, what means that $\exists y\ (j < y \land y < k)$. This is a contradiction. So $\exists z\,(z \subseteq i \land z \subseteq x)$ follows by **LIN**. Then $z \subseteq i$ and $i < k$. So, by **MON**, $z < k$. On the other hand, $j < x$ and $z \subseteq x$. So, by **MON**, $j < z$. Thus $j < z$ and $z < k$, so $\exists y\,(j < y \land y < k)$. This is a contradiction. Thus $\forall x\, \neg(j < x \land x < l)$.
A proof of the equivalence in the opposite direction follows in the same way.

□

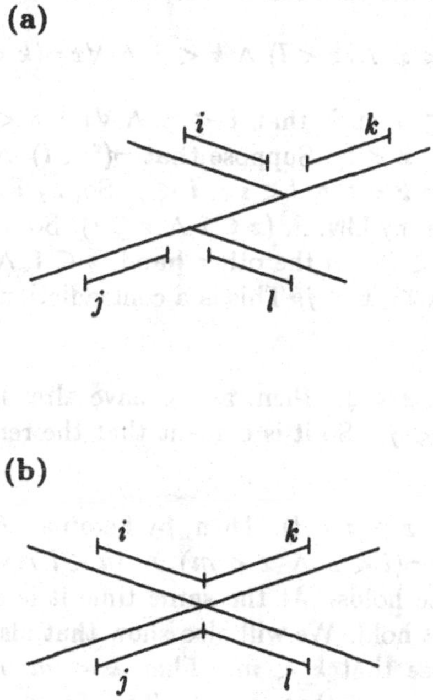

Figure 7.6 Relations of precedence and meeting of intervals in partially ordered structures.

Digression It seems interesting that in the case of a partial order, i.e. with the axiom **LIN** which was often used during the proof abandoned, $\xi(\mathrm{M1})$ cannot be proved though it should hold. This results from the exceptionality of the

case of meeting intervals, which is not taken into considerations in the classical approach. So, if there is $i < k$, $j < k$ and $j < l$, then it is not necessary for $i < l$ (see Fig. 7.6a), and in the case of meeting intervals it is just so (see Fig. 7.6b).
As follows from the figure 7.6(a), in the case of the left linear order it should be possible to perform a proof of this property.

$$\begin{aligned}
\xi\,(\text{M3}) = \;& \forall i,j,k,l(i < j \wedge \forall x\neg(i < x \wedge x < j) \wedge k < l \wedge \\
& \forall x\neg(k < x \wedge x < l) \rightarrow \\
& (i < l \wedge \forall x\neg(i < x \wedge x < l)) \text{ XOR} \\
& \exists m\,(i < m \wedge \forall x\neg(i < x \,\&\, x < m) \wedge m < l \wedge \\
& \forall x\neg(m < x \wedge x < l)) \text{ XOR} \\
& \exists n\,(k < n \wedge \forall x\neg(k < x \wedge x < n) \wedge n < j \wedge \\
& \forall x\neg(n < x \wedge x < j)))
\end{aligned}$$

Evidently, in the first case we have $i \parallel j \wedge k \parallel l \wedge i \parallel l$. So, by M1, M2, $k \parallel j$, hence the translation of the case can be extended to:

$$i < l \wedge \forall x\neg(i < x \wedge x < l) \wedge k < j \wedge \forall x\neg(k < x \wedge x < j)$$

Consider any $i,j,k,l \in I$ such that $i < j \wedge \forall x\neg(i < x \wedge x < j)$ and $k < l \wedge \forall x\neg(k < x \wedge x < l)$. Suppose that $\neg(i < l) \wedge \neg(k < j)$. Suppose also that $l < i$. We have $k < l \wedge l < i \wedge i < j$. So, by P_TRANS, $k < j$. This is a contradiction. Thus, by LIN, $\exists z\,(z \subseteq i \wedge z \subseteq l)$. So we have $z \subseteq i \wedge i < j$. Therefore, by MON, $z < j$. On the other hand, $z \subseteq l \wedge k < l$, so by MON, $k < z$. Then, by P_TRANS, $k < j$. This is a contradiction. Thus $i < l \vee k < j$. Assume that $i < l$.

1. If $\forall x\neg(i < x \wedge x < l)$, then, as we have already shown, $k < j$ and $\forall x\neg(k < x \wedge x < j)$. So it is evident that the remaining two cases do not hold.

2. Otherwise $\exists x\,(i < x \wedge x < l)$. Then, by Lemma 7.6, there exists m such that $i < m \wedge \forall x\neg(i < x \wedge x < m) \wedge m < l \wedge \forall x\neg(m < x \wedge x < l)$, so the second case holds. At the same time it is evident that now the first case does not hold. We will also show that also the third case does not hold. Suppose that $k < m$. Then $k < m \wedge m < l$. This is a contradiction. Suppose, that $m < k$. Then $m < k \wedge k < l$. This is a contradiction. So, by LIN, $\exists u\,(u \subseteq k \,\&\, u \subseteq m)$. Suppose that $k < j$. So we have $u \subseteq k \wedge k < j$. Hence, by MON, $u < j$. On the other hand, $i < m \wedge u \subseteq m$, so by MON, $i < u$. It means that $i < u \wedge u < j$. This is a contradiction. Thus $\neg(k < j)$, so the third case does not hold.

Assume that $k < j$. If $\forall x\neg(k < x \wedge x < j)$, then again we have item 1.

3. Otherwise $\exists x\,(k < x \wedge x < j)$. Then, by Lemma 7.6, there exists n such that $k < n \wedge \forall x\neg(k < x \wedge x < n) \wedge n < j \wedge \forall x\neg(n < x \wedge x < j)$, so

the third case holds. Also it is now evident that the first case does not hold. A proof that the second case does not hold proceeds analogously as in item 2.

$$\xi(\text{M4}) = \forall i \exists j,k\,(j < i \wedge \forall x \neg(j < x \wedge x < i) \wedge i < k \wedge \forall x \neg(i < x \wedge x < k))$$

Consider any $i \in I$. It follows (by SUCC) that there exist u, v such that $u < i$ and $i < v$. Then it follows (by NEIGH) that there exist j, k such that $j < i \wedge \forall x \neg(j < x \wedge x < i)$ and $i < k \wedge \forall x \neg(i < x \wedge x < k)$.

$$\begin{aligned}\xi\,(\text{M5}) = \quad & \forall i,j\,(i < j \wedge \forall x \neg(i < x \wedge x < j) \quad \rightarrow \\ & \exists k,l,m\,((k < i \wedge \forall x \neg(k < x \wedge x < i) \wedge \\ & i < j \wedge \forall x \neg(i < x \wedge x < j) \wedge \\ & j < l \wedge \forall x \neg(j < x \wedge x < l)) \wedge \\ & (k < m \wedge \forall x \neg(k < x \wedge x < m) \wedge \\ & m < l \wedge \forall x \neg(m < x \wedge x < l)))\end{aligned}$$

Consider any i, j such that $i < j \wedge \forall x \neg(i < x \,\&\, x < j)$. Then by SUCC there exist u, v such that $u < i$ and $j < v$. Then by NEIGH there exist k, l such that $k < i \wedge \forall x \neg(k < x \wedge x < i)$ and $j < l \wedge \forall x \neg(j < x \wedge x < l)$. Thus by P_TRANS we have $k < j$ and $i < l$. We have $k < i \wedge k < j$, so by MOND $\exists m(i \subseteq m \wedge j \subseteq m \,\&\, k < m \wedge \forall v\,(isubseteqv \wedge j \subseteq v \rightarrow m \subseteq v))$. As we also have $i < l \wedge j < l$, by MOND additionally $m < l$ holds. Suppose that $\exists x\,(k < x \wedge x < m)$. Then we have $x < m \wedge i \subseteq m$, so by MON $x < i$, which contradicts $\forall x \neg(k < x \wedge x < i)$. We can show that $\forall x \neg(m < x \,\&\, x < l)$ in a similar way.

$$\begin{aligned}\xi\,(\text{M6}) = \quad & \forall i,j,k,l\,((i < k \wedge \forall v \neg(i < v \wedge v < k) \wedge \\ & k < j \wedge \forall v \neg(k < v \wedge v < j) \wedge \\ & i < l \wedge \forall v \neg(i < v \wedge v < j) \wedge \\ & i < j \wedge \forall v \neg(l < v \wedge v < j)) \rightarrow k = l)\end{aligned}$$

Consider any $i, j, k, l \in I$ such that $i < k \,\&\, \forall v \neg(i < v \wedge v < k) \wedge k < j \wedge \forall v \neg(k < v \wedge v < j) \wedge i < l \wedge \forall v \neg(i < v \wedge v < j) \wedge l < j \wedge \forall v \neg(l < v \wedge v < j)$. Consider any $z \subseteq k$. Then, by MON, $i < z$ and $z < j$. Suppose that $z < l$. Then $\exists v\,(i < v \wedge v < l)$. This is a contradiction. Suppose that $l < z$. Then $\exists v\,(l < v \wedge v < j)$. This is a contradiction. Thus, by LIN, $\exists u\,(u \subseteq l \wedge u \subseteq z)$. Therefore, by FREE, $k \subseteq l$. In a similar way $l \subseteq k$ can be proved. Then, by I_ANTIS, we have $l = k$.

Therefore the translation of all the axioms of Allen & Hayes' theory $\mathcal{T}_A$ are satisfied in all models of the classical theory T_C. □

Since the translation of all the axioms of the theory $\mathcal{T}_A$ are satisfied in all models of the theory $\mathcal{T}_C$, so are the translations of all theorems of the theory $\mathcal{T}_A$. As a result, translations of all theorems of the theory $\mathcal{T}_A$ are theorems of the theory $\mathcal{T}_C$.

Corollary: Allen & Hayes' theory $\mathcal{T}_A$ is interpretable in the classical theory $\mathcal{T}_C$. □

It is easy to see that for the proof of the translations of Allen & Hayes' axioms we have to use many classical axioms that do not belong to the basic theory $\mathcal{T}_{CB}$, even for the proof of the axioms from the basic theory $\mathcal{T}_{AB}$. This is partially justified by differences between approaches being used. The basic Allen & Hayes' theory (even considering only axioms M1 and M3 and ignoring M4″!) requires satisfaction of the classical axioms LIN, NEIGH, CONJ and MOND (all except the first were used in the proof of axiom M3 only). The need to apply NEIGH is obvious, as it is the main property of intervals in $\mathcal{T}_A$. For the proof of the other axioms of the theory $\mathcal{T}_A$, the axiom SUCC should also be satisfied. Note that SUCC is used not only in the proof of its counterpart M4, but also to prove M5. However, this is not the case for its weaker counterpart M5′.

It is interesting that some of the axioms of the basic theory $\mathcal{T}_{CB}$ were not used in the above proof. These axioms are I_TRANS and I_REF. It is easy to see that these are the axioms connected with "looking inside intervals". Moreover, the axiom I_ANTIS is used only to prove the additional axiom M6. However, the latter is actually a counterpart of the formulae describing uniqueness of intervals occupying the same place in time.

Because the axiom LIN had to be satisfied, we considered only structures satisfying the axiom CONV. Thus, the translation of the theory that does not contain a convexity condition holds only in structures of convex intervals of the other one. It is possible, however, that if we had a weaker linearity condition then such a strange situation would not appear.

7.4.2 A translation of the classical theory $\mathcal{T}_C$ into Allen & Hayes' theory $\mathcal{T}_A$

Now we try to perform the opposite operation, i.e. to perform a translation of the classical theory $\mathcal{T}_C$ into Allen & Hayes' theory $\mathcal{T}_A$. Unfortunately, the latter is too weak to perform this operation, i.e. we are not able to express the relation of inclusion of intervals in it. It results from the fact already mentioned several times that Allen & Hayes' theory considers only endings, meeting places of intervals, without "looking inside them". To avoid a need for "looking inside intervals" we have to restrict ourselves to the class of structures of convex intervals. In what follows we will talk about convex intervals only, unless it is explicitly formulated otherwise.

Let $\varrho' : Z_C \longrightarrow Z_A$ be a function transforming the set of variables of the classical theories to the set of variables of Allen & Hayes' theories. We define a function $\xi' : \mathcal{F}_C \longrightarrow \mathcal{F}_A$ such that:

- $\xi'(x < y) = \varrho'(x) \parallel \varrho'(y) \vee \exists i (\varrho'(x) \parallel i \wedge i \parallel \varrho'(y))$

- $\xi'(x \subseteq y) = \exists i, j\,(i \parallel \varrho'(y) \wedge \varrho'(y) \parallel j \wedge (i \parallel \varrho'(x) \vee \exists k(i \parallel k \wedge k \parallel \varrho'(x)) \wedge (\varrho'(x) \parallel j \vee \exists k\,(\varrho'(x) \parallel k \wedge k \parallel j))$

Evidently $x, y \in Z_C$, $i, j, k \in Z_A$. Similarly, as before, we will not differentiate between the standard logical symbols in the theories.

As we already have the translations in both directions, we are able to carry out more scrupulous analysis of these translations. As in the previous section, we omit the symbol ϱ and ϱ' in the following discussion.

Theorem 7.5 Axiom M5 of Allen & Hayes' theory $\mathcal{T}_A$ implies that

$$\xi'(\xi(i \parallel j)) \leftrightarrow i \parallel j.$$

Proof:

- $\xi(i \parallel j) = i < j \wedge \forall x \neg(i < x \wedge x < j)$
- $\xi'(i < j \wedge \forall x \neg(i < x \wedge x < j)) = (i \parallel j \vee \exists k\,(i \parallel k \wedge k \parallel j) \wedge \forall x \neg((i \parallel x \vee \exists k\,(i \parallel k \wedge k \parallel x)) \wedge (x \parallel j \vee \exists k\,(x \parallel k \wedge k \parallel j)))$

Consider any structure $\mathcal{J} = \langle J, \parallel \rangle$ such that it satisfies axiom M5. Consider any $i, j \in J$. Suppose that $i \parallel j$. Evidently $i \parallel j \vee \exists k\,(i \parallel k \wedge k \parallel j)$. Consider any $x \in J$. Assume that $i \parallel x$. If also $x \parallel j$, then we have $i \parallel x \wedge x \parallel j$, which contradicts the assumption that $i \parallel j$. Consider such a k', that $x \parallel k' \wedge k' \parallel j$. So we have $i \parallel x \wedge x \parallel k' \wedge k' \parallel j$, and then, by M5, there exists l such that $i \parallel l \wedge l \parallel j$. Thus $\neg(i \parallel x \wedge (x \parallel j \vee \exists k'(x \parallel k' \wedge k' \parallel j)))$. Analogously we can show that $\neg(\exists k\,(i \parallel k \wedge k \parallel x) \wedge (x \parallel j \vee \exists k'(x \parallel k' \wedge k' \parallel j)))$. Thus we have shown that $i \parallel j \rightarrow (i \parallel j \vee \exists k\,(i \parallel k \wedge k \parallel j) \wedge \forall x \neg((i \parallel x \vee \exists k\,(i \parallel k \wedge k \parallel x)) \wedge (x \parallel j \vee \exists k\,(x \parallel k \wedge k \parallel j))))$, i.e. we have the only-if part ($\leftarrow$) of our theorem. We have also to prove the if part ($\rightarrow$) of the theorem.

Suppose that $\exists k\,(i \parallel k \wedge k \parallel j)$. It contradicts the statement $\forall x \neg(i \parallel x \wedge x \parallel j)$, and thus the statement $\forall x \neg((i \parallel x \vee \exists k\,(i \parallel k \wedge k \parallel x)) \wedge (x \parallel j \vee \exists k\,(x \parallel k \wedge k \parallel j)))$. Thus $i \parallel j$. The fact that it is consistent with the rest of the expression follows from the first part of the proof. □

Theorem 7.6 The axioms P_TRANS, NEIGH, MOND and CONJ of the classical theory $\mathcal{T}_C$ imply that $\xi(\xi'(x < y)) \leftrightarrow x < y$.

Proof:

- $\xi'(x < y) = x \parallel y \vee \exists i\,(x \parallel i \wedge i \parallel y)$
- $\xi(x \parallel y \vee \exists i\,(x \parallel i \wedge i \parallel y)) = x < y \wedge \forall z \neg(x < z \wedge z < y) \vee \exists i\,(x < i \wedge \forall z \neg(x < z \wedge z < i) \wedge i < y \wedge \forall z \neg(i < z \wedge z < y))$

Consider any structure $\Im = \langle I, <, \subseteq \rangle$ such that it satisfies the axioms P_TRANS, NEIGH, MOND and CONJ. Consider any $x, y \in I$. Suppose that $x < y$. By Lemma 7.6 we have $\forall z \neg(x < z \wedge z < y) \vee \exists i (x < i \wedge \forall z \neg(x < z \wedge z < i) \wedge i < y \wedge \forall z \neg(i < z \wedge z < y))$, so the only-if part ($\leftarrow$) of our theorem is satisfied. So, the proof of the if ($\rightarrow$) part remains. If $x < y \wedge \forall z \neg(x < z \wedge z < y)$, then evidently $x < y$. And if $\exists i (x < i \wedge \forall z \neg(x < z \wedge z < i) \wedge i < y \wedge \forall z \neg(i < z \wedge z < y))$, then by P_TRANS $x < y$. □

The necessity of using axiom M5 and Lemma 7.6 in the above proofs results from the way the precedence relation $<$ has been translated into Allen & Hayes' theory: there should be exactly one interval meeting any two disjoint intervals, i.e. not just any (possibly even infinite) sequence of intervals.

As the inclusion relation $\subseteq$ has not been used in any of the above translation, so these theorems assure the mutual correctness of translations of the classical precedence relation $<$ and Allen & Hayes' meeting relation $\|$.

Theorem 7.7 The axioms P_TRANS, MON, SUCC, NEIGH, LIN and FREE of the classic theory $\mathcal{T}_C$ entail $\xi(\xi'(x \subseteq y)) \leftrightarrow x \subseteq y$.

Proof: Consider any structure $\Im = \langle I, <, \subseteq \rangle$ which satisfies the axioms P_TRANS, MON, SUCC, NEIGH, LIN and FREE.

$$\begin{aligned}
\xi'(x \subseteq y) = \; & \exists i, j (i \| y \wedge y \| j \wedge (i \| x \vee \exists k (i \| k \wedge k \| x)) \wedge \\
& (x \| j \vee \exists k (x \| k \wedge k \| j)))
\end{aligned}$$

$$\begin{aligned}
\xi(\exists i, j (i \| y \wedge y \| j \wedge (i \| x \vee \exists k (i \| k \wedge k \| x)) \wedge & \\
(x \| j \vee \exists k (x \| k \wedge k \| j)))) = & \\
\exists i, j ((i < y \wedge \forall u \neg(i < u \wedge u < y)) \wedge & \\
(y < j \wedge \forall u \neg(y < u \wedge u < y)) \wedge & \\
(i < x \wedge \forall u \neg(i < u \wedge u < x) \vee & \\
\exists k (i < k \wedge \forall u \neg(i < u \wedge u < k) \wedge k < x \wedge & \\
\forall u \neg(k < u \wedge u < x))) \wedge & \\
(x < j \wedge \forall u \neg(x < u \wedge u < j) \vee & \\
\exists k (x < k \wedge \forall u \neg(x < u \wedge u < k) \wedge k < j \wedge & \\
\forall u \neg(k < u \wedge u < j)))) &
\end{aligned}$$

From the above we can infer, using P_TRANS, that $\exists i, j (i < y \wedge \forall u \neg(i < u \wedge u < y) \wedge y < j \wedge \forall u \neg(y < u \wedge u < y) \wedge i < x \wedge x < j)$. By Theorem 7.5 these formulas are equivalent.

Note that the inclusion relation $\subseteq$ does not appear in this formula. It follows from the fact that it does not appear in the translation of the relation of meeting of intervals, $\|$.

Suppose that $x \subseteq y$. By SUCC there exist i', j' such that $i' < y \wedge y < j'$. Then, by NEIGH, there exist i, j such that $i < y \wedge \forall u \neg(i < u \wedge u < y)$ and $y < j \wedge \forall u \neg(y < u \,\&\, u < j)$. On the other hand, by MON, $i < x \wedge x < j$. Consider i, j such that $i < y \wedge \forall u \neg(i < u \wedge u < y)$ and $i < j \wedge \forall u \neg(y <$

$u \wedge u < j)$. Suppose that $\neg(x \subseteq y)$. By **FREE** there exists z such that: $z \subseteq x \wedge \forall v \neg(v \subseteq z \wedge v \subseteq y)$. Consider any $z \subseteq x$. By **MON**, $i < z$ and $z < j$. Suppose that $z < y$. Then $\exists u\,(i < u \wedge u < y)$. This is a contradiction. Suppose that $y < z$. Then $\exists u\,(y < u \wedge u < j)$. This is a contradiction. Thus, by **LIN**, $\exists u\,(u \subseteq y \wedge u \subseteq z)$. Therefore, by **FREE**, $x \subseteq z$. □

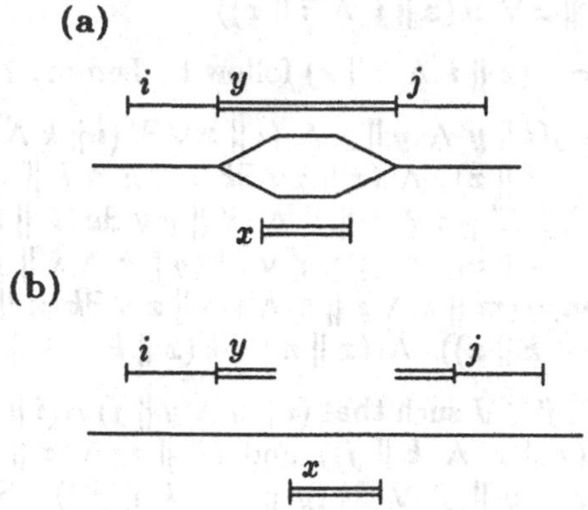

Figure 7.7 The translation of the relation ⊆ into Allen & Hayes' theory in comparison with the properties of interval structures

In the above proof we have used such nonbasic axioms as **SUCC** and **LIN**. It turns out that for such a definition of the inclusion relation ⊆, the convexity of intervals is not sufficient—the linearity of the structure is needed (see Fig. 7.7). Unfortunately, a more adequate translation of the inclusion relation onto Allen & Hayes' theory cannot be defined.

Theorem 7.8 Translations of the axioms of the classical theory T_C are satisfied in all models of Allen & Hayes' theory T_A.

Proof: Consider any structure $\mathcal{J} = \langle J, \| \rangle$ such that it is a model of the theory T_A.

$$\xi'(\mathsf{P\_TRANS}) = \forall x, y, z\,((x \| y \vee \exists i(x \| i \wedge i \| y)) \wedge (y \| z \vee \exists i(y \| i \wedge i \| z)) \rightarrow (x \| z \vee \exists i(x \| i \wedge i \| z)))$$

Consider any $x, y, z \in J$ such that $x \| y \vee \exists i\,(x \| i \wedge i \| y)$ and $y \| z \vee \exists i\,(y \| i \wedge i \| z)$. Let $x \| y$.

1. If $y \| z$, then $\exists i\,(x \| i \wedge i \| z)$.

2. Otherwise $\exists i\,(y \| i \wedge i \| z)$. By M5 there exists m such that $x \| m \wedge m \| z$. Otherwise $\exists i\,(x \| i \wedge i \| y)$.

3. If $y \parallel z$, then the reasoning proceeds as in the item 2.

4. Otherwise $\exists j\,(y \parallel j \wedge j \parallel z)$. We have $x \parallel i \wedge i \parallel y \wedge y \parallel j \& j \parallel z$. By M5 there exists k such that $x \parallel k \wedge k \parallel j$. Then, by M5, there exists m such that $x \parallel m \wedge m \parallel z$.

$$\xi'(\mathsf{P\_IRREF}) = \quad \exists x\, \neg(x \parallel x \vee \exists i\,(x \parallel i \wedge i \parallel x))$$

Both formulae $\neg(x \parallel x)$ and $\neg\exists i\,(x \parallel i \wedge i \parallel x)$ follow by Lemma 7.4.

$$\begin{aligned}\xi'(\mathsf{I\_TRANS}) = \quad & \forall x, y, z(\exists i, j(i \parallel y \wedge y \parallel j \wedge (i \parallel x \vee \exists k(i \parallel k \wedge \\ & \quad k \parallel x)) \wedge (x \parallel j \vee \exists k\,(x \parallel k \wedge k \parallel j))) \wedge \\ & \exists i', j'\,(i' \parallel z \wedge z \parallel j' \wedge (i' \parallel y \vee \exists k\,(i' \parallel k \wedge \\ & \quad k \parallel y)) \wedge (y \parallel j' \vee \exists k\,(y \parallel k \wedge k \parallel j'))) \rightarrow \\ & \exists m, n\,(m \parallel z \wedge z \parallel n \wedge (m \parallel x \vee \exists k\,(n \parallel k \wedge \\ & \quad k \parallel x)) \wedge (x \parallel n \vee \exists k\,(x \parallel k \wedge k \parallel n))))\end{aligned}$$

Consider $x, y, z \in J$ and $i, j, i', j' \in J$ such that $(i \parallel y \wedge y \parallel j) \wedge (i \parallel x \vee \exists k\,(i \parallel k \wedge k \parallel x)) \wedge (x \parallel j \vee \exists k\,(x \parallel k \wedge k \parallel j))$ and $(i' \parallel z \wedge z \parallel j') \wedge (i' \parallel y \vee \exists k\,(i' \parallel k \wedge k \parallel y)) \wedge (y \parallel j' \vee \exists k\,(y \parallel k \wedge k \parallel j'))$. So we have $i \parallel y \wedge y \parallel j \wedge i' \parallel z \wedge z \parallel j'$. Let $i \parallel x$ and $i' \parallel y$. Then $i \parallel x \wedge i \parallel y \wedge i' \parallel y$. So, by M2, $i' \parallel x$. Thus $i' \parallel x \wedge i' \parallel z$, hence $\exists m\,(m \parallel z \wedge m \parallel x)$.

Let $x \parallel j$.

1. If $y \parallel j'$, then we have $x \parallel j \wedge y \parallel j \wedge y \parallel j'$. So, by M1, $x \parallel j'$. Then $x \parallel j' \wedge z \parallel j'$, hence $\exists n\,(x \parallel n \wedge z \parallel n)$.

2. Otherwise $\exists k\,(y \parallel k \wedge k \parallel j')$. Then $x \parallel j \wedge y \parallel j \wedge y \parallel k$. So, by M1, $x \parallel k$. Thus $z \parallel j' \wedge \exists k\,(x \parallel k \wedge k \parallel j')$, hence $\exists n\,(z \parallel n \wedge \exists k\,(x \parallel k \wedge k \parallel n))$. Otherwise $\exists k\,(x \parallel k \wedge k \parallel j)$.

3. If $y \parallel j'$, then we have $y \parallel j \wedge k \parallel j \wedge y \parallel j'$. So, by M1, there holds $k \parallel j'$. Thus $z \parallel j' \wedge \exists k\,(x \parallel k \wedge k \parallel j')$.

4. Otherwise $\exists k'\,(y \parallel k' \wedge k' \parallel j')$. Then $k \parallel j \wedge y \parallel j \wedge y \parallel k'$. So, by M1, $k \parallel k'$. Then $x \parallel k \wedge k \parallel k' \wedge k' \parallel j'$. So, by M5, there exists l such that $x \parallel l \wedge \exists l\,(x \parallel l \wedge l \parallel j')$.

Thus in all the above cases the consequent of the implication is satisfied. The further course of the proof is analogous to the part already done, but we should use axiom M2 instead of M1 while considering interdependencies between left endings of intervals.

$$\begin{aligned}\xi'(\mathsf{I\_REF}) = \quad & \forall x \exists i, j\,(i \parallel x \wedge \ \parallel j \wedge (i \parallel x \vee \exists k\,(i \parallel k \wedge \\ & \quad k \parallel x)) \wedge (x \parallel j \vee \exists k\,(x \parallel k \wedge k \parallel j)))\end{aligned}$$

Consider any $x \in J$. By M4 there exist $i, j \in J$ such that $i \parallel x \wedge x \parallel j$. Thus in the obvious way the next two conjuncts are satisfied.

$$\xi'(\mathsf{I\_ANTIS}) = \forall x, y(\exists i, j\,(i \parallel y \wedge y \parallel j \wedge (i \parallel x \vee \exists k\,(i \parallel k \wedge k \parallel x)) \wedge (x \parallel j \vee \exists k\,(x \parallel k \wedge k \parallel j))) \wedge \exists i', j'\,(i' \parallel x \wedge x \parallel j' \wedge (i' \parallel y \vee \exists k\,(i' \parallel k \wedge k \parallel y)) \wedge (y \parallel j' \vee \exists k(y \parallel k \wedge k \parallel j'))) \rightarrow x = y)$$

Consider $x, y \in J$ and $i, j, i', j' \in J$ such that $i \parallel y \wedge y \parallel j \wedge (i \parallel x \vee \exists k\,(i \parallel k \wedge k \parallel x)) \wedge (x \parallel j \vee \exists k\,(x \parallel k \wedge k \parallel j))$ and $i' \parallel x \wedge x \parallel j' \wedge (i' \parallel y \vee \exists k\,(i' \parallel k \wedge k \parallel y)) \wedge (y \parallel j' \vee \exists k\,(y \parallel k \wedge k \parallel j'))$. So we have $i \parallel y \wedge y \parallel j \wedge i' \parallel x \wedge x \parallel j'$. Then we also have $i \parallel x \wedge i \parallel y \wedge i' \parallel x$. So, by M2, $i' \parallel y$. Let $i \parallel x$.

1. Let $x \parallel j$. Then we have $x \parallel j \wedge y \parallel j \wedge x \parallel j'$. So, by M1, $y \parallel j'$. And then there holds $i \parallel x \wedge x \parallel j \wedge i \parallel y \wedge y \parallel j$. So, by M6, $x = y$.

2. Otherwise $\exists k\,(x \parallel k \wedge k \parallel j)$. Suppose that $y \parallel j'$. We have $x \parallel k \wedge x \parallel j' \wedge y \parallel j'$. So, by M2, $y \parallel k$. Thus we have $y \parallel k \wedge k \parallel j \wedge y \parallel j$. It contradicts the anti transitivity of $\parallel$ (Lemma 7.4.). Otherwise $\exists k'\,(y \parallel k' \wedge k' \parallel j')$. We have $x \parallel j' \wedge k' \parallel j' \wedge x \parallel k$. So, by M1, $k' \parallel k$. Therefore we have $y \parallel k' \wedge k' \parallel k \wedge k \parallel j$. So, by M5, there exists l such that $y \parallel l \wedge l \parallel j$. And then we have $y \parallel l \wedge l \parallel j \wedge y \parallel j$, which contradicts the anti transitivity of $\parallel$ again.

Otherwise, $\exists k\,(i \parallel k \wedge k \parallel x)$. As $i' \parallel y \vee \exists k'\,(i' \parallel k' \wedge k' \parallel y)$, with the same argument as in item 2, we obtain a contradiction again.

Thus for the proof of I_ANTIS — the axiom from the basic classical theory $\mathcal{T}_{CB}$ the additional axiom M6 was needed. On the other hand, it seems evident that I_ANTIS of $\mathcal{T}_C$ and M6 of $\mathcal{T}_A$ are the counterparts of each other in these theories (in Theorem 7.4 I_ANTIS was used for the proof of M6 only).

$$\xi'(\mathsf{MON}^1) = \forall x, y((x \parallel y \vee \exists k(x \parallel k \wedge k \parallel y)) \rightarrow \exists z\,(\exists i, j(i \parallel x \wedge x \parallel j \wedge (i \parallel z \vee \exists k\,(i \parallel k \wedge k \parallel z)) \wedge (z \parallel j \vee \exists k\,(z \parallel k \wedge k \parallel j))) \rightarrow (z \parallel y \vee \exists k\,(z \parallel k \wedge k \parallel y))))$$

Consider any $x, y \in J$ such that $x \parallel y \vee \exists k\,(x \parallel k \wedge k \parallel y)$ and any $z \in J$ such that $\exists i, j\,(i \parallel x \wedge x \parallel j \wedge (i \parallel z \vee \exists k\,(i \parallel k \wedge k \parallel z)) \wedge (z \parallel j \vee \exists k\,(z \parallel k \wedge k \parallel j)))$. Thus we have $i \parallel x \wedge x \parallel j$. Let $x \parallel y$.

1. Let $z \parallel j$. Then we have $x \parallel j \wedge z \parallel j \wedge x \parallel y$. So, by M1, $z \parallel y$, so the consequent of the implication is satisfied.

2. Otherwise $\exists k\,(z \parallel k \wedge k \parallel j)$. We have $x \parallel j \wedge k \parallel j \wedge x \parallel y$. So, by M1, $k \parallel y$. Thus $\exists k\,(z \parallel k \wedge k \parallel y)$, so the consequent of the implication is satisfied. Otherwise $\exists k\,(x \parallel k \wedge k \parallel y)$.

3. Let $z \parallel j$. Then we have $x \parallel j \wedge z \parallel j \wedge x \parallel k$. So, by M1, $z \parallel k$. Thus $\exists k\,(z \parallel k \wedge k \parallel y)$, so the consequent of the implication is satisfied.

4. Otherwise $\exists k'(z \parallel k' \wedge k' \parallel j)$. We have $x \parallel k \wedge x \parallel j \wedge k' \parallel j$. So, by M2, $k' \parallel k$. Therefore $z \parallel k \wedge k' \parallel k \wedge k \parallel y$. So, by M5, $\exists l(z \parallel l \wedge l \parallel y)$, hence the consequent of the implication is satisfied.

$$\xi'(\mathsf{MON}^2) = \forall x, y((x \parallel y \vee \exists k\,(x \parallel k \wedge k \parallel y)) \rightarrow \exists z(\exists i, j(i \parallel y \wedge y \parallel j \wedge (i \parallel z \vee \exists k(i \parallel k \wedge k \parallel z)) \wedge (z \parallel j \vee \exists k\,(z \parallel k \wedge k \parallel j))) \rightarrow (x \parallel z \vee \exists k\,(x \parallel k \wedge k \parallel z))))$$

The proof is analogous (symmetrical) to $\xi'(\mathsf{MON}^1)$.

$$\begin{aligned}\xi'(\mathsf{CONJ}) = \forall x, y(&\exists u\,(\exists i, j(i \parallel x \wedge x \parallel j \wedge (i \parallel u \vee \exists k\,(i \parallel k \wedge k \parallel u)) \wedge (u \parallel j \vee \exists k\,(u \parallel k \wedge k \parallel j))) \wedge \\ &\exists i', j'(i' \parallel y \wedge y \parallel j' \wedge (i' \parallel u \vee \exists k(i' \parallel k \wedge k \parallel u)) \wedge (u \parallel j' \vee \exists k\,(u \parallel k \wedge k \parallel j')))) \rightarrow \\ &\exists z(\exists i, j(i \parallel x \wedge x \parallel j \wedge (i \parallel z \vee \exists k(i \parallel k \wedge k \parallel z)) \wedge (z \parallel j \vee \exists k\,(z \parallel k \wedge k \parallel j))) \wedge \\ &\exists i', j'(i' \parallel y \wedge y \parallel j' \wedge (i' \parallel z \vee \exists k(i' \parallel k \wedge k \parallel z)) \wedge (z \parallel j' \vee \exists k\,(z \parallel k \wedge k \parallel j'))) \wedge \\ &\forall v(\exists i, j(i \parallel x \wedge x \parallel j \wedge (i \parallel v \vee \exists k(i \parallel k \wedge k \parallel v)) \wedge (v \parallel j \vee \exists k\,(v \parallel k \wedge k \parallel j))) \wedge \\ &\exists i', j'(i' \parallel y \wedge y \parallel j' \wedge (i' \parallel v \vee \exists k\,(i' \parallel k \wedge k \parallel v)) \wedge (v \parallel j' \vee \exists k\,(v \parallel k \wedge k \parallel j'))) \rightarrow \\ &\exists m, n(m \parallel z \wedge z \parallel n \wedge (m \parallel v \vee \exists k\,(m \parallel k \wedge k \parallel v)) \wedge (v \parallel n \vee \exists k\,(v \parallel k \wedge k \parallel n))))))\end{aligned}$$

Consider $x, y \in J$ and $i, j, i', j' \in J$ such that $i \parallel x \wedge x \parallel j$ and $i' \parallel y \wedge y \parallel j'$. So we have $i \parallel x \wedge i' \parallel y$ and $x \parallel j \wedge y \parallel j'$. We will consider all the possibilities following from M3.

Let $i \parallel y$. Then we have $i' \parallel x$.

1. Let $y \parallel j$. Hence we have $x \parallel j'$. Consider $z = x$. Then $i \parallel z \wedge z \parallel j$. At the same time $i \parallel z \wedge i \parallel y \wedge i' \parallel y$. So, by M2, $i' \parallel z$. On the other hand $z \parallel j \wedge y \parallel j \wedge y \parallel j'$. So, by M1, $z \parallel j'$. Consider any v such that $(i \parallel v \vee \exists k\,(i \parallel k \wedge k \parallel v)) \wedge (v \parallel j \vee \exists k\,(v \parallel k \wedge k \parallel j)) \wedge (i' \parallel v \vee \exists k\,(i' \parallel k \wedge k \parallel v)) \wedge (v \parallel j' \vee \exists k\,(v \parallel k \wedge k \parallel j'))$. If $i \parallel v$, then $i \parallel v \wedge i \parallel z$, so $\exists m\,(m \parallel z \wedge m \parallel v)$. Otherwise $\exists k\,(i \parallel k \wedge k \parallel v)$, so $\exists m\,(m \parallel z \wedge \exists k\,(m \parallel k \wedge k \parallel v))$. If $v \parallel j$, then $v \parallel j \wedge z \parallel j$, so $\exists n(z \parallel n \wedge v \parallel n)$. Otherwise $\exists k\,(v \parallel k \wedge k \parallel j)$, so $\exists m(z \parallel n \wedge \exists k\,(v \parallel k \wedge k \parallel n))$. Eventually we can see that such a z satisfies the consequent of the implication.

2. Let $\exists p(y \parallel p \wedge p \parallel j)$. Consider $z = y$. Then $i \parallel z \wedge i' \parallel z \wedge z \parallel i' \wedge \exists k\,(z \parallel k \wedge k \parallel j)$. Consider any v such that $(i \parallel v \vee \exists k\,(i \parallel k \wedge k \parallel v)) \wedge (v \parallel j \vee \exists k\,(v \parallel k \wedge k \parallel j)) \wedge (i' \parallel v \vee \exists k\,(i' \parallel k \wedge k \parallel v)) \wedge (v \parallel j' \vee \exists k\,(v \parallel k \wedge k \parallel j'))$. Performing an analogous reasoning as in item 1 (for i', j' instead of i, j) we obtain the remaining conditions which show that such a z satisfies the consequent of the implication.

3. Let $\exists p\,(x \parallel p \wedge p \parallel j')$. Consider $z = x$. This is the case analogous to item 2. Let $\exists p\,(i' \parallel p \wedge p \parallel x)$.

4. Let $y \parallel j$. Then we have $x \parallel j'$. Consider $z = x$. This is the case analogous to item 2.

5. Let $\exists q\,(y \parallel q \wedge q \parallel j)$. We have $p \parallel x \wedge y \parallel q$. Let us consider all the possibilities following from M3.

   (i) Let $y \parallel x$. Hence we have $p \parallel q$. Then $i \parallel x \wedge y \parallel x \wedge y \parallel j'$. So, by M1, $i \parallel j'$. Suppose that there exists u such that $(i \parallel u \vee \exists k\,(i \parallel k \wedge k \parallel u)) \wedge (u \parallel j \vee \exists k\,(u \parallel k \wedge k \parallel j))$ and $(i' \parallel u \vee \exists k\,(i' \parallel k \wedge k \parallel u)) \wedge (u \parallel j' \vee \exists k\,(u \parallel k \wedge k \parallel j'))$. If $i \parallel u \wedge u \parallel j'$, then it is contrary the anti transitivity of $\parallel$ (Lemma 7.4). And if $i \parallel u \wedge \exists k\,(u \parallel k \wedge k \parallel j)$, then by M5 $\exists l\,(i \parallel l \wedge l \parallel j)$, which is contrary with anti transitivity of $\parallel$. In a similar way we can prove the remaining cases to be contrary with anti transitivity of $\parallel$. Thus the consequent of the implication is satisfied.

   (ii) Let $\exists r\,(y \parallel r \wedge r \parallel x)$. Suppose that there exists u such that $(i \parallel u \vee \exists k\,(i \parallel k \wedge k \parallel u)) \wedge (u \parallel j \vee \exists k\,(u \parallel k \wedge k \parallel j))$ and $(i' \parallel u \vee \exists k\,(i' \parallel k \wedge k \parallel u)) \wedge (u \parallel j' \vee \exists k\,(u \parallel k \wedge k \parallel j'))$. Suppose that $i \parallel u$. Then $i \parallel x \wedge r \parallel x \wedge i \parallel u$. So, by M1, $r \parallel u$. So we have $y \parallel r \wedge r \parallel u$. Suppose that $u \parallel j'$. Thus we have $y \parallel r \wedge r \parallel u \wedge u \parallel j'$, which contradicts (by M5 and the anti transitivity of $\parallel$) with the fact that $y \parallel j'$. Otherwise $\exists k\,(u \parallel k \wedge k \parallel j)$. Analogously, we get a contradiction. Otherwise $\exists k\,(i \parallel k \wedge k \parallel u)$. Then $i \parallel x \wedge r \parallel x \wedge i \parallel k$. So, by M1, $r \parallel k$. So we have $y \parallel r \wedge r \parallel k \wedge k \parallel u$. As before, we can show a contradiction with the fact that $u \parallel j' \vee \exists k'\,(u \parallel k' \wedge k' \parallel j')$. So the antecedent of the implication is not satisfied.

   (iii) Let $\exists r\,(p \parallel r \wedge r \parallel q)$. Consider $z = r$. We have $p \parallel z \wedge z \parallel q$. Thus $i \parallel x \wedge p \parallel x \wedge p \parallel z$. So, by M1, $i \parallel z$. We have $y \parallel q \wedge y \parallel j' \wedge z \parallel q$. So, by M2, $z \parallel j'$. Moreover, $z \parallel q \wedge q \parallel j$, thus $\exists k\,(z \parallel k \wedge k \parallel j)$ and $i' \parallel p \wedge p \parallel z$, hence $\exists k\,(i' \parallel k \wedge k \parallel z)$. Consider any v such that $(i \parallel v \vee \exists k\,(i \parallel k \wedge k \parallel v)) \wedge (v \parallel j \vee \exists k\,(v \parallel k \wedge k \parallel j)) \wedge (i' \parallel v \vee \exists k\,(i' \parallel k \wedge k \parallel v)) \wedge (v \parallel j' \vee \exists k\,(v \parallel k \wedge k \parallel j'))$. With the same argument as in item 1 we can show that such a z satisfies the consequent of the implication.

6. Let $\exists q\,(x \parallel q \wedge q \parallel j')$. Consider $z = x$. Then $i \parallel z \wedge p \parallel z \wedge z \parallel q$. So we have $i' \parallel p \wedge p \parallel z \wedge z \parallel q \wedge q \parallel j'$, so $\exists k\,(i' \parallel k \wedge k \parallel z)$ and $\exists k\,(z \parallel k \wedge k \parallel j')$. Consider any v such that $(i \parallel v \vee \exists k\,(i \parallel k \wedge k \parallel v)) \wedge (v \parallel j \vee \exists k\,(v \parallel k \wedge k \parallel j)) \wedge (i' \parallel v \vee \exists k\,(i' \parallel k \wedge k \parallel v)) \wedge (v \parallel j' \vee \exists k\,(v \parallel k \wedge k \parallel j'))$. As before, we can show that such a z satisfies the consequent of the implication.

Let $\exists p\,(i \parallel p\ \wedge\ p \parallel y)$. Cases 7, 8 and 9 are analogous to cases 4, 6 and 7, respectively (the symmetry between x and y). All the cases are presented in Fig. 7.8.

$$\begin{aligned}\xi'(\mathsf{CONV}) = \forall x,y,z\,(&(x \parallel y \vee \exists k\,(x \parallel k\ \wedge\ k \parallel y))\ \wedge\\ &(y \parallel z\ \vee\ \exists k\,(y \parallel k\ \wedge\ k \parallel z)) \to\\ &\forall u\,(\exists i,j(i \parallel u \wedge u \parallel j \wedge (i \parallel x \vee \exists k(i \parallel k \wedge k \parallel x)) \wedge\\ &\quad (x \parallel j \vee \exists k\,(x \parallel k\ \wedge\ k \parallel j))) \wedge\\ &\quad \exists i,j\,(i \parallel u\ \wedge\ u \parallel j\ \wedge\ (i \parallel z \vee \exists k\,(i \parallel k \wedge k \parallel z)) \wedge\\ &\quad (z \parallel j \vee \exists k\,(z \parallel k\ \wedge\ k \parallel j))) \to\\ &\quad \exists i,j\,(i \parallel u\ \wedge\ u \parallel j\ \wedge\ (i \parallel y \vee \exists k\,(i \parallel k \wedge k \parallel y)) \wedge\\ &\quad (y \parallel j \vee \exists k\,(y \parallel k\ \wedge\ k \parallel j)))))\end{aligned}$$

Consider $x, y, z \in J$ such that $(x \parallel y \vee \exists k\,(x \parallel k\ \wedge\ k \parallel y))$ and $(y \parallel z \vee \exists k\,(y \parallel k\ \wedge\ k \parallel z))$ and $u, i, j \in J$ such that $i \parallel u\ \wedge\ u \parallel j$ and $(i \parallel x \vee \exists k\,(i \parallel k\ \wedge\ k \parallel x)) \wedge (x \parallel j \vee \exists k\,(x \parallel k \wedge k \parallel j))$ and $(i \parallel z \vee \exists k\,(i \parallel k \wedge k \parallel z)) \wedge (z \parallel j \vee \exists k\,(z \parallel k\ \wedge\ k \parallel j)) \wedge (i \parallel y \vee \exists k\,(i \parallel k\ \wedge\ k \parallel y)) \wedge (y \parallel j \vee \exists k(y \parallel k\ \wedge\ k \parallel j))$. We have $i \parallel u\ \wedge\ u \parallel j$. Let $x \parallel y$ and $y \parallel z$ and $i \parallel z$.

1. Let $z \parallel j$. Then $i \parallel x\ \wedge\ x \parallel y\ \wedge\ y \parallel z\ \wedge\ z \parallel j$, so $\exists k\,(i \parallel k\ \wedge\ k \parallel y)$ and $\exists k\,(y \parallel k\ \wedge\ k \parallel j)$.
2. Otherwise $\exists k\,(z \parallel k \wedge k \parallel j)$. Then $i \parallel x \wedge x \parallel y \wedge y \parallel z \wedge z \parallel k \wedge k \parallel j$. Therefore, by M5, $\exists l\,(y \parallel l\ \wedge\ l \parallel j)$, and evidently $\exists k\,(i \parallel k\ \wedge\ k \parallel y)$.

In the remaining cases the reasoning proceeds in a similar way—a sequence of meeting intervals can be different, but using M5 (one or more times) we can prove the thesis in each case.

Note that $\xi'(\mathsf{CONV})$ is valid even though structures of unconvex intervals can constitute models of Allen & Hayes' theory. But actually $\xi'(\mathsf{CONV})$ does not ensure the convexity of intervals—it follows from the way the inclusion relation $\subseteq$ is translated. The translation makes sense only for structures of convex intervals-for other structures it does not preserve the meaning of the relation.

$$\begin{aligned}\xi'(\mathsf{LIN}) = \forall x,y\,(&x \parallel y \vee \exists k(x \parallel k\ \wedge\ k \parallel y) \vee y \parallel x \vee \exists k(y \parallel k\ \wedge\ k \parallel x) \vee\\ &\exists z\,(\exists i,j\,(i \parallel x\ \wedge\ x \parallel j\ \wedge\ (i \parallel z \vee \exists k\,(i \parallel k\ \wedge\ k \parallel z)) \wedge\\ &\quad (z \parallel j \vee \exists k\,(z \parallel k\ \wedge\ k \parallel j))) \wedge\\ &\quad \exists i',j'\,(i' \parallel y\ \wedge\ y \parallel j'\ \wedge\ (i' \parallel z \vee \exists k\,(i' \parallel k \wedge k \parallel z)) \wedge\\ &\quad (z \parallel j' \vee \exists k\,(z \parallel k\ \wedge\ k \parallel j')))))\end{aligned}$$

Consider any $x, y \in J$. By M4 there exist $i, j, i', j' \in J$ such that $i \parallel x\ \wedge\ x \parallel j$ and $i' \parallel y \wedge y \parallel j'$. So we have $i \parallel x\ \wedge\ i' \parallel y$ and $x \parallel j\ \wedge\ y \parallel j'$. We will consider all the possibilities following from M3. Let $i \parallel y$. Then we have $i' \parallel x$.

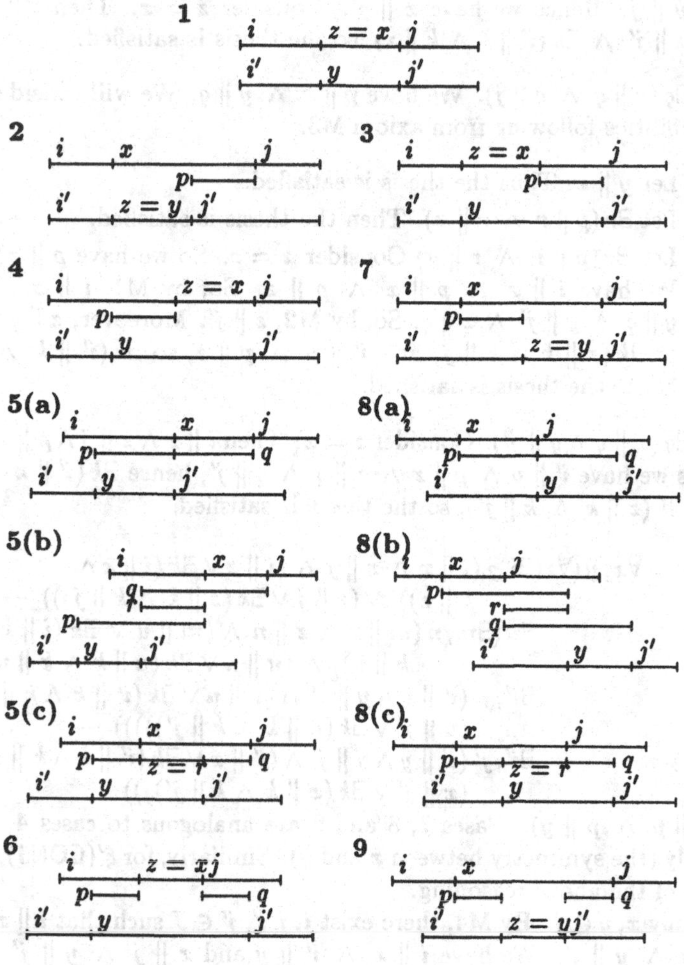

Figure 7.8 Existence of an intersection of two intervals x and y with regard to their mutual location.

1. Let $y \parallel j$. Hence we have $x \parallel j'$. Consider $z = x$. Then $i \parallel z \wedge z \parallel j \wedge i' \parallel z \wedge z \parallel j'$, so the thesis is satisfied.

2. Let $\exists p\,(y \parallel p \wedge p \parallel j)$. Consider $z = y$. Then $i \parallel z \wedge i' \parallel z \wedge z \parallel i' \wedge \exists k\,(z \parallel k \wedge k \parallel j)$, so the thesis is satisfied.

3. Let $\exists p\,(x \parallel p \wedge p \parallel j')$. Consider $z = x$. Then $i \parallel z \wedge z \parallel j \wedge i' \parallel z \wedge \exists k\,(z \parallel k \wedge k \parallel j')$, so the thesis is satisfied.

   Let $\exists p\,(i' \parallel p \wedge p \parallel x)$.

4. Let $y \parallel j$. Hence we have $x \parallel j'$. Consider $z = x$. Then $i \parallel z \wedge z \parallel j \wedge z \parallel j' \wedge \exists k\,(i' \parallel k \wedge k \parallel z)$, so the thesis is satisfied.

5. Let $\exists q\,(y \parallel q \wedge q \parallel j)$. We have $p \parallel x \wedge y \parallel q$. We will consider all the possibilities following from axiom M3.

   (i) Let $y \parallel x$. Thus the thesis is satisfied.
   (ii) Let $\exists r\,(y \parallel r \wedge r \parallel x)$. Then the thesis is satisfied.
   (iii) Let $\exists r\,(p \parallel r \wedge r \parallel q)$ Consider $z = r$. So we have $p \parallel z \wedge z \parallel q$. We have $i \parallel x \wedge p \parallel x \wedge p \parallel z$. So, by M1, $i \parallel z$. We have $y \parallel q \wedge y \parallel j' \wedge z \parallel q$. So, by M2, $z \parallel j'$. Moreover, $z \parallel q \wedge q \parallel j$, so $\exists k\,(z \parallel k \wedge k \parallel j)$ and $i' \parallel p \wedge p \parallel z$, so $\exists k\,(i' \parallel k \wedge k \parallel z)$, hence the thesis is satisfied.

6. Let $\exists q\,(x \parallel q \wedge q \parallel j')$. Consider $z = x$. Then $i \parallel z \wedge z \parallel j \wedge p \parallel z \wedge z \parallel q$. Thus we have $i' \parallel p \wedge p \parallel z \wedge z \parallel q \wedge q \parallel j'$, hence $\exists k\,(i' \parallel k \wedge k \parallel z)$ and $\exists k\,(z \parallel k \wedge k \parallel j')$, so the thesis is satisfied.

$$
\begin{aligned}
\xi'(\mathsf{FREE}) = \forall x, y\,(\forall z(\exists i, j\,(i \parallel x \wedge x \parallel j \wedge (i \parallel z \vee \exists k\,(i \parallel k \wedge{} \\
k \parallel z)) \wedge (z \parallel j \vee \exists k\,(z \parallel k \wedge k \parallel j))) \rightarrow{} \\
\exists u\,(\exists m, n\,(m \parallel z \wedge z \parallel n \wedge (m \parallel u \vee \exists k\,(i \parallel k \wedge{} \\
k \parallel u)) \wedge (u \parallel n \vee \exists k\,(u \parallel k \wedge k \parallel n))) \wedge{} \\
\exists i', j'\,(i' \parallel y \wedge y \parallel j' \wedge (i' \parallel u \vee \exists k\,(i' \parallel k \wedge k \parallel u)) \wedge{} \\
(u \parallel j' \vee \exists k\,(u \parallel k \wedge k \parallel j'))))) \rightarrow{} \\
\exists i', j'\,(i' \parallel y \wedge y \parallel j' \wedge (i' \parallel x \vee \exists k\,(i' \parallel k \wedge k \parallel x)) \wedge{} \\
(x \parallel j' \vee \exists k\,(x \parallel k \wedge k \parallel j'))))
\end{aligned}
$$

Let $\exists p\,(i \parallel p \wedge p \parallel y)$. Cases 7, 8 and 9 are analogous to cases 4, 6 and 7, respectively (the symmetry between x and y). Similarly, for $\xi'(\mathsf{CONJ})$, Fig. 7.8. illustrates of the above reasoning.
Consider any $x, y \in J$. By M4, there exist $i, j, i', j' \in J$ such that $i \parallel x \wedge x \parallel j$ and $i' \parallel y \wedge y \parallel j'$. We have $i \parallel x \wedge i' \parallel y$ and $x \parallel j \wedge y \parallel j'$. We will consider all the possibilities following from M3. Let $i \parallel y$. Then $i' \parallel x$.

1. Let $y \parallel j$. Then $x \parallel j'$. Thus $i' \parallel x \wedge x \parallel j'$, hence the thesis is satisfied.

2. Let $\exists p\,(y \parallel p \wedge p \parallel j)$. We have $i \parallel y \wedge y \parallel p$, so $\exists k\,(i \parallel k \wedge k \parallel p)$. We can consider $z = p$, for then $\exists k\,(i \parallel k \wedge k \parallel z)$. Consider any u, m, n such that $m \parallel z \wedge z \parallel n \wedge (m \parallel u \vee \exists k\,(i \parallel k \wedge k \parallel u)) \wedge (u \parallel j \vee \exists k\,(u \parallel k \wedge k \parallel n))$. Suppose that $m \parallel u$. We have $m \parallel u \wedge m \parallel z \wedge y \parallel z$. Hence, by M2, $y \parallel u$. Suppose that $u \parallel j'$. We have $y \parallel u \wedge u \parallel j'$. So, by the antitransitivity of $\parallel$ (Lemma 7.4), $y \parallel j'$ is impossible. This is a consideration. Otherwise $\exists k\,(u \parallel k \wedge k \parallel j')$. Then we have $y \parallel u \wedge u \parallel k \wedge k \parallel j'$. Thus, by M5, and the antitransitivity of $\parallel y, \parallel j'$ is impossible. This is a consideration. Otherwise $\exists k\,(m \parallel k \wedge k \parallel u)$. Then we have $m \parallel k \wedge m \parallel z \wedge y \parallel z$. So, by M2, $y \parallel k$. Suppose that

$u \parallel j'$. We have $y \parallel k \wedge k \parallel u \wedge u \parallel j$. As before, it is contradictory to the fact that $y \parallel j'$ (by M5 and the antitransitivity of $\parallel$). Otherwise $\exists k' (u \parallel k' \wedge k' \parallel j')$. Then we have $y \parallel k \wedge k \parallel u \wedge u \parallel k' \wedge k' \parallel j'$. Analogously, we have a contradiction. Therefore the premise (having the form of an implication) of the theorem is not satisfied.

3. Let $\exists p (x \parallel p \wedge p \parallel j')$. Then $i' \parallel x \wedge \exists k (x \parallel k \wedge k \parallel j')$, so the thesis is satisfied. Let $\exists p (i' \parallel p \wedge p \parallel x)$.

4. Let $y \parallel j$. Then $x \parallel j'$. Thus $x \parallel j' \wedge \exists k (i' \parallel k \wedge k \parallel x)$, so the thesis is satisfied.

5. Let $\exists q (y \parallel q \wedge q \parallel j)$. We have $p \parallel x \wedge y \parallel q$. We consider all the possibilities following from M3.

   (i) Let $y \parallel x$. We can consider $z = x$, as then $i \parallel z \wedge z \parallel j$. Then $y \parallel z$ holds. Consider any u, m, n such that $m \parallel z \wedge z \parallel n \wedge (m \parallel u \vee \exists k (i \parallel k \wedge k \parallel u)) \wedge (u \parallel j \vee \exists k (u \parallel k \wedge k \parallel n))$. Suppose that $m \parallel u$. We have $m \parallel z \wedge m \parallel u \wedge y \parallel z$. So, by M2, $y \parallel u$. Then the rest of the proof is analogous to item 2. Otherwise $\exists k (m \parallel k \wedge k \parallel u)$. Then we have $m \parallel z \wedge m \parallel k \wedge y \parallel z$. So, by M2, $y \parallel k$. Then again the rest of the proof is analogous to item 2. So the premise of the theorem is not satisfied.

   (ii) Let $\exists r (y \parallel r \wedge r \parallel x)$. We can consider $z = x$, for then $i \parallel z \wedge z \parallel j$. Then $\exists r (y \parallel r \wedge r \parallel z)$ holds. Consider any u, m, n such that $m \parallel z \wedge z \parallel n \wedge (m \parallel u \vee \exists k (i \parallel k \wedge k \parallel u)) \wedge (u \parallel j \vee \exists k (u \parallel k \wedge k \parallel n))$. Suppose that $m \parallel u$. We have $m \parallel z \wedge m \parallel u \wedge y \parallel r$. So, by M2, $y \parallel r$. Suppose that $u \parallel j'$. We have $y \parallel r \wedge r \parallel u \wedge u \parallel j'$. So, by M5 and the anti-transitivity of $\parallel$, there is a contradiction with the fact that $y \parallel j'$. The remaining cases are analogous. So the premise of the theorem is not satisfied.

   (iii) Let $\exists r (p \parallel r \wedge r \parallel q)$. We have $p \parallel x \wedge i \parallel x \wedge p \parallel r$. So, by M1, $i \parallel r$. Thus we can consider $z = q$, since $\exists k (i \parallel k \wedge k \parallel z)$ and $z \parallel j$. Additionally, we have $y \parallel z$. Consider any u, m, n such that $m \parallel z \wedge z \parallel n \wedge (m \parallel u \vee \exists k (i \parallel k \wedge k \parallel u)) \wedge (u \parallel j \vee \exists k (u \parallel k \wedge k \parallel n))$. The rest of the proof is analogous to item 2. Thus the premise of the theorem is not satisfied.

6. Let $\exists q (x \parallel q \wedge q \parallel j')$. Then $p \parallel x \wedge x \parallel q$. So we have $i' \parallel p \wedge p \parallel x \wedge x \parallel q \wedge q \parallel j'$, hence $\exists k (i' \parallel k \wedge k \parallel x)$ and $\exists k (x \parallel k \wedge k \parallel j')$, so the thesis is satisfied. Let $\exists p (i \parallel p \wedge p \parallel y)$.

7. Let $y \parallel j$. Then $x \parallel j'$. We have $p \parallel y \wedge y \parallel j$, so $\exists k (p \parallel k \wedge k \parallel j)$. We can consider $z = p$, as then $i \parallel z \wedge \exists k (z \parallel k \wedge k \parallel j)$. The case is analogous to item 2 (the symmetry w.r.t. the time arrow; i' should

be considered instead of j'). Thus the premise of the theorem is not satisfied.

8. Let $\exists q\,(x \parallel q \;\wedge\; q \parallel j')$. We have $p \parallel y \;\wedge\; x \parallel q$. We will consider all the possibilities following from M3.

   (i) Let $x \parallel y$. Thus $p \parallel q$. We can consider $z = x$, for then $i \parallel z \;\wedge\; z \parallel j$. Then $z \parallel y$ also holds. The case is analogous to item 5(i) (a symmetry w.r.t. the time arrow).

   (ii) Let $\exists r\,(x \parallel r \;\wedge\; r \parallel y)$. Then we can consider $z = x$, since $i \parallel z \wedge z \parallel j$. The case is analogous to item 5(ii) (the symmetry w.r.t. the time arrow).

   (iii) Let $\exists r\,(p \parallel r \;\wedge\; r \parallel q)$. We have $x \parallel q \;\wedge\; x \parallel j \;\wedge\; r \parallel q$. So, by M2, $r \parallel j$. So we can consider $z = p$, since $i \parallel p \wedge \exists r\,(p \parallel r \;\wedge\; r \parallel j)$. The case is analogous to item 5(iii) (the symmetry w.r.t. the time arrow).

9. Let $\exists q\,(y \parallel q \;\wedge\; q \parallel j)$. We have $i \parallel p \;\wedge\; p \parallel y \;\wedge\; y \parallel q$. So, by M5, $\exists k\,(i \parallel k \;\wedge\; k \parallel q)$. Moreover $q \parallel j$, so we can consider $z = q$. The rest of the proof is analogous to item 2.

Eventually, for all the cases either the premise was false or the thesis was true. Figure 7.8 can be treated as an illustration for the above reasoning, too.

$$\begin{aligned}\xi'(\mathsf{NEIGH}^1) = \;& \forall x, y((x \parallel y \vee \exists k\,(x \parallel k \;\wedge\; k \parallel y)) \rightarrow \\ & \quad \exists z\,((x \parallel z \vee \exists k\,(x \parallel k \;\wedge\; k \parallel z)) \;\wedge \\ & \quad\quad \forall u \neg((x \parallel u \vee \exists k\,(x \parallel k \;\wedge\; k \parallel u)) \;\wedge \\ & \quad\quad\quad (u \parallel z \vee \exists k\,(u \parallel k \;\wedge\; k \parallel z)))))\end{aligned}$$

By Theorem 7.5 it is equivalent to the following formula:

$$\forall x, y((x \parallel y \vee \exists k\,(x \parallel k \wedge k \parallel y)) \rightarrow \exists z\,(x \parallel z))$$

The consequent of the implication holds by M4.

$$\begin{aligned}\xi'(\mathsf{NEIGH}^2) = \;& \forall x, y((y \parallel x \vee \exists k\,(y \parallel k \;\wedge\; k \parallel x)) \rightarrow \\ & \quad \exists z\,((z \parallel x \vee \exists k\,(z \parallel k \;\wedge\; k \parallel x)) \;\wedge \\ & \quad\quad \forall u \neg((z \parallel u \vee \exists k\,(z \parallel k \;\wedge\; k \parallel u)) \;\wedge \\ & \quad\quad\quad (u \parallel x \vee \exists k\,(u \parallel k \;\wedge\; k \parallel x)))))\end{aligned}$$

This formula is valid analogously to the previous one.

$$
\begin{aligned}
\xi'(\mathsf{DISJ}) = \forall x, y\, (\exists u\, (&\exists a, b\, (a \parallel u \ \wedge\ u \parallel b \ \wedge\ (a \parallel x \vee \exists k\, (a \parallel k \ \wedge \\
&\quad k \parallel x)) \wedge (x \parallel b \vee \exists k\, (x \parallel k \ \wedge\ k \parallel b))) \wedge \\
&\exists a, b\, (a \parallel u \ \wedge\ u \parallel b \ \wedge\ (a \parallel y \vee \exists k\, (a \parallel k \wedge \\
&\quad k \parallel y)) \wedge (y \parallel b \vee \exists k\, (y \parallel k \ \wedge\ k \parallel b)))) \rightarrow \\
&\exists z\, (\exists a, b\, (a \parallel z \ \wedge\ z \parallel b \ \wedge\ (a \parallel x \vee \exists k\, (a \parallel k \ \wedge\ k \parallel x)) \wedge \\
&\quad (x \parallel b \vee \exists k\, (x \parallel k \ \wedge\ k \parallel b))) \wedge \\
&\quad \exists a, b\, (a \parallel z \ \wedge\ z \parallel b \wedge (a \parallel y \vee \exists k\, (a \parallel k \wedge k \parallel y)) \wedge \\
&\quad (y \parallel b \vee \exists k\, (y \parallel k \ \wedge\ k \parallel b))) \wedge \\
&\quad \forall v\, (\exists m, n\, (m \parallel v \wedge v \parallel n \ \wedge\ (m \parallel x \vee \exists k\, (m \parallel k \wedge \\
&\qquad k \parallel x)) \wedge (x \parallel n \vee \exists k\, (x \parallel k \wedge k \parallel n))) \wedge \\
&\quad \exists m, n\, (m \parallel v \ \wedge\ v \parallel n \wedge (m \parallel y \vee \exists k\, (m \parallel k \wedge \\
&\qquad k \parallel y)) \ \wedge\ (y \parallel n \vee \exists k\, (y \parallel k \ \wedge\ k \parallel n))) \rightarrow \\
&\quad \exists m, n\, (m \parallel v \ \wedge\ v \parallel n \wedge (m \parallel z \vee \exists k\, (i \parallel k \wedge \\
&\qquad k \parallel z)) \ \wedge\ (z \parallel n \vee \exists k\, (z \parallel k \ \wedge\ k \parallel n))))))
\end{aligned}
$$

Consider any $x, y \in J$. By M4, there exist $i, j, i', j' \in J$ such that $i \parallel x \wedge x \parallel j$ and $i' \parallel y \wedge y \parallel j'$. We have $i \parallel x \wedge i' \parallel y$ and $x \parallel j \wedge y \parallel j'$. We will consider all the possibilities following from M3. Let $i \parallel y$. Then $i' \parallel x$.

1. Let $y \parallel j$. Then $x \parallel j'$. Consider $z = x$, $a = i$, $b = j$. Thus $a \parallel z \wedge z \parallel b \wedge a \parallel x \wedge x \parallel b \wedge a \parallel y \wedge y \parallel b$. Consider any v, m, n such that $m \parallel v \wedge v \parallel n$. Suppose that $m \parallel x$. Then $\exists m\, (m \parallel v \wedge m \parallel z)$. Otherwise $\exists k\, (m \parallel k \wedge k \parallel x)$. Then $\exists m\, (m \parallel v \wedge \exists k\, (m \parallel k \wedge k \parallel z))$. Suppose that $x \parallel n$. Hence $\exists n\, (v \parallel n \wedge z \parallel n)$. Otherwise $\exists k\, (x \parallel k \wedge k \parallel n)$. Then $\exists n\, (v \parallel n \wedge \exists k\, (z \parallel k \wedge k \parallel n))$. As we can see, in all the cases z satisfies the required conditions.

2. Let $\exists p\, (y \parallel p \wedge p \parallel j)$. Consider $z = x$, $a = i$, $b = j$. Then $a \parallel z \wedge z \parallel b \wedge a \parallel x \wedge x \parallel b \wedge a \parallel y \wedge \exists k\, (y \parallel k \wedge k \parallel b)$. Consider any v, m, n such that $m \parallel v \wedge v \parallel n$. The reasoning is analogous to item 1.

3. Let $\exists p\, (x \parallel p \wedge p \parallel j')$. Consider $z = y$, $a = i'$, $b = j'$. Then $a \parallel z \wedge z \parallel b \wedge a \parallel x \wedge \exists k\, (x \parallel k \wedge k \parallel b) \wedge a \parallel y \wedge y \parallel b$. Consider any v, m, n such that $m \parallel v \wedge v \parallel n$. Suppose that $m \parallel y$. Then $\exists m\, (m \parallel v \wedge m \parallel z)$. Otherwise $\exists k\, (m \parallel k \wedge k \parallel y)$. Thus $\exists m\, (m \parallel v \wedge \exists k\, (m \parallel k \wedge k \parallel z))$. Suppose that $y \parallel n$. Then $\exists n\, (v \parallel n \wedge z \parallel n)$. Otherwise $\exists k\, (y \parallel k \wedge k \parallel n)$. Then $\exists n\, (v \parallel n \wedge \exists k\, (z \parallel k \wedge k \parallel n))$. As we can see, in all the cases z satisfies the required conditions. Let $\exists p\, (i' \parallel p \wedge p \parallel x)$.

4. Let $y \parallel j$. Thus $x \parallel j'$. Consider $z = y$, $a = i'$, $b = j'$. Then $a \parallel z \wedge z \parallel b \wedge \exists k\, (a \parallel k \wedge k \parallel x) \wedge x \parallel b \wedge a \parallel y \wedge y \parallel b$. Consider any v, m, n such that $m \parallel v \wedge v \parallel n$. The reasoning is analogous to item 3.

5. Let $\exists q\, (y \parallel q \wedge q \parallel j)$. We have $p \parallel x \wedge y \parallel q$. We will consider all the possibilities following from M3.

(i) Let $y \parallel x$. Then we have $i' \parallel y \wedge y \parallel x \wedge x \parallel j$. So, by M5, there exists z such that $i' \parallel z \wedge z \parallel j$. Consider $a = i'$, $b = j$. We have $a \parallel z \wedge z \parallel b \wedge \exists p (a \parallel p \wedge p \parallel x) \wedge x \parallel b \wedge a \parallel y \wedge \exists q (y \parallel q \wedge q \parallel j)$. Consider any v, m, n such that $m \parallel v \wedge v \parallel n$. The first part of the proof is analogous to item 1, and the second to item 2.

(ii) Let $\exists r (y \parallel r \wedge r \parallel x)$. Then we have $i' \parallel y \wedge y \parallel r \wedge r \parallel x \wedge x \parallel j$. Hence, by M5 used twice, there exists z such that $i' \parallel z \wedge z \parallel j$. Consider $a = i'$, $b = j$. The reasoning is analogous to part (i).

(iii) Let $\exists r (p \parallel r \wedge r \parallel q)$. We have $i' \parallel p \wedge p \parallel r \wedge r \parallel q \wedge q \parallel j$. Hence, by M5 used twice, there exists z such that $i' \parallel z \wedge z \parallel j$. Consider $a = i'$, $b = j$. We have $a \parallel z \wedge z \parallel b \wedge \exists p (a \parallel p \wedge p \parallel x) \wedge x \parallel b \wedge a \parallel y \wedge \exists q (y \parallel q \wedge q \parallel b)$. The rest of the proof proceeds analogously as before.

6. Let $\exists q (x \parallel q \wedge q \parallel j')$. Consider $z = y$, $a = i'$, $b = j'$. Then $a \parallel z \wedge z \parallel b \wedge \exists k (a \parallel k \wedge k \parallel x) \wedge a \parallel y \wedge y \parallel b \wedge \exists k (x \parallel k \wedge k \parallel b)$. The rest of the proof proceeds analogously as before.

Let $\exists p (i \parallel p \wedge p \parallel y)$.

The cases 7, 8 and 9 are analogous to cases 4, 5 and 6, respectively (symmetry between x and y). Although intervals composing a union of the intervals x and y are not depicted in Figure 7.8, the figure can help with analyzing the above reasoning.

$$\begin{aligned} \xi'(\mathsf{DIR}) = \quad & \forall x, y (\exists z (\exists i, j (i \parallel z \wedge z \parallel j \wedge (i \parallel x \vee \exists k (i \parallel k \wedge \\ & \qquad k \parallel x)) \wedge (x \parallel j \vee \exists k (x \parallel k \wedge k \parallel j))) \wedge \\ & \quad \exists i, j (i \parallel z \wedge z \parallel j \wedge (i \parallel y \vee \exists k (i \parallel k \wedge k \parallel y)) \wedge \\ & \qquad (y \parallel j \vee \exists k (y \parallel k \wedge k \parallel j))))) \end{aligned}$$

This is a counterpart of part of the thesis of ξ'(DISJ) (or of part of its premise). Both the premise and the thesis of ξ'(DISJ) are valid in all possible cases.

$$\begin{aligned} \xi'(\mathsf{SUCC}) = \quad & \forall x \exists y (x \parallel y \vee \exists k (x \parallel k \wedge k \parallel y)) \\ & \forall x \exists y (y \parallel x \vee \exists k (y \parallel k \wedge k \parallel x)) \end{aligned}$$

Both the formulae follow evidently from axiom M4.

$$\begin{aligned}\xi'(\mathsf{MOND}^1) = \quad & \forall x, y, z\, ((x \parallel z \vee \exists k\, (x \parallel k \wedge k \parallel z)) \wedge \\ & \quad (y \parallel z \vee \exists k\, (y \parallel k \wedge k \parallel z)) \rightarrow \\ & \exists v (\exists m, n (m \parallel v \wedge v \parallel n \wedge (m \parallel x \vee \exists k\, (m \parallel k \wedge \\ & \qquad k \parallel x)) \wedge (x \parallel n \vee \exists k\, (x \parallel k \wedge k \parallel n))) \wedge \\ & \quad \exists m, n\, (m \parallel v \wedge v \parallel n \wedge (m \parallel y \vee \exists k\, (m \parallel k \wedge \\ & \qquad k \parallel y)) \wedge (y \parallel n \vee \exists k\, (y \parallel k \wedge k \parallel n))) \wedge \\ & \qquad (v \parallel z \vee \exists k\, (v \parallel k \wedge k \parallel z)) \wedge \\ & \forall u\, (\exists m', n' (m' \parallel u \wedge u \parallel n' \wedge \\ & \qquad (m' \parallel x \vee \exists k\, (m' \parallel k \wedge k \parallel x)) \wedge \\ & \qquad (x \parallel n' \vee \exists k\, (x \parallel k \wedge k \parallel n'))) \wedge \\ & \quad \exists m', n'\, (m' \parallel u \wedge u \parallel n' \wedge \\ & \qquad (m' \parallel y \vee \exists k\, (m' \parallel k \wedge k \parallel y)) \wedge \\ & \qquad (y \parallel n' \vee \exists k\, (y \parallel k \wedge k \parallel n'))) \rightarrow \\ & \quad \exists m', n'\, (m' \parallel u \wedge u \parallel n' \wedge \\ & \qquad (m' \parallel v \vee \exists k\, (m' \parallel k \wedge k \parallel v)) \wedge \\ & \qquad (v \parallel n' \vee \exists k\, (v \parallel k \wedge k \parallel n'))))))\end{aligned}$$

Consider any $x, y \in J$. By M4, there exist $i, j, i', j' \in J$ such that $i \parallel x \wedge x \parallel j$ and $i' \parallel y \wedge y \parallel j'$. We have $i \parallel x \wedge i' \parallel y$ and $x \parallel j \wedge y \parallel j'$. We will consider all the possibilities following from M3. Let v be the union of the intervals x and y as it was defined (for each case) in the proof of $\xi'(\mathsf{CONJ})$ (it was called z there). Additionally, we should prove that $v \parallel z \vee \exists k\, (v \parallel k \wedge k \parallel z)$. Let $i \parallel y$. Then $i' \parallel x$.

1. Let $y \parallel j$, then $x \parallel j'$. We consider $z = x$. Therefore $v \parallel z \vee \exists k\, (v \parallel k \wedge k \parallel z)$, so the thesis is valid.

2. Let $\exists p\, (y \parallel p \wedge p \parallel j)$. We consider $z = x$, and then $v \parallel z \vee \exists k\, (v \parallel k \wedge k \parallel z)$, so the thesis is valid.

3. Let $\exists p\, (x \parallel p \wedge p \parallel j')$. We consider $z = y$, and then $v \parallel z \vee \exists k\, (v \parallel k \wedge k \parallel z)$, so the thesis is valid. Let $\exists p\, (i' \parallel p \wedge p \parallel x)$.

4. Let $y \parallel j$. Then $x \parallel j'$. We consider $z = y$, and then $v \parallel z \vee \exists k\, (v \parallel k \wedge k \parallel z)$, so the thesis is valid.

5. Let $\exists q\, (y \parallel q \wedge q \parallel j)$. We have $p \parallel x \wedge y \parallel q$. We consider all the possibilities following from M5.

   (i) Let $y \parallel x$. We have $i' \parallel y \wedge y \parallel x \wedge x \parallel j$. Thus, by M5, there exists v such that $i' \parallel v \wedge v \parallel j$. If $x \parallel z$, then we have $x \parallel z \wedge x \parallel j \wedge v \parallel j$. So, by M2, $v \parallel z$. Otherwise $\exists k\, (x \parallel k \wedge k \parallel z)$. Then we have $x \parallel k \wedge x \parallel j \wedge v \parallel j$. So, by M2, $v \parallel k$, hence $\exists k\, (x \parallel k \wedge k \parallel lz)$. Thus the thesis is valid.

   (ii) Let $\exists r\, (y \parallel r \wedge r \parallel x)$. We have $i' \parallel y \wedge y \parallel r \wedge r \parallel x \wedge x \parallel j$. Thus, by M5 used twice, there exists v such that $i' \parallel v \wedge v \parallel j$. The reasoning is analogous as before.

(iii) Let $\exists r\,(p \parallel r \ \wedge \ r \parallel q)$. We have $i' \parallel p \ \wedge \ p \parallel r \ \wedge \ r \parallel q \wedge q \parallel j$. Thus, by M5 used twice, there exists v such that $i' \parallel v \ \wedge \ v \parallel j$. The reasoning is analogous as before.

6. Let $\exists q\,(x \parallel q \ \wedge \ q \parallel j')$. We consider $z = y$, and then $v \parallel z \vee \exists k\,(v \parallel k \ \wedge \ k \parallel z)$, hence the thesis is satisfied.

Let $\exists p\,(i \parallel p \ \wedge \ p \parallel y)$.
Cases 7, 8 and 9 are analogous to the cases 4, 5 and 6, respectively (symmetry between x and y).

$$
\begin{aligned}
\xi'(\mathsf{MOND}^2) = \ & \forall x, y, z\,((z \parallel x \vee \exists k\,(z \parallel k \wedge k \parallel x)) \wedge \\
& \quad (z \parallel y \vee \exists k\,(z \parallel k \wedge k \parallel y)) \rightarrow \\
& \exists v\,(\exists m, n\,(m \parallel v \wedge v \parallel n \wedge (m \parallel x \vee \exists k\,(m \parallel k \wedge \\
& \qquad k \parallel x)) \wedge (x \parallel n \vee \exists k\,(x \parallel k \wedge k \parallel n))) \wedge \\
& \exists m, n\,(m \parallel v \wedge v \parallel n \wedge (m \parallel y \vee \exists k\,(m \parallel k \wedge \\
& \qquad k \parallel y)) \wedge (y \parallel n \vee \exists k\,(y \parallel k \wedge k \parallel n))) \wedge \\
& \quad (z \parallel v \vee \exists k\,(z \parallel k \wedge k \parallel v)) \wedge \\
& \forall u\,(\exists m', n'\,(m' \parallel u \wedge u \parallel n' \wedge \\
& \qquad (m' \parallel x \vee \exists k\,(m' \parallel k \wedge k \parallel x)) \wedge \\
& \qquad (x \parallel n' \vee \exists k\,(x \parallel k \wedge k \parallel n'))) \wedge \\
& \exists m', n'\,(m' \parallel u \wedge u \parallel n' \wedge \\
& \qquad (m' \parallel y \vee \exists k\,(m' \parallel k \wedge k \parallel y)) \wedge \\
& \qquad (y \parallel n' \vee \exists k\,(y \parallel k \wedge k \parallel n'))) \rightarrow \\
& \exists m', n'\,(m' \parallel u \wedge u \parallel n' \wedge \\
& \qquad (m' \parallel v \vee \exists k\,(m' \parallel k \wedge k \parallel v)) \wedge \\
& \qquad (v \parallel n' \vee \exists k\,(v \parallel k \wedge k \parallel n'))))))
\end{aligned}
$$

The proof is analogous to the case of $\xi'(\mathsf{MOND}^1)$.

Therefore the translation of all the axioms of the classical theory $\mathcal{T}_C$ is satisfied in all models of Allen & Hayes' theory $\mathcal{T}_A$. □

For the proof of the axioms of the classical theory $\mathcal{T}_C$, all the axioms of Allen & Hayes' theory $\mathcal{T}_A$ were needed (M6 only for the proof of LANTIS). This concerns the basic theory $\mathcal{T}_{CB}$, too.

Since the translations of all the axioms of theory $\mathcal{T}_C$ are satisfied in all models of theory $\mathcal{T}_A$, so are translations of all theorems of theory $\mathcal{T}_C$. As a result, translations of all theorems of theory $\mathcal{T}_C$ are theorems of theory $\mathcal{T}_A$.

Corollary: Allen & Hayes' theory $\mathcal{T}_C$ is interpretable in the classical theory $\mathcal{T}_A$.

7.4.3 A translation of Tsang's theory $\mathcal{T}_T$ into the classical theory $\mathcal{T}_C$

Now we draw a comparison between Tsang's theory $\mathcal{T}_T$ and the classical theory $\mathcal{T}_C$. These theories are much more similar than the theories $\mathcal{T}_A$ and $\mathcal{T}_C$—the precedence relation $<$ is the same for both theories. Because of this, some axioms are also identical or very similar.

Let $\varrho : Z_T \longrightarrow Z_C$ be a function transforming the set of variables of Tsang's theories into to the set of variables of the classical theories. We define a function $\xi : \mathcal{F}_T \longrightarrow \mathcal{F}_C$ such that:

$$\begin{aligned} \xi(x < y) &= \varrho(x) < \varrho(y) \\ \xi(x \mathcal{O} y) &= \exists u (u \subseteq \varrho(x) \wedge u \subseteq \varrho(y)) \end{aligned}$$

Evidently $x, y \in Z_T$, $u \in Z_C$. Remaining formulae are translated in the obvious way. As before, we will not differentiate between the standard logic symbols in both theories and we will omit the symbol ϱ. Since the meaning of the precedence relation is the same in both theories, it will be denoted by the same symbol in both theories—the context is always univocal.

As Tsang has used the auxiliary relation *in*, we present a useful lemma before we start to analyze the axioms of his theory. Its validity follows from the fact that the definition of Tsang's relation *in* is the same as our translation of the classical relation $\subseteq$ into his theory.

Lemma 7.7 The axioms I_TRANS and FREE of the classic theory $\mathcal{T}_C$ imply that $\xi(x \ in \ y) \leftrightarrow x \subseteq y$ holds.

Proof:

$$\xi(x \ in \ y) = \forall u (\exists v (v \subseteq u \wedge v \subseteq x) \rightarrow \exists v (v \subseteq u \wedge v \subseteq y))$$

Let $\Im = \langle I, <, \subseteq \rangle$ be a structure satisfying the axioms I_TRANS and FREE. Consider any $x, y \in I$. Consider $z \in I$ such that $z \subseteq x$. Evidently $z \subseteq z \wedge z \subseteq x$, hence $\exists v (v \subseteq z \wedge v \subseteq x)$. Then $\exists v (v \subseteq z \wedge v \subseteq y)$. Thus we have $\exists z (z \subseteq x \rightarrow \exists v (v \subseteq z \wedge v \subseteq y))$. Therefore, by FREE, $x \subseteq y$.

Suppose that $x \subseteq y$. Consider any u such that $\exists v (v \subseteq u \wedge v \subseteq x)$. Consider such a v. We have $v \subseteq x \wedge x \subseteq y$. So, by I_TRANS, $v \subseteq y$. Thus $\exists v (v \subseteq u \wedge v \subseteq y)$. Eventually we have $\forall u (\exists v (v \subseteq u \wedge v \subseteq x) \rightarrow \exists v (v \subseteq u \wedge v \subseteq x))$. So, considered equivalence holds in both directions. □

Theorem 7.9 Translations of all the axioms of Tsang's theory $\mathcal{T}_T$ are satisfied in all models of the classical theory $\mathcal{T}_C$.

Proof: Let $\Im = \langle I, <, \subseteq \rangle$ be a model of theory $\mathcal{T}_C$.

ξ (E1) $= \forall x, y (x < y \leftarrow \neg(y < x))$
Consider any $x, y \in I$. Suppose that $x < y \wedge y < x$. Then, by P_TRANS, $x < x$. It contradicts P_IRREF.

ξ (E2) $= \forall x, y, z (x < y \wedge y < z \rightarrow x < z)$
This is the classical axiom P_TRANS.

ξ (E3) $= \forall x, y (\exists u (u \subseteq x \wedge u \subseteq y) \rightarrow \exists u (u \subseteq y \wedge u \subseteq x))$
Consider any $x, y \in I$. Consider $u \in I$ such that $u \subseteq x \wedge u \subseteq y$. Then, by the commutativity of $\wedge$, we obtain $u \subseteq y \wedge u \subseteq x$.

ξ (E4) $= \forall x \exists u (u \subseteq x \wedge u \subseteq x)$
Consider any $x \in I$. Then, by I_REF, $x \subseteq x$, hence $\exists u (u \subseteq x)$.

ξ (E5) $= \forall x, y (x < y \rightarrow \neg \exists u (u \subseteq x \wedge u \subseteq y))$
Consider any $x, y \in I$ such that $x < y$. Consider any $u \subseteq x$. Then, by **MON**, $u < y$. And then, by Lemma 7.1, we have $\neg(u \subseteq y)$.

ξ (E6) $= \forall x, y, z, u (x < y \wedge \exists v (v \subseteq y \wedge v \subseteq z) \wedge z < u \rightarrow x < u)$
Consider any $x, y, z, u, v \in I$ such that $x < y \wedge v \subseteq y \wedge v \subseteq z \wedge z < u$. We have $x < y \wedge v \subseteq y$. So, by **MON**, $x < v$. On the other hand $v \subseteq z \wedge z < u$. So, by **MON**, $v < u$. So we have $x < v \wedge v < u$. Hence, by **P_TRANS**, $x < u$.

ξ (E7) $= \forall x, y (x < y \vee \exists u (u \subseteq x \wedge u \subseteq y) \vee y < u)$
This is the classical axiom **LIN**.

ξ (E8) $= \forall x \exists y (y < x \wedge \neg \exists u (y < u \wedge u < x))$

ξ (E9) $= \forall x \exists y (x < y \wedge \neg \exists u (x < u \wedge u < y))$
These are direct consequences of the classical axioms **SUCC** and **NEIGH**.

By Lemma 7.7 we will write $x \subseteq y$ in the place of $\xi(x \textit{ in } y)$ straight off.

$$\xi \text{ (E10)} = \forall x, y (\exists v (v \subseteq x \wedge v \subseteq y) \rightarrow \exists z (z \subseteq x \wedge z \subseteq y) \wedge \\ \forall u (u \subseteq x \wedge u \subseteq y \rightarrow u \subseteq z)))$$

This is the classical axiom **CONJ**.

$$\xi \text{ (E11)} = \forall x, y \exists z (x \subseteq z \wedge y \subseteq z \wedge \forall u (u < x \wedge u < y \rightarrow \\ u < z) \wedge \forall u (x < u \wedge y < u \rightarrow z < u))$$

The first part of the above formula—$\forall x, y \exists z (x \subseteq z \wedge y \subseteq z)$—constitute the axiom **DIR**. By **DISJ** there exists $z \in I$ such that, moreover, $\forall v (x \subseteq v \wedge y \subseteq v \rightarrow z \subseteq v)$. Consider any u such that $u < x \wedge u < y$. Then, by **MOND**, $u < z$. Consider any u such that $x < u \wedge y < u$. Then, by **MOND**, $z < u$.

Therefore the translation of all the axioms of Tsang's theory $\mathcal{T}_T$ are satisfied in all models of the classical theory $\mathcal{T}_C$. □

Since the translation of all the axioms of theory $\mathcal{T}_T$ are satisfied in all models of theory $\mathcal{T}_C$, so are translations of all theorems of the theory $\mathcal{T}_T$. As a result, translations of all theorems of theory $\mathcal{T}_T$ are theorems of theory $\mathcal{T}_C$.

Corollary: Tsang's theory $\mathcal{T}_T$ is interpretable in the classical theory $\mathcal{T}_C$.

The axioms **P_TRANS**, **P_IRREF**, **I_REF**, **I_TRANS**, **MON**, **FREE** were used for a proof of the translations of the axioms of the basic Tsang's theory $\mathcal{T}_{TB}$ as well as **LIN** for the proof of the linearity axiom E7. This axiom belongs to the basic theory $\mathcal{T}_{TB}$ since it is an original Kamp's axiom. However, Tsang himself considers theories without this axiom. Since the axiom **FREE** does not belong to the basic classical theory $\mathcal{T}_{CB}$, an interpretability of the basic Tsang's theory

$\mathcal{T}_{TB}$ in the basic classical theory $\mathcal{T}_{CB}$ does not occur, even after abandoning the linearity axiom E7. To prove the remaining axioms, the classical axioms SUCC, NEIGH, DIR, DISJ and MOND were also needed. The only axiom of the basic theory $\mathcal{T}_{CB}$ which has not been used is I_ANTIS.

7.4.4 A translation of the classical theory $\mathcal{T}_C$ into Tsang's theory $\mathcal{T}_T$

Now we perform the inverse operation, i.e. a translation of the classical theory $\mathcal{T}_C$ into Tsang's theory $\mathcal{T}_T$.

Let $\varrho' : Z_C \longrightarrow Z_T$ be a function transforming the set of variables of the classical theories into the set of variables of Tsang's theories. We define a function $\xi' : \mathcal{F}_C \longrightarrow \mathcal{F}_T$ such that:

$$\begin{aligned} \xi'(x < y) &= \varrho'(x) < \varrho'(y) \\ \xi'(x \subseteq y) &= \forall u\,(u\,\mathcal{O}\,\varrho'(x) \rightarrow u\,\mathcal{O}\,\varrho'(y)) \end{aligned}$$

where $x, y \in Z_C$, $u \in Z_T$. As before, we will not differentiate between the standard logical symbols and the symbol of the precedence relation $<$ in the theories, and we will omit the symbol ϱ'.

As we have already defined the translations in both directions, we will perform a more precise analysis of these translations, as in Section 7.4.2.

Theorem 7.10 The axioms I_TRANS and FREE of the classical theory $\mathcal{T}_C$ imply that $\xi(\xi'(x \subseteq y)) \leftrightarrow x \subseteq y$ holds.

Proof: It is the direct consequence of Lemma 7.7. □

Theorem 7.11 Axioms E2–E5 and E7–E11 of Tsang's theory imply that $\xi'(\xi(x\,\mathcal{O}\,y) \leftrightarrow x\,\mathcal{O}\,y$ holds.

Proof:

$$\xi(x\,\mathcal{O}\,y) = \exists z\,(z \subseteq x \wedge z \subseteq y)$$

$$\xi'(\exists z\,(z \subseteq x \wedge z \subseteq y)) = \exists z\,(\forall u\,(u\,\mathcal{O}\,z \rightarrow u\,\mathcal{O}\,x) \wedge \forall u\,(u\,\mathcal{O}\,z \rightarrow u\,\mathcal{O}\,y))$$

Using other notation,

$$\xi'\,(\exists z\,(z \subseteq x\ \wedge\ z \subseteq y)) = \exists z\,(z\ in\ x\ \wedge\ z\ in\ y)$$

Consider any structure $\mathcal{G} = \langle G, <, \mathcal{O} \rangle$ which satisfies axioms E2–E5 and E7–E11. Consider any $x, y \in G$ such that $x\,\mathcal{O}\,y$. Then, by E10, $\exists z(z\ in\ x$ and $z\ in\ y)$. Consider any $x, y \in G$. Suppose that there exists z such that $z\ in\ x \wedge z\ in\ y$. Evidently, by E4 and the definition of *in*, we have $z\,\mathcal{O}\,x \wedge z\,\mathcal{O}\,y$. Suppose that $x < y$. By E9 there exists u such that $y < u$. Consider such a u.

Then, by E2, $x < u$. By E11 there exists v such that $y \, in \, v \wedge u \; in \; v \wedge \forall p (p < y \wedge p < u \rightarrow p < v)$. Therefore, since $x < y \wedge x < u$, we have $x < v$. On the other hand, by E4 and the definition of *in*, we have $y \mathcal{O} v \wedge u \mathcal{O} v$. Thus, by the definition of *in*, since $z \mathcal{O} y \wedge y \; in \; v$, we have $z \mathcal{O} v$. Then, by E3, we have $v \mathcal{O} z$. So, by the definition of *in*, since $z \; in \; x \wedge v \mathcal{O} z$, we have $v \mathcal{O} x$. This, together with E5, contradicts the fact that $x < v$. With the same argument, we can prove that $\neg(y < x)$. Thus, by E7, $x \mathcal{O} y$. □

To show the correctness of these translations in the classical theory, the axioms I_TRANS and FREE were needed, which are the basic properties of the inclusion relation. But in Tsang's theory almost all the axioms (without E1 and E6) were needed, and several of them were not basic ones.

Theorem 7.12 The translations of almost all the axioms of the classical theory $\mathcal{T}_C$ (except I_ANTIS) are satisfied in all models of Tsang's theory $\mathcal{T}_T$.

Proof: Let $\mathcal{G} = \langle G, <, \mathcal{O} \rangle$ be a model of the theory $\mathcal{T}_T$.

$\xi'(\text{P\_TRANS}) = \quad \forall x, y, z \, (x < y \wedge y < z \rightarrow x < z)$

This is Tsang's axiom E2.

$\xi'(\text{P\_IRREF}) = \quad \forall x \, \neg(x < x)$

Suppose that $x < x$. Then, by E1, $\neg(x < x)$. This is a contradiction.

$$\xi'(\text{I\_TRANS}) = \quad \forall x, y (\forall u \, (u \mathcal{O} x \rightarrow u \mathcal{O} y) \wedge \forall u \, (u \mathcal{O} y \rightarrow u \mathcal{O} z) \rightarrow \forall u \, (u \mathcal{O} x \rightarrow u \mathcal{O} z))$$

Consider any $u \in G$ such that $u \mathcal{O} x$. Then $u \mathcal{O} y$, and then $u \mathcal{O} z$. Thus $\forall u \, (u \mathcal{O} x \rightarrow u \mathcal{O} z)$.

$\xi'(\text{I\_REF}) = \quad \forall x \forall u \, (u \mathcal{O} x \rightarrow u \mathcal{O} x)$

This is obvious.

$\xi'(\text{I\_ANTIS}) = \quad \forall x, y (x \; in \; y \wedge y \; in \; x \rightarrow x = y)$

Unfortunately, it is possible that this formula is not satisfied in a model of Tsang's theory. It results from the fact that the translation of $\subseteq$ is too weak (in other words, the definition of the relation *in* is too weak). The structure presented is a counterexample.

$\xi'(\text{MON}^1) = \quad \forall x, y (x < y \rightarrow \forall z \, (\forall u \, (u \mathcal{O} z \rightarrow u \mathcal{O} x) \rightarrow z < y))$

Consider $x, y \in G$ such that $x < y$. Consider any z such that $\forall u \, (u \mathcal{O} z \rightarrow u \mathcal{O} x)$. Then, by E4, we have $z \mathcal{O} x$. Suppose that $y < z$. Then we have $y < z \wedge z \mathcal{O} x \wedge x < y$. So, by E6, $y < y$. It contradicts E1 (see $\xi'(\text{P\_IRREF})$). Suppose that $y \mathcal{O} z$. Then $y \mathcal{O} x$ (because z has been chosen in such a way). By E5 we have a contradiction with $x < y$. Thus, by E7, $z < y$.

$\xi'(\text{MON}^2) = \quad \forall x, y (x < y \rightarrow \forall z \, (\forall u \, (u \mathcal{O} z \rightarrow u \mathcal{O} y) \rightarrow x < z))$

The reasoning is analogous to $\xi'(\text{MON}^1)$.

$$\xi'(\mathsf{CONJ}) = \forall x, y(\exists u\,(u\ in\ x \wedge u\ in\ y) \rightarrow \exists z\,(z\ in\ x \wedge z\ in\ y \wedge \forall u\,(u\ in\ x \wedge u\ in\ y \rightarrow u\ in\ z))$$

By Theorem 7.11 it is equivalent to the formula

$$\forall x, y(x \mathcal{O} y \rightarrow \exists z\,(z\ in\ x \wedge z\ in\ y \wedge \forall u(u\ in\ x \wedge u\ in\ y \rightarrow u\ in\ z))$$

This is axiom E10.

$$\xi'(\mathsf{LIN}) = \forall x, y(x < y \vee \exists u\,(u\ in\ x \wedge u\ in\ y) \vee y < x)$$

By Theorem 7.11 it is equivalent to the formula

$$\forall x, y(x < y \vee x \mathcal{O} y \vee y < x)$$

This is axiom E7.

$$\xi'(\mathsf{FREE}) = \forall x, y(\forall z\,(z\ in\ x \rightarrow \exists u(u\ in\ z \wedge u\ in\ y)) \rightarrow x\ in\ y)$$

By Theorem 7.11 the translation is equivalent to the formula $\forall x, y$ $(\forall z\,(z\ in\ x \rightarrow z \mathcal{O} y) \rightarrow x\ in\ y)$ so, using the other notation, $\forall x, y\,(\forall z\,(\forall u\,(u \mathcal{O} z \rightarrow u \mathcal{O} x) \rightarrow z \mathcal{O} y) \rightarrow \forall u(u \mathcal{O} x \rightarrow u \mathcal{O} y))$. Consider any $x, y \in G$. Consider any $u \in G$ such that $u \mathcal{O} x$. Then, by E3, $x \mathcal{O} u$. By E10, there exists z such that $z\ in\ u \wedge z\ in\ x$. Suppose that $u < y$. Then we have $z\ in\ u \wedge u < y$, so, since the validity of $\xi'(\mathsf{MON})$ was shown, $z < y$ holds. But we should have $\forall z\,(z\ in\ x \rightarrow z\ in\ y)$, and we have $z\ in\ x \wedge z < y$, so the antecedent of the implication being proved does not hold. Suppose that $y < u$. Analogously we can show that the antecedent of the implication does not hold. Thus, by E7, we have $u \mathcal{O} y$. Therefore we have $\forall u\,(u \mathcal{O} x \rightarrow u \mathcal{O} y)$, if only the antecedent of the implication is satisfied.

$$\xi'(\mathsf{CONV}) = \forall x, y, z\,(x < y \wedge y < z \rightarrow \forall u(x\ in\ u \wedge z\ in\ u \rightarrow y\ in\ u))$$

Consider any $x, y, z \in G$ such that $x < y \wedge y < z$. Consider any $u \in G$ such that $x\ in\ u \wedge z\ in\ u$. Then $x \mathcal{O} u \wedge z \mathcal{O} u$. Consider any $v \in G$ such that $v \mathcal{O} y$. Suppose that $v < u$. Suppose also that $v \mathcal{O} x$. Then (by the definition of u) $v \mathcal{O} u$. This contradicts E5. Suppose that $x < v$. Then $v < u \wedge u \mathcal{O} x \wedge x < v$. So, by E6, $v < v$. This contradicts E1. Thus, by E7, $v < x$. Then $v < x \wedge x < y$. So, by E2, $v < y$. By E5 it contradicts that $v \mathcal{O} y$. Suppose that $u < v$. With the same argument, we can prove that it contradicts that $v \mathcal{O} y$. Thus, by E7, $v \mathcal{O} u$. Therefore for any $v \in G$ such that $v \mathcal{O} y$ we have shown that $v \mathcal{O} u$, which means that $y\ in\ u$.

$$\xi'(\mathsf{NEIGH}^1) = \forall x, y(x < y \rightarrow \exists z\,(x < z \wedge \forall u \neg(x < u \wedge u < z)))$$

The consequent of the implication is equivalent to axiom E9.

$$\xi'(\mathsf{NEIGH}^2) = \forall x, y(y < x \rightarrow \exists z\,(z < x, \wedge \forall u \neg(z < u \wedge u < x)))$$

The consequent of the implication is equivalent to axiom E8.

$$\xi'(\mathsf{DISJ}) = \forall x, y\,(\exists u\,(x\ in\ u \wedge y\ in\ u) \rightarrow \exists z\,(x\ in\ z \wedge y\ in\ z \wedge \forall v\,(x\ in\ v \wedge y\ in\ v \rightarrow z\ in\ v)))$$

Consider any $x, y \in G$. By E11, there exists $z \in G$ such that $x \; in \; z \wedge y \; in \; z \wedge \forall u\,(u < x \wedge u < y \rightarrow u < z) \wedge \forall u\,(x < u \wedge y < u \rightarrow z < u)$. Consider such a z. Consider $v \in G$ such that $x \; in \; v \wedge y \; in \; v$. Then, by E4 and the definition of *in*, we have $x \mathcal{O} v \wedge y \mathcal{O} v$. So, by E3, we also have $v \mathcal{O} x \wedge v \mathcal{O} y$. Consider any $r \in G$ such that $r \mathcal{O} z$. Suppose that $r < v$. Suppose also that $x < r$. Then we have $r < v \wedge v \mathcal{O} x \wedge x < r$. So, by E6, $r < r$. This contradicts E1. Suppose that $x \mathcal{O} r$. As we have $x \; in \; v$, by the definition of *in* and E3, $r \mathcal{O} v$ holds. This contradicts E5. Thus, by E7, $r < x$. Using the same argument we can prove that $r < y$. And then by the definition of z we have $r < z$. By E5, this contradicts that $r \mathcal{O} z$. Suppose that $v < r$. Analogously, this contradicts that $r \mathcal{O} z$. Thus, by E7, we have $r \mathcal{O} v$.

Therefore we have proved that for any r such that $r \mathcal{O} z$, there holds $r \mathcal{O} v$, which is equivalent to $z \; in \; v$.

$$\xi'(\mathsf{DIR}) = \quad \forall x, y \exists z\,(x \; in \; z \wedge y \; in \; z)$$

This is a simple consequence of E11.

$$\xi'(\mathsf{SUCC}) = \quad \forall x \, \exists y\,(x < y)$$
$$\forall x \, \exists y\,(y < x)$$

These are simple consequences of E8 and E9.

$$\xi'(\mathsf{MOND}^1) = \quad \forall x, y, z\,(x < z \wedge y < z \rightarrow \exists v\,(x \; in \; v \wedge y \; in \; v \wedge v < z \wedge \forall u\,(x \; in \; u \wedge y \; in \; u \rightarrow v \; in \; u)))$$

Instead of the above formula, we can write the stronger one:

$$\forall x, y \exists v\,(x \; in \; v \wedge y \; in \; v \wedge \forall z\,(x < z \wedge y < z \rightarrow v < z) \wedge \forall u\,(x \; in \; u \wedge y \; in \; u \rightarrow v \; in \; u))$$

The first part of this formula follows from E11. The second part of it is equivalent to the formula $\xi'(\mathsf{DISJ})$, which has been already proved.

$$\xi'(\mathsf{MOND}^2) = \quad \forall x, y, z\,(z < x \wedge z < y \rightarrow \exists v\,(x \; in \; v \wedge y \; in \; v \wedge z < v \wedge \forall u\,(x \; in \; u \wedge y \; in \; u \rightarrow v \; in \; u)))$$

The proof is analogous to $\xi'(\mathsf{MOND}^1)$.

Therefore the translations of all the axioms of the classical theory $\mathcal{T}_C$ (except I_ANTIS) are satisfied in all models of Tsang's theory $\mathcal{T}_T$. □

To prove the axioms of the basic classical theory $\mathcal{T}_{CB}$ (except CONJ) we have needed only the axioms from the basic Tsang's theory $\mathcal{T}_{TB}$. However, for the proof of CONJ, all the remaining axioms were needed (because Theorem 7.12 was used).

Since there exists an axiom from the classical theory $\mathcal{T}_C$ (and its basic subtheory $\mathcal{T}_{CB}$) that is not satisfied in some models of Tsang's theory $\mathcal{T}_T$, we can speak neither about the satisfiability of theorems of theories $\mathcal{T}_C$ and $\mathcal{T}_{CB}$ in models of theory $\mathcal{T}_T$, nor about the interpretability of theory $\mathcal{T}_C$ in theory $\mathcal{T}_T$. However, there hold both interpretability of theory $\mathcal{T}_C - \{\text{I\_ANTIS}\}$ in theory $\mathcal{T}_T$, and interpretability of theory $\mathcal{T}_{CB} - \{\mathsf{I\_ANTIS}, \mathsf{CONJ}\}$ in theory $\mathcal{T}_{TB}$.

It is worth mentioning here that for the proof of some, quite elementary, classical axioms it was necessary to use many, often not elementary, Tsang's axioms. For instance, axiom E7 was used in the proofs of translations of the axioms MON, CONJ, FREE, CONV, DISJ, MOND and, certainly, LIN. Thus removal of the linearity condition brings into question such important properties as monotonicity, freedom and convexity.

7.5 Conclusions

In this chapter we do not consider translations between Allen & Hayes' and Tsang's theories, because such translations were considered by Tsang [19]. The translation of Allen & Hayes' formula $x \parallel y$ into Tsang's theory is the same as our translation of this formula into the classical theory: $x < y \wedge \neg\exists z\,(x < z \wedge z < y)$. Moreover, as we might expect, the translation of Tsang's formula $x < y$ into Allen & Hayes' theory is identical to our translation of its classical counterpart into this theory: $x \parallel y \vee \exists z\,(x \parallel z \wedge z \parallel y)$. However, Tsang bases the translation of the formula $x\,\mathcal{O}\,y$ on the above translation together with axiom E7: $\neg(x < y) \wedge \neg(y < x)$. Hence, this translation assumes the satisfiability of both the linearity and the convexity condition in the structures being described. However, though Allen & Hayes' theory imposes the linearity condition, it does not impose the convexity of intervals condition, as we have mentioned many times. Thus this translation makes sense only for structures of convex intervals. On the other hand, defining a translation of the formula $x\,\mathcal{O}\,y$ directly would not help us to avoid these problems, because they are immanent features of Allen & Hayes' theory and they also appear while defining the translation from the classical theory into Allen & Hayes' one. But we can say that the above translation was defined for a theory with one predicate $<$, because the translation of the predicate $\mathcal{O}$ is defined by means of it.

As follows from the above considerations, the validity of translations of axioms of one theory into another so strongly depends on the form of the translation (which, on the other hand, depends on the capability provided by theories) that speaking about equivalence of these theories seems to be a misuse.

Tsang considers Allen & Hayes' theory $\mathcal{T}_{A^\circ}$, without axiom M6, hence the translation of it is not valid in his theory, similarly with the translation of the classical axiom I_ANTIS. This does not mean that Tsang's theory cannot be extended in such a way that the appropriate translations of axioms would be satisfied. It should be mentioned that the lack of the condition of antisymmetry of the inclusion relation in Tsang's theory is a conscious manipulation—Tsang actually wants to consider event structures, not interval structures, and there is possible for many events to occur at the same time. But, unfortunately, as we have shown, this assumption causes other undesirable effects.

As a main advantage of his theory over that of Allen & Hayes, Tsang considers that Allen & Hayes' axiom M3 contains much more than linearity only, so we cannot describe nonlinear structures in it. However, the translation of the classical theory into Tsang's one shows that E7 also implies validity of several other properties (even though it is not to the same extent as M3). Expressing these properties directly often demands the use of the auxiliary relation *in*. Even Tsang, in his considerations, sometimes claims that two overlapping intervals have a common subinterval, so in fact he does not treat the relation $\mathcal{O}$ as a primitive one. In my opinion, all the above problems which appear while defining the inclusion relation by means of the overlapping relation, are caused by the simple fact that the inclusion relation is actually more primitive than the overlapping one.

The aim of Allen & Hayes was the creation of a common-sense theory of time. But it is not obvious why the meeting relation $\|$ is more natural for human reasoning than the precedence relation $<$. Finally, we think that the precedence relation $<$ and the inclusion relation $\subseteq$ characterize the nature of intervals in the most natural way. Therefore, the classical theories describe interval temporal structures in the best way. It is also worth mentioning that removing the linearity axiom LIN causes least harm to the characteristics of a structure (especially as van Benthem considers the convexity condition CONV separately). We should also pay attention to the fact that the classical approach contains more different axioms, thus it allows a description of more different classes of structures, hence it is the most flexible one.

Acknowledgements

I would like to thank Prof. Ewa Orlowska and Prof. Leonard Bolc for their very helpful discussions about this work.

References

[1] Allen, J.F. 1983. Maintaining knowledge about temporal intervals. *Communications of ACM* **26**(11), 832–43.

[2] Allen, J. F. & P. J. Hayes 1985. A common-sense theory of time, In *Proceedings of the 9th International Joint Conference on Artificial Intelligence*, 528–31. Los Altos, CA: Morgan Kaufmann.

[3] Allen, J.F. & P. J. Hayes 1987. Short time periods. In *Proceedings of the 10th International Joint Conference on Artificial Intelligence*, 981–83. Los Altos, CA: Morgan Kaufmann.

[4] Allen, J.F. & P. J. Hayes 1989. Moments and points in an interval-based temporal logic. *Computational Intelligence* **5**, 225–38.

[5] van Benthem, J.F.A.K. 1983. *The Logic of Time*. Dordrecht: D. Reidel.

[6] Eberle, K. 1988. Extensions of event structures. In *Proceedings of the 8th European Conference on Artificial Intelligence*, 241–46. Los Altos, CA: Morgan Kaufmann.

[7] Hajnicz, E. 1989. *Formalization of the inferential system on temporal dependencies between events.* ICS PAS report no. 658, Institute of Computer Science, Polish Academy of Sciences, Warsaw.

[8] Hajnicz, E. 1991. Another approach to formalizing the point and interval calculi. Forthcoming in *International Journal of Men–Machine Studies.*

[9] Kamp, H. 1979. Instants and temporal reference. In *Semantics from different points of view*, von Stechow (ed), 376–417. Berlin: Springer.

[10] Kamp, H. 1980. Some remarks on the logic of change, Part I. In *Proceedings of the Stuttgart Conference on the Logic of Tense and Quantification*, Guenthner F. (ed), 135–79. Amsterdam: North Holland.

[11] Kowalski, R. & M. Sergot 1986. A logic-based calculus of events. *New Generating Computing* **4**, 67–95.

[12] Ladkin, P. B. 1986. Primitives and units for time specification. In *Proceedings of the 5th AAAI Conference*, 354-59. Los Altos, CA: Morgan Kaufmann.

[13] Ladkin, P. B. 1987. Models of axioms for time intervals. In *Proceedings of the 6th AAAI Conference*, 234-39. Los Altos, CA: Morgan Kaufmann.

[14] Ladkin, P.B. & R. D. Maddux 1987. *The algebra of convex time intervals.* Kestrel Institute Technical Report KES.U.87.2, Palo Alto, CA.

[15] McDermott, D. 1982. A temporal logic for reasoning about processes and plans. *Cognitive Science* **6**, 101–55.

[16] McTaggart, J.M.E. 1908. The unreality of time, *Mind*, 457–74.

[17] McTaggart, J.M.E. 1927. *The nature of existence.* Cambridge.

[18] Tsang, E.P.K. 1986. *The interval structure of Allen's logic.* Technical Report CSCM-24, University of Essex.

[19] Tsang, E.P.K. 1987. Time structures for AI. In *Proceedings of the 10th International Joint Conference on Artificial Intelligence*, 456–61. Los Altos, CA: Morgan Kaufmann.

[20] Vilain, M. B. & H. Kautz 1986. Constraint propagation algorithms for temporal reasoning. In *Proceedings of the 5th AAAI Conference*, 377-92. Los Altos, CA: Morgan Kaufmann.

Index